# XML Data Mining:

## Models, Methods, and Applications

Andrea Tagarelli
*University of Calabria, Italy*

| | |
| --- | --- |
| Managing Director: | Lindsay Johnston |
| Senior Editorial Director: | Heather Probst |
| Book Production Manager: | Sean Woznicki |
| Development Manager: | Joel Gamon |
| Development Editor: | Michael Killian |
| Acquisitions Editor: | Erika Gallagher |
| Typesetters: | Michael Brehm, Deanna Zombro |
| Print Coordinator: | Jamie Snavely |
| Cover Design: | Nick Newcomer |

Published in the United States of America by
Information Science Reference (an imprint of IGI Global)
701 E. Chocolate Avenue
Hershey PA 17033
Tel: 717-533-8845
Fax: 717-533-8661
E-mail: cust@igi-global.com
Web site: http://www.igi-global.com



Library of Congress Cataloging-in-Publication Data

XML data mining : models, methods, and applications / Andrea Tagarelli, editor.
p. cm.
Includes bibliographical references and index.
Summary: "This book is a collection of knowledge from experts of database, information retrieval, machine learning, and knowledge management communities in developing models, methods and systems for XML data mining that can be used to address key issues and challenges in XML data mining"--Provided by publisher.
ISBN 978-1-61350-356-0 (hardcover) -- ISBN 978-1-61350-357-7 (ebook) -- ISBN 978-1-61350-358-4 (print & perpetual access) 1. XML (Document markup language) 2. Data mining. I. Tagarelli, Andrea, 1976-
QA76.76.H94X4184 2011
006.3'12--dc23

2011018558

British Cataloguing in Publication Data
A Cataloguing in Publication record for this book is available from the British Library.

## Editorial Advisory Board



## List of Reviewers



*Each contributing author has also participated in the evaluation process of the other authors' manuscripts*

# Table of Contents

# Foreword

XML is the de-facto standard for data interchange and document representation. The popularity of XML stems from the fact that its semi-structured nature allows the modeling of a wide variety of data as XML documents. XML data thus forms an important data mining domain. However, until now there has been no single book that discusses the myriad challenges and opportunities of mining XML data. This information is usually scattered in various journal, conference, and workshop articles.

This edited volume on XML Data Mining by Andrea Tagarelli brings together for the first time models, methods, and applications of XML mining in a single source. The book covers all the major data mining tasks such as similarity search, frequent pattern mining, classification, and clustering in the context of XML data. The distinguishing features of the book include the focus on cutting edge challenges such as modeling and mining uncertain XML data, approximate matching, leveraging the structure, content as well as semantics for the various XML mining tasks, and handling evolving or streaming XML data.

I am confident that this timely volume will be the go-to reference for finding the latest methods and developments in XML data mining. It will be an invaluable resource for students, researchers, and practitioners in the field.

*Mohammed J. Zaki*
*Rensselaer Polytechnic Institute, USA*

***Mohammed J. Zaki** is a Professor of Computer Science at Rensselaer Polytechnic Institute, Troy, New York. He received his Ph.D. degree in computer science from the University of Rochester in 1998. His research interests focus on developing novel data mining techniques, especially in bioinformatics. He has published over 200 papers and book-chapters on data mining and bioinformatics. He is the founding co-chair for the BIOKDD series of workshops. He is currently Area Editor for Statistical Analysis and Data Mining, and an Associate Editor for Data Mining and Knowledge Discovery, ACM Transactions on Knowledge Discovery from Data, Knowledge and Information Systems, ACM Transactions on Intelligent Systems and Technology, Social Networks and Mining, and International Journal of Knowledge Discovery in Bioinformatics. He was the program co-chair for SDM'08, SIGKDD'09, and PAKDD'10. He received the National Science Foundation CAREER Award in 2001 and the Department of Energy Early Career Principal Investigator Award in 2002. He is a senior member of the IEEE, and was named an ACM Distinguished Scientist in 2010.*

# Preface

Data mining is concerned with the generalized problem of digging out "the hidden gold" in form of knowledge patterns from massive amounts of data. The information overload, which characterizes the digital era we are living in, is further exasperated due to the textual nature of the majority of data available in existing information sources. Moreover, text data have a "semistructured" nature in most of such sources, primarily over the Web but also in digital libraries, company data repositories, and scientific databases.

Semistructured text data is the connection point between the natural language written text and the rigidly structured tuples of typed data—for example, a news article may contain a few structured fields (such as, news channel, headline, author, location, publication date) but also a largely unstructured text component (the article body). Semistructured data also enables the representation and description of complex real-life objects and their relationships, thus unleashing a potentially unlimited number of possibilities for human-machine-human communication.

XML is the preeminent form of representation of semistructured data. In contrast to most of the Web pages which are encoded as HTML documents, XML is well-defined and flexible, and markup is used to put emphasis on structuring and modeling data, rather than on presentation and layout issues, and to encode semantics. While the counterpart HTML is designed primarily for human-readable documents, XML supports the exchange of machine-readable data. Using XML, information representation is separated from information rendering, making documents to be presented by different views.

XML makes it possible to define complex document structures, such as unbounded nesting and object-oriented hierarchies, and to specify not only data but also the data structures, how elements are nested, and their content models. The flexible nature of XML syntax simplifies the definition and deployment of arbitrary languages for domain-specific markup, enabling automatic authoring and processing of networked data. It has been recognized that an important role of XML vocabularies is the ability of modeling a large variety of data types and their many interrelationships, and being flexible enough to support new information as it is discovered. XML is indeed conceived to couple data with its context (metadata) through an extensible, hierarchical tag structure, which is essential to handle taxonomies (as in life sciences) or other conceptual structures. As a consequence, XML has rapidly become the preferred meta-language for disseminating information in on-line databases, digital libraries, scientific and financial data repositories, multimedia, and many others. All these features, and much more, have made the impact of XML significant not only in research contexts but also in industry: publishing information sources in XML is ever attractive for organizations that want to easily interoperate and provide their information in a format processable by other applications especially on the Web. XML technologies have also been coupled with relational databases to solve business problems. As a matter of fact, encoding data into XML provides benefits in decreasing the translation overheads of communication within and between organizations.

The widespread use of XML has prompted the development of methodologies, techniques, and systems for effectively and efficiently mining XML data. Since the early years of XML, database vendors have responded to these information management needs raised by XML, and the actual scenario offers a variety of approaches which include object-oriented database systems and native XML database systems. All of this has increasingly attracted the attention of various research communities, including databases, information retrieval, Web intelligence, machine learning, and data mining from which myriad proposals have been offered to address problems in XML data management and knowledge discovery.

Mining XML data has its roots in semistructured data management. Therefore, most of the application domains of interest, such as integration of data sources and query processing, were initially focused on structure information available from XML data. In this context, they raised the demand for effective and efficient solutions to any problem concerned with structural comparison of semistructured data. For this purpose, a corpus of study has been borrowed from related research problems; important research contributions have especially regarded pattern matching, change detection, similarity search and detection, and document summarization. Schema matching was initially an important issue in relational models, but has rapidly gained momentum in the XML context. For instance, schema matching algorithms have been developed to support the clustering of structurally similar DTDs, the classification of XML documents with respect to a set of XML-Schemas, and the evolution of a schema based on structural information extracted from classes/clusters of XML documents. Identifying structural similarities between XML documents, rather than XML schemas, is also central in semistructured data mining in part because most real-life XML documents are schema-less. Defining a suitable distance or similarity measure between XML documents requires considering at least the features upon which documents are identified as similar and the method of pattern matching that is used according to the model chosen for representing an XML document. Early approaches to structural document similarity detection are based on tree edit distances, whereas most recent approaches range from vectorial or transactional representations to probabilistic models of XML data. The detection of structural similarities can be a valid support to recognize different sources providing the same kind of information, or for query processing in semistructured data; in addition, the capability of summarizing sets of XML documents can further help to estimate the selectivity of path expressions and devising indexing techniques for clusters to eventually improve the construction of query plans. Also, mining frequent patterns and association rules in XML data is useful to explore relationships between structure elements (e.g., tag names), such as their frequency of co-occurrence within the same collection of XML documents.

Mining XML data according to both structure and content information has become essential in an increasing number of tasks for which it is relevant to consider the types of structure in the documents as well as the topics that can be inferred from the textual content of XML elements. However, the definition of content features makes any mining task inherit some problems faced in traditional knowledge discovery from text data, while new ones arise as XML content is contextually dependent of the XML (logical) structure. The increase in volume and heterogeneity of XML-based application scenarios also makes XML data sources exhibit different ways of semantically annotating their information. Thanks to the inherent subjectivity in the definition of markup tags, XML documents that are different by structure and content may however be semantically related at a certain degree. Several "semantic questions" arise in this context, and hence there is an urgent need for developing semantics-aware representation models and devising suitable notions of semantic features and semantic relatedness measures for XML data. In this respect, semantic organization of XML data has become one of the hardest challenges in XML knowledge discovery and management.

## OBJECTIVES AND MISSION

This book is intended to collect and distil the knowledge from experts of database systems, information retrieval, machine learning, Web intelligence and knowledge management communities in developing models, methods, and systems for XML data mining. Within this view, the book addresses key issues and challenges in XML data mining, offering insights into the various existing solutions and best practices for modeling, processing, and analyzing XML data. It explores algorithmic, theoretical, and practical issues regarding mining tasks specific for XML data, and is also concerned with XML-based data mining applications.

At the time of writing, this book also represents the *first* editorial opportunity to provide a single reference focused on Data Mining & XML. Indeed, most notable book publications have addressed separately such XML related fields as semistructured data management and relational databases, XML data management and XML-enabled database systems, XML and the Semantic Web, while none of the existing references on knowledge discovery and data mining focuses on semistructured data and XML. In some cases, the latter are at most treated marginally as related technologies for Web structure and content mining; analogously, no book reference on XML and related technologies focuses on the need for organizations to efficiently access and share data, extracting information from data and making a competitive use of them by resorting to knowledge discovery and data mining solutions. Therefore, the anticipated mission of this book was to fill this lack of a book concerned with data mining and XML in a unified way.

## PROSPECTIVE AUDIENCE AND POTENTIAL USES

This book is targeted to both researchers and practitioners in XML data mining and related fields, including Web mining, information retrieval, and knowledge management.

As a textbook, it aims to provide a guide to and through classic and challenging topics in knowledge discovery and data mining which are particularly concerned with the realm of XML. Therefore, the book could be used as a supplement of basic courses on either of the aforementioned disciplines, or as a reference for upper-level courses on advances in databases, information retrieval, and machine learning.

From an industry perspective, the book would be a reference for professionals in XML/database technologies for e-business and e-commerce. In this respect, the book provides insights into benefits, issues, and challenges of data mining solutions for developing XML-based intelligent management and analysis systems.

## ORGANIZATION OF THE BOOK

The book is laid out as follows:

- Section 1: Models and Measures
- Section 2: Clustering and Classification
- Section 3: Association Mining
- Section 4: Semantics-Aware Mining
- Section 5: Applications

Each of the parts is comprised of a set of chapters that are coherent with respect to a major topic of interest in XML data mining. Although the parts are self-contained, the reader will may find useful to go beyond this underlying main classification of the chapters, and follow the cross-references between chapters (possibly located in different parts) to obtain further information about a topic.

The content of the parts is summarized as follows.

*Section 1*: *Models and Measures*. The success of an XML data mining method strongly relies on the choice of a model for representing XML data. This in turn influences the choice for the proximity measures and methods that are essential to compare XML data. The first part of this book is hence concerned with representation models (Chapters 1 and 2) and proximity measures (Chapters 3 and 4) that are well-suited for XML data.

Chapter 1 by Kutty, Nayak, and Tran provides a systematization to the many concepts around the context of XML models according to three main lines: the representations, the ways these representations are used for the various mining tasks, and the issues and challenges. The chapter also provides interesting pointers to future directions of research in XML modeling for data mining.

Kharlamov and Senellart address the very challenging problem of mining uncertain XML data in Chapter 2, where uncertainty essentially refers to the inherent impreciseness in automatic processes, and is usually represented as the probability the data is correct. The authors discuss how uncertainty is modeled in relational data before moving on to presenting uncertain XML models. Starting from lessons learned from probabilistic XML querying, the authors propose specific probabilistic models for XML documents and show how these models can be applied to XML mining tasks.

Madria and Viyanon overview similarity detection in XML documents in Chapter 3. Their description covers not only similarity and distance measures according to structure and content features of XML documents for mining, but also discusses the challenging problem of detecting semantically similar XML documents.

In Chapter 4, Wang, Li, and Li focus on effective and scalable solutions to approximate search and join on ordered trees for purposes of similarity detection in large and high-dimensional XML datasets. Within this view, they improve upon the known pq-gram method by introducing a randomized data structure and effective approximate join strategies.

*Section 2: Clustering and Classification*. Two of the most attractive research topics in XML data mining are considered in this part. Chapter 5, by Xing, presents solutions for computing approximate matching between XML documents and schemas to support the tasks of XML classification and clustering. The author investigates tree edit based measures and related algorithms to determine how well an XML document conforms to a schema, and demonstrates how the proposed methods can effectively be applied to structural classification and clustering of XML data.

Like Chapter 5, both XML schemas and instances are considered in Chapter 6, by De Meo, Nocera, Ursino, and Fiumara. They however focus on aspects related specifically to the clustering of XML structures, and their discussion of popular methods for structural clustering is organized to distinguish between the intensional data level (DTDs and XML Schemas) and the extensional data level (XML document structures).

Chapter 7 by Antonellis overviews the main literature on XML clustering algorithms by taking into account documents only. The author explores the various facets of XML document clustering according to structure and/or content information, also including the more recent semantic XML clustering.

Collectively, Chapters 6 and 7 cover a breadth of approaches and algorithms for XML clustering. Fuzzy clustering has not been largely investigated so far in the XML domain. The study presented in

Chapter 8 by Kozielski is a first attempt to attract the attention of researchers in the clustering field towards the potentialities of fuzzy methods for grouping structurally similar XML documents. Particularly, the author leverages the importance of adopting a fuzzy approach for encoding XML structures and a "multilevel" clustering method that enables to better handle the various hierarchy levels when clustering XML documents.

In Chapter 9, Bifet and Gavaldà propose a framework for the classification of XML trees in the challenging domain of data streams. The evolving nature of such data is handled by adaptively mining closed tree patterns from the streams and combining them with a classifier to reduce the dimensionality in the classification task.

In Chapter 10, Hagenbuchner, Tsoi, Kc, and Zhang address the novel problem of link prediction in XML document sets. The key idea of their work is to encode graph-structured XML information using an unsupervised learning approach based on one particular class of neural networks, and exploit it for prediction in an inter-linked domain. The authors argue that self-organizing maps are well-suited for the challenging task at hand, and therefore propose the first extension of self-organizing map algorithms for predicting incoming and outgoing links in XML document collections.

*Section 3: Association Mining.* The third part of this book is concerned with frequent pattern and association rule mining in XML data. State-of-the-art research on these closely related problems is overviewed in Chapter 11, by Ding and Sundarraj. They introduce the challenges in content-based and structure-based mining of XML frequent patterns and association rules, discuss the various existing approaches, and finally highlight open issues in the field.

In Chapter 12, Mazuran, Quintarelli, Rauseo, and Tanca describe their experience in applying tree mining techniques to extract summarized views of content and structure in XML documents. Here the objective is to facilitate the query-answering process by enabling the user to query the extracted, concise tree-shaped XML patterns in addition to the original dataset.

Chapter 13 by Cagliero, Cerquitelli, and Garza is focused on the problem of extracting generalized association rules to mine higher correlations from XML data. The proposed approach entails the conversion of XML data to a transactional format, and the use of a taxonomy to organize item features at different granularity levels; this taxonomy is then evaluated to guide the generalization of the extracted association rules.

*Section 4: Semantics-Aware Mining.* This part is devoted to the presentation of works that, in one way or another, address semantic aspects in XML data mining. The first chapter in this part bridges the studies on Semantic Web and mining XML data, whereas the other two chapters respectively focus on exploiting interschema knowledge for XML integration and exploration, and on knowledge matching for the detection of structural/conceptual relationships in XML knowledge representations.

In Chapter 14, Berlanga and Nebot discuss the importance and feasibility of combining knowledge resources in data mining processes towards semantics-aware knowledge discovery. They discuss the benefits provided by semantic annotations and knowledge representation formalisms as a common layer for integrating heterogeneous data sources. Through an exhaustive review of the literature, the authors describe how semantic features have been incorporated and dealt with mining complex structured and semistructured data.

Chapter 15 by De Meo, Nocera, and Ursino presents a framework that extracts interschema properties from XML sources, builds up a hierarchy to represent the sources at different abstraction levels, and then exploits this hierarchy to organize and explore the sources. Although the authors describe a general, component-based framework with the aforementioned characteristics, they also provide implementations of the three layers of the framework that are focused on the intensional aspect of XML data.

Pan, Hadzic, and Dillon address the challenging problem of conceptual and structural matching in heterogeneous knowledge representations in Chapter 16. They prove that frequent tree mining algorithms, being capable of efficiently extracting common substructures in tree-structured knowledge representations, are useful to automatically model the knowledge shared by different XML data for a specific domain.

*Section 5: Applications*. The final part of this book contains an interesting mix of application-oriented studies: content characterization of geographical maps based on tag annotations provided by social network users, collaborative document clustering in P2P networks, and frequent subtree mining applied to credit risk assessment data.

In Chapter 17, Roglia, Meo, and Ponassi present an appealing application scenario for online mapping services like OpenStreetMap and Google Map. By exploiting information in tag-based cartographic annotations, the authors propose an approach based on a statistical test on the frequency of the annotations to characterize the map contents in a concise yet meaningful way.

Gullo, Ponti, and Greco describe a collaborative distributed framework for clustering XML documents in Chapter 18. They pose their attention on distributed environments implemented as P2P systems to introduce the novel element of collaborativeness in the task of XML document clustering. The proposed centroid-based partitional clustering method is shown to be suitable for efficiently organizing XML documents distributed across peers.

Chapter 19 by Ikasari, Hadzic, and Dillon is aimed at filling the lack of mining approaches that exploit qualitative information in credit risk assessment. XML is used in this endeavour to model quantitative as well as qualitative information of small-medium enterprises in loan applications. Frequent tree mining algorithms are then applied to the resulting XML data to discover potentially useful associations for supporting loan granting decision making.

*Andrea Tagarelli*
*University of Calabria, Rende, Italy–February 2011*

# Acknowledgment

In January 2010, when I was invited by IGI Global to edit a book in the data mining area, I realized that the thought of editing a book on XML data mining was appealing and daunting at the same time, due to the wide range of problems and topics that have been addressed in the past years. Hence I decided to face the challenge of creating a multi-authored book that captured the collective expertise of researchers in the field. Therefore, my first thank-you goes to the authors who welcomed and contributed to this project, trying their best to fulfill the organizational and content guidelines that I provided in advance for the various parts of the book and, in most cases, for the individual chapters.

I am very grateful to the external reviewers, who carefully scrutinized the assigned chapters and made many valuable suggestions for improvements.

My special thanks are for the editorial advisory board members, who kindly supported me through the editing process, especially in reviewing the chapter proposals and handling submission cases where conflicting reviews occurred.

I am also grateful to Mohammed J. Zaki, who wrote the foreword of this book. It was like receiving an unexpected and invaluable gift.

I wish to thank Mike Killian, who has been my assistant development editor at IGI Global. He has been everything I could hope for. I also wish to thank Salvatore Romeo, whose careful reading of the references led to a number of corrections and improvements.

This book is dedicated to my wife, Monica, for tolerating the editing process (I promise her not to take on new grand projects, at least not immediately), and to my son, Alessandro G., my very pride and joy.

*Andrea Tagarelli*
*University of Calabria, Rende, Italy–February 2011*

# Section 1
# Models and Measures

# Chapter 1
# A Study of XML Models for Data Mining:
## Representations, Methods, and Issues

**Sangeetha Kutty**
*Queensland University of Technology, Australia*

**Richi Nayak**
*Queensland University of Technology, Australia*

**Tien Tran**
*Queensland University of Technology, Australia*

## ABSTRACT

*With the increasing number of XML documents in varied domains, it has become essential to identify ways of finding interesting information from these documents. Data mining techniques can be used to derive this interesting information. However, mining of XML documents is impacted by the data model used in data representation due to the semi-structured nature of these documents. In this chapter, we present an overview of the various models of XML documents representations, how these models are used for mining, and some of the issues and challenges inherent in these models. In addition, this chapter also provides some insights into the future data models of XML documents for effectively capturing its two important features, structure and content, for mining.*

## INTRODUCTION

Due to the increased popularity of XML in varied application domains, a large number of XML documents are found in both organizational intranets and Internet. Some of the popular datasets such as English Wikipedia contains 3.1 million web documents in XML format with 1.74 billion words, and the ClueWeb dataset used in Text Retrieval Conference (TREC) tracks contains 503.9 million XML documents collected from the web in January and February 2009. In order to discover useful knowledge from these large amount of XML documents, researchers have used data mining techniques (Nayak, 2005). XML data mining techniques have gained great deal of

DOI: 10.4018/978-1-61350-356-0.ch001

interest among researchers due to their potential to discover useful knowledge in diverse fields such as bioinformatics, telecommunication network analysis, community detection, information retrieval, social network analysis (Nayak, 2008).

Unlike structured data where the structure is fixed because the data is stored in structured format as in relational tables, XML data has flexibility in its structure as the users are allowed to use custom-defined tags to represent the data. An XML document contains tags and the data is enclosed within those tags. A tag usually describes a meaningful name to the content it represents. Moreover, tags present in the document are organised in hierarchical order showing the relationships between elements of the document. Usually, the hierarchical ordering of tags in an XML document is called as the *document structure* and the data enclosed within these tags is called as the *document content.*

XML data can be modelled in various forms namely vectors (or transactional data models), paths, trees and graphs based on its structure and/or content. The focus of this chapter is to present an overview of the various models that can be used to represent XML documents for the process of mining. This chapter also addresses some of the issues and challenges associated with each of these models.

Organisation of this chapter is as follows. In the next section, it explains various XML data models in detail. The third section discusses about the roles of models in diverse mining tasks such as frequent pattern mining, association rules mining, clustering and classification. The chapter then details about the issues and the challenges in using these models for mining. It concludes with the needs and opportunities of new models for mining on XML documents.

## DATA MODELS FOR XML DOCUMENT MINING

To suit the objectives and the needs of XML mining algorithms, XML data has been represented in various forms. Figure 1 gives taxonomy of XML data showing various data models that facilitate XML mining with different features that exist in the XML data.

There are two types of XML data: *XML document* and *XML schema definition*. An XML schema definition contains the structure and data definitions of XML documents (Abiteboul, Bun-

*Figure 1. Data models facilitating mining of XML data*

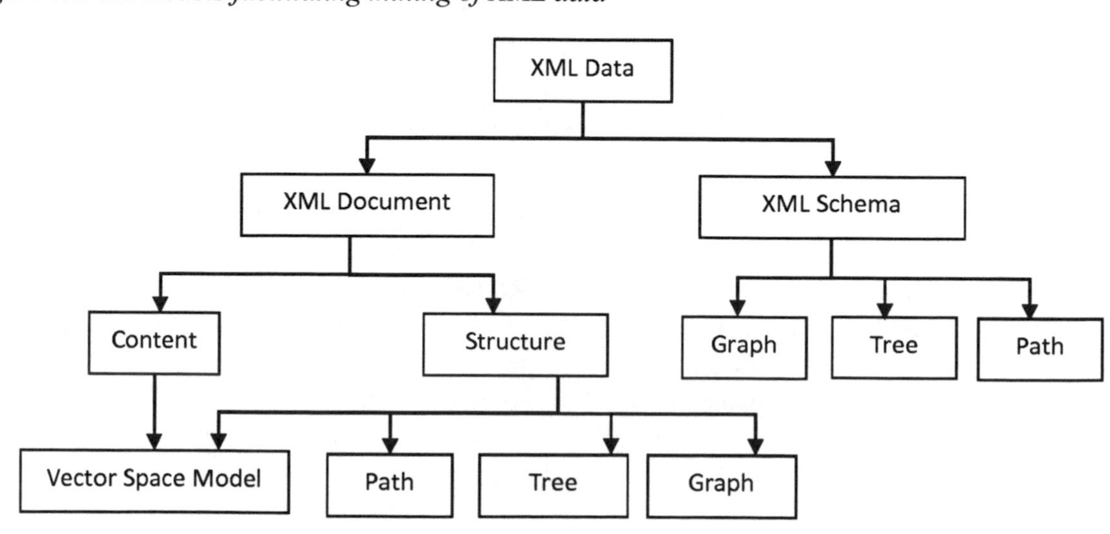

*Figure 2. An example of a DTD schema (conf.dtd)*

```
<!ELEMENT conf (id, title, year, editor?, paper*)>
<!ATTLIST conf id ID #REQUIRED>
<!ELEMENT title (#PCDATA)>
<!ELEMENT year (#PCDATA)>
<!ELEMENT editor (person*)>
<!ELEMENT paper (title, author, references?)>
<!ELEMENT author (person*)>
<!ELEMENT person (name, email)
<!ELEMENT name (#PCDATA)>
<!ELEMENT email (#PCDATA)>
<!ELEMENT references (paper*)>
```

eman, & Suciu, 2000). An XML document, on the other hand, is an instance of the XML schema that contains the data content represented in a structured format.

The provision of the XML schema definition with XML documents makes it different from the other types of semi-structured data such as HTML and BibTeX. The schema imposes restrictions on the syntax and structure of XML documents. The two most popular XML document schema languages are Document Type Definition (DTD) and XML-Schema Definition (XSD). Figures 2 and 3 show DTD and XSD examples respectively. An example of a simple XML document conforming to the schemas from Figure 2 and 3 is shown in Figure 4.

An XML document can belong to one of the followings, *ill-formed*, *well-formed*, and *valid*, according to how it abides the XML schema definition. An ill-formed document does not have a fixed structure meaning it does not conform to the XML syntax rules such as lack of XML declaration statement and it contain more than one root element. A well-formed document conforms to the XML syntax rules and may have a document schema but the document does not conform to it. It contains exactly one root element, and sub-elements are properly nested within each other. Finally, a valid XML document is a well-formed document which conforms to a specified XML schema definition (Stuart, 2004). The document as shown in Figure 4 is an example of valid document.

Each XML document can be divided into two parts, namely *markup constructs* and *content*. A markup construct consists of the characters that are marked up using “<” and “/>”. The content is the set of characters that is not included in markup. There are two types of markup constructs, tags (or elements) and attributes. Tags are the markup constructs which begin with a start tag “<” and end with an end tag “/>” such as *conf, title, year, editor,* for the *conf.xml* document in Figure 4. On the other hand, the attributes are markup constructs consisting of a name/value pair that exists within a start-tag. In the running example, *id* is the attribute and “SIAM10” is its value. Examples of content are “SIAM Data Mining Conference”, “2010”, “Bing Liu”.

Having discussed about the preliminaries of XML, now let us look into the various models, namely Vector Space or Transactional data models, Path, Tree and Graph models for XML data for mining in the following subsections.

## Transactional Data Model or Vector Space Model

A way to represent an XML dataset is using the Transactional Data Model (TDM) or Vector Space Model (VSM) in which each document in the dataset is represented as transaction or vector. The TDM or VSM of an XML document can be represented based on either its tags or its content.

Firstly, let us look at converting the tags of an XML document into a transactional data model or bag of words (as used in VSM). The XML document is first parsed using a SAX (Simple API for XML) parser and the resulting information is pre-processed and then transformed into a TDM with the XML tags as the items in the transaction along with their number of occurrences as shown in Figure 5.

One problem of applying the mining techniques on the TDM is that this model does not preserve the hierarchical relationship between the tags. Hence, the data mining methods applied on the

*Figure 3. An example of an XSD schema (conf.xsd)*

```
<?xml version="1.0" encoding="UTF-8"?>
<xsd:schema xmlns:xsd=http://www.w3.org/2001/XMLSchema,
targetNamespace=http://www.conferences.org,
xmlns=http://www.conferences.org, elementFormDefault="qualified">
  <xsd:element name="conf">
    <xsd:complexType>
      <xsd:sequence>
        <xsd:element ref="title" minOccurs="1" maxOccurs= "1"/>
        <xsd:element ref="year" minOccurs="1" maxOccurs= "1"/>
        <xsd:element ref="editor" minOccurs="0" maxOccurs= "unbounded"/>
        <xsd:element ref="paper" minOccurs="1" maxOccurs= "unbounded"/>
      </xsd:sequence>
      <xsd:attribute ref="id" use="required"/>
    </xsd:complexType>
  </xsd:element>
  <xsd:element name="editor">
    <xsd:complexType>
      <xsd:sequence>
        <xsd:element ref="person" minOccurs="1" maxOccurs="unbounded"/>
      </xsd:sequence>
    </xsd:complexType>
  </xsd:element>
  <xsd:element name="paper">
    <xsd:complexType>
      <xsd:sequence>
        <xsd:element ref="title" minOccurs="1" maxOccurs="1"/>
        <xsd:element ref="author" minOccurs="1" maxOccurs="1"/>
        <xsd:element ref="references" minOccurs="0" maxOccurs="unbounded"/>
      </xsd:sequence>
    </xsd:complexType>
  </xsd:element>
  <xsd:element name="author">
    <xsd:complexType>
      <xsd:sequence>
        <xsd:element ref="person" minOccurs="1" maxOccurs="unbounded"/>
      </xsd:sequence>
    </xsd:complexType>
  </xsd:element>
  <xsd:element name="person">
    <xsd:complexType>
      <xsd:sequence>
        <xsd:element ref="name" minOccurs="1" maxOccurs="1"/>
        <xsd:element ref="email" minOccurs="1" maxOccurs="1"/>
      </xsd:sequence>
    </xsd:complexType>
  </xsd:element>
  <xsd:element name="references">
    <xsd:complexType>
      <xsd:sequence>
        <xsd:element ref="paper" minOccurs="1" maxOccurs="unbounded"/>
      </xsd:sequence>
    </xsd:complexType>
  </xsd:element>
  <xsd:attribute name="id" type="xsd:string"/>
  <xsd:element name="title" type="xsd:string"/>
  <xsd:element name="year" type="xsd:string"/>
  <xsd:element name="name" type="xsd:string"/>
  <xsd:element name="email" type="xsd:string"/>
</xsd:schema>
```

*Figure 4. An example of XML document (conf.xml)*

```xml
<?xml version="1.0"?>
<!DOCTYPE conf SYSTEM "conf.dtd">
<conf id="SIAM10">
   <title> SIAM Data Mining Conference</title>
   <year> 2010 </year>
   <editor>
      <person>
         <name>Bing Liu</name>
         <email>b.liu</email>
      </person>
   </editor>
   <paper>
      <title>MACH: Fast Randomized Tensor Decompositions</title>
      <author>
         <person>
            <name>Charalampos E. Tsourakakis</name>
            <email>ctsourak@cs.cmu.edu</email>
         </person>
      </author>
      <references>
         <paper>
            <title>Unsupervised multiway data analysis: A literature survey</title>
            <author>
               <person>
                  <name>Acar E</name>
                  <email>acare@cs.rpi.edu</email>
               </person>
            </author>
         </paper>
      </references>
   </paper>
</conf>
```

*Figure 5. Transactional data model generated from the structure of XML document given in Figure 4.*

| Transaction Id | Tags |
|---|---|
| 1 | conf 1 title 3 year 1 editor 1 person 4 name 2 email 4 paper 2 author 3 reference 1 |

transaction models may not provide accurate results. A simple example to illustrate this problem is given in Figure 6. The fragment *<craft> boat </craft>* appearing in Figure 6(a) and the fragment *<craft> boat building </craft>* appearing in Figure 6(b) show that they both have the same tag; however, the former refers to a *vessel* and the latter to an *occupation*.

Application of a frequent pattern mining technique on this document set would yield *<craft></craft>* as a frequent structure result. However, *<craft></craft>* is not a frequent structure as its parents are different. This is due to the reason that hierarchical relationships are not considered while modelling the XML data as a transactional model.

*Figure 6. (a) XML document A, and (b) XML document B*

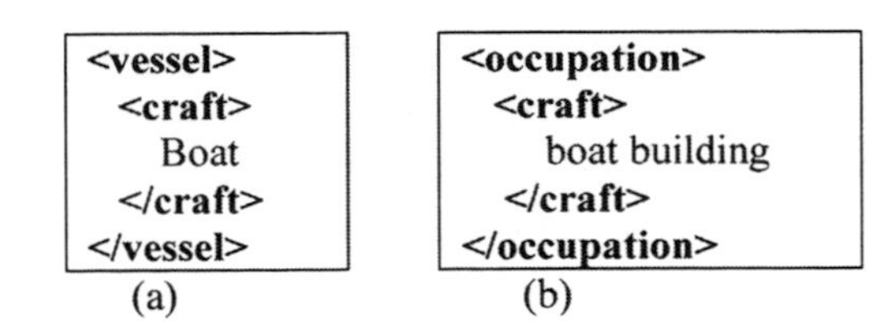

*Figure 7. Transactional data model generated from the content of the XML document given in Figure 4*

| Transaction Id | Content |
|---|---|
| 1 | siam10 1 siam 1 data 1 mineng 1 2010 1 bing 1 liu 1<br>liub 1 mach 1 fast 1 random 1 tensor 1 decomposition 1 charalampos 1 tsourakakis 1 ctsourak 1 cmu 1<br>unsupervised 1 multiwai 1 data 1 analysis 1 literature 1 survei 1 acar 1 acare 1 cs 3 rpi 2 edu 3 yener 2 |

Now let us consider modelling the content of the XML document which is often modelled as transactional data similar to the tag representation. Some of the common pre-processing techniques such as stop-word removal and stemming are applied on the content to identify the unique words that could be represented in TDM. Each unique word in the content of the XML document corresponds to an item and the document is considered as a transaction. An example is illustrated in Figure 7 using the XML document in Figure 4 which shows that the words such as "on", "for", "a", "of" and many others are removed as they are stop words and then the stemmed words are generated. The words do not include the tag names in the XML document; therefore, it is not clear whether the name "bing" refers to an author or an editor of the paper. This may result in imprecise knowledge discovery. Thus, it is essential not only to include the structure hierarchical relationships among the data items but also the content while mining for XML documents.

## Paths

A path is an expression that contains edges in sequential order from the root node labelled $r$ to a node labelled $m$ in an XML document, $(n_r, n_1)$, $(n_1, n_2)$, ..., $(n_{m-1}, n_m)$ where. The length of the path is the number of nodes in the path. A path could be either a partial path or a complete path. A partial path contains the edges in sequential order from the root node to an internal node in the document; a complete path (or unique path) contains the edges in sequential order from the root node to a leaf node. A leaf node is a node that encloses the content or text. Figures 8, (a) and (b) show an example of a complete and a partial path model respectively for the structure of the XML document using its tags. A complete path can have more than one partial path with varying lengths.

As shown in Figure 8(c), paths can be used to model both the structure and the content by considering the leaf node as the text node. However, this kind of model results in repeated paths for different text nodes. For instance, if there is another editor "Malcom Turn" for this conference proceedings, then the path with the text node for this editor will have the same path as that of the editor "Bing Liu" and the only difference will be in the text node. Hence, to reduce the redundancy in the structure and to capture the sibling relationships, XML documents are commonly modelled as trees.

## Trees

Often XML data occurs naturally as trees or can easily be converted into trees using a node-splitting methodology (Anderson, 2000). Figure 9 shows the tree model of the XML document depicted in Figure 4 using only its structure that is obtained by parsing an XML document with a Document Object Model (DOM) parser (Hégaret, Wood, & Robie, 2000).

A tree is denoted as $T = (V, E, f)$, where (1) $V$ is the set of vertices or nodes; (2) $E$ is the set of edges in the tree $T$; and (3) $f$ is a mapping function $f: E \rightarrow V \times V$.

Most of the XML documents are rooted labelled trees where vertices represent tags, edges represent the element-sub-element or element-attribute relationships, and the leaf vertices represent the contents within the tags or instances. Based on

*Figure 8. (a) A complete path, (b) a partial path, and (c) a full path with text node model for our running example*

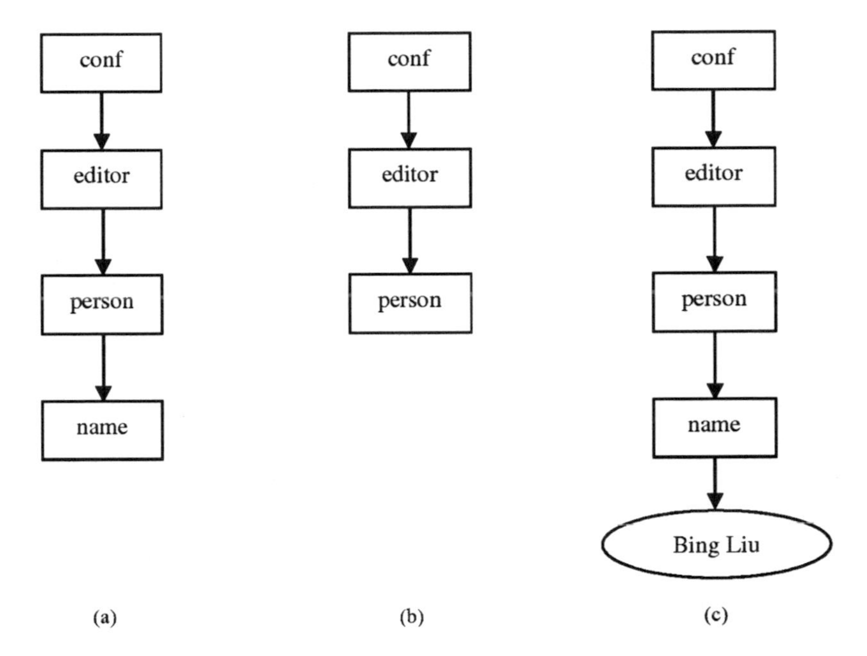


*Figure 9. Tree representation of the XML document shown in Figure 4 using only its structure*

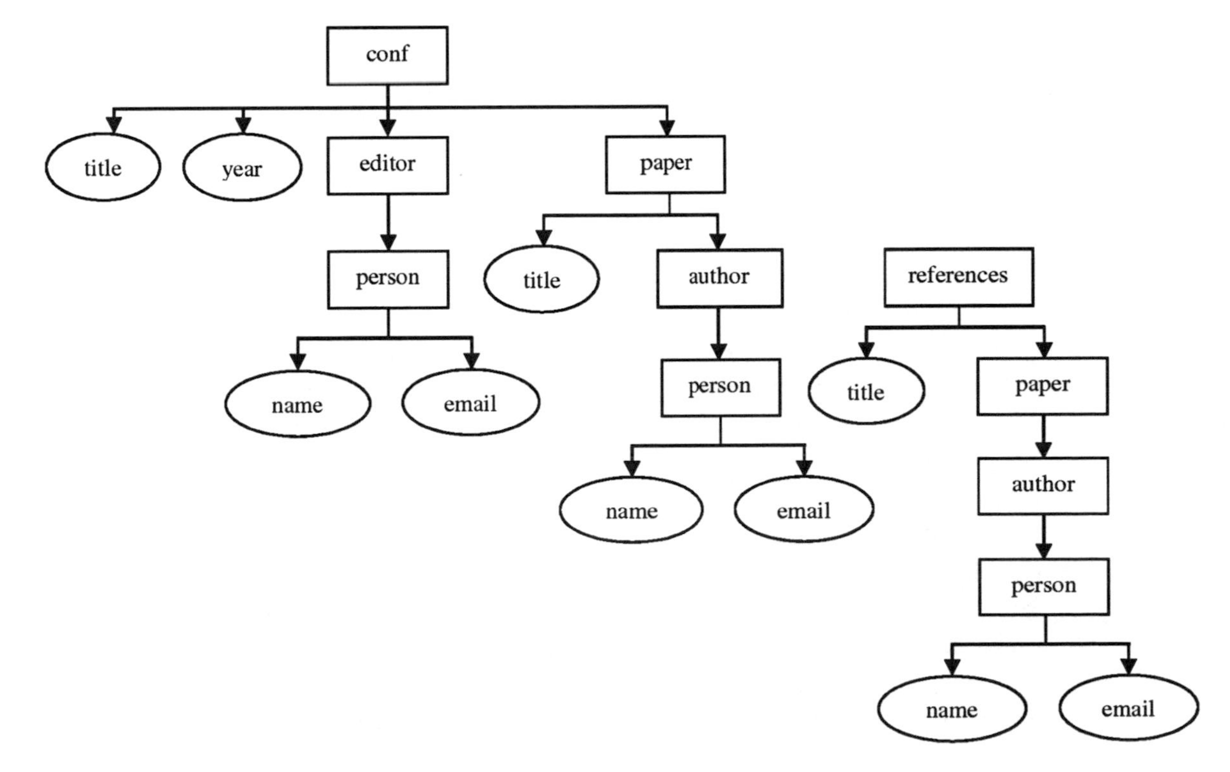

*Figure 10. (a) A rooted tree, (b) a labelled tree, and (c) a directed tree*

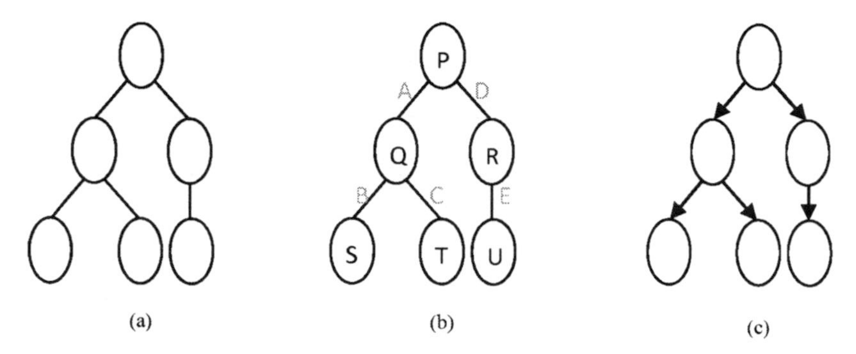


the existence of a root vertex and ordering among the vertices of trees, they are divided into different types.

Some of the common types of trees are free, rooted, labelled tree or unlabelled tree, directed or undirected tree, and connected or disconnected tree. A tree is free if its edges have no direction, i.e., it is an undirected graph. Therefore, the tree has no predefined root. Figure 10 illustrates examples of rooted, labelled and directed trees. A rooted tree has the form $T=(V, v_0, E, f)$, where $v_0$ is the root vertex which does not have any edges entering in it. In the *conf.xml* document, the root vertex is *conf*. The labelled tree in Figure 10(b) can be denoted by $(V, E, f, \Sigma, L)$, since it contains an alphabet $\Sigma$ which represents the vertex (*P*, *Q*, *R*, *S*, *T*, *U*) and edge labels (*A*, *B*, *C*, *D*, *E*) with a labelling function *L* to assign the labels to the vertices and edges. A tree is directed or undirected if it indicates the ordering in which the vertices are connected among each other with the edge labels, or not. If all the vertices are connected with at least one edge then it is a connected graph otherwise unconnected.

Also, there are two canonical representations that could be used for these trees for mining namely *pre-order string encoding* and *level-wise encoding*. The pre-order string and level-wise encoding for the labelled tree in Figure 10 (b) are *PQS$T$$RU$* and *P$QR$STU$* respectively. The $ sign is used to mark the end of the nodes in that level and to indicate backtracking.

A tree model can successfully model an XML document; however, it cannot be used to model the relationships in an XML schema due to the presence of cyclic relationships between the elements in a schema. Hence, the graph models have also been used to represent XML data.

## Graphs

A graph can be defined as a triple $G=(V, E, f)$ where $V$ representing the set of vertices and an edge set $E$ with a mapping function $f: E \rightarrow V \times V$. The vertices are the elements in XML documents and the edge set $E$ corresponds to the links that connect the vertices for representing parent-child relationships.

There are different types of graphs similar to trees except that cycles also need to be considered. A cyclic graph is the one in which the first and last vertices in the path are the same as shown in Figure 11 which has vertices *S* and *U* connected to the first vertex *P*. On the other hand, an acyclic graph is a tree. If all the vertices are connected with at least one edge then it is a connected graph, otherwise unconnected.

Often graph models are used in representing the schema of an XML document rather than the XML document itself due to the presence of cyclic relationships in a schema. The labelled graph representation of the schema as shown in Figure 2 is given in Figure 12. It can be noted from the

*Figure 11. A connected, directed, cyclic, labelled graph*

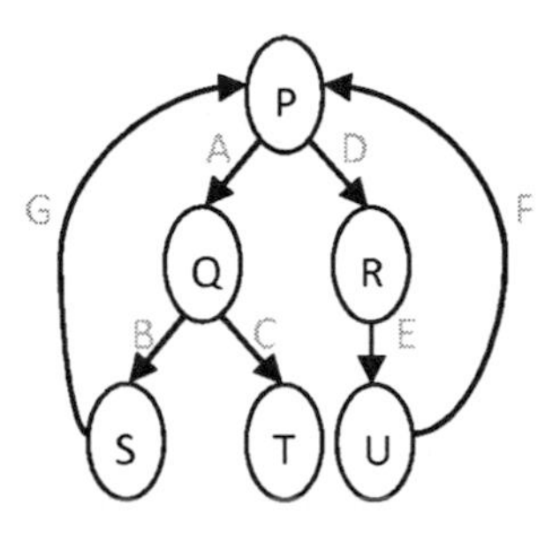


graph representation that there is a cyclic reference to the element paper from the element *reference*.

## Other Models

Apart from the vector, path, tree and graph models mentioned above, there are other types of models such as time-series models (Flesca, Manco, Masciari, Pontieri, Pugliese, 2005) and multi-dimensional models that have been used to model XML documents for mining. In the time-series models, the structure of each XML document is represented as discrete time signal in which numeric values summarise relevant features of the elements enclosed within documents. The Discrete Fourier Transformation Theory (DFTT) is applied to compare the encoded documents which are represented as signals for mining purpose.

Another model which addresses both the structure and the content of the XML documents is BitCube (Yoon, Raghavan, Chakilam, & Kerschberg, 2001). BitCube model was used to cluster and query the XML documents. Paths, words and document ids represent the three dimensions of the BitCube where each entry in the cube presents either the presence or absence of a given word in the path of a given document.

*Figure 12. Graph representation of conf.dtd*

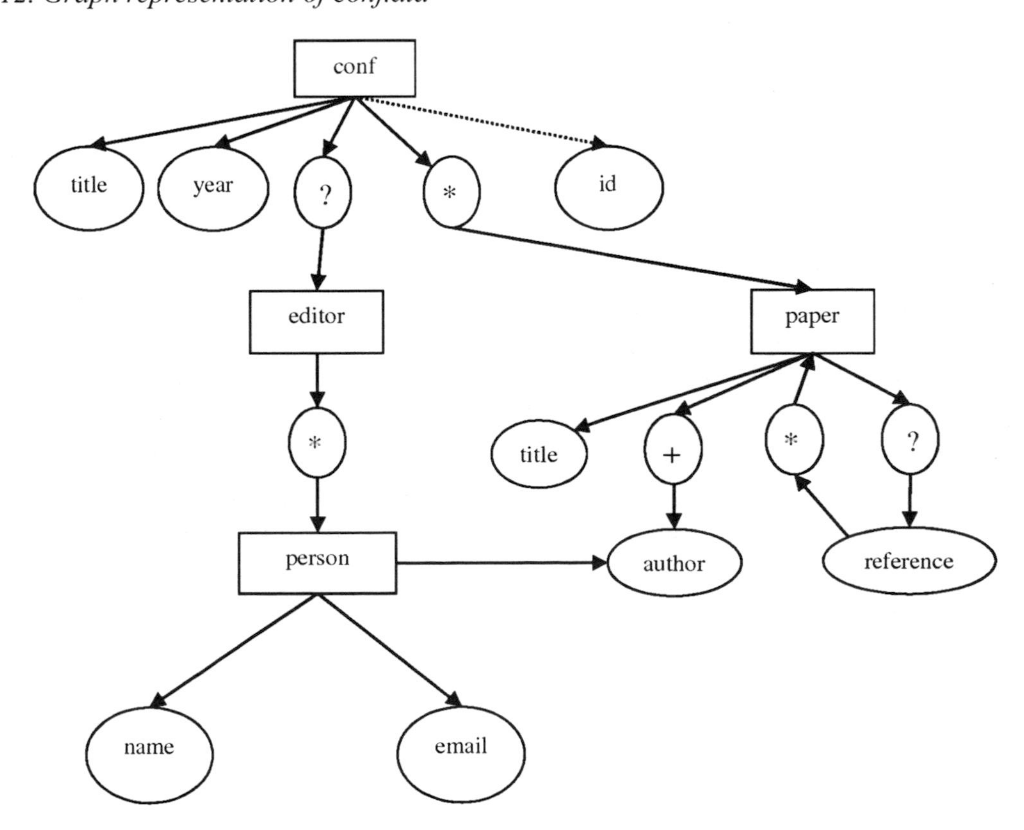

## DATA MINING TASKS USING THE VARIOUS MODELS

There are various types of data mining tasks namely frequent pattern mining, association rule mining, classification and clustering that can be applied to XML data sets using the different types of data models as described in the preceding section. This section details how each of these models could be used for the various data mining tasks.

### Frequent Pattern Mining

XML frequent pattern mining is one of the well-researched area (Paik, Shin, & Kim, 2005; Termier et al., 2005; Win & Hla, 2005; Zhang, Liu, & Zhang, 2004). Frequent pattern mining on XML documents involves mining of structures as well as their content (Nayak, 2005). The element tags and their nesting dictate the *structure* of an XML document (Abiteboul et al., 2000). Identifying frequently occurring structures in the dataset is the essence of XML structure mining. On the other hand, application of frequent pattern mining on the content which is the text enclosed within the tags contributes to content mining.

#### Using Transactional Data Model (TDM)

Inspired by frequent itemset mining, the tags/content are represented in a transactional data format to identify frequent tags/content patterns from XML databases (Gu, Hwang, & Ryu, 2005). As shown in Figures 5 and 7, tags or content of an XML document are modelled as items in a transaction.

A standard frequent pattern mining process can be applied on an XML dataset represented as TDM. The TDM considers the XML dataset as a fixed structured dataset. The process begins with a complete scan of the transactional data to identify 1-length frequent tags/content with a length of 1 and they are tested for support greater than the user-defined support threshold (*min_supp*). Then the 1-length frequent tags/content are combined together to form 2-length candidate tags/content in order to verify whether they are frequent or not. The process of forming *n*-length candidate and frequent tags/content is repeated until there is no more frequent tags/content combinations that could be found. This type of frequent pattern generation is referred to as *generate-and-test* (Agrawal, Mannila, Srikant, Toivonen, & Verkamo, 1996) as the *k*+1-length candidates is *generated* by joining the frequent *k*-length candidates and these candidates are *tested* whether the generated candidates are frequent. However, this technique incurs a huge overhead for dense datasets in which there exist a very large number of candidates, and testing each of them is expensive.

To overcome this disadvantage, a novel approach called pattern-growth as used in FP-growth algorithm (Han, Pei, & Yin, 2000) was proposed which adopts the "divide-and-conquer" heuristic to recursively partition the dataset based on the frequent patterns generated and then it mines them for frequent patterns in each of the partitions. This technique is less expensive as it scans only the projections of the datasets based on the frequent patterns and not the entire dataset. Also, it generates 1-length candidates for frequent patterns only from the projections and hence counting of their support is simple. Despite all the benefits, this type of methods is memory-intensive compared to Apriori-based algorithms due to the need of projections being resided in the memory.

Application of frequent pattern mining on the TDMs for XML documents faces a serious problem as the TDMs ignore the hierarchical relationship between the tags and the content of the XML document in order to represent a transaction.

#### Using Paths

The ability of a path model to capture the hierarchical relationship between the tags has facilitated the use of this model for frequent pattern mining. Often the path model is used to represent only the structure of the XML document. Given a collection of paths extracted from dataset $D$, the problem is to find a partial path $p$ such that $freq(p) \geq min\_supp$, where $freq(p)$ is the percentage of paths in $D$ that contain $p$.

In this data model, every XML document in the dataset is represented as a bag of paths with each path corresponding to an item in transactional data format. Similar to the frequent tag/content pattern mining, the first scan of the dataset is conducted to identify the frequent 1-length path which will be just a node. The frequent 1-length paths are then combined to form candidate 2-length paths. Testing is then carried out to verify how often these candidate paths occur in the dataset; if they occur more than the *min_supp* then the paths are considered as frequent. The difference between the frequent pattern mining using the TDM and the paths is that while checking the support of the paths, the hierarchical structure is also verified against the dataset which is not in the case of TDM.

This technique is much more suitable for partial paths than complete paths as the frequency of complete paths could often be very low and hence there might not be sufficient frequent paths to output. Often there is a large set of partial paths generated especially for lower support thresholds or from dense datasets. To reduce the number of common partial paths, a new threshold called *maximum support threshold* (*max_supp*) has been introduced to avoid the generation of very common partial paths as these very common subpaths do not provide any interesting or new knowledge (Aggarwal, Ta, Wang, Feng, & Zaki, 2007).

## Using Trees

As XML documents are often modelled as trees, several frequent tree mining algorithms have been developed. These frequent tree mining techniques can be divided into two broad categories based on their candidate generation, namely *generate-and-test* and *pattern-growth* technique. The *generate-and-test* generates the candidates and tests for their support. On the other hand, *pattern-growth* generates subtrees by partitioning the dataset based on the frequent subtrees generated in the previous iteration. The former technique requires less memory as the patterns are generated on-the-fly but are not suitable for datasets having high branching factor (more than 100 branches out of a given node). The latter technique is memory intensive, as a result, several algorithms have been developed to efficiently store the dataset and partition it.

In frequent tree mining of XML data, it has been noted that often the entire tree will not be frequent, rather there is a good possibility that parts of the tree would be frequent. The parts of such trees are referred to as subtrees. There are different notions about subtrees and we discuss some of them below.

### Induced Subtree

For a tree $T$ with edge set $E$ and a vertex set $V$, a tree $T'$ with vertex set $V'$, edge set $E'$ is an induced subtree of $T$ if and only if (1) $V' \subseteq V$; (2) $E' \subseteq E$; (3) the labelling of vertices of $V'$ in $T'$ is preserved in $T$; (4) $(v_1,v_2) \in E$, where $v_1$ is the parent of $v_2$ in $T'$ if and only if $v_1$ is the parent of $v_2$ in $T$; and (5) for $v_1$, $v_2 \in V'$, $preorder(v_1) < preorder(v_2)$ in $T'$ if and only if $preorder(v_1) < preorder(v_2)$ in $T$. In other words, an induced subtree $T'$ preserves parent-child relationship among the vertices of the tree $T$ (Kutty, Nayak, & Li, 2007).

### Embedded Subtree

For a tree $T$ with edge set $E$ and a vertex set $V$, a tree $T'$ with vertex set $V'$, edge set $E'$ is an embedded subtree of $T$ if and only if (1) $V' \subseteq V$; (2) $E' \subseteq E$; and (3) the labelling of vertices of $V'$ and $E'$ in $T'$ is preserved in $T$. In simpler terms, an embedded subtree $T'$ is a subtree which preserves ancestor-descendent relationship among the vertices of the tree, $T$. Figure 13 shows the induced and embedded subtrees generated from a tree. As can be seen, Figure 13(b) preserves

*Figure 13. (a) A tree, (b) an induced subtree, and (c) an embedded subtree*

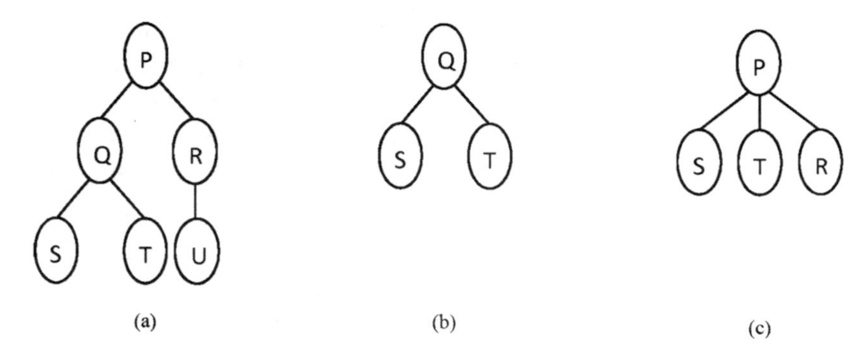


the parent-child relationship, and in Figure 13(c) the ancestor-descendent relationship is preserved (Kutty et al., 2007).

Often, the number of frequent subtrees generated from XML documents is too large and to derive useful and interesting knowledge from these patterns becomes a challenge (Chi, Nijssen, Muntz, & Kok, 2005). In order to control the number of frequent subtrees, two popular concise representations were proposed, namely *closed* and *maximal*. These concise representations not only reduce the redundancy of having all the frequent subtrees but also do not suffer much from information loss due to the reduction.

Given an XML dataset *D* modelled as *T* trees and a user-defined support threshold *min_supp*, a subtree *T'* is said to be closed if there exists no superset of *T'* with the same support as that of *T'*. On the other hand, a subtree, *T'* is said to be maximal if there exists no superset of *T'* which is frequent. They can be formally defined as follows. In a given tree dataset, $D = \{T_1, \ldots, T_n\}$, let there exist two frequent subtrees *T'* and *T"*: (1) *T'* is said to be maximal of *T"* if and only if for every $T' \supseteq T''$, $supp(T') \leq supp(T'')$; and (2) *T'* is closed of *T"* if and only if, for every $T' \supseteq T''$, $supp(T') = supp(T'')$. Based on the definition, it is clear that $M \leq C \leq F$, where *M*, *C*, and *F* denote the number of maximal frequent subtrees, closed frequent subtrees, and frequent subtrees, respectively.

The benefit of generating closed or maximal frequent subtrees is two-fold. Firstly, these concise representations result in a reduced number of subtrees and hence ease the analysis of the subtrees with no information loss. Secondly, a subset of the frequent subtrees is identified and candidates are generated on them, therefore it results in improved performance when compared to mining all the frequent subtrees (Kutty et al., 2007).

According to various trees and subtrees representations, several tree mining algorithms have been developed. Table 1 provides an outline of such algorithms.

The rooted unordered or ordered tree mining algorithms can easily be applied for mining XML documents and the free trees for mining XML Schema or element(s) that exhibit cyclic relationships. Chi (2005) provides an overview of most of these algorithms in detail and an interested reader can refer to it.

## Using Graphs

Frequent graph mining is more commonly applied on XML schema datasets. This type of graph mining can also be applied on the XML dataset in which various documents are linked to each other or a given document has elements having a cyclic relationship. An example of such dataset is INEX (Initiative for Evaluation of XML Retrieval) 2009 Wikipedia dataset[1] with categories having cyclic

*Table 1. Classification of frequent tree mining algorithms for various representations*

| Models | Types | Algorithms |
|---|---|---|
| *Tree representation* | Free Tree | FreeTreeMiner (Chi, Yang, & Muntz, 2003) |
| | Rooted Unordered Tree | uFreqt (Nijssen & Kok, 2003), Unot (Asai, Arimura, Uno, & Nakano, 2003), HybridTreeMiner (Chi, Yang, & Muntz, 2004). |
| | Rooted Ordered Tree | TreeMiner (Zaki, 2005), FREQT (Asai et al., 2002). |
| *Subtree representation* | Induced subtree | FREQT(Asai et al., 2002), uFreqt (Nijssen & Kok, 2003), HybridTreeMiner (Chi, Yang, & Muntz, 2004), Unot (Asai et al., 2003) |
| | Embedded Subtree | TreeMinerV (Zaki, 2005) |
| *Canonical representation* | Pre-order string encoding | TreeMinerV (Zaki, 2005) |
| | Level-wise encoding | HybridTreeMiner (Chi, Yang, & Muntz, 2004) |
| *Concise representations* | Closed | PCITMiner (Kutty et al., 2007), PCETMiner (Kutty, Nayak, & Li, 2009b), CMTreeMiner (Chi, Yang, Xia, & Muntz, 2004) |
| | Maximal | CMTreeMiner, PathJoin (Xiao, Yao, Li, & Dunham, 2003) |

relationships as well as documents are connected via various elements appearing in documents.

The frequent graph mining problem can be defined as follows. Given a graph dataset $D$, find a subgraph $g$ such that $freq(g) \geq min\_supp$ where $freq(g)$ is the percentage of graphs in $D$ that contain $g$. The basic of a graph mining algorithm is checking for *subgraph isomorphism*, i.e., deciding if there is a subgraph of one graph which is *isomorphic* to another graph. Two graphs are isomorphic if there is a one-to-one correspondence between their vertices and there is an edge between two vertices of one graph if and only if there is an edge between the two corresponding vertices in the other graph. Determining a subgraph isomorphism is often considered to be expensive for graphs.

Let us now analyse the cost of frequent subgraphs to understand why graph mining is expensive. There are three types of costs as given below:

$$\text{Cost} \propto \sum_{\propto} \left| D_{\propto} \right| G_{\propto}^{iso}$$

where $\sum_{\propto}$ represents the number of candidates, $D_{\propto}$ represents the data and the $G_{\propto}^{iso}$ indicates the costs in subgraph isomorphism checking (Garey & Johnson, 1979). Due to the presence of cyclic relationships in graphs, the testing of candidate subgraphs is expensive. Due to the huge number of candidate checks required, it takes exponential time to identify frequent subgraphs. This problem becomes computationally expensive for larger graphs with many nodes and for large-sized datasets.

There has been a myriad of frequent graph mining techniques developed. There also exists some improved techniques such as Biased Apriori-based Graph Mining (B-AGM) (Inokuchi, Washio, & Motoda, 2005) and CI-GBI that could provide results in acceptable time period by introducing bias for generating only specific graphs and greedy algorithms respectively. Table 2 presents some of the graph mining algorithms with a focus on the underlying data models.

These techniques can be split upon various factors such as types of graphs, concise representations similar to frequent tree mining techniques. Also, based on the approaches used for solving the subgraph isomorphism, the graph mining algorithms can be classified into Apriori-based Graph Mining (AGM) and Graph Based Induction (GBI) (Matoda, 2007). AGM family searches for all possible spaces efficiently devising a good data structure using an adjacency matrix with

*Table 2. Frequent graph mining algorithms*

| Models | Types | Algorithms |
|---|---|---|
| *Type of Graphs* | Unconnected graphs | UGM (Unconnected Graph Mining) (Skonieczny, 2009) |
| | Connected graphs | FSG (Deshpande, Kuramochi, & Karypis, 2003), AcGM (Apriori-based connected Graph Mining algorithm) (Inokuchi, Washio, Nishimura, & Motoda, 2002), MFC (Maximal Frequent Connected Graphs) |
| *Concise representations* | Maximal and Closed graphs | CloseGraph (Xifeng & Jiawei, 2003) MFC (Maximal Frequent Connected Graphs) MARGIN (Thomas, Valluri, & Karlapalem, 2006) SPIN (Jun et al., 2004) |
| *Approaches* | AGM | AcGM (Apriori-based connected Graph Mining algorithm) (Inokuchi, Washio, Nishimura, & Motoda, 2002), B-AGM (Inokuchi et al., 2005) |
| | GBI | CI-GBI (Nguyen, Ohara, Motoda, & Washio, 2005), DT-GBI (Geamsakul et al., 2004) |

appropriate indexing. On the contrary, GBI avoids exhaustive search using a greedy algorithm which recursively chunks two adjoining nodes, thus generating fairly large subgraphs at an early stage of search.

In the same line as frequent tree mining, frequent graph mining techniques also employ concise representations such as closed and maximal graph patterns in order to reduce the size of generated frequent graph patterns. Closed frequent graph utilizes the heuristic that a frequent graph *G* is closed if there exists no supergraph of *G* that contains the same support as that of *G*. A frequent graph *G* is said to be maximal if there exists no supergraph of *G* that is frequent. The CloseGraph (Xifeng & Jiawei, 2003) method employs a pattern-growth approach and terminates the growth of *G* which is a subgraph of *G* if in any part of graphs in the dataset where *G* occurs, *G'* also occurs as the supergraphs of *G* will be included by *G'*.

In spite of the advances in graph-mining algorithms, these methods have often been criticized due to the difficulty in interpreting the results because of the existence of a massive number of patterns. Due to the large pattern set, it will lead to more knowledge, hence perplexing users in utilising the knowledge for further discovery such as clustering, classification, and indexing (Chen, Lin, Yan, & Han, 2008).

### Association Rule Mining

Association rule mining for XML documents derives its main motivation from market-basket analysis. The two steps in determining association rules are:

1. Finding frequent pattern based on *min_supp*
2. Using these frequent patterns and applying the user defined minimum confidence (*min_conf*) constraint to form rules.

We have discussed the process and algorithms of frequent pattern mining using *min_supp* in the previous section. We will now discuss about the second step. The support values for the frequent patterns are stored and then their confidence (*conf*) values are calculated with the following equation $conf = supp(X \cup Y) / supp(X)$, where $X$ and $Y$ denote items or structures in the dataset according to which data model is used in the process of frequent mining. If the *conf* value is greater than *min_conf* then $X \Rightarrow Y$, which implies that for a given document, if $X$ items/structures occur then it is likely that $Y$ items/structures also occur.

### Using Transactional Data Model

Researchers have predominantly used TDM for association rule mining, with some exceptions. Association rule mining for XML documents was initially proposed by Braga, Campi, Ceri, Klemettinen, and Lanzi (2002) using the XMINE rule operator to extract association rules from XML documents in a SQL-like format. The XML tags are mapped to a TDM then association rules are extracted. Wan and Dobbie (2004) used XQuery expressions to extract association rules from XML data.

This technique has its limitations in the sense that it does not take into account the structure of XML data. For more complex XML data, transformations may be required before applying the XQuery expressions, though this type of mapping XML tags to TDM enables to represent the data easily and allows for efficient management and analysis of the data. Nevertheless, this model ignores the hierarchical structure while generating frequent patterns and hence could result in poor accuracy or incorrect results, as identified in the "craft" example provided in Figure 6.

### Using Trees

Approaches using trees for association rule mining used either the fragments of XML documents or tree summaries. Association rules based on fragments have implications of the form $X \Rightarrow Y$, where $X$ and $Y$ are fragments of XML documents given $X$ and $Y$ is disjoint. The tree summarisation of XML documents can be used in either graph-based summarised patterns or used frequent subtrees of the XML tree model (Mazuran, Quintarelli, & Tanca, 2009).

## Clustering

Clustering is a process for grouping unknown data into smaller groups having some commonalities (Jain & Dubes, 1988). The generic clustering process involves three stages. The first stage is data modelling. This stage is to represent the input data using a common data model that can capture the semantic or/and structure information inherent in the input data. The second stage is similarity computation, which is to determine the most appropriate measure to compute the similarity between the models of two documents. The final stage is to choose an algorithm to group the input data into clusters.

XML clustering is useful for many applications such as data warehouse, information retrieval, data/schema integration and many more. The clustering process of XML documents can be performed on its content, its structure or on both the content and the structure. The following sections present some of the recent XML clustering approaches in relation to the various data models explained earlier.

### Using Transactional Data Model or Vector Space Model

In clustering, the TDM is often referred to as Vector Space Model (VSM) (Salton, 1975). VSM is a model for representing text documents or any objects as vectors of identifiers, for example, terms. When using the VSM model for XML clustering, feature of the document content is a set of terms, and the feature of the document structure is a set of substructure such as tags, paths, subtrees, or subgraphs.

There exist various techniques to compute the weights of features in VSM. The most popular one is the *term frequency-inverse document frequency* (*tf-idf*) weighting. The key intuition is that the more frequent a feature (term) in a particular document, and the less common a feature in the document collection, the higher its weight. This weighting prevents a bias toward longer documents and gives a measure of the importance of a feature $f_i$ within a particular document $d_j$. Given a collection $D$ of documents, the weight vector for any document $d_j \in D$ is defined as:

$$tf\text{-}idf(f_i, d_j) = tf_{i,j} \log \frac{|D|}{|\{d : f_i \in d\}|}$$

Above, $tf_{i,j}$ is called term-frequency of the feature $f_i$ in the document $d_j$, and denotes the number of occurrences of $f_i$ in $d_j$. The logarithmic term is called inverse-document-frequency, with the numerator denoting the number of documents in the collection and the denominator denoting the number of documents in which the feature $f_i$ appears (at least once). For an XML dataset, the feature $f_i$ is either referred to a content feature or a substructure feature of the XML documents.

Another popular weighting scheme is Okapi BM-25 which works on utilising similar concepts as that of *tf-idf* but has two tuning parameters, namely $k_1$ and $b$, which influence the effect of feature frequency and document length, respectively. The default values are $k_1 = 2$ and $b = 0.75$. The BM-25 weighting depends on three factors:

- the Collection Frequency Weight (*CFW*), which is defined for the feature *f* as:

$$CFW = \log(|D| - \log(|D: f \in D|))$$

- the feature frequency $ff_f$ (i.e., the term-frequency as in the *tf-idf* function)
- the Normalized Document Length (*NDL*), which is defined for the given document *d* as:

$$NDL(d) = DL(d) / \text{avg}(DL(D))$$

where $DL(d)$ is the length of the document (in words) and avg($DL(D)$) denotes the average document length in the collection.

BM25 weighting for a given feature *f* is given by the following formula:

$$B_f = \frac{CFW\ ff_f\ (k_1 + 1)}{k_1\ ((1 - b) + (b\ NDL(d))) + ff_f}$$

In the VSM representation, the matrix cell value is the weight of the feature if the feature is present in the document. The cell value is zero if a document does not contain the feature. There are two VSM representations for representing the data distribution, dense and sparse. The sparse VSM representation retains only the non-zero values along with the feature id. This improves the efficiency in computation especially for sparse datasets where the number of non-zeroes is less compared to the number of zeroes. Figure 14 gives examples of a dense and a sparse representation using only the frequency of the feature. It can be seen that the size of the sparse representation is smaller than the dense representation. Clustering using the sparse representation is more efficient when the number of zeroes is more; however, if there is more number of non-zeroes then the sparse representation could incur in additional overhead as the feature indices are also stored.

The VSM model is commonly used by XML clustering methods that focus on content features (Salton & McGill, 1986). Some attempts (Tran, Nayak, & Bruza, 2008; Yang & Chen, 2002) have

*Figure 14. An example of (a) dense and (b) sparse representation of an XML dataset modelled in VSM using feature frequencies*

| | $f_1$ | $f_2$ | $f_3$ | $f_4$ | $f_5$ | $f_6$ |
|---|---|---|---|---|---|---|
| $d_1$ | 1 | 0 | 0 | 2 | 6 | 0 |
| $d_2$ | 3 | 1 | 0 | 2 | 0 | 0 |
| $d_3$ | 1 | 7 | 3 | 2 | 1 | 1 |

(a)

| | |
|---|---|
| $d_1$ | **1 1 4 2 5 6** |
| $d_2$ | **1 3 2 1 4 2** |
| $d_3$ | **1 1 2 7 3 3 4 2 5 1 6 1** |

(b)

been made to model and mine both the content and the structure of XML documents for the clustering tasks. Tran et al. approach (2008) models the structure and the content of XML document in different VSM models. Structure similarity and content similarity is calculated independently for each pair of documents and then these two similarity components are combined using a weighted linear combination approach to determine a single similarity score between documents. Another representation which can link the content and the structure together is the Structured Link Vector Model (SLVM) (Yang & Chen, 2002) that represents both the structure and the content information of XML documents using vector linking. For instance in the SLVM model, given an XML document $d$, it is defined as a matrix $d \in R^{n \times m}$ such that $d = [d(1), \ldots, d(m)]$, where $m$ is the number of elements, $d(i) \in R^n$ is the *tf-idf* feature vector representing the element $e_i$, given as $d(i) = tf(t_j, d, e_i)\ idf(t_j)$ (for all $j$=1 to $n$), where $tf(t_j, d, e_i)$ is the frequency of the term $t_j$ in the element $e_i$ of $d$.

## Using Paths

The path model represents the document's structure as a collection of paths. A clustering method using this path model measures the similarity between XML documents by finding the common paths (Nayak, 2008; Nayak & Iryadi, 2006). One of the common techniques for identifying the common paths is to apply frequent pattern mining on the collection of paths to extract the frequent paths of a constrained length and using these frequent paths as representatives for the cluster. This technique has been utilised by Hwang and Ryu (2005) and XProj (Aggarwal et al., 2007).

Another simple method of finding XML data similarity according to common paths is by treating the paths as feature for VSM model (Doucet & Ahonen-Myka, 2002; Yao & Zerida, 2007). Other approaches such as XSDCluster (Nayak & Xia, 2004), PCXSS (Nayak & Tran, 2007) and XClust (Lee, Yang, Hsu, & Yang, 2002) adopt the concept of schema matching for finding the similarity between paths. The path similarity is obtained by considering the semantic and structure similarity of a pair of elements appearing in two paths. The path measures in these approaches are computationally expensive as it considers many attributes of the elements such as data type and their constraints.

The above described methods usually ignore the content that the nodes in the path may contain. Some researchers have made attempt to include the text along with the path representation in order to cluster XML documents using both structure and content features. However, such methods are computationally expensive due to the presence of repeated paths for various text nodes. Previous works by Vercoustre, Fegas, Gul, and Lechevallier (2005) and Yao & Zerida (2007) have shown that this type of data representation and clustering technique is not effective for paths with lengths greater than 3. In this model, the increase in the length imposes strict restriction and often results in poor accuracy. Another approach that combines the structure and the content is that using the Boolean representation model of BitCube; here, the XML document collection is first partitioned using the top down approach into small bitcubes based on the paths and then the smaller bitcubes are clustered using the bit-wise distance and their popularity measures.

## Using Trees

This is one of the well-established fields of XML clustering methods. Several approaches modelling the XML data as trees have been developed to determine XML data similarity. The reputed methods of tree edit distance are extended to compute the similarity between the XML documents.

The tree edit distance is based on dynamic programming techniques for string-to-string correction problem (Wagner & Fischer, 1974). The tree edit distance essentially involves three edit operations for the trees involved namely changing, deleting, and inserting a vertex to transform one tree into another tree. The tree edit distance between two trees is the minimum cost between the costs of all possible tree edit sequences based on a cost model. The basic intuition behind this technique is that the XML documents with the minimum distance are likely to be similar and hence they can be clustered together. Some of the clustering techniques that use the tree-edit distance are Dalamagas, Cheng, Winkel, and Sellis (2006) and Nierman and Jagadish (2002).

Besides mining the structure similarity of the whole tree, other techniques have also been developed to mine the frequent pattern in subtrees from a collection of trees (Termier et al., 2005; Zaki, 2005). Termier et al. (2005) approach consists of two steps; first it clusters the trees based on the occurrence of the same pairs of labels in the ancestor relation using the Apriori algorithm. After the trees are clustered, a maximal common tree is computed to measure the commonality of each cluster to all the trees.

To avoid modifying the tree structure as in tree edit distance methods, other clustering techniques involve breaking the paths of tree-structured data into a collection of macro-path sequences where each macro-path contains a tag name, its attribute, data types and content. A matrix similarity of XML documents is then generated based on the macro-path similarity technique. Clustering of XML documents is then performed based on the similarity matrix with the support of approximate tree inclusion and isomorphic tree similarity (Shen & Wang, 2003). Many other approaches have also utilised the idea of tree similarity for XML document change detection (DeWitt & Cai, 2003) and for extracting the schema information from an XML document such as those proposed in Garofalakis, Gionis, Rastogi, Seshadri, and Shim (2000) and Moh, Lim, and Ng (2000).

Majority of these methods focuses on clustering the XML documents by identifying structure similarity between them. However, as pointed out earlier in the chapter, for some datasets it becomes essential to include both the structure and the content similarity for identifying clusters. Recently, some researchers have focused on combining content and structure for the clustering process (Kutty, Nayak, & Li, 2009a; Tagarelli & Greco, 2010). The SemXClust method (Tagarelli & Greco, 2010) represents XML documents into a collection of tree tuples with the structure and the content features enriched by the support of an ontology knowledge base to create a set of semantically cohesive and smaller-sized documents. These tree tuples are then modelled as transactions and transactional clustering algorithms are then applied. The HCX method (Kutty et al., 2009a) includes both the structure and the content information of XML documents in producing clusters in order to improve the accuracy and meaning of the clustering solution. HCX first determines the structure similarity in the form of frequent subtrees as a constraint and then uses these frequent subtrees to represent the content of the XML documents. In other words, the content included in the nodes of frequent tree is only used in clustering process and hence it is a constrained content. By using only the constrained content corresponding to the frequent subtrees results, it not only combines the structure and the content effectively but also reduces the huge overhead of the combination.

## Using Graphs

The clustering algorithms on graph data can be categorised into two types: node clustering and graph clustering. Flake, Tsioutsiouliklis, and Tarjan (2002) and Aggarwal and Wang (2010) give a good overview of graph clustering algorithms. The node clustering algorithms attempt to group the underlying nodes with the use of a distance (or similarity) value on the edges. In this case, the edges of the graph are labelled with a numerical distance values. These numerical distance values are used to create clusters of nodes. On the other hand, the graph clustering algorithms use the underlying structure as a whole and calculate the similarity between two different graphs. This task is more challenging than the node clustering tasks because of the need to match the structures of the underlying graphs, and then use these structures for clustering purposes.

A popular graph clustering algorithm for XML document is S-GRACE (Lian, Cheung, Mamoulis, & Siu-Ming, 2004) which computes the distance between two graphs by measuring the common set of nodes and edges. It first scans the XML documents and computes their s-graphs. S-graph of two documents is the sets of common nodes and edges. The s-graphs of all documents are then stored in a structure table called SG, which contains two fields of information: a bit string representing the edges of an s-graph and the ids of all the documents whose s-graphs are represented by this bit string. Once the SG is constructed, clustering can be performed on the bit strings. S-GRACE is a hierarchical clustering algorithm that uses the ROCK method (Guha, Rastogi, & Shim, 1999) to exploit the link (common neighbours) between s-graphs to select the best pair of clusters to be merged in the hierarchical merging process.

## Classification

The concept of classification on XML documents was first introduced by XRules (Zaki & Aggarwal, 2003). Though there had not been many techniques developed for XML classification rules since the initial work, the classification data mining challenge (Nayak, De Vries, Kutty, Geva, Denoyer, & Gallinari, 2010) in the INEX forum has attracted a great deal of interest among researchers in extending the supervised machine learning techniques for XML documents classification. Let us now look at how different models were used for the XML classification task.

### Using Transactional Data Model or Vector Space Model

As the XML documents are often considered as text documents, they could be represented in a VSM and standard mining methods for classification tasks may well be applied. A simple and the most commonly used method is the nearest neighbour method that could be applied for small number of class labels. However, in many cases, the classification behaviour of the XML document is hidden in the structure information available inside the document. In these situations, classifiers using IR based representations are likely to be ineffective for XML documents.

A recent technique attempted to represent the XML documents is SLVM which includes not only the content but also the structure (Yang & Wang, 2010). The frequent structure of the XML documents is captured and their content is represented in this model similar to the ideas of HCX (Kutty et al., 2009a) in clustering.

### Using Paths

To our best knowledge, we have not come across any XML classification method that utilised paths models in its representation.

### Using Trees

XRules (Zaki & Aggarwal, 2003) classifier utilises a rule based classification of XML data by using frequent discriminatory subtrees within the XML documents collection. Some of the other approaches that utilise the tree structures for not only modelling the structure but also to the content for the purpose of classification utilise the concept of tree-edit distance to compute the minimal cost involved in changing a source tree to a destination tree. The cost information is then provided to a *k*-NN classifier to classify the XML documents based on the structure and the content (Bouchachia & Hassler, 2007). Also, the concise frequent subtrees have been be used to combine the structure and the content of XML documents in reduced search space for classification (Yang & Chen, 2002).

### Using Graphs

Graphs models have been used to model the XML documents that have links amongst them and then generate the classifications (Chidlovskii, 2010; Tsoi, Hagenbuchner, Chau, & Lee, 2009). The links between the documents were captured using graph structures. By doing so, not only content analysis but also link mining could be performed to improve the accuracy of the classification.

## CURRENT ISSUES AND CHALLENGES IN MODELLING XML DOCUMENTS FOR MINING

Some of the current issues and challenges in XML mining for the various models are:

1. How to effectively model both the structure and content features for mining XML documents? Though there have been several attempts to combine the structure and the content features for mining XML documents, it often resulted in decreased quality of mining results. For instance, the BitCube model was used to cluster and query the XML documents. However, this approach suffers from the typical disadvantages inherent in Boolean representation models, such as the lack of partial matching criteria and natural measures of document ranking. Also, it was evident from the experimental results that it is an expensive task to project a document into small bitcubes based on their paths and, hence, the application of this type of approach to large datasets containing about thousands of documents is questionable. This calls for a multi-dimensional representation of XML documents using not all the content features but more significant content features. Defining what is significant is a critical problem.
2. How to combine the structure and content features, in these different types of models which do not affect the scalability of the mining process? Not only the effectiveness of combining the features of structure and content is important but also the impact of this combination on the scalability of the mining process is also an issue. For example, BitCube can capture the relationship between the structure and the content however it is expensive in terms of memory usage. Another example is the CRP and 4RP approach by Yao and Zerida (2007) with VSM model using path representation. Each path contains the edges in sequential order from a node *i* to a term in the data content. This approach creates a large number of features, for instance, if there are 5 distinct terms in a document, and 5 of these distinct terms are in two different paths then there will be 10 different features altogether. Techniques like random indexing (Achlioptas & Mcsherry, 2007) can be used to reduce the large number of features.
3. How to integrate background knowledge into the model for mining – using high utility data for mining? In the presence of very large number of XML documents, data models and mining techniques, it is now essential to mine patterns which are of much use and can be referred to as "high utility patterns". To create high utility patterns background knowledge should be included in mining process. SemXClust (Tagarelli & Greco, 2010) utilises WordNet ontology to derive semantically rich and smaller XML documents for the purpose of clustering. WordNet could be used for enriching the tags as in YAWN (Schenkel, Suchanek, & Kasneci, 2007). These enriched tags could

be used while modelling XML documents to assist in providing these high utility patterns. Also, ontologies could be incorporated into the mining models to provide more useful and interesting results.

4. How to capture the semantic relationships using the models? Due to the flexibility of the XML language, XML users can define their own schema definitions. Therefore, the document heterogeneity does not lie in the content but also in the element tag's name. To address this problem, approaches such as XSDCluster (Nayak & Xia, 2004), PCXSS (Nayak & Tran, 2007) and XClust (Lee et al., 2002) use external resources such as WordNet (Fellbaum, 1998) to find the semantic meaning between element tag names for finding common paths. To find the semantic between element tag names, many research have been made in the area of schema matching (Madhavan, Bernstein, & Rahm, 2001). Other techniques such as the Latent Semantic Kernel (LSK) (Cristianini, Shawe-Taylor, & Lodhi, 2002) which is based on LSI can construct a "semantic" space wherein terms and documents that are closely associated are placed near one another, which reflects major associative patterns in the data and ignores less important patterns. The advantage of finding semantic relationships is that it allows the mining process to be more accurate; however, it is the trade-off between the accuracy and the scalability as many features are considered in the mining process.

## FUTURE MODELS OF XML DOCUMENTS AND THEIR OPPORTUNITIES

The forthcoming models can utilise the relationship within the content of the XML documents represented in a TDM. To model the sequential relationship within the content of XML documents, the terms in the document can be combined to form bigrams, trigrams and *n*-grams. For the *conf.xml* some of the bigrams are "international conference", "conference data", "data mining" that could be represented in TDM.

TDM can also be used as a simple model to represent the link relationship between XML documents. For instance, if there are two Wikipedia documents which discuss about the same subject they may have links between them. There are two types of links: inbound link and outbound link: an inbound link is a link coming into a given Wikipedia document from another Wikipedia document, whereas an outbound is a link going out of the given Wikipedia document. When the documents are represented in a pair-wise matrix, then the presence of a link between two documents can be indicated using a non-zero value. Figure 16 shows the transactional data model for the links in the sample Wikipedia documents given in Figure 15.

Consider the three Wikipedia documents in Figure 15, which contain outbound and inbound links. These links are used to build the link-based transactional data model. For every document in the document corpus, if there is an outbound link from document $d_i$ to document $d_j$, the cell value of $(i, j)$ is entered as 1 and if there is an inbound link from $d_i$ to $d_j$, the cell value of $(j, i)$ is entered as 1.

The TDM could easily store these links without much preprocessing efforts, especially for smaller datasets. However, it should be noted that when the number of documents is very large as in many real-life datasets, the transactional data model will be of size $n^2$ where $n$ is the number of documents. Hence, it is essential to have efficient structures which could reduce the redundancy in situations when the number of links between documents is sparse.

Also, the future models of XML documents should include multiple features regarding structure and content. Also, with the increasing number

*Figure 15. Examples of Wikipedia XML documents with links: (from top to bottom, and left to right) 1.xml, 2.xml, and 3.xml files*

```
<article xmlns:xlink="http://www.w3.org/1999/xlink">
  <header>
    <categories>
      <category>Nigerian dramatists and playwrights
      </category>
    </categories>
  </header>
  <bdy>
    <b>Sam Ukala</b> is a
    <link xlink:type="simple"  xlink:href="4.xml">Nigerian
    </link>
        playwright, poet.
    <location wordnetid="100027167" confidence="0.8">
      <link xlink:type="simple" xlink:href="2.xml">
        Edo State
      </link>
    </location>
  </bdy>
</article>
```

```
<article xmlns:xlink="http://www.w3.org/1999/xlink">
  <header>
    <title>Edo State</title>
    <categories>
      <category>States of Nigeria</category>
    <categories>
  </header>
  <bdy>
    <country>
      <link xlink:type="simple"  xlink:href="4.xml">
        Nigeria
      </link>.
        Also known as
      <link xlink:type="simple"  xlink:href="3.xml">
        Nigeria
      </link>.
    </country>
  </bdy>
</article>
```

```
<article xmlns:xlink="http://www.w3.org/1999/xlink">
  <header>
    <title>List of Nigerian States nicknames</title>
    <categories>
      <category>States of Nigeria</category>
    <categories>
  </header>
  <bdy>
    Listing of
  <country wordnetid="108544813" confidence="0.9508927676800064">
    <link xlink:type="simple" xlink:href="4.xml">Nigeria
    </link>locations
  </country>nicknames.
  <country wordnetid="108544813" confidence="0.8">
    <location wordnetid="100027167" confidence="0.8">
      <link xlink:type="simple" xlink:href="2.xml">Edo State</link>
    </location>
  </country>
     Heart Beat of Nigeria
  </bdy>
</article>
```

of XML documents, the future models should include the link also as one of its dimensions. Initial work by BitCube representation using the paths used only the binary representation of the feature corresponding to its path. However, it used all the paths and hence might incur in heavy computational complexity. It is essential to identify the common subtrees similar to the work by

*Figure 16. Link-based transactional data model built using the sample Wikipedia XML documents given in Figure 15*

| | 1.xml | 2.xml | 3.xml |
|---|---|---|---|
| 1.xml | 1 | 1 | 0 |
| 2.xml | 0 | 1 | 1 |
| 3.xml | 0 | 1 | 1 |

XProj (Aggarwal et al., 2007) and HCX (Kutty et al., 2009a) to reduce the number of subtrees for clustering.

One of the common multi-dimensional models is the *tensor space model* which has been successfully used to model in signal processing (Damien & Salah, 2007), web mining (Mirzal, 2009) and many other fields. By modelling XML documents in a tensor space model, multi-way data analysis could be conducted to study the interaction between the features of the XML documents.

## CONCLUSION

With the growing importance of XML documents as a means to represent data, there has been extensive effort on devising new technologies to process, query, transform and integrate various XML documents. Our focus on this chapter has been to overview the various models that has been used for XML mining in order to accomplish various XML data applications. In spite of the abundance of the models for XML mining, the unprecedented growth in the size of XML data has resulted in several challenges for the XML data modelling and mining techniques that are yet to be addressed by future researches.

## REFERENCES

Abiteboul, S., Buneman, P., & Suciu, D. (2000). *Data on the Web: From relations to semistructured data and XML*. San Francisco, CA: Morgan Kaufmann Publishers.

Aggarwal, C. C., Ta, N., Wang, J., Feng, J., & Zaki, M. J. (2007). XProj: A framework for projected structural clustering of XML documents. In P. Berkhin, R. Caruana, & X. Wu (Eds.), *Proceedings of the 13th ACM SIGKDD International Conference on Knowledge Discovery and Data Mining (KDD),* (pp. 46-55). ACM.

Aggarwal, C. C., & Wang, H. (2010). Graph data management and mining: A survey of algorithms and applications. In Aggarwal, C. C., & Wang, H. (Eds.), *Managing and mining graph data* (pp. 13–68). London, UK: Kluwer Academic Publishers. doi:10.1007/978-1-4419-6045-0_2

Agrawal, R., Mannila, H., Srikant, R., Toivonen, H., & Verkamo, A. I. (1996). Fast discovery of association rules. In Fayyad, U. M., Piatetsky-Shapiro, G., Smyth, P., & Uthurusamy, R. (Eds.), *Advances in knowledge discovery and data mining* (pp. 307–328). Menlo Park, CA: American Association for Artificial Intelligence.

Anderson, R. (2000). *Professional XML*. Birmingham, UK: Wrox Press Ltd.

Asai, T., Abe, K., Kawasoe, S., Arimura, H., Sakamoto, H., & Arikawa, S. (2002). Efficient substructure discovery from large semi-structured data. In R. L. Grossman, J. Han, V. Kumar, H. Mannila, & R. Motwani (Eds.), *Proceedings of the Second SIAM International Conference on Data Mining*. SIAM.

Asai, T., Arimura, H., Uno, T., & Nakano, S. (2003). Discovering frequent substructures in large unordered trees. In G. Grieser, Y. Tanaka, and A. Yamamoto (Eds.), *Lecture Notes in Computer Science: Vol. 2843, Discovery Science, 6th International Conference,* (pp. 47-61). Springer.

Bouchachia, A., & Marcus, H. (2007). Classification of XML documents. In *Proceedings of the IEEE Symposium on Computational Intelligence and Data Mining, part of the IEEE Symposium Series on Computational Intelligence (CIDM)*, (pp. 390-396). IEEE.

Braga, D., Campi, A., Ceri, S., Klemettinen, M., & Lanzi, P. L. (2002). A tool for extracting XML association rules.In *Proceedings of the 14th IEEE International Conference on Tools with Artificial Intelligence (ICTAI),* (p. 57). IEEE Computer Society.

Chen, C., Lin, C. X., Yan, X., & Han, J. (2008). On effective presentation of graph patterns: A structural representative approach. In J. G. Shanahan, S. Amer-Yahia, I. Manolescu, Y. Zhang, D. A. Evans, A. Kolcz, K.-S. Choi, & A. Chowdhury (Eds.), *Proceedings of the 17th ACM Conference on Information and Knowledge Management (CIKM),* (pp. 299-308). ACM.

Chi, Y., Nijssen, S., Muntz, R. R., & Kok, J. N. (2005). Frequent subtree mining - An overview. *Fundamenta Informaticae, 66*(1-2), 161–198.

Chi, Y., Yang, Y., & Muntz, R. R. (2003). Indexing and mining free trees. In *Proceedings of the 3rd IEEE International Conference on Data Mining (ICDM),* (pp. 509-512). IEEE Computer Society.

Chi, Y., Yang, Y., & Muntz, R. R. (2004). HybridTreeMiner: An efficient algorithm for mining frequent rooted trees and free trees using canonical forms. In *Proceedings of the 16th International Conference on Scientific and Statistical Database Management (SSDBM),* (pp. 11-20). IEEE Computer Society.

Chi, Y., Yang, Y., Xia, Y., & Muntz, R. R. (2004). CMTreeMiner: Mining both closed and maximal frequent subtrees. In H. Dai, R. Srikant, & C. Zhang (Eds.), *Advances in Knowledge Discovery and Data Mining, 8th Pacific-Asia Conference (PAKDD), Lecture Notes in Computer Science: Vol. 3056* (pp. 63-73). Springer.

Chidlovskii, B. (2010). Multi-label Wikipedia classification with textual and link features. In S. Geva, J. Kamps & A. Trotman (Eds.), *Focused Retrieval and Evaluation, 8th International Workshop of the Initiative for the Evaluation of XML Retrieval (INEX): Vol. 6203. Lecture Notes in Computer Science* (pp. 387-396). Springer.

Cristianini, N., Shawe-Taylor, J., & Lodhi, H. (2002). Latent semantic kernels. *Journal of Intelligent Information Systems, 18*(2-3), 127–152. doi:10.1023/A:1013625426931

Dalamagas, T., Cheng, T., Winkel, K.-J., & Sellis, T. (2006). A methodology for clustering XML documents by structure. *Information Systems, 31*(3), 187–228. doi:10.1016/j.is.2004.11.009

Damien, M., & Salah, B. (2007). Survey on tensor signal algebraic filtering. *Signal Processing, 87*(2), 237–249. doi:10.1016/j.sigpro.2005.12.016

Deshpande, M., Kuramochi, M., & Karypis, G. (2003). Frequent sub-structure-based approaches for classifying chemical compounds. In *Proceedings of the 3rd IEEE International Conference on Data Mining* (ICDM), (pp.35-42). IEEE Computer Society.

DeWitt, D. J., & Cai, J. Y. (2003). X-Diff: An effective change detection algorithm for XML documents. In U. Dayal, K. Ramamritham, & T. M. Vijayaraman (Eds.), *Proceedings of the 19th International Conference on Data Engineering (ICDE),* (pp. 519-530). IEEE Computer Society.

Doucet, A., & Ahonen-Myka, H. (2002). *Naive clustering of a large XML document collection.* Paper presented at the Initiative for the Evaluation of XML Retrieval (INEX) Workshop

Doucet, A., & Ahonen-Myka, H. (2002). Naïve clustering of a large XML document collection. In N. Fuhr, N. Gövert, G. Kazai, & M. Lalmas (Eds.) *Proceedings of the First Workshop of the Initiative for the Evaluation of XML Retrieval (INEX),* (pp. 81-87).

Fellbaum, C. (Ed.). (1998). *WordNet: An electronic lexical database*. Massachusetts, USA: MIT Press.

Flake, G. W., Tsioutsiouliklis, K., & Tarjan, R. E. (2002). *Graph clustering techniques based on minimum cut trees*. Princeton, NJ: NEC.

Flesca, S., Manco, G., Masciari, E., Pontieri, L., & Pugliese, A. (2005). Fast detection of XML structural similarity. *IEEE Transactions on Knowledge and Data Engineering, 17*(2), 160–175. doi:10.1109/TKDE.2005.27

Garey, M. R., & Johnson, D. S. (1979). *Computers and intractability: A guide to the theory of NP-completeness*. W.H. Freeman and Company.

Garofalakis, M., Gionis, A., Rastogi, R., Seshadri, S., & Shim, K. (2000). XTRACT: A system for extracting document type descriptors. In W. Chen, J. F. Naughton, & P. A. Bernstein (Eds.), *Proceedings of the 2000 ACM SIGMOD International Conference on Management of Data* (pp. 165-176). ACM.

Geamsakul, W., Yoshida, T., Ohara, K., Motoda, H., Yokoi, H., & Takabayashi, K. (2004). Constructing a decision tree for graph-structured data and its applications. *Fundamenta Informaticae*, *66*(1-2), 131–160.

Gu, M. S., Hwang, J. H., & Ryu, K. H. (2005). Designing the ontology of XML documents semi-automatically. In D.-S. Huang, X.-P. Zhang, & G.-B. Huang (Eds.), *Advances in Intelligent Computing, International Conference on Intelligent Computing (ICIC) Lecture Notes in Computer Science: Vol. 3644* (pp. 818-827). Springer.

Guha, S., Rastogi, R., & Shim, K. (1999). ROCK: A robust clustering algorithm for categorical attributes. *Proceedings of the 15th International Conference on Data Engineering (ICDE)*, (pp. 512-521). IEEE Computer Society Press.

Han, J., Pei, J., & Yin, Y. (2000). Mining frequent patterns without candidate generation. In W. Chen, J. F. Naughton, & P. A. Bernstein (Eds.), *Proceedings of the 2000 ACM SIGMOD International Conference on Management of Data* (pp. 1-12). ACM.

Hégaret, P. L., Wood, L., & Robie, J. (2000). What is the document object model? *Document Object Model (DOM) Level 2 Core Specification*. Retrieved from http://www.w3.org/TR/DOM-Level-2-Core/introduction.html

Hwang, J. H., & Ryu, K. H. (2005). Clustering and retrieval of XML documents by structure. In Gervasi, O., Gavrilova, M. L., Kumar, V., Laganà, A., Lee, H. P., & Mun, Y. (Eds.), *Computational Science and Its Applications (ICCSA) Lecture Notes in Computer Science* (*Vol. 3481*, pp. 925–935). Springer.

Inokuchi, A., Washio, T., & Motoda, H. (2005). A general framework for mining frequent subgraphs from labeled graphs. *Fundamenta Informaticae*, *66*(1-2), 53–82.

Inokuchi, A., Washio, T., Nishimura, K., & Motoda, H. (2002). *A fast algorithm for mining frequent connected subgraphs*. Tokyo, Japan: IBM Research, Tokyo Research Laboratory.

Kutty, S., Nayak, R., & Li, Y. (2007). *PCITMiner: Prefix-based closed induced tree miner for finding closed induced frequent subtrees*. In P. Christen, P. J. Kennedy J. Li, I. Kolyshkina, & G. J. Williams (Eds.), *Proceedings of the Sixth Australasian Data Mining Conference: Vol. 70. Conferences in Research and Practice in Information Technology* (pp. 151-160). Australian Computer Society.

Kutty, S., Nayak, R., & Li, Y. (2009a). HCX: An efficient hybrid clustering approach for XML documents. In U. M. Borghoff, & B. Chidlovskii (Eds.), *Proceedings of the 2009 ACM Symposium on Document Engineering* (pp. 94-97). ACM.

Kutty, S., Nayak, R., & Li, Y. (2009b). XCFS: An XML documents clustering approach using both the structure and the content. In D. W.-L. Cheung, I.-Y. Song, W. W. Chu, X. Hu, & J. J. Lin (Eds.), *Proceedings of the 18th ACM Conference on Information and Knowledge Management (CIKM),* (pp. 1729-1732). ACM.

Lee, M. L., Yang, L., Hsu, W., & Yang, X. (2002). XClust: Clustering XML schemas for effective integration. In *Proceedings of the International Conference on Information and Knowledge Management (CIKM),* (pp. 292–299). ACM.

Lian, W., Cheung, D. W. L., Mamoulis, N., & Yiu, S.-M. (2004). An efficient and scalable algorithm for clustering XML documents by structure. *IEEE Transactions on Knowledge and Data Engineering*, *16*(1), 82–96. doi:10.1109/TKDE.2004.1264824

Madhavan, J., Bernstein, P. A., & Rahm, E. (2001). Generic schema matching with Cupid. In P. M. G. Apers, P. Atzeni, S. Ceri, S. Paraboschi, K. Ramamohanarao, & R. T. Snodgrass (Eds.), *Proceedings of 27th International Conference on Very Large Data Bases (VLDB),* (pp. 49-58). Morgan Kaufmann.

Mazuran, M., Quintarelli, E., & Tanca, L. (2009). Mining tree-based frequent patterns from XML. In Andreasen, T., Yager, R., Bulskov, H., Christiansen, H., & Larsen, H. (Eds.), *Flexible Query Answering Systems Lecture Notes in Computer Science* (*Vol. 5822*, pp. 287–299). Springer. doi:10.1007/978-3-642-04957-6_25

Mirzal, A. (2009). Weblog clustering in multilinear algebra perspective. *International Journal of Information Technology*, *15*(1), 108–123.

Moh, C.-H., Lim, E.-P., & Ng, W.-K. (2000). *DTD-Miner: A tool for mining DTD from XML documents*. In The Second International Workshop on Advance Issues of E-Commerce and Web-Based Information Systems (WECWIS). IEEE Computer Society.

Nayak, R. (2005). Discovering knowledge from XML documents. In Wong, J. (Ed.), *Encyclopedia of data warehousing and mining* (pp. 372–376). Hershey, PA: Idea Group Publications. doi:10.4018/978-1-59140-557-3.ch071

Nayak, R. (2008). Fast and effective clustering of XML data using structural information. *Knowledge and Information Systems*, *14*(2), 197–215. doi:10.1007/s10115-007-0080-8

Nayak, R., De Vries, C., Kutty, S., Geva, S., Denoyer, L., & Gallinari, P. (2010). Overview of the INEX 2009 XML mining track: Clustering and classification of XML documents. In S. Geva, J. Kamps, & A. Trotman (Eds.), *Focused Retrieval and Evaluation, 8th International Workshop of the Initiative for the Evaluation of XML Retrieval, Lecture Notes in Computer Science: Vol. 6203* (pp. 366-378). Springer.

Nayak, R., & Iryadi, W. (2006). XMine: A methodology for mining XML structure. In X. Zhou, J. Li, H. Shen, M. Kitsuregawa, & Y. Zhang (Eds.), *Frontiers of WWW Research and Development, 8th Asia-Pacific Web Conference (APWeb), Lecture Notes in Computer Science: Vol. 3841* (pp. 786-792). Springer.

Nayak, R., & Tran, T. (2007). A progressive clustering algorithm to group the XML data by structural and semantic similarity. *International Journal of Pattern Recognition and Artificial Intelligence*, *21*(3), 1–21.

Nayak, R., & Xia, F. B. (2004). Automatic integration of heterogenous XML-schemas. In S. Bressan, D. Taniar, G. Kotsis, & I. K. Ibrahim (Eds.), *Proceedings of the Sixth International Conference on Information Integrationand Web-based Applications Services (iiWAS)*. Austrian Computer Society.

Nguyen, P. C., Ohara, K., Motoda, H., & Washio, T. (2005). Cl-GBI: A novel approach for extracting typical patterns from graph-structured data. In T. B. Ho, D. Cheung & H. Liu (Eds.), *Proceedings of the Advances in Knowledge Discovery and Data Mining, 9th Pacific-Asia Conference (PAKDD), Lecture Notes in Computer Science: Vol. 3518*. (pp. 639-649). Springer.

Nierman, A., & Jagadish, H. V. (2002). Evaluating structural similarity in XML documents. In *Proceedings of the ACM SIGMOD WebDB Workshop* (pp. 61-66).

Nijssen, S., & Kok, J. N. (2003). Efficient discovery of frequent unordered trees. In *Proceedings of First International Workshop on Mining Graphs, Trees, and Sequences* (pp. 55-64).

Paik, J., Shin, D. R., & Kim, U. (2005). EFoX: A scalable method for extracting frequent subtrees. In V. S. Sunderam, G. D. van Albada, P. M. A. Sloot, & J. Dongarra (Eds.), *Proceedings of the Computational Science, 5th International Conference (ICCS) Lecture Notes in Computer Science: Vol. 3516.* (pp. 813-817). Springer.

Salton, G., & McGill, M. J. (1986). *Introduction to modern information retrieval.* New York, NY: McGraw-Hill Inc.

Schenkel, R., Suchanek, F. M., & Kasneci, G. (2007). YAWN: A semantically annotated Wikipedia XML corpus. In A. Kemper, H. Schoning, T. Rose, M. Jarke, T. Seidl, C. Quix, & C. Brochhaus (Eds.), *Datenbanksysteme in Business, Technologie und Web (BTW 2007): Vol. 103.* LNI (pp. 277-291). GI.

Shen, Y., & Wang, B. (2003). Clustering schemaless XML documents. In Meersman, R., Tari, Z., & Schmidt, D. C. (Eds.), *On The Move to Meaningful Internet Systems 2003: CoopIS, DOA, and ODBASE, Lecture Notes in Computer Science* (*Vol. 2888*, pp. 767–784). Springer. doi:10.1007/978-3-540-39964-3_49

Skonieczny, Ł. (2009). Mining for unconnected frequent graphs with direct subgraph isomorphism tests. In Cyran, K., Kozielski, S., Peters, J., Stanczyk, U., & Wakulicz-Deja, A. (Eds.), *Man-machine interactions* (*Vol. 59*, pp. 523–531). Springer. doi:10.1007/978-3-642-00563-3_55

Stuart, I. (2004). XML schema, a brief introduction. Retrieved from http://lucas.ucs.ed.ac.uk/tutorials/xml-schema/

Tagarelli, A., & Greco, S. (2010). Semantic clustering of XML documents. *ACM Transactions on Information Systems, 28*(1), 1–56. doi:10.1145/1658377.1658380

Termier, A., Rousset, M.-C., Sebag, M., Ohara, K., Washio, T., & Motoda, H. (2005). Efficient mining of high branching factor attribute trees. In *Proceedings of the 5th IEEE International Conference on Data Mining (ICDM)*, (pp. 785-788). IEEE Computer Society.

Tran, T., Nayak, R., & Bruza, P. (2008). Document clustering using incremental and pairwise approaches. In N. Fuhr, J. Kamps, M. Lalmas & A. Trotman (Eds.), *Focused Access to XML Documents, 6th International Workshop of the Initiative for the Evaluation of XML Retrieval (INEX) Lecture Notes in Computer Science: Vol. 4862.* (pp. 222-233). Springer.

Tsoi, A., Hagenbuchner, M., Chau, R., & Lee, V. (2009). Unsupervised and supervised learning of graph domains. In Bianchini, M., Maggini, M., Scarselli, F., & Jain, L. (Eds.), *Innovations in Neural Information Paradigms and Applications, Studies in Computational Intelligence* (*Vol. 247*, pp. 43–65). Springer. doi:10.1007/978-3-642-04003-0_3

Vercoustre, A.-M., Fegas, M., Gul, S., & Lechevallier, Y. (2005). A flexible structured-based representation for XML document. In *Mining Advances in XML Information Retrieval and Evaluation* [Springer.]. *Lecture Notes in Computer Science, 3977*, 443–457.

Wagner, R. A., & Fischer, M. J. (1974). The string-to-string correction problem. *Journal of the ACM, 21*(1), 168–173. doi:10.1145/321796.321811

Wan, J. W. W., & Dobbie, G. (2004). Mining association rules from XML data using XQuery. In J. M. Hogan, P. Montague, M. K. Purvis, & C. Steketee (Eds.), *Proceedings of the Second Workshop on Australasian Information Security, Data Mining and Web Intelligence, and Software Internationalisation: Vol. 32. ACSW Frontiers* (pp. 169-174). Australian Computer Society.

Xiao, Y., Yao, J.-F., Li, Z., & Dunham, M. H. (2003). Efficient data mining for maximal frequent subtrees. In *Proceedings of the 3rd IEEE International Conference on Data Mining (ICDM),* (pp. 379-386). IEEE Computer Society.

Xifeng, Y., & Jiawei, H. (2003). CloseGraph: Mining closed frequent graph patterns. In L. Getoor, T. E. SenatoR, & P. Domingos (Eds.), *Proceedings of the Ninth ACM SIGKDD International Conference on Knowledge Discovery and Data Mining (KDD)*, (pp. 286-295). ACM.

*XML Schema*. (n.d.). Retrieved from http://www.w3.org/XML/Schema

Yang, J., & Chen, X. (2002). A semi-structured document model for text mining. *Journal of Computer Science and Technology*, *17*(5), 603–610. doi:10.1007/BF02948828

Yang, J., & Wang, S. (2010). Extended VSM for XML document classification using frequent subtrees. In S. Geva, J. Kamps & A. Trotman (Eds.), *Focused Retrieval and Evaluation, 8th International Workshop of the Initiative for the Evaluation of XML Retrieval (INEX) Lecture Notes in Computer Science: Vol. 6203.* (pp. 441-448). Springer.

Yao, J., & Zerida, N. (2007). Rare patterns to improve path-based clustering. In N. Fuhr, J. Kamps, M. Lalmas, & A. Trotman (Eds.), *Proceedings of the 6th International Workshop of the Initiative for the Evaluation of XML Retrieval (INEX)*. Springer.

Yoon, J. P., Raghavan, V., Chakilam, V., & Kerschberg, L. (2001). BitCube: A three-dimensional bitmap indexing for XML documents. [Kluwer Academic Publishers.]. *Journal of Intelligent Information Systems*, *17*(2-3), 241–254. doi:10.1023/A:1012861931139

Zaki, M. J. (2005). Efficiently mining frequent trees in a forest: Algorithms and applications. *IEEE Transactions on Knowledge and Data Engineering*, *17*(8), 1021–1035. doi:10.1109/TKDE.2005.125

Zaki, M. J., & Aggarwal, C. C. (2003). XRules: An effective structural classifier for XML data. *Proceedings of the Ninth ACM SIGKDD International Conference on Knowledge Discovery and Data Mining (KDD),* (pp. 316-325). ACM.

Zhang, W.-S., Liu, D.-X., & Zhang, J.-P. (2004). A novel method for mining frequent subtrees from XML data. In Z. R. Yang, R. M. Everson, & H. Yin (Eds.), *Intelligent Data Engineering and Automated Learning (IDEAL): Vol. 3177. Lecture Notes in Computer Science (pp. 300-305).* Springer.

## ENDNOTE

1 http://www.inex.otago.ac.nz//tracks/wiki-mine/wiki-mine.asp

# Chapter 2
# Modeling, Querying, and Mining Uncertain XML Data

**Evgeny Kharlamov**
*Free University of Bozen-Bolzano, Italy & INRIA Saclay, France*

**Pierre Senellart**
*Télécom ParisTech, France*

## ABSTRACT

*This chapter deals with data mining in uncertain XML data models, whose uncertainty typically comes from imprecise automatic processes. We first review the literature on modeling uncertain data, starting with well-studied relational models and moving then to their semistructured counterparts. We focus on a specific probabilistic XML model, which allows representing arbitrary finite distributions of XML documents, and has been extended to also allow continuous distributions of data values. We summarize previous work on querying this uncertain data model and show how to apply the corresponding techniques to several data mining tasks, exemplified through use cases on two running examples.*

## INTRODUCTION

Though traditional database applications, for instance, bank account management, have no room for uncertainty, more recent applications, such as information extraction from the Web, automatic schema matching in information integration, or information gathering from sensor networks are inherently imprecise. This uncertainty is sometimes represented as the *probability* that the data is correct, as with conditional random fields in information extraction (Lafferty, McCallum, & Pereira, 2001), or uncertain schema mappings in information integration (Dong, Halevy, & Yu, 2009). In other cases, only *confidence* in the information is provided by the system, which can be seen after renormalization as an approximation of the probability. More rarely, some applications do not provide any form of preference among possible uncertain choices (think, for example, of missing data in a data recovery application), or only some unweighted preferences (like the

DOI: 10.4018/978-1-61350-356-0.ch002

core solution in data exchange (Fagin, Kolaitis, & Popa, 2005) or a minimal repair in managing inconsistent databases (Chomicki & Libkin, 2000; Lopatenko & Bertossi, 2007)).

Usually, data uncertainty is not formally taken into account: only the most likely interpretation is kept for future processing, or all probable choices above a threshold are maintained. We claim this is not sufficient. There is a need for managing the imprecision in this data more rigorously. The need is even stronger when the uncertain data is manipulated by other systems, potentially uncertain themselves. A good example of that is data mining. Consider a scenario where some dataset (say, a list of emails) was acquired, cleaned, and enriched, by a variety of systems (information extraction, deduplication, data integration, natural language analysis, sentiment analysis, etc.). We now want to mine this dataset, for instance to construct from it a list of popular keywords, or to build a social network of individuals, where the friendship links between two persons is derived from their recorded interactions. An application that would make use of the inherent uncertainty in the dataset would be able to discover much more knowledge than one that would ignore it altogether. Besides, in the mining task the confidence annotation in the data could also be used to derive the confidence of the resulting (mined) data.

A number of models and systems for managing uncertain data have been proposed in the literature and a high-level picture of some of them is presented in this chapter. We focus, however, on the particular case of XML data, adapted in the cases where the information is either not strictly constrained by a schema (e.g., Web data), or inherently tree-like (mailing lists, parse trees of natural language sentences, etc.). We also mostly discuss probabilistic models, which have the advantage, in addition to being suited to a number of tasks that provide probability or probability-like confidence scores, of allowing extensive mathematical manipulations (more so than models based on fuzzy logic (Galindo, Urrutia, & Piattini, 2006), that are not discussed in this chapter).

The objective of our chapter is thus to bridge the studies on uncertain XML and data mining. On the one hand, we want to introduce different models of uncertain data to the data mining community. On the other hand, we want to study different data mining tasks for probabilistic XML. Recent studies of probabilistic XML (Abiteboul, Kimelfeld, Sagiv, & Senellart, 2009; Kimelfeld, Kosharovsky, & Sagiv, 2009; Kharlamov, Nutt, & Senellart, 2010) focus on query answering and updates, but mining, that has been studied in the context of relational probabilistic data (Aggarwal, 2009; Bernecker, Kriegel, Renz, Verhein, & Züfle, 2009), has not received attention in the semistructured case. Note that the change of representation format from tables to trees also makes data mining tasks different (Nayak, 2005). In this chapter we propose methods for mining probabilistic XML data (frequent items, correlations, summaries of data values, etc.) that rely on the existing literature on probabilistic XML querying (Kimelfeld et al., 2009; Abiteboul, Chan, Kharlamov, Nutt, & Senellart, 2010).

In the following part of this chapter we discuss several main approaches to uncertainty modeling. We start with uncertain relational databases and present examples and intuitions of incomplete and probabilistic tables. We discuss how these approaches were adapted to the semistructured setting and illustrate incomplete XML trees and two probabilistic XML models: with local and global probabilistic relationships. The next section is devoted to a formal presentation of these probabilistic XML models; we present the syntax and semantics of discrete and continuous probabilistic XML. We then summarize known results about probabilistic XML querying, both for Boolean and aggregate queries, that are at the basis of the data mining approaches we present in a subsequent section, where we give examples and develop computation techniques for mining frequent, co-occurring, or popular items, or for summarizing continuous distributions.

## MODELS OF UNCERTAINTY

In this section, we discuss how to formally model the uncertainty that arises in applications. Unsurprisingly, there is a trade-off between expressiveness and succinctness of the model on one hand and its simplicity and the ability to efficiently use it for query processing on the other hand. We first discuss relational data then see how these relational uncertain data models can be adapted to XML, which we will focus on in the rest of this chapter. Historically, uncertain relational data models precede semistructured ones and these heavily rely on the ideas developed for the relational setting. Moreover, translating probabilistic XML into relations is a way to manage it, as shall be discussed further. Due to this historical and practical importance of relational uncertain models, we present them in detail.

### Relational Models of Uncertain Data

The relational model, proposed by Codd (1970) is the most commonly used data representation model today. The need for modeling uncertainty in relational tables has been felt as early as the mid-1970s (Codd, 1975) and has led to the notion of *null* values implemented in System R, one of the first relational DBMS, a few years afterwards (Date, 1981). We first present this way of representing uncertain data and look next to more expressive models.

#### Codd Tables

The first works mentioning the problem of incompleteness in relational models are by Codd (1975, 1979). Codd proposed to augment relational tables with special constants, called *nulls* and usually denoted @, assumed to be different from all other data values. A null is meant to be a syntactic substitute for a missing or uncertain value. Relational tables with tuples that may contain @ are called *Codd tables* or *naïve tables* (Abiteboul, Hull, & Vianu, 1995). For example, one can use @ as a value for the unknown telephone number of Mary in Table 1.

*Table 1. Codd table $T_{ex}$*

| Id | Name | Tel_nr |
|---|---|---|
| 1 | Mary | @ |

Codd proposed a semantics for query evaluation over tables with nulls based on three-valued logics. According to this semantics, logical expressions involving nulls are evaluated using “true”, “false” and “unknown”, e.g., (@ > 5) is unknown, (@ > 5) ∧ (5 < 3) is false, while (@ > 5) ∨ (3 < 5) is true. Codd’s semantics for nulls is the current standard in SQL (ISO/IEC, 2008) and implemented in the main relational DBMSs. However, it can produce counterintuitive results, as noted by Grant (1977):

```
evaluating a query
SELECT * FROM T_ex WHERE tel_
nr='333111' OR tel_nr <> '333111'
over T_ex returns no answers, while
one might expect the tuple about
"Mary".
```

An alternative semantics of Codd tables, that will be helpful for other uncertain data models as well, is given by *sets of possible worlds* (Abiteboul et al., 1995). From the incomplete data about Mary in our example we can only guess what her missing phone number is. Each guess gives one completion of the data, that is, one complete database, and all the possible guesses give a set of data completions and, consequently, a set of corresponding databases, or *worlds*. When the *domain* (the set of legal values) for a given attribute is infinite, there can be infinitely many such worlds. The actual database is assumed to be one of these possible worlds. In the following we use the term *incomplete database* to refer to such a set of possible worlds, denoted as *D*. Formalisms to represent sets of possible databases, such as Codd tables, are called *representations systems*.

From the point of view of possible-world semantics, nulls are treated as variables, and different occurrences of a null value correspond to different variables. The semantics of a Codd table *T* is the set of all databases *rep*(*T*) (where *rep* stands for *represents*) obtained from it by substituting every occurrence of @ with a data value from the corresponding domain. Looking back to the previous example, we have: $rep(T_{ex})$ = {{1, Mary, 111333}, {1, Mary, 333444}, …}.

Codd tables have serious limitations in representing incomplete databases, in particular when one wants to model additional knowledge about the unknown data values (Imieliński & Lipski, 1984). Consider the following incomplete database: "Mary" and "John", spouses, have the same unknown telephone number, which might be different from the unknown telephone number of a third person "Bob". In addition we may have constraints on the unknown values, for instance, that "Mary"'s age is between 30 and 35 and that she is younger than "John" and older than "Bob". This incomplete database cannot be represented as a Codd table, since we need the ability to have coreferences across null values, and to express constraints on unknown values. To overcome these limitations, Imieliński and Lipski (1984) introduced the representation system of *c-tables* ("c" stands for "conditional").

## C-Tables

In c-tables, nulls are labeled with subscripts such that two nulls with the same label always denote the same value. C-tables are also equipped with an extra column to store (local) boolean conditions of the form $@_1 < c$ or $@_1 < @_2$ on labeled nulls and constants. Table 2 is an example of a c-table representing the incomplete database discussed in the previous paragraph.

*Table 2.*

| Id | Name | Tel_nr | Age | Cond |
|---|---|---|---|---|
| 1 | Mary | $@_1$ | $@_3$ | $@_3 \in (30, 35)$ |
| 2 | John | $@_1$ | $@_4$ | $@_3 < @_4$ |
| 3 | Bob | $@_2$ | $@_5$ | $@_5 < @_3$ |

Note that a c-table where every labeled null occurs only once and with an empty condition column is a Codd table. The possible-world semantics of c-tables is similar to that of Codd tables, with the difference that one substitutes all occurrences of the same labeled null with the same constant, and afterwards deletes from the resulting table each tuple whose attributes do not satisfy the conditions associated to the tuple.

Evaluation of a query *Q* over an incomplete database *D* is defined point-wise: one queries all the databases in *D* separately and then considers the set of query results, which is an incomplete database, as the output *Q*(*D*), that is, $Q(D) = \{Q(d) \mid d \in D\}$. An important question studied for different representation systems is to understand under which query languages they are *closed*, i.e., given a representation *T* and a query *Q*, whether it is possible to represent *Q*(*rep*(*T*)) in the same formalism as *T* (Sarma, Benjelloun, Halevy, & Widom, 2006). It was shown (Imieliński & Lipski, 1984) that Codd tables are closed under the *project-union* fragment of the relational algebra, but are not closed under *select* or *join*. In contrast, c-tables are closed under the whole relational algebra, i.e., selection, projection, join, difference, union, and (attribute) renaming. Interestingly, these closure results also give polynomial-time algorithms for directly constructing a representation of *Q*(*rep*(*T*)) by evaluating *Q* over *T*, treating nulls as constants, and (for c-tables) combining the conditions with Boolean operators that depend on the operation performed over the corresponding tuples. Details can be found in (Imieliński & Lipski, 1984).

## Probabilistic Models

Modeling uncertainty by incomplete databases is not enough: it is often useful to have some indication of the likelihood of possible worlds, or of the confidence we have in a piece of information. This can be done by adding probabilities to incomplete database models. A *probabilistic database* is a probabilistic distribution over a set of possible worlds. As for incomplete databases, we are interested in compact representation systems for such probabilistic distributions. We are thus looking for probabilistic counterparts to the incomplete database representation systems described earlier.

A first model, inspired by Codd tables, is that of *p-Codd tables* (Lakshmanan, Leone, Ross, & Subrahmanian, 1997). They assume that each attribute inside each tuple has a separate finite distribution of values. Consider a tuple whose value of the Name attribute is either "Mary" with probability $p = 0.3$ or "John" with $p = 0.7$; the phone number is either "111 333" with $p = 0.2$, or "333 444" with $p = 0.8$. The corresponding p-Codd table can be represented as shown in Table 3.

Every world of a p-Codd table has an associated probability that is equal to the product of the probabilities of every choice taken to obtain that world. For example, the probability of the world {1, Mary, 111333} is $0.3 \times 0.2 = 0.06$.

Another early probabilistic model has been independently introduced by Fuhr and Rölleke (1997) and Zimányi (1997). A so-called *tuple-independent* database is a probabilistic database where the probability of each tuple is given, and where the existence of a tuple is independent of the existence of the other tuples. The model was further extended by Ré, Dalvi, and Suciu (2006) to the so-called *block-independent* databases (BIDs), by regrouping tuples of a relation into independent blocks, with mutually exclusive tuples inside a given block, as shown in Table 4.

The semantics of BIDs chooses at most one tuple in each block, and choices across blocks are independent. In this example, the tuple (1, Mary, 30) can be kept with probability 0.3, the tuple (1, Mary, 32) with 0.5, and (1, Mary, 35) with 0.2, and these tuples are mutually exclusive. Independently from this choice, one of the two tuples (2, John, 37) or (2, John, 40) can be chosen with uniform probability.

Both p-Codd tables and BIDs assume that occurrences of attribute values or tuples in a given world are independent from each other. Due to this assumption the models cannot capture complex probabilistic dependencies across data items. This limitation is similar to the limitations of Codd tables with respect to c-tables. A very general probabilistic model is thus an extension of c-tables to *probabilistic c-tables* (Green & Tannen, 2006), where every variable in a table is treated as a random variable.

Recently a number of systems to support probabilistic relational databases were developed, they include *Trio* at Stanford (Widom, 2005), *MYSTIQ* at U. Washington (Boulos et al., 2005), *MayBMS* at Cornell and U. Oxford (Huang, Antova, Koch, & Olteanu, 2009), and *PrDB* at U. Maryland (Sen, Deshpande, & Getoor, 2009). The Trio system implements probabilistic variants of *or-sets* (Imieliński, Naqvi, & Vadaparty, 1991; Libkin & Wong, 1996), and *?-sets* (Sarma et al., 2006),

*Table 3.*

| Id | Name | tel_nr |
|---|---|---|
| 1 | Mary ($p = 0.3$) | 111333 ($p = 0.2$) |
| | Mary ($p = 0.7$) | 333444 ($p = 0.8$) |

*Table 4.*

| Id | Name | Age | Prob. |
|---|---|---|---|
| 1 | Mary | 30 | 0.3 |
| | | 32 | 0.5 |
| | | 35 | 0.2 |
| 2 | John | 37 | 0.5 |
| | | 40 | 0.5 |

which can be seen as c-tables with correlations within tuples only. In addition, Trio supports data provenance in order to trace the origin of query results. MYSTIQ implements BIDs. MayBMS is an extension of PostgreSQL and implements so called *world-set decompositions* (Antova, Koch, & Olteanu, 2007), that are probabilistic c-tables where the domains of labeled nulls are finite and dependencies (conditions) on variables and data items are of a limited form. The dependencies are encoded using the cross product of probabilistic tables. PrDB is based on graphical models to capture uncertain data, which are a well known probabilistic modeling technique coming from the statistics and machine learning community. PrDB captures both tuple and attribute uncertainty together with complex probabilistic correlations among tuples and attributes, encoded as factored join distributions.

For further reading on probabilistic databases we refer the reader to (Green & Tannen, 2006; Sarma et al., 2006), where there is a nice overview of some probabilistic models.

## Semistructured Models of Uncertain Data

Semistructured models of uncertain data have been much less studied than relational ones. As we shall see, the models proposed so far are, unsurprisingly, semistructured counterparts of the relational models discussed above. However, they are still worthwhile to study on their own, since they are used to represent different kinds of uncertain data and that typical query languages over trees have different expressive power from that over relations (tree-pattern queries vs. conjunctive queries, XPath vs SQL).

### Incomplete XML

Barceló, Libkin, Poggi, and Sirangelo (2009) proposed a model of incomplete XML that is inspired by c-tables and tree-pattern queries. In the

*Figure 1. An incomplete XML document*

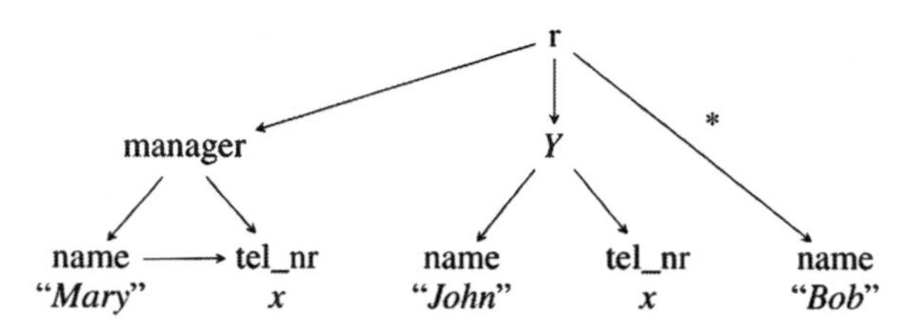


spirit of c-tables, their model allows representing unknown labels, using variables. Besides that, their model also supports structural uncertainty, which is not possible in c-tables, but is common when data is queried through tree-patterns queries. It is thus possible to model uncertainty along horizontal (sibling) and vertical (descendant, child) navigational axes. To illustrate, consider the uncertain XML document about people in a company of Figure 1. The first person is a manager with name "Mary" and unknown phone number, denoted $x$. The second person is "John", his position is unknown, denoted as the variable $Y$, and his telephone is unknown but the same as of "Mary". The third person has name "Bob". It is also known that (the node storing) "Mary"'s phone number is the following sibling of (the node storing) her name and (the node storing) "Bob"'s name is a descendant of the root. No further structural information is known.

Problems over uncertain XML documents studied in (Barceló et al., 2009) are consistency of partial descriptions (i.e., whether there is an XML document satisfying a given description), representability of complete documents by incomplete ones, and query answering. They also show how schema information, the presence of node identifiers, and missing structural information affect the complexity of these main computational problems, and they identify tractable query classes over incomplete XML descriptions.

*Figure 2. PrXML$^{mux,det}$ p-document $P_{MBOX\text{-}L}$: Mailbox organized in threads*

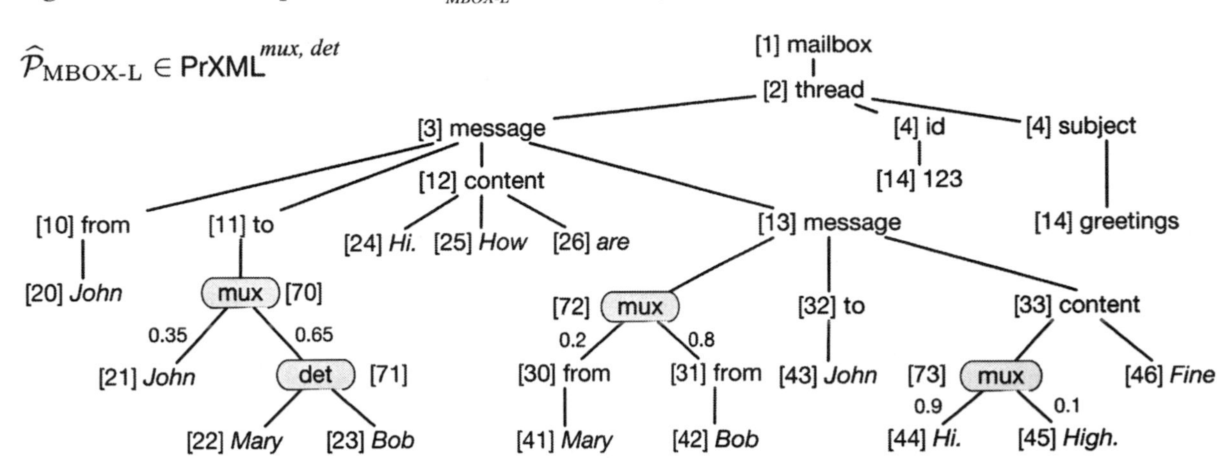


## Probabilistic XML

Similarly as in the relational setting, a probabilistic semistructured database is a probability distribution over regular XML documents. A number of models (Nierman & Jagadish, 2002; Hung, Getoor, & Subrahmanian, 2003a, 2003b; Keulen, Keijzer, & Alink, 2005; Abiteboul & Senellart, 2006) have been proposed for compact representation of probabilistic XML databases. The model we focus here is called PrXML. It was introduced in (Kimelfeld, Kosharovski, & Sagiv, 2008; Abiteboul et al., 2009) and it uses *p-documents* as representations. Practically all probabilistic XML models proposed in the literature can be defined by means of p-documents. P-documents are trees with two types of nodes: *ordinary* and *distributional.* A p-document can be thought of as a probabilistic process that generates a random XML document in a conceptually simple way, namely, each distributional node chooses a subset of its children (see next section). Therefore, each distributional node of a p-document should specify the probability distribution of choosing a subset of its children in the above random process. There are several types of distributional nodes that differ from one another in how they specify probabilities. An example of a p-document is presented in Figure 2. This p-document, denoted $P_{\text{MBOX-L}}$, represents a mailbox organized in threads. It contains one (uncertain) thread with two (uncertain) messages. The possible worlds of this probabilistic XML document follow the DTD of Figure 3 (left). The following fragments of data are uncertain in $P_{\text{MBOX-L}}$: the recipient of the first message, the sender of the second, and a part of the content of the second message; we will come back to this example in the next section and explain it in more detail. We consider four types of distributional nodes:

- **det:** for deterministic (every child is chosen with probability 1);

*Figure 3. (on the left) Mailbox DTD, and (on the right) Electricity Consumption DTD*

```
<!ELEMENT mailbox (thread)*>
<!ELEMENT thread (message, id, subject) >
<!ELEMENT message (from, to, content, subject)>
<!ELEMENT from (#PCDATA)>
<!ELEMENT to (#PCDATA)>
<!ELEMENT content (#PCDATA)>
<!ELEMENT subject (#PCDATA)>
```

```
<!ELEMENT electr-cons (room1, room2)>
<!ELEMENT room1 (measurement)* >
<!ELEMENT room2 (measurement)* >
<!ELEMENT measurement (date, value)>
<!ELEMENT date (#PCDATA)>
<!ELEMENT value (#PCDATA)>
```

- **ind:** for independent (every child can be chosen independently from another, according to the corresponding assigned probability);
- **mux:** for mutually exclusive (at most one child can be chosen);
- **cie:** for conjunction of independent events (each child is chosen according to a conjunction of probabilistically independent events, which can be used globally throughout the p-document).

It may seem that using *det* nodes is redundant, but actually they increase expressive power when used in conjunction with some of the other types.

We define different families of p-documents in terms of the types of distributional nodes that are allowed. $\text{PrXML}^{C}$, where $C \subseteq \{mux, ind, det, cie\}$, denotes the family of p-documents that use the types appearing in the subset *C*. We ignore here the *exp* distributional nodes from (Abiteboul et al., 2009) that are a generalization of *mux* nodes with less practical interest.

$\text{PrXML}^{mux,ind}$ is a local probabilistic model, that is, it allows for dependencies between siblings only, or, in other words, for hierarchical dependencies. In this respect, $\text{PrXML}^{mux,ind}$ is a semistructured counterpart of BIDs. It is easy to see that any $\text{PrXML}^{mux,ind}$ p-document can actually be transformed into an equivalent and as succinct $\text{PrXML}^{mux,det}$ p-document. Therefore, we shall ignore in the following *ind* distributional nodes. On the other hand, $\text{PrXML}^{cie}$ is global since it allows for complicated probabilistic relationships between data items. Thus, $\text{PrXML}^{cie}$ is a semistructured counterpart of probabilistic c-tables.

The PrXML data model has been extended to represent continuous distributions of data values (Abiteboul et al., 2010), and to capture infinite probability spaces of documents where the depth or the width of the possible worlds is unbounded (Benedikt, Kharlamov, Olteanu, & Senellart, 2010). We focus in this chapter on the standard PrXML model together with continuous distributions, that we formally introduce in the next section.

An alternative probabilistic XML representation system is that of Cohen, Kimelfeld, and Sagiv (2008). The idea is to add, on top of a simple PrXML description, external *constraints* (defined by aggregate tree-pattern queries) restricting the validity of possible worlds. For instance, constraints may only allow possible worlds where at least *n* nodes of a given type are present. This is related to the coupling of probabilistic XML documents with schema validation, discussed in (Cohen, Kimelfeld, & Sagiv, 2009).

## PROBABILISTIC XML

In this section, we present more formally the syntax and semantics of the PrXML model. We first focus on a discrete model (to represent discrete probability distributions) and then extend it to allow continuous data values.

### Discrete Probabilistic XML

We model XML documents as unranked, unordered, labeled trees. Not taking into account the order between sibling nodes in an XML document is a common but non-crucial assumption. The same modeling can be done for ordered trees, without much change to the theory. A *finite probability space* over documents, *px-space* for short, is a pair $(D, \Pr)$, where $D$ is a finite set of documents and Pr maps each document to a probability $\Pr(d)$ such that the sum of probabilities $\Pr(d)$ over all $d \in D$ is equal to 1.

#### Syntax of p-Documents

The PrXML model from (Kimelfeld et al., 2009; Abiteboul et al., 2009) uses *p-documents* to represent px-spaces in a compact way. As already discussed, a p-document is similar to a document, with the difference that it has two types of nodes:

ordinary and distributional. Distributional nodes are used for defining the probabilistic process that generates random documents but they do not actually occur in these. Ordinary nodes have labels and they may appear in random documents. We require the leaves and the root to be ordinary nodes.

More precisely, we assume given a set $X$ of independent Boolean random variables with some specified probability distribution $\Delta$ over them. A p-document, denoted by $P$, is an unranked, unordered, labeled tree. Each node has a unique identifier $u$ and a label $\mu(u)$ in $L \cup \{cie(E)\}_E \cup \{mux(\mathrm{Pr})\}_{\mathrm{Pr}} \cup \{det\}$, where $L$ are labels of ordinary nodes, and the others are labels of distributional nodes. We consider three kinds of the latter labels: $cie(E)$ (for conjunction of independent events), $mux(\mathrm{Pr})$ (for mutually exclusive), and $det$ (for deterministic). If a node $u$ is labeled with $cie(E)$, then $E$ is a function that assigns to each child of $u$ a conjunction $e_1 \wedge \ldots \wedge e_k$ of literals ($x$ or $\neg x$, with $x \in X$). If $u$ is labeled with $mux(\mathrm{Pr})$, then Pr assigns to each child of $u$ a probability with the sum across children at most 1.

## Example 1

Two p-documents are shown in Figures 2 and 4. The first one belongs to PrXML$^{mux,det}$ since it has only *mux* and *det* distributional nodes. The p-document stores one thread with two messages and the subject "greetings". The first message is sent by John and addressed to either himself or to both Mary and Bob. The reason why we may have this uncertainty in the recipient is that we try to identify the persons' name using email addresses. We know that John sent a message to two email addresses that either both belong to John himself with the probability $\Pr(n_{21}) = 0.35$, or to Mary and Bob with the probability $\Pr(n_{71}) = 0.65$. This probabilistic ambiguity is modeled with the *mux* distributional node $n_{70}$, since the two options are represented as sub-documents rooted at this node. Note that the *det* distributional node $n_{71}$ is needed to account for both Mary and Bob as the second probabilistic option for the recipient. Another kind of uncertainty is in the content of the second message. This message contains a voice record for which automatic speech recognition is ambiguous. In the p-document of Figure 2, under the node $n_{73}$ we have two possible interpretations of a word from a voice record: "Hi" and "High". In our example the interpretation "Hi" has a higher probability, i.e., 0.85. The p-document of Figure 4, belongs to PrXML$^{cie}$ since it has only *cie* distributional nodes. For example, node $n_{70}$ has the label $cie(E)$ and three children $n_{21}$, $n_{22}$, and $n_{23}$, such that the event formulas labeling the nodes are, respectively, $E(n_{21}) = z$, $E(n_{22}) =$

*Figure 4. PrXML$^{cie}$ p-document $P_{MBOX\text{-}G}$: Mailbox organized in threads*

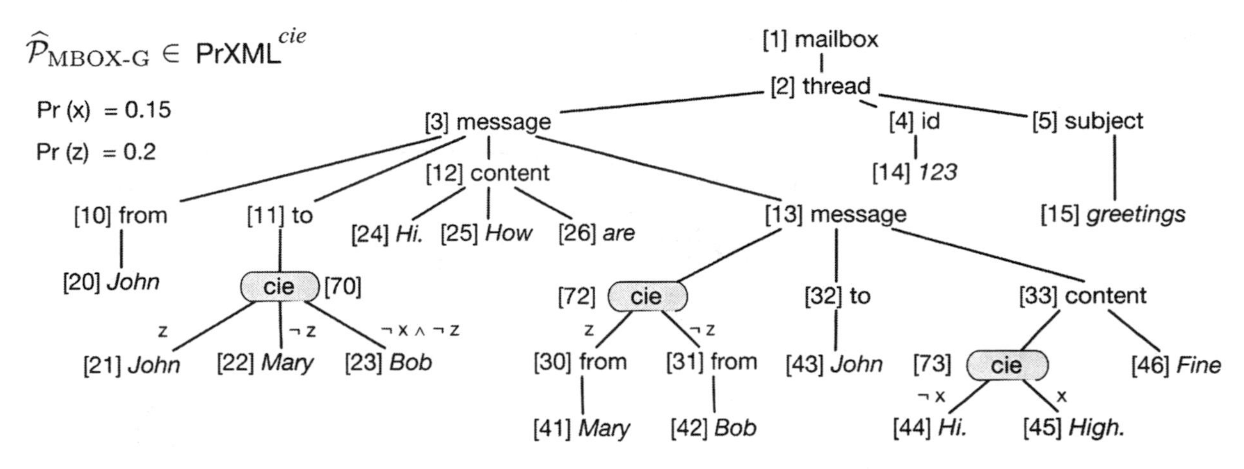

$\neg z$, and $E(n_{23}) = \neg x \wedge \neg z$. The probabilities of the event variables are $Pr(x) = 0.15$ and $Pr(z) = 0.2$.

## Semantics of p-Documents

The semantics of a p-document $P$, denoted by $[|P|]$, is a px-space over documents, where the documents are obtained from $P$ following a randomized three-step process (Abiteboul et al., 2009).

1. We choose a valuation $v$ of the variables $x$ in $X$. The probability of this choice, according to the distribution $\Delta$, is

$$p_v = \Sigma_{v(x)=true}\ \Delta(x) \times \Sigma_{v(x)=false}\ (1-\Delta(x)).$$

2. For each *cie* node labeled *cie*($E$), we delete its children $u$ where $v(E(u))$ is false, and their descendants. Then, independently for each *mux* node $u$ labeled *mux*(Pr), we select one of its children $u'$ according to the corresponding probability distribution Pr and delete the other children and their descendants, the probability of the choice is $Pr(u')$. We do not delete any of the children of *det* nodes.
3. We then remove in turn each distributional node, connecting each ordinary child $u$ of a deleted distributional node with its lowest ordinary ancestor $u'$.

The result of this third step is a random document $P^{rand}$. The probability of a random generation is defined by the probabilities of the choices done during the generation and it is the product of $p_v$, the probability of the variable assignment we chose in the first step, with all $Pr(u')$, the probabilities of the choices made in the second step for the *mux* nodes. The probability $Pr(P^{rand})$ is the sum of the probabilities across all possible random generations that yield $P^{rand}$.

## Example 2

One can obtain the document $d_{MBOX}$ in Figure 5 by applying the randomized process to either of the p-documents $P_{MBOX-L}$ and $P_{MBOX-G}$.

For $P_{MBOX-L}$ in Figure 2 this can be done by making three choices, namely, (1) the right branch of the node $n_{70}$ with probability 0.65, (2) the right branch of $n_{72}$ with probability 0.8, and finally (3) the left branch of the node $n_{73}$ with probability 0.9. Then the probability of $d_{MBOX}$ is the product of the probabilities of the choices $Pr(d) = 0.65 \times 0.8 \times 0.9 = 0.468$.

For $P_{MBOX-G}$ in Figure 4 this can be done by assigning $v = \{x/false, z/false\}$. According to $v$, the nodes $n_{21}$, $n_{30}$, and $n_{45}$, which are children of *cie* distributional nodes, are to be deleted from the p-document $P_{MBOX-G}$ and do not occur in the resulting document, since the edges incoming to these

*Figure 5. XML document $d_{MBOX}$: Mailbox organized in threads*

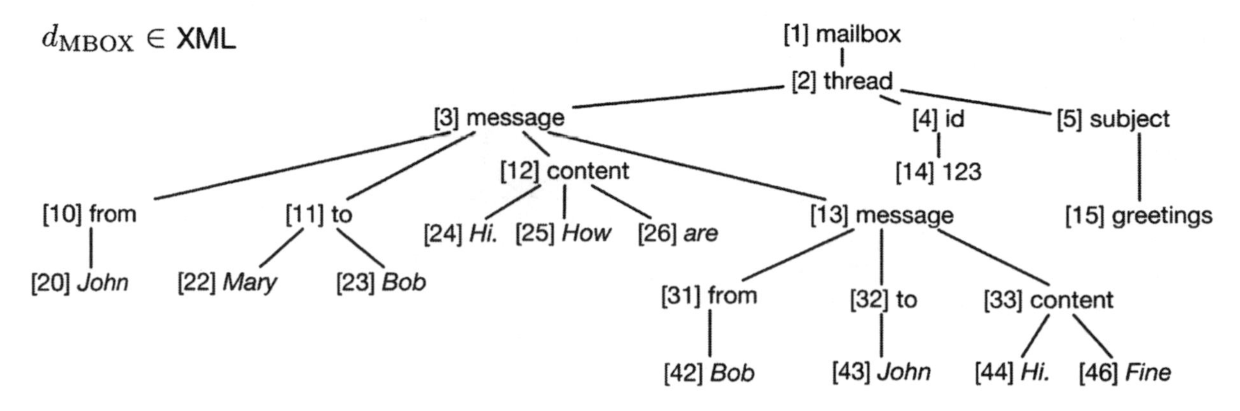

nodes are labeled with formulas evaluated by $v$ to false. The other children of the *cie* distributional nodes remain in the resulting document, since the edges incoming to these nodes are labeled with formulas evaluated by $v$ to true. This is the only valuation leading to the result document $d_{\text{MBOX}}$, thus the probability of this document is the product of the probabilities of the assignments for each variable, that is, of $\Pr(\neg x) = 0.85$ and $\Pr(\neg z) = 0.8$, and it is equal to $\Pr(d) = 0.85 \times 0.8 = 0.68$.

PrXML$^{cie}$ and PrXML$^{mux,det}$ are both capable of representing any discrete px-space. However, they correspond to different trade-offs between succinctness and query efficiency. As shown in (Abiteboul et al., 2009), PrXML$^{cie}$ is an exponentially more compact representation system than PrXML$^{mux,det}$, which itself is as compact as PrXML$^{mux,ind}$. On the other hand, Kimelfeld et al. (2008, 2009) have shown that there exists a polynomial-time algorithm (in data complexity) for computing the probability of all *tree-pattern queries* over PrXML$^{mux,det}$, while all non-trivial queries are #P-complete over PrXML$^{cie}$.

## Continuous Probabilistic XML

We generalize p-documents to documents whose leaves are labeled with (representations of) probability distributions over the reals, instead of single values. We give semantics to such documents in terms of continuous distributions over documents with real numbers on their leaves.

In the discrete case, a p-document defines a finite set of trees and probabilities assigned to them. In the continuous case, a p-document defines an uncountably infinite set of trees with a continuous distribution, which assigns probabilities to (typically infinite) sets of trees, the possible events. In order to support such a model we now consider only documents whose leaves are labeled with real numbers. Let $D$ be the set of all documents where the values of the leaves range over the reals.

Then, a *continuous px-space* is a continuous distribution over $D$. We refer to a textbook on measure and probability theory such as (Ash & Doléans-Dade, 2000) for the definitions of the concepts used in this section.

To support (possibly continuous) distributions on leaves, we extend the syntax of p-documents by an additional type of distributional nodes, the *cont* nodes. A *cont* node has the form *cont*($D$), where $D$ is a representation of a probability distribution over the real numbers. In contrast to the distribution nodes introduced earlier, a *cont* node can only appear as a leaf.

### Example 3

Consider the probabilistic XML document $P_{\text{CONS}}$ in Figure 6 that belongs to PrXML$^{cont,mux}$, since it has two types of distributional nodes, namely *cont* and *mux*. Documents represented by this p-document follow the DTD in Figure 3 on the right. The p-document collects results of electricity-consumption monitoring by sensors installed in two rooms: room 1 and room 2. The data in the first room is measured during September 3 and 4. The consumption on September 3 is reported to be 15 units. This measurement is imprecise, but we know (from the sensor's manufacturer) that the error is normally distributed around the reported value with variance 3. We represent this fact by a continuous node $n_{25}$ labeled *cont*($N$(15,3)). On September 4 there is a communication problem with this sensor and the reported consumption is either 50 units with probability 0.1, or 52 units with probability 0.9. Moreover, when the consumption is higher than 30, the variance of the measurement imprecision is getting higher and equal to 5. This data is represented using the mux distributional node $n_{27}$ with two children that are labeled with continuous distributions *cont*($N$(50,5)) and *cont*($N$(52,5)). In the second room we have uncertainty on the date when the measurement stored in the node $n_{29}$ was collected.

*Figure 6. PrXML$^{cont,mux}$ p-document $P_{CONS}$: Electricity consumption*

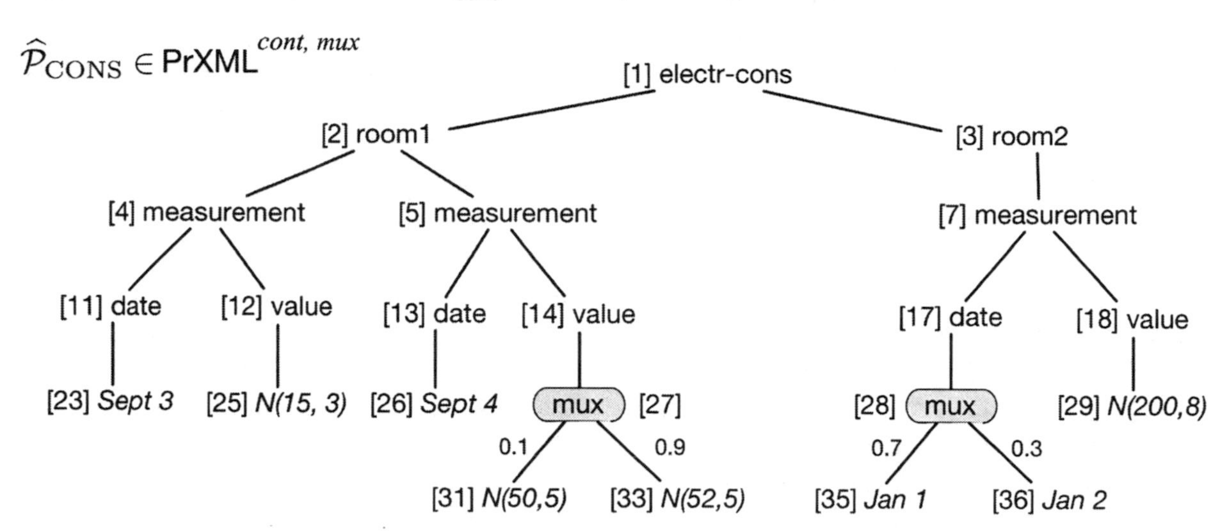


Any finitely representable distribution can appear in a *cont* node: uniform distributions, piecewise polynomials, Poisson distributions, etc. We consider in more detail the example of *normal* or *Gaussian distributions*, that were used in the example above. The probability density function of a Gaussian distribution $N(\mu, \sigma^2)$ of mean $\mu$ and variance $\sigma^2$ is:

$$f(x) = \frac{1}{\sqrt{2\pi\sigma^2}} e^{-(x-\mu)^2/(2\sigma^2)}.$$

The density function has a shape of a bell centered in the mean value $\mu$ with variance $\sigma^2$.The Gaussian distribution is often used to describe, at least approximately, measurements that tend to cluster around the mean. For example, if a sensor indicates a temperature of 30, then the real value might be slightly different from 30, but not too much. The further the value is from 30, the lower the chance that this is the actual temperature. This behavior can be nicely captured by a Gaussian distribution with mean of 30 and a small variance.

We define the semantics $[|P|]$ of continuous p-documents of PrXML$^{cont,cie,mux,det}$ as a continuous px-space described by a probability distribution function $\Pr_P$. More precisely, the semantics is defined in two steps (Abiteboul et al., 2010):

1. Let $P \in$ PrXML$^{cont,cie,mux,det}$ and $P' \in$ PrXML$^{cie,mux,det}$ be the p-document obtained from $P$ by replacing every continuous node with an arbitrary value, say, 0. $P'$ is a (discrete) px-space $(\{(d_1, p_1), \ldots, (d_n, p_n)\})$ with the sum of probabilities $p_i$ over all $i$ $(1 \leq i \leq n)$ equal to 1. For a given $i$, we consider the document $P_i$ of PrXML$^{cont}$ obtained by putting back in $d_i$ the continuous nodes of $P$, where the corresponding leaves still exist.
2. Let $D_{i1}, \ldots, D_{ik}$ be the $k$ probability distributions over the real numbers represented in the *cont* nodes of $P_i$. We define then a continuous probability distribution $\Pr_i$ over $R^k$ as the product distribution (Ash & Doléans-Dade, 2000) of the distributions $D_{ij}$, i.e., the unique distribution such that $\Pr_i (X_1 \times \ldots \times X_k) = D_{i1}(X_1) \times \ldots \times D_{ik}(X_k)$. Let $D_i \subseteq D$ be all the documents that have the same structure as $d_i$, that is, that may differ from $d_i$ on the values of the leaves only. Then, the probability of every subset $D' \subseteq D$ defined by $\Pr_P$ is equal to the sum of the probabilities $p_i \Pr_i (D' \cap D_i)$, for all $i = 1..n$.

## QUERYING PROBABILISTIC XML

We explain here how p-documents can be queried, and what the complexity of this operation is, depending on the query language considered. Most of the results from this section are from (Kimelfeld et al., 2009; Abiteboul et al., 2010). They will be useful in understanding the kind of mining tasks that are tractable, as detailed in the next section. We start by introducing standard tree-pattern queries, before moving to aggregate queries, which are of special interest in mining tasks that involve data values. We first define how these queries apply to regular documents, and then explain how to query probabilistic documents.

### Tree-Pattern Queries

A *tree pattern*, denoted $Q$, is a tree with two types of edges: child edges and descendant edges. The nodes of the tree are labeled by a labeling function with either labels or variables (e.g., $x, y, z$), such that no variable occurs more than once, that is, *join variables* are not allowed.

A *tree-pattern query* has the form $Q[ntuple]$, where $Q$ is a tree pattern and *ntuple* is a tuple of nodes of $Q$ (defining its output). We sometimes identify the query with the pattern and simply write $Q$ instead of $Q[ntuple]$ if the tuple *ntuple* is not important or clear from the context. If *ntuple* is the empty tuple, we say that the query is Boolean. If the set of edges of a query is a linear order, the query is called a *single-path query*. We denote the set of all tree-pattern queries as TP, and the subclass of single-path queries as SP.

### Example 4

Consider the two queries in Figure 7, ignoring for now the aggregate functions *countd* and *sum*. The left query is over the mailbox DTD and the right one over the electricity consumption DTD, both can be found in Figure 3. Descendant edges are marked with double lines. The left query is a TP query since it has branching; it asks for people that received messages inside a given thread $t$. The right query is in SP since it has no branching; it returns all electricity consumption values recorded in the document.

*Figure 7. Two types of queries: TP query $Q^{countd}_{\text{Recpts}}$ and SP query $Q^{sum}_{\text{ElCon}}$*

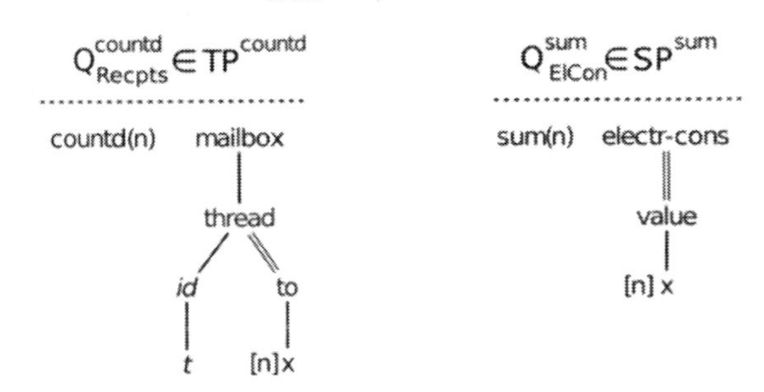


A *valuation* maps query nodes to document nodes. A document *satisfies* a query if there exists a *satisfying* valuation, which maps query nodes to the document nodes in a way that is consistent with the edge types and the labeling. That is,

1. nodes connected by child/descendant edges are mapped to nodes that are children/descendants of each other;
2. query nodes with label $a$ are mapped to document nodes with label $a$.

We define that applying a query $Q[ntuple]$ to a document $d$ returns a set of tuples of nodes:

```
Q(d):= {v(ntuple) | v satisfying
valuation for Q}.
```

### Aggregate Functions

An *aggregate function* maps a finite bag of values (e.g., rationals) into some domain (possibly the same or different). In particular, we assume that any aggregate function is defined on the empty bag. We consider here standard aggregate functions: *sum*, *count*, *min*, *countd* (count distinct), and *avg* (average) under their usual semantics. Our results easily extend to *max* and *topk*.

Aggregate functions can be naturally extended to work on documents $d$: the result $\alpha(d)$ is $\alpha(B)$ where $B = \{|l_1, \ldots, l_n|\}$ is the bag of the labels of all leaves in $d$. This makes the assumption that all leaves are of the type required by the aggregate function, e.g., rational numbers for *sum*. Again to simplify, we ignore this issue here and assume they all have the proper type. It is straightforward to extend this model and the corresponding results with a more refined treatment of typing.

A class of aggregate functions that play an important role in our investigation are *monoid* ones (Cohen, Nutt, & Sagiv, 2006), because they can be handled by a divide-and-conquer strategy. It turns out that *sum*, *count*, *min*, *max*, and *topk* are monoid aggregate functions. For example, *sum* can be handled as

$$sum(\{|l_1, \ldots, l_n|\}) = sum(\{|l_1|\}) + \ldots + sum(\{|l_n|\}) = l_1 + \ldots + l_n.$$

On the other hand, it is easy to check that neither *avg* nor *countd* are monoid aggregate functions and, as we see further, in general it is more difficult to handle them.

## Aggregate Queries over Documents

An *aggregate* TP-query has the form $Q[\alpha(n)]$, where $Q$ is a tree pattern, $n$ is a node of $Q$, and $\alpha$ is an aggregate function. The semantics of such an aggregate query $Q[\alpha(n)]$ is given by this three-step evaluation:

1. Evaluate the non-aggregate query $Q' := Q[n]$ over $d$ and obtain a set of nodes $Q'(d)$.
2. Compute the *bag* $B$ of labels of $Q'(d)$, that is $B := \{|\varphi(n) \mid n \in Q'(d)|\}$, where $\varphi$ is the labeling function of $d$.
3. Finally, apply $\alpha$ to $B$.

We denote the value resulting from evaluating an aggregate query $Q$ over $d$ as $Q(d)$. If $Q[n]$ is a non-aggregate query and $\alpha$ an aggregate function, we use the shorthand $Q^\alpha$ to denote the aggregate query $Q[\alpha(n)]$. More generally, we denote the set of aggregate queries obtained from queries in SP, TP, and some function $\alpha$, as $SP^\alpha$ and $TP^\alpha$, respectively.

### Example 5

Consider the two aggregate queries in Figure 7, where the aggregation nodes are marked with $[n]$. The query $Q^{countd}_{Recpts} \in TP^{countd}$ asks for the number of different persons receiving messages inside a given thread $t$. The evaluation of this query over the document $d_{MBOX}$ from Figure 5 with $t = 123$ returns the value 3, since there are three distinct persons concerned, namely Mary, Bob and John. The query $Q^{sum}_{ElCon} \in SP^{sum}$ returns the total electricity consumption across all rooms.

The syntax and semantics above can be generalized in a straightforward fashion to aggregate queries with an SQL-like GROUP BY operator.

## Queries over Probabilistic Documents

We have defined the semantics of queries over regular documents. We now define their semantics over a p-document using the possible-world semantics of p-documents.

First, consider a Boolean query $Q$. The semantics of $Q$ over $P$, denoted $Q(P)$ is defined as the probability that $Q$ evaluates to true in the possible-world semantics of $P$:

$$Q(P) = \Pr(Q(d) \mid d \in [|P|]).$$

Similarly, since an aggregate query $Q^\alpha$ maps elements of the probability space $[|P|]$ to values in the range of $\alpha$, we can see $Q^\alpha(P)$ as a random variable. We therefore define the result of applying $Q^\alpha$ to $P$ as the distribution of this random variable:

$$(Q^\alpha(P))(c) = \Pr(Q^\alpha(d) = c \mid d \in [|P|])$$

for $c$ in the range of α. Note that if the non-aggregate part $Q$ does not match a document $d$, then we define $Q^\alpha(d)$ depending on the type of α. If α is a monoid function, we define $Q^\alpha(d)$ as the neutral element corresponding to α, e.g., 0 for sum, $-\infty$ for max. If α is countd or avg, we set $Q^\alpha(d) = 0$.

Observe that for the case of continuous p-documents the probability defining $(Q^\alpha(P))(c)$ is equal to zero, unless there are Dirac functions labeling the leaves of $P$. A more appropriate definition for continuous p-documents would be on an interval, rather than a single point:

$$(Q^\alpha(P))(c_1, c_2) = \Pr(Q^\alpha(d) \in (c_1, c_2) \mid d \in [|P|])$$

for $c_1$ and $c_2$ in the range of α.

We use the notation $Q(P)$ or $Q^\alpha(P)$ to denote the random variable corresponding to the application of query $Q$ or $Q^\alpha$ over the random document $P^{rand}$ associated to a p-document $P$.

## Example 6

The evaluation of the query $Q^{countd}_{Recpts}$ over the mux-det p-document $P_{MBOX\text{-}L}$ gives the distribution:

$$Q^{countd}_{Recpts}(P_{MBOX\text{-}L}) = \{(1, 0.35), (3, 0.65)\}.$$

Indeed, $P_{MBOX\text{-}L}$ has three mux distributional nodes, $n_{70}$, $n_{72}$ and $n_{73}$ with two children each; therefore, there are eight possible worlds for this p-document. It is easy to see that in this example all generations yield different documents. Observe that the document $d_{MBOX}$ can be generated by choosing the right branch of $n_{70}$, the right branch of $n_{72}$, and the left branch of $n_{73}$. Considering these distributional nodes as the vector $(n_{70}, n_{72}, n_{73})$, the eight possible worlds are $w_1 = (l, l, l)$, $w_2 = (r, l, l)$, $w_3 = (l, r, l)$, $w_4 = (l, l, r)$, $w_5 = (r, r, l)$, $w_6 = (r, l, r)$, $w_7 = (l, l, r)$, $w_8 = (r, r, r)$, where $l$ (resp. $r$) stands for the choice of the left (resp. right) child of the corresponding mux node. Note that only the choice in node $n_{70}$ has an influence over the result of the aggregate query $Q^{countd}_{Recpts}$. One can see that the probabilities of the worlds are, for example, $\Pr(w_1) = 0.35 \times 0.2 \times 0.9$ and $\Pr(w_8) = 0.65 \times 0.8 \times 0.1$. The probability that there are three distinct recipients is:

$$\Pr(Q^{countd}_{Recpts}(P_{MBOX\text{-}L}) = 3) = \Pr(w_2) + \Pr(w_5) + \Pr(w_6) + \Pr(w_8) = 0.65$$

and otherwise, there is only one recipient (John).

Similarly, one can check that the evaluation of the query $Q^{countd}_{Recpts}$ over the PrXML$^{cie}$ p-document $P_{MBOX\text{-}G}$ gives the distribution:

$$Q^{countd}_{Recpts}(P_{MBOX\text{-}G}) = \{(1, 0.2), (2, 0.12), (3, 0.68)\}$$

by considering all possible valuations of the variables $x$ and $z$.

## Complexity of Querying and Aggregating p-Documents

We now summarize complexity results for both querying and aggregating probabilistic XML, from (Kimelfeld et al., 2009; Abiteboul et al., 2010). We are interested in *data complexity* (Vardi, 1982), i.e., the complexity is measured with respect to the size of the input document, the query being fixed. To simplify, we do not consider continuous distributions here, see (Abiteboul et al., 2010) for details. We are interested in three computational problems. (see Table 5)

The first problem is the computation of the probability:

$$\Pr(P^{rand} \models Q)$$

*Table 5. Worst-case data complexity of computation problems for $PrXML^{mux,det}$: the probability of a query match for a $Pr(P^{rand} \models Q)$ Boolean query Q; the probability of an aggregate value $Pr(Q^{\alpha}(P^{rand}) = c)$, and the moment $E^k(Q^{\alpha}(P^{rand}))$ of degree k for an aggregate query $Q^{\alpha}$ where $\alpha \in$ {count, sum, min, countd, avg}*

| | |
|---|---|
| $\Pr(P^{rand} \models Q)$ | PTIME |
| $\Pr(Q^{\alpha}(P^{rand}) = c)$ | *count, min* in PTIME |
| | *sum, avg, countd* in $FP^{\#P}$-complete |
| $E^k(Q^{\alpha}(P^{rand}))$ | SP in PTIME |
| | TP *avg* in $FP^{\#P}$<br>TP others in PTIME |

that a given Boolean query $Q$ matches a random document $P^{rand}$ of a given probabilistic document $P$. The second problem is the computation of the probability:

$$\Pr(Q^{\alpha}(P) = c)$$

that the value of a given aggregate query $Q^{\alpha}$ over a random document $P^{rand}$ of a given probabilistic document $P$ is equal to a given value $c$. The third problem is the computation of moments:

$$E^k(Q^{\alpha}(P))$$

of degree $k$ for a given aggregate query $Q^{\alpha}$ and a natural number $k$ (moments are useful summaries of probabilistic distributions, e.g., the moment of degree 1 is the expected value).

For the $PrXML^{cie}$ model all problems are intractable, namely $FP^{\#P}$-complete ($FP^{\#P}$ is a class of computational problems that are defined using counting counterparts of NP problems.) with the exception of the computation of moments for $SP^{sum}$ and $SP^{count}$, which is polynomial-time.

For $PrXML^{mux,det}$, the situation is more involved and is described in Table 1. The probability of a query match can be computed in polynomial time for TP. Note that for relational databases, computational problems for aggregate queries are usually more difficult than for non-aggregate queries (Cohen et al., 2006). This situation also holds for $PrXML^{mux,det}$ when considering the complexity of a probability of an aggregate value for $TP^{countd}$ or $TP^{avg}$ queries, that is, for queries with non-monoid aggregate functions. For $TP^{count}$ or $TP^{min}$ the complexity of aggregate value probability computation is the same as for the query match problem. Moment computation is tractable for $SP^{\alpha}$ with every considered $\alpha$ and even for $TP^{\alpha}$ when $\alpha \in \{count, sum, min, countd\}$.

**System issues.** Most existing work on probabilistic XML is at the theoretical level. At the time of this writing, an actual full-fledged system that supports the management of probabilistic XML is still missing. There are, however, several attempts at meeting this need. A first approach relies on encoding XML data into relations (Hollander & Keulen, 2010): a probabilistic XML database thus becomes encoded as a probabilistic relational database, that can then be managed using a system such as MayBMS, for which efficient query evaluation algorithms have been developed, both exact and approximate. The downside of the approach is that relational databases do not exploit the specific characteristics of tree-like data encoded into databases, that for instance makes tree-pattern queries over local models tractable. Another direction is to natively process tree-pattern queries over XML data: this is what is done in the implementation of the EvalDP algorithm (Kimelfeld et al., 2008; Kimelfeld et al., 2009) for $PrXML^{mux,det}$ and this is also the idea behind ProApproX (Senellart & Souihli, 2010a; Senellart & Souihli, 2010b), which implements approximate query answering using various schemes of sampling methods (Kimelfeld et al., 2009), on top of a native XML query processor. Either approach has ignored the specific aspects of indexing and storage of probabilistic XML. An actual system would need to reduce the number of disk and memory accesses to data and probabilistic annotations. A first observation is that it is sometimes more efficient to store the marginal probabilities of nodes in a document rather than the probabilities of nodes conditioned by the existence of their parent (Li, Shao, & Chen, 2006).

## MINING INFORMATION FROM PROBABILISTIC XML

In this section we show how techniques developed for query answering over probabilistic XML can be applied to data mining tasks. We illustrate the techniques on a number of use cases, for our two example scenarios: a collection of emails (such as the one from $P_{MBOX\text{-}G}$ or $P_{MBOX\text{-}L}$) and data collected from sensors (e.g., $P_{CONS}$).

### Mining Frequent Items

Frequent itemsets play an essential role in many data mining tasks that look for interesting patterns in databases, such as association rules, correlations, sequences, episodes, classifiers, clusters. Association rule mining, especially, is one of the most common data mining task, originally motivated by *market basket* analysis. This problem assumes that a number of items, like bread or milk, are bought by customers who fill their market baskets with (subsets of) these items. The task is to learn which items people usually buy together, this information being valuable to position items on market shelves and influence the way typical customers browse stores. Mining frequent itemsets is used as the basis of association rules mining since they guarantee that the rules are based on sets of items with a high *support* (Tan, Steinbach, & Kumar, 2005). In our mailbox example scenario, a traveling agency might want to find cities that are often mentioned in messages and then use this information for targeted advertisement. The following request checks for frequent terms in the mailbox repository: *Find a word that with probability higher than θ occurs more than k times in emails across all the threads*, where $\theta$ is the quality of frequent item prediction.

One possible strategy for running this request is to check for each city which is operated by the agency whether this city is frequently discussed in the mailbox repository. That is, for a given word $w$ and a p-document $P$, this request could be formulated as the decision problem $\Pr(Q^{count}(P) \geq k) \geq \theta$ for the following $SP^{count}$ aggregate query written in XPath notation:

$$Q^{count} = count(//\text{content}/w) \qquad (1)$$

For every p-document $P$, the range of the random variable $Q^{count}(P)$ (i.e., the number of different values with non-zero probability) is bounded by the number of leaves in $P$, that is, by the size $|P|$ of $P$. Therefore, taking into account that the probabilistic events $Q^{count}(P) = n_1$ and $Q^{count}(P) = n_2$ (where $n_2 n_1 \neq n_2$) are disjoint, we obtain that $\Pr(Q^{count}(P) \geq k)$ is equal to the sum of probabilities $\Pr(Q^{count}(P) = n)$, for all $n = k..\,|P|$. This sum can be computed in polynomial time as far as the computation of every component is polynomial. In the previous section we discussed that the tractability of probability computation $\Pr(Q^{count}(P) = n)$ for a given aggregate value depends on the type of the p-document $P$. For $P \in \text{PrXML}^{cie}$ the computation is hard, but for $P \in \text{PrXML}^{mux,det}$ the computation is indeed tractable for $TP^{count}$.

In the case when $Q \in TP$, the computation of $\Pr(Q^{count}(P) = n)$ can be done using the techniques of (Cohen et al., 2008) that are based on dynamic programming and boil down to computing the probability of a query match under aggregation constraints. In the case when $Q \in SP$, the computation of $\Pr(Q^{count}(P) = n)$ can be done using techniques from (Abiteboul et al., 2010), which allow for computing the entire distribution $Q^{count}(P)$ in one bottom-up scan of $P$, computing thus convex sums and convolutions of distributions.

### Example 7

We now compute the probability $\Pr(Q^{count}(P_{MBOX\text{-}L}) \geq 2)$ for the query of (1) and $w$ = "Hi". One can see that the probability $\Pr(Q^{count}(P_{\text{MBOX-L}}) = 1)$ is the same as the probability to choose the right child of the node $n_{73}$, that is, equal to 0.1. The probability of $\Pr(Q^{count}(P_{\text{MBOX-L}}) = 2)$ is equal to the probability of the left-side child, that is, to 0.9. Moreover, for $n > 2$, $\Pr(Q^{count}(P_{\text{MBOX-L}}) = n)$ is equal to 0. Therefore, $\Pr(Q^{count}(P_{\text{MBOX-L}}) \geq 2) = \Pr(Q^{count}(P_{\text{MBOX-L}})=2)=0.9$. Assuming the required quality of frequent item prediction $\theta$ is 0.8, then the word "Hi" is a frequent item, since it has high frequency and has the probability $0.9 > 0.8$.

## Mining Co-Occurring Items

Another important application of frequent itemset mining is the extraction of social-network graphs from communication traces. These graphs are used, for example, in recommender systems or social search applications, when one wants to use the social network of an individual to personalize recommendations or search results. Mining a social-network graph in our mailbox setting can be carried out in the following way: *Find all pairs of people that with probability higher than θ are emailing in the same thread.*

Every such pair can be interpreted as an edge of the social network. We could go further and also require that two persons have exchanged a minimum number of messages to categorize them as "friends", for instance, but let us consider this simple request for now.

One possible strategy for running this request is to check for each pair of names $(w_1, w_2)$ mentioned in a p-document whether their probability of co-occurrence is high enough. That is, for a p-document $P$ this request can be formulated as the decision problem $\Pr(P \models Q) \geq \theta$ for the Boolean TP query:

$$Q = // \text{thread}[.//\text{from} = w_1 \text{ and} .//\text{from} = w_2] \quad (2)$$

The probability of a Boolean query match for TP queries can be computed efficiently over PrXML$^{mux,det}$ p-documents using the techniques of (Kimelfeld et al., 2008). On the other hand, the computation is intractable over PrXML$^{cie}$ p-documents.

## Example 8

We now compute the probability $\Pr(P \models Q) \geq \theta$ for the query of (2), persons $w_1$ = "John", $w_2$ = "Mary" and threshold $\theta = 0.7$. The probability $\Pr(P \models Q)$ is the same as the probability to choose the left child of node $n_{72}$ and thus equal to 0.2, which is less than the threshold. We conclude that John and Mary are not friends. Besides, if $w_2$ = "Bob", then $\Pr(P \models Q) = 0.8$ and since $0.8 > 0.7$ we conclude that John and Bob are friends.

## Mining Popular Items

In applications such as recommender systems an important task is to find popular items (Ricci, Rokach, Shapira, & Kantor, 2010). A classic example of a recommender system is *Amazon*, where products like books or electronics are recommended to people. These recommendations are based on both the popularity of items and the purchase history of individual customers. Popular items are products that either have high users' ratings or have been chosen by many customers. In the mailbox example, an item could be a thread and its popularity could be measured by the number of people that received messages sent within the thread. An example of a request for popular threads is the following: *Find all threads that with probability higher than θ attract more than k different recipients.*

This request can be formulated as an aggregate query. For a given thread identifier $t$ and a p-document $P$, decide whether $\Pr(Q^{countd}(P) \geq k) \geq \theta$ holds where $Q^{countd}$ is the aggregate query:

$$Q^{countd} = countd(// \text{thread}[\text{id} = t]//\text{to}). \quad (3)$$

As in the case of $Q^{countd}(P)$, the range of the random variable $Q^{countd}(P)$ is limited by the number of leaves in $P$ and we can reformulate this query as $\Pr(Q^{countd}(P) \geq k)$ which is equal to the sum of probabilities $\Pr(Q^{countd}(P) = n)$, for all $n = k..\ |P|$. We are again in the case where the tractability of the mining task depends on the tractability of the probability computation $\Pr(Q^{countd}(P) = n)$. This time the aggregate function is *countd*, that is, a non-monoid function, and consequently, the probability computation is intractable in both models $\text{PrXML}^{cie}$ and $\text{PrXML}^{mux,det}$, even for $\text{SP}^{countd}$ queries. This means that the only known way to compute the probability is to construct the whole probability space of p-documents $[|P|]$ represented by $P$, then to evaluate the aggregate query $Q^{countd}$ in each document of $[|P|]$ separately and, finally, to sum the probabilities of the documents $d \in [|P|]$, where $Q^{countd}(d) = n$.

## Example 9

We compute the probability $\Pr(Q^{countd}(P_{\text{MBOX-G}}) \geq 3)$ for the query of (3) and $t$ = "greetings". As discussed in Example 6, there are four documents in $P_{\text{MBOX-G}}$ corresponding to different assignments of the variables $x$ and $z$. One can see that the only world where there are at least three different people subscribed to the thread "greetings" is when both $x$ and $z$ are assigned to false. The three recipient in this case are Mary, Bob, (who received the first message) and John (who received the second message). The probability of such a world is $0.85 \times 0.8 = 0.68$, therefore $\Pr(Q^{countd}(P_{\text{MBOX-G}}) \geq 3) = 0.68$. Assume that the required quality of popular item prediction $\theta$ is again 0.8. Then the thread "greetings" is not a popular item, since its popularity has lower probability.

## Mining Continuous Data

One application that motivated the introduction of a continuous model for probabilistic data is monitoring in sensor networks (Cheng, Kalashnikov, & Prabhakar, 2003; Abiteboul et al., 2010). A typical example of sensor network is sensors installed in a river to measure either the temperature, or the level of water, or the concentration of different chemical components to predict floods of poisoning of the river. Another example is sensors that measure consumption of, say, electricity or Internet bandwidth. In sensor networks, monitoring of measurements' behavior is the main task. One wants to be alerted whenever the level of water in the river is growing too fast, or when the electricity consumption is higher than expected. In this case one can make actions to avoid flooding or to repair, substitute the equipment that is wasting the electricity. Coming back to the continuous p-document $P_{CONS}$ we would like to perform the following monitoring task: *Find all rooms where the expected value of the total electricity consumption is more than v units.*

For a given room $r$, p-document $P$, and an expected electricity consumption of $v$ units this request can be reformulated as the decision problem $E(Q^{sum}(P)) \geq v$ for the aggregate query:

$$Q^{sum} = sum(/*/r/*/\text{value}) \tag{4}$$

The expected value $E(Q^{sum}(P))$ can be computed in polynomial time for continuous p-documents from $\text{PrXML}^{cont,mux,det}$ as long as one is able to compute the expected values of the continuous distributions stored on the leaves of p-documents (Abiteboul et al., 2010). The computation proceeds exactly in the same way as for discrete documents.

## Example 10

Let us compute the expected value $E(Q^{sum}(P))$ for the query of (4), room $r$ = "room1" and threshold $v = 150$. This can be done by separately computing the expected values of the sum in the left and in the right child of $n_{27}$, and then by combining the values as the convex sum with the corresponding coefficients 0.1 and 0.9; see (Abiteboul et al., 2010) for details. The expected value of a Gaussian is obviously its mean. The result is,

$E(Q^{sum}(P)) = 15 + (0.1 \times 50 + 0.9 \times 52) = 66.8.$

Since the expected value is below the threshold, we conclude that the electricity consumption in "room 1" is fine.

## CONCLUSION AND FUTURE RESEARCH

As shown in the previous section, a number of data mining tasks are indeed possible over probabilistic XML data, and it is possible to use probabilistic characterizations (probability higher than a threshold, expected value, etc.) to define these tasks. The efficiency of the proposed methods critically depends on the kind of data model considered (especially, global vs. local models) and on the tractability of querying over these models, for a query language (Boolean vs. aggregate queries, single-path vs. tree-pattern) that depends of the task considered.

The foundations of probabilistic XML are now quite well established. The connection between local and global models is well-understood, and the complexity of querying these models with tree-pattern queries has been investigated in length. Challenges in modeling and querying lie in more expressive models (such as the recursive Markov chains of (Benedikt et al., 2010)), more expressive query languages (especially, involving value joins, cf. (Senellart & Abiteboul, 2007; Abiteboul et al., 2010)), and understanding better how results from the relational and XML settings relate to each other. An important missing aspect is the building of an actual system that leverage the knowledge brought by theoretical studies of probabilistic XML. We have already pointed at several works in that direction.

On the mining side, however, much remains to be done. The approaches for mining probabilistic XML data proposed in this chapter directly rely on a reformulation of the problem as a query or a set of queries. In some cases, this might not be the most efficient technique. Consider for instance the problem of discovering frequent itemsets. Obviously, an approach that would consider all possible itemsets of a bounded size and evaluate a query for each of these would be impractical on large data even though this may amount to running a polynomial-time algorithm. It would make sense, in the spirit of (Bernecker et al., 2009) for relational data, of first evaluating the frequency of one-item sets, and then use this information as a basis to discover itemsets of larger cardinality, making use of the probability scores for top-$k$ retrieval. In other words, this chapter has described how to model probabilistic XML data, query it, and use this query capability as a general tool for various mining tasks. Further work could elaborate efficient algorithms for a specific mining task without necessary relying on the existing querying techniques.

## ACKNOWLEDGMENT

This work would not have been possible without the previous joint work (Abiteboul et al., 2010) on aggregate queries with Serge Abiteboul, T.-H. Hubert Chan, and Werner Nutt. This work was supported by the European Research Council grant Webdam (under FP7), grant agreement 226513, and by the Dataring project of the French ANR. We are also grateful to the anonymous reviewers and the editor of this book, whose comments were of great help in improving the chapter.

## REFERENCES

Abiteboul, S., Chan, T.-H. H., Kharlamov, E., Nutt, W., & Senellart, P. (2010). Aggregate queries for discrete and continuous probabilistic XML. In L. Segoufin (Ed.), *Proceedings of the 13th International Conference on Database Theory (ICDT)*, (pp. 50-61). ACM.

Abiteboul, S., Hull, R., & Vianu, V. (1995). *Foundations of databases*. Addison-Wesley.

Abiteboul, S., Kimelfeld, B., Sagiv, Y., & Senellart, P. (2009). On the expressiveness of probabilistic XML models. *The VLDB Journal, 18*(5), 1041–1064. doi:10.1007/s00778-009-0146-1

Abiteboul, S., & Senellart, P. (2006). Querying and updating probabilistic information in XML. In Y. E. Ioannidis, M. H. Scholl, J. W. Schmidt, F. Matthes, M. Hatzopoulos, K. Böhm, A. Kemper, T. Grust, & C. Böhm (Eds.), *Proceedings of the 10th International Conference on Extended Database Technology (EDBT),* (pp. 1059-1068). ACM.

Aggarwal, C. C. (Ed.). (2009). *Managing and mining uncertain data*. Springer.

Antova, L., Koch, C., & Olteanu, D. (2007). World-set decompositions: Expressiveness and efficient algorithms. In T. Schwentick, & D. Suciu (Eds.), *Proceedings of the 11th International Conference on Database Theory (ICDT),* (pp. 194-208). ACM.

Ash, R. B., & Doléans-Dade, C. A. (2000). *Probability & measure theory*. San Diego, CA: Academic Press.

Barceló, P., Libkin, L., Poggi, A., & Sirangelo, C. (2009). XML with incomplete information: Models, properties, and query answering. In *Proceedings of the 28th Symposium on Principles of Database Systems (PODS),* (pp. 237-246). ACM.

Benedikt, M., Kharlamov, E., Olteanu, D., & Senellart, P. (2010). Probabilistic XML via Markov chains. *Proceedings of the VLDB Endowment, 3*(1), 770–781.

Bernecker, T., Kriegel, H.-P., Renz, M., Verhein, F., & Züfle, A. (2009). Probabilistic frequent itemset mining in uncertain databases. In *Proceedings of the 15th Knowledge Discovery and Data Mining (KDD),* (pp. 119-128). ACM.

Boulos, J., Dalvi, N. N., Mandhani, B., Mathur, S., Ré, C., & Suciu, D. (2005). MYSTIQ: A system for finding more answers by using probabilities. In *Proceedings of the International Conference on Management of Data (SIGMOD),* (pp. 891-893). ACM.

Cheng, R., Kalashnikov, D. V., & Prabhakar, S. (2003). Evaluating probabilistic queries over imprecise data. In A. Y. Halevy, Z. G. Ives, & A. Doan (Eds.), *Proceedings of the International Conference on Management of Data (SIGMOD),* (pp. 551-562). ACM.

Chomicki, J., & Libkin, L. (2000). Aggregate languages for constraint databases. In *Proceedings of the Constraint Databases* (pp. 131-154). Springer.

Codd, E. F. (1970). A relational model of data for large shared data banks. *Communications of the ACM, 13*(6), 377–387. doi:10.1145/362384.362685

Codd, E. F. (1975). Understanding relations (Installment #7). *FDT - Bulletin of ACM SIGMOD, 7*(3), 23-28.

Codd, E. F. (1979). Extending the database relational model to capture more meaning. *ACM Transactions on Database Systems, 4*(4), 397–434. doi:10.1145/320107.320109

Cohen, S., Kimelfeld, B., & Sagiv, Y. (2008). Incorporating constraints in probabilistic XML. In M. Lenzerini, & D. Lembo (Eds.), *Proceedings of the 27th Symposium on Principles of Database Systems (PODS),* (pp. 109-118). ACM.

Cohen, S., Kimelfeld, B., & Sagiv, Y. (2009). Running tree automata on probabilistic XML. In J. Paredaens, & J. Su (Eds.), *Proceedings of the 28th Symposium on Principles of Database Systems (PODS),* (pp. 227-236). ACM.

Cohen, S., Nutt, W., & Sagiv, Y. (2006). Rewriting queries with arbitrary aggregation functions using views. *ACM Transactions on Database Systems, 31*(2), 672–715. doi:10.1145/1138394.1138400

Date, C. J. (1981). *An introduction to database systems* (3rd ed.). Addison-Wesley.

Dong, X. L., Halevy, A. Y., & Yu, C. (2009). Data integration with uncertainty. *The VLDB Journal, 18*(2), 469–500. doi:10.1007/s00778-008-0119-9

Fagin, R., Kolaitis, P. G., & Popa, L. (2005). Data exchange: Getting to the core. *ACM Transactions on Database Systems, 30*(1), 174–210. doi:10.1145/1061318.1061323

Fuhr, N., & Rölleke, T. (1997). A probabilistic relational algebra for the integration of information retrieval and database systems. *ACM Transactions on Information Systems, 15*(1), 32–66. doi:10.1145/239041.239045

Galindo, J., Urrutia, A., & Piattini, M. (2006). *Fuzzy databases: Modeling, design and implementation*. Hershey, PA: IGI Global.

Grant, J. (1977). Null values in a relational data base. *Information Processing Letters, 6*(5), 156–157. doi:10.1016/0020-0190(77)90013-8

Green, T. J., & Tannen, V. (2006). Models for incomplete and probabilistic information. In *Proceedings of the Extended Database Technology (EDBT Workshops): Vol. 4254. Lecture Notes in Computer Science* (pp. 278-296). ACM.

Hollander, E., & van Keulen, M. (2010). Storing and querying probabilistic XML using a probabilistic relational DBMS. In *Proceedings of the 4th International Workshop on Management of Uncertain Data (MUD).*

Huang, J., Antova, L., Koch, C., & Olteanu, D. (2009). MayBMS: A probabilistic database management system. In *Proceedings of the ACM SIGMOD International Conference on Management of Data (SIGMOD)* (pp. 1071-1074). ACM.

Hung, E., Getoor, L., & Subrahmanian, V. S. (2003a). Probabilistic interval XML. In D. Calvanese, M. Lenzerini, & R. Motwani (Eds.), *Proceedings of the International Conference on Database Theory (ICDT) Lecture Notes in Computer Science: Vol. 2572* (pp. 358-374). ACM.

Hung, E., Getoor, L., & Subrahmanian, V. S. (2003b). PXML: A probabilistic semistructured data model and algebra. In Umeshwar Dayal, K. Ramamritham, & T. M. Vijayaraman (Eds.), *Proceedings of the International Conference on Data Engineering (ICDE),* (p. 467). IEEE Computer Society.

Imieliński, T., & Lipski, W. Jr. (1984). Incomplete information in relational databases. *Journal of the ACM, 31*(4), 761–791. doi:10.1145/1634.1886

Imieliński, T., Naqvi, S. A., & Vadaparty, K. V. (1991). Querying design and planning databases. In *Proceedings of the International Conference on Deductive and Object-Oriented Databases (DOOD),* (pp. 524-545). Springer.

ISO/IEC. (2008). *ISO/IEC 9075: SQL*. Geneva, Switzerland: International Standards Organization.

Kharlamov, E., Nutt, W., & Senellart, P. (2010). Updating probabilistic XML. In *Proceedings of the Extended Database Technology (EDBT Workshops).* ACM.

Kimelfeld, B., Kosharovski, Y., & Sagiv, Y. (2008). Query efficiency in probabilistic XML models. In *Proceedings of the ACM SIGMOD International Conference on Management of Data (SIGMOD),* (pp. 701-714). ACM.

Kimelfeld, B., Kosharovsky, Y., & Sagiv, Y. (2009). Query evaluation over probabilistic XML. *The VLDB Journal, 18*(5), 1117–1140. doi:10.1007/s00778-009-0150-5

Lafferty, J., McCallum, A., & Pereira, F. (2001). Conditional random fields: Probabilistic models for segmenting and labeling sequence data. In C. E. Brodley, & A. Pohoreckyj Danyluk (Eds.), *Proceedings of the 18th International Conference on Machine Learning (ICML),* (pp. 282-289). Morgan Kaufmann.

Lakshmanan, L. V. S., Leone, N., Ross, R. B., & Subrahmanian, V. S. (1997). ProbView: A flexible probabilistic database system. *ACM Transactions on Database Systems, 22*(3), 419–469. doi:10.1145/261124.261131

Li, T., Shao, Q., & Chen, Y. (2006). Pepx: A query-friendly probabilistic XML database. In P. S. Yu, V. J. Tsotras, E. A. Fox, & B. Liu (Eds.), *Proceedings of the International Conference on Information and Knowledge Management (CIKM),* (pp. 848-849). *ACM.*

Libkin, L., & Wong, L. (1996). Semantic representations and query languages for or-sets. *Journal of Computer and System Sciences, 52*(1), 125–142. doi:10.1006/jcss.1996.0010

Lopatenko, A., & Bertossi, L. E. (2007). Complexity of consistent query answering in databases under cardinality-based and incremental repair semantics. In T. Schwentick, & D. Suciu (Eds.), *Proceedings of the 11th International Conference on Database Theory (ICDT) Lecture Notes in Computer Science: Vol. 4353.* (pp. 179-193). Springer.

Nayak, R. (2005). Discovery knowledge from XML documents. In *Encyclopaedia of data warehousing and mining* (pp. 372–376). Hershey, PA: IGI Global. doi:10.4018/978-1-59140-557-3.ch071

Nierman, A., & Jagadish, H. V. (2002). ProTDB: Probabilistic data in XML. In *Proceedings of the 28th International Conference on Very Large Data Base (VLDB),* (pp. 646-657). Morgan Kaufmann.

Ré, C., Dalvi, N. N., & Suciu, D. (2006). Query evaluation on probabilistic databases. *A Quarterly Bulletin of the Computer Society of the IEEE Technical Committee on Data Engineering, 29*(1), 25–31.

Ricci, F., Rokach, L., Shapira, B., & Kantor, P. (Eds.). (2010). *Recommender systems handbook.* Springer.

Sarma, A. D., Benjelloun, O., Halevy, A. Y., & Widom, J. (2006). Working models for uncertain data. In L. Liu, A. Reuter, K.-Y. Whang, & J. Zhang (Eds.), *Proceedings of the 22nd International Conference on Data Engineering (ICDE),* (p. 7). IEEE Computer Society.

Sen, P., Deshpande, A., & Getoor, L. (2009). PrDB: Managing and exploiting rich correlations in probabilistic databases. *The VLDB Journal, 18*(5), 1065–1090. doi:10.1007/s00778-009-0153-2

Senellart, P., & Abiteboul, S. (2007). On the complexity of managing probabilistic XML data. In L. Libkin *(Ed.), Proceedings of the Symposium on Principles of Database Systems (PODS),* (pp. 283-292). ACM.

Senellart, P., & Souihli, A. (2010a). ProApproX: A lightweight approximation query processor over probabilistic trees. In *Proceedings of the ACM SIGMOD International Conference on Management of Data.* ACM.

Senellart, P., & Souihli, A. (2010b). Un système de gestion de données XML probabilistes. In *Bases de Données Avancées.* BDA.

Tan, P.-N., Steinbach, M., & Kumar, V. (2005). *Introduction to data mining.* Addison Wesley.

van Keulen, M., de Keijzer, A., & Alink, W. (2005). A probabilistic XML approach to data integration. In *Proceedings of the 21st International Conference on Data Engineering (ICDE),* (pp. 459-470). IEEE Computer Society.

Vardi, M. Y. (1982). The complexity of relational query languages (Extended Abstract). In *Proceedings of the 14th Symposium on Theory of Computing (STOC),* (pp. 137-146). ACM.

Widom, J. (2005). Trio: A system for integrated management of data, accuracy, and lineage. In *Proceedings of the Conference on Innovative Data Systems Research (CIDR)* (pp. 262-276). Online Proceedings.

Zimányi, E. (1997). Query evaluation in probabilistic relational databases. *Theoretical Computer Science, 171*(1-2), 179–219. doi:10.1016/S0304-3975(96)00129-6

## ADDITIONAL READING

Abiteboul, S., Chan, T.-H. H., Kharlamov, E., Nutt, W., & Senellart, P. (2010). Aggregate Queries for Discrete and Continuous Probabilistic XML. In *Proceeding of the 13th International Conference on Database Theory (ICDT),* (pp. 50-61). ACM.

Abiteboul, S., Hull, R., & Vianu, V. (1995). *Foundations of Databases*. Addison Wesley.

Abiteboul, S., Kimelfeld, B., Sagiv, Y., & Senellart, P. (2009). On the Expressiveness of Probabilistic XML Models. *The VLDB Journal, 18*(5), 1041–1064. doi:10.1007/s00778-009-0146-1

Aggarwal, C. C. (Ed.). (2009). *Managing and Mining Uncertain Data*. Springer.

Kimelfeld, B., Kosharovsky, Y., & Sagiv, Y. (2009). Query Evaluation over Probabilistic XML. *The VLDB Journal, 18*(5), 1117–1140. doi:10.1007/s00778-009-0150-5

# Chapter 3
# XML Similarity Detection and Measures

**Sanjay Kumar Madria**
*Missouri University of Science and Technology, USA*

**Waraporn Viyanon**
*Missouri University of Science and Technology, USA*

## ABSTRACT

*XML similarity detection plays an important role in facilitating many applications such as data integration, document classification/clustering, querying, and change management. In this chapter, we present an overview on XML document syntactic and semantic similarity/distance measures along with existing research related to XML similarity detection. The measures are classified into two main categories: structural similarity, and structural and content similarity. We review similarity detection approaches proposed in the literature and discuss some of the challenges and future directions for research on XML similarity detection and related fields.*

## INTRODUCTION

In recent years, the number of various multi-dimensional data generated and distributed in various information sources as well as the number of users that use these information sources has been increasing. These sources usually use different models for the representation of data, such as the relational model, semistructured models on the web, text files, etc. For efficient data management and exchange, XML has been increasing its relevance as a fundamental standard. As the widespread use of XML for describing and exchanging data on the web is increasing, XML based comparison becomes a central issue in the database and information retrieval. The use of XML similarity in a wide range of applications such as data integration, change management, classification/clustering of XML documents and XML querying is needed (Tekli, Chbeir, & Yetongnon, 2009).

DOI: 10.4018/978-1-61350-356-0.ch003

The objective of data integration is to identify similar XML documents originated from different data source to be integrated so that users can access more complete information. Typically the individuals doing the integration are not experts of the data; they must first understand the nature of the data, what data is available and how good it is. They must determine how the data is represented in the application and decide how to normalize data across the data sources. Data integration task is not easy. A good similarity measurement is required to improve the result of the data integration, otherwise users might discover problems such as unexpected or missing results appear and they have to look through the whole process.

The purpose of change management is to discover changes by finding dissimilarity among documents which helps the user tell what has been inserted, updated, or deleted from the last version. This can be applied in many applications, such as version control or index maintenance. Classification of XML documents can be exploited to improve storage, retrieval and indexing facilities. Only structures of XML documents are measured for the similarity to solve the problem of recognizing different sources providing the same kind of information. For XML query processing, similarity among documents will be calculated to find and rank results according to their similarity in order to retrieve the best results as possible. This is obvious that all of these applications require similarity measurement.

XML similarity detection for XML documents can be classified into two main categories: (i) structural similarity and (ii) structural and content similarity. In addition, semantic similarity becomes important in document similarity particularly in information retrieval and information integration as it supports the detection of conceptually close (but not identical) entities.

The rest of this chapter is organized as follows: Section "Background" introduces background knowledge on views and benefits of using XML, whereas the subsequent section outlines significant challenges in XML similarity detection. Section "Similarity Measures" overviews similarity measures from both syntactic and semantic viewpoints. Section "XML similarity" describes existing approaches and the use of XML similarity. Finally, the chapter ends with a section containing concluding remarks and a discussion on open issues concerning XML similarity detection.

## BACKGROUND

### Views of XML

XML documents can be classified as having either a *document-centric* (*text-centric*) view or a *data-centric* view (Bourret, 2005).

Data-centric documents are used to transport data. As such, they are highly structured data marked up with XML tags. Most data-centric XML documents are generated from structured sources such as RDBMS. The data-centric view emphasizes on XML structure since the meaning of a data-centric XML document depends only on the structured data represented inside it, and is usually used to exchange data in a structured form.

Document-centric documents focus on application-relevant objects. They are loosely structured documents marked-up with XML tags, and their meaning depends on the document as a whole. Their structure is more irregular, and their data are heterogeneous. Such documents might not even have a document-type declaration (DTD) or XML schema. For this view, text is a higher priority than structure. Figure 1 shows examples of both document-centric and data-centric documents.

### Benefits of XML

In (Daly, 2003) the main benefits of XML are outlined, explaining why it is an effective solution for the design of a wide range of applications.

*Figure 1. Two types of XML documents: (a) text-centric document, and (b) data-centric document*

```
<FlightInfo>
   <Airline>ABC  Airways</Airline>
         provides
   <Count>three</Count>
         non-stop flights daily from
   <Origin>Dallas</Origin>
         to
   <Destination>Fort Worth</Destination>.
         Departure times are
   <Departure>09:15</Departure>,
   <Departure>11:15</Departure>,
         and
   <Departure>13:15</Departure>.
         Arrival times are minutes later.
</FlightInfo>
```

(a)

```
<Flights>
   <Airline>ABC Airways</Airline>
   <Origin>Dallas</Origin>
   <Destination>Fort Worth</Destination>
   <Flight>
      <Departure>09:15</Departure>
      <Arrival>09:16</Arrival>
   </Flight>
   <Flight>
      <Departure>11:15</Departure>
      <Arrival>11:16</Arrival>
   </Flight>
   <Flight>
      <Departure>13:15</Departure>
      <Arrival>13:16</Arrival>
   </Flight>
</Flights>
```

(b)

1. **XML is simple.** It codes information coded in a format that is easy for humans to read and understand, and easy for applications to process.
2. **XML is extensibility.** It has no fixed set of fields. New fields can be created as needed.
3. **XML is self-describing.** In traditional databases, data records require schemas set up by the database administrator. Because they contain meta-data in the form of fields and attributes, XML documents can be stored without such definitions. XML also provides a basis for author identification and versioning at the element level. Any XML field can possess an unlimited number of attributes, such as author or version.
4. **XML is a World Wide Web Consortium (W3C) standard endorsed by software industry market leaders.**
5. **XML supports multilingual documents and Unicode.** It is appropriate for the international applications.
6. **XML facilitates the comparison and aggregation of data.** The tree structure of XML documents allows documents to be compared and aggregated efficiently, element-by-element.
7. **XML can embed multiple data types.** XML documents can contain any possible data type - from multimedia data (image, sound, and video) to active components (Java applets, ActiveX).
8. **XML can embed existing data.** Mapping existing data structures like file systems or relational databases to XML is simple. XML supports multiple data formats and can cover all existing data structures.

## CHALLENGES IN XML SIMILARITY DETECTION

Some of the major challenges that can be identified in XML similarity detection are here described as follows.

**Performance:** Generally, XML similarity detection relies on a large number of comparisons among subtrees in DOM (Document Object Model) trees. To identify simple and reasonable properties of the match and merge functions, efficient processing and optimal algorithms are needed.

**Scalability:** Most XML documents, particularly in XML data integration, are large (e.g., such as protein sequence data sets). Efficient matching and merging functions require that the data sets are loaded, which may not allow them to fit into the main memory to fetch and write results to disk as efficiently as possible. Secondary storage may be required in this case. One possible solution is to store XML documents in a relational database, which requires a mapping technique to maintain the structure and content of the XML documents.

**Similarity notion and measures:** Similarity measures play a key role in analyzing XML similarity. Selecting or building a similarity approach is important for accuracy. Many approaches measuring similarity must be compared and improved for efficiency.

## SIMILARITY MEASURES

The concept of similarity has been the subject of research in the fields of computer science, psychology, artificial intelligence, and linguistics. Typically, such studies have focused on the similarity between vectors, strings, trees, or objects. In our context, the input data comes from two documents, $X$ and $Y$, and any similarity measure considered is presented as a function $X$ and $Y$ indicating the degree of similarity between documents $X$ and $Y$. The similarity value is typically a number between 0 and 1; in general, the similarity is minimized only if the two documents share nothing in common, and it is maximized only if the two documents are identical. In order to decide which pair of documents is similar, a threshold is usually defined. In the following, we briefly recall the most popular similarity/distance measures used for documents, which include measures defined in a Vector-space model, those defined for strings, and those defined as semantics-aware based on the use of a knowledge base. The interested reader can find exhaustive descriptions of distance/similarity functions in (Deza & Deza 2009; Cha, 2007), and detailed information on string matching in (Gusfield, 1997); moreover, (Budanitsky & Hirst, 2006) provides an interesting review of WordNet-based measures for lexical semantic similarity.

### Vector-Space Data Similarity

In the Vector-space data model (Salton, Wong, & Yang, 1975), given a collection $D$ of documents, a set of terms (vocabulary) $V$, any document $d \in D$ is represented by an $m$-dimensional vector ($m = |V|$) such that the $i$-th element in the vector measures the importance of the term $t_i \in V$ as a valid descriptor of the content of document $d$. The "importance" is usually quantified on the basis of a combination of the frequency of occurrence of the term with respect to the document (local term frequency) and to the whole collection (global term frequency). The *term frequency-inverse document frequency* function represents the most popular term relevance weighting scheme (see Chapter "A Study of XML Models for Data Mining: Representations, Methods, and Issues").

The relevance of a document to a query, or to another document, is evaluated as a measure of *proximity* between their respective vectors. A measure of proximity must satisfy at least the properties of non-negativity, reflexivity, symmetry, and transitivity. A natural way to quantify the proximity between generic (numerical) data vectors is to resort to a *distance* function, or *metric*, defined on a geometrical (Euclidean) space, for which the triangle inequality property also holds. A very common class of distance functions includes the L1 norm (also known as Manhattan or city-block distance) and the L2 norm (also known as Euclidean distance). Given two data vectors $X$ and $Y$ of length $m$, these two norms are defined as:

$$L_1(X,Y) = \sum_{i=1}^{m} | x_i - y_i |$$

$$L_2(X,Y) = \sqrt{\sum_{i=1}^{m} (x_i - y_i)^2}$$

However, the use of metrics turns out to be inappropriate for documents: indeed, the direct use of metrics does not address the issue of text length normalization, so that long documents would be more similar to each other by virtue of length (instead of topic); moreover, in these metrics there is a tendency of the largest scaled attributes to dominate the others, therefore attribute scaling and standardization or attribute weighting might be required to use such metrics.

The Vector space model proposes to quantify the proximity between documents by computing a function of similarity, typically expressed as the *cosine* of the angle between their respective vectors:

$$\cos(\theta) = \frac{| X | \cdot | Y |}{|| X || \times || Y |} = \frac{\sum_i x_i y_i}{\sqrt{\sum_i x_i^2}\sqrt{\sum_i y_i^2}}$$

The cosine similarity provides the measure of the angle between the two documents to check whether the two documents point to the same direction or not. We can also transform this measure in set notation:

$$sim_{cosine}(X,Y) = \frac{| X \cap Y |}{\sqrt{| X | \cdot | Y |}}$$

The above set notation allows us to easily compare the cosine similarity and other popular similarity functions, namely *Jaccard* and *Dice* similarity:

$$sim_{Jaccard}(X,Y) = \frac{| X \cap Y |}{| X \cup Y |}$$

$$sim_{Dice}(X,Y) = \frac{2 | X \cap Y |}{| X \cup Y |}$$

Similarity solutions in a Vector-space model are easy to implement, although this model suffers from several limitations. For instance, the order in which the terms appear in a document is lost, as well as the phrase structure and other structure information. Moreover, semantic information is missing, since only syntactic information (i.e., term frequency) is stored.

## String Similarity

String matching is important in the domain of text processing. It involves identifying a place where one or several strings are found within a text. String matching algorithms generally scan the text with the help of a *window*. A typical scheme, called *sliding window*, essentially works as follows: first, the left ends of the window and the text are aligned, then the characters of the window (called patterns) are compared; after a whole matching of the pattern, or after a mismatch, the window is shifted to the right, and the same procedure is repeated until the right end of the window goes beyond the right end of the text.

Longest common subsequence (LCS) (Maier, 1978) determines the longest subsequences that can be obtained by deleting zero or more symbols from each of two given sequences of characters. This is an NP-hard problem. Given two sequences $X = (x_1, \ldots, x_i, \ldots, x_n)$ and $Y = (y_1, \ldots, y_j, \ldots, y_m)$ having possibly different lengths, let $X_i$ and $Y_j$ denote the $i$-th and the $j$-th prefixes of $X$ and $Y$, respectively. For any two prefixes $X_i$ and $Y_j$, the set of longest common subsequences is defined as shown in Exhibit 1.

This method is suitable for biological data integration applications (Gusfield, 1997), where exact string matching often fails to associate a

*Exhibit 1.*

$$LCS(X_i, Y_j) = \begin{cases} \varnothing & \text{if } i = 0 \text{ or } j = 0 \\ (LCS(X_{i-1}, Y_{j-1}), x_i) & \text{if } x_i = y_j \\ longest(LCS(X_i, Y_{j-1}), LCS(X_{i-1}, Y_j)) & \text{if } x_i \neq y_j \end{cases}$$

name with its biological concept (e.g., ID or accession number in the database) due to seemingly small differences between names. Soft string matching could permit identification of relevant information by considering the similarity between names; however, the accuracy of soft matching depends heavily on the similarity measure used.

## Semantic Similarity

Semantic similarity rests on the concept that a set of documents, or terms within a term list, can be assigned a metric based on the relatedness of their semantic content. Semantic similarity methods (Resnik, 1995), (Jiang & Conrath, 1997), (Li, Bandar, & McLean, 2003), (Lin, 1998), (Pirro & Seco, 2008) have been introduced to capture the meaning of words. Generally, these methods can be categorized into two main groups: edge-counting-based methods (Rada, Mili, Bicknell, & Blettner, 1989) and information-corpus-based methods.

Semantic similarity requires a lexical database. One large lexical database used in many natural language processing (NLP) applications is WordNet. WordNet (Fellbaum, 1998) includes most English nouns, verbs, adjectives, and adverbs, and is organized by meaning: words in close proximity are semantically similar. It is classified in terms of "synsets", or unordered sets of roughly synonymous word or multi-word phases. Each synset expresses a distinct meaning/concept. Figure 2(a) shows the synsets for the term *pipe*, one per row, where each row contains synonym words and meaning.

A taxonomy is represented in a hierarchal form consisting of nodes and edges. Each node represents a synset, and each edge indicates a semantic relationship between synsets, namely hyperonymy, hyponymy, holonymy, meronymy, coordinate term, troponymy, or entailment. Figure 2(b) depicts the relations among synsets.

## Node and Edge Metrics

### Edge-Counting Based Metric

The edge-based approach is a simple and intuitive way of evaluating semantic similarity in a taxonomy. This approach estimates the distance between nodes corresponding to the concepts being compared. This geometric distance can be measured. Rada, Mili, Bicknell, and Blettner (1989) showed that the simplest means of determining the distance between two concept nodes, *A* and *B*, is identifying the shortest path that links *A* and *B*, or the minimum number of edges that separate *A* and *B*.

Jiang and Conrath (1997) have noted that the distance between any two adjacent nodes is not necessarily equal; therefore, this approach is not sensitive to the problem of varying link distances. Edge weight can be considered in order to solve this problem. It is related to the number of children, the depth of a node in the hierarchy, the type of link (such as is-a, part-of, or substance-of links), the network density, and the strength of an edge link.

*Figure 2. (a) WordNet's synsets, (b) portion of WordNet*

**Noun**
{pipe, tobacco pipe} (a tube with a small bowl at one end; used for smoking tobacco)
{pipe, pipage, piping} (a long tube made of metal or plastic that is used to carry water or oil or gas etc.)
{pipe, tube} (a hollow cylindrical shape)
{pipe} (a tubular wind instrument)
{organ pipe, pipe, pipework} (the flues and stops on a pipe organ)
**Verb**
{shriek, shrill, pipe up, pipe} (utter a shrill cry)
{pipe} (transport by pipeline) "pipe oil, water and gas into the desert"
{pipe} (play on a pipe) "pipe a tune"
{pipe} (trim with piping) "pipe the skirt"

(a)

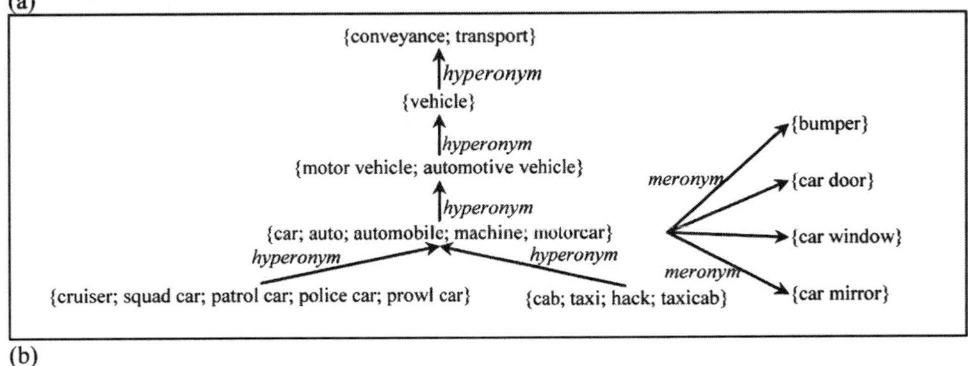


(b)

## Path Length Metric

Leacock and Chodorow's measure of similarity (Leacock & Chodorow, 1998) relies on the length $len(c_1, c_2)$ of the shortest path between two synsets:

$$sim_{LC}\left(c_1, c_2\right) = -\log \frac{len(c_1, c_2)}{2 \times DEPTH}$$

where *DEPTH* is the overall depth of the taxonomy. This measure is limited by its attention to *is-a* links and to the scale of the path length, or the depth of the taxonomy.

## Node Depth Metric

This method measures the depth of two concepts in a taxonomy and the depth of their *least common subsumer*. It then combines these properties into a similarity score:

$$sim_{WP}\left(c_1, c_2\right) = \frac{2 \times depth(lcs(c_1, c_2))}{depth(c_1) + depth(c_2)}$$

where *lcs*() computes the lowest common subsumer and *depth*() computes the depth of a concept node in the hierarchy.

## Information Corpus-Based Methods

Several research groups (Resnik, 1995), (Jiang & Conrath, 1997) and (Lin, 1998) have proposed information-content (IC) based measures of semantic similarity between terms. These measures were designed mainly for WordNet.

## Resnik's Measure

This measure calculates the semantic similarity between two concepts $c_1$, $c_2$ in a given ontology (e.g., WordNet) as the *information content* (IC) of the least common subsumer between $c_1$ and $c_2$. The idea behind this measure is that the semantic relatedness of two concepts is proportional to the amount of information they share in common The IC of a concept $c$ can be quantified in terms of the probability of its occurrence, and hence estimated in terms of its relative frequency of occurrence:

$$sim_{Resnik}\left(c_1, c_2\right) = IC(lcs(c_1, c_2)) = -\log(\Pr(c))$$

The probability Pr($c$), where $c$ represents $lcs(c_1, c_2)$, is defined as the probability that a randomly selected word in a corpus is an instance of the concept $c$. This can also be rewritten as:

$$\Pr(c) = \frac{\sum_{w \in words(c)} count(w)}{N}$$

where $words(c)$ is the set of words subsumed by concept $c$, and $N$ is the total number of words in the corpus.

### Jiang and Conrath Distance

Intuitively, the more differences between $A$ and $B$, the less similar they are. Conversely, the more $A$ and $B$ have in common, the more similar they are. Jiang and Conrath distance uses the notion of information content and the probability of encountering an instance of a child-synset given an instance of an LCS. Thus, the information content of the two nodes, as well as that of their most specific subsume, plays a part:

$$dist_{JC}\left(c_1, c_2\right) = 2 \times \log \Pr(lcs(c_1, c_2)) - (\log \Pr(c_1) + \log \Pr(c_2))$$

Note that the output for this equation is the distance, the inverse of similarity.

### Lin's Measure

Lin's similarity measure follows from his theory of similarity between arbitrary objects. It uses the same elements as Jiang and Conrath distance, but in a different fashion:

$$sim_{Lin}\left(c_1, c_2\right) = \frac{2 \times \log \Pr(lcs(c_1, c_2))}{\log \Pr(c_1) + \log \Pr(c_2)}$$

## XML SIMILARITY

Much work has addressed similarity in XML data. XML similarity can in principle be computed at different layers of abstraction; at the data layer (i.e., similarity between data), at the type layer (i.e., similarity between types, also referred to as schema, models, or structures, depending on the application domain), or between the two layers (i.e., similarity between data and types). XML similarity can be categorized as either of two approaches: (1) structural similarity; or (2) content and structural similarity. The XML documents thus compared are data-centric documents.

### Structural Similarity

Structural similarity focuses mainly on document classification or schema mapping in order to generate a global schema. A global schema is generated based on formal merge ontology as a basis for integration and to resolve heterogeneity problems during integration. Buttler (2004) summarized three approaches to structural similarity: *tag similarity*, *tree edit distance* (TED), and *Fourier transform similarity*.

### Tag Similarity

This is the simplest way to measure the structural similarity of documents. It measures how close element names from two XML documents are. Documents that use similar element names are likely to have similar schema. This measure evaluates the number of intersected elements from the compared documents and it is divided by the union. In addition, the overlap can be calculated by applying taxonomy to observe how similar element names are.

However, tag similarity is not suitable for several reasons. One critical problem is that documents conforming to the same schema may have only a limited number of element names; one document may contain a large number of a particular element name, whereas the other may contain relatively few occurrences of the tag. Moreover, tag similarity completely ignores the structure of documents, thus yielding low clustering or classification quality.

## Tree Edit Distance

Because XML documents can be represented in tree form, one popular technique is to determine the edit operations that can transform one tree into another with minimum cost. Edit operations can be classified in two groups: atomic edit operations and complex edit operations. An atomic edit operation can be either the deletion of an inner or leaf node, the insertion of an inner or leaf node, or the update of one node by another node. A complex edit operation is the insertion, deletion, or update of a whole subtree. Tai (1979) introduced the first non-exponential algorithm that has complexity $O(|T_1||T_2|\ depth(T_1)^2 depth(T_2)^2)$ when finding the minimum edit distance between trees $T_1$ and $T_2$. Here, $|T_1|$ and $|T_2|$ denote the number of nodes in $T_1$ and $T_2$, respectively, and *depth*() computes the depth of a tree.

Figure 3 shows an example of tree edit distance (TED) calculation between trees $T_1$ and $T_2$. If nodes *b*, *c*, and *d* are inserted in the sequence, then $T_1$ can transformed into $T_2$ and the distance calculated is equal to 3.

Previously, edit operations (insertion, deletion, substitution) have been allowed on single nodes

*Figure 3. Atomic tree edit distance calculation*

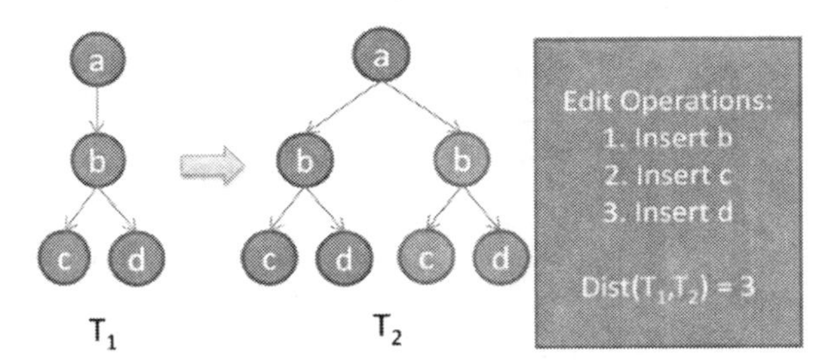


only. If the distance between trees is computed by applying atomic edit operations as in Figure 4, the distance between $T_A$ and $T_B$ is equal to 5 as calculated from the cost of inserting node *h*, *b*, *c*, *d*, and *h*. This cost is equal to the distance between $T_A$ and $T_C$ the cost of inserting *h*, *e*, *f*, *g*, and *h*. In other words, $T_B$ and $T_C$ have the same distance from $T_A$. Obviously, $T_B$ is more similar to $T_A$ based on subtree structural commonalities (the complex tree edit operations) marked as circles in the XML tree comparisons in Figure 4.

Chawathe's approach (Chawathe, 1999) considers the insertion and deletion operations at the leaf-node level and allows replacement of node labels anywhere in the tree, but disregards the move operation. The overall complexity of Chawathe's algorithm is expressed as $O(N^2)$, where $N$ is the maximum number of nodes in the trees being compared. This method is computationally expensive and has a prohibitively high run time; therefore, it is not practical for similarity matching over large XML data repositories.

Shasha and Zhang (1997) propose a TED metric that permits the addition and deletion of single nodes anywhere in the tree, not just at the leaves. However, entire subtrees cannot be inserted or deleted in one step. The complexity of this approach is expressed as $O(|T_1|\ |T_2|\ depth(T_1)\ depth(T_2))$.

Nierman and Jagadish (2002) emphasize the identification of subtree structural similarities. Their edit operations are similar to those defined by Chawathe, but they add two new operations: "insert tree" and "delete tree". To determine sub-

*Figure 4. Examples of tree edit distance between three XML trees*

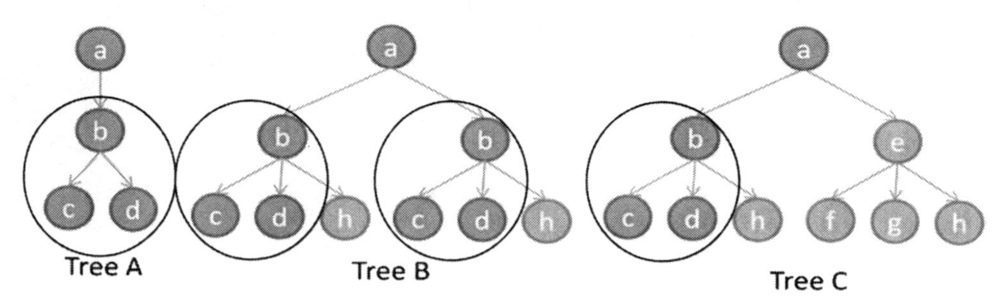


tree similarities, they introduce containment in the relationship between trees or subtrees. A tree $T_1$ is said to be *contained* in a tree $T_2$ if all nodes of $T_1$ occur in $T_2$ with the same parent/child edge relationship and node order. The overall complexity of this algorithm is expressed as $O(N^2)$. This approach proved to be more accurate in detecting XML structural similarities than those of either Chawathe or Shasha.

## Fourier Transform Similarity

Essentially, Fourier transform similarity (Rafiei & Mendelzon, 1998) removes all the information from a document except for its start and end tags, leaving only its skeleton, which represents its structure. The structure is then converted into a sequence of numbers, which is viewed as a time series, and a Fourier transform is applied to convert the data into a set of frequencies. Finally, the distance between two documents is computed by calculating the difference in the magnitudes of the two signals.

The approach proposed in (Flesca, Manco, Masciari, Pontieri, & Pugliese, 2005) for detecting structural similarity between XML documents is based on graph-matching algorithms and consists in linearizing the structure of each XML document by representing it as a numerical sequence using the Discrete Fourier Transform of the associated signals. Then, it compares the encoded documents (i.e., signals) in the domain of frequencies.

There are several requirements to match the tag mapping and pre-compute the maximum depth of the compared documents. Buttler (2004) proved that this algorithm is the least accurate of all approximation algorithms, and performs poorly because Fourier transform does not discriminate sufficiently between very similar documents.

## Edge Matching

(Lian, Cheung, Mamoulis, & Yiu, 2004) represented XML document structures as directed graphs called *s-graphs*, and define a distance metric that captures the number of edges common to the graph representations of two XML documents:

$$dist\left(G_1, G_2\right) = \frac{1 - |\, Edges(G_1) \cap Edges(G_2)\,|}{\max\{Edges(G_1), Edges(G_2)\}}$$

This metric is more effective than others based on TED, in separating documents that are structurally different. It can be applied not only to tree-structured documents but also to document collections of arbitrary (graph) structures.

## Path Similarity

Path expressions can be used in measuring the similarity of paths of XML documents (Rafiei, Moise, & Sun, 2006). A path is defined as a list of connected nodes starting at the root and terminating at a leaf node. Path similarity can be measured in several different ways: binary (where a path is either equivalent or not), partial (where the number of comparable nodes in each path is determined), or weighted (where the nodes are weighted according to their distance from the root). In (Rafiei, Moise, & Sun, 2006), two XML documents are similar if they share a large fraction of the paths in their path sets. The path set includes all root paths (from the root to leaf nodes) and all possible subpaths. The time complexity in terms of number of string comparisons is expressed as $O(nl^2)$, where $n$ is the number of root paths and $l$ is the length of each path. Buttler (2004) showed that the path similarity method provides fairly accurate results compared to TED.

### Substructure Based Similarity

(Aggarwal, Ta, Wang, Feng, & Zaki, 2007) proposed a clustering algorithm for XML data which uses substructures of the documents in order to gain the important underlying structure. A key subject is to find frequent substructure representatives by using approximate mining techniques. An approximate data representation is used to remove or simplify the graph isomorphism problem, while its structural relationship is still maintained. The edge sequence representation is introduced to represent the parent-child relationship and the ordering among the sibling nodes by using the sequence of pre-order depth-first traversal of the tree edges. Selection of high quality substructure representatives reduces the computation of comparing the similarity between documents. One way of achieving this goal is to simply select the top-K most frequent substructures. This results in an efficient approach which can be used over very large data sets.

In (Kutty, Nayak, & Li, 2009a) a hybrid clustering approach for XML documents (HCX) determines the structural similarity in the form of frequent subtrees first and then uses these frequent subtrees to represent the constrained content of the XML documents to determine the content similarity. HCX uses the common substructures of XML documents using frequent subtrees to characterize the structural similarity among them. It uses the frequent subtrees to extract the content and represent it in VSM. The dimensionality of the content is reduced by eliminating the content corresponding to infrequent substructures. Experimental results show that it improves accuracy and can efficiently work for very large data sets.

### XML/DTD Similarity

XML structural similarity can also be detected by comparing document type definitions (DTDs) with XML documents. In (Bertino, Guerrini, & Mesiti, 2004) a matching algorithm is proposed for measuring the structural similarity between an XML document and a DTD. By comparing the document structure with that required by the DTD, the matching algorithm is able to identify commonalities and differences. Differences can be the occurrence of extra elements beyond those required by the DTD, or the absence of required elements. The degree of similarity can be evaluated based on the element's properties, such as level or weight. Elements at higher levels are considered more relevant than those at lower levels. The authors state that their approach is of exponential complexity.

## Structure and Content Similarity

In many real-world scenarios, structural similarity cannot be sufficient to distinguish, or classify, or integrate XML documents. Therefore, not only the structure of XML documents but also their contents must be handled in order to determine whether any two XML documents can be considered similar. Especially in recent years, researchers have proposed several methods to measure the similarity of XML content and structure. Most of existing methods can be grouped into the following categories.

## Subtree Similarity

To integrate XML documents, many methods begin by with identifying objects in a data source that may represent real-world objects by clustering them into small fragments or subtrees. This method is called *entity resolution* (ER), also known as duplication or record linkage. A well-clustered subtree should satisfy the following requirements: (1) each subtree represents one independent item, (2) each independent item is clustered into one subtree, and (3) the leaf nodes belonging to that item should be included in the subtree.

Liang and Yokota (2005) present an approach called *leaf-clustering based approximate XML join* (LAX). This method consists of two main steps, by which similarity computation is carried out after fragmenting the XML documents into subtrees. More precisely, LAX first divides XML trees into subtrees by considering a clustering point from the height (distance from the furthest child) and the number of link branches of XML trees. A link branch is a link between two candidate elements that have at least two children, or the distance of which to its furthest child is at least three. The subtree can be generated by deleting the link branch below the clustering point. The clustering point is calculated from the maximum weighting factor of the multiplication between the height level and the number of link branches. After clustering the documents, the clustered subtrees are compared at the leaf-node levels using the percentage of matched leaf nodes in the subtrees. The overall complexity of this approach is expressed as $O(N^2)$, where $N$ is the maximum number of nodes in the XML documents. The authors found that when LAX is applied after fragmenting documents, the matched subtrees selected from the output pair of fragmented documents with a high degree of similarity among trees might not be the subtrees appropriate for integration. To solve this problem, they introduced SLAX (an improved LAX to Integrate XML data at subtree classes) (Liang & Yokota, 2006). SLAX divides XML documents into smaller portions by parsing them into $k$ document trees. In each document tree, SLAX applies the weighting factor from LAX to find points for subtree clustering. Since the clustering method relies on the number of link branches and the document's depth, this method may not perform well for deep and complex XML structures.

Viyanon and Madria have recently developed a number of methods for comparing XML documents by structure and content similarity (2008, 2009a, 2009b). To increase scalability and circumvent the difficulty of loading very large XML trees into the main memory, XML documents are stored in a relational database using XRel. Their algorithms generate more complete information by integrating similar documents. The first algorithm, XDoI (Viyanon, Madria, & Bhowmick, 2008), offers a data-centric approach to clustering XML documents into subtrees using leaf-node parents. The clustered subtrees are considered as individual objects. The key of a subtree is modeled as an XML attribute which is one of the leaf nodes in a subtree. It has a unique value compared to other nodes with the same path and is able to identify other attributes of its subtree. The unique leaf node is considered as the key which can identify its subtree. The subtree keys play an important role to discover the best match among the XML documents. It reduces dramatically the number of subtrees to be matched, thus improving the degree of similarity by reducing false positives. Due to complex structures of XML documents, the clustering method in XDoI may produce a huge number of subtrees which would affect the computation time in subtree comparison. The second algorithm, called XDI-CSSK (Viyanon & Madria, 2009a), introduces filtering methods to prune the unnecessary clustered subtrees that are primarily responsible for the high computation costs of similarity measurement in XDoI. The algorithm uses leaf-node parents as clustering points and validates them using the concept of instance statistics, along with a taxonomic analyzer. The information thus required is used to purge subtrees in one document that are unrelated to those in the other document. The execution time for this approach is better than that of XDoI because semantic similarity plays a crucial role in precise computational similarity measures. XML-SIM (2009b) is a further improvement over XDoI and XDI-CSSK. It focuses on the semantics associated with the child nodes in a subtree, thus reducing the number of subtree comparisons to be made. The main improvement of this approach is that it determines content similarity based on structural similarity, which in turn is determined using semantics. The execution time for XML-SIM makes it a dramatic improvement over XDI-CSSK and XDoI. The complexity of each approach is $O(N^2)$.

## Document List Similarity

Kade and Heuser (2008) presented a different approach, called XSIM, that uses information from both structure and content of XML documents. In order to compute the similarity between two nodes of XML trees, three types of information are involved: the content of the elements and the names and path of the nodes. The comparison has two main steps: node matching and document matching. First, the document tree is traversed to produce a set of tuples each containing a pair (path, content), which is called a document list for subtrees. Second, the tuples of the document lists are compared and searched for matching nodes based on similarity of textual content, node label and node path. The similarity between two elements is computed as the average of textual content, element name, and path similarity values without considering semantics.

## Probabilistic Model Similarity

In (de Keijzer, 2006), XML uncertainty is managed in order to support unattended information integration in probabilistic form using a probabilistic database approach. A major problem in using probabilistic databases for data integration is how to determine the probabilities. Many schema matching techniques suitable for data integration, however, quantify the degree of matching. For example, instance-based matchers use classification techniques. If two data items from different information sources referring to the same real-world object conflict on some attribute value, and one of those values is classified with less certainty that the other in the class corresponding to the attribute, then that attribute value is less likely to be correct and should receive a smaller probability. The same holds for techniques that use dictionaries or thesauri: if a possible data value is not present in the corresponding dictionary, it should receive a smaller probability. The document tree contains two new kinds of nodes: probability nodes and possibility nodes. Comparison is based on the probability associated with possibility nodes that can compute a possible representation of the matched real-world object. To determine the probability that two XML elements refer to the same real-world object, knowledge rules are applied. These rules can be generic or domain-specific. The amount of uncertainty can be reduced after applying the rules.

The probabilistic model in (Leitão, Calado, & Weis, 2007) uses a Bayesian network to effectively detect duplicates in hierarchical and semistructured XML data. This approach combines the probabilities that children and descendents in a given pair of XML subtrees are duplicates. To compare two candidate XML elements, a maximum overlay between the two trees is computed. Two non-leaf nodes can be matched if they are ancestors of two matched leaves. Once a maximum overlay has been determined, its cost is computed by a string distance function. Results presented in (Leitão, Calado, & Weis, 2007) show that this model provides great flexibility in its configuration, allowing the use of various similarity measures for the field values and various conditional probabilities to combine the similarity probabilities of the XML elements. The primary disadvantage of Bayesian techniques is their computational complexity.

### Object Description Similarity

Weis and Naumann (2005) proposed a method, called DogmatiX, for comparing XML elements based on their data values, parents, children, and structure. The method comprises three steps: (1) candidate detection, which specifies what objects to compare, (2) object identification, which defines what information is part of a candidate's description, and (3) similarity computation. The method starts by taking an XML document and mapping its elements to real-world entities. Objects, or elements, are then described. An object description comprises a set of tuples (name, value) that can be identified by heuristics and conditions. Heuristics include *r*-distant ancestors, *r*-distant descendants, and *k*-closest descendants. The conditions that can be used to refine the selection descriptions are content model, string data type, mandatory elements, and singleton elements. The last step is similarity comparison. Similarities in textual values are compared using a variation of string edit distance. Element similarities are evaluated by a variation of the inverse document frequency (IDF) score. Experimental results show that DogmatiX is effective in identifying real and synthetic duplicate XML elements and documents. This method however relies on the manual mapping between the elements of schema and real-world entities.

### Tree Serialization Similarity

Wen, Amagasa, and Kitagawa (2009) proposed an approach to tree serialization similarity developed in the context of data integration. Because the tree structure representation of XML data makes it difficult to measure similarity, that is converted into node sequences by traversing the tree in a particular order (e.g., pre- and post-order). After serialization, the XML data becomes one long node sequence. This sequence is extracted into sub-sequences corresponding to the XML subtree using parameters such as the smallest number of the text nodes, the maximum number of text nodes, and the least height from the leaf node that a subsequence should have. The similarity measure used in this approach takes into account a comparison of textual information using the Jaccard similarity coefficient and a comparison of structural information based on edit similarity. The comparison process is accelerated by a Bloom filter (Gong, Qian, Yan, & Zhou, 2005), which provides a probabilistic way to determine if an element is a member of a given set. The authors state that the results are accurate and effective; however, they do not compare their approach with other existing approaches.

### Similarity on Collection of Values

In (Dorneles, Heuser, Lima, da Silva, & de Moura, 2004), a set of similarity metrics is described for manipulating collections of values occurring in XML documents. XML nodes can be considered atomic (when contain single values such as numbers, texts, and dates) or complex (when contain nested node structures). In addition, the authors divide the complex nodes into two categories: tuple elements and collection elements. A tuple element contains multiple sub-elements, whereas a collection element contains a duplicate of the sub-element. The similarity measures apply to atomic and complex values recursively. The evaluation of XML element similarities requires that the elements to be compared share the same contexts and have similar children.

## Semantic XML Similarity

Semantic similarity plays an important role in finding the similarity in meaning or semantic content. Syntactic similarity measures have performed strongly with resources containing large amounts of text, but they cannot appropriately cope with syntactic and semantic heterogeneity and ambiguity if the semantics of the terms are not explicitly available.

Hybrid similarity methods in XML data aim to combine both semantic and syntactic similarity measures to effectively determine the similarity among documents. In principle, hybrid approaches can easily be developed by combining the various semantic and syntactic similarity measures using average, maximum, additive, or weighted sum functions: the average, maximum and additive functions may be simpler to use than weighted sum functions, however the latter should work better although they may require the involvement of a domain expert to suitably choose the weights.

An early work on semantic similarity measures for XML data is (Nayak, 2006). Here, while syntactic measures involving the hierarchical structure and relationship between elements were found useful for supporting XML document clustering, semantic measures did not introduce any significant improvement. This finding, however, was justified in that the affect of semantic measure incorporation in clustering may be not significant in some applications where the documents are varied due to little semantic difference. On the contrary, in those applications, it may be advisable to apply semantic computation after applying structural computation.

Nayak and Iryadi (2007) presented a methodology, called XMine, for clustering XML schemas according to structural and semantic information of elements. The element structural similarity is measured based on the element level hierarchy positions and depends on the identification of maximal similar paths, whereas the element semantic similarity combines linguistic and constraint similarities between the elements contained only in the maximal large paths. Experiments have demonstrated the effectiveness of XMine to categorize heterogeneous schemas into the relevant classes that ease the generalization of a schema class hierarchy.

Formica (2008) compared some of the methods described in the previous section on semantic similarity measures. She pointed out that Resnik, Wu and Palmer, and Lin measures have been conceived to determine semantic similarity of hierarchically organized concepts without addressing the structures. The results show a higher correlation of Lin's approach with human judgment, however in various contexts the structural approach is adopted, whose similarity scores significantly differ from Lin. To reduce the distances between these approaches, a hybrid approach is introduced in (Formica, 2008) to address both the taxonomy and the concept structures. Precisely, a method is proposed for determining semantic similarity of XML Schema elements in the presence of type hierarchies. Such a method is defined by combining and revisiting (1) the information content approach, and (2) a method for comparing the structural components of type declarations, which is inspired by the maximum weighted matching problem in bipartite graphs. Results have shown that the proposed hybrid approach overcomes the limitations of those similarity measures when directly applied to XML Schema elements.

In (Kutty, Nayak, & Li, 2009b), a study in the INEX 2009 XML Mining track context is proposed to drive the extraction of XML content with the support of frequent subtrees for clustering XML documents. These documents were also marked up using Wikipedia tags and contained categories derived by using the YAGO ontology (Suchanek, Kasneci, & Weikum, 2007).

In (Tagarelli, Longo, & Greco, 2009), element names are mapped to appropriate lexical meanings based on a word sense disambiguation task. The objective of that work was to investigate semantic relatedness measures for XML data in order to extract structural features coupled with semantic information. Two basic methods for computing semantic relatedness were defined and combined, namely gloss-overlap-based and ontology-path-based: the former exploits a Lesk-based scoring mechanism for comparing the glosses of the synsets associated to the element names, whereas the latter utilizes node depth metrics like Wu and Palmer to compute the synset distances in the reference ontology. This study on XML semantic features was also exploited in (Tagarelli & Greco, 2010), where an approach, called SemXClust, is proposed for clustering related documents according to structure as well as content features which are semantically enriched with the support of a lexical ontology (WordNet).

## Applications of XML Similarity

Applications of XML similarity are numerous and they range mainly over (1) data integration, (2) change management, (3) classification/clustering of XML documents, and (4) XML query systems.

### XML Data Integration

With the recent explosive spread of XML, a growing amount of XML data represents similar contents but with dissimilar structures. XML documents from heterogeneous sources might have the same or similar information but may be constructed using different structures or have some information added/deleted/modified. XML similarity plays an important role in evaluating affinities between XML documents in order to integrate data so that the user can get easily access to more complete and useful information.

XML data integration can be effectively performed by measuring the similarity between two XML documents, using one of the approaches described in the previous section. Given two XML sources, $S_1$ and $S_2$, a user defined threshold $\tau$, and a similarity function $sim(d_1, d_2)$ that evaluates the similarity between any two documents $d_1 \in S_1$ and $d_2 \in S_2$, if $sim(d_1, d_2) \geq \tau$ then the documents are considered a match and can be integrated.

The integration of multiple sources aims to give users and applications the illusion of interacting with one single information system. The integration of various sources can be categorized into two general approaches: (1) materialized integration, and (2) virtual integration (Zhou, Hull, King, & Franchitti, 1995).

Materialized integration is similar to materialized views in database concepts. Essentially, all data from different sources are stored locally first and an integration process is carried out to generate the integrated information. *Data warehousing* is a well-known example of materialized integration, which is suitable for situations when data changes infrequently. Virtual integration aims to offer the same result without storing and updating all data from all sources. The integrated schema (global schema) acts as a mediator. A global schema provides mappings of the relevant parts of all data model schemas. Queries issued over it are rewritten at runtime and redirected to the original data sources.

Virtual integration requires finding the similarity of XML documents based on their structures in order to have a global schema. On the other hand, materialized integration not only involves structural similarity but also content similarity, so that the similar content can be integrated.

Schema matching has been extensively researched, and many matching systems have been developed. Loosely speaking, a schema matcher tries to discover schema elements which model the same real-world object or concept, and the overall similarity is measured by comparing the similarity between objects (see, for instance, Chapter "The Role of Schema and Document Matchings in XML Source Clustering").

### Change Management

Data publication in XML data warehouses is constantly increasing. Users are often not only interested in the current values of documents and query answers but also in changes. They want to see changes as information that can be used to learn about the evolution of information. The management of versions is essential for a number of reasons ranging from traditional support for temporal queries to more specific ones, such as index maintenance or support for query subscriptions (Marian, Abiteboul, Cobena, & Mignet,

2001). Change detection serves many purposes in such XML warehouse environments, as described in the following:

- **Versions:** A user may want to version a particular document, or the results of a continuous query can be in the form of versions. This is the most standard use of versions, namely recording history of results. Version control systems (VCSs) serve as a basis for the management of changes. A VCS can be characterized as a system which tracks the history of file and directory changes over time. All version-controlled files and directories reside as a tree structure in a system and both can have version-controlled meta-data. Changes to such a tree are transactional resulting in a new snapshot (aka. revision) of the whole tree including all recent changes made in that commit operation as well as all the previous unchanged data.
- **Resource sharing:** Different users may be simultaneously updating (off-line) the same XML document. Deltas turn out to be useful to synchronize the respective versions. The changes describe the modifications and facilitate the detection of potential conflicts. This is in the style of CVS (CVS: Concurrent Version System), a version control system software that keeps track of all work and all changes in a set of files.
- **Querying the past:** A user might ask a query about the past, e.g., to find the value of some particular element at some previous time. Also, one might want to query changes, e.g., ask for the list of all items recently introduced in a catalog.
- **Learning about changes:** The changes between any two subsequent versions can be explained to the user and also track how the old version gets updated. This is in the character of the Information and Content Exchange protocol (Webber et al., 1998).
- **Monitoring changes:** To detect changes of interest in XML documents, e.g., whether a new product has been added to a particular catalog, a new version of some data is computed to evaluate the delta and verify if some of the changes that have been detected are relevant to some subscriptions. Subscription systems mentioned in (Yan & Garcia-Molina, 1999) and (Altinel & Franklin, 2000) that use filtering tools for information dissemination can be used in this case.
- **Indexing:** In a huge XML data warehouse like the Xyleme project (Abiteboul et al., 2001), a full-text index over a large volume of XML documents is required. To support queries using the structure of data, structural information needs to be stored for every indexed word of the document (Aguilera, Cluet, Veltri, Vodislav, & Wattez, 2000). The use of the delta is considered in maintaining such indexes.

## XML Classification and Clustering

Classification and clustering of XML documents play a major role in organizing and indexing documents due to two main reasons: (1) a user query can be satisfied by means of different possible answers, so that closely associated documents tend to be relevant to the same requests, and (2) retrieval systems and web mining tools are generally operational in the same environment. The aim is to discover structural and content patterns shared by XML documents of the same class in order to group XML documents of similar structures together. These patterns are mainly expressed in terms of their tags (node labels), contents, and inter-relationships.

Loosely speaking, classifying and clustering XML documents can be substantially done in three ways: (1) using exclusively the textual contents of documents as usually done in traditional text categorization and clustering systems, (2) using exclusively the structure of documents, and (3) using both the contents and the structure in a hybrid manner (Bouchachia & Marcus, 2007). See also Section 2 of this book.

## XML Retrieval

XML query languages are significant in order to retrieve XML information according to user's queries. There are many XML query languages such as XML-QL (Deutsch, Fernandez, Florescu, Levy, & Suciu, 1998), XQL (Robie, Lapp, & Schach, 1999), XML-GL (Ceri, Comai, Damiani, Fraternali, Paraboschi, & Tanca, 1999), and XQuery (Boag, et al., 2002). They provide complex queries but only browse for exact matches. Therefore, *ranked XML query* comes in to a picture to extend these query languages to look for relevant results. This requires that XML similarity techniques are properly applied.

Ranking in XML retrieval can incorporate both content relevance and structural similarity, which is a resemblance between the structure given in the query and the structure of the document. Also, the retrieval units resulting from an XML query may not always be entire documents, but can be any deeply nested XML elements, i.e., dynamic documents. The aim is to find the smallest retrieval unit that is highly relevant. Relevance can be defined according to the notion of specificity, which is the extent to which a retrieval unit focuses on the topic of request (Malik, Trotman, Lalmas, & Fuhr, 2007).

In (Baeza-Yates, Navarro, Vegas, & De La Fuente, 2002), the use of result ranking is proposed for structured queries. For this purpose, a simple query language and a generic ranking model are introduced. Queries are logical formulas consisting of presence and inclusion operators. The score computed for each document is the sum of all occurrences of the content terms specified by the query. However, the distribution of substructures is not considered, and the document concept is static.

Many retrieval techniques adopt the similarity measure in a vector space model (Salton, Wong, & Yang, 1975) and incorporate the document structure, and support structured queries. In (Schlieder & Meuss, 2002), the query model is based on tree matching cooperating with weighting of keywords by treating substructures as terms to measure the similarity between the query and documents.

Keyword search querying is one of the most effective paradigms for information retrieval. One of the key advantages of keyword search querying is its simplicity since users do not have to learn a complex query language and can issue queries without any prior knowledge about the structure of the underlying data. Queries may not always be precise and can return a large number of query results, especially in large documents collections. In (Guo, Shao, Botev, & Shanmugasundaram, 2003), the authors presented the XRANK system, which supports ranked XML keyword search. The system can return deeply nested XML elements that contain the desired keywords. Some systems also support ranked XML keyword search, such as XIRQL (Fuhr & Großjohann, 2001), which is an extension of XQL that incorporates the concepts of term weights and vague predicates, and XXL (Theobald & Weikum, 2002), which uses term occurrences and ontological similarity for ranking.

We summarize in Table 1 main XML similarity approaches and their characteristics discussed in this chapter. Notations corresponding to the complexity aspects in Table 1 are described using the following:

- $N$ is the number of nodes in an XML document
- $n$ is the number of leaf nodes in an XML document
- $M$ is the number of nodes

*Table 1. Comparison of XML similarity approaches*

| Approach | Characteristics | Complexity | Application |
|---|---|---|---|
| Layered approach (Kim, Peng, Kulvatunyou, Ivezic, & Jones, 2008) | Schema mapping<br>Divides data elements into layers<br>Measures semantic similarity using layer specific metrics | - | XML data integration |
| Path similarity (Rafiei, Moise, & Sun, 2006) | Structure of an XML document modeled as a set of paths<br>Computes the number of common paths between two XML documents | $O(pl^2)$ | XML clustering |
| Matching algorithm (Bertino, Guerrini, & Mesiti, 2004) | Measures the structural similarity between an XML document and a DTD<br>Identifies commonalities and differences<br>Level of the element and weight of the element considered in evaluating similarity | $O(\Gamma^2 (N+M))$ | XML clustering |
| S-GRACE (Lian, Cheung, Mamoulis, & Yiu, 2004) | XML documents represented as directed graphs<br>Edge matching (computing the number of common edges between the graphs) | $O(N^2)$ | XML clustering |
| XProj (Aggarwal, Ta, Wang, Feng, & Zaki, 2007) | Measures the structural similarity between XML documents using substructure<br>Edge sequence representation characterizes the parent-child relationship<br>Selects the top-K most frequent substructures to reduce computation cost of comparison | - | XML clustering |
| HCX (Kutty, Nayak, & Li, 2009a) | Determines the structural similarity in the form of frequent subtrees<br>Uses these frequent subtrees to represent the constrained content of the XML documents to determine the content similarity | - | XML clustering |
| SemXClust (Tagarelli & Greco, 2010) | Computes the similarity between XML tree tuple items<br>Uses two parameters: the amount of structure (or content) and the uncertainty in similarity detection | - | XML clustering |
| LAX (Liang & Yokota, 2005) | Subtree similarity<br>Clusters XML documents into subtrees based on link branch (edge) and node's height | $O(N^2)$ | XML data integration |
| XML-SIM (Viyanon & Madria, 2009) | Subtrees are clustered by leaf node's parents<br>Similarity detected using "subtree keys", semantic structural similarity, and leaf node similarity | $O(pl^2 + n^2)$ | XML data integration |
| XSIM (Kade & Heuser, 2008) | Node matching and document matching<br>Similarity based on textual content, node's label, and node's path | - | XML data integration |
| Probabilistic XML model (de Keijzer, 2006) | Comparison based on a probabilistic database<br>Exploits knowledge rules to determine probability | - | XML data integration |
| Probabilistic XML model (Leitão, Calado, & Weis, 2007) | Uses Bayesian network to combine the probabilities of children and descendents being duplicates | $O(N^2)$ | XML data integration |
| DogMatiX (Weis & Naumann, 2005) | Comparing XML elements based on their data values, parent, children and structure<br>Mapping between the elements of schema and real world entities | - | XML data integration |
| Tree serialization (Wen, Amagasa, & Kitagawa, 2009) | Converts the tree structure into node sequences<br>Similarity based on comparing tree serialization<br>The approach is accelerated by Bloom filter | $O(N^2)$ | XML data integration |
| Collection of values (Dorneles, Heuser, Lima, da Silva, & de Moura, 2004) | XML nodes considered as atomic values<br>Complex nodes categorized into tuple and collection elements | - | XML retrieval and XML data integration |
| Tree matching (Schlieder & Meuss, 2002) | Tree matching cooperating with weighting of keywords | - | XML retrieval |
| XXL (Theobald & Weikum, 2002) | Exploits term occurrences and ontological similarity for ranking | - | XML retrieval |
| XRANK (Guo, Shao, Botev, & Shanmugasundaram, 2003) | Integrates keyword search with structured XML querying to compute the ranking for XML keyword search queries | - | XML retrieval |

- $l$ is the length of the longest path (the number of nodes from the root to the leaf node in the longest path)
- $p$ is the number of root paths
- $\Gamma$ is the maximum number of edges outcoming from a node of the document.

## CONCLUSION AND DISCUSSION

In this chapter, we presented an overview of existing research related to the problem of XML similarity detection according to XML document structure as well as content features. Besides syntactic similarity, semantic similarity were also presented since they also play an important role to evaluate documents' similarities by determining relations between words or concepts. We discussed the various approaches that could be used for finding similarity in XML data, focusing on the major applications of XML similarity detection, such as XML data integration and XML document classification/clustering.

XML data integration, classification/clustering and change detection require accurate XML similarity methods so that they can produce better results in terms of more complete information, higher quality classification, and more precise change detection, respectively. From a structure viewpoint, most existing methods for these application areas refer to measures based on edit distance, edge matching, path similarity, semantic similarity and hybrid approaches. On the other hand, a major concern for XML querying is performance due to users' expectations that would like to have relevant results in a very short period of time. Hence, especially from a content viewpoint, most approaches focus on the popular TF-IDF relevance weighting scheme and the vector space model.

Since the work by (Nierman & Jagadish, 2002), the tree edit distance has shown to be an effective metric for measuring the structural similarity in XML documents However, tree edit distances are considered as very expensive in terms of computational complexity, so their application is not feasible in practice when XML documents are huge. This can partly be solved by applying filters that aim to reduce the size of the documents being compared.

To evaluate the similarity between items in XML documents, clustering of XML documents is useful; however, it is not easy to automatically cluster an XML document tree into subtree representing independent items without assisting from domain experts. A well-clustered document may require that: (1) each subtree represents only one independent item; a subtree does not include any information of other items, (2) one independent item is clustered into one subtree; one item does not have more than one corresponding subtrees, and (3) each subtree includes the information as much as possible; the leaf nodes belonging to that item should be included in the subtree as much as possible.

The DOM trees of large XML data sets to be compared may not be fit into the main memory, and hence storing XML documents into a relational database could provide the basis for a scalable approach to similarity detection. Therefore, some benefits could be derived by approaches like XRel (Yoshikawa, Amagasa, Shimura, & Uemura, 2001) proposed for storage and retrieval of XML documents using relational databases.

Since XML applications must deal with the heterogeneity of data, recent research work are trying to solve this issue by incorporating semantic similarity. Semantic similarity could be integrated in multiple ways while comparing XML data. The semantic complexity issue is currently an open problem: indeed, semantic similarity measures are dependent on a corpus, or dictionary, or ontology, and the presence or absence of a concept therein; therefore, if a concept is not found in the reference knowledge base, the value of information content tends to become zero or infinity, and hence the semantic similarity measure may not reflect the actual information content of the concept well.

## REFERENCES


Abiteboul, S., Aguilera, V., Ailleret, S., Amann, B., Arambarri, F., & Cluet, S. ... Westmann, T. (2001). Xyleme, a dynamic warehouse for XML data of the Web. In M. E. Adiba, C. Collet, & B. C. Desai (Eds.), *Proceedings of the International Database Engineering & Applications Symposium (IDEAS),* (pp. 3-7). IEEE Computer Society Press.

Aggarwal, C. C., Ta, N., Wang, J., Feng, J., & Zaki, M. J. (2007). XProj: A framework for projected structural clustering of XML documents. In P. Berkhin, R. Caruana, & X. Wu (Eds.), *Proceedings of the 13th ACM SIGKDD International Conference on Knowledge Discovery and Data Mining (KDD),* (pp. 46-55). ACM.

Aguilera, V., Cluet, S., Veltri, P., Vodislav, D., & Wattez, F. (2000). Querying XML documents in Xyleme. In *Proceedings of the ACM-SIGIR 2000 Workshop on XML and Information Retrieval.* ACM.

Altinel, M., & Franklin, M. (2000). Efficient filtering of XML documents for selective dissemination of information. In A. E. Abbadi, M. L. Brodie, S. Chakravarthy, U. Dayal, N. Kamel, G. Schlageter, & K.-Y. Whang (Eds.), *Proceedings of the 26th International Conference on Very Large Data Bases (VLBD)*, (pp. 53-64). Morgan Kaufmann.

Baeza-Yates, R. A., Navarro, G., Vegas, J., & De La Fuente, P. (2002). A model and a visual query language for structured text. In *Processing of the String Processing and Information Retrieval: A South American Symposium (SPIRE),* (pp. 7-13).

Bertino, E., Guerrini, G., & Mesiti, M. (2004). A matching algorithm for measuring the structural similarity between an XML document and a DTD and its applications. *Information Systems, 29*(1), 23–46. doi:10.1016/S0306-4379(03)00031-0

Boag, S., Chamberlin, D., Fernández, M., Florescu, D., Robie, J., & Siméon, J. (Eds.). (2002). *XQuery 1.0: An XML query language.* W3C Working Draft.

Bouchachia, A., & Marcus, H. (2007). Classification of XML documents. In *Proceedings of the IEEE Symposium on Computational Intelligence and Data Mining, part of the IEEE Symposium Series on Computational Intelligence (CIDM)*, (pp. 390-396). IEEE Computer Society.

Bourret, R. (2005, September). *XML and databases.* Retrieved March 2010, from http://www.rpbourret.com/xml/XMLAndDatabases.htm

Budanitsky, A., & Hirst, G. (2006). Evaluating WordNet-based measures of lexical semantic relatedness. *Computational Linguistics, 32*(1), 13–47. doi:10.1162/coli.2006.32.1.13

Buttler, D. (2004). A short survey of document structure similarity algorithms. In H. R. Arabnia, & O. Droegehorn (Eds.), *Proceedings of the International Conference on Internet Computing (IC): Vol. 1* (pp. 3-9). CSREA Press.

Ceri, S., Comai, S., Damiani, E., Fraternali, P., Paraboschi, S., & Tanca, L. (1999). XML-GL: A graphical language for querying and restructuring XML documents. *Computer Networks, 31*(11-16), 1171-1188.

Cha, S.-H. (2007). Comprehensive survey on distance/similarity measures between probability density functions. *International Journal of Mathematical Models and Methods in Applied Sciences, 1*(4), 300–307.

Chawathe, S. (1999). Comparing hierarchical data in external memory. In M. P. Atkinson, M. E. Orlowska, P. Valduriez, S. B. Zdonik, & M. L. Brodie (Eds.), *Proceedings of 25th International Conference on Very Large Data Bases (VLDB)*, (pp. 90-101). Morgan Kaufmann.

CVS. *Concurrent Version System*. (n.d.). Retrieved March 2010, from http://www.cvshome.org/eng/

Daly, P. G. (2003, December 8). XML basics and benefits. *Intranet Jounal: Building the Corporate Enterprise*. Retrieved August 4, 2010, from http://www.intranetjournal.com/articles/200312/ij_12_08_03a.html

de Keijzer, A. (2006). Probabilistic XML in information integration. In J. Shim, & F. Casati (Eds.), *Proceedings of the VLDB 2006 Ph.D. Workshop.* CEUR Workshop Proceedings.

Deutsch, A., Fernandez, M., Florescu, D., Levy, A., & Suciu, D. (1998). *XML-QL: A query language for XML*. Retrieved March 2010, from http://www.w3.org/TR/NOTE-xml-ql/

Deza, M. M., & Deza, E. (2009). *Encyclopedia of distances*. Springer. doi:10.1007/978-3-642-00234-2

Dorneles, C., Heuser, C., Lima, A., da Silva, A., & de Moura, E. (2004). Measuring similarity between collection of values. In A. H. F. Laender, D. Lee, & M. Ronthaler (Eds.) *Proceedings of the Sixth ACM CIKM International Workshop on Web Information and Data Management (WIDM 2004)*, (pp. 56-63). ACM.

Fellbaum, C. (Ed.). (1998). *WordNet: An electronic lexical database*. Massachusetts, USA: MIT Press.

Flesca, S., Manco, G., Masciari, E., Pontieri, L., & Pugliese, A. (2005). Fast detection of XML structural similarity. *IEEE Transactions on Knowledge and Data Engineering*, *17*(2), 160–175. doi:10.1109/TKDE.2005.27

Formica, A. (2008). Similarity of XML-schema elements: A structural and information content approach. *The Computer Journal*, *51*(2), 240–254. doi:10.1093/comjnl/bxm051

Fuhr, N., & Großjohann, K. (2001). XIRQL: A query language for information retrieval in XML documents. In W. B. Croft, D. J. Harper, D. H. Kraft, & J. Zobel (Eds.), *Proceedings of the 24th Annual International Conference on Research and Development in Information Retrieval (SIGIR)*, (pp. 172-180). ACM.

Gong, X., Qian, W., Yan, Y., & Zhou, A. (2005). Bloom filter-based XML packets filtering for millions of path queries. In *Proceedings of the 21st International Conference on Data Engineering (ICDE)*, (pp. 890-901). IEEE Computer Society Press.

Guo, L., Shao, F., Botev, C., & Shanmugasundaram, J. (2003). XRANK: Ranked keyword search over XML documents. In A. Y. Halevy, Z. G. Ives, & A. Doan (Eds.), *Proceedings of the 2003 ACM International Conference on Management of Data (SIGMOD)*, (pp. 16-27). ACM.

Gusfield, D. (1997). *Algorithms on strings, trees, and sequences: Computer science and computational biology*. USA: Cambridge University Press. doi:10.1017/CBO9780511574931

Jain, A. K., & Dubes, R. C. (1988). *Algorithms for clustering data*. New Jersey: Prentice-Hall.

Jiang, J. J., & Conrath, D. W. (1997). Semantic similarity based on corpus statistics and lexical taxonomy. In *Proceedings of International Conference Research on Computational Linguistics*.

Kade, A., & Heuser, C. (2008). Matching XML documents in highly dynamic applications. In M. d.G. C. Pimentel, D. C. A. Bulterman, & Luiz F. G. Soares (Eds.), *Proceedings of the 2008 ACM Symposium on Document Engineering* (pp. 191-198). ACM.

Kim, J., Peng, Y., Kulvatunyou, S., Ivezic, N., & Jones, A. (2008). A layered approach to semantic similarity analysis of XML schemas. In *Proceedings of the IEEE International Conference on Information Reuse and Integration (IRI),* (pp. 274-279). IEEE Systems, Man, and Cybernetics Society.

Kriegel, H., & Schönauer, S. (2003). Similarity search in structured data. In Y. Kambayashi, M. K. Mohania, & W. Wöß (Eds.), *Data Warehousing and Knowledge Discovery, 5th International Conference (DaWaK)*, (pp. 309-319). Springer.

Kutty, S., Nayak, R., & Li, Y. (2009a). HCX: An efficient hybrid clustering approach for XML documents. In U. M. Borghoff, & B. Chidlovskii (Eds.), *Proceedings of the 2009 ACM Symposium on Document Engineering* (pp. 94-97). ACM.

Kutty, S., Nayak, R., & Li, Y. (2009b). Utilising semantic tags in XML clustering. In S. Geva, J. Kamps, and A. Trotman (Eds.), *Focused Retrieval and Evaluation, 8th International Workshop of the Initiative for the Evaluation of XML Retrieval (INEX) Lecture Notes in Computer Science: Vol. 6203.* (pp. 416-425). Springer.

Leacock, C., & Chodorow, M. (1998). Combining local context and WordNet similarity for word sense identification. In Fellbaum, C. (Ed.), *WordNet: An electronic lexical database* (pp. 265–283). Massachusetts, USA: MIT Press.

Leitão, L., Calado, P., & Weis, M. (2007). Structure-based inference of XML similarity for fuzzy duplicate detection. In M. J. Silva, A. H. F. Laender, R. A. Baeza-Yates, D. L. McGuinness, B. Olstad, Ø. H. Olsen, & A. O. Falcão (Eds.), *Proceedings of the Sixteenth ACM Conference on Information and Knowledge Management (CIKM),* (pp. 293-302). ACM.

Li, Y., Bandar, Z., & McLean, D. (2003). An approach for measuring semantic similarity between words using multiple information sources. *IEEE Transactions on Knowledge and Data Engineering, 15*(4), 871–882. doi:10.1109/TKDE.2003.1209005

Lian, W., Cheung, D., Mamoulis, N., & Yiu, S. (2004). An efficient and scalable algorithm for clustering XML documents by structure. *IEEE Transactions on Knowledge and Data Engineering, 16*(1), 82–96. doi:10.1109/TKDE.2004.1264824

Liang, W., & Yokota, H. (2005). LAX: An efficient approximate XML join based on clustered leaf nodes for XML data integration. In M. Jackson, D. Nelson, & S. Stirk (Eds.), *Database: Enterprise, Skills and Innovation, 22nd British National Conference on Databases (BNCOD) Lecture Notes in Computer Science: Vol. 3567* (pp. 82-97). Springer.

Liang, W., & Yokota, H. (2006). SLAX: An improved leaf-clustering based approximate XML join algorithm for integrating XML data at subtree classes. *IPSJ Digital Courier, 2*, 382–392. doi:10.2197/ipsjdc.2.382

Lin, D. (1998). An information-theoretic definition of similarity. In J. W. Shavlik (Ed.), *Proceedings of the Fifteenth International Conference on Machine Learning (ICML),* (pp. 296-304). Morgan Kaufmann.

Maier, D. (1978). The complexity of some problems on subsequences and supersequences. [JACM]. *Journal of the ACM, 25*(2), 322–336. doi:10.1145/322063.322075

Malik, S., Trotman, A., Lalmas, M., & Fuhr, N. (2007). Overview of INEX 2006. In N. Fuhr, M. Lalmas, and A. Trotman (Eds.), *Comparative Evaluation of XML Information Retrieval Systems, 5th International Workshop of the Initiative for the Evaluation of XML Retrieval (INEX) Lecture Notes in Computer Science: Vol. 4518* (pp. 1-11). Springer.

Marian, A., Abiteboul, S., Cobena, G., & Mignet, L. (2001). Change-centric management of versions in an XML warehouse. In P. M. G. Apers, P. Atzeni, S. Ceri, S. Paraboschi, K. Ramamohanarao, & R. T. Snodgrass (Eds.), *Proceedings of 27th International Conference on Very Large Data Bases (VLDB),* (pp. 581-590). Morgan Kaufmann.

Nayak, R. (2006). Investigating semantic measures in XML clustering. In *Proceedings of IEEE/WIC/ACM International Conference on Web Intelligence (WI),* (pp. 1042-1045). IEEE Computer Society Press.

Nayak, R., & Iryadi, W. (2007). XML schema clustering with semantic and hierarchical similarity measures. *Knowledge-Based Systems, 20*(4), 336–349. doi:10.1016/j.knosys.2006.08.006

Nierman, A., & Jagadish, H. V. (2002). Evaluating structural similarity in XML documents. *Proceedings of the Fifth International Workshop on the Web and Databases (WebDB),* (pp. 61-66).

Pirro, G., & Seco, N. (2008). Design, implementation and evaluation of a new semantic similarity metric combining features and intrinsic information content. In Meersman, R., & Tari, Z. (Eds.), *On the Move to Meaningful Internet Systems: OTM 2008 Lecture Notes in Computer Science* (*Vol. 5332*, pp. 1271–1288). Springer. doi:10.1007/978-3-540-88873-4_25

Rada, R., Mili, H., Bicknell, E., & Blettner, M. (1989). Development and application of a metric on semantic nets. *IEEE Transactions on Systems, Man, and Cybernetics, 19*(1), 17–30. doi:10.1109/21.24528

Rafiei, D., & Mendelzon, A. (1998). *Fourier transform based techniques in efficient retrieval of similar time sequences*. PhD thesis, University of Toronto, Canada.

Rafiei, D., Moise, D., & Sun, D. (2006). Finding syntactic similarities between XML documents. In *17th International Workshop on Database and Expert Systems Applications (DEXA 2006),* (pp. 512-516). IEEE Computer Society Press.

Resnik, P. (1995). Using information content to evaluate semantic similarity in a taxonomy. In *Proceedings of the 14th International Joint Conference on Artificial Intelligence (IJCAI '95 Vol. 2)*, (pp. 448-453). Morgan Kaufmann.

Robie, J., Lapp, J., & Schach, D. (1999). *XQL (XML query language)*. Retrieved April 2010, from ibiblio: the public's library and digital archive: http://www.ibiblio.org/xql/xql-proposal.html

Salton, G., Wong, A., & Yang, C. S. (1975). A vector space model for automatic indexing. *Communications of the ACM, 18*(11), 613–620. doi:10.1145/361219.361220

Schlieder, T., & Meuss, H. (2002). Querying and ranking XML documents. *Journal of the American Society for Information Science and Technology, 53*(6), 489–503. doi:10.1002/asi.10060

Shasha, D., & Zhang, K. (1997). Approximate tree pattern matching. In Apostolico, A., & Galil, Z. (Eds.), *Pattern matching in strings, trees and arrays* (pp. 341–371). Oxford University Press.

Suchanek, F. M., Kasneci, G., & Weikum, G. (2007). Yago: A core of semantic knowledge. In C. L. Williamson, M. E. Zurko, P. F. Patel-Schneider, & P. J. Shenoy (Eds.), *Proceedings of the 16th International Conference on World Wide Web (WWW)*, (pp. 697-706). ACM.

Tagarelli, A., & Greco, S. (2010). Semantic clustering of XML documents. [TOIS]. *ACM Transactions on Information Systems, 28*(1), 1–56. doi:10.1145/1658377.1658380

Tagarelli, A., Longo, M., & Greco, S. (2009). Word sense disambiguation for XML structure feature generation. In L. Aroyo, P. Traverso, F. Ciravegna, P. Cimiano, T. Heath, E. Hyvönen, R. Mizoguchi, E. Oren, M. Sabou, & E. P. B. Simperl (Eds.), *Proceedings of the 6th European Semantic Web Conference on The Semantic Web: Research and Applications (ESWC) Lecture Notes in Computer Science: Vol. 5554* (pp. 143-157). Springer.

Tai, K. (1979). The tree-to-tree correction problem. [JACM]. *Journal of the ACM, 26*(3), 422–433. doi:10.1145/322139.322143

Tekli, J., Chbeir, R., & Yetongnon, K. (2009). An overview on XML similarity: Background, current trends and future directions. *Computer Science Review*, *3*(3), 151–173. doi:10.1016/j.cosrev.2009.03.001

Theobald, A., & Weikum, G. (2002). The XXL search engine: Ranked retrieval of XML data using indexes and ontologies. In M. J. Franklin, B. Moon, & A. Ailamaki (Eds.), *Proceedings of the 2002 ACM International Conference on Management of Data (SIGMOD Conference),* (p. 615). ACM.

Viyanon, W., & Madria, S. K. (2009a). A system for detecting XML similarity in content and structure using relational database. In D. W.-L. Cheung, I.-Y. Song, W. W. Chu, X. Hu, J. J. Lin (Eds.), *Proceedings of the 18th ACM Conference on Information and Knowledge Management (CIKM),* (pp. 1197-1206). ACM.

Viyanon, W., & Madria, S. K. (2009b). XML-SIM: Structure and content semantic similarity detection using keys. In R. Meersman, T. S. Dillon, & P. Herrero (Eds.), *Proceeding of the 8th International Conference on Ontologies, DataBases, and Applications of Semantics (ODBASE 2009) Lecture Notes in Computer Science: Vol. 5871.* (pp. 1183-1200). Springer.

Viyanon, W., Madria, S. K., & Bhowmick, S. S. (2008). XML data integration based on content and structure similarity using keys. In R. Meersman, & Z. Tari (Eds.), *On the Move to Meaningful Internet Systems (OTM 2008) Lecture Notes in Computer Science: Vol. 5331.* (pp. 484-493). Springer.

Webber, N., O'Connell, C., Hunt, B., Levine, R., Popkin, L., & Larose, G. (1998). *The information and content exchange (ICE) protocol.* Retrieved March 2010, from http://www.w3.org/TR/NOTE-ice

Weis, M., & Naumann, F. (2005). DogmatiX tracks down duplicates in XML. In F. Özcan (Ed.), *Proceedings of the 2005 ACM International Conference on Management of Data (SIGMOD),* (pp. 431-442). ACM.

Wen, L., Amagasa, T., & Kitagawa, H. (2009). An approach for XML similarity join using tree serialization. In J. R. Haritsa, K. Ramamohanarao, & V. Pudi (Eds.), *Database Systems for Advanced Applications, 13th International Conference (DASFAA): Vol. 4947. Lecture Notes in Computer Science* (pp. 562-570). Springer.

Yan, T., & Garcia-Molina, H. (1999). The SIFT information dissemination system. *ACM Transactions on Database Systems*, *24*(4), 529–565. doi:10.1145/331983.331992

Yoshikawa, M., Amagasa, T., Shimura, T., & Uemura, S. (2001). XRel: A path-based approach to storage and retrieval of XML documents using relational databases. *ACM Transactions on Internet Technology*, *1*(1), 110–141. doi:10.1145/383034.383038

Zhou, G., Hull, R., King, R., & Franchitti, J.-C. (1995). Using object matching and materialization to integrate heterogeneous databases. In S. Laufmann, S. Spaccapietra, & T. Yokoi (Eds.), *Proceedings of the 3rd International Conference on Cooperative Information Systems (CoopIS'95)*, (pp. 4-18). IEEE Computer Society Press.

# Chapter 4
# Efficient Identification of Similar XML Fragments Based on Tree Edit Distance

**Hongzhi Wang**
*Harbin Institute of Technology, China*

**Jianzhong Li**
*Harbin Institute of Technology, China*

**Fei Li**
*Harbin Institute of Technology, China*

## ABSTRACT

*Similarity detection between large XML fragment sets is broadly used in many applications such as data integration and XML de-duplication. Extensive methods are used to find similar XML fragments, such as the pq-gram state-of-the-art method which allows for relatively high join quality and efficiency. In this chapter, we propose pq-hash as an improvement to pq-grams. As the base of pq-hash, a randomized data structure, pq-array, is developed. With pq-array, large trees are represented as small fixed sized arrays. To efficiently perform similarity join on XML fragment sets, in this chapter we propose a cluster-based partition strategy as well as a sort-merge & hash join strategy to avoid nested loop join. Both our theoretical analysis and experimental results confirm that, while retaining high join quality, pq-hash gains much higher efficiency than pq-grams, and our strategies for approximate join are effective.*

## INTRODUCTION

Thanks to its ability to represent data from a wide variety of sources, XML has rapidly emerged as the new standard for data representation and exchange on the Internet. Given the flexibility of XML, data in autonomous sources which represent the same real-world object may not be exactly the same. Thus, similarity detection techniques are often applied to find XML fragments representing the same real-world object. In this chapter we refer to a real-world application in the Municipality of Bozen in order to illustrate the use of techniques for detecting similar XML fragments. In this con-

DOI: 10.4018/978-1-61350-356-0.ch004

text, the GIS office in that municipality maintains maps of the city area, so that one would like to enrich such maps with information retrieved from various databases of the municipality as well as external institutions. Residential addresses turn out to play a pivotal role in this process since they have to be used to access and link relevant information. However, performing exact join on the street names would yield poor results since street names are different in different databases due to, e.g., spelling mistakes, different naming conventions, and renamed streets which are not always updated in all databases. Moreover, in the bilingual region of Bozen, each street has typically two names, and these are often used interchangeably. Since these data can be modeled as ordered, labeled trees, methods for the detection of similar XML fragments can be used to effectively match the data representing the same real-world data.

A widely used approach to the evaluation of similarity between XML documents is to compute their *edit distance* (Cobena, Abiteboul, & Marian, 2002; Guha, Jagadish, Koudas, Srivastava, & Yu, 2002; Lee, Choy, & Cho 2004). Since XML documents are often modeled as ordered, labeled trees, the tree edit distance between any two such trees is defined as the minimum number of node insertions, deletions and relabelings to transform a tree into another (Tai, 1979). It is well-known that the edit distance behaves well but is computationally expensive. Many works such as (Zhang & Shasha, 1989; Klein, 1998; Chen, 2001; Demaine, Mozes, Rossman, & Weimann, 2007) have been proposed to improve the efficiency in the computation of tree edit distance. However, all of them have more than $O(n^3)$ runtime, where $n$ is the tree size, and hence they do not scale to large trees. Since it is hard to improve the efficiency fundamentally by optimizing the tree edit algorithms independently, transformation-based methods are often adopted in order to transform trees into other data structures whose similarities are easier to evaluate.

An example of computation of tree edit distance is shown in Figure 1. To transform the XML fragment $T$ to the XML fragment $T_3$, the following operations are made: insertion of node $i$, relabeling of node $c$ with $x$, and deletion of node $g$. Since this is the minimum cost transformation sequence, the tree edit distance between $T$ and $T_3$ is equal to 3.

The *pq-gram* method is known as an effective and efficient transformation-based tree similarity detection method (Augsten, Böhlen, & Gamper, 2005). In this method, each tree is split into a small subtree bag. The *pq*-distance between the *pq*-bags is used to describe the distance between their corresponding trees. Both theoretical analysis and experimental results confirm the detection quality based on *pq-grams*. An "optimized join" (Augsten, Böhlen, Dyreson, & Gamper, 2008) was also presented to accelerate the detection process by taking advantage of the diversity of trees in a forest. However, this optimized join

*Figure 1. Example of computation of tree edit distance computation: the left-most tree is transformed into the right-most tree*

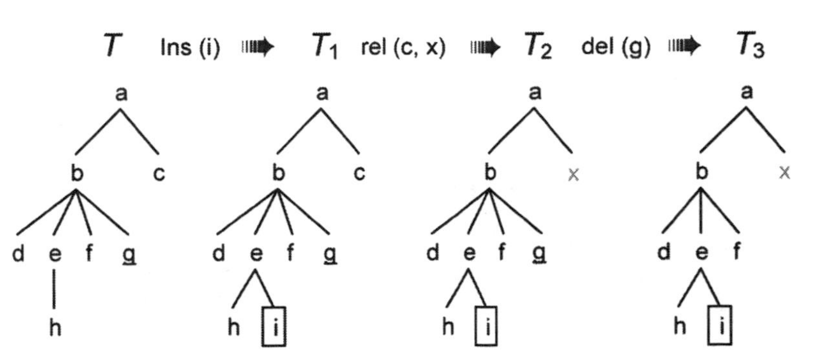

cannot always improve efficiency. In many cases, such as the cases in which a large part of tree pairs (in the Cartesian product of any two tree sets) show high similarity, the efficiency of the optimized join is nearly as low as that of the nested loop join.

To perform approximate matching efficiently even in the worst case, we propose a method called *pq*-hash and a randomized data structure called a *pq*-arrays which allows for faster comparisons. In our method *pq*-hash, trees are first transformed into bags of *pq*-grams and then hashed into *pq*-arrays. Min-wise hashes (Broder, Charikar, Frieze, & Mitzenmacher, 1998) are applied for the generation of these *pq*-arrays with small fixed size. As a result, two trees are considered similar if the numbers in most positions in their corresponding *pq*-arrays equal. Note that since counting the number of such positions can be done in time $O(1)$, the similarity detection is performed efficiently even using nested-loop join. Instead of nested-loop join, we perform sort-merge and hash join operations on these *pq*-arrays to further improve the efficiency. Experimental results show that even with very high efficiency, the quality of matches based on *pq*-array is good. To summarize, the main contributions of this chapter include:

- we introduce a randomized data structure called *pq*-array;
- based on *pq*-array, we propose a new method called *pq*-hash for efficient similarity detection on large XML fragment sets;
- the similarity detection process is accelerated by two strategies, the one based on XML clustering and the other one is based on sort-merge and hash join;
- our theoretical analysis and experimental results have confirmed that *pq*-hash retains the detection quality of *pq-grams* and improves the efficiency significantly in any cases when the number of trees in both sources is large and the trees are huge.

The rest of this chapter is organized as follows. The next two sections briefly discuss related work and introduce background knowledge, respectively. Section "A randomized structure for the estimation of tree edit distance" presents the randomized data structure *pq*-array and the method *pq*-hash. Based on *pq*-array, the algorithms of two important operators, similarity search and similarity join, are proposed in Section "Similarity detection algorithms for XML fragments" and Section "Similarity detection algorithms for XML fragment sets", respectively. The methods in this chapter are tested experimentally in Section "Experimental results". In Section "Future research directions" we discuss pointers for future research and, in the final section, we draw the conclusions.

## RELATED WORK

As previously mentioned, tree matching techniques have been widely applied to compute similarity between trees. Let us denote with let $n$, $l$ and $d$ the node number, the leaf number and the depth of a tree, respectively. The first algorithm for computing tree edit distance was proposed by Tai (1979) and worked in time $O(n^2l^4)$, with a worst-case running time of $O(n^6)$. Zhang & Shasha (1989) improved this result to an $O(n^2 \min^2(l, d))$ running time algorithm which in worst-case has an $O(n^4)$ time complexity. Klein (1998) further improved this result to a worst-case $O(n^3 \log n)$ time algorithm. Both (Klein, 1998) and (Zhang & Shasha, 1989) achieved their improvements based on closely related dynamic programs, presenting different ways of computing only a subset of relevant subproblems. Chen (2001) presented a different approach based on the results of fast matrix multiplication and proposed an algorithm with $O(n^{3.5})$ worst-case runtime. A recent development is by Demaine, Mozes, Rossman, and Weimann (2007) which described an algorithm running in $O(n^3)$ time.

Obviously, the tree edit distance computation is expensive and is not scalable for similarity search on large trees in huge datasets. Therefore, most work aims to transform trees into other data structures whose similarities are easier to evaluate. In (Guha et al., 2002), XML documents are transformed into their corresponding preorder and postorder traversal sequences. Then the maximum of the string edit distance of the two sequences is used as the lower bound of the tree edit distance. Other works including (Akutsu, 2006; Akutsu, Fukagawa, & Takasu, 2006) discuss approximate tree edit distance using string edit distance.

(Multi-)Set is a kind of data structure whose similarity is easy to evaluate. In the method of *pq*-gram (Augsten, Böhlen, & Gamper, 2005), each tree is transformed into a set of *pq*-grams (a small subtree in a specific shape). By this transformation, the similarity between trees can be evaluated in time $O(n \log n)$. In (Augsten, Böhlen, Dyreson, & Gamper, 2008), the *pq*-gram method is extended to evaluate the similarity between unordered trees. The authors also provided an optimized join algorithm which in many cases can avoid the nested-loop join. It has $O(Nn \log n + Nn \log Nn)$ runtime in the best case, where $N$ is the number of trees in each dataset. However, in many other cases (especially when many tree pairs show high degree of similarity), the time complexity is near to the nested-loop join $O(Nn \log n + N^2 n)$.

Another set-transformation based method is presented in (Tatikonda & Parthasarathy, 2010). Each tree is transformed into a set of pivots, where a pivot is a tuple $(lca, u, v)$ where $u$ and $v$ are nodes and $lca$ is the lowest common ancestor of $u$ and $v$. In the case of unordered trees, that method can better approximate tree edit distance than *pq*-gram. However, as the number of the pivots is potentially quadratic in the tree size while the number of *pq*-grams is linear in the tree size, the efficiency might be lower than *pq*-gram when the datasets are large.

The detection of similar XML fragments have also been combined with other techniques recently. In (Yuan, Sha, Wang, Yang, Zhou, & Yang, 2010), similar XML fragments techniques are combined with MapReduce. In (Yuan, Wang, Sha, Gao, & Zhou, 2010), GRAMS3 is introduced as an efficient framework for XML structural similarity detection.

Differently from approximately matching of trees, another solution for searching trees based on the structure approximately is the query relaxation for XML data. Amer-Yahia, Cho, and Srivastava (2002) presented a method to find proper queries that has query results and is similar to the given query. As an extension to the tree-structured data query, (Fazzinga, Flesca, & Furfaro, 2010) have recently proposed a rule-based method for the XPath queries.

## BACKGROUND

In this section, we provide basic notions and definitions that will be used through this chapter. This background knowledge particularly includes the definition of detection of similar XML fragments and of *pq*-grams.

### Definition 1 (Detection of Similar XML Fragments)

Given any two XML fragment sets $F_1$ and $F_2$, the similarity detection on them is to retrieve the set $\{(T_i, T_j) \mid T_i \in F_1, T_j \in F_2, sim(T_i, T_j)\}$, where $sim(T_i, T_j)$ is true if and only if $T_i$ and $T_j$ are similar in a predefined evaluation.

### Example 1

Figure 2 shows two XML fragment sets $F_1 = \{T_1^{F_1}, T_2^{F_1}\}$ and $F_2 = \{T_1^{F_2}, T_2^{F_2}\}$. Suppose that the predefined similarity evaluation corresponds to having a tree edit distance (Tai, 1979) lower than 2. In this case, only $(T_1^{F_1}, T_1^{F_2})$ and $(T_2^{F_1}, T_2^{F_2})$ fit that evaluation. Therefore, the result of similar

*Figure 2. Example of XML fragment similarity detection*

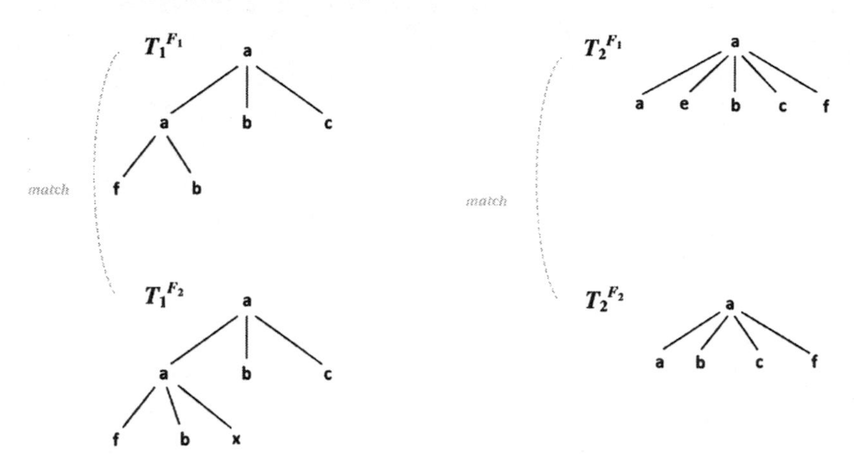


XML fragment detection on the input sets is represented by the set $\{(T_1^{F_1}, T_1^{F_2}), (T_2^{F_1}, T_2^{F_2})\}$.

The *pq*-gram method was introduced in (Augsten, Böhlen, & Gamper, 2005) as an effective method for similarity evaluation between ordered, labeled trees. Intuitively, a *pq*-gram *g* is a small subtree with a specific shape. It consists of an anchor node with its *p*-1 ancestors and its *q* children. The *anchor node* and its *p*-1 ancestors form the *stem* while the *q* children form the *base*.

In order to make sure that each node in an input tree appears in at least one *pq*-gram as the anchor node, the input tree is extended with *dummy nodes* by a special label *. The *pq-extended tree* $T^{pq}$ of a given tree is constructed by carrying out the following three steps:

- *p*-1 ancestors are appended to the root node;
- *q* children are inserted into each leaf;
- *q*-1 children are added before the first and after the last child of each non-leaf node.

## Example 2

In Figure 3, $T_1^{F_1}$ is extended to its 2,3-extended tree. Figure 4 shows some 2,3-grams of the 2,3-extended tree.

## Definition 2 (*pq*-Bag)

Given a tree *T*, the pq-bag of *T* is the bag of the form $\{g \mid g \text{ is a } pq\text{-gram of the extended tree of } T\}$. We use the symbol $S_T^{pq}$ to denote the *pq*-bag of *T*.

## Example 3

Figure 5 shows the 2,3-bags of $T_1^{F_1}$ and $T_1^{F_2}$. For the sake of brevity, each *pq*-gram is represented as a tuple consisting of all the labels in that *pq*-gram in preorder.

As discussed in (Augsten, Böhlen, & Gamper, 2005), some important properties of *pq*-grams are as follows:

- the size of a *pq*-bag is *O*(*n*), where *n* is the tree size.
- all the *pq*-grams in a tree can be generated in *O*(*n*) time;
- experimental results have shown the quality of matches based on *pq*-grams.

As a result of the transformation, all the trees are represented as large *pq*-bags with *O*(*n*) *pq*-grams for each. *O*(*n*) time is needed for the similarity evaluation between a pair of sorted *pq*-bags. When joining any two tree sets, all their tree pairs have to be compared. For the sake of clarity of

*Figure 3. pq-Extended tree of $T_1^{F_1}$, with p=2 and q=3.*

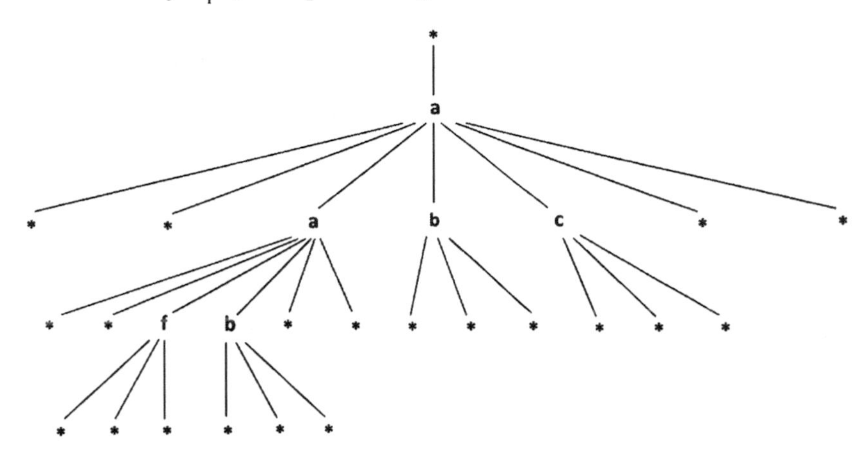

*Figure 4. Some 2,3-grams of $T_1^{F_1}$*

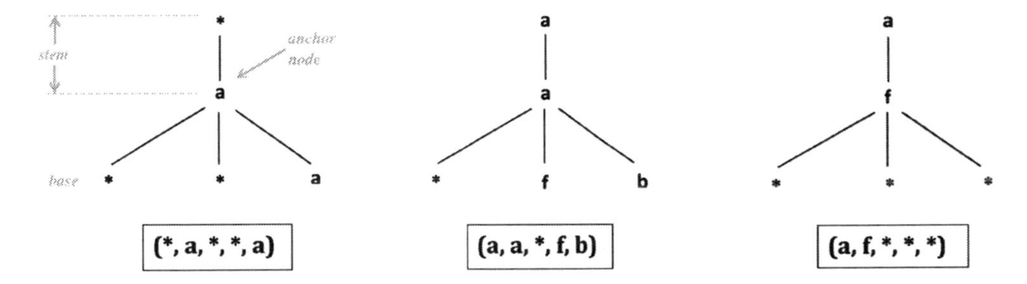


presentation, we can assume that both of the two tree sets have $N$ trees and each tree in a set has $O(n)$ nodes. That is, $N^2$*pq*-bag pairs are needed to be compared in nested-looped join, so altogether $O(N^2n)$ time is needed. Therefore, *pq*-gram does not scale when the tree sets are large. To solve this problem, an optimized join method was provided in (Augsten, Böhlen, Dyreson, & Gamper, 2008) to avoid the nested-loop join. However, as we will analyze later, in many cases the optimized join method can not accelerate the similarity detection when many tree pairs are similar. In this respect, the goal of the study presented in this chapter is to accelerate the comparisons between these *pq*-bags. Since Jaccard coefficient (Metwally, Agrawal, & Abadi, 2007) serves as one of the standard metrics for bag similarity evaluation, it is used in this chapter as the measure of similarity between any two *pq*-bags:

$$\text{sim}(T_1, T_2) \approx \text{Jaccard}(S_{T_1}^{pq}, S_{T_2}^{pq}) = | S_{T_1}^{pq} \cap S_{T_2}^{pq} | / | S_{T_1}^{pq} \cup S_{T_2}^{pq} |$$

### Example 4

Consider the 2,3-bags of $T_1^{F_1}$ and $T_1^{F_2}$ in Figure 5. The Jaccard coefficient between them is equal to 11/17.

## A RANDOMIZED STRUCTURE FOR THE ESTIMATION OF TREE EDIT DISTANCE

In this section, we present a randomized data structure called *pq*-array which is used for efficiently comparing *pq*-bags. In our method *pq*-hash, each *pq*-bag is converted into a fixed sized

*Figure 5. The 2,3-bags of $T_1^{F_1}$ and $T_1^{F_2}$*

| pq-bag $T_1^{F_1}$ |
|---|
| (*, a, *, *, a) |
| (a, a, *, *, f) |
| (a, f, *, *, *) |
| (a, a, *, f, b) |
| (a, b, *, *, *) |
| (a, a, f, b, *) |
| (a, a, b, *, *) |
| (*, a, *, a, b) |
| (a, b, *, *, *) |
| (*, a, a, b, c) |
| (a, c, *, *, *) |
| (*, a, b, c, *) |
| (*, a, c, *, *) |

| pq-bag $T_1^{F_2}$ |
|---|
| (*, a, *, *, a) |
| (a, a, *, *, f) |
| (a, f, *, *, *) |
| (a, a, *, f, b) |
| (a, b, *, *, *) |
| (a, a, f, b, x) |
| (a, x, *, *, *) |
| (a, a, b, x, *) |
| (a, a, x, *, *) |
| (*, a, *, a, b) |
| (a, b, *, *, *) |
| (*, a, a, b, c) |
| (a, c, *, *, *) |
| (*, a, b, c, *) |
| (*, a, c, *, *) |

*pq*-array by means of three hash functions: two transformation-hash functions and a signature-hash function. The former transform a *pq*-bag into a number-set by hashing each *pq*-gram into a unique integer, whereas the latter hashes each large number-set into a small fixed sized *pq*-array.

## Transformation Hash Function

Each *pq*-gram $g_i \in S_T^{pq}$ is first hashed into an integer as follows:

$$h(g_i) = a_1 g_i(1) + \ldots + a_{p+q}\, g_i(p+q) \bmod M_1$$

where $M_1$ and the $a$'s are large prime numbers. Each *pq*-bag is also hashed into a number-bag. To compute the Jaccard coefficient between these number bags more efficiently, we hash each number bag into a number set using the method described in (Haveliwala, Gionis, & Indyk, 2000), which is briefly recalled as follows: Let $f$ be the frequency with which an element $w$ appears, and $h_2(w) = (b_1 w + b_2) \bmod M_2$ be a linear hash function. Each $w$ is hashed into $f$ numbers $w_1, \ldots, w_i, \ldots, w_f$, where $w_1 = w$ and $w_{i+1} = h_2(w_i)$. Once these hash functions are computed, a number set called *pq*-set is generated. From now on, we use the symbol $S_T^{pq}$ to denote the *pq*-set transformed from $T$. According to (Haveliwala, Gionis, & Indyk, 2000), the Jaccard coefficient between *pq*-bags is equal to the Jaccard coefficient between their corresponding *pq*-sets.

## Signature Hash Function

Since the size of *pq*-sets is linear in the tree size, the merge and intersection operations between two sorted *pq*-sets have costs $O(n)$. Since there are be $N^2$ pairs of sets to be compared, the overall similarity detection needs a lot of time. To compare the similarity between these *pq*-sets efficiently, we use the *min-hash* technique (Broder, Charikar, Frieze, & Mitzenmacher, 1998; Haveliwala, Gionis, & Indyk, 2000). We propose the signature hash function to transform each *pq*-set into a fixed size array called *pq*-array. The computation of the Jaccard coefficient between *pq*-sets can be approximated in $O(1)$ time using these *pq*-arrays.

Given a *pq*-set $S_T^{pq}$ transformed from tree $T$, let $\pi(x) = (c\,x + d) \bmod M$ be a random linear permutation, where $c$, $d$ and $M$ are all large prime numbers. Let $S' = \{\pi(x) \mid x \in S_T^{pq}\}$. Only the minimal element in $S'$ is recorded; thus, the set $S_T^{pq}$ is hashed into a minimum number denoted with $\min_{\pi(T)}$. According to (Broder, Charikar, Frieze, & Mitzenmacher, 1998), for two *pq*-sets $S_{T_1}^{pq}$ and $S_{T_2}^{pq}$, the probability of $\min_{\pi(T_1)} = \min_{\pi(T_2)}$ is equal to the Jaccard coefficient. Therefore, the problem is transformed to computing the probability of $\min_{\pi(T_1)} = \min_{\pi(T_2)}$. In order to estimate this probability, $k$ random linear permutations $\pi_1(x), \ldots, \pi_k(x)$ are chosen and the hash function is performed independently for $k$ times. Thus, for any given tree, an array with $k$ entries is generated. Such array is called *pq*-array. Its formal definition is given in Definition 3, whereas the notion of *equal ratio* for computing the similarity between *pq*-arrays is given in Definition 4.

### Definition 3 (*pq*-Array)

Let $T$ be a tree and $\Pi = \pi_1(x), \ldots, \pi_k(x)$ be $k$ independent random linear permutations. The *pq*-array $A_\Pi^T$ is an array with each entry $A_\Pi^T[i] = \min(\pi_i(S_T^{pq}))$.

### Definition 4 (Equal Ratio)

Given a permutation set $\Pi$ and two trees, the equal ratio $\gamma$ is the ratio between the frequency that the minimum numbers equal and the size of $\Pi$.

It can be proven that the probability of $\min_{\pi(T_1)} = \min_{\pi(T_2)}$ is approximated by $\gamma$ in a bounded ratio with high probability. From Definition 4, $\gamma$ is computed in $O(|\Pi|)$. Since the size of $\Pi$ is a constant independent of $T_1$ and $T_2$, such approximation can be computed in constant time.

## SIMILARITY DETECTION ALGORITHMS FOR XML FRAGMENTS

Using the algorithmic framework described in (Augsten, Böhlen, & Gamper, 2005), our hash algorithms for computing *pq*-arrays are shown in Algorithm 1, Algorithm 2, and Algorithm 3.

*Algorithm 1. Compute-pq-array*

```
Input: T, p, q, k
Output: pq-Array

1: Let Π be the k random linear functions in pq-hash
2: Let h1 be the function to hash a pq-bag into a number bag
3: Let h2 be the function to hash a number bag into pq-set
4: pq-Bag and pq-Set are initialized as null
5: pq-Array is initialized with k random large numbers
6: stem:= initialize stem register full with *
7: pq-Bag = compute-pq-Bag(T, root(T), p, q, pq-Bag, stem)
8: pq-Set = h2 (pq-Bag)
9: pq-Array = MinHash(pq-Set, k)
10: return pq-Array
```

For purposes of efficient transformation, two shift registers, *stem* and *base*, are used in the algorithms to store the stem and base of the current *pq*-gram. The operation *shift*(*reg*, *el*) returns *reg* with its oldest element dequeued and *el* enqueued. For example, *shift*((*a*,*b*,*c*),*x*) returns (*b*,*c*,*x*). The operation *stem*∘*base* returns the *pq*-gram with a stem of *stem* and a base of *base*. The hash function *h* hashes *pq*-grams into *pq*-numbers.

The compute-*pq*-Array algorithm (Algorithm 1) takes as input a tree and the three values *p*, *q* and *k*, and returns the *pq*-array of the input tree. This algorithm calculates the *pq*-grams starting from the root node of the tree (line 7), then it hashes *pq*-bag into *pq*-set (line 8) and transforms *pq*-set to *pq*-array (line 9).

The compute-*pq*-Bag function (Algorithm 2) first shifts the label of the anchor node *r* into the *stem*, which corresponds to moving the *pq*-grams one step down. Now *stem* contains the labels of *r* and its *p*-1 ancestors. The loop at line 7 in Algorithm 2 moves the register *base* from left to right over the children of *r* in order to produce all the *pq*-grams with anchor *r*.

*Algorithm 2. Compute-pq-Bag*

```
Input: T, r, p, q, pq-Bag, stem
Output: pq-Bag
 1: stem:= shift(stem, r)
 2: base:= initialize base register full filled with *
 3: if r is a leaf node then
 4:   pq-number = h(stem∘base) //compute the hash value
 5:   pq-Bag = pq-Bag ∪ pq-number //add the number to the pq-Bag
 6: else
 7:   for all children c (from left to right) of r do
 8:      base = shift(base, c)
 9:      pq-number = h(stem∪base) //compute the hash value for the base
10:       pq-Bag = pq-Bag ∪ pq-number
11:       pq-Bag = compute-pq-Bag(T, r, p, q, pq-Bag, stem)
12:   for j=1 to q-1 do
13:      base = shift(base, *) //obtain new base for the q values
14:      pq-number = h(stem∪base) //compute the hash value for the new base
15:      pq-Bag = pq-Bag ∪ pq-number
16: return pq-Bag
```

*Algorithm 3. MinHash*

```
Input: pq-Set, k
Output: pq-Array

1: for all the pq-numbers in pq-Set do
2:   for all the pq-numbers in pq-Set do
3:      minh = π_i(pq-number)
4:      if minh < pq-Array[i] then
5:         pq-Array[i] = minh
6: return pq-Array
```

Finally, the MinHash function (Algorithm 3) calculates the minimum number for each entry in *pq*-array. After the transformation, each entry only stores the minimum number after the corresponding random hash function.

## SIMILARITY DETECTION ALGORITHMS FOR XML FRAGMENT SETS

Using the algorithms previously presented, all the trees in any two tree sets can be transformed into their corresponding *pq*-arrays. Although the equal ratio between *pq*-arrays takes only $O(1)$ time, a nested-loop detection between the *pq*-array may still take a long time when $N$ (i.e., the size of each of the tree sets) is very large. Therefore, we adopt two strategies for the similarity detection on XML fragment sets, namely an XML clustering based strategy and a min-number filtering based strategy.

### XML Fragment Set Clustering Strategy

An obvious issue in the naïve algorithm for similarity detection in XML fragment sets is that, regardless of how an XML fragment is different from other XML fragments, *pq*-array has to be generated, and consequently all pairs of *pq*-arrays should be compared. When the XML sets are very large, especially when only a few XML fragments are similar, most time is spent for useless computation and comparisons.

We use an example to illustrate this problem. Consider two sets of XML fragments $A$ and $B$ each with 100 XML fragments, of which only 10% of XML fragments in $A$ are similar as 10% documents in $B$. In order to compute the similarity between $A$ and $B$, 10,000 comparisons of *pq*-arrays are to be performed but only 100 comparisons are actually useful.

To address this problem, we propose a new strategy where the basic idea is to cluster the fragment sets and apply join on the clusters efficiently. The clustering framework hence consists in building a *signature* for each XML fragment and aggregating the XML fragments (that belong to two given sets) with similar signatures together. We now introduce the structure of this signature and then present the clustering process based on the signature.

### XML Fragment Index

To efficiently perform the clustering of XML fragment sets, we choose some representatives in each XML fragment. By using these representatives, the similarity of two XML fragments is estimated efficiently. Intuitively, the impact of a node on an XML fragment corresponds to its impact on the similarity between the fragment and the other ones. Based on this observation, we define the notion of impact of a node on the comparison of similarity.

### Definition 5 (Impact)

Given a node $n$ of an XML fragment, let $PT$ be the number of all *pq*-grams of the XML fragment, and $Pn$ be the number of *pq*-grams containing $n$. The impact of $n$ is defined as $t = Pn/PT$.

Based on the above notion, some particular nodes are hence chosen as the index of an XML fragment. Moreover, some properties that hold for XML fragments put the basis for the design of the strategy of index selection: non-leaf nodes cover all *pq*-grams, and the impacts of non-leaf nodes are higher than the impact of leaf nodes.

*Algorithm 4. GetIndex*

```
Input: An XML fragment T and a node n in T
Output: Its corresponding index IT

1: IT is initialized as null
2: if n is a leaf then
3:    return null
4: IT = IT ∪ GetIndex(T, n)
5: for all child c of n do
6:    IT = IT ∪ GetIndex(T, n)
7: return IT
```

Within this view, we choose all non-leaf nodes as index to make the index selection simple and efficient. Algorithm 4 computes the index of each XML fragment, denoted by *IT*. This algorithm processes every node in the XML fragment recursively choosing non-leaf nodes as the index.

## XML Fragment Clustering

Our proposed XML fragment clustering strategy is based on the index previously presented, and on a function of similarity which is described next.

### Definition 6 (XML Fragment Similarity)

Given two XML fragments $T_1$ and $T_2$, let $IT_1$ and $IT_2$ denote their respective indexes. The similarity between $T_1$ and $T_2$ is computed as the ratio between the number of common nodes in the indexes and the sum of the sizes of the indexes.

Given a threshold *param* (between 0 and 1), if the similarity between any two XML fragments is greater than or equal to this threshold, then the fragments are considered as similar, and hence assigned to the same cluster.

Our clustering strategy is based on the observation that if two XML fragments share many same non-leaf nodes and each non-leaf node affects many *pq*-grams, then the two XML fragments share many *pq*-grams and the probability of matching is large. Moreover, if the indexes of two trees are not similar, their probability of matching is low.

Suppose the two XML fragment sets to be joined are $F_1$ and $F_2$. Based on the clustering, the fragments in $F_1$ and $F_2$ are partitioned into some chunks. Similarity detection is performed only on the XML fragments in corresponding chunks.

The XML fragment clustering algorithm is shown in Algorithm 5. To accelerate the preliminary clustering, a bitmap with each bit as a tag is used. Given a cluster *C*, *bitmap(C)* is its corresponding cluster and for a XML fragment *T*, *bitmap(T)* is the bitmap of its index. In this algorithm, for each XML fragment *T*, with the function *find_bitmap*, the cluster $C_T$ with the most similar bitmap is selected. If the similarity between *T* and $C_T$ is larger than a threshold, *T* is added to $C_T$. Otherwise, a new cluster is created with only *T*.

We use an example to illustrate the execution of Algorithm 5. Let $\{A_1, A_2, A_3\}$ and $\{B_1, B_2, B_3, B_4\}$ be two sets of XML fragments. Suppose the indexes of $A_1$, $A_2$, and $A_3$ are $(a, b, c)$, $(a, b, c, d)$ and $(g, h, i)$ with bitmaps 1110000000, 1101000000, 0000001110, respectively, and the indexes of $B_1$, $B_2$, $B_3$, and $B_4$ are $(a, b, b, c)$, $(a, b, b, d)$, $(g, h, i, j)$, and $(g, h, i)$ with bitmaps 1110000000, 1101000000, 0000001111, and 0000001110, respectively. By setting *param*=3,

*Algorithm 5. XML Fragment Clustering*

```
Input: XML fragment sets F1, F2, and threshold param
Output: a set S of clusters containing XML fragments from F1
and F2

 1: S is initialized as null
 2: for all fragment T ∈ F1 ∪ F2 do
 3:    Cx = find_bitmap(bitmap(T),S)
 4:    if sim(bitmap(T), bitmap(CT)) < param then
 5:       add T to CT
 6:       bitmap(CT) = bitmap(CT) AND bitmap(T)
 7:    else
 8:       create a cluster C
 9:       add T to C
10:       bitmap(C) = bitmap(T)
11:       add C to S
12: return S
```

which means that any two bitmaps in the same cluster should share at least 3 same bits. $A_1$ is first processed and a cluster is created for $A_1$. Then, when $B_1$ is processed, since its bitmap is the same as $A_1$, it is assigned to the same cluster as $A_1$. When $B_2$ is processed, since it shares only 2 bits as that of $B_1$ and $A_1$, a new cluster for $B_2$ is created. Other fragments are clustered in the same manner and the final cluster result is $\{\{A_1, B_1\}, \{A_2, B_2\}, \{A_3, B_3, B_4\}\}$.

### Min-Number Filtering Strategy

In our second strategy, when detecting similar trees between two tree sets, we check for each min-number in which pairs of *pq*-arrays appear, instead of computing the equal ratio between each pair of *pq*-arrays independently. In this way, we can apply sort-merge and hash join to optimize this detection.

After the process of *pq*-hash, each tree is transformed into a *pq*-array with $k$ numbers. We denote each min-number by a tuple (*treeId, value, position*). *TreeId* records which tree the min-number belongs to, while *value* records the value of that min-number. The *position* records the min-number's position in its *pq*-array. We put all these tuples in a source together to form a *List*. Then we sort the *List* by the value of the min-number. Using the Algorithm 6, the equal ratio between each pair of *pq*-arrays can be computed without nested-loop.

*Algorithm 6. Optimized join for pq-arrays*

**Input:** two sorted *Lists*, $k$, $\tau$
**Output:** join result

1: $List_1 \leftarrow \rho_{treeId / treeId_1}$
2: $List_2 \leftarrow \rho_{treeId / treeId_2}$
3: $List' = List_1 \rhd\lhd List_2$
4: $List'' = \Gamma_{treeId_1, treeId_2, COUNT/k \rightarrow EqualRatio} (List')$
5: **return** $\pi_{treeId_1, treeId_2} (\sigma_{EqualRatio \geq \tau} (List''))$

In Algorithm 6, $\rho_{treeId / treeId_i}$ means that attribute *treeId* is renamed as $treeId_i$; $List_1 \rhd\lhd List_2$ denotes the natural join operation applied to $List_1$ and $List_2$; $\Gamma_{treeId_1, treeId_2, COUNT/k \rightarrow EqualRatio} (List')$ computes the equal ratio for each tree pair; finally, $\Gamma_{treeId_1, treeId_2, COUNT/k \rightarrow EqualRatio} (List')$ is returned to output all the tree pair whose equal ratio above a predefined threshold $\tau$.

## COMPUTATIONAL ANALYSIS

### Efficiency Analysis

For the sake of simplicity, we assume that, given any two tree sets $F_1$ and $F_2$, both of them have $N$ trees and each tree in them has $O(n)$ nodes. The matching on these tree sets $F_1$ and $F_2$ based on *pq*-array consists of three steps:

1. All the trees in $F_1$ and $F_2$ are transformed into *pq*-sets.
2. $k$-MinHash functions are used to hash all *pq*-sets into *pq*-arrays.
3. Optimized join between these *pq*-arrays is performed and the set $\{(T_i, T_j) \mid T_i \in F_1, T_j \in F_2, \gamma(T_i, T_j) \geq \tau\}$ is outputted, where $\tau$ is the threshold.

In step 1, the transformation for a *pq*-set takes $O(n \log n)$ time. Since there are $2N$ trees in $F_1$ and $F_2$, generating all the *pq*-sets totally costs $O(Nn \log n)$ time. In step 2, $O(kn)$ time is needed to transform a *pq*-set into its *pq*-array. The total cost in this step is $O(kNn)$ since there are $2N$ *pq*-sets to transform. Since $k$ is a constant independent of the input, the time cost in this step is $O(Nn)$. In step 3, different from the nested-loop detection, our detection algorithm takes advantage of the diversity of trees in a forest. In the best case, when no *pq*-array has equal minimum number in the same position, the runtime is $O(N \log N)$.

Even in the worst cases, when the forests consist of identical copies of the same tree, our detection algorithm still has a $O(N^2)$ time complexity. Note that the detection result are $N^2$ tree pairs in the worst cases, thus no algorithm can improve on the quadratic runtime.

To summarize, our algorithm has an $O(Nn \log n + N \log N)$ total time cost in the best case while an $O(Nn \log n + N^2)$ total time cost in the worst case.

## Random Error Analysis

In our method, we use many hash functions: we use $h_1$ to transform a *pq*-gram into a number, $h_2$ to transform each *pq*-bag to a *pq*-set, and *k*-Minhash. In this subsection, we will analyze the random error in each hash function.

### Collision in Each Hash Function

Since all the parameters (i.e., $a_1, \ldots, a_{p+q}, M_1$ in $h_1$; $b_1, b_2, M_2$ in $h_2$; all the $c$, $d$, $M$ in each $\pi$) are random large prime numbers, the probability of collision is very low (Gionis, Indyk, & Motwani, 1999). The random error in this step is almost 0 with carefully selected parameters.

### Random Error in k Min-Hash Functions

The main random error results in using equal ratio between *pq*-arrays to approximate the Jaccard coefficient between the corresponding *pq*-sets. The core of this approximation is using the frequency of *k* Bernoulli trials to estimate the probability. We use *r* to denote the random error. For a random linear hash function $\pi$, we use *P* to denote the probability of $\min_{\pi(T_1)} = \min_{\pi(T_2)}$.

In our method, *pq*-hash is performed independently for *k* times with *k* linear permutations. This process is a series of Bernoulli trials. By counting the times *t* that event $\min_{\pi(T_1)} = \min_{\pi(T_2)}$ occurs, the equal ratio $t/k$ is used to approximate *P*. We use random error to describe the difference between $t/k$ and *P*.

By denoting the random variable in the Bernoulli trials as *X*, since Bernoulli trials are independent of each other, *X* fits the binomial distribution with parameters of *k* and *P* as follows:

$$\Pr(X/k = t/k) = \Pr(X = t)\ \mathrm{B}(k, t)\ P^t\ P^{k-t},\ (t = 0..k)$$

where $\mathrm{B}(k, t)$ denotes the binomial coefficient with parameters *k* and *t*. When *k* is a finite constant, the average random error is computed by summing $\Pr(X = t)$ for all $t = k(P-v)..\ k(P+v)$, which is equal to the sum $\mathrm{B}(k, t)\ P^t\ P^{k-t}$ for all $t = k(P-v)..\ k(P+v)$.

When *P* and *k* are fixed, the average value of random error can be computed as mentioned above. Intuitively, the average random error decreases by increasing *k*. Here, we show the impact of *k* on the average random error under some values of *P* in Figure 6.

When *k* is larger than 400, the average random error of this approximation is smaller than 0.02, regardless of the value of the Jaccard coefficient *P*. It means that, with 400-MinHashes, the average random error is smaller than 0.02. Thus, we choose 400 as our recommended value for *k*.

## EXPERIMENTAL RESULTS

In this section, we present efficiency and effectiveness results obtained by the proposed algorithms in an extensive experimental evaluation.

## Efficiency

We compare our approach with the optimized join using *pq*-grams in (Augsten, Böhlen, Dyreson, & Gamper, 2008) and (Augsten, Böhlen, & Gamper, 2005); we obtained the source code from the authors and we modified their code to apply the "optimize join" on ordered trees. We chose the values for our parameters as $p$=2, $q$=3, $k$=400. Since the first step in both methods is to

*Figure 6. The relationship between average random error and k*

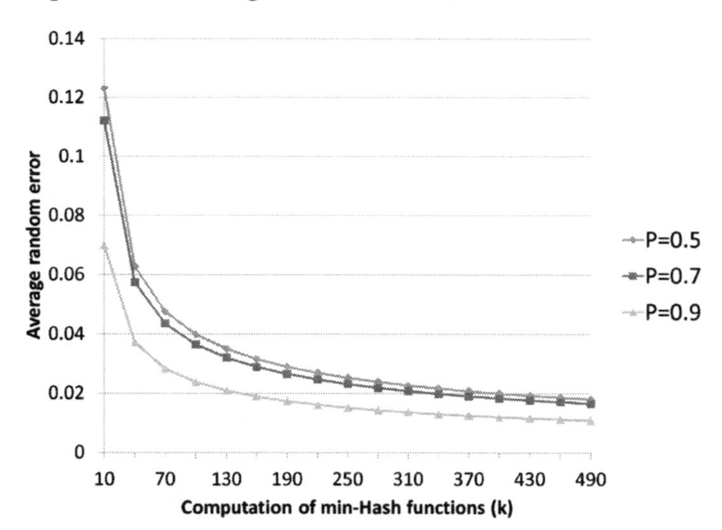


transform each tree to *pq*-bags and these *pq*-bags can be updated incrementally, we did not take the time in that step into account. The result is shown in Figure 7(a)-7(c).

We used the Swissprot[1] (bioinformatics), Treebank[2] (linguistics) and DBLP[3] (bibliography) XML databases to generate large tree sets. In each database, the top-level XML tags were removed to generate a set of small (sub) documents. Large trees are generated by combining these small documents randomly. Here, the large trees we deal with have about 5000 nodes for each. Note that the three XML sources used for our experiments are very different. Indeed, the large trees we combined from Swissprot share many *pq*-grams (more than 25% on average), while those

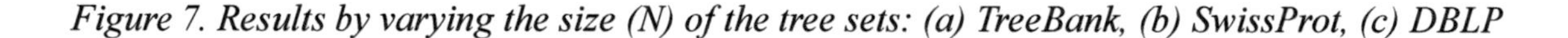

*Figure 7. Results by varying the size (N) of the tree sets: (a) TreeBank, (b) SwissProt, (c) DBLP*

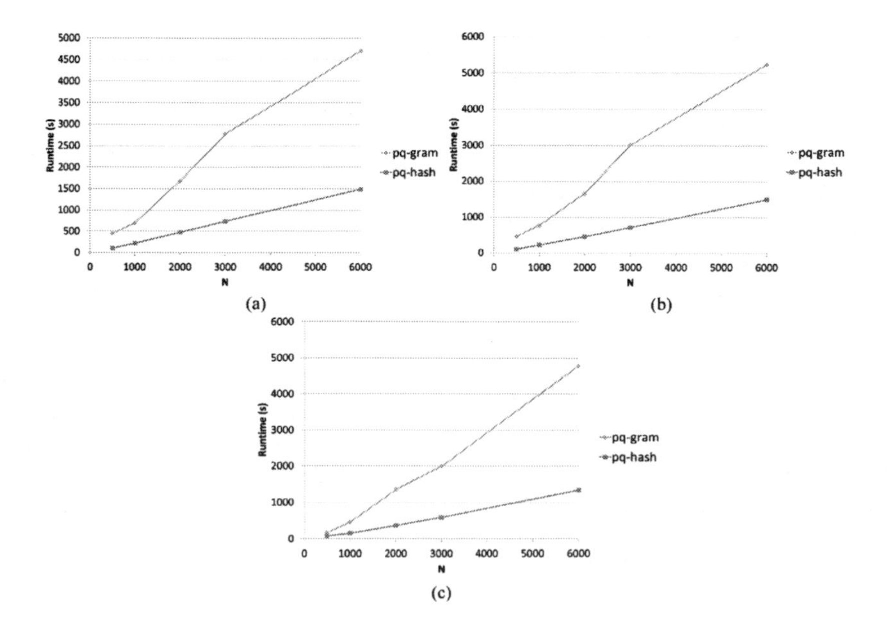

combined from Treebank have much fewer *pq*-grams in common (about 12% on average) and the trees combined from DBLP share very few *pq*-grams (about 5% on average). As previously mentioned, in the cases that trees share large numbers of *pq*-grams, the efficiency of optimized join would near to the nested-looped join. However, since the list we merge in Algorithm 6 is $O(N)$ whereas the index in the method *pq*-gram is $O(Nn)$, our method outperforms *pq*-gram significantly in bad cases.

In the worst case, the joined forests consist of identical copies of the same tree. Two tree sets, each of which with $N$ trees, are joined. All the trees are identical copies of a tree (5000 nodes) generated by *xmlgen*. The *xmlgen* generator models the behavior of an online auction site and is useful for controlled experiments. The size of data trees is controlled by the *scaling factor*, an input to the generator. It produces one large single tree. We removed the top-level XML tags such as site, regions, closed auctions to generate a number of small trees. We further combine these small trees until we get the tree with proper size. The result is shown in Figure 8(a). The optimized join based on *pq*-arrays significantly outperforms the optimized join based on *pq*-grams in the worst case. As we discussed in Section "Similarity detection algorithms for XML fragment sets", the average random error decreases while the time cost increases with the increase of $k$. The impact of $k$ on join cost in the worst case is shown in Figure 8 (b). It can be seen that the run time increases linear with $k$. When both the efficiency and accuracy have to be considered, the recommended value of $k$ is 400.

## Effectiveness

We add noise to several publicly available XML data sets (spelling mistakes and missing elements). We approximately join the original and the noisy sets. Analogously to the efficiency analysis, we used the Swissprot, Treebank and DBLP databases, in which top-level XML tags were removed to generate a set of small (sub) documents. A number of documents were chosen from each set for our experiments: 160 for Swissprot, 165 for Treebank, and 950 for DBLP. The resulting document sets were very different: Swissprot documents contain on average 109 nodes with about 3.6 depth on average; Treebank documents have deep recursive structure (48 nodes and 6.7 depth on average); DBLP contains small and flat documents (16 nodes and 2.0 depth on average).

We randomly relabeled and deleted a number of nodes on the original documents. Node relabels simulate spelling mistakes while node deletions simulate missing elements or attributes and modify the structure of the document.

For each original document $d$, we match if $d$ has only one nearest neighbor in the modified set. We define the *precision* criterion as the ratio between correct matches and all the matches. The

*Figure 8. Results on identical tree sets*

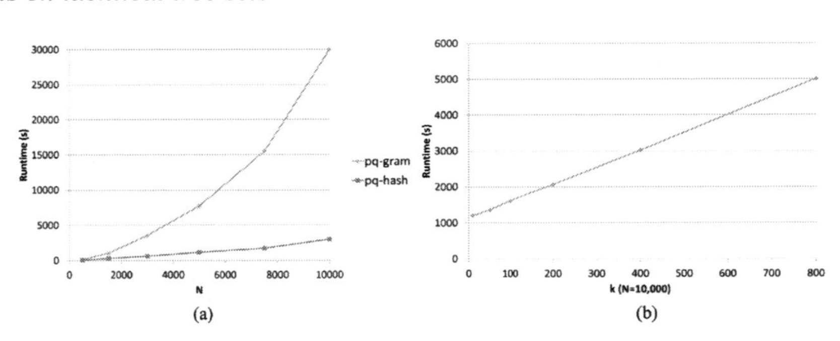

*recall* ratio is defined as the ratio between correct matches and the number of the documents.

Figure 9 shows precision and recall for different percentages of changed nodes in different databases. We compared precision and recall with the competing *pq*-gram method (Augsten, Böhlen, & Gamper, 2005). In our method, we chose 400-MinHashes. As we can observe from Figure 9, our method behaved as well as *pq*-gram.

## Matchmaking with Real Data

To test the accuracy of our method on real-world data, we used an application data discussed in the Introduction; we obtained the data from the authors of (Augsten, Böhlen, & Gamper, 2005). The Office there wanted to integrate data about apartments stored in two databases and display that information on a map. We denote the two sources as R and L. For each document in R, we found the tree in L with the highest equal-ratio and then matched them.

We computed a mapping result using the *pq*-gram distance (Augsten, Böhlen, & Gamper, 2005). We also computed a mapping using the embedded strategy without level presented in (Tatikonda & Parthasarathy, 2010) and other methods like Tree-embedding (Minos, Garofalakis, & Kumar, 2005), Bottom up Distance (Valiente, 2001) and Binary Branch (Yang, Kalnis, & Tung,

*Figure 9. Precision and Recall results: (a), (d) TreeBank, (b), (e) SwissProt, and (c), (f) DBLP*

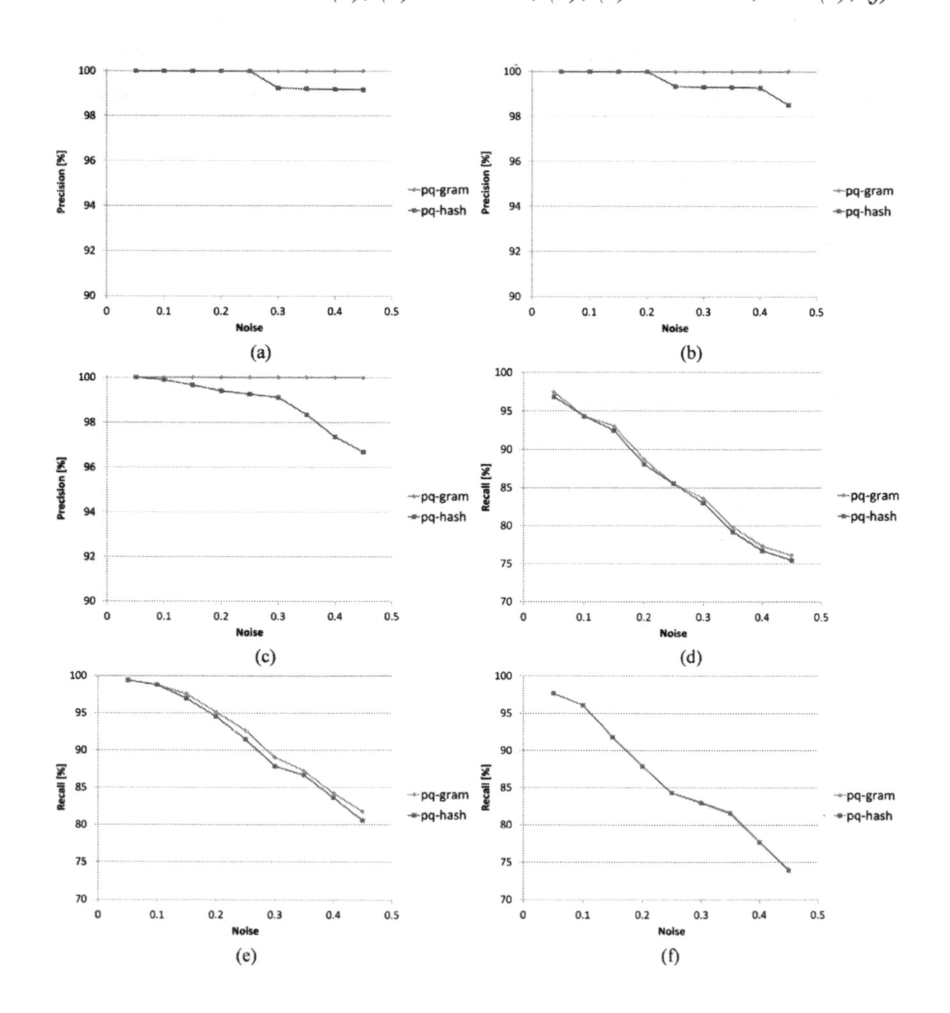

*Table 1. Join quality in different methods*

| | correct | false | Recall |
|---|---|---|---|
| Edit distance | 247 | 9 | 82.6% |
| *pq*-hash (*k*=400) | 231 | 5 | 77.0% |
| *pq*-gram (*p*=2, *q*=3) | 232 | 4 | 77.3% |
| Tree-embedding | 206 | 8 | 68.9% |
| Binary branch | 193 | 14 | 64.5% |
| Hashing tree | 162 | 14 | 54.2% |
| Bottom-up | 148 | 12 | 49.5% |

2005). Results are shown in Table 1. We can see that our accuracy is nearly as good as *pq*-gram when we use 400-MinHashes, and better than other efficient methods.

As we analyzed, the random error $r$ decreases when we increase the parameter $k$. We tested the impact of $k$ on accuracy using the data above. The results are shown in Figure 10. When $k$ is small, the accuracy increased significantly by increasing $k$. Note that in both cases of efficiency and accuracy evaluation, we chose 400 for $k$ as a recommended value.

## Evaluation of the Clustering Strategy

In this subsection, we used the street data to assess our clustering strategy. To generate trees with high degree of similarity, for each tree, we performed some basic operations (i.e., edit labels, delete/insert nodes) on them to obtain a series of trees. The trees modified from the same tree were similar in a high degree.

For each source, we clustered the trees into some clusters by setting a threshold (here we chose equal ratio higher than 0.5). In the join process, we first compared the representation trees between L and R and outputted the similar cluster pairs. Then, for each cluster pair, we computed the equal ratio between all the tree pairs in them and outputted the similar tree pairs as our final join result.

We compared the runtime for cluster efficiency with the non-cluster join, as shown in Figure 11. We can observe in the figure that the cluster join method outperforms non-cluster join significantly in efficiency.

Figure 12 shows the runtimes by distinguishing the time needed for the cluster creation and the time needed for the cluster comparisons. It can be observed that the clustering part takes the lion's share. In many cases such as similarity search, the clustering needs to be performed only when the databases are updated. Thus, the cluster method for XML documents would be more suitable for similarity search.

We also tested the accuracy of the result of the clustering-based join method. Since the cluster method has no false positives but some false negatives, we tested the false negative rate. We compared all the tree pairs using nested-loop join and output the join result (here we denote it as $M_m$). We also computed the join result using our cluster method (denoted by $M_c$). The cluster accuracy is defined as $|(M_m \cup M_c)| / |M_m|$ and the false negative

*Figure 10. Street matching results with different k*

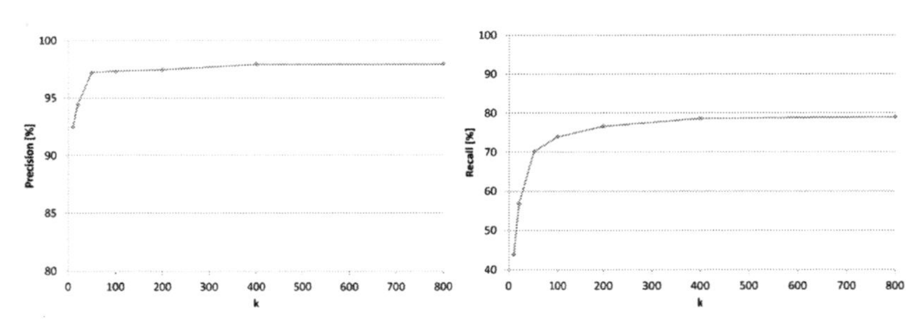

*Figure 11. Cluster join vs. non-cluster join*

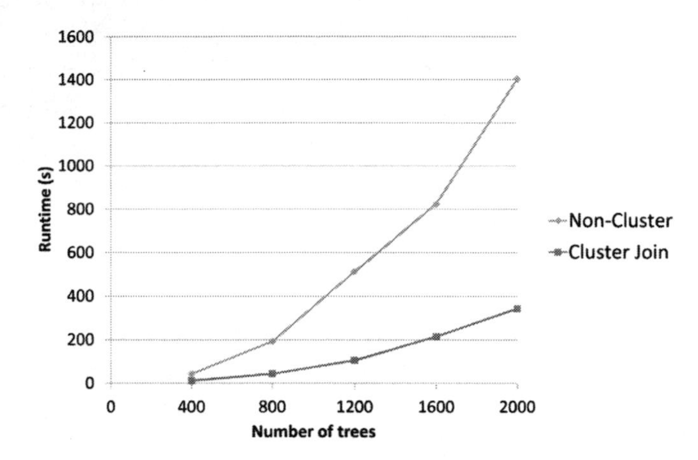


*Figure 12. Cluster creation time vs. cluster comparison time*

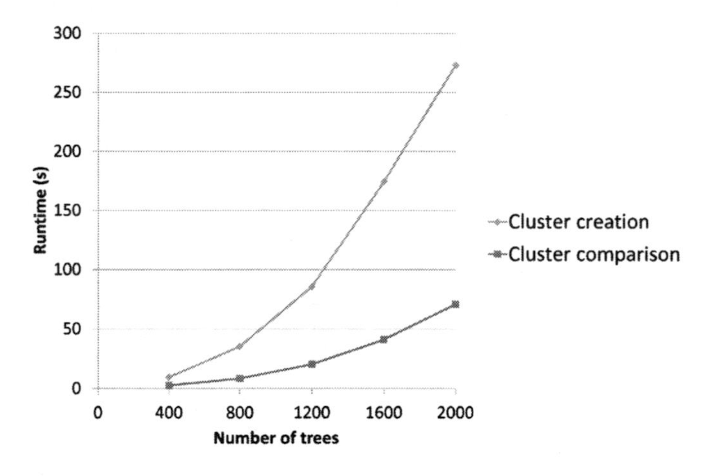


*Figure 13. Cluster join accuracy*

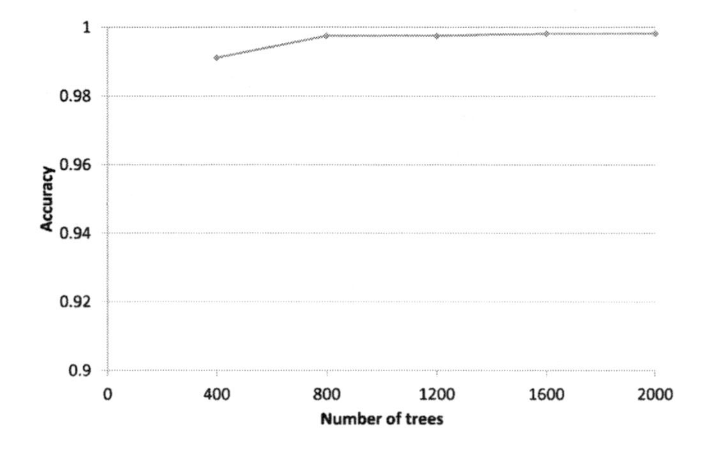

is defined as $|(M_m \setminus M_c)| / |M_m|$. The result is shown in Figure 13. We observe that the cluster accuracy of our method is always close to 1.

## FUTURE RESEARCH DIRECTIONS

The development of effective and efficient approximate search and join operations on (large) XML fragments is challenging and especially for large XML fragments is valuable to be studied further Because of the widely application in duplication detection, object identification and information integration. In this respect, we think that some future research directions should concern the following topics:

- Parallel approximate search and join algorithms on massive XML fragment sets.
- Effective and efficient approximate search and join algorithms on a broader range of hierarchical data such as unordered trees, free trees and directed acyclic graphs.
- Efficient clustering algorithms for XML clustering based on tree edit distance.
- Approximate search and join techniques for XML clustering algorithms focusing on approximations concerning not only the structure information but also the content information in XML data.

## CONCLUSION

In this chapter, we proposed an effective and efficient method of *pq*-hash for the approximate search and join on ordered trees. The basic idea of our method is to transform trees into fixed-size *pq*-arrays whose equal-ratios are used to evaluate the similarity between their corresponding trees. We theoretically analyze that our method outperforms the *pq*-gram method significantly in efficiency when the number of trees in each source are large and trees are huge. Instead of computing the equal-ratio between each pair of *pq*-arrays, we designed a cluster-based strategy and a min-number filtering strategy to accelerate the approximate join based *pq*-arrays. Experimental results confirmed the result quality of the optimized join based on *pq*-array and suggest that our techniques are both effective and scalable.

## ACKNOWLEDGMENT

This research is partially supported by National Science Foundation of China (No. 61003046), the NSFC-RGC of China (No. 60831160525), National Grant of High Technology 863 Program of China (No. 2009AA01Z149), Key Program of the National Natural Science Foundation of China (No. 60933001), National Postdoctoral Foundation of China (No. 20090450126, No. 201003447), Doctoral Fund of Ministry of Education of China (No. 20102302120054), Postdoctoral Foundation of Heilongjiang Province (No. LBH-Z09109), Development Program for Outstanding Young Teachers in Harbin Institute of Technology (No. HITQNJS.2009.052).

## REFERENCES

Akutsu, T. (2006). A relation between edit distance for ordered trees and edit distance for Euler strings. *Information Processing Letters*, *100*(3), 105–109. doi:10.1016/j.ipl.2006.06.002

Akutsu, T., Fukagawa, D., & Takasu, A. (2006). Approximating tree edit distance through string edit distance. In T. Asano (Ed.), *International Society for Augmentative and Alternative Communication (ISAAC) Lecture Notes in Computer Science: Vol. 4288* (pp. 90-99). Springer.

Amer-Yahia, S., Cho, S., & Srivastava, D. (2002). Tree pattern relaxation. In C. S. Jensen, K. G. Jeffery, J. Pokorný, S. Saltenis, E. Bertino, K. Böhm, & M. Jarke (Eds.), *Proceedings of the 8th International Conference on Extending Database Technology (EDBT) Lecture Notes in Computer Science: Vol. 2287* (pp. 496-513). Springer.

Augsten, N., Böhlen, M. H., Dyreson, C. E., & Gamper, J. (2008). Approximate joins for data-centric XML. In *Proceedings of the 24th International Conference on Data Engineering (ICDE)*, (pp. 814-823). IEEE Computer Society.

Augsten, N., Böhlen, M. H., & Gamper, J. (2005). Approximate matching of hierarchical data using pq-grams. In K. Böhm, C. S. Jensen, L. M. Haas, M. L. Kersten, P. Larson, & B. C. Ooi (Eds.), *Proceedings of the 31st International Conference on Very Large Data Bases (VLDB)*, (pp. 301-312). ACM.

Augsten, N., Böhlen, M. H., & Gamper, J. (2010). The *pq*-gram distance between ordered labeled trees. *ACM Transactions on Database Systems, 35*(1), 1–36. doi:10.1145/1670243.1670247

Bille, P. (2005). A survey on tree edit distance and related problems. *Theoretical Computer Science, 337*(1-3), 217–239. doi:10.1016/j.tcs.2004.12.030

Broder, A. Z., Charikar, M., Frieze, A. M., & Mitzenmacher, M. (1998). Min-wise independent permutations (extended abstract). In *ACM Symposium on Theory of Computing (STOC)*, (pp. 327-336).

Chen, W. (2001). New algorithm for ordered tree-to-tree correction problem. *Journal of Algorithms, 40*(2), 135–158. doi:10.1006/jagm.2001.1170

Chow, Y. S., & Teicher, H. (1978). *Probability* (4th ed.). New York, NY: Springer.

Cobena, G., Abiteboul, S., & Marian, A. (2002). Detecting changes in XML documents. In *Proceedings of the 18th International Conference on Data Engineering (ICDE)*, (pp. 41-52). IEEE Computer Society.

Cohen, E., Datar, M., Fujiwara, S., Gionis, A., Indyk, P., & Motwani, R. (2001). Finding interesting associations without support pruning. *IEEE Transactions on Knowledge and Data Engineering, 13*(1), 64–78. doi:10.1109/69.908981

Demaine, E. D., Mozes, S., Rossman, B., & Weimann, O. (2007). An optimal decomposition algorithm for tree edit distance. In L. Arge, C. Cachin, T. Jurdzinski, & A. Tarlecki (Eds.), *Proceedings of 34th International Colloquium on Automata, Languages and Programming (ICALP) Lecture Notes in Computer Science: Vol. 4596.* (pp. 146-157). Springer.

Fazzinga, B., Flesca, S., & Furfaro, F. (2010). XPath query relaxation through rewriting rules. *IEEE Transactions on Knowledge and Data Engineering*, 99.

Garofalakis, M. N., & Kumar, A. (2005). XML stream processing using tree-edit distance embeddings. *ACM Transactions on Database Systems, 30*(1), 279–332. doi:10.1145/1061318.1061326

Gionis, A., Indyk, P., & Motwani, R. (1999). Similarity search in high dimensions via hashing. In M. P. Atkinson, M. E. Orlowska, P. Valduriez, S. B. Zdonik, & M. L. Brodie (Eds.), *Proceedings of 25th International Conference on Very Large Data Bases (VLDB)*, (pp. 518-529). Morgan Kaufmann.

Guha, S., Jagadish, H. V., Koudas, N., Srivastava, D., & Yu, T. (2002). Approximate XML joins. In M. J. Franklin, B. Moon, & A. Ailamaki (Eds.), *Proceedings of the 2002 International Conference on Management of Data (ACM SIGMOD)*, (pp. 287-298). ACM.

Haveliwala, T. H., Gionis, A., & Indyk, P. (2000). Scalable techniques for clustering the web. In *International Workshop on the Web and Databases (WebDB)*, (pp. 129-134).

Karp, R. M., & Rabin, M. O. (1987). Efficient randomized pattern-matching algorithms. *IBM Journal of Research and Development, 31*(2), 249–260. doi:10.1147/rd.312.0249

Klein, P. N. (1998). Computing the edit-distance between unrooted ordered trees. In G. Bilardi, G. F. Italiano, A. Pietracaprina, & G. Pucci (Eds.), *6th Annual European Symposium on Algorithms (ESA) Lecture Notes in Computer Science: Vol. 1461* (pp. 91-102). Springer.

Lee, K. H., Choy, Y. C., & Cho, S. B. (2004). An efficient algorithm to compute differences between structured documents. *IEEE Transactions on Knowledge and Data Engineering, 16*(8), 965–979. doi:10.1109/TKDE.2004.19

Metwally, A., Agrawal, D., & Abbadi, A. E. (2007). Detectives: Detecting coalition hit inflation attacks in advertising networks streams. In C. L. Williamson, M. E. Zurko, P. F. Patel-Schneider, & P. J. Shenoy (Eds.), *Proceedings of the 16th International Conference on World Wide Web (WWW)*, (pp. 241-250). ACM.

Tai, K.-C. (1979). The tree-to-tree correction problem. *Journal of the ACM, 26*(3), 422–433. doi:10.1145/322139.322143

Tatikonda, S., & Parthasarathy, S. (2010). Hashing tree-structured data: Methods and applications. In F. Li, M. M. Moro, S. Ghandeharizadeh, J. R. Haritsa, G. Weikum, M. J. Carey, F. Casati, E. Y. Chang, I. Manolescu, S. Mehrotra, U. Dayal, & V. J. Tsotras (Eds.), *Proceedings of the 26th International Conference on Data Engineering (ICDE)*, (pp. 429-440). IEEE Computer Society.

Valiente, G. (2001). An efficient bottom-up distance between trees. *In Symposium on String Processing and Information Retrieval*, (pp. 212-219).

Yang, R., Kalnis, P., & Tung, A. K. H. (2005). Similarity evaluation on tree-structured data. In F. Özcan (Ed.), *Proceedings of the International Conference on Management of Data (SIGMOD Conference)*, (pp. 754-765). ACM.

Yuan, P., Sha, C., Wang, X., Yang, B., Zhou, A., & Yang, S. (2010). XML structural similarity search using MapReduce. In L. Chen, C. Tang, J. Yang, & Y. Gao (Eds.), *Web-Age Information Management, 11th International Conference (WAIM) Lecture Notes in Computer Science: Vol. 6184* (pp. 169-181). Springer.

Yuan, P., Wang, X., Sha, C., Gao, M., & Zhou, A. (2010). GRAMS: An efficient framework for XML structural similarity search. In M. Yoshikawa, X. Meng, T. Yumoto, Q. Ma, L. Sun, & C. Watanabe (Eds.), *15th International Conference on Database Systems for Advanced Applications, Lecture Notes in Computer Science: Vol. 6193.* (pp. 422-433). Springer.

Zhang, K., & Shasha, D. (1989). Simple fast algorithms for the editing distance between trees and related problems. *SIAM Journal on Computing, 18*(6), 1245–1262. doi:10.1137/0218082

## ADDITIONAL READING

Li, F., Wang, H., Hao, L., Li, J., & Gao, H. (2010). *pq*-Hash: An Efficient Method for Approximate XML Joins. *Workshop of Web-Age Information Management (WAIM 2010 Workshops)*, LNCS 6185, pp. 125–134.

## ENDNOTES

1. http://us.expasy.org/sprot/
2. http://www.cis.upenn.edu/~treebank/
3. http://dblp.uni-trier.de

# Section 2
# Clustering and Classification

# Chapter 5
# Approximate Matching Between XML Documents and Schemas with Applications in XML Classification and Clustering

**Guangming Xing**
*Western Kentucky University, USA*

## ABSTRACT

*Classification/clustering of XML documents based on their structural information is important for many tasks related with document management. In this chapter, we present a suite of algorithms to compute the cost for approximate matching between XML documents and schemas. A framework for classifying/clustering XML documents by structure is then presented based on the computation of distances between XML documents and schemas. The backbone of the framework is the feature representation using a vector of the distances. Experimental studies were conducted on various XML data sets, suggesting the efficiency and effectiveness of our approach as a solution for structural classification/clustering of XML documents.*

## INTRODUCTION

The eXtensible Markup Language (XML) (Bray, Paoli, Sperberg-McQueen, Maler, & Yergeau, 2004) has become the standard format for data exchange on the Internet, providing interoperability between different business applications. Such wide use results in large volumes of heterogeneous XML data, i.e., XML documents conforming to different schemas. XML documents are naturally tree structured, and may contain atomic and complex structures. XML documents are also semistructured as they incorporate both structural informa-

DOI: 10.4018/978-1-61350-356-0.ch005

tion and content (Abiteboul, 1997). Dealing with structure information is important to XML data storage and management (Jagadish et al., 2002), and the presence of a schema can significantly simplify the processing of XML documents. For example, elements from different documents with similar structures can be stored together, resulting in reduced storage and faster query processing. However, processing XML documents based on the schemas may not be feasible in practice, since most XML documents are schema-less.

Studying the problem of *approximate matching* between an XML document and a schema and its applications in XML data management and mining is not only theoretically interesting, but also critical to many real-world scenarios. For instance, similarly structured XML documents can be stored in relational databases more efficiently than documents with arbitrary structures. As discussed in (Bertino, Castano, Ferrari, & Mesiti, 2004), the distance between an XML document and a DTD can be effective for classifying Web documents. When schemas are not available, meaningful schemas can be inferred from XML documents as explained in the XTRACT system (Garofalakis, Gionis, Rastogi, Seshadri, & Shim, 2000). The framework to compute edit distances between XML documents and inferred schemas provides an alternative to the traditional algorithms for tree-to-tree edit distance in evaluating structural similarity between XML documents (Nierman & Jagadish, 2002). Moreover, with the rapid growth of XML documents on the Internet, disseminating XML documents to a large group of information consumers is becoming more and more important. This typically involves applying XSLT to present related information to the end users, which requires that the XML documents are grouped based on the similarity of their tree structures. The approximate matching between XML documents and schemas is also useful for evaluating schema-based queries over sources of XML documents. Other applications in literature include selective dissemination of XML documents (Stanoi, Mihaila, & Padmanabhan, 2003), information extraction from Web documents (Reis, Golgher, Silva, & Laender, 2004), database integration (Parent & Spaccapietra, 1998), stream processing and document integration (Garofalakis & Kumar, 2005), and protection of XML documents (Bertino, Castano, Ferrari, & Mesiti, 2002).

In this chapter, we present a suite of algorithms for computing approximate matching between XML documents and schemas. Our proposed methods are close to the work in (Suzuki, 2005), which describes how to compute a sequence of edit scripts to transform an XML document to conform to a DTD with the minimum cost. In particular, the algorithm described in Suzuki (2005) is very similar to the unrestricted tree editing method which will be presented in this chapter, however our method achieves similar results with better time efficiency. Bertino, Castano, Ferrari and Mesiti (2008) also considered similarity between XML documents and DTDs by viewing a DTD as a special tree with nodes labeled with special operators and then applying traditional tree matching algorithms. The key differences between the algorithms in this chapter and other methods are the use of the edit distance between an ordered labeled tree and regular tree grammar. The regular tree grammar is more general than most other schema languages used in similar distance (Murata, Lee, Mani, & Kawaguchi, 2005), and the edit distance provides a precise measure on how well an ordered tree (XML document) conforms to the regular tree grammar (schema).

One of the most important applications of the above mentioned algorithms is document classification and clustering, which is also essential to XML data storage, data integration, query processing, and schema matching. Traditionally, although not exclusively, the problems of XML document classification and clustering have been addressed based on some variants of tree edit distances. However, when the document sizes vary significantly, the performance of tree edit distance based algorithms becomes unpractical.

Nierman and Jagadish (2002) proposed using tree edit distance on XML trees, which takes into account of XML issues such as optional and repeating elements. Like most edit distance algorithms, it takes $O(|T_1||T_2|)$ time to compute the distance, where $|T_1|$ and $|T_2|$ are the sizes of the XML trees, which are smaller than the corresponding sizes of documents. In the year 2006, the INEX XML Mining Challenge (Denoyer, Gallinari, & Vercoustre, 2006) attracted a few researchers, and different methodologies, such as (Maes, Denoyer, & Gallinari, 2006; Tran & Nayak, 2006; Xing, Xia, & Guo, 2006), were proposed to classify/cluster XML documents based on structural information. Since then, while INEX still represents an important forum for researchers in XML retrieval and mining, several approaches and methods have been developed concerning both XML classification and clustering. More recently, clustering based on the semantics of XML documents (combination of text and structural information enriched with ontological knowledge) has also been studied (Tagarelli & Greco, 2010).

Similarity measures for XML schemas have also been studied in various contexts. XClust (Lee, Yang, Hsu, & Yang 2002) introduced a matching algorithm based on a DTD tree, considering linguistic and structural information of DTD elements and also the context of a DTD element defined by its ancestors and descendents. Formica (2008) has shown that the differences between content and structural information often lead to incomparable similarity scores. This necessitates a similarity measure that combines and reconciles the differences between the content approach and the structural approach. McCann, Shen and Doan (2008) studied schema similarity in the context of communication in online communities. Most research on schema similarities has focused on ontology mapping for documents from different resources, while the work in this chapter focuses on a suite of algorithms on document and schema matching. These algorithms can be used in document classification/clustering and other XML document management systems.

As mentioned earlier, the main objective of this chapter is to present a suite of algorithms for approximate matching between XML documents and schemas, and their applications in document clustering/classification. The main contributions of the work presented in this chapter can be summarized as follows:

- A set of measures to determine how well an XML document conforms to a schema. These measures can be valuable for many applications related to XML document management.
- A framework for structurally classifying/clustering XML documents. With schema extraction, the framework described in this chapter provides an effective alternative for classifying/clustering XML documents.

The remainder of this chapter is organized as follows. The next section gives an introduction to the background of this work and formally defines the problem. Section "Tree matching algorithms" presents our proposed methods to determine approximate matching using top-down editing, unrestricted editing, and tree-alignment editing; the section also covers edit script tracing, the effects of tag similarity, and schema extraction heuristics. The fourth section presents the applications of the algorithms in document classification/clustering. The fifth section presents the results of our experimental studies, demonstrating the efficiency and effectiveness of the algorithms presented in this chapter. Directions of future research and concluding remarks are given at the end of this chapter.

## BACKGROUND

### Similarity Between XML Documents Based on Tree Edit Distance

As XML documents can be viewed as rooted ordered labeled trees, early XML classification/

*Figure 1. Example of tree edit operations*

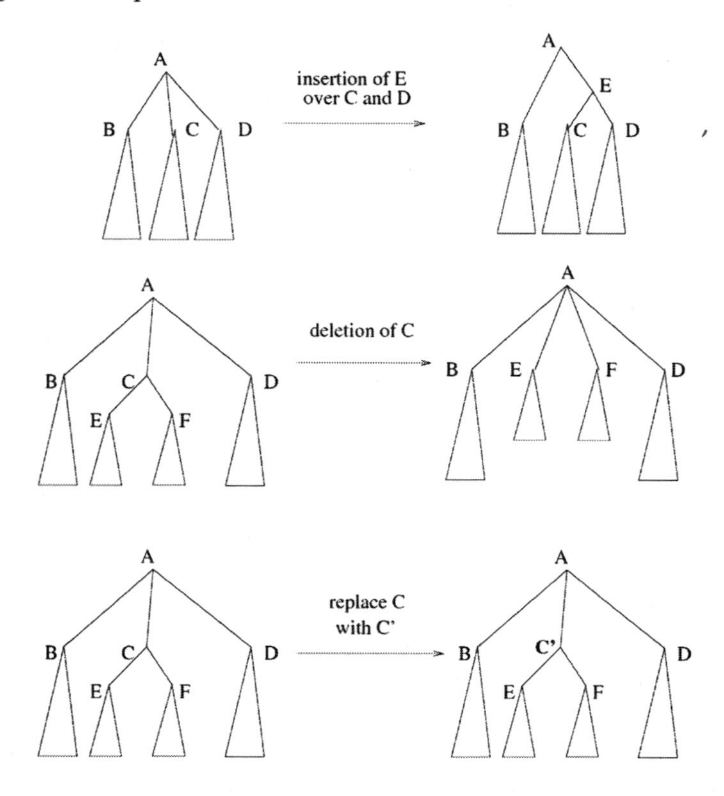


clustering methods have used some variants of tree edit distance to measure the similarity between XML documents. Shasha and Zhang (1997) discussed three types of elementary editing operations for ordered labeled forests, namely insert, delete, and replace, which are illustrated in Figure 1.

A cost is assigned to each edit operation, and it is assumed that each operation is of unit cost in this chapter. To identify the nodes in a tree, the nodes are labeled based on post-order traversal. Given a tree $T$ and an integer $i$, the following notations will be used (Figure 2 illustrates some of these notations):

- $t[i]$ or $i$ represents the node of $T$ whose post-order is $i$;

*Figure 2. Illustration of basic notations for tree representation*

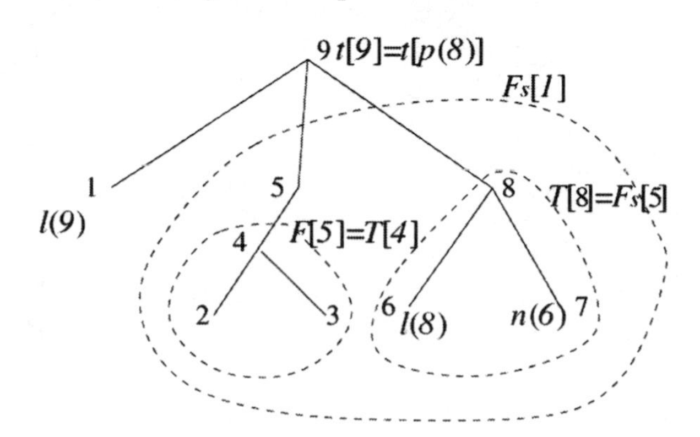

- $t[i]$ or $i$ refers to the label of the node when there is no confusion;
- $T[i]$ represents the subtree rooted at node $t[i]$;
- $F[i]$ represents the sub-forest obtained by deleting node $t[i]$ from the tree $T[i]$;
- $p(i)$ refers to the order of the parent node of $t[i]$;
- $\ell(i)$ refers to the order of the left most child node of $t[i]$;
- $n(i)$ refers to the order of the right sibling of $t[i]$;
- $F_s[i]$ denotes the suffix-forest obtained by deleting the left sibling(s) of $t[i]$ from $F[p(i)]$.

We now review some basic results for the ordered tree matching problem as introduced in the survey paper by Shasha and Zhang (1997). Instead of working on edit sequences directly, a *mapping* was studied as a graphical specification of which edit operations apply to each node in two trees (or two ordered forests). $M(T_1,T_2)$ was used to denote a mapping from $T_1$ to $T_2$, where $M$ is any set of pair of integers $(i, j)$ satisfying the following properties:

1. $1 \leq i \leq |T_1|$, $1 \leq j \leq |T_2|$.
2. For any pair $(i_1,j_1)$ and $(i_2,j_2)$ in $M$
   a. $i_1 = i_2 \Leftrightarrow j_1 = j_2$ (one to one)
   b. $t_1[i_1]$ is to the left of $t_1[i_2] \Leftrightarrow t_2[j_1]$ is to the left of $t_2[j_2]$ (sibling order preserved)
   c. $t_1[i_1]$ is an ancestor of $t_1[i_2] \Leftrightarrow t_2[j_1]$ is an ancestor of $t_2[j_2]$ (ancestor order preserved).

For any sequence of edit operations transforming tree $T_1$ to $T_2$, there is a corresponding mapping between $T_1$ and $T_2$, which is illustrated in Figure 3.

There are the following operations on the source tree from the mapping in Figure 3:

- Six replacements, which can be represented as (1, 1), (2, 2), (3, 3), (5, 4), (6, 6), and (7, 7). There is one non-identical replacement (1, 1), which has a cost of 1. The other five are identical replacements, which are 0-cost edit operations.
- One deletion: deleting node 4. This can be represented as $(4, \lambda)$ in the mapping.
- One insertion: inserting node 5 (in target tree) over node 2, 3, and 5 (in source tree). This can be represented as $(\lambda, 5)$ in the mapping.

A cost function $\delta$ can be associated with the edit operations (mapping). The costs for (1, 1), $(4, \lambda)$, and $(\lambda, 5)$ can be represented as $\delta(t_1[1] \rightarrow t_2[2])$, $\delta(t_1[4] \rightarrow \lambda)$, and $\delta(\lambda \rightarrow t_2[5])$ respectively. In general, the cost of the edit operations trans-

*Figure 3. Illustration of tree mappings*

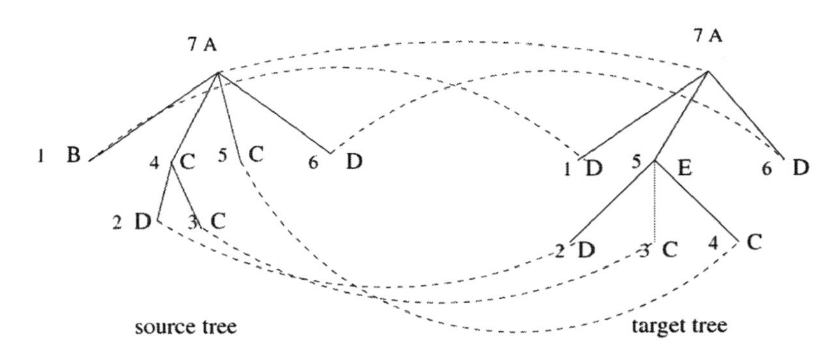

forming the source tree to the target tree can be determined by the following formula:

$$\delta(M) = \underbrace{\sum_{(i,j)\in M} \delta(t_1[i] \rightarrow t_2[j])}_{\text{replace cost}} + \underbrace{\sum_{\{i|\neg\exists j(i,j)\in M\}} \delta(t_1[i] \rightarrow \lambda)}_{\text{deletion cost}} + \underbrace{\sum_{\{l|\neg\exists i(i,j)\in M\}} \delta(\lambda \rightarrow t_2[j])}_{\text{insertion cost}}$$

## Different Tree Edit Distances

Various algorithms for tree edit distances have been proposed (Lu, 1979; Selkow, 1977; Tai, 1979; Tanaka & Tanaka, 1988), and the best known result for ordered trees was proposed by Zhang and Shasha (1989). Given two ordered trees $T_1$ and $T_2$, their algorithm finds optimal editing scripts (thus, edit distance) in $O(|T_1||T_2| \min\{depth(T_1), leaves(T_1)\} \min\{depth(T_2), leaves(T_2)\})$ time, where $|T|$ denotes the number of nodes in a tree $T$, $depth(T)$ denotes the depth or height of $T$, and $leaves(T)$ denotes the number of leaves of $T$. Edit distance for unordered trees has also been investigated by Zhang, Statman and Shasha (1992) and it was proved to be an NP-complete problem.

The mapping problem in its generic formulation may prevent its use in many applications due to its complexity in terms of running time. There are practical applications that can be modeled using restricted edit operations. There are four classical restricted formulations: tree alignment distance (Jiang, Wang, & Zhang 1994), isolated subtree distance (Tanaka & Tanaka, 1988), top-down distance (Selkow, 1977), and bottom-up distance (Valiente, 2001). In this chapter, we consider edit distances based on the following three variants of edit operations:

- *Unrestricted edit operation*,
- *Top-down edit operation*, and
- *Tree alignment*.

A mapping $M$ between a tree $T_1$ and a tree $T_2$ is said to be top-down only if for every pair $(i_1, i_2) \in M$ there is also a pair $(p(i_1), p(i_2)) \in M$, where $i_1$ and $i_2$ are non-root nodes of $T_1$ and $T_2$, respectively. Based on this definition, the mapping in Figure 3 is not a top-down mapping, as $(2,2)\in M$, but $(p(2), p(2))=(4, 6)\notin M$. It is easy to see that the insertions and deletions can only occur at the leaf level in a top-down mapping.

Tree alignment distance corresponds to a restricted edit distance where all insertions must be performed before any deletions. The difference between unrestricted tree editing and tree alignment editing can be illustrated by Figure 4 and Figure 5. In Figure 4, the source tree can be transformed into the target tree by two edit operations: delete node $b$, and insert node $e$ over $d$ and $c$. In Figure 5, however, as the insert operations must come before the delete operations, two extra operations are involved: delete node $d$ in the source tree and insert node $d$ in the target tree.

*Figure 4. Unrestricted tree editing*

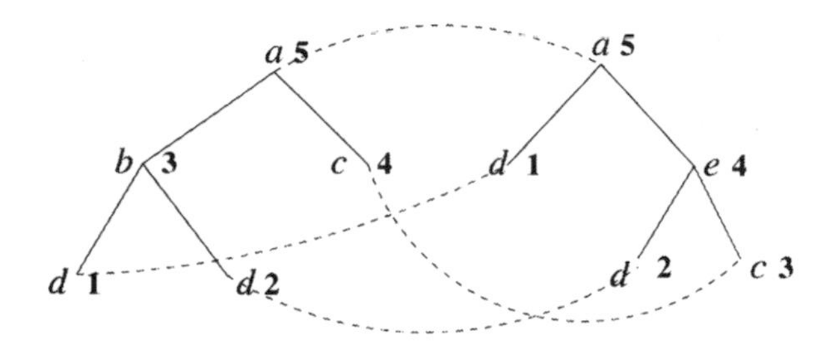

Figure 5. Tree editing using alignment

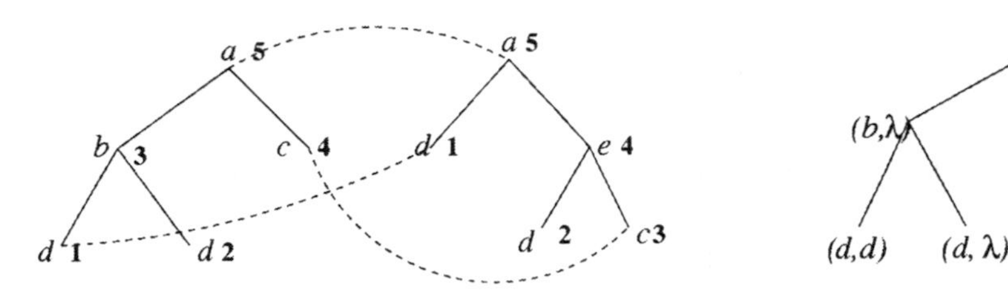


## Tree Grammars

To describe XML data, various schema languages have been proposed. Among them, DTD (Bray et al., 2000), W3C XML Schema (Sperberg-McQueen & Thompson, 2000) and RELAX NG (Clark & Murata, 2001) are widely used in business applications. To formally capture schemas, regular tree grammar or tree automata theory have been recently used by many researchers (Murata et al., 2005).

A *regular tree grammar* (*RTG*) is a 4-tuple $G = (N, T, S, P)$, where:

- $N$ is finite set of non-terminals,
- $T$ is the set of terminals,
- $S$ is a set of start symbols, where $S$ is a subset of $N$,
- $P$ is the set of production rules of the form $X \rightarrow a\langle r\rangle$, where $X \in N$ is the left-hand side of the rule, $a \in T$ and $a\langle r\rangle$ is the right-hand side of the rule, and $r$ is a regular expression over $N$ which is called the content model of this production rule.

As explained by Myers (1995) in computing the approximate matching between Context Free Grammar and strings, using a normalized grammar makes the understanding of our algorithm much easier. In this chapter, our algorithms are based on a normalized regular tree grammar, which can be defined as follows.

A *normalized regular tree grammar* (*NRTG*) is a 5-tuple $(\Sigma, V_T, V_F, P, S)$, where:

- $\Sigma$ is a finite set of terminals,
- $V_T$ is a finite set of tree variables,
- $V_F$ is a finite set of forest variables.
- $P$ is a finite set of production rules, each of which takes one of the four forms as below:
  a. $v_t \rightarrow x$, where $v_t$ is a tree variable in $V_T$, and $x$ is a terminal in $\Sigma$. This rule is used to generate a tree with a single node.
  b. $v_t \rightarrow a\langle v_f\rangle$ where $v_t$ is a tree variable in $V_T$, $a$ is a terminal in $\Sigma$, $v_f$ is a variable forest in $V_F$. This rule is used to put a new node $a$ as a new root of the forest

Figure 6. Top-down tree editing

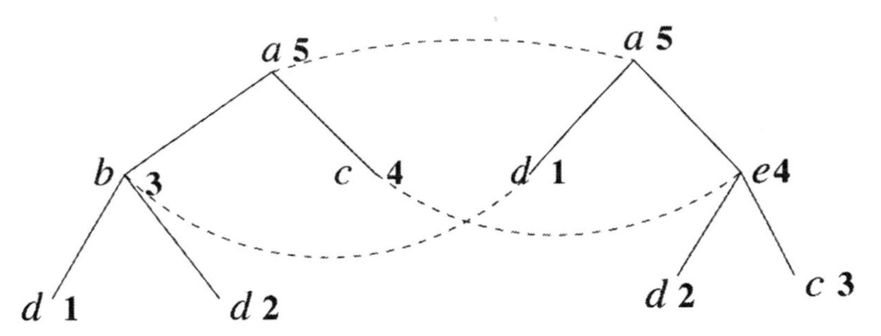

that is generated by the forest variable $v_f$.

c. $v_f \rightarrow v_t$; where $v_t$ is a tree variable in $V_T$ and $v_f$ is a variable forest in $V_F$. This rule is the base case to generate a tree in a forest.

d. $v_f \rightarrow v_t\, v_f'$, where $v_t$ is a tree variable in $V_T$, and $v_f$, $v_f'$ are variable forests in $V_F$. This rule is used to append a forest to a tree, forming a larger forest.

- $S$ is the set of the starting tree variables.

It can be shown that any regular tree grammar can be converted to a normalized regular tree grammar by following the same procedure for converting a context free grammar to the corresponding Chomsky Normal Form (Hopcroft, Motwani, & Ullman, 2006, p. 272).

## TREE MATCHING ALGORITHMS

In this section, we present three approximate matching algorithms based on (1) top-down tree editing, (2) unrestricted tree editing, and (3) tree alignment. We discuss how to enhance the three distance algorithms to obtain the edit scripts, and how tag similarity can be used to enable the algorithms to deal with real-world data sets. We begin our presentation with the top-down algorithm, as it is easier to understand than the other two.

### Top-Down Algorithm

Top-down edit distance for XML documents is considered as it is generally accepted that the nodes closer to the root node are more important than the nodes closer to the leaf level.

We use $C[v_t, T[i]]$ to denote the minimum cost to transform a tree $T[i]$ to conform to a tree variable $v_t$. This means

$$C[v_t, T[i]] = \min\{\delta(t, T[i]) \mid v_t \rightarrow {}^*t\}.$$

Similarly, we have

$$C[v_f, F[i]] = \min\{\delta(f, F[i]) \mid v_f \rightarrow {}^*f\}$$

to denote the minimum cost to transform a forest $F[i]$ to conform to a forest variable $v_f$.

The main theorem on top-down matching algorithm that is revised from Xing (2006) can be stated as shown in Theorem 1.

The theorem shows the recursion to compute the minimum cost to transform each subtree to each tree variable, and each suffix forest to each forest variable. The correctness of the theorem can be proved by showing that the left hand side of the equation is smaller or equal to the right hand side, and then the right hand side is smaller or equal to the left hand side. The complete details of the proof can be found in Xing (2006).

*Theorem 1.*

For each $v_t \in V_T$ and each subtree $T[i]$:

$$C[v_t, T[i]] = \min\left\{\begin{array}{lll} v_t \rightarrow x & \delta(x, T[i]) & (1) \\ v_t \rightarrow a\langle v_f\rangle & \delta(\lambda, T[i]) + C[v_t, \lambda] & (2) \\ v_t \rightarrow a\langle v_f\rangle & C[v_f, F[i]] + \delta(a, t[i]) & (3) \end{array}\right\}$$

and for each $v_f \in V_F$ and sub-forest $F_S[i]$ which can be represented as $F_S[i] =$ $T[i]\ F_S[n(i)]$:

$$C[v_t, F_S[i]] = \min\left\{\begin{array}{lll} v_f \rightarrow v_t & C[v_t, T[i]] + \delta(\lambda, F_S[n(i)]) & (4) \\ & \delta(\lambda, T[i]) + C[v_f, F_S[n(i)]] & (5) \\ v_f \rightarrow v_t v_f' & C[v_t, T[i]] + C[v_f', F_S[n(i)]] & (6) \\ v_f \rightarrow v_t v_f' & C[v_t, \lambda] + C[v_f', F_S[i]] & (7) \end{array}\right\}$$

*Figure 7. Computing the minimum size of tree (forest) variables*

```
1:  int minSize[n] ← ∞
2:  boolean known[n] ← false
3:  boolean inComputing[n] ← false;
4:  function compute(int v)
5:      intComputing[v] = true
6:      for each rule p with v as LHS
7:          size = ∞
8:          if p = v ⟶ x then
9:              size = 1
10:         else if p = v ⟶ v_t then
11:             if known[v_t]
12:                 size = minSize[v_t]
13:             else if not inComputing[v_t]
14:                 size = compute(v_t)
15:             endIf
16:         else if p = v ⟶ a⟨v_f⟩ then
17:             if known[v]
18:                 size = 1 + minSize[v_f]
19:             else if not inComputing[v_t]
20:                 size = 1 + compute(v_f)
21:             endIf
22:         else if p = v ⟶ v_t v_f′ then
23:             if known[v_t] and known[v_f′]
24:                 size = minSize[v_t] + minSize[v_f′]
25:             else if not inComputing[v′_f] and known[v_t]
26:                 size = minSize[v_t] + compute(v_f′)
27:             else if not inComputing[v_t] and known[v_f′]
28:                 size = minSize[v_f′] + compute(v_t)
29:             else if not inComputing[v_f′] and not inComputing[v_t]
30:                 size = compute(v_t) + compute(v_f′)
31:             endIf
32:         endIf
33:         if size ≤ minSize[v] then
34:             minSize[v] = size
35:         endIf
36:     endFor
37:     known[v] = true
38:     return minSize[v]
39: end
```

## Computing the Minimum Size of Tree and Forest Variables

$C[v_t, \lambda]$ and $C[v_f, \lambda]$ are two base cases that we must handle. Based on the previous definitions, $C[v_t, \lambda]$ equals to the size of the tree with fewest nodes that can be derived from $v_t$, and $C[v_f, \lambda]$ equals to the size of the tree with fewest node that can be derived from $v_f$. Our proposed procedure for computing $C[v_t, \lambda]$ and $C[v_f, \lambda]$ is shown in Figure 7.

## Computing the Distance Between a Suffix Forest and a Forest Variable

The recursion given in the scheme of Figure 7 can be implemented using straightforward dynamic programming, except that $C[v_f, F_S[i]]$ may depend on itself based on rule (7) in Theorem 1. In this section, we will show how to use dynamic programming to compute $C[v_f, F_S[i]]$, for each $v_f \in V_F$ and each suffix forest $F_S[i]$.

As explained in Myers (1995), the value $C[v_f, F_S[i]]$ may potentially depend on itself. This precludes a direct use of dynamic programming. We may use the shortest path algorithm to circumvent this problem.

First, we consider the three cases that lead to smaller cases of the problem. (see Exhibit 1)

Then, we consider the case (7) in Theorem 1 that leads to a forest with the same size. A *dependency graph* can be constructed as follows:

1. The set of vertices consists of a source vertex, *start*, and $C[v_f, F_S[i]]$ for each forest variable $v_f$.
2. The edges are added based on one of the following rules:
   a. Add an edge from start to each vertex with the weight of the edge as $K[v_f, F_S[i]]$.

*Exhibit 1.*

$$K[v_f, F_S[i]] = \min \begin{Bmatrix} v_f \to v_t & C[v_t, T[i]] + \delta(\lambda, F_S[n(i)]) & (4) \\ & \delta(\lambda, T[i]) + C[v_f, F_S[n(i)]] & (5) \\ v_f \to v_t v_f^{'} & C[v_t, T[i]] + C[v_f^{'}, F_S[n(i)]] & (6) \end{Bmatrix}$$

b. Add an edge from $C[v_f, F_s[i]]$ to $C[v_f', F_s[i]]$ with weight $C[v_t, \lambda]$ for each rule (7) in the form of $v_f \rightarrow v_t\, v_f'$.

As an example, suppose there are four forest variables $v_{f1}$, $v_{f2}$, $v_{f3}$, and $v_{f4}$, and the following two rules: $v_{f1} \rightarrow v_{t1}v_{f2}$ and $v_{f2} \rightarrow v_{t2}v_{f4}$. The dependency graph can be constructed as shown in Figure 8.

There are at most $O(|V_F|)$ vertices and $O(|V_F|)$ edges in the graph. As there is no negative weight edge in this graph, the Dijkstra's shortest path algorithm (Cormen, Leiserson, Rivest, Ronald, & Stein, 2001) can be used to get the minimum

*Figure 8. Example of construction of dependency graph*

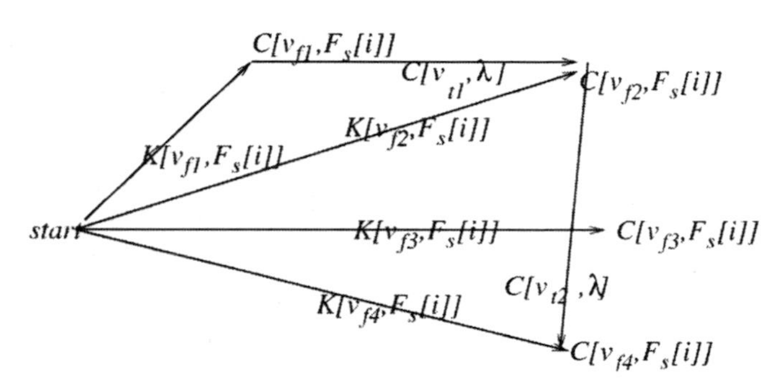


*Figure 9. Algorithm for top-down edit distance*

```
1:  procedure topDownDistance(G,T)
2:  Input: NRTG G and T that is post-order traversed
3:  Output: C[n..F[1../T/]] matrix
4:  Ct[/VT/][n]: cost matrix holds C[vt, T[i]]
5:  Cf[/VF/][n]: cost matrix holds C[vf, Fs[i]]
6:  for i = 1 to /VT/ do
7:      for j = 1 to n do
8:          Ct [i, j] = ∞
9:  for i = 1 to /VF/ do
10:     for j = 1 to n do
11:         Ct [i, j] = ∞
12: for1 s = 0 to n do
13:     for2 all tree T[i] of size s do
14:         for3 all vt ∈ VT do
15:             compute C[vt, T[i]]
16:     for4 all forest Fs [i] of size s do
17:         for5 all vf ∈ VF do
18:             C[vf, Fs [i]] = K[vf, Fs [i]]
                // add all distances from start to C[vf, Fs[i]] into the heap h
19:         h ← heap of C[vf, Fs [i]]
20:         while not h.empty()
21:             C[vf, Fs [i]] ←h.extract_min()
                // the same as for each edge from vertex C[vf, Fs [i]] in Dijkstra's algorithm
22:             for each vf' → vt vf
23:                 C[vf', Fs [i]] ←min {C[vf', Fs [i]], δ(vt, λ) + C[vf', Fs [i]]}
24:                 h.decrease(C[vf', Fs [i]])
25:             endFor
26:         endWhile
```

for each $C[v_f, F_S[i]]$ which is the length from the source vertex *start* to all other vertices in the graph. Since the time needed to complete the Dijkstra's shortest path algorithm is $O(|V| \log|V| + |E|)$ (on a graph with vertices $V$ and edges $E$), the overall time to compute $C[v_f, F_S[i]]$ for all $v_f \in V_F$ is $O(|V_F| \log|V_F|)$. Please note that this graph is never constructed explicitly, which will be explained in the algorithm (lines 21 and 22) in Figure 9.

For a tree with $n$ nodes, and a grammar with $t$ tree variables, $f$ forest variables, and $p$ production rules, the time needed for the algorithm as shown in Figure 9 is $O(n\, p \log p)$, which can be analyzed as follows (the pseudo-code is highlighted into blocks):

- The two **for** loops of lines 6 to 11 runs in $O(n\,(t + f))$ times.
- Considering the **for**[1] loop from line 12 to line 26, there are two blocks:
  - **for** loop from line 13 to line 15. As there are $n$ number of nodes in the tree, we need to compute $C[v_t, T[i]]$ for $n\ t$ times. The time to compute $C[v_t, T[i]]$ is constant. So the overall time to compute $C[v_t, T[i]]$ from line 13 to line 15 is $O(n\ t)$.
  - **for**[4] loop from line 16 to line 26. For the block from line 16 to line 26, there are $n$ iterations of two sub-blocks: for loop from line 17 to line 18, and the while loop from line 20 to line 26. The block from line 17 to line 18 takes $O(f\,n)$ time in the worst case, but as there are at most $n$ subtrees, so the overall time for the block from line 17 to line 18 is $O(f\,n)$. The block from line 20 to line 26 takes $O(f \log f + p)$ time. So the overall time for the code block from line 16 to 26 is $O(f \log f)$.

As $f = O(p)$ and $t = O(p)$ (the number of tree variables and forest variables in normalized regular tree grammar will be smaller than the number of rules), the algorithm runs in $O(n\ p \log p)$ time.

## Unrestricted Edit Distance

The top-down edit operation simplifies the matching by considering only the subtrees for a given tree. When the edit operations are unrestricted, however, sub-forests that are not covered by the suffix-forests have to be considered.

Let us consider the source document as shown in Figure 10 and the following grammar:

$v_{tA} \rightarrow A\langle v_{f1} \rangle$

$v_{tB} \rightarrow B$

$v_{tC} \rightarrow C,\ v_{tC} \rightarrow C\langle v_{f2} \rangle$

$v_{tD} \rightarrow D$

$v_{tE} \rightarrow E\langle v_{f3} \rangle$

$v_{f1} \rightarrow v_{tB}\ v_{f4}$

$v_{f4} \rightarrow v_{tD},\ v_{f4} \rightarrow v_{tE}\ v_{f4}$

$v_{f2} \rightarrow v_{tC},\ v_{f2} \rightarrow v_{tC}\ v_{f2}$

$v_{f3} \rightarrow v_{tD}\ v_{f3},\ v_{f3} \rightarrow v_{f5}$

$v_{f5} \rightarrow v_{tC}\ v_{f5},\ v_{f5} \rightarrow v_{tC}$

In order to transform the source tree to conform to the target tree, the following operations are needed:

1. Delete node 4,
2. Insert a node with label $E$ over nodes 2, 3, 5.

*Figure 10. Illustration of tree and schema matching with non-leaf level insertions/deletions*

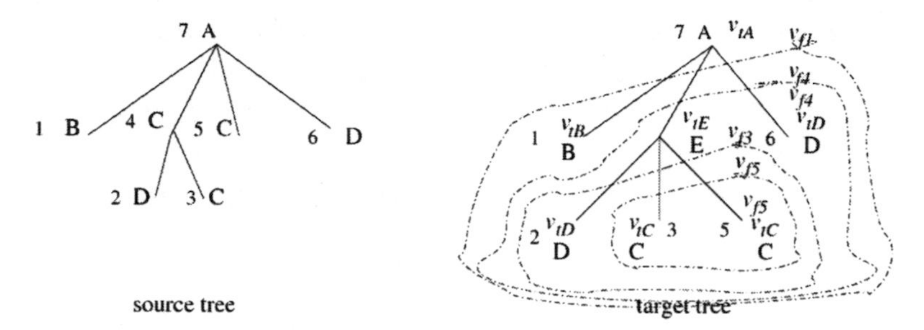


This implies that the suffix forest used in top-down mapping is not sufficient to handle a mapping when there is no restriction. It is necessary to consider all possible sub-forests in the source tree.

Based on this observation, we use *leaf forest* $F[i..j]$ to refer the sub-forests in our algorithm (Canfield & Xing, 2005). A *leaf forest* $F[i..j]$ to represent a forest with nodes $k$ satisfying the following two properties:

1. $i \leq k \leq j$
2. $k$ is either a leaf node or a node with all leaf descendants between $i$ and $j$.

It is called leaf forest because it only includes those nodes whose leaf descendants are all in this forest. From the definition, we know that not all nodes between $i$ and $j$ are necessarily in the forest $F[i..j]$. Figure 11 illustrates leaf forests $F[2..8]$, $F[9..11]$ and $F[9..12]$. As shown in Figure 11, leaf forests $F[9..11]$ and $F[9..12]$ are identical. For a given tree with $n$ nodes, there are $O(n^2)$ leaf forests.

*Figure 11. Illustration of leaf forests*

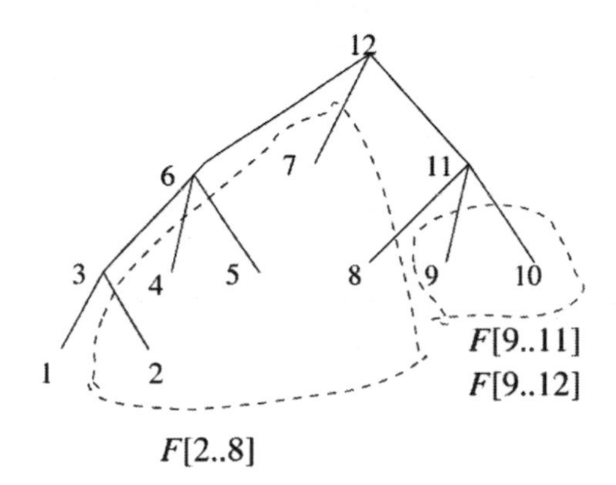


For each node $k$ in leaf forest $F[i..j]$, in which $i \leq k \leq j$, we use the following procedure to determine whether or not node $k$ belongs to $F[i..j]$:

1. Starting from node $i$, find the first leaf element $i'$.
2. Iterate on each element $k$ from $j$ down to $i'$, determine whether or not $k - size(k) \geq i'$.
   - If yes, then $k \in F[i..j]$;
   - If no, then $k \notin F[i..j]$.

It is easy to show that the above procedure can be completed in $O(j\text{-}i)$ time.

Another property about $F[i..j]$ is that it may not be equal to the concatenation of $F[i..k]$ and $F[k+1..j]$, because some nodes may be deleted when $F[i..j]$ is divided into two sub-forests $F[i..k]$ and $F[k+1..j]$.

We use $\delta(F[i..j], F[i..k]F[k+1..j])$ to denote the cost of dividing the forest $F[i..j]$ into two sub-forests $F[i..k]$ and $F[k+1..j]$, and $\delta(F[i..j], F[i..k]F[k+1..j])$ can be computed in $O(j\text{-}i)$ time using the above procedure.

For edit distance based on unrestricted edit operations, we have Theorem 2 (Canfield & Xing 2005).

The correctness of Theorem 2 can be proved in the same way as the proof for Theorem 1 by going through all the cases. The detailed proof of the theorem can be found in (Canfield & Xing, 2005).

*Theorem 2.*

For each $v_t \in V_T$, and each sub-forest $F[i..j]$:

$$C[v_t, F[i..j]] = \min \begin{cases} v_t \to x & \delta(x, F[i..j]) & (1) \\ v_t \to a\langle v_f \rangle & C[v_f, F[i..j]] + \delta(a, \lambda) & (2) \\ v_t \to a\langle v_f \rangle & C[v_t, F[i..j-1]] + \delta(\lambda, j) & (3) \\ v_t \to a\langle v_f \rangle & C[v_t, F[j - size(j)..j] + \delta(\lambda, F[i..j - size(j) - 1]) & (4) \end{cases}$$

and for each $v_f \in V_F$ and sub-forest $F[i..j]$:

$$C[v_f, F[i..j]] = \min \begin{cases} & C[v_f, F[i..j-1]] + \delta(\lambda, j) & (5) \\ v_f \to v_t & C[v_t, F[i..j]] & (6) \\ v_f \to v_t v'_f & C[v_t, F[i..k]] + C[v'_f, F[k+1..j]] + & (7) \\ i-1 \le k \le j & \delta(F[i..j], F[i..k]F[k+1..j]) & \end{cases}$$

The above recursion can be implemented using dynamic programming in a very similar fashion as shown in Figure 9. The major differences are:

- Instead of using $T[i]$ and $F_s[i]$, $F[i..j]$ is used to go through all subtrees and sub-forests.
- An inner loop is need to try all possibilities to divide $F[i..j]$ into $F[i..k\text{-}1]$ and $F[k..j]$ in case (7).
- The overall time needed is $O(T^2P(T + \log P))$, where $T$ is the size of the tree, and $P$ is the size of the grammar.
- The space requirement for this algorithm is $O(F^2P)$.

## Tree Alignment

As previously explained, the difference between tree alignment and the unrestricted tree editing is that the insert operations should precede the delete operations in a tree alignment. This means that there is no need to consider the child list from different nodes, and only have to consider all the sub-forests constructed from consecutive siblings in the tree. Based on this observation, we have Theorem 3 to compute the distance between a document and a schema based on tree alignment.

In Theorem 3, $F[i][l,r]$ is used to denote the consecutive sequence of subtrees, which are illustrated in Figure 12, where the sub-forest (in bold as shown in Figure 12) with three consecutive subtrees rooted at node 16, 24, and 40 can be represented as $F[55][2,4]$.

The correctness of Theorem 3 can also be proved in a same way as the proof for Theorem 1. The above recursion can be implemented using dynamic programming in a very similar fashion as shown in Figure 9 with the following differences:

- Instead of using $T[i]$ and $F_s[i]$, $T[i]$ and $F[i][l,r]$ is used to go through all subtrees and sub-forests.

- The overall time needed is:

$$O\left(\sum_{1 \le i \le n} deg_i^2 P(T + \log P)\right)$$

where $deg_i$ is the degree of node $i$, $T$ is the size of the tree, and $P$ is the size of the grammar.

The space needed for storing the distance table is bounded by

$$O\left(\sum_{1 \le i \le n} deg_i^2 P\right)$$

*Theorem 3.*

For each $v_t \in V_T$ *and* $v_f \in V_F$, and each sub-forest (subtree) $F[i][l..r]$, we have:

$$C[v_t / v_f, F[i][l,r]] = \min \begin{cases} v_t \rightarrow x & \delta(x, F[i][l,r]) & (1) \\ v_t \rightarrow a\langle v_f \rangle & \delta(a,\lambda) + C[v_f, F[i][l,r]] & (2) \\ v_t / v_f & C[v_t / v_f, F[i][l+1,r]] + \delta(\lambda, F[i][l,l]) & (3) \\ v_t / v_f & C[v_t / v_f, F[i][l,r-1]] + \delta(\lambda, F[i][r,r]) & (4) \\ v_f \rightarrow v_t & C[v_t, F[i][l,r]] & (5) \\ v_f \rightarrow v_t v_f' & C[v_t, T[c(i,l)]] + C[v_f', F[i][l+1,r]] & (6) \end{cases}$$

and for each $v_t \in V_T$ *and* $v_f \in V_F$, and each subtree

$$T[i]: C[v_t / v_f, T[i]] = \min \begin{cases} v_t / v_f & \delta(\lambda, t[i]) + C[v_t / v_f, F[i]] & (7) \\ v_t \rightarrow x & \delta(x, T[i]) & (8) \\ v_t \rightarrow a\langle v_f \rangle & \delta(a, t[i]) + C[v_f, F[i]] & (9) \\ v_t \rightarrow a\langle v_f \rangle & \delta(a,\lambda) + C[v_f, T[i]] & (10) \\ v_f \rightarrow v_t & C[v_t, T[i]] & (11) \\ v_f \rightarrow v_t v_f' & C[v_t, T[i]] + C[v_f', \lambda] & (12) \\ v_f \rightarrow v_t v_f' & C[v_t, \lambda] + C[v_f', T[i]] & (13) \end{cases}$$

*Figure 12. Illustration of F[i][l,r]*

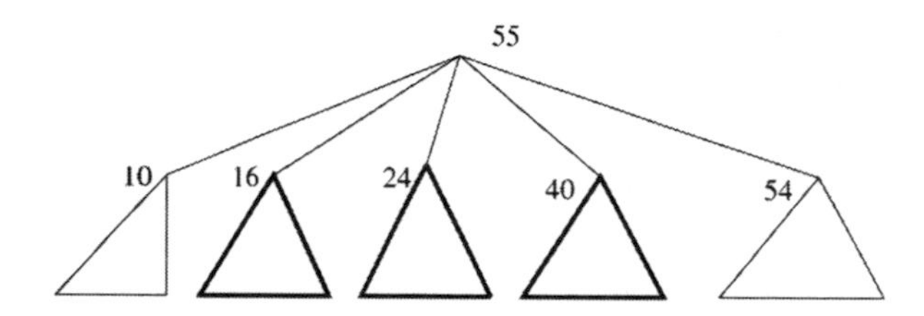


## Tracing the Edit Operations

As discussed in Suzuki (2005), obtaining the sequence of edit scripts with the minimum cost is important to many applications. Tracing the edit operations is straightforward from our algorithm, and does not increase the running time asymptotically. In unrestricted editing, for each variable (tree variable or forest variable), and sub-forest $F[i..j]$, the case that yields the minimum is recorded with the following information:

- The rule and the case (1 to 7) that lead to the minimum value for $C[v, F[i..j]]$;
- The $k$ that divides $F[i..j]$ to $F[i..k]$ and $F[k+1..j]$ when the case 7 is used.

Minor changes are needed for top-down and tree-alignment. Just as other dynamic programming algorithms, only those actions that help yield the optimal edit sequence will be traced after the computation of the action tables. So tracing the edit scripts will not increase the time complexity of the algorithms presented above.

## Tag Similarity

In XML documents, two tags match if they are identical. But synonyms are widely used in different business applications. As an example, a tag similarity measure was proposed by Bertino, Guerrini and Mesiti (2008), which considers synonym and syntactically similar tags.

Consider the two documents in Figure 13. Both of them contain information about the article "Semantic Clustering of XML documents", but the document on the left side is in DBLP format, while the document on the right side is part of RSS feed from Computer Science Bibliographies (CSB). Clearly, the author in the DBLP document is a synonym for the creator in the RSS document. Taking account of tag similarity reconciles the

*Figure 13. XML documents with different tags for the same content*

```
<dblp>
  <article key="journals/tois/TagarelliG10" mdate="2010-02-25">
    <author>Andrea Tagarelli</author>
    <author>Sergio Greco</author>
    <title>Semantic clustering of XML documents.</title>
    <year>2010</year>
    <volume>28</volume>
    <journal>ACM Trans. Inf. Syst.</journal>
    <number>1</number>
    <ee>http://doi.acm.org/10.1145/1658377.1658380</ee>
    <url>db/journals/tois/tois28.html#TagarelliG10</url>
  </article>
</dblp>
```

```
<rss version="2.0">
  <channel xmlns:dc="http://purl.org/dc/elements/1.1/">
    <item>
      <link>http://liinwww.ira.uka.de/searchbib/index?query=....
        &amp;results=bibtex&amp;mode=dup&amp;rss=1
      </link>
      <dc:creator>Andrea Tagarelli</dc:creator>
      <dc:title>Semantic clustering of XML documents</dc:title>
      <title>[2010] Semantic clustering of XML documents (by: Andrea Tagarelli, Sergio
          Greco)
      </title>
      <dc:date>2010</dc:date>
      <description><p>Author: Andrea Tagarelli, Sergio Greco;<br />
          Title: Semantic clustering of XML documents; <br />Year: 2010; <br />URLs
          available (possible fulltext access); <br />2 records for this title/author
          combination available.</p>
      </description>
    </item>
  </channel>
</rss>
```

difference between the structural view and content view of XML documents.

We propose a general function of distance between two tags $\tau_1$ and $\tau_2$, which is expressed by the formula shown in Exhibit 2.

One important advantage of using $\delta(\tau_1,\tau_2)$ is that we can use $\alpha$ and $\beta$ to adjust the cost of the edit operations in different applications. We also believe that $\alpha$ and $\beta$ could be adjusted based on ontology learning methods (Buitelaar, Cimiano, & Magnini, 2005). Distance functions defined as above can easily be plugged into our algorithms without any modification to the implementation.

## Schema Extraction

Our algorithms require that XML documents are associated with available schemas. However, schemas are often missing in XML documents, especially in many real-world document collec-

*Exhibit 2.*

$$\delta(\tau_1,\tau_2) = \begin{cases} 0 & \text{if } \tau_1 = \tau_2 \\ \alpha & \text{if } \tau_1 \text{ is a synonym of } \tau_2 \\ \beta & \text{syntactical difference between} \tau_1 \text{ and } \tau_2 \\ 1 & \text{otherwise} \end{cases}$$

tions. Therefore, the task of *schema extraction* is a prerequisite for our algorithms.

Inferring regular expressions from a set of strings has been well studied in XTRACT (Garofalakis et al., 2000). One novel contribution by XTRACT is the introduction of Minimum Length Description (MLD) to rank candidate expressions. In general, the MLD principle states that the best grammar (schema) to infer from a set of data is the one that minimizes the sum of $L_g$ and $L_d$, where $L_g$ is the length of the grammar and $L_d$ is the length of the data when it is encoded with the grammar.

As the number of elements in a given training set is generally very large, it is impractical to extract the schema out of every document. We choose to select a small set of elements that are possible good representatives from the training set. When selecting the representatives, we require that the size of the document is not too small or too large, as the structure of those documents may not be common in the set of documents. For the remaining documents, we randomly select a small subset (representative) for schema extraction. The extracted schemas are then merged.

Although XTRACT is very effective to infer schema from an XML document, inferring a schema from a large collection of XML documents is challenging: as we need to balance the following two factors:

- **precision:** the extracted pattern precisely describes the sample documents while doesn't cover those documents (with different structures) outside of the sample set.
- **generality:** the extracted pattern should be general enough to cover those documents that share similar structure with those in the sample set.

We found the following heuristics useful to extract the schema:

1. The frequencies of the child sequences are evaluated. Sequences with low frequencies may not be covered by the inferred grammar. This would help reduce the negative effects of noises in the classification process.
2. Instead of using $L = L_g + L_d$ as suggested in XTRACT, $L = \lambda L_g + L_d$ is used as the object function to minimize. The parameter $\lambda$ is used to balance the precision and generality of the inferred schema.

A DTD is the output of the XTRACT system, which can be further processed to generate a normalized regular tree grammar.

## APPLICATIONS IN XML DOCUMENT CLASSIFICATION/CLUSTERING

In this section, we will briefly discuss how to apply the approximate matching algorithms in the contexts of document clustering and classification. In this respect, a major issue is how to compute tree edit similarity between documents and schemas, and hence how to represent XML documents using the tree distances.

### Similarity Measures Using Edit Distances

The edit distances defined in the previous section depend on the size of the document, as a larger document tends to have larger distance to a schema even if it conforms to the schema better than a small document. To overcome this, we use *normalized edit distance*. For a document *doc* and a schema *r*, the normalized edit distance can be defined by the following formula:

$$\hat{d}(r, doc) = \frac{C[v_S, F[1..|doc|]]}{|doc| + \min(r)}$$

where $|doc|$ denotes the size of the document, and $\min(r)$ denotes the size of the smallest document that can be generated by the schema *r* from the starting symbol $v_s$ in *r*. Based on the definition of $C[v_S, F[1..|doc|]]$, the normalized edit distance ranges between 0 and 1, where 0 means the document *doc* conforms to schema *r*, and 1 means a complete deletion of *doc* and a rebuilding of a new document from *r*.

Given a document $doc_i$, a collection of documents *D*, and the corresponding schema *s*(*D*) for *D*, we define the distance between $doc_i$ and *D* as

$$\delta_{i,D} = \hat{d}(s(D), doc_i).$$

Similarly, the pair-wise distance of documents $d_i$ and $d_j$ is defined as

$$\delta(doc_i, doc_j) = \frac{(\delta_{i,\{doc_j\}} + \delta_{j,\{doc_i\}})}{2}.$$

The value of $\delta(doc_i, doc_j)$ lies between 0 and 1. A smaller $\delta(doc_i, doc_j)$ indicates the two documents being structurally more similar. In the case of a document clustering task, a matrix of pair-wise distances may be used to feed the clustering algorithm.

## XML Document Representation for Classification

Suppose there are *n* classes of objects in the training set, one obvious solution is to have one unified schema for each class. For each document, a distance vector $\langle d_1, d_2, \ldots, d_n \rangle$, which represents the distance between each document and the schema of the class, is computed and fed into a machine learning algorithm to train a classifier.

Although XTRACT is a very effective in inferring a schema from a collection of XML documents, it is subject to noise data, which can significantly degrade the performance of a classifier. Dalamagas, Cheng, Winkel, and Sellis (2006) proposed to use a kNN classifier based on the accumulated distances with all the training documents. We use a similar approach, but with a smaller number of schemas. The procedure to obtain the schemas for each group can be described as follows:

1. We only infer the schema from a subset of training documents to eliminate the effects of noise documents. The documents in each class of the training data are ranked based on the following score:

$$score = \sum_{1 \le i \le n} 1 - \delta(d_i, d_j)$$

Since noise documents tend to have a large difference with respect to the remaining documents in the same class, they will be discarded from the pool of documents for inferring the schemas.

2. XTRACT will take multiple XML documents to extract the schema. This helps the grammar inference engine to generalize the sample sequence to obtain the pattern. Instead of having one single schema as the centroid of a class, a number of schemas is used to characterize the class. This also reduces the number of distance computations. The exact number of documents to be used for inferring a schema depends on a specific application, and tuning is needed to get the optimal solution.

Each document can then represented by a distance vector of the form $\langle \delta(d,s_{1,1}), \delta(d,s_{1,2}), \ldots, \delta(d,s_{1,k}), \ldots \rangle$, where *k* is the number of schemas from each class. From this point, training and classification are performed in a standard way and straightforwardly for most classification software systems.

*Figure 14. Evaluation framework: Main modules and data flows*

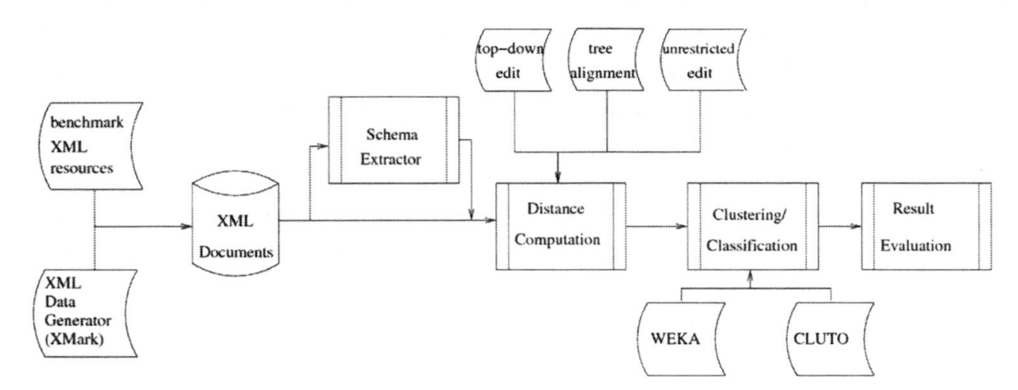


## EXPERIMENTAL EVALUATION

We now investigate the efficiency, effectiveness, and scalability of the algorithms presented in this chapter on various data sets. Experiments were carried out on a Mac computer with Intel Core 2 Duo processor and 4GB memory.

Figure 14 shows the main modules and data flows of the framework used for the evaluation of our algorithms. For this purpose, we collected synthetically generated data using XMark (Schmidt et al., 2002) and benchmark documents available from XML Mining Challenge (Denoyer, Gallinari, & Vercoustre, 2006) in order to:

1. Assess the feasibility of automatic document classification/clustering using our proposed algorithms.
2. Show that the distance between an XML document and a schema is an effective similarity measure for XML documents.
3. Assess how different distances may affect the performance of a classification/clustering system.

### Efficiency

Table 1 shows information about the seven test cases we generated for evaluating the time performances of our algorithms. Each test case is

*Table 1. Test cases for evaluating time performance*

| Test Case | Parameter $f$ | #Nodes |
|---|---|---|
| 1 | 0.001 | 367 |
| 2 | 0.002 | 1691 |
| 3 | 0.005 | 3371 |
| 4 | 0.01 | 4178 |
| 5 | 0.02 | 4879 |
| 6 | 0.03 | 4989 |
| 7 | 0.05 | 5166 |

*Figure 15. Number of sub-forests considered in each algorithm*

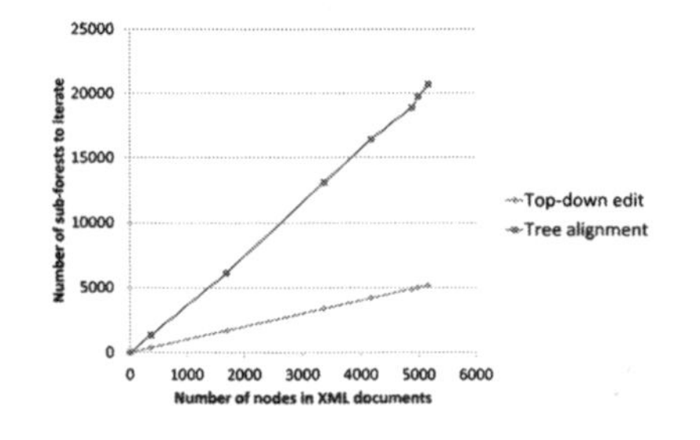


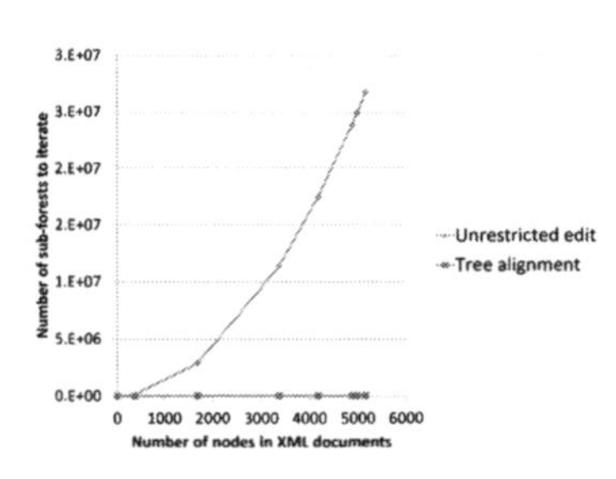

*Table 2. Comparison of running times (in ms)*

| | Parsing | Summary/Schema Extraction | Distance Computation |
|---|---|---|---|
| Original Tree | 2049 | N/A | 1754647 |
| Tree Summary | 2230 | 117 | 68484 |
| Top-down | 492 | 3012 | 375293 |
| Tree-alignment | 542 | 3122 | 3637655 |
| Unrestricted | 536 | 3248 | > 24 hours |

characterized by a different parameter to control the size of the test data, which is set up in XMark (Schmidt et al., 2002).

We have designed the following experiments to show the relation between the size of document and the number of sub-forests (trees) that the algorithms need to go through (the running time is linear to this number). Although the worst case for tree alignment distance is the same as unrestricted, Figure 15 clearly shows that tree alignment is practical for the benchmark data.

To study the feasibility of using our algorithms for XML classification/clustering tasks, we conducted experiments on the data set from XML Mining Challenge (Denoyer & Gallinari, 2007) using the following methods: original tree distance, tree summary distance as described in (Dalamagas et al., 2006), and our top-down tree-schema, tree

*Table 3. Comparison of clustering results*

| *Clustering Using Original Tree Distance* | | | | | | | | |
|---|---|---|---|---|---|---|---|---|
| **Cid** | **Size** | **A** | **B** | **C** | **D** | **E** | **F** | **G** |
| **A** | 26 | 14 | 0 | 0 | 9 | 0 | 3 | 0 |
| **B** | 13 | 0 | 8 | 0 | 0 | 5 | 0 | 0 |
| **C** | 11 | 0 | 0 | 11 | 0 | 0 | 0 | 0 |
| **D** | 13 | 6 | 0 | 0 | 7 | 0 | 0 | 0 |
| **E** | 34 | 0 | 9 | 0 | 0 | 14 | 0 | 11 |
| **F** | 20 | 0 | 0 | 0 | 3 | 0 | 17 | 0 |
| **G** | 23 | 0 | 3 | 9 | 1 | 1 | 0 | 9 |
| | Entropy: 0.429, Purity: 0.571 | | | | | | | |

| *Clustering Using Tree Summary Distance* | | | | | | | | |
|---|---|---|---|---|---|---|---|---|
| **Cid** | **Size** | **A** | **B** | **C** | **D** | **E** | **F** | **G** |
| **A** | 26 | 20 | 0 | 0 | 0 | 0 | 0 | 6 |
| **B** | 30 | 0 | 12 | 0 | 10 | 0 | 8 | 0 |
| **C** | 20 | 0 | 0 | 20 | 0 | 0 | 0 | 0 |
| **D** | 20 | 0 | 2 | 0 | 10 | 0 | 8 | 0 |
| **E** | 20 | 0 | 0 | 0 | 0 | 20 | 0 | 0 |
| **F** | 10 | 0 | 6 | 0 | 0 | 0 | 4 | 0 |
| **G** | 14 | 0 | 0 | 0 | 0 | 0 | 0 | 14 |
| | Entropy: 0.265, Purity: 0.729 | | | | | | | |

| *Clustering Using Top-down Distance* | | | | | | | | |
|---|---|---|---|---|---|---|---|---|
| **Cid** | **Size** | **A** | **B** | **C** | **D** | **E** | **F** | **G** |
| **A** | 21 | 12 | 0 | 9 | 0 | 0 | 0 | 0 |
| **B** | 25 | 0 | 19 | 0 | 0 | 0 | 0 | 6 |
| **C** | 19 | 7 | 0 | 11 | 1 | 0 | 0 | 0 |
| **D** | 20 | 1 | 0 | 0 | 19 | 0 | 0 | 0 |
| **E** | 20 | 0 | 0 | 0 | 0 | 20 | 0 | 0 |
| **F** | 20 | 0 | 0 | 0 | 0 | 0 | 20 | 0 |
| **G** | 15 | 0 | 1 | 0 | 0 | 0 | 0 | 14 |
| | Entropy: 0.190, Purity: 0.821 | | | | | | | |

| *Clustering Using Tree Alignment Distance* | | | | | | | | |
|---|---|---|---|---|---|---|---|---|
| **Cid** | **Size** | **A** | **B** | **C** | **D** | **E** | **F** | **G** |
| **A** | 20 | 20 | 0 | 0 | 0 | 0 | 0 | 0 |
| **B** | 22 | 0 | 20 | 0 | 1 | 1 | 0 | 0 |
| **C** | 20 | 0 | 0 | 20 | 0 | 0 | 0 | 0 |
| **D** | 17 | 0 | 0 | 0 | 14 | 0 | 0 | 3 |
| **E** | 19 | 0 | 0 | 0 | 0 | 19 | 0 | 0 |
| **F** | 20 | 0 | 0 | 0 | 0 | 0 | 20 | 0 |
| **G** | 22 | 0 | 0 | 0 | 5 | 0 | 0 | 17 |
| | Entropy: 0.102, Purity: 0.929 | | | | | | | |

alignment tree-schema, and unrestricted tree-schema distances.

The parsing time, summary/schema extraction time, and the time for computing pair-wise distance between 140 documents are shown in Table 2.

In Table 2, we observe that the parsing time and schema (summary) extraction time is relatively small compared with the time needed for computing the distances. The experiments clearly show that tree summary method is the most efficient, followed by top-down method, and then tree-alignment method. It also shows that the unrestricted distance is not suitable for classification/clustering. Hence our experiments on effectiveness will focus on the comparison of the first four methods.

## Effectiveness

We performed a clustering task on the testing corpus from (Denoyer & Gallinari, 2007), in which the documents are organized in seven classes, each containing 20 documents. In our experiments, the CLUTO[1] toolkit (repeated Bisection with 10 iteration refinement) was applied on the pair-wise distance matrices to obtain the clustering results.

We have studied XML documentation classification as well as clustering. The implementation had several improvements over what we did in Xing et al. (2007). SOM (Self-organizing map) package in WEKA[2] was used in the implementation of the classifier. The same testing corpus from XML Data Mining (Denoyer & Gallinari, 2007) is used in our study. Each group in the training set has 55 documents. The results of the classification using top-down distance and tree-alignment distance is the same, so we only the result of classification using top-down distance in Table 4.

Compared with the results from different research groups as reported in (Denoyer & Gallinari, 2007), the results in Table 4 suggest that our method is effective for XML classification.

## FUTURE RESEARCH DIRECTIONS

We have identified some research directions that are worth to be further investigated, as described in the following:

- **Defining further versions of edit distance:** As suggested in previous sections, edit operations can be restricted to have different formulation of edit distance. It would be interesting to study the edit distance using isolated tree mapping, and bottom-up edit operations. We believe that the time complexity of the top-down edit distance is the lower bound while the time complexity for unrestricted edit operations is the upper bound.
- **Combining our algorithms with tree summary algorithms such as (Dalamagas et al., 2006):** As the tree summary significantly reduces the size of an XML tree, it will offer significant improvements on time efficiency of our algorithms.
- **Estimating edit distance:** Time efficiency is important for applications like document classification/clustering. As indicated in our experimental studies, tree-alignment edit distance algorithms run much slower than top-down distance algorithm. It would be interesting to study how to obtain an es-

*Table 4. Classification results using top-down distance*

| Cid | Size | A | B | C | D | E | F | G |
|---|---|---|---|---|---|---|---|---|
| A | 20 | 20 | 0 | 0 | 0 | 0 | 0 | 0 |
| B | 22 | 0 | 20 | 0 | 2 | 0 | 0 | 0 |
| C | 20 | 0 | 0 | 20 | 0 | 0 | 0 | 0 |
| D | 19 | 0 | 0 | 0 | 18 | 0 | 0 | 1 |
| E | 20 | 0 | 0 | 0 | 0 | 20 | 0 | 0 |
| F | 20 | 0 | 0 | 0 | 0 | 0 | 20 | 0 |
| G | 19 | 0 | 0 | 0 | 0 | 0 | 0 | 19 |
| | Precision: 0.971 | | | | | | | |

timate of the edit distance that is close to the tree-alignment (and even unrestricted) distance in linear with respect to the size of the document.

- **Tree matching with gap penalty:** When a sequence of nodes with the same label are inserted or deleted, instead of using constant cost for each node, a function $\varphi(n)$ is used, where $n$ is the numbers of nodes with the same label. Using different types of $\varphi(n)$ (e.g., linear, quadratic), the time complexity will be different. This is a complete analogy to edit distance for strings. We may also consider the functions suggested in (Rice, Bunke, & Nartker, 1997).
- **Developing algorithms with low space complexity:** The space complexity of the algorithms in this chapter is $O(f\,p)$, where $f$ is the number of forests in consideration, and $p$ is the number of variables. When the size of an XML document becomes large, how to reduce the space complexity (still maintaining practical time complexity) is a challenging problem to study.

## CONCLUSION

The work in this chapter was mainly motivated by classifying/clustering XML documents by structure. Faced with the task to quantify the structural similarity among different clusters, we proposed a suite of algorithms for computing the edit distance between XML documents (ordered labeled tree) and schemas (regular tree grammars). Based on different restrictions, three types of edit distance were studied: top-down edit distance, tree alignment distance, and unrestricted edit distance. For a tree with $t$ nodes, and a grammar with $p$ production rules, the top-down edit distance can be computed in $O(t\,p\log p)$ the tree-alignment distance can be computed in $O(\sum d_i^2 p(t+\log p))$, and the unrestricted edit distance can be computed in $O(t^2 p(t+\log p))$. Applications of the algorithms in XML document classification/clustering were then presented. Heuristics on schema extraction, effects of tag similarity, and feature representation using edit distances were also discussed.

To validate the proposed methods, we implemented a prototype system and tested it on various data sets. Experimental results have shown that the top-down algorithm performed well in terms of running time and classification/clustering accuracy. Although the time performance of the tree alignment algorithm is not as good, the higher accuracy makes it a good alternative for XML clustering. We also suggested a list of topics that are suitable for future studies based on the work in this chapter.

## ACKNOWLEDGMENT

The author would like to thank Theodore Dalamagas for providing the implementation of tree summary for evaluation of the algorithms in this chapter. We would also like to thank the reviewers for helpful suggestions in improving the presentation of this chapter.

## REFERENCES

Abiteboul, S. (1997). Querying semi-structured data. In F.N. Afrati, & P. G. Kolaitis (Eds.), *Proceedings of the Database Theory - 6th International Conference (ICDT) Lecture Notes in Computer Science: Vol. 1186* (pp. 1-18). Springer.

Bertino, E., Castano, S., Ferrari, E., & Mesiti, M. (2002). Protection and administration of XML data sources. *Data & Knowledge Engineering, 43*(3), 237–260. doi:10.1016/S0169-023X(02)00127-1

Bertino, E., Guerrini, G., & Mesiti, M. (2004). A matching algorithm for measuring the structural similarity between an XML document and a DTD and its applications. *Information Systems, 29*(1), 23–46. doi:10.1016/S0306-4379(03)00031-0

Bertino, E., Guerrini, G., & Mesiti, M. (2008). Measuring the structural similarity among XML documents and DTDs. *Journal of Intelligent Information Systems*, *30*(1), 55–92. doi:10.1007/s10844-006-0023-y

Bray, T., Paoli, J., Sperberg-McQueen, C. M., Maler, E., & Yergeau, F. (2004). *Extensible markup language* (XML) 1.0 (3rd ed). Retrieved from http://www.w3.org/TR/2004/REC-xml-20040204/

Buitelaar, P., Cimiano, P., & Magnini, B. (Eds.). (2005). *Ontology learning from text: Methods, evaluation and applications*. Amsterdam, The Netherlands: IOS Press.

Canfield, R., & Xing, G. (2005). Approximate matching of XML document with regular hedge grammar. *International Journal of Computer Mathematics*, *82*(10), 1191–1198. doi:10.1080/00207160412331336053

Clark, J., & Murata, M. (2001). *RELAX NG specification*. Retrieved from http://www.relaxng.org/spec-20011203.html

Cormen, T. H., Leiserson, C. E., Rivest, R. L., & Stein, C. (2001). 3: Dijkstra's algorithm. In *Introduction to algorithms* (2nd ed., pp. 595–601). MIT Press.

Dalamagas, T., Cheng, T., Winkel, K., & Sellis, T. K. (2006). A methodology for clustering XML documents by structure. *Information Systems*, *31*(3), 187–228. doi:10.1016/j.is.2004.11.009

Denoyer, L., Gallinari, P., & Vercoustre, A. (2006). Report on the XML mining track at INEX 2005 and INEX 2006. In Fuhr, N., Lalmas, M., & Trotman, A. (Eds.), *Proceedings of the Comparative Evaluation of XML Information Retrieval Systems, 5th International Workshop of the Initiative for the Evaluation of XML Retrieval (INEX) Lecture Notes in Computer Science: Vol. 4518.* (pp. 432-443). Springer.

Formica, A. (2008). Similarity of XML-schema elements: A structural and information content approach. *The Computer Journal*, *51*(2), 240–254. doi:10.1093/comjnl/bxm051

Garofalakis, M., & Kumar, A. (2005). XML stream processing using tree-edit distance embeddings. *ACM Transactions on Database Systems*, *30*(1), 279–332. doi:10.1145/1061318.1061326

Garofalakis, M. N., Gionis, A., Rastogi, R., Seshadri, S., & Shim, K. (2000). XTRACT: A system for extracting document type descriptors from XML documents. In W. Chen, J. F. Naughton, & P. A. Bernstein (Eds.), *Proceedings of the International Conference on Management of Data (SIGMOD Conference),* (pp. 165-176). ACM.

Hopcroft, J. E., Motwani, R., & Ullman, J. D. (2006). *Introduction to automata theory, languages, and computation* (3rd ed.). Boston, MA: Addison-Wesley.

Jagadish, H. V., Al-Khalifa, S., Chapman, A., Lakshmanan, L., Nierman, A., & Paparizos, S. (2002). Timber: A native XML database. *The VLDB Journal*, *11*(4), 274–291. doi:10.1007/s00778-002-0081-x

Jiang, T., Wang, L., & Zhang, K. (1994). Alignment of trees - An alternative to tree edit. In M. Crochemore, & D. Gusfield (Eds.), *Proceedings of the 5th Annual Symposium on Combinatorial Pattern Matching, Lecture Notes in Computer Science: Vol. 807* (pp. 75-86). Springer.

Lu, S. Y. (1979). A tree to tree instance and its applications to cluster analysis. *IEEE Transactions on Pattern Analysis and Machine Intelligence*, *1*, 219–224.

Maes, F., Denoyer, L., & Gallinari, P. (2006). XML structure mapping. In N. Fuhr, M. Lalmas & A. Trotman (Eds.), *Proceedings of the Comparative Evaluation of XML Information Retrieval Systems, 5th International Workshop of the Initiative for the Evaluation of XML Retrieval (INEX) Lecture Notes in Computer Science: Vol. 4518* (pp. 540-551). Springer.

McCann, R., Shen, W., & Doan, A. (2008). Matching schemas in online communities: A Web 2.0 approach. In *Proceedings of the 24th International Conference on Data Engineering (ICDE)*, (pp. 110-119). IEEE Computer Society.

Murata, M., Lee, D., Mani, M., & Kawaguchi, K. (2005). Taxonomy of XML schema languages using formal language theory. *ACM Transactions on Internet Technology*, *5*(4), 660–704. doi:10.1145/1111627.1111631

Myers, G. (1995). Approximately matching context free languages. *Information Processing Letters*, *54*(2), 85–92. doi:10.1016/0020-0190(95)00007-Y

Nayak, R., & Iryadi, W. (2007). XML schema clustering with semantic and hierarchical similarity measures. *Knowledge-Based Systems*, *20*(4), 336–349. doi:10.1016/j.knosys.2006.08.006

Nayak, R., & Xu, S. (2006). XCLS: A fast and effective clustering algorithm for heterogeneous XML documents. In W.K. Ng, M. Kitsuregawa, J. Li, & K. Chang (Eds.), *Proceedings of the Advances in Knowledge Discovery and Data Mining, 10th Pacific-Asia Conference* (*PAKDD*) *Lecture Notes in Computer Science: Vol. 3918* (pp. 292-302). Springer.

Nierman, A., & Jagadish, H. V. (2002). Evaluating structural similarity in XML documents. In *Proceedings of the Fifth International Workshop on the Web and Databases (WebDB)*, (pp. 61-66).

Parent, C., & Spaccapietra, S. (1998). Issues and approaches of database integration. *Communications of the ACM*, *41*(5), 166–178. doi:10.1145/276404.276408

Reis, D. C., Golgher, P. B., Silva, A. S., & Laender, A. F. (2004). Automatic Web news extraction using tree edit distance. In S. I. Feldman, M. Uretsky, M. Najork, & C. E. Wills (Eds.), *Proceedings of the 13th International Conference on World Wide Web (WWW)*, (pp 502-511). ACM.

Rice, S. V., Bunke, H., & Nartker, T. A. (1997). Classes of cost functions for string edit distance. *Algorithmica*, *18*(2), 271–280. doi:10.1007/BF02526038

Schlieder, T. (2001). Similarity search in XML data using cost-based query transformations. In G. Mecca & J. Siméon (Eds.), *Proceedings of the International Workshop on Web and Databases* (pp. 19-24). ACM.

Schmidt, A., Waas, F., Kersten, M. L., Carey, M. J., Manolescu, I., & Busse, R. (2002). XMark: A benchmark for XML data management. In *Proceedings of the 28th International Conference on Very Large Data Bases (VLDB)*, (pp. 974-985). Morgan Kaufmann.

Selkow, S. M. (1977). The tree-to-tree editing problem. *Information Processing Letters*, *6*(6), 184–186. doi:10.1016/0020-0190(77)90064-3

Shasha, D., & Zhang, K. (1990). Fast algorithms for the unit cost editing distance between trees. *Journal of Algorithms*, *11*(4), 581–621. doi:10.1016/0196-6774(90)90011-3

Shasha, D., & Zhang, K. (1997). Approximate tree pattern matching. In Apostolico, A., & Galil, Z. (Eds.), *Pattern matching in strings, trees and arrays* (pp. 341–371). Oxford University Press.

Sperberg-McQueen, C. M., & Thompson, H. (2000). XML schema. Retrieved from http://www.w3.org/XML/Schema.html

Stanoi, I., Mihaila, G., & Padmanabhan, S. (2003). A framework for the selective dissemination of XML documents based on inferred user profiles. In U. Dayal, K. Ramamritham, & T. Vijayaraman (Eds.), *Proceedings of the19th International Conference on Data Engineering (ICDE),* (pp. 531–542). IEEE Computer Society.

Suzuki, N. (2005). Finding an optimum edit script between an XML document and a DTD. In L. M. Liebrock (Ed.), *Proceedings of the 2005 ACM Symposium on Applied Computing (SAC),* (pp. 647-653). ACM.

Tagarelli, A., & Greco, S. (2010). Semantic clustering of XML documents. [TOIS]. *ACM Transactions on Information Systems, 28*(1), 1–56. doi:10.1145/1658377.1658380

Tai, K.-C. (1979). The tree-to-tree correction problem. *Journal of the ACM, 26*(3), 422–433. doi:10.1145/322139.322143

Tanaka, E., & Tanaka, K. (1988). The tree-to-tree editing problem. *Journal of Pattern Recognition and Artificial Intelligence, 2*(2), 221–240. doi:10.1142/S0218001488000157

Tran, T., & Nayak, R. (2006). Evaluating the performance of XML document clustering by structure only. In N. Fuhr, M. Lalmas, & A. Trotman (Eds.), *Comparative Evaluation of XML Information Retrieval Systems, 5th International Workshop of the Initiative for the Evaluation of XML Retrieval, Lecture Notes in Computer Science: Vol. 4518* (pp. 473-484). Springer.

Valiente, G. (2001). An efficient bottom-up distance between trees. In G. Navarro (Ed.), *Proceedings of the 8th International Symposium on String Processing and Information Retrieval* (pp. 212-219). IEEE Computer Science Press.

Xing, G. (2006). Fast approximate matching between XML documents and schemata. In X. Zhou, J. Li, H. Shen, M. Kitsuregawa, & Y. Zhang (Eds.), *Frontiers of WWW Research and Development, 8th Asia-Pacific Web Conference (APWeb) Lecture Notes in Computer Science: Vol. 3841* (pp. 425-436). Springer.

Xing, G., Guo, J., & Xia, Z. (2006). Classifying XML documents based on structure/content similarity. In N. Fuhr, M. Lalmas & A. Trotman (Eds.), *Comparative Evaluation of XML Information Retrieval Systems, 5th International Workshop of the Initiative for the Evaluation of XML Retrieval (INEX) Lecture Notes in Computer Science: Vol. 4518* (pp. 444-457). Springer.

Xing, G., Xia, Z., & Guo, J. (2007). Clustering XML documents based on structural similarity. In R. Kotagiri, P. R. Krishna, M. Mohania, & E. Nantajeewarawat (Eds.), *Proceedings of the 12th international Conference on Database Systems For Advanced Applications (DASFAA) Lecture Notes in Computer Science: Vol. 4443* (pp. 905-911). Springer.

Zhang, K. (1993). A new editing based distance between unordered labeled trees. In A. Apostolico, M. Crochemore, Z. Galil, & U. Manber (Eds.), *Proceedings of the 4th Annual Symposium on Combinatorial Pattern Matching (CPM) Lecture Notes in Computer Science: Vol. 684* (pp. 110–121). Springer.

Zhang, K., & Shasha, D. (1989). Simple fast algorithms for the editing distance between trees and related problems. *SIAM Journal on Computing, 18*(6), 1245–1262. doi:10.1137/0218082

Zhang, K., Statman, R., & Shasha, D. (1992). On the editing distance between unordered labeled trees. *Information Processing Letters, 42*(3), 133–139. doi:10.1016/0020-0190(92)90136-J

## ADDITIONAL READING

Amer-Yahia, S., Koudas, N., & Srivastava, D. (2003). Approximate Matching in XML. In U. Dayal, K. Ramamritham, and T.M. Vijayaraman (Eds.), *Proceedings of the 19th International Conference on Data Engineering (ICDE),* (p. 803). IEEE Computer Society.

Cobena, G., Abiteboul, S., & Marian, A. (2002). Detecting Changes in XML Documents. In *Proceedings of the 18th International Conference on Data Engineering (ICDE),* (pp. 41–52). IEEE Computer Society.

Deutsch, A., Fernandez, M., & Suciu, D. (1999). Storing Semistructured Data with STORED. In A. Delis, C. Faloutsos, and S. Ghandeharizadeh (Eds.), *Proceedings of the International Conference on Management of Data (SIGMOD Conference),* (pp. 431-442). ACM.

Do, H.-H., Melnik, S., & Rahm, E. (2003). Comparison of Schema Matching Evaluations. In A. Chaudhri, M. Jeckle, E. Rahm, and R. Unland (Eds.), *Web, Web-Services, and Database Systems: Vol. 2593. Lecture Notes in Computer Science* (pp. 221-237). Springer.

Do, H.-H., & Rahm, E. (2002). COMA - A System for Flexible Combination of Schema Matching Approaches. In J. Freytag, P.C. Lockemann, S. Abiteboul, M. Carey, P. Selinger and A. Heuer (Eds.), *Proceedings of the 28th International Conference on Very Large Databases (VLDB),* (pp. 610–621). Morgan Kaufmann.

Flesca, S., Manco, G., Masciari, E., Pontieri, L., & Pugliese, A. (2002). Detecting Structural Similarities between XML Documents. In M.F. Fernandez and Y. Papakonstantinou (Eds.), *Proceedings of the Fifth International Workshop on Web and Databases (WebDB),* (pp. 55–60).

Guerrini, G., Mesiti, M., & Bertino, E. (2006). Structural Similarity Measures in Sources of XML Documents. In Darmont, J., & Boussaid, O. (Eds.), *Processing and Managing Complex Data for Decision Support* (pp. 247–279). Idea Group. doi:10.4018/978-1-59140-655-6.ch009

Guerrini, G., Mesiti, M., & Sanz, I. (2007). An Overview of Similarity Measures for Clustering XML Documents. In Vakali, A., & Pallis, G. (Eds.), *Web Data Management Practices: Emerging Techniques and Technologies* (pp. 56–78). Idea Group.

Lee, M. L., Yang, L., Hsu, W., & Yang, X. (2002). XClust: Clustering XML Schemas for Effective Integration. In *Proceedings of the International Conference on Information and Knowledge Management (CIKM),* (pp. 292–299). ACM.

Madhavan, J., Bernstein, P., & Rahm, E. (2001). Generic Schema Matching with Cupid. In *Proceedings of the 27th International Conference on Very Large Databases (VLDB '02),* (pp. 49–58). Morgan Kaufmann.

Moh, C., Lim, E., & Ng, W. (2000). Re-engineering Structures from Web Documents. In *Proceedings of ACM Digital Library (ACM DL),* (pp. 67-76). ACM.

Nestorov, S., Abiteboul, S., & Motwani, R. (1998). Extracting Schema from Semistructured Data. In L. M. Haas, and A. Tiwary (Eds.), *Proceedings of the International Conference on Management of Data (SIGMOD Conference),* (pp. 295-306). ACM.

Nierman, A., & Jagadish, H. (2002). Evaluating Structural Similarity in XML Documents. In *Proceedings of the International Workshop on Web and Databases (WebDB),* (pp. 61-66).

Rahm, E., & Bernstein, P. A. (2001). A Survey of Approaches to Automatic Schema Matching. *The VLDB Journal, 10*(4), 334–350. doi:10.1007/s007780100057

Wang, K., & Liu, H. (1998). Discovering Typical Structures of Documents: A Road Map Approach. In *Proceedings of the 21st Annual International Conference on Research and Development in Information Retrieval (SIGIR '98),* (pp. 146–154). ACM.

Wang, Y., DeWitt, D. J., & Cai, J.-Y. (2003). X-Diff: An Effective Change Detection Algorithm for XML Documents. In U. Dayal, K. Ramamritham, and T.M. Vijayaraman (Eds.), *Proceedings of the 19th International Conference on Data Engineering (ICDE),* (pp. 574–580). IEEE Computer Society.

Zhang, K., Shasha, D., & Wang, J.-L. (1994). Approximate Tree matching in the Presence of Variable Length Don't Cares. *Journal of Algorithms, 16*(1), 33–66. doi:10.1006/jagm.1994.1003

## ENDNOTES

[1] http://glaros.dtc.umn.edu/gkhome/views/cluto/

[2] http://wekaclassalgos.sourceforge.net/

# Chapter 6
# The Role of Schema and Document Matchings in XML Source Clustering

**Pasquale De Meo**
*University of Messina, Italy*

**Giacomo Fiumara**
*University of Messina, Italy*

**Antonino Nocera**
*University Mediterranea of Reggio Calabria, Italy*

**Domenico Ursino**
*University Mediterranea of Reggio Calabria, Italy*

## ABSTRACT

*In recent years, there has been an increase in the volume and heterogeneity of XML data sources. Moreover, these information sources are often comprised of both schemas and instances of XML data. In this context, the need of grouping similar XML documents together has led to an increasing research on clustering algorithms for XML data. In this chapter, we present an overview of the most popular methods for clustering XML data sources, distinguishing between the intensional data level and the extensional data level, depending whether the sources to cluster are DTDs and XML schemas, or XML documents; in the latter case, we focus on the structural information of the documents. We classify and describe techniques for computing similarities among XML data sources, and discuss methods for clustering DTDs/XML schemas and XML documents.*

DOI: 10.4018/978-1-61350-356-0.ch006

## INTRODUCTION

The eXtensible Markup Language (XML) has emerged as the de-facto standard for the representation and the diffusion of data both on the Web and within organizations (De Meo, Quattrone, Terracina, & Ursino, 2006; Lee, Yang, Hsu, & Yang, 2002; Thompson, Beech, Maloney, & Mendelsohn, 2004).

Today, various vendors propose software tools to manage native XML (i.e., they use XML documents as the core storage unit) (Tamino, 2010), whereas some software companies, like Oracle, propose tools based on relational database technologies to efficiently store, navigate, and query XML data (Oracle XML DB, 2010). As a result, XML databases are rapidly proliferating and there are significant research efforts devoted to develop scalable techniques for efficiently handling the huge amount of XML data.

An effective solution to organize XML data sources relies on *clustering* techniques, which are applied based on the XML structural similarities. Clustering is an active research area in data mining (Han & Kamber, 2006). The goal of a clustering algorithm is to group objects into clusters such that objects within a cluster share similar features whereas objects associated with different clusters are dissimilar. Clustering XML data sources is useful to organize data in an unsupervised way and, ultimately, this is important to make the process of retrieving and browsing data easier.

Some of the activities that can benefit from the clustering of XML data sources are *data integration* and *retrieval*. The rapid growth of XML data sources explains the need of specific tools for integrating these data sources, i.e., the task of merging data coming from disparate sources with the goal of providing end-users with a unified view of these data (Lee, Yang, Hsu, & Yang, 2002). Data integration hence plays a key role in a wide range of domains, ranging from life sciences to Web mining and e-commerce (De Meo, Quattrone, Terracina, & Ursino, 2007). As soon as the size and complexity of the XML sources to integrate increases, the data integration task must be automatized as much as possible; for this purpose, there is a demand for tools capable of automatically detecting whether portions of two data sources represent the same concepts and of grouping sources describing the same piece of reality into homogeneous clusters. Moreover, the computation of the similarity degree of XML data is useful for designing tools capable of better ranking XML documents on the basis of their similarity with respect to a user query. The final outcome is an increase in terms of both accuracy and completeness of the answers generated for a given user query (Tagarelli & Greco, 2010).

The process of clustering XML data is a nontrivial task as it poses some challenging research issues which are not present when flat data or textual sources are considered. A first research problem regards which data model is to be adopted to represent XML data sources. In the literature, a large variety of data models have been introduced, such as rooted and labeled trees (Dalamagas, Cheng, Winkel, & Sellis, 2006), (weighted) graphs (De Meo, Quattrone, Terracina, & Ursino, 2006), arrays/matrices (Theobald, Schenkel, & Weikum, 2003), or sequential data (Flesca, Manco, Masciari, Pontieri, & Pugliese, 2005).

The second research problem regards the definition of suitable techniques to compute the similarity degree of two XML data sources. This last problem has been considered in the literature at two different levels, specifically:

- At the *intensional* level (also known as *schema-level*), DTDs or XML Schemas are taken into account (De Meo, Quattrone, Terracina, & Ursino, 2006; Lee, Yang, Hsu, & Yang, 2002). Moreover, the research line devoted to extract semantic similarities between two DTDs/XML Schemas is part of a more general research activity known as *schema matching* (Kementsietsidis, 2009; Rahm & Bernstein, 2001).

- At the *extensional* level (also known as *instance-* or *data-level*), XML documents only are considered (Chawathe, Rajaraman, Garcia-Molina, & Widom, 1996; Cobéna, Abiteboul, & Marian, 2002).

In both cases, the XML data clustering problem is difficult, and often it is necessary to consider information at both the schema and the instance levels. In other words, two XML Schemas (resp., documents) may represent the same application domain but with different granularity levels (e.g., the first Schema may present an almost flat structure whereas the second one may present a deep level of nesting of its elements). Analogously, two XML Schemas (resp., documents) describing the same piece of reality may differ because they use different tags to identify the same concepts, and hence an activity devoted to interpret the meaning of a tag is required.

Finally, the third research problem regards the algorithm to cluster XML data sources either at the intensional or the extensional level. Some approaches suggest to apply any off-the-shelf algorithm (e.g., hierarchical agglomerative or partitional clustering algorithms) (Algergawy, Schallehn, & Saake, 2009; De Meo, Quattrone, Terracina, & Ursino, 2007), whereas other ones provide ad-hoc algorithms (Aggarwal, Ta, Wang, Feng, & Zaki, 2007).

In this chapter, we present an overview of XML data clustering approaches at both intensional and extensional levels. In the next two sections, we first consider the intensional similarity computation problem and provide a classification of the corresponding approaches; then, we discuss the extensional similarity computation problem and, also in this case, we provide a taxonomy of the corresponding approaches. In the second part of the chapter, we focus on the XML data source clustering problem and we investigate it at the intensional level and the extensional one in two separate sections. Since we assume that the presence of both schemas and documents is important in XML data sources, we address the similarity computation and clustering problems mainly from a structural viewpoint.

## COMPUTING SIMILARITIES BETWEEN XML SCHEMAS/DTDS

### The Schema Matching Problem

*Schema matching* is the process of analyzing two data sources with the goal of identifying pairs of objects which are semantically related (Rahm & Bernstein, 2001). Derived relationships are often known in the literature as *semantic matchings* or *interschema properties* (Batini & Lenzerini, 1986; Palopoli, Saccà, Terracina, & Ursino, 2003). The most common types of semantic matchings are *synonymies*, *homonymies*, *hyponymies* and *hyperonymies*. More precisely, given two elements $e_1$ of a schema $S_1$ and $e_2$ of a schema $S_2$ we say that:

- $e_1$ and $e_2$ are *synonyms* if they have the same meaning even if they could have different names;
- $e_1$ and $e_2$ are *homonyms* if they have different meanings even if they have the same name;
- $e_1$ is a *hyponym* of $e_2$ (which, in its turn, is a *hyperonym* of $e_1$) if $e_1$ has a more specific meaning than $e_2$ (e.g., $e_1$ may be the element "PhD student" whereas $e_2$ may be the element "student").

Schema matching is a central research theme in database and artificial intelligence areas as it plays a key role in many application scenarios like data integration (Melnik, Rahm, & Bernstein, 2003), data management in peer-to-peer systems (Kantere, Tsoumakos, Sellis, & Roussopoulos, 2009), ontology alignment and mapping (Euzenat & Shvaiko, 2007), Semantic Web (Dhamankar, Lee, Doan, Halevy, & Domingos, 2004), data warehousing (Madhavan, Bernstein, & Rahm,

2001). There is a rich literature on this theme and some research papers provide an excellent description of many of the existing approaches (Kementsietsidis, 2009; Rahm & Bernstein, 2001; Shvaiko & Euzenat, 2005); we refer the reader to (Algergawy, Nayak, & Saake, 2010), in which a detailed classification of schema matching approaches along with an experimental comparison is reported. The goal of this section is to focus on schema matching methods explicitly conceived to handle DTDs/XML Schemas, or which at least include some specific functionalities to handle them.

Before introducing XML-specific approaches, we briefly recall the main properties of schema matching algorithms (often known as *matchers*). In particular, existing algorithms can be classified as follows.

## Schema-Level Matchers vs. Instance-Level Matchers (Shvaiko & Euzenat, 2005;Rahm & Bernstein, 2001)

*Schema-level matchers* assume that each available data source is provided with a schema capable of representing it. This schema can be an E/R diagram (if involved sources are relational databases) or a DTD/XML Schema (if involved sources are XML documents). The schema of a data source provides a rich body of information necessary to carry out matching activities. For instance, it allows the extraction of the *name* of schema elements, of their *data types* and, sometimes, of some of their *constraints* (e.g., cardinality constraints expressed by the minOccurs and the maxOccurs attributes in XML Schemas); this information can be extremely useful in schema matching tasks.

*Instance-level matchers* analyze the extensional component of a data source to infer semantic matchings. Instance-level approaches are generally very precise because they look at the actual content of the involved sources, and hence they are able to better interpret their content; however, they are computationally expensive since they must examine the whole extensional component of the involved sources (which in some cases may be huge). These matchers often use techniques coming from Information Retrieval and linguistics to discover potential matches. For instance, they could compute the frequency at which two strings $s_1$ and $s_2$ co-occur with a third string $s_3$ to determine whether $s_1$ and $s_3$ (or $s_2$ and $s_3$) define a semantic matching.

In real cases, instance-level matchers are often used in conjunction with schema-level matchers to filter out false matchings and to learn similarities among schema elements on the basis of the values of the corresponding instances. The schema matching algorithms that adopt this strategy are known as *hybrid matchers* because they use both intensional and extensional information (Rahm & Bernstein, 2001; Kementsietsidis, 2009). The overall result is an accuracy increase in the discovery of semantic matchings; however, as in the case of pure instance-level matchers, the amount of data to process is usually huge and, therefore, the computational effort can be significantly high. Hybrid matchers often use machine learning algorithms to compute semantic matchings. For instance, SemInt (Li & Clifton, 2000) uses Self-Organizing Maps (Kohonen, 1988) to reduce the dimensionality of the data to analyze; LSD (Doan, Domingos, & Halevy, 2001) and GLUE (Doan, Madhavan, Domingos, & Halevy, 2002) use a multi-strategy learning approach and the stacking algorithm (Wolpert, 1992); finally, the approach of (Jeong, Lee, Cho, & Lee, 2008) uses least square regression.

## Simple Matchers vs. Complex Matchers (Rahm & Bernstein, 2001)

Matching algorithms can also be classified on the basis of the *cardinality* of the matchings they are able to find. To better illustrate this concept, let us consider two Schemas $S_1$ and $S_2$; the following types of matchers can be defined:

- **Simple matchers.** These approaches aim at finding all pairs of elements $<e_1,e_2>$ such that $e_1 \in S_1$, $e_2 \in S_2$ and a semantic matching exists between them. Most of these approaches derive synonymies but some of them consider also hyperonymies or hyponymies (De Meo, Quattrone, Terracina, & Ursino, 2007; Gal, Anaby-Tavor, Trombetta, & Montesi, 2005). Simple matchings are also known as *1:1 matchings*.
- **Complex matchers.** These approaches find all pairs of the form $<G_1, G_2>$ being $G_1$ and $G_2$ two groups of elements extracted from $S_1$ and $S_2$, respectively. For instance, $G_1$ could be an element "address" whereas $G_2$ could be a pair of elements "street", "zip". In such a case, there exists a complex matching because the set of elements "street" and "zip" of $S_2$ is semantically similar to the element "address" of $S_1$. Complex matchings are also known as *sub-schema similarities* (De Meo, Quattrone, Terracina, & Ursino, 2004a) or *m:n matchings*.

A large part of schema matching algorithms consider only 1:1 matchings (see, for instance, (Doan, Domingos, & Halevy, 2001; Do & Rahm, 2002) and (Giunchiglia, Yatskevich, & Shvaiko, 2007)). However, there are few examples of systems devoted to handle complex matchings, like iMAP (Dhamankar, Lee, Doan, Halevy, & Domingos, 2004), DCM (He & Chang, 2006), INDIGO (Idrissi & Vachon, 2007) and XIKE (De Meo, Quattrone, Terracina, & Ursino, 2004a).

Some of these approaches use data mining and artificial intelligence techniques to discover complex matchings. For instance, in iMAP the complex matching computation problem is seen as a *search problem*. A set of searchers is exploited to explore the space of all possible groups of schema elements candidate to form a complex matching. In order to reduce the computational complexity, the search space is pruned by taking domain knowledge into account.

In DCM, the complex matching discovery problem is solved by analyzing patterns of co-occurrence in input data. In particular, the authors hypothesize the presence, for each application domain, of a *hidden schema model* which acts as a unified generative model describing how Schemas are generated from a finite vocabulary.

INDIGO uses a variety of techniques like linguistic matchers or the WHIRL algorithm (Cohen & Hirsch, 1998), which has been developed in the context of text classification and is capable of matching concepts on the basis of their shared instances.

In XIKE, pairs of *promising groups* of elements are preliminarily detected. Two groups of elements are said promising if there is a high chance that they can form a complex matching. To avoid the explosion of computational costs, XIKE adopts a suitable heuristics in which groups of elements are selected on the basis of the number of 1:1 matchings they share. Promising groups are then analyzed to verify which of them really form complex matchings. The computational complexity of the approach underlying XIKE is polynomial against the size of input schemas, and this makes it suitable to effectively handle large Schemas.

The two criteria illustrated above are valid for all matchers existing in the literature, and, in particular, they can be applied to matchers operating on DTDs and XML Schemas. However, the specificities of the XML data model have inspired many researchers to design ad-hoc approaches for the extraction of semantic matchings. In particular, the main features of the XML data model which can be used in the schema matching process are the following:

- **Constraints on data types and cardinalities.** The XML data model provides a rich set of primitive and built-in data types. As a consequence, the compatibility of the data types associated with two elements

is a useful indicator to assess whether two elements actually form a semantic matching or not. Constraints on data types can be *hard* (if they cannot be violated in any case) or *soft* (if they can be relaxed). An example of hard constraints is the translation of a string into a real. On the contrary, an example of soft constraint is the translation of an integer into a longinteger. A further constraint regards the cardinality associated with the instance of an element in a document. In fact, in a DTD/XML Schema *S*, an element *e* can be declared as *optional* or not; in the former case, an instance of *e* could not appear in a document *D* associated with *S*, whereas in the latter case, one or even more instances of *e* appear in *D*. The cardinality of an element in an XML Schema is declared by means of the attributes minOccurs and maxOccurs and it can be used in the semantic matching discovery. For instance, a matching between two elements $e_1$ and $e_2$ could be recognized as a false positive if the value of the maxOccurs attribute associated with $e_1$ is smaller than the value of the minOccurs attribute associated with $e_2$.
- **Constraints on the structure.** The XML data model is hierarchical and different designers may decide to represent the same piece of reality at different granularity levels. The hierarchical organization of a DTD/XML Schema, besides reflecting the personal standpoint of a human designer, heavily influences the schema matching process. As a matter of fact, the role of the hierarchical structure of DTDs/XML Schemas in the semantic matching process is investigated in the LSD system (Doan, Domingos, & Halevy, 2001). Here the authors suggest to *serialize* an XML document and to analyze the frequency at which tags appear. This is used to train a Naïve Bayes classifier. However, experimental trials have shown that the semantic matchings discovered by this classifier are poor in terms of accuracy, therefore the authors also suggest to continue to use the Naïve Bayes classifier while proposing a more refined encoding of an XML document, in which the nesting level of each data instance is considered. This encoding influences the training phase of the Bayesian classifier and yields a meaningful increase in accuracy.

The above ideas suggest to introduce a new classification criterion orthogonal with respect to the two ones mentioned above. In particular, a first group of matchers takes information about elements (e.g., constraints on data types) into account. We shall call them as *element-level matchers*. A second group of matchers takes advantage of structural information coming from DTDs and XML Schemas. These matchers define the concept of *context* of an element; for instance, if an XML Schema is modeled as a tree, the context of an element is represented by the set of its descendants and ancestors; there exists a semantic matching between two nodes if there exists a matching between their contexts. Approaches belonging to this category are called *context-level matchers*.

Since the previous criteria have been largely investigated in the literature, in the following we shall examine this new criterion in detail and classify schema matching approaches operating on XML sources according to it.

## Element-Level Matching

Approaches in this category use information about elements of a DTD/XML Schema to compute semantic similarities. In particular, the usually considered information regards the names of the elements (expressed as strings), their data types and constraints on their cardinalities. Each of this information provides a basic similarity metric.

All these metrics are described in detail in the following subsections.

## Name Similarity

Name similarity techniques are based on the following intuition: the more similar the names of two XML elements are, the higher the similarity level of the corresponding XML elements is. In order to measure the similarity degree of two strings, various methods, like *prefix*, *suffix*, *edit distance*, *Jaro distance* and *n-gram* (Algergawy, Schallehn, & Saake, 2009; Giunchiglia & Yatskevich, 2004) have been proposed in the literature.

*Prefix* receives two strings and checks whether the first one starts with the second one. Prefix is efficient in recognizing *acronyms* (e.g., it recognizes that terms like "int" or "integer" form a semantic matching). Some systems that adopt this method are those reported in (Do & Rahm, 2002; Madhavan, Bernstein, & Rahm, 2001; Melnik, Garcia-Molina, & Rahm, 2002).

*Suffix* receives two strings and checks whether the first one ends with the second one (e.g., "phone" and "telephone"). Systems using suffix are again presented in (Do & Rahm, 2002; Madhavan, Bernstein, & Rahm, 2001; Melnik, Garcia-Molina, & Rahm, 2002).

The edit distance technique receives two strings and computes the shortest sequence of operations capable of transforming the first one into the second one. Operations usually considered are the insertion of a character in a string, the deletion of a character, and the substitution of a character. Edit distance has been used in, e.g., (Do & Rahm, 2002).

The *Jaro* distance (Jaro, 1995) is a metric proposed to compute the similarity degree of two strings. In particular, given two strings $s_1$ and $s_2$, their Jaro distance is defined as follows:

$$d = 1/3*(m/|s_1| + m/|s_2| +(m-t)/m)$$

where $m$ is the number of matching characters between $s_1$ and $s_2$, $t$ is the number of *transpositions* of the characters, i.e., the number of matching characters but in different order present in $s_1$ and $s_2$, $|s_1|$ and $|s_2|$ are the length of $s_1$ and $s_2$, respectively. Jaro distance has been used in (Quix, Kensche, & Li, 2007).

An *n-gram* is a sequence of $n$ consecutive characters in a string. For instance, given the string "house", an $n$-gram of length 3 (often known as *trigram*) is "ous". In approaches relying on $n$-grams, the distance between two strings is computed by comparing the number of $n$-grams they share. In the context of Schema Matching, examples of approaches exploiting $n$-grams are reported in (Do & Rahm, 2002, Giunchiglia, Shvaiko, & Yatskevich, 2005).

An experimental comparison of various metrics for string matching is reported in (Cohen, Ravikumar, & Fienberg, 2003).

## Language-Based Similarity

Language-based techniques use natural language processing techniques to compute the similarity degree of two elements. These techniques often carry out some pre-processing tasks on the data sources to analyze (Madhavan, Bernstein, & Rahm, 2001; Giunchiglia, Yatskevich, & Shvaiko, 2007). For instance, popular pre-processing activities are tokenization (i.e., the names of the entities are parsed and symbols like punctuation, blank characters or digits are detected) and removal of words (i.e., some tokens like prepositions or articles are filtered out).

Most of these techniques rely on the use of *external sources*, such as dictionaries or thesauri. A popular tool is *WordNet*, a lexical database for English language developed at the University of Princeton (Miller, 1995). WordNet groups English words into sets of synonyms (called *synsets*), and hence it provides a plenty of facilities also for schema matching purposes. In this context, WordNet has been used in the *S-Match* system (Giunchiglia, Yatskevich& Shvaiko, 2007; Shvaiko, Giunchiglia, & Yatskevich, 2010) as a background knowledge source that returns semantic relations between element names. In particular, S-Match uses WordNet not only to find pairs of elements having the same meaning but also to check whether the meaning of a term is more general than the one of another term. As a further example, in (De Meo, Quattrone, Terracina, & Ursino, 2006; De Meo, Quattrone, Terracina, & Ursino, 2004b; De Meo, Quattrone, Terracina, & Ursino, 2007) the authors suggest to query WordNet to find syntactic correspondences between the elements of two XML Schemas; these correspondences are then used to discover a broad range of semantic correspondences like synonymies, homonymies, hyponymies and hyperonymies.

Other approaches like COMA++ (Do & Rahm, 2007) and PORSCHE (Saleem, Bellahsene, & Hunt, 2008) suggest to use domain specific dictionaries; sometimes, these dictionaries are manually built up.

### Data Type Similarity

Some authors suggest that an analysis of the data types associated with two elements of two XML Schemas is useful to reveal false matchings. In fact, it may happen that two elements share the same name but they represent completely different concepts. These false positives can be sometimes detected by checking if a type compatibility is violated.

XML provides a rich data model and supports 44 primitive and derived built-in data types (Thompson, Beech, Maloney, & Mendelsohn, 2004). As a consequence, it offers to human designers a broad range of options to model complex scenarios; in this context, the issue of checking whether a form of compatibility exists between two different data types is an interesting problem.

In (Nayak & Tran, 2007) the authors develop a compatibility table that indicates whether two data types are not compatible (e.g., string and float) or if a weak form of compatibility can be recognized (e.g., integer and longinteger). An analogous study is presented in (De Meo, Terracina, & Ursino, 2004b) in the context of XML DTDs.

### Cardinality Constraint Similarity

Another source of information which is useful to reveal the similarity between two elements of a schema is given by *cardinality constraints*. For this purpose XML Schemas provide the minOccurs and maxOccurs attributes. A cardinality table for DTD constraints has been proposed in (Lee, Yang, Hsu, & Yang, 2002). Nayak and Tran (2007) have adapted this table for the case of XML Schemas.

## Context-Level Matching

In context-level matching approaches, a DTD/XML Schema is usually represented as a tree $T$ or a graph $G$ and each of its elements corresponds to a node in $T$ or $G$. The *context* of a node $n$ in $T$ (resp., $G$) is represented by all the nodes of $T$ (resp., $G$) which are "close" to $n$. For instance, if a tree-based representation is exploited, the context of $n$ may consist of all its ancestors/descendants. Analogously, in case of a graph-based representation, the context of $n$ may consist of its *neighbor nodes* (e.g., those nodes adjacent to $n$ or tied to $n$ through paths up to a fixed length $k$).

The context of a node $n$ is exploited to better interpret the meaning of the element represented by $n$, and this information is definitely useful in carrying out schema matching tasks. In fact, the intuition behind context-level matching approaches is the following: if two elements are similar, their contexts might also be somehow similar. As a consequence, the task of determining whether two elements are similar requires to check if their contexts are similar. Such an idea was first introduced in (Fankhauser, Kracker, & Neuhold, 1991) and it was later applied in other fields including data mining (Jeh & Widom, 2002), Web Search (Jeh

& Widom, 2003), and Social Network Analysis (Liben-Nowell & Kleinberg, 2003).

In the following we shall discuss in detail the main features of context-level matching approaches; for this purpose, we classify them into two categories, namely *tree-based* and *graph-based approaches*, depending whether a dtd/xml schema is modeled as a tree or a graph, respectively. A graphical comparison of such approaches is shown in Figure 1.

## Tree-Based Approaches

Some approaches suggest to map DTD/XML Schemas into trees and to use tree matching algorithms to identify pairs of similar elements. The context of a node usually coincides with the set of its ancestors and descendants. This implies that similarities are computed only for non-leaf nodes (in fact, a leaf node is not provided with descendants and it has only one parent). Tree-based algorithms can be classified as follows (Algergawy, Nayak, & Saake, 2010):

- **Child similarity.** These approaches take a non-leaf node and identify its children. Two non-leaf elements are then classified as similar if their sets of children present a high matching degree. The set of children of two nodes could by compared by applying the Jaccard coefficient or other analogous methods. An implementation of this strategy can be found in the Cupid system (Madhavan, Bernstein, & Rahm, 2001).
- **Leaf similarity.** In these approaches any non-leaf node is considered as the root of a subtree and the set of leaf nodes associated with this subtree is extracted. The similarity degree between two non-leaf nodes $n_1$ and $n_2$ is computed by comparing the sets of leaf nodes belonging to the subtrees rooted in $n_1$ and $n_2$. As an example, the approach of (Algergawy, Schallehn, & Saake, 2009) suggests to map the set of leaf nodes into arrays whose entries are real numbers. The similarity of these arrays is then computed by applying the cosine similarity measure.
- **Sibling similarity.** In these approaches, for each element $e_i$, the set consisting of both preceding and following siblings of $e_i$ is extracted. We recall that the siblings of a node $e_i$ in a tree are the nodes which are at the same level of the node $e_i$ itself. According to the procedure adopted to visit a tree (e.g., pre-order or post-order) some siblings of $e_i$ can be visited before $e_i$ itself (preceding siblings) of after it (following siblings). For each pair of siblings belonging to the two sets above, the similarity is computed; then, the matching pairs with the highest similarity scores are selected (*best matching pairs*). The similarity degree of two nodes is defined as the average of the similarities of the best matching pairs.
- **Ancestor similarity.** In these approaches, the ancestor context of a node is considered to compute similarities. In particular, given an element $e_i$ in an XML tree and the path $p(e_i)$ joining the root with $e_i$, the set of nodes composing $p(e_i)$ is called the *ancestor context* of $e_i$. Some authors (Algergawy, Schallehn, & Saake, 2009) suggest to use refined techniques (like *Prufer sequences*) to efficiently encode these paths; finally,

*Figure 1. Classification of context-level matching approaches*

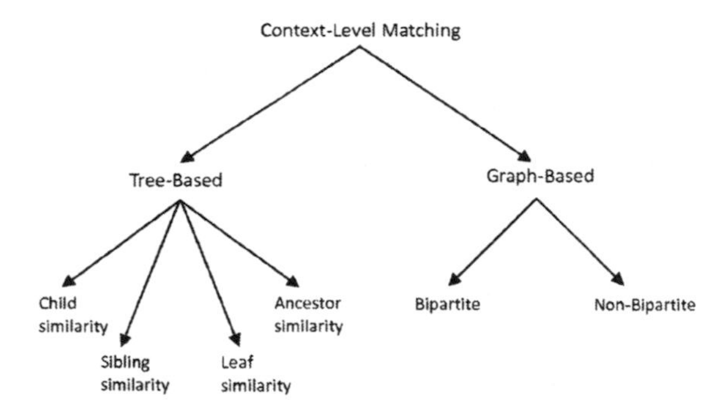

the ancestor contexts of two nodes $e_i$ and $e_j$ are compared to define the degree of similarity between $e_i$ and $e_j$.

Recently, some authors (Wojnar, Mlynkova, & Dokulil, 2010) have suggested to map XML Schemas onto trees and to apply some suitable rules to simplify the structure of these trees; next, they compute the edit distance between simplified trees. The similarity degree of two DTDs/XML Schemas coincides with the value of their edit distance. Edit distance has been largely exploited to determine the matching degree of two XML documents but its usage in the context of XML Schemas is still largely unexplored.

## Graph-Based Approaches

Graph-based techniques consider the input schemas as labeled and often weighted graphs. Such a representation is useful and intuitive because relationships between elements of a schema can be interpreted in terms of structural properties, like edges or paths, of a graph.

In particular, given two nodes $n_1$ and $n_2$ in a graph $G$ corresponding to a schema $S$, the notion of distance between $n_1$ and $n_2$ can be defined by considering the paths joining $n_1$ and $n_2$. For instance, in the approach of (De Meo, Quattrone, Terracina, & Ursino, 2006), the distance between two nodes in $G$ is interpreted as the length of the shortest path joining them.

Assuming that a notion of distance between two elements of a schema is available, the notion of *neighborhood* of a node can be introduced as follows: given a node $n_1$ in $G$, the ε-neighborhood associated with $n_1$ consists of the set of the nodes of $G$ whose distance from $n_1$ is less than ε, being ε a pre-fixed integer or real number. Once the neighborhoods of $n_1$ and $n_2$ have been built, they can be compared to determine if there exists a matching between $n_1$ and $n_2$. A popular comparison strategy consists of applying graph matching algorithms (Galil, 1986). For instance, in (De Meo, Quattrone, Terracina, & Ursino, 2006) given two nodes $n_1$ (coming from a schema $S_1$) and $n_2$ (coming from a schema $S_2$) and an integer $u$ (called *severity level*), the authors suggest to build a bipartite graph $BG = < N_1 \cup N_2, E>$ such that:

- $N_1$ coincides with the $u$-neighborhood of $n_1$,
- $N_2$ coincides with the $u$-neighborhood of $n_2$, and
- an edge $e \in E$ links a node of $N_1$ with a node of $N_2$ if there exists a *syntactic matching* (revealed by querying WordNet) between the two nodes.

A *maximum weight matching problem* is then solved on $BG$; if the value of a suitable objective function is higher than a predefined threshold then it is possible to conclude that a similarity between $n_1$ and $n_2$ exists. It should be noted that the approach in (De Meo, Quattrone, Terracina, & Ursino, 2006) is parametric against the severity level $u$ (in the sense that a human user is allowed to freely fix it depending on its information needs); in addition, it is scalable because the size of $BG$ is usually small.

Other interesting approaches are those described in (Euzenat & Valtchev, 2004; Melnik, Garcia-Molina, & Rahm, 2002). These approaches differ from the one of (De Meo, Quattrone, Terracina, & Ursino, 2006) because the graphs to match are not bipartite, and hence the problem of finding semantic matchings between two graphs requires to determine if an isomorphism between them exists (Ullmann, 1976). Such a problem is computationally intractable, therefore heuristics are needed. For instance, in (Euzenat & Valtchev, 2004; Melnik, Garcia-Molina, & Rahm, 2002), the task of finding semantic matchings between two graphs (representing schemas or portion of schemas) is seen as an optimization problem. This problem is solved by applying an iterative and fix-point algorithm which, at each iteration, tries to improve the current optimal solution and ends when no further improvement is possible. Experimental studies show that these algorithms are computationally competitive on large schemas too.

## COMPUTING SIMILARITIES BETWEEN XML DOCUMENTS

The problem of computing similarities between XML documents has attracted the interest of many researchers mainly in the areas of database systems and information retrieval. A wide range of methods for comparing XML documents has been proposed in the literature, which are usually classified depending on the model and data structures used to represent XML documents, i.e., tree-based, graph-based, vector-based, and sequence-based. A graphical classification of main existing approaches is reported in Figure 2.

In the following we overview the key ideas and concepts underlying each of the main XML document similarity approaches in the literature, and when possible we also provide pointers to the clustering algorithms (discussed in the next section) that use specific similarity methods.

### Tree Matching

Tree matching approaches model XML documents as labeled trees. Originally, such approaches have been largely and successfully applied to detect changes between two different versions of an XML document. Often, tree matching approaches use *dynamic programming* techniques to find the distance of two trees; here, the idea is that the distance of two trees coincides with the minimum number of operations (called *edit operations*) capable of transforming the former tree into the latter one. Edit operations can be carried out at the node level (i.e., they may be applied only on nodes) or at the subtree level (i.e., they may involve entire subtrees extracted from an XML tree). Within this view, tree matching approaches can be divided in two categories, namely *node-level matching* and *subtree-level matching.*

Edit operations performed on any tree at node level refer to atomic tree operations, i.e., changing the label of a node, deleting a node, and inserting a node as a child of another node. Complex tree operations can also be used; they are defined as sequences of atomic tree operations. For instance, the insertion of a whole subtree in a tree can be regarded as a complex tree operation; it consists of a sequence of atomic node insertion operations. We can assign a *cost* to each atomic operation. The cost of a complex operation is usually defined as the sum of the costs of its constituent atomic operations.

In tree matching approaches, the distance between any two trees $T_1$ and $T_2$ is regarded as the tree edit minimum distance between the trees, which is the cost of a sequence of edit operations capable of transforming $T_1$ into $T_2$ with the minimum cost. The first non-exponential algorithm to compute the edit distance between ordered labeled trees was proposed in (Tai, 1979), whereas a significant computational improvement was given by the Shasha-Zhang algorithm (Shasha & Zhang, 1995) (Table 1). However, both these algorithms were

*Figure 2. Classification of document similarity detection approaches*

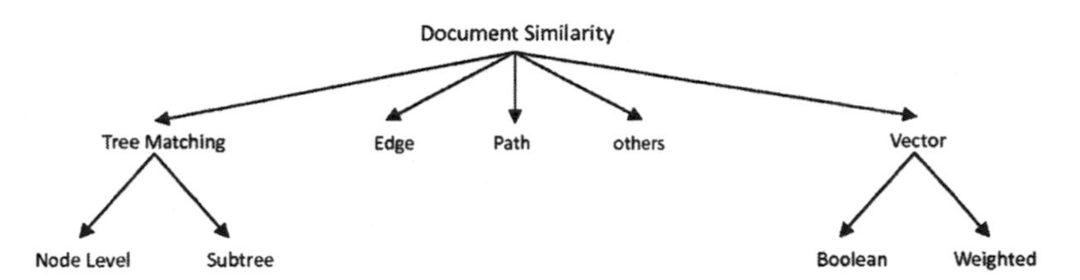

not conceived for XML documents and, therefore, they might not provide significant results. In fact, both the algorithms allow nodes to be arbitrarily deleted, inserted or re-labeled independently of their position in the document. By contrast, as observed by some authors (Dalamagas, Cheng, Winkel, & Sellis, 2006), elements of an XML source may have different relevance levels on the basis of their position in the hierarchical structure of the source itself. As a consequence, deleting nodes on the top of the document hierarchy has not the same effect of deleting nodes at leaf level. For this purpose, (Dalamagas, Cheng, Winkel, & Sellis, 2006) proposed to use the edit distance in conjunction with some suitable constraints; for instance, the deletion of an internal node $n$ in an XML document tree requires a path going from $n$ to a leaf node $m$ to be identified and all nodes of this path to be deleted.

The first approach explicitly developed to handle XML documents appeared in (Cobéna, Abiteboul, & Marian, 2002). In this approach the authors restricted insertion and deletion operations only to leaf nodes. In addition, a *move* operator, capable of moving a whole subtree, was introduced; the resulting algorithm uses dynamic programming techniques and its worst-case computational complexity is $O(N \log N)$.

A significant example of an algorithm relying on the edit distance computation is the *Chawathe's algorithm* (Chawathe, 1999). In this algorithm, XML trees are represented as a sequence of pairs (called *ld* pairs) of the form $<l, d>$, being $l$ the label of a node and $d$ its depth. The distance between two *ld* pairs (and, ultimately, of the XML trees represented by them) is carried out by applying the Wagner-Fisher algorithm (Wagner & Fisher, 1974). The worst case time complexity of the Chawathe's algorithm is $O(N^2)$, being $N$ the total number of nodes in the documents to match.

Approaches based on the edit distance at node level would fail to recognize documents that, although conforming to the same DTD, may significantly differ from each other due to repeated or optional occurrences of elements. Subtree-level matching approaches aim to overcome this limitation by considering the edit distance between document subtrees, i.e., edit operations are applied to subtrees rather than only to single nodes.

(Nierman & Jagadish, 2002) introduced the first structural similarity approach for two XML documents generated from the same DTD. Besides the traditional edit operations (i.e., insert, delete, change), this approach also includes two additional operations: *InsertTree,* which allows a subtree to be inserted, and *DeleteTree,* which allows a subtree to be deleted. However, the *InsertTree* and *DeleteTree* operations can be applied only if some specific constraints are satisfied. In particular, given two XML trees $T_1$ and $T_2$, whose similarity degree must

*Table 1. A comparison of node level matching approaches*

| Algorithm | Allowed operations | Nodes | Description | Time Complexity |
|---|---|---|---|---|
| Tai, 1979 | • insertion<br>• deletion<br>• substitution | Both internal and leaf nodes | Dynamic Programming | $O(\|T_1\|\|T_2\|\ depth(T_1)^2 depth(T_2)^2)$ |
| Shasha & Zhang, 1995 | • insertion<br>• deletion<br>• substitution | Both internal and leaf nodes | Dynamic Programming | $O(\|T_1\|\|T_2\|\ depth(T_1)\ depth(T_2))$ |
| Cobéna, Abiteboul, & Marian, 2002 | • insertion<br>• deletion<br>• substitution<br>• move | Only leaf nodes | Dynamic Programming | $O(N \log N)$ |
| Chawathe, 1999 | Map a tree onto a sequence of *ld*-pairs | Both internal and leaf nodes | Wagner-Fisher algorithm | $O(N^2)$ |

be computed, the insertion of a tree $A$ in $T_1$ (or $T_2$), as well as the deletion of a tree $A$ from $T_1$ (or $T_2$), can be executed if and only if $T_1$ and $T_2$ share $A$. The overall complexity of the algorithm presented in (Nierman & Jagadish, 2002) is $O(N^2)$, being $N$ the total number of nodes in the trees to match. Experimental results showed that the algorithm in (Nierman & Jagadish, 2002) is more accurate than the Chawathe's algorithm, although it is conceptually more complex and requires a heavy pre-computation phase. Subtree-level matching has been adopted in clustering methods such as (Dalamagas, Cheng, Winkel, & Sellis, 2006).

## Edge Matching

Edge matching requires to transform XML documents into directed graphs and to compute the similarity of two documents based on their common edges. An early approach belonging to this category is provided in (Kriegel & Schönauer, 2003): given two documents $D_1$ and $D_2$, these are mapped to two labeled graphs $G_1 = <N_1, E_1>$ and $G_2 = <N_2, E_2>$, and a bipartite graph $G^* = <E_1 \cup E_2, E^*>$ is built, where an edge $e^* \in E^*$ links two nodes in $G^*$ if there exists a match between the corresponding edges in $G_1$ and $G_2$. A maximum weight matching problem is then defined on $G^*$, and the distance between the input documents is finally set as the value of the corresponding objective function.

Edge matching methods have been employed in XML document clustering algorithms such as (Lian, Cheung, Mamoulis, & Yiu, 2004; Costa, Manco, Ortale, & Tagarelli, 2004; Nayak, 2008; Antonellis, Makris, & Tsirakis, 2008; Alishahi, Naghibzadeh, & Aski, 2010).

## Path Matching

An XML document can also be modeled as a set of paths, each starting from the root of the document and ending in a leaf node, therefore the similarity between two XML documents can be computed based on the sets of paths associated with them (Butler, 2004; Rafiei, Moise, & Sun, 2006). Experimental trials show that path matching techniques are highly accurate and, sometimes, they work better than approaches based on the edit distance (Butler, 2004; Rafiei, Moise, & Sun, 2006).

Unfortunately,path matching techniques can be time-expensive when large documents must be handled. In order to obtain a fast computation, some authors suggest to use approximate techniques (Butler, 2004). One of the most popular techniques relies on the idea of *shingles* (Broder, 1997). A shingle is a data structure which uses hash functions to represent the objects of a collection. The main idea of (Butler, 2004) is to use shingles of fixed length to represent the paths of an XML document. Since the length of shingles is fixed, the worst case time complexity of the approach illustrated in (Butler, 2004) is $O(1)$. However, a pre-processing phase is required to extract shingles from documents, and this phase may be computationally expensive.

In (Joshi, Agrawal, Krishnapuram, & Negi, 2003), the authors consider two kinds of paths: generic paths (i.e., nodes tied only by parent/child relationships) and paths derived from XPath expressions. The distance between two documents is computed by identifying the paths they share. Experiments showed that the use of paths derived from XPath expressions yields better results whose quality is higher than the one obtained by using generic paths only (Joshi, Agrawal, Krishnapuram, & Negi, 2003).

## Vector Based Approaches

Vector based approaches gained a large popularity in the context of information retrieval. They essentially aim to map XML documents onto vectors of an $n$-dimensional feature space. To produce such a mapping, vector based approaches can use both the structure and the content of a document or, alternatively, only information about the structure of the document itself; in this section, we consider only approaches using information on the structure of the documents.

The simplest feature that can be considered is the label of an element in a document. Of course, more complex features could also be considered. For instance, each element could be encoded as a pair of the form $<l, d>$, being $l$ its name and $d$ its depth in the document. Finally, features can be designed to take the different levels of structural granularities allowed by an XML document into account. This means that, rather than describing an XML document in terms of the elements composing it, we can represent it by considering the paths starting from the root (also known as XML *twigs*). As shown in (Theobald, Schenkel, & Weikum, 2003), the representation of an XML document by means of its paths is useful to better capture its semantics. However, the identifications of all the paths existing in an XML document is exponential against the number of its elements. As a consequence, near-exponential costs would be necessary to map an XML document onto the feature space and to store this representation. For these reasons, some authors (e.g., (Theobald, Schenkel, & Weikum, 2003)) suggest to consider paths up to a fixed length $k$. Once features have been extracted, suitable tools are applied to compare two documents. For instance, the simplest comparison criterion requires the computation of the *inner product* of the vectors associated with the two documents.

Other approaches to compute the similarity of two documents rely on notions from probability and information theory. Intuitively, these approaches assume that a document $D$ may contain a particular feature with a certain probability. As a consequence, the $i$-th component of the vector associated with $D$ is set equal to the probability $p_i$ that $D$ contains the $i$-th feature. The computation of the similarity degree of two documents is performed by comparing two probability distributions. A popular metric carrying out this task is the Kullback-Leibler divergence (Kullback & Leibler, 1951).

We can classify vector-based approaches in the following categories:

- **Boolean approaches.** In this case, an XML document $D$ is represented by an $n$-dimensional boolean array whose $i$-th component is 1 if the $i$-th feature is present in $D$, and 0 otherwise. In some cases, multidimensional matrices are exploited instead of arrays. For instance, in some approaches 3-D matrices are introduced to represent relationships among documents, elements and paths. The generic element $M[i, j, k]$ is set to 1, if the document $D_i$ contains the element $e_j$ in the path $p_k$, and to 0 otherwise. Some variations have also been considered, such as focusing only on paths going from the root to the leaves.
- **Weighted approaches.** In this case, an XML document $D$ is represented by an $n$-dimensional boolean array such that its $i$-th component is equal to a value $r_i$ ranging in a closed interval (e.g., the interval [0,1]). Intuitively, the higher $r_i$, the more relevant the contribution of the $i$-th feature in the construction of $D$.

In (Yoon, Raghavan, & Chakilam, 2001), the similarity degree of two XML documents is directly proportional to the number of e-paths shared by them, where an e-path is defined as a set of nested elements labeled with the same tag. In (Yang, Cheung, & Chen, 2005), the authors introduce a model called *Structured Link Vector Model*, to represent a set of XML documents. This approach assumes that the XML documents are generated from a set of $m$ elements, and consequently the degree of similarity of two documents depends on the similarity of the elements composing it. A matrix storing the similarities between all pairs of elements is then learned by applying an iterative algorithm. The approach of (Yang, Kalnis, & Tung,

2005) first represents an XML document as a full binary tree (i.e., a binary tree in which each node has exactly zero or two children), where a binary branch consists of a node along with its children. A generic XML document can be mapped onto a multi-dimensional vector (*binary branch vector)* such that the $j$-th component of is equal to the number of occurrences of the $j$-th branch in it. The distance $\delta$ between two XML documents $D_1$ and $D_2$ is computed as the Manhattan distance of the corresponding binary branch vectors.

## Other Approaches

In (Flesca, Manco, Masciari, Pontieri, & Pugliese, 2005), an XML document is seen as a sequence of real numbers (a *time series*), and the evaluation of the similarity degree between two XML documents is performed by comparing the corresponding time series based on their *Discrete Fourier Transform*. The worst case time complexity of this approach is $O(N \log N)$, being $N$ the size of the largest document.

In (Helmer, 2007), the notion of *entropy* is used to compute the similarity of two XML documents $D_1$ and $D_2$. First, structural information like tags, edges or paths are extracted from the documents. This information is stored in two separate files $F_1$ and $F_2$; each of these files is compressed by applying the GNU zip software; let $S(F_1)$ and $S(F_2)$ be the sizes of $F_1$ and $F_2$ after compression. $F_1$ and $F_2$ are then concatenated into a new file $F_{12}$ which, in its turn, is compressed again. Let $S(F_{12})$ be the size of the compressed version of $F_{12}$. The similarity between $D_1$ and $D_2$ is computed as follows:

$$sim(D_1, D_2) = \{S(F_{12}) - \min\{S(F_1), S(F_2)\}\} / \max\{S(F_1), S(F_2)\}$$

Intuitively, this algorithm relies on the idea that the higher the similarity of two documents, the higher their overlap; and, the higher the overlap of two documents, the better their compression ratio. The time complexity of the algorithm presented in (Helmer, 2007) is $O(N)$, being $N$ the number of objects in a file.

# CLUSTERING DTDS AND XML SCHEMAS

Existing approaches to clustering DTDs or XML Schemas can be classified according to the strategy they exploit to model schemas. In Table 2 we report a brief summary of the approaches we shall present in the following.

A first category of approaches (De Meo, Quattrone, Terracina, & Ursino, 2007; Qian, Zhang, Liang, Qian, & Jin, 2000) considers XML Schemas as points of a high dimensional space and maps them onto points of a lower dimensional space. The approach of De Meo et al. (2007) uses semantic matchings to perform the clustering of XML Schemas. In particular, given a set of schemas $S$, it builds a multi-dimensional vectorial space $V$, which is generated by the elements appearing in the Schemas of $S$; two elements involved in a semantic matching (e.g., two synonymous elements) are collapsed onto a unique dimension of $V$. An arbitrary Schema $S_i \in S$ can be mapped onto a point $P_i$ of $V$. As a consequence, the computation of the distance between two XML Schemas $S_i$ and $S_j$ implies the computation of the Euclidean distance of the points $P_i$ and $P_j$ representing them. This eventually allows the construction of a similarity matrix $M$. Once $M$ has been obtained, any clustering algorithm like K-Means (MacQueen, 1967) or Expectation-Maximization (Dempster, Laird, & Rubin, 1977) can be applied on it.

Qian et al. (2000) propose an approach to cluster DTDs, which operates as follows. In the first stage, it clusters the elements of all available DTDs on the basis of their linguistic similarity. Such a clustering task can be interpreted as a *dimensionality reduction* activity in which the set of the elements generating the available DTDs is mapped onto a lower dimensional space. In this

*Table 2. Description of approaches to clustering XML DTDs/Schemas*

| Approach | Schema Representation | Main Features |
|---|---|---|
| De Meo, Quattrone, Terracina, & Ursino, 2007 | Vector | - Each XML Schema is mapped onto a point on the basis of inter-schema properties<br>- Distance between two Schemas is computed as the Euclidean distance of the points representing them |
| Qian, Zhang, Liang, Qian, & Jin, 2000 | Vector | - Elements of all XML DTDs are clustered on the basis of linguistic similarities<br>- An arbitrary DTD is mapped onto an array having one component for each cluster obtained before |
| Lee, Yang, Hsu, & Yang, 2002 | Tree | - Linguistic matchers are applied to compute the similarity degree of two DTDs<br>- A hierarchical clustering algorithm is applied |
| Nayak & Iryadi, 2007 | Tree | - A thesaurus (e.g., WordNet/ user-defined thesaurus) is used to compute the similarity degree of two XML DTDs/ Schemas.<br>- An arbitrary clustering algorithm is applied |

new space, an arbitrary DTD can be represented as an array having one component for each cluster; the *i*-th component of this array indicates how many elements of the corresponding DTD belong to the *i*-th cluster. Experimental tests showed that these approaches are able to achieve a high level of accuracy; however, the preliminary mapping phase plays a central role and potential inaccuracies/mistakes in it can negatively influence the whole clustering process.

A further category of approaches models XML Schemas as trees (Lee, Yang, Hsu, & Yang, 2002; Nayak & Iryadi, 2007). Structural properties of trees are used, in conjunction with linguistic matchers, to compute the similarity degree of two schemas.

Lee et al. (2002) presents the XClust system. In XClust, a procedure to compute the similarity degree of two DTDs is adopted. This procedure models a DTD as a tree; thanks to this choice, the neighborhood of an element consists of the set of its ancestors and descendants. This neighborhood is used along with linguistic matchers to determine the similarity degree of two DTDs. Finally, a hierarchical clustering algorithm (Han & Kamber, 2006) is applied to obtain the final clusters.

In (Nayak & Iryadi, 2007) the authors introduce the XMine system to cluster both XML Schemas and DTDs. XMine represents DTDs/XML Schemas as rooted and labeled trees. This representation is used to compute the similarity degree of two schemas, with the support of external thesauri (WordNet and a user-defined dictionary to identify abbreviations/acronyms). Once schema similarities have been computed, an arbitrary clustering algorithm can be applied. Approaches based on trees are effective because they consider both the structure and the content of an DTD/XML Schema. However, schemas may be large and the computation of the similarity degree of two schemas may require the corresponding trees to be traversed more times. Such an operation can be computationally expensive and some authors (Algergawy, Schallehn, & Saake, 2008) suggested to reduce computational costs by exploiting suitable data structures (in particular, Prufer sequences (Prufer, 1918)) instead of trees.

## CLUSTERING XML DOCUMENTS

Main existing methods for clustering XML documents can be classified as follows:

- *Graph and tree based approaches*, which model a set of XML documents as labeled graphs/trees, whose nodes represent documents and edges specify the similarity degree of the corresponding documents. Graph and tree algorithms, like the Prim algorithm or tree matching algorithms, are applied to partition the set of nodes into disjoint clusters.

- *Frequent itemsets/substructure mining approaches,* which find frequent subtrees shared by the documents to cluster and exploit these subtrees to perform the clustering task.
- *Semantic approaches,* which use semantic tools, like ontologies, to carry out the clustering task.

In the following we shall describe each of these categories.

## Graph and Tree Based Approaches

Liu, Wang, Hsu, and Herbert (2004) present an approach to cluster XML documents referring to the same "piece of reality". An XML document $D$ is represented as an unordered and labeled tree $T_D$, which is then mapped into a vector of a high-dimensional Euclidean space. The approach requires tools based on the Principal Component Analysis (Jolliffe, 2002) to reduce the dimensionality of these arrays.

In (Costa, Manco, Ortale, & Tagarelli, 2004), the structural clustering of XML documents is based on tree matching and merging algorithms. Tree matching is used to identify the structural similarities existing among the XML document trees; in this way, available documents can be partitioned into homogeneous classes. Then, for each class, a tree (called XML cluster representative) is defined to summarize the main characteristics of the documents belonging to that class. Finally, this partitioning is refined by applying a suitable hierarchical clustering algorithm called XRep.

The importance of summarizing (sets of) XML documents was first raised in (Lian, Cheung, Mamoulis, & Yiu, 2004). Given an XML document $D$, this approach constructs a directed graph $sg(D)$ called *structural graph* (s-graph). It also defines the distance between two structural graphs $sg(D_1)$ and $sg(D_2)$ as the ratio of the number of common edges between $sg(D_1)$ and $sg(D_2)$ and the maximum between the number of the edges of $sg(D_1)$ and $sg(D_2)$. The distance between structural graphs is then exploited to cluster the input XML documents based on a hierarchical clustering algorithm, called S-Grace, derived by the ROCK algorithm (Guha, Rastogi, & Shim, 2000). The authors show that the proposed metric is efficient in the context of XML document clustering, if compared with the methods based on the computation of tree edit distance. In particular, they show that the worst case time complexity of this approach is $O(N^2)$, being $N$ the maximum number of the nodes of the structural graphs to compare. However, some criticisms can be found in the approach of (Lian, Cheung, Mamoulis, & Yiu, 2004); in particular, as observed in (Costa, Manco, Ortale, & Tagarelli, 2004), two documents could share the same structural graph despite they present significant structural differences. A further drawback is that if two documents do not share any edge, their similarity measure is zero even if they could have some elements with the same labels.

In (Dalamagas, Cheng, Winkel, & Sellis, 2006), the authors also suggest to extract a structural summary of an XML document. The structural summary of an XML document is a modified tree in which the redundancies due to repeated and nested nodes are eliminated. The similarity between two XML documents is computed by applying the Chawathe's algorithm on the corresponding structural summaries; the time complexity of such a task is $O(N^2)$, being $N$ the total number of nodes in the trees to match. Next, a labeled graph $G$ is constructed, where the nodes represent XML documents and the edges denote the corresponding similarity degrees; the Prim algorithm is finally applied to partition the set of nodes of $G$ and associates a cluster with each partition.

In XCLS (*XML Clustering by Level Structure*) (Nayak, 2008), a multilevel array is used to represent an XML document; in particular, at the level 0 the array stores the root, whereas at level *i* the array stores the elements whose distance from the root (expressed as the number of edges going from the root to an arbitrary element) is equal to *i*. A suitable function (called *LevelSim*) uses the multilevel array to compute the degree of similarity between two elements; intuitively, LevelSim assigns a high degree of similarity to elements which share a large number of ancestors. In addition, LevelSim considers the level of similarity between an XML document and a cluster of XML documents. XCLS progressively groups the XML documents of a collection by assigning each document to the cluster with the maximum level similarity. Experiments show that XCLS is able to produce fast and accurate results.

An improvement of XCLS algorithm is given by the XCLS+ algorithm (Alishahi, Naghibzadeh, & Aski, 2010). In XCLS+, a more refined data structure to represent an XML document is provided; specifically, a multilevel array is used to represent both the element names and their parents. Such a data structure is useful to represent an XML document both at structural and content level. Experimental trials show that XCLS+ provides more accurate results and is faster than XCLS.

Antonellis, Makris, and Tsirakis (2008) propose XEdge, a clustering algorithm capable of handling both homogeneous and heterogeneous XML documents. Two XML documents are said homogeneous (resp., heterogeneous) if they are generated by the same (resp., different) DTDs. Like XCLS and XCLS+, in XEdge, a multilevel array is used to model the content of an XML document, and a metric is used to compute the similarity degree of two LevelEdge representations. Similarities between XML documents to cluster are stored in a matrix and a suitable partitional clustering algorithm is applied on this matrix.

## Frequent Itemsets/Substructure Mining Approaches

The approaches belonging to this category consider a large collection of XML documents and try to find *substructures* (like paths or subtrees) which frequently co-occur. The rationale behind these approaches is that the use of substructures allows a more robust and accurate similarity computation than that achieved by techniques considering only element/sub-element relationships.

A relevant example of approaches belonging to this category is XProj (Aggarwal, Ta, Wang, Feng, & Zaki, 2007). In order to understand the behavior of this algorithm let us assume that an XML document $D_i$ can be represented through an ordered and labeled tree $T_i$. A substructure $S$ extracted from $T_i$ is defined as an undirected and labeled graph such that: for each node $n_S$ in $S$ there is a node $n_T$ in $T$ and the labels of $n_S$ and $n_T$ coincide; parent-child relationships in $T$ are preserved in $S$; $S$ is a connected and acyclic graph.

Given a collection of XML documents $D$, a substructure $S$ and a real threshold *min_sup*, we say that $S$ is *frequent* if it appears in at least *min_sup* fractions of the documents of $D$. The main idea of XProj consists of building a set of possible frequent substructures and using them to represent available documents. Clearly, it may happen that a document $D_i$ is not perfectly adherent to a substructure $S$ in the sense that it contains only a fraction of the nodes of $S$. In such a case, the similarity degree of $D_i$ and $S$ is computed on the basis of the number of nodes in $S$ which are also nodes in $D_i$. In order to find frequent substructures, XProj uses a variant of BIDE (Wang & Han, 2004), a sequential pattern mining algorithm. In addition, to reduce the computational load, the size of a substructure is kept fixed to a constant value $l$ and an approximate technique for substructure mining is adopted.

In (Kutty, Nayak, & Li, 2009), the authors propose a hybrid clustering approach for XML documents called HCX. In HCX, frequent subtrees are extracted from a collection of XML documents and used to determine the degree of similarity of XML documents. The authors also proposed an extension of HCX, called HCXC (Hybrid Clustering of XML documents using Constraints) (Kutty, Nayak, & Li, 2010). HCXC was presented in the context of the INEX 2009 XML Mining Track; the dataset exploited in that track was a corpus of 2.7 millions of XML pages coming from Wikipedia and written in English. In HCXC, frequent subtrees are extracted from XML documents to generate their content, which is used to cluster documents. Experiments showed that HCHX combines information at structural and content level in a non-linear fashion.

## Semantic Approaches

Semantic approaches represent quite a novel (and, in our opinion, promising) research area. In fact, they combine an in-depth analysis of both content and structural properties of an XML source, which in principle is useful to enhance the accuracy of the clustering process. Most of the approaches falling within this category represent the content and the structure of an XML document by means of a vector; for this reason, semantic approaches could also be classified as vector-based approaches, although they emphasize the role of semantics in the clustering process.

In (Tran, Nayak, & Bruza, 2008), the authors describe both a structural and a content similarity measure for XML documents. Given a collection $D$ of XML documents and a set $P$ of paths extracted from $D$, each document $D_i$ in $D$ is mapped onto a vector $v_i$ such that each the $l$-th component of $v_i$ reflects the frequency with which the path $p_l$ appears in $d_i$. The structural distance of two documents $D_i$ and $D_j$ is then computed as the Euclidean distance of the vectors $v_i$ and $v_j$. As for content similarity analysis, Singular Value Decomposition is applied on $D$ in such a way as to map each document onto an array of concepts; next, the cosine similarity is applied to measure the degree of content similarity of two documents. A weighted mean of structural and content similarity values is computed to determine the overall similarity degree of two documents. Experiments proved that content similarity produces a better solution in the case of homogeneous documents (i.e., documents coming from the same DTD); in case of heterogeneous documents (i.e., document generated by different DTDs) the combination of structural and content similarity measures achieves the best results.

A similar approach is proposed in (Nagwani & Bhansali, 2010). In this approach, structural similarity of two XML documents is defined as their tree edit distance, and a range of techniques (like Jaccard Coefficient and TF-IDF) is used to detect the similarity of two documents on the basis of their content. Structural and content similarity measures are then combined for calculating the distance between any two homogeneous XML documents.

A combination of structural and content-based features is used in (Yongming, Dehua, & Jiajin, 2008) to compute a similarity measure between any pair of XML documents, whereas a hierarchical clustering algorithm is used to group documents into clusters.

A very notable approach belonging to the category of semantic approaches is SemXClust (Tagarelli & Greco, 2010). This approach constructs a description of available XML data both at the content and the structural levels. Information at the content level is extracted from textual elements, whereas structural information is derived from the analysis of tag paths. These two kinds of information are enriched with the knowledge provided by an external lexical ontology and are exploited to determine if two documents are semantically related. An important feature of SemXClust is the definition of an XML representation model (called *tree tuple*) that allows XML document trees to be mapped onto transactional data. XML transactions are then provided as input to a suitable transactional clustering algorithm. As for the clustering technique to be adopted, even if SemXClust has been conceived to be parametric against any existing clustering algorithm, the authors propose two new algorithms; the first exploits a centroid-based partitional method, whereas the second uses frequent (XML) itemsets to compute clusters and to build a hierarchy upon them.

In Table 3 we summarize the main features of the approaches discussed in this section. Note that, as for the Frequent itemsets/subtrees category, we do not report the corresponding clustering algorithms because in this approach the phase devoted to compute document similarity and the phase of clustering documents are not independent to each other.

## FURTHER RESEARCH DIRECTIONS

Despite a large body of work have been done in the fields of XML Schema/DTD matching, XML document similarity computation and clustering of XML Schemas and documents, a significant number of problems regarding the efficiency and accuracy in the clustering of XML data sources still remain open. In addition, many authors are investigating applications that benefit from the clustering of XML data sources. In the following, we shall briefly discuss a list of future research directions in the area of XML data clustering.

### Defining Collaborative Clustering Approaches

Most of the existing approaches to clustering XML documents rely on centralized algorithms. Recently, some authors suggested a collaborative

*Table 3. A summary of the features of approaches to clustering XML documents*

| Category | Approach | Similarity Computation | Clustering Algorithm |
|---|---|---|---|
| *Graph & Tree Based* | Dalamagas, Cheng, Winkel & Sellis, 2006 | Dynamic Programming | Prim algorithm |
| | Liu, Wang, Hsu, & Herbert, 2004 | Vector Similarity | Principal Component Analysis |
| | Costa, Manco, Ortale, & Tagarelli, 2004 | Tree Matching | Hierarchical Clustering (XRep) |
| | Lian, Cheung, Mamoulis, & Yiu, 2004 | Path Matching | Hierarchical Clustering (similar to ROCK) |
| | Antonellis, Makris, & Tsirakis, 2008 | Multilevel Array Similarity | Partitional Clustering |
| *Frequent itemsets/subtrees* | Aggarwal, Ta, Wang, Feng, & Zaki, 2007 | Frequent Substructures plus the Bide algorithm (Wang & Han, 2004) | - |
| | Kutty, Nayak, & Li, 2009 | Frequent subtrees | - |
| *Semantic approaches* | Tran, Nayak, & Bruza, 2008 | Path Similarity plus Singular Value Decomposition | Any clustering algorithm can be applied |
| | Nagwani & Bhansali, 2010 | Tree Edit Distance plus content similarity (TF-IDF, Jaccard, etc.) | Any clustering algorithm can be applied |
| | Yongming, Dehua, & Jiajin, 2008 | Structural plus Content-Based analysis | Hierarchical Clustering |
| | Tagarelli & Greco, 2010 | Structure and Content Analysis plus Lexical Ontology | Transactional Clustering |

approach to data clustering (Hammouda & Kamel, 2009). The rationale behind these approaches is that there are scenarios in which a centralized clustering algorithm yields result which are in opposition with the end-user expectations. For instance, let us consider the case of multiple digital libraries, each owing a collection of documents and assume that the collections of two different libraries may partially overlap. In such a case, we would not like all the documents were clustered and stored in a single location; instead, a more natural solution is that each digital library is allowed to cluster its own collection of documents. To better perform clustering, independent libraries could exchange information.

In collaborative approaches, the clustering task can be performed by independent computers (*peers*). Each peer in the network is allowed to compute a local clustering solution over its own data, and to exchange information with other peers. In detail, each peer exchanges a data structure with other peers; such a data structure summarizes the main features of the local clustering solution a peer would produce. For instance, in the approach of (Hammouda & Kamel, 2009) such a summary consists of a set of vectors; in the approach of (Greco, Gullo, Ponti, & Tagarelli, 2009), which is specialized for XML documents, the summary is the set of centroids of the clusters to generate. Exchanged information plays the role of recommendations offered by a peer to other peers. As a consequence, the overall clustering activity can be depicted as a collaborative process in which peers exchange recommendation to produce a global clustering solution. Experimental trials show that collaborative approaches are effective in raising the accuracy of clustering process; in addition, the network load generated by the exchange of messages among the various peers is relatively small (Greco, Gullo, Ponti & Tagarelli, 2009).

## Using Structural Properties in Ontology Learning Process

In the past years, several approaches have suggested to use machine learning techniques in conjunction with Semantic Web tools. For instance, a popular research field is *ontology learning* (Maedche & Staab, 2001); in ontology learning a corpus of text documents is processed by means of techniques coming from Natural Language Processing in order to extract relevant entities from text; classification or clustering algorithms are often applied to automatically learn relations between two documents. More recently, many researchers are focusing on the ontology learning process in the context of Social Web applications; in particular, in the context of Social Web a rapidly growing phenomenon is given by *folksonomies* (i.e., data structures in which users are allowed to label and classify resources of various type like photos or videos by applying tags). Some authors (Specia & Motta, 2007; De Meo, Quattrone, & Ursino, 2009, 2010) describe methods for extracting knowledge from a folksonomy and organize it in a taxonomic form.

The rapid growth of XML document explains the need of ad-hoc methods for learning ontologies from a corpus of XML documents. In fact, the knowledge of the structure of a document can provide a meaningful benefits to the learning process and it could effectively complement Natural Language Processing techniques.

## Improving the Performance of an Information Retrieval Engine

According to the Jardine and van Rijsbergen hypothesis (Jardine & van Rijsbergen, 1971), the relevance for a given user query is similar for documents that belong to the same cluster. Based on this assumption, the solution of a document clustering algorithm can be used to answer the user query more efficiently: once a user submits a query, we do not longer need to search in a whole collection of documents but we could forward the query to a small number of clusters of documents. The final outcome is an increase of the throughput of an Information Retrieval system as the time elapsed between a user submits a query and the answer returned is much lower. Recently, at the INEX 2010 XML Mining track (INEX, 2010), researchers from data mining, information retrieval, machine learning and XML communities have proposed and tested their XML data clustering algorithms on significant volumes of data to assess whether the Jardine and van Rijsbergen hypothesis holds on very large datasets. In particular, the organizers of INEX track provided a corpus of 144,625 documents extracted from Wikipedia.

In the context of e-government (De Meo, Hind, Quattrone, & Ursino, 2006) suggest to model e-government service providers as XML databases and apply clustering algorithms to group governmental data sources into clusters. Experiments showed that the task of grouping XML government databases yields an improvement in the accuracy of query answering process.

## CONCLUSION

Clustering XML sources is a very important research problem with relevant applications in many practical domains like information retrieval, data integration, Web mining and XML query processing. In this chapter, we proposed a survey on the extraction of interschema properties from heterogeneous XML sources and on their role in XML source clustering.

Initially, we showed that the knowledge of the relationships involving objects belonging to the XML sources to cluster can significantly help the clustering process. We investigated the XML source clustering problem at two different levels, namely the intensional one (which involves DTDs and XML Schemas) and the extensional one (which involves XML documents). We also described a large number of approaches that construct relationships involving objects belonging to different XML sources. Finally, we presented various approaches that exploit derived relationships to perform XML source clustering at the intensional level and the extensional one.

## REFERENCES

Aggarwal, C. C., Ta, N., Wang, J., Feng, J., & Zaki, M. J. (2007). XProj: A framework for projected structural clustering of XML documents. In P. Berkhin, R. Caruana, & X. Wu (Eds.), *Proceedings of the 13th ACM SIGKDD International Conference on Knowledge Discovery and Data Mining (KDD),* (pp. 46-55). ACM.

Algergawy, A., Nayak, R., & Saake, G. (2010). Element similarity measures in XML schema matching. *Information Sciences, 180*(24), 4975–4998. doi:10.1016/j.ins.2010.08.022

Algergawy, A., Schallehn, E., & Saake, G. (2008). A schema matching-based approach to XML schema clustering. In *Proceedings of the International Conference on Information Integration and Web-based Application and Services (iiWAS)*, (pp. 131-136). ACM.

Algergawy, A., Schallehn, E., & Saake, G. (2009). Improving XML schema matching using Prufer sequences. *Data & Knowledge Engineering, 68*(8), 728–747. doi:10.1016/j.datak.2009.01.001

Alishahi, M., Naghibzadeh, M., & Aski, B. S. (2010). Tag name structure-based clustering of XML documents. *International Journal of Computer and Electrical Engineering, 2*(1).

Antonellis, P., Makris, C., & Tsirakis, N. (2008). XEdge: Clustering homogeneous and heterogeneous XML documents using edge summaries. In R. L. Wainwright & H. Haddad (Eds.), *Proceedings of the 2008 ACM Symposium on Applied Computing (SAC)*, (pp. 1081-1088). ACM.

Batini, C., & Lenzerini, M. (1984). A methodology for data schema integration in the entity/relationship model. *IEEE Transactions on Software Engineering, 10*(6), 650–664. doi:10.1109/TSE.1984.5010294

Broder, A. Z. (1997). On the resemblance and containment of documents. In *Proceedings of the International Conference on the Compression and Complexity of Sequences (SEQUENCES)*, (pp. 21-29). IEEE Computer Society.

Buttler, D. (2004). A short survey of document structure similarity algorithms. In H. R. Arabnia & O. Droegehorn (Eds.), *Proceedings of the International Conference on Internet Computing (IC)*, (pp. 3-9). CSREA Press.

Chawathe, S. (1999). Comparing hierarchical data in external memory. In M. P. Atkinson, M. E. Orlowska, P. Valduriez, S. B. Zdonik, & M. L. Brodie (Eds.), *Proceedings of the International Conference on Very Large Databases (VLDB),* (pp. 90-101). Morgan Kaufmann.

Chawathe, S., Rajaraman, A., Garcia-Molina, H., & Widom, J. (1996). Change detection in hierarchically structured information. In H. V. Jagadish, & I. S. Mumick (Eds.), *Proceedings of the ACM International Conference on Data Management (SIGMOD)*, (pp. 26-37). ACM.

Cobéna, G., Abiteboul, S., & Marian, A. (2002). Detecting changes in XML documents. In *Proceedings of the 18th IEEE International Conference on Data Engineering (ICDE)*, (pp. 41-52). IEEE Computer Society.

Cohen, W., & Hirsh, H. (1998). Joins that generalize: Text classification using Whirl. In *Proceedings of the 4th International Conference on Knowledge Discovery and Data Mining (KDD),* (pp. 169-173). AAAI Press.

Cohen, W., Ravikumar, P., & Fienberg, S. (2003). A comparison of string metrics for matching names and records. In *Proceedings of the International Workshop on Data Cleaning and Object Consolidation at the International Conference on Knowledge Discovery and Data Mining (KDD),* (pp. 73-78). ACM.

Costa, G., Manco, G., Ortale, R., & Tagarelli, A. (2004). A tree-based approach to clustering XML documents by structure. In J.-F. Boulicaut, F. Esposito, F. Giannotti, & D. Pedreschi (Eds.), *Proceedings of the European Conference on Principles of Knowledge Discovery in Databases (PKDD) Lecture Notes in Computer Science: Vol. 3202* (pp. 137-148). Springer.

Dalamagas, T., Cheng, T., Winkel, K., & Sellis, T. K. (2006). A methodology for clustering XML documents by structure. *Information Systems, 31*(3), 187–228. doi:10.1016/j.is.2004.11.009

De Meo, P., Fadil, H., Quattrone, G., & Ursino, D. (2006). A multi-agent system for efficiently managing query answering in an e-government scenario. In Hisham Haddad (Ed.), *Proceedings of the ACM Symposium on Applied Computing (SAC),* (pp. 308-312). ACM.

De Meo, P., Quattrone, G., Terracina, G., & Ursino, D. (2004a). Deriving sub-schema similarities from semantically heterogeneous XML sources. In *Proceedings of the International Conference on Cooperative Information Systems (CoopIS)* [Springer.]. *Lecture Notes in Computer Science, 3290*, 209–226.

De Meo, P., Quattrone, G., Terracina, G., & Ursino, D. (2004b). Extraction of synonymies, hyponymies, overlappings and homonymies from XML schemas at various "severity" levels. In *Proceedings of the International Database Engineering and Applications Symposium (IDEAS)*, (pp. 389-394). IEEE Computer Society.

De Meo, P., Quattrone, G., Terracina, G., & Ursino, D. (2006). Integration of XML schemas at various "severity" levels. *Information Systems*, *31*(6), 397–434. doi:10.1016/j.is.2004.11.010

De Meo, P., Quattrone, G., Terracina, G., & Ursino, D. (2007). An approach to extracting interschema properties from XML schemas at various severity levels. *Informatica*, *31*(2), 217–232.

De Meo, P., Quattrone, G., Terracina, G., & Ursino, D. (2007). Semantics-guided clustering of heterogeneous XML schemas. *Journal on Data Semantics*, *9*, 39–81.

De Meo, P., Quattrone, G., & Ursino, D. (2009). Exploitation of semantic relationships and hierarchical data structures to support a user in his annotation and browsing activities in folksonomies. *Information Systems*, *34*(6), 511–535. doi:10.1016/j.is.2009.02.004

De Meo, P., Quattrone, G., & Ursino, D. (2010). A query expansion and user profile enrichment approach to improve the performance of recommender systems operating on a folksonomy. *User Modeling and User-Adapted Interaction*, *20*(1), 41–86. doi:10.1007/s11257-010-9072-6

De Meo, P., Terracina, G., & Ursino, D. (2004). X-Global: A system for the "almost automatic" and semantic integration of XML sources at various flexibility levels. *Journal of Universal Computer Science*, *10*(9), 1065–1109.

Dempster, A. P., Laird, N. M., & Rubin, D. B. (1977). Maximum likelihood from incomplete data via the EM algorithm. *Journal of the Royal Statistical Society. Series B. Methodological*, *39*(1), 1–38.

Dhamankar, R., Lee, Y., Doan, A., Halevy, A., & Domingos, P. (2004). iMAP: Discovering complex semantic matches between database schemas. In *Proceedings of the ACM International Conference on Management of Data (SIGMOD)*, (pp. 383-394). ACM.

Do, H., & Rahm, E. (2002). COMA - A system for flexible combination of schema matching approaches. In *Proc. of the International Conference on Very Large Databases* (*VLDB 2002*), (pp. 610–621). Hong Kong, China, 2002. VLDB Endowment.

Do, H., & Rahm, E. (2002). COMA: A system for flexible combination of schema matching approaches. In *Proceedings of the 28th International Conference on Very Large Data Bases* (*VLDB*), (pp. 610-621).

Do, H., & Rahm, E. (2007). Matching large schemas: Approaches and evaluation. *Information Systems*, *32*(6), 857–885. doi:10.1016/j.is.2006.09.002

Doan, A., Domingos, P., & Halevy, A. Y. (2001). Reconciling schemas of disparate data sources: A machine-learning approach. In *Proceedings of the ACM International Conference on Management of Data (SIGMOD)*, (pp. 509-520). ACM.

Doan, A., Madhavan, J., Domingos, P., & Halevy, A. Y. (2002). Learning to map between ontologies on the Semantic Web. In *Proceedings of the ACM International Conference on World Wide Web (WWW)*, (pp. 662-673). ACM.

Duchateau, F., Bellahsene, Z., & Roche, M. (2007). A context-based measure for discovering approximate semantic matching between schema elements. In C. Rolland, O. Pastor, & J.-L. Cavarero (Eds.), *Proceedings of the 1st International Conference on Research Challenges in Information Science (RCIS)*, (pp. 9-20).

Euzenat, J., & Shvaiko, P. (2007). *Ontology matching*. Springer.

Euzenat, J., & Valtchev, P. (2004). Similarity-based ontology alignment in OWL-lite. In *Proceedings of the 16th European Conference on Artificial Intelligence (ECAI)*, (pp. 333-337). IOS Press.

Fankhauser, P., Kracker, M., & Neuhold, E. J. (1991). Semantic vs. structural resemblance of classes. *SIGMOD Record*, *20*(4), 59–63. doi:10.1145/141356.141383

Flesca, S., Manco, G., Masciari, E., Pontieri, L., & Pugliese, A. (2005). Fast detection of XML structural similarity. *IEEE Transactions on Knowledge and Data Engineering*, *17*(2), 160–175. doi:10.1109/TKDE.2005.27

Gal, A., Anaby-Tavor, A., Trombetta, A., & Montesi, D. (2005). A framework for modeling and evaluating automatic semantic reconciliation. *The VLDB Journal*, *14*(1), 50–67. doi:10.1007/s00778-003-0115-z

Galil, Z. (1986). Efficient algorithms for finding maximum matching in graphs. *ACM Computing Surveys*, *18*(1), 23–38. doi:10.1145/6462.6502

Giunchiglia, F. Shvaiko., P., & Yatskevich, M. (2005). Semantic schema matching. *Proceedings of the International Conference on Cooperative Information Systems (CoopIS) Lecture Notes in Computer Science: Vol. 3760.* (pp. 347-365). Springer.

Giunchiglia, F., & Yatskevich, M. (2004). Element level semantic matching. In *Proceedings of the International Meaning Coordination and Negotiation Workshop co-located with 3rd International Semantic Web Conference (ISWC)*, (pp. 37-48).

Giunchiglia, F., Yatskevich, M., & Shvaiko, P. (2007). Semantic matching: Algorithms and implementation. *Journal on Data Semantics*, *9*, 1–38.

Greco, S., Gullo, F., Ponti, G., & Tagarelli, A. (2009). Collaborative clustering of XML documents. In *Proceedings of the International Conference on Parallel Processing Workshops (ICPP Workshops)*, (pp. 579-586). IEEE Computer Society.

Guha, S., Rastogi, R., & Shim, K. (2000). ROCK: A robust clustering algorithm for categorical attributes. *Information Systems*, *25*(5), 345–366. doi:10.1016/S0306-4379(00)00022-3

Hammouda, K. M., & Kamel, M. S. (2009). Hierarchically distributed peer-to-peer document clustering and cluster summarization. *IEEE Transactions on Knowledge and Data Engineering*, *21*(5), 681–698. doi:10.1109/TKDE.2008.189

Han, J., & Kamber, M. (2006). *Data mining: Concepts and techniques*. Morgan Kaufman.

He, B., & Chang, K. C.-C. (2006). Automatic complex schema matching across web query interfaces: A correlation mining approach. *ACM Transactions on Database Systems*, *31*(1), 346–395. doi:10.1145/1132863.1132872

Helmer, S. (2007). Measuring the structural similarity of semistructured documents using entropy. In *Proceedings of the 33rd International Conference on Very Large Data Bases (VLDB)*, (pp. 1022-1032). ACM.

Idrissi, Y. B., & Vachon (2007). A context-based approach for the discovery of complex matches between database sources. In R. Wagner and N. Revell, & G. Pernul (Eds.), *Proceedings of the International Conference on Database and Expert Systems Applications (DEXA) Lecture Notes in Computer Science: Vol. 4653* (pp. 864-873). Springer.

INEX. (2010). *INEX 2010 XML mining track.* Retrieved from http://www.inex.otago.ac.nz/tracks/wiki-mine/wiki-mine.asp

Jardine, N., & van Rijsbergen, C. J. (1971). The use of hierarchic clustering in information retrieval. *Information Storage and Retrieval*, *7*(5), 217–240. doi:10.1016/0020-0271(71)90051-9

Jaro, M. A. (1995). Probabilistic linkage of large public health data file. *Statistics in Medicine*, *14*(5-7), 491–498. doi:10.1002/sim.4780140510

Jeh, G., & Widom, J. (2002). SimRank: A measure of structural-context similarity. *Proc. of the ACM Conference on Knowledge Discovery and Data Mining (KDD)*, (pp. 538-543). ACM.

Jeh, G., & Widom, J. (2003). Scaling personalized web search. *Proceedings of the ACM Conference on World Wide Web (WWW)*, (pp. 271-279). ACM.

Jeong, B., Lee, D., Cho, H., & Lee, J. (2008). A novel method for measuring semantic similarity for XML schema matching. *Expert Systems with Applications*, *34*(3), 1651–1658. doi:10.1016/j.eswa.2007.01.025

Jolliffe, I. T. (2002). *Principal component analysis* (2nd ed.). Springer.

Joshi, S., Agrawal, N., Krishnapuram, R., & Negi, S. (2003). A bag of paths model for measuring structural similarity in web documents. In L. Getoor, T. E. Senator, P. Domingos, & C. Faloutsos (Eds.), *Proceedings of the ACM Conference on Knowledge Discovery and Data Mining (KDD)*, (pp. 577-582). ACM.

Kantere, V., Tsoumakos, D., Sellis, T. K., & Roussopoulos, N. (2009). GrouPeer: Dynamic clustering of P2P databases. *Information Systems*, *34*(1), 62–86. doi:10.1016/j.is.2008.04.002

Kementsietsidis, A. (2009). Schema matching. In Liu, L., & Özsu, M. T. (Eds.), *Encyclopedia of database systems* (pp. 2494–2497). Springer, US.

Kohonen, T. (1988). *Self-organization and associative memory*. Springer.

Kriegel, H.-P., & Schönauer, S. (2003). Similarity search in structured data. In *Proceedings of the 5$^{th}$ International Conference on Data Warehousing and Knowledge Discovery (DaWaK)* [Springer.]. *Lecture Notes in Computer Science*, *2737*, 309–319. doi:10.1007/978-3-540-45228-7_31

Kullback, S., & Leibler, R. A. (1951). On information and sufficiency. *Annals of Mathematical Statistics*, *22*(1), 79–86. doi:10.1214/aoms/1177729694

Kutty, S., Nayak, R., & Li, Y. (2009). HCX: An efficient hybrid clustering approach for XML documents. In U. M. Borghoff, & B. Chidlovskii (Eds.), *Proceedings of the 2009 ACM Symposium on Document Engineering (DocEng)*, (pp. 94-97). ACM.

Kutty, S., Nayak, R., & Li, Y. (2009). Utilising semantic tags in XML clustering. In S. Geva, J. Kamps, & A. Trotman (Eds.), *Focused Retrieval and Evaluation, 8th International Workshop of the Initiative for the Evaluation of XML Retrieval (INEX) Lecture Notes in Computer Science: Vol. 6203* (pp. 416-425). Springer.

Lee, M. L., Yang, L. H., Hsu, W., & Yang, X. (2002). XClust: Clustering XML schemas for effective integration. In *Proceedings of the International Conference on Information and Knowledge Management (CIKM)*, (pp. 292–299). ACM.

Li, W. S., & Clifton, C. (2000). SEMINT: A tool for identifying attribute correspondences in heterogeneous databases using neural networks. *Data & Knowledge Engineering*, *33*(1), 49–84. doi:10.1016/S0169-023X(99)00044-0

Lian, W., Cheung, D. W., Mamoulis, N., & Yiu, S. (2004). An efficient and scalable algorithm for clustering XML documents by structure. *IEEE Transactions on Knowledge and Data Engineering*, *16*(1), 82–96. doi:10.1109/TKDE.2004.1264824

Liben-Nowell, D., & Kleinberg, J. M. (2003). The link prediction problem for social networks. *Proceedings of the ACM International Conference on Information and Knowledge Management (CIKM)*, (pp. 556-559). ACM.

Liu, J., Wang, J. T. L., Hsu, W., & Herbert, K. G. (2004). XML clustering by principal component analysis. In *Proceedings of the 16th IEEE International Conference on Tools with Artificial Intelligence (ICTAI)*, (pp. 658–662). IEEE Computer Society.

MacQueen, J. B. (1967). Some methods for classification and analysis of multivariate observations. In *Proceedings of the International Symposium on Mathematics, Statistics and Probability*, (pp. 281-297). University of California Press.

Madhavan, J., Bernstein, P. A., & Rahm, E. (2001). Generic schema matching with Cupid. In P. M. G. Apers, P. Atzeni, S. Ceri, S. Paraboschi, K. Ramamohanarao, & R. T. Snodgrass (Eds.), *Proceedings of the International Conference on Very Large Data Bases (VLDB)*, (pp. 49-58). Morgan Kaufmann.

Maedche, A., & Staab, S. (2001). Ontology learning for the Semantic Web. *IEEE Intelligent Systems*, *16*(2), 72–79. doi:10.1109/5254.920602

Melnik, S., Garcia-Molina, H., & Rahm, E. (2002). Similarity flooding: A versatile graph matching algorithm and its application to schema matching. In *Proceedings of the IEEE International Conference on Data Engineering (ICDE)*, (pp. 117-128). IEEE Computer Society.

Melnik, S., Rahm, E., & Bernstein, P. A. (2003). Rondo: A programming platform for generic model management. In A. Y. Halevy, Z. G. Ives, & A. Doan (Eds.), *Proceedings of the International Conference on Management of Data (SIGMOD)*, (pp. 193-204). ACM.

Miller, G. A. (1995). WordNet: A lexical database for English. *Communications of the ACM*, *38*(11), 39–41. doi:10.1145/219717.219748

Myers, E. (1986). An *O(ND)* difference algorithm and its variations. *Algorithmica*, *1*(2), 251–266. doi:10.1007/BF01840446

Nayak, R. (2008). Fast and effective clustering of XML data using structural information. *Knowledge and Information Systems*, *14*(2), 197–215. doi:10.1007/s10115-007-0080-8

Nayak, R., & Iryadi, W. (2007). XML schema clustering with semantic and hierarchical similarity measures. *Knowledge-Based Systems*, *20*(4), 336–349. doi:10.1016/j.knosys.2006.08.006

Nayak, R., & Tran, T. (2007). A progressive clustering algorithm to group the XML data by structural and semantic similarity. *International Journal of Pattern Recognition and Artificial Intelligence*, *21*(4), 723–743. doi:10.1142/S0218001407005648

Nierman, A., & Jagadish, H. V. (2002). Evaluating structural similarity in XML documents. In *Proceedings of the International Workshop on the Web and Databases (WebDB)*, (pp. 61-66).

Oracle, X. M. L. D. B. (2010). *Database features*. Retrieved from http://www.oracle.com/technetwork/database/features/xmldb/index.html

Palopoli, L., Saccà, D., Terracina, G., & Ursino, D. (2003). Uniform techniques for deriving similarities of objects and subschemes in heterogeneous databases. *IEEE Transactions on Knowledge and Data Engineering*, *15*(2), 271.294.

Prufer, H. (1918). Neuer Beweis eines Satzes uber Permutationen. *Archiv fur Mathematik und Physik*, *27*, 742–744.

Qian, W., Zhang, L., Liang, Y., Qian, H., & Jin, W. (2000). A two-level method for clustering DTDs. In H. Lu, & A. Zhou (Eds.), *Proceedings of the International Conference on Web-Age Information Management (WAIM) Lecture Notes in Computer Science: Vol. 1846* (pp. 41-52). Springer.

Quix, C., Kensche, D., & Li, X. (2007). Matching of ontologies with XML schemas using a generic metamodel. In *Proceedings of the International Conference on Cooperative Information Systems (CoopIS)* [Springer.]. *Lecture Notes in Computer Science*, *4803*, 1081–1098. doi:10.1007/978-3-540-76848-7_71

Rafiei, D., Moise, D. L., & Sun, D. (2006). Finding syntactic similarities between XML documents. In *Proceedings of the International Conference on Database and Expert Systems Applications (DEXA)*, (pp. 512-516). IEEE Computer Society.

Rahm, E., & Bernstein, P. A. (2001). A survey of approaches to automatic schema matching. *The VLDB Journal*, *10*(4), 334–350. doi:10.1007/s007780100057

Saleem, K., Bellahsene, Z., & Hunt, E. (2008). PORSCHE: Performance oriented schema mediation. *Information Systems*, *33*(7-8), 637–657. doi:10.1016/j.is.2008.01.010

Shasha, D., & Zhang, K. (1997). Approximate tree pattern matching. In Apostolico, A., & Galil, Z. (Eds.), *Pattern matching in strings, trees and arrays* (pp. 341–371). Oxford University Press.

Shvaiko, P., & Euzenat, J. (2005). A survey of schema-based matching approaches. *Journal of Data Semantics*, 146-171.

Shvaiko, P., Giunchiglia, F., & Yatskevich, M. (2010). Semantic matching with S-Match. In De Virgilio, R., Giunchiglia, F., & Tanca, L. (Eds.), *Semantic Web information management: A model-based perspective* (pp. 183–202). Springer.

Tagarelli, A., & Greco, S. (2010). Semantic clustering of XML documents. *ACM Transactions on Information Systems*, *28*(1), 1–56. doi:10.1145/1658377.1658380

Tai, K.-C. (1979). The tree-to-tree correction problem. *Journal of the ACM*, *26*(3), 422–433. doi:10.1145/322139.322143

Tamino. (2010). The XML database–Software AG. Retrieved from http://www.softwareag.com/Corporate/products/wm/tamino

Tansalarak, N., & Claypool, K. T. (2007). QMatch – Using paths to match XML schemas. *Data & Knowledge Engineering*, *60*(2), 260–282. doi:10.1016/j.datak.2006.03.002

Theobald, M., Schenkel, R., & Weikum, G. (2003). Exploiting structure, annotation, and ontological knowledge for automatic classification of XML data. In *Proceedings of the 6th International Workshop on the Web and Databases (WebDB)*, (pp. 1-6).

Thompson, H. S., Beech, D., Maloney, M., & Mendelsohn, N. (Eds.). (2004). *XML schema part 1: Structures*. W3C recommendation. Retrieved from http://www.w3.org/TR/xmlschema-1

Tran, T., Nayak, R., & Bruza, P. (2008). Combining structure and content similarities for XML document clustering. *In Proceedings of the Australasian Data Mining Conference (AusDM)*, (pp. 219-226).

Wagner, R. A., & Fisher, M. J. (1974). The string-to-string correction problem. *Journal of the ACM*, *21*(1), 168–173. doi:10.1145/321796.321811

Wang, J., & Han, J. (2004). BIDE: Efficient mining of frequent closed sequences. *Proceedings 20th International Conference on Data Engineering (ICDE)*, (pp. 79-90). IEEE Computer Society.

Wojnar, A., Mlynkova, I., & Dokulil, J. (2010). Structural and semantic aspects of similarity of document type definitions and XML schemas. *Information Sciences*, *180*(10), 1817–1836. doi:10.1016/j.ins.2009.12.024

Wolpert, D. H. (1992). Stacked generalization. *Neural Networks*, *5*(2), 241–259. doi:10.1016/S0893-6080(05)80023-1

Yang, J., Cheung, W. K., & Chen, X. (2005). Learning the kernel matrix for XML document clustering. In *Proceedings of the IEEE International Conference on e-Technology, e-Commerce and e-Service (EEE)*, (pp. 353-358). IEEE Computer Society.

Yang, R., Kalnis, P., & Tung, A. K. H. (2005). Similarity evaluation on tree-structured data. In *Proceedings of the ACM International Conference on Management of Data (CIKM)*, (pp. 754-765). ACM.

Yongming, G., Dehua, C., & Jiajin, L. (2008). Clustering XML documents by combining content and structure. In *Proceedings of the International Symposium on Information Science and Engineering (ISISE)* (pp. 583-587).

Yoon, J. P., Raghavan, V., & Chakilam, V. (2001). BitCube: A three-dimensional bitmap indexing for XML documents. In *Proc. of the International Conference on Scientific and Statistical Database Management (SSDBM)*, (pp. 158-167). IEEE Computer Society.

Ziv, J., & Lempel, A. (1978). Compression of individual sequences via variable-rate coding. *IEEE Transactions on Information Theory, 24*(5), 530–536. doi:10.1109/TIT.1978.1055934

Ziv, J., & Merhav, N. (1993). A measure of relative entropy between individual sequences with application to universal classification. *IEEE Transactions on Information Theory, 39*(4), 1270–1279. doi:10.1109/18.243444

# Chapter 7
# XML Document Clustering:
## An Algorithmic Perspective

**Panagiotis Antonellis**
*University of Patras, Greece*

## ABSTRACT

*The wide use of XML as the de facto standard of storing and exchanging information through Internet has led a wide spectrum of heterogeneous applications to adopt XML as their information representation model. The heterogeneity of XML data sources has brought up the problem of efficiently clustering a set of XML documents. However, traditional clustering algorithms cannot be applied due to the semistructured nature of XML, which contains both structure and content features. Hence, special techniques should be used that would take into account the XML semantics in order to address the problem of XML clustering. The described approaches, based on either the structure or the content or both, manage to successfully address the problem and can be applied efficiently in real-world applications.*

## INTRODUCTION

The wide acceptance of the Web as a means of information and data exchange combined with the growth of native XML databases has designated the problem of efficient data mining techniques on semistructured data. Traditional approaches have proven inefficient as they are mainly oriented to well- structured data, like relational databases, while Web data and XML databases are based on semistructured formats.

*Clustering* (Jain & Dubes, 1988) is a major exploratory task in data mining which uses an unsupervised learning approach to divide a set of items into subsets (called clusters) so that items in the same cluster are similar in some sense. As an advanced statistical data analysis approach, clustering has been widely adopted in several applications and research contexts, including machine learning, pattern recognition, image

DOI: 10.4018/978-1-61350-356-0.ch007

analysis and bioinformatics. An important step in every clustering approach is to define a notion of proximity between the items to be clustered. Proximity functions include both distance and similarity measures, such as the well-known Euclidean distance and Manhattan distance (typically used in geometrical data spaces), the cosine similarity (particularly suitable for clustering high dimensional data, including text data), and the Hamming distance, which measures the minimum number of substitutions required to change one item into another (see Chapter "XML Similarity Detection and Measures").

The Jardine and van Rijsbergen cluster hypothesis (1971) states that documents that are clustered together have a similar relevance to a given query. If the cluster hypothesis holds, and if a suitable clustering can be achieved, then a clustering solution will minimise the number of clusters that need to be searched to satisfy any given query. If only a small fraction of clusters (hence documents) need to be searched for, then the throughput of an information retrieval system will be greatly improved. Documents belonging to the same cluster will likely refer to same topic or contain similar text information. Although there exist various measures for computing the proximity between a pair of documents, such measures are always defined on the text content within each document. Most existing document clustering approaches rely on the Vector Space Model (VSM) representation, and hence use an appropriate similarity measure between the vectorial representations of the documents (for example, the cosine similarity).

With the rapid growth of the size of XML information exchanged, data management and processing issues, such as storage, mining and retrieval of large collections of XML documents have also arisen. Clustering of XML documents improves the process of management and retrieval as it organizes the massive amounts of XML documents into groups without prior knowledge. This grouping may boost the process of querying by applying the user queries only to related groups of XML documents.

Unlike the clustering of text documents, XML document clustering is an intricate process which introduces some new challenges. The new challenges can be summarized as follows:

- XML documents contain structural features (that is, element tags/attributes and their nesting therein) as well as their text data (content features). Regarding the application domain, either the structural features or the content features may be important. However, there are cases in which both the structure and the contents should be considered during clustering in order to achieve meaningful results. Traditional clustering algorithms are tuned for clustering text documents, thus they cannot be straightforwardly generalized in order to capture structural features as well.
- The structural features of a set of XML documents usually have high dimensionality, due to different tags and nesting relationships. In such cases, techniques for reducing the number of dimensions should be used in order to efficiently cluster the corresponding XML documents.
- Most clustering algorithms rely on the idea of "cluster representative", which represents all the objects belonging to the underlying cluster. The objects are checked against the cluster representatives in order to be assigned to the most appropriate cluster. Defining a cluster representative of a set of XML documents, which should summarize all the structural or/and content features of the corresponding XML documents, is not obvious.
- Due to the wide variety and heterogeneity of data sources used to generate XML information, each data source may utilize different structures and contents. Markup tags, which play a basic role to impose the

structure of a document, reflect subjective factors that brand the authorship in coding information. As a consequence, differently annotated XML data may be "semantically related" at a certain degree.

The problem of XML clustering has been well studied over the last years and the related bibliography is rapidly growing. The existing algorithms can be divided in two major categories:

- **Structure-based.** The clustering algorithms of this category concentrate only on the structural features of the XML documents, thus totally ignoring the content of the documents.
- **Content-based.** The clustering algorithms of this category rely on the content of the XML documents and utilize techniques similar to clustering flat text documents. Some of them take also into account a subset of the documents' structural features, thus may be considered as *hybrid*.

However, as mentioned before, XML documents originated from different data sources, usually utilize totally different markup tags and content. For example, some XML documents storing information about cars may use the markup tag "car", while some others from a different source may use the tag "automobile". In such cases the clustering results will not be correct. This problem has recently gained great attention and new approaches have been proposed to utilize semantic analysis to match different tags/text that have similar semantics. *Semantic XML clustering* refers to both structure and content and may be considered as an evolution of structural/content XML clustering approaches.

The remainder of this chapter is organized as follows. XML clustering by-structure methods are presented in the next section. Section "Content-based and hybrid XML clustering" describes methods to cluster XML documents according to content information solely or in addition to structure information. Section "Semantic XML clustering" is devoted to the clustering of semantically related documents. The chapter ends with Section "Application domains" before giving concluding remarks.

## STRUCTURE-BASED XML CLUSTERING

XML documents have diverse types of structural information in different refinement levels, e.g., attribute/element labels, edges, paths, twigs, etc. When defining the distance/similarity measure between two documents, the section of a simple structural component (e.g., label, edge) as a *feature* would make clustering fast. On the other hand, a measure based on too refined components could make clustering less efficient, and hence unpractical.

Structure-based XML clustering is the most well-studied category of XML clustering, featuring lots of approaches and algorithms. All the existing approaches choose a subset of the structural features and define a proximity function based on that subset; this function is then suitably combined with a clustering algorithm tailored to XML data to group the documents into related clusters. The tricky issue on those approaches is the trade-off between efficiency and complexity of the distance metric. Due to the large number of XML documents, the computation of the distance/similarity between two XML documents should be fast and precise, which is not trivial in case of large-sized documents.

Since there is a large number of algorithms, we have tried to group similar approaches together and discuss the most representative algorithms of each category. To the best of our knowledge, the structure-based XML clustering algorithms can be divided in the following three groups:

- **Tree-edit distance.** Algorithms that model each XML document as an unordered tree and define a metric based on the well-known tree-edit distance. The main differences between existing algorithms regard which edit operations are allowed, the cost of each operation, and the employed clustering algorithm.
- **Subtree mining and matching.** Algorithms that use mining techniques to identify common subtrees between a pair of XML documents and define the distance measure based on the coverage of the common subtrees. They differ on how the subtrees are identified and calculated and on the utilized distance measure.
- **Edge/Node summaries.** A totally different set of techniques that either utilize only the node information or only the edge information of each XML document. The distance computation is usually very fast, thus making such algorithms quite efficient in case of large-scaled XML documents.

## Algorithms Based on Tree-Edit Distance

An XML document is typically modeled as a rooted ordered labeled tree $T$. Each node in this tree corresponds to an element in the document and is labeled with the element tag name. Each edge in this tree represents inclusion of the element corresponding to the child node under the element corresponding to the parent node in the XML document. An *atomic tree edit operation* on a rooted ordered labeled tree is either the deletion of a node, or the insertion of a node, or the replacement of a node by another one. A *complex tree edit operation* is a set of atomic tree edit operations, treated as one single operation. An example of a complex tree edit operation is the insertion of a whole tree as a subtree in another tree, which is actually a sequence of atomic node insertion operations.

Given two rooted ordered labeled trees $T_1$ and $T_2$, a *tree edit sequence* is a sequence of tree edit operations that transform $T_1$ to $T_2$. Assuming a cost model to assign costs for every tree edit operation, the *tree edit distance* between $T_1$ and $T_2$ is the minimum cost between the costs of all possible tree edit sequences that transform $T_1$ to $T_2$.

In order to define a proper distance metric between two trees (and the corresponding XML documents), each type of tree edit operation should be assigned with a specific cost $c \geq 0$. Assuming that there is such a cost model, calculating the tree edit distance comes down to identifying the tree edit sequence with the smallest cost.

Different approaches have been developed to determine tree edit sequences and tree edit distances (Selkow, 1977; Shasha & Zhang, 1997; Chawathe & Molina, 1997; Chawathe, 1999; Nierman & Jagadish, 2002; Dalamagas, Cheng, Winkel, & Sellis, 2006). Some of them are applied to general trees, while some others are specialized on XML. All utilize similar tree edit operations with minor variations. Before discussing the various algorithms in detail, we present a general form of the basic atomic tree edit operations with the variations that the aforementioned algorithms use. Some examples of the basic atomic operations are displayed in Figure 1.

- **Insert node.**
  - **Variation I.** Given a node $x$, $Insert^1_T(x, y, i)$ is a node operation applied to $T$ that inserts $x$ as the $i$-th child of node $y$. The node $x$ can only be inserted as a leaf. In the new tree $T'$ produced after inserting the node $x$, the node $y$ will have $y_1, \ldots, y_{i-1}, x, y_i, y_{i+1}, \ldots, y_n$ as children.
  - **Variation II.** The restriction that a new node can be inserted only as a leaf is relaxed. $Insert_T(x, y, i)$ is a node operation applied to $T$ that inserts $x$ as the $i$-th child of node $y$. The node $x$ takes a subsequence of the children of

*Figure 1. Examples of basic atomic tree operations: (a) original tree, (b) Insert[1](D, C, 1), (c) Insert(F, B, 2), (d) Delete[1](E), (e) Delete(B), and (f) Replace(B, C)*

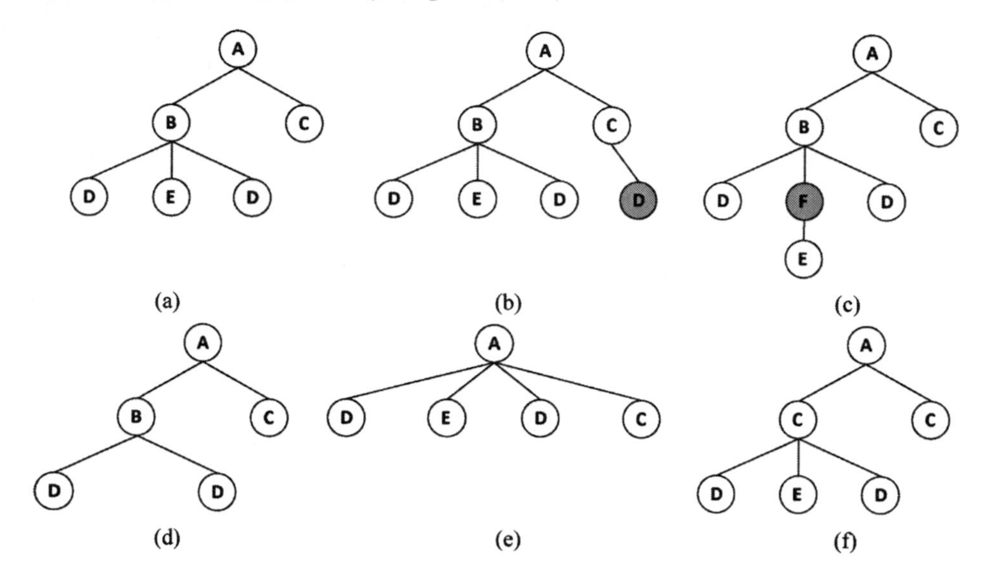


$y$ as its own children. Given $p$, in the new tree $T'$ produced after inserting the node $x$, the node $y$ will have $y_1, \ldots, y_{i-1}, x, y_p, y_{p+1}, \ldots, y_n$ as children and the node $x$ will have $y_i, y_{i+1}, \ldots, y_p$ as children.

We denote by $c_{ins}(x)$ the cost of the insert node operation.

- **Delete node.**
  - **Variation I.** Only leaf nodes can be deleted. Given a node $x$, $Delete^1_T(x)$ is a node operation applied to $T$ that deletes $x$ from the tree. Let $y$ be the parent of $x$ with children $y_1, y_2, \ldots, y_n$ and let $x$ be the $i$-th child of $y$ (i.e., $x = y_i$). In the new tree $T'$ produced after deleting the node $x$, node $y$ will have $y_1, \ldots, y_{i-1}, y_{i+1}, \ldots, y_n$ as children.
  - **Variation II.** Deletion can be applied to any node. Given a node $x$, $Delete_T(x)$ is a node operation applied to $T$ that deletes $x$ from the tree. Let $y$ be the parent of the $x$ with children $y_1, y_2, \ldots, y_n$ and let $x$ be the $i$-th child of $y$ (i.e., $x = y_i$) with $x_1, x_2, \ldots, x_m$ as its children. In the new tree $T'$ produced after deleting the node $x$, node $y$ will have $y_1, \ldots, y_{i-1}, x_1, \ldots, x_m, y_{i+1}, \ldots, y_n$ as children.

We denote by $c_{del}(x)$ the cost of the delete node operation.

- **Replace node.** Given a node $x$, $Replace_T(x, y)$ is the node operation applied to $T$ that replaces node $x$ with a new node $y$. In the new tree $T'$ produced after replacing $x$ with $y$, the node $y$ will have the same parent and the same children as $x$ in $T$. We denote by $c_{rep}(x, y)$ the cost of the replace node operation.

A generic algorithm for calculating the tree edit distance can in principle be combined with a traditional clustering algorithm to group them into clusters. However, due to the semantics of XML, there are some restrictions of which types of tree edit operations are allowed. Below, we concentrate only on the XML-specific algorithm for calculating the tree edit distance between the tree representations of two XML documents and the corresponding clustering algorithm that the authors propose.

The algorithm presented in (Nierman & Jagadish, 2002) is one of the first approaches to structure-based XML clustering and the authors discuss an algorithm for calculating the tree edit distance tailored to XML data. Besides the previously described basic atomic tree edit operations, this algorithm allows the following two complex operations:

- **Insert tree.** Given a tree $A$, $InsertTree_T(A, i)$ is an insert tree operation applied to $T$ that inserts the tree $A$ as the $i$-th child of the root node of $T$.
- **Delete tree.** The operation $DeleteTree_T(T_i)$ removes the subtree positioned under the $i$-th child of the root node of $T$.

The proposed algorithm assigns unit costs both to atomic and complex edit operations, which is simple and straightforward but can lead to invalid results. For example, inserting a whole tree costs the same as inserting a single node, which is not valid according to the XML semantics. In addition, the cost of deleting a node is the same, no matter the node's level; hence, deleting a leaf node costs the same as deleting a node just below the root node. Although this may be valid for general trees, XML semantics impose that nodes closer to the root are more important than lower-level nodes. Thus, it would be more precise to dynamically calculate the cost of a delete operation in relation with the node's level. The same stands for the rest of atomic operations (*insert* and *replace*).

When identifying the edit sequences, the authors introduce some extra constraints in order to simplify the process:

- The insertion of a tree is only allowed if the tree to be inserted already occurs in the source tree, while the deletion of a tree is only allowed if the tree occurs in the destination tree.
- A tree that has been inserted may not subsequently have additional nodes inserted. A tree that has been deleted may not previously have had children nodes deleted.

The first restriction limits the use of insert/delete tree operations to when the subtree that is being inserted (or deleted) is shared between the source and destination tree. The second restriction provides an efficient means for computing the costs of inserting and deleting the subtrees found in the destination and source trees, respectively.

The algorithm in (Nierman & Jagadish, 2002) uses a dynamic programming formulation in order to calculate the tree edit distance between a source tree $A$ and a destination tree $B$. In order to do this, it calculates the cost of inserting every subtree of $B$ and the cost of deleting every subtree of $A$.

Let us denote by $Cost_{Graft}(T_i)$ the cost of inserting a subtree $T_i$. This could be done with a single *InsertTree* operation (if it is allowable), or with some combination of *InsertTree* and *Insert* operations. There is a cost associated with each possible sequence of *InsertTree* and *Insert* operations that result in the construction of the subtree $T_i$. The minimum of these costs is $Cost_{Graft}(T_i)$. Similarly, $Cost_{Prune}(T_i)$ is the minimum cost sequence of *Delete* and *DeleteTree* operations needed to remove a subtree.

An overview of the algorithm in (Nierman & Jagadish, 2002) is presented in Figure 2. The algorithm works on two stages. After aligning the labels of the roots of the two input trees, on the first stage the graft and prune costs are calculated; the complexity of this stage is proved to be $O(|A|\times|B|)$. On the second stage, the *editDistance* procedure is called once for each pair of vertices at the same depth in the input trees $A$ and $B$; hence the complexity of the second stage is $O(|A|\times|B|)$ as well.

Having defined the distance metric between any pair of XML documents, the authors utilize a hierarchical agglomerative clustering, adopting

*Figure 2. Algorithm for calculating the tree edit distance in (Nierman & Jagadish, 2002)*

```
Algorithm: EDITDISTANCENJ02
Input: two trees A and B
Output: the tree edit distance between A and B

 1: int M = degree(A)
 2: int N = degree(B)
 3: int[][] dist = new int[0..M][0..N]
 4: dist[0][0] = CostRelabel(root(A), root(B))
 5: for (int j = 1; j ≤ N; j++)
 6:     dist[0][j] = dist[0][j-1] + CostGraft(Bj)
 7: for (int i = 1; i ≤ M; i++)
 8:     dist[i][0] = dist[i-1][0] + CostPrune(Ai)
 9: for (int i = 1; i ≤ M; i++)
10:     for (int j = 1; j ≤ N; j++)
11:         dist[i][j] = min(dist[i-1][j-1] + editDistanceNJ02(Ai, Bj),
                             dist[i][j-1] + CostGraft(Bj),
                             dist[i-1][j] + CostPrune(Ai))
12: return dist[M][N]
```

the Unweighted Pair Group Averaging Method (UPGMA) as the distance between any pair of clusters. Therefore, the distance between clusters $C_i$ and $C_j$ is computed as follows:

$$dist\left(C_i, C_j\right) = \frac{\sum_{k=1}^{|C_i|}\sum_{l=1}^{|C_j|} \delta\left(doc_k^{C_i}, doc_l^{C_j}\right)}{|C_i||C_j|}$$

where $doc_k^{C_i}$ (resp. $doc_l^{C_j}$) is the $k$-th (resp. $l$-th) document of cluster $C_i$ (resp. $C_j$).

Due to the high cost of calculating the edit distance between a pair of trees, the algorithm's complexity lies on calculating the distance between two XML documents or two clusters. Compared to other general algorithms for computing the edit distance, this approach performs the same as the measure provided in (Chawathe & Molina, 1997) and slightly better than the measure described in (Shasha & Zhang, 1997).

Dalamagas et al. (2006) provide a methodology for clustering XML documents by structure, based on the tree-edit distance between XML documents. Instead of directly calculating the distance between two XML documents, they introduce the idea of *structural summaries*. These summaries maintain the structural relationships between the elements of an XML document and at the same time have minimal processing requirements instead of the original trees representing the XML documents. The motivation behind structural summaries is the increasing complexity of real-world XML documents. Indeed, real XML documents tend to have many repeated elements. As a result, the trees representing XML documents can be large and deeply nested, and may have quite different size and structure even if they are based on the same DTD or XML Schema. Repetition and nesting affect the performance of the tree edit algorithms, since the involved trees can be too large. Moreover, repetition and nesting is a reason for having inaccurate results concerning the tree edit distance calculation. A tree edit algorithm will output a large distance between two XML documents which are based on the same schema, with one of the two being quite long due to many repeated elements.

The algorithm proposed in (Dalamagas et al., 2006) performs nesting reduction and repetition reduction to extract the structural summaries for rooted ordered labeled trees which represent XML documents.

- **Nesting reduction.** During this phase, the tree is traversed using pre-order traversal. For the current node, the algorithm checks whether there is an ancestor with the same label. If there is no such ancestor, it goes on to the next node. If there is such ancestor, then it moves all current node's subtrees to that ancestor. The subtrees are added at the end of the ancestor's child list so that it will traverse these nodes later. Nothing will be moved if the current node is a leaf.
- **Repetition reduction.** During this phase, the tree is also traversed using pre-order traversal. At each node, the algorithm checks whether the path from the root to the node already exists or not by looking it up in a hash table keeping the paths. If there is no such a path, it stores this node in the hash table, with its path being the index. If there is already one such path in the hash table, then this node is a repeated node, and in that case:
  1. all its subtrees are moved to the destination node that is found on the hash table by using the path as index,
  2. the subtrees are added at the end of the destination node's child list to traverse these trees later, and
  3. the current node is deleted and the algorithm starts to traverse the subtrees which have been moved to the destination node.

After traversing all the nodes that have been moved, the algorithm goes on to traverse the right sibling of the node which is deleted. If there is no such node, the traversal ends.

Figure 3 illustrates an example of structural summary extraction. Applying the nesting reduction phase on $T_1$, we obtain $T_2$, where there are no nested/repeated nodes. Applying the repetition reduction on $T_2$, we obtain $T_3$, which is the structural summary tree without nested/repeated and repeated nodes.

The algorithm for calculating the tree edit distance between two structural summaries uses a dynamic programming algorithm which is close to (Chawathe, 1999) in terms of the tree edit operations that are allowed. However, the recurrence that it is used does not need the costly edit graph calculation of the latter. An *insert node* operation is permitted only if the new node becomes a leaf. A *delete node* operation is permitted only at leaf nodes. Any node can be updated using the *replace node* operation. Therefore, the set of permitted tree edit operations is,

$$\{Insert^1_T(x, y, i), Delete^1_T(x), Replace_T(x, y)\}$$

with costs $c_{ins}(x)$, $c_{del}(x)$, and $c_{rep}(x, y)$ all equal to 1. The cost of inserting a whole subtree $t_2$ is the number of nodes in $t_2$. The cost of deleting a whole subtree $t_2$ anywhere in a tree $t_1$, is also the number of nodes in $t_2$.

Given $T_1$ and $T_2$, with roots $s$ and $t$ respectively, the algorithm for calculating their tree edit distance is shown in Figure 4, where:

*Figure 3. Example of structural summary extraction*

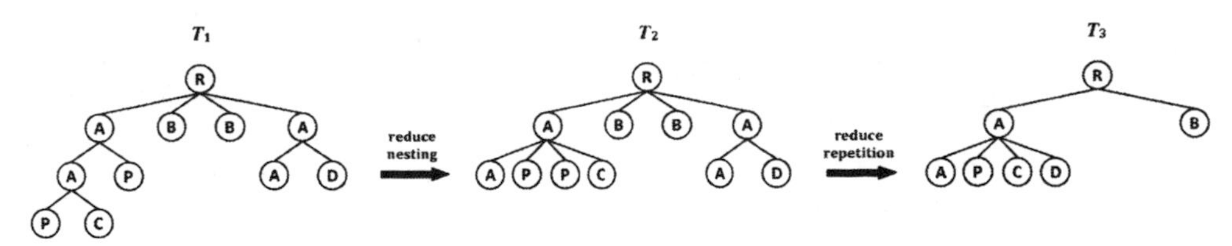

*Figure 4. Algorithm for calculating the distance between two structural summaries in (Dalamagas, Cheng, Winkel, & Sellis, 2006)*

```
Algorithm: EDITDISTANCEDCWS06
Input: two tree nodes s and t
Output: the distance between the structural summaries corresponding to s and t

1: int[][] dist = new int[numOfChildren(s)+1][numOfChildren(t)+1]
2: dist[0][0] = UpdateCost(LabelOf(s), LabelOf(t))
3: for (int i = 1; i ≤ numOfChildren(s); i++)
4:    dist[i][0] = dist[i-1][0] + numOfNodes(s_i)
5: for (int j = 1; j ≤ numOfChildren(t); j++)
6:    dist[0][j] = dist[0][j-1] + numOfNodes(t_j)
7: for (int i = 1; i ≤ numOfChildren(s); i++)
8:    for (int j = 1; j ≤ numOfChildren(t); j++)
9:        dist[i][j] = min(dist[i][j-1] + numOfNodes(t_j),
                           dist[i-1][j] + numOfNodes(s_i),
                           dist[i-1][j-1] + editDistanceDCWS06(s_i,t_j))
10: return dist[numOfChildren(s)][numOfChildren(t)]
```

- $s_i$ is the *i*-th child of node *s* and $t_j$ is the *j*-th child of node *t*.
- *numOfChildren*(*s*) returns the number of child nodes of node *s*.
- *numOfNodes*(*s*) returns the number of nodes of the subtree rooted at *s* (including *s*).
- *LabelOf*(*s*) returns the label of node *s*.
- *UpdateCost*(*LabelOf*(*s*), *LabelOf*(*t*)) returns the cost $c_{rep}(s,t)$ to make the label of node *s* the same as the label of node *t*: 1 if the labels are different, 0 otherwise.

Based on the calculated tree edit distance, the authors define the structural distance *S* between two structural summaries $T_1$ and $T_2$ for rooted ordered labeled trees that represent XML documents as follows:

$$S\left(T_1,T_2\right)=\frac{dist\left(T_1,T_2\right)}{dist'\left(T_1,T_2\right)}$$

where $dist(T_1, T_2)$ denotes the tree edit distance between $T_1$ and $T_2$, and $dist'(T_1, T_2)$ is the cost to delete all the nodes from $T_1$ and insert all the nodes of $T_2$. The structural distance is:

- equal to 0 when the trees have exactly the same structure and the same labels in their matching nodes,
- equal to 1 when the trees have totally different structure and not even two pairs of matching nodes with the same ancestor/descendant relationship,
- low when the trees have similar structure and high percentage of matching nodes, and
- high when the trees have different structure and low percentage of matching nodes.

This distance is much more accurate than the one utilized in (Nierman & Jagadish, 2002) and can be calculated faster as it is applied to structural summaries and not to the original trees. However, allowing the replacement of any node in the tree with cost 1 may result in invalid results. For example, if two large structural summaries differ only in their root node, their structural distance would be 1. On the other hand, if two large structural summaries differ only in 2 leaf nodes, their structural distance would be 2 (greater than the first case). According to the XML semantics, the XML documents in the second case are probably more similar than in the first case.

Having defined the distance metric between any pair of XML documents, Dalamagas et al. (2006) employ a single-link hierarchical clustering algorithm to group the XML documents into clusters. In this algorithm, the distance between two non-singleton clusters is defined as the minimum of the distances between all pairs of elements so that one element is in the first cluster and the other element is in the second cluster.

Given $n$ structural summaries of rooted labeled trees that represent XML documents, the algorithm forms a fully connected graph $G$ with $n$ vertices and $n(n-1)/2$ weighted edges. The weight of an edge corresponds to the structural distance between the vertices (trees) that this edge connects. The next step is to compute the minimum spanning tree (MST) of $G$. The single link clusters at a *clustering level* $l_1$ can be identified by deleting all the edges with weight greater than or equal to $l_1$ from the MST of $G$. The connected components of the remaining graph are the single link clusters. The stopping rule adopted is the $C$-index (Hubert & Levin, 1976), adapted for a hierarchical clustering procedure.

## Algorithms Based on Subtree Mining and Matching

Algorithms in this category (Aggarwal, Feng, Ta, & Zaki, 2007; Kutty, Tran, Nayak, & Li, 2007), are also based on the tree representation of XML documents. However, instead of calculating the tree edit distance between any pair of XML documents, which is quite inefficient in case of large XML documents, they quantify the proximity in terms of *containment* of frequent substructures (e.g., subtrees, paths). These frequent substructures are utilized to measure the similarity between particular groups of documents. Thus, a group of documents is defined to be most similar, when it results in a large number of similar substructures at a specified support level. The complexity of such an approach lies in the complexity of mining the frequent substructures which, again in case of large XML documents, might turn out inefficient. The algorithm discussed next tries to address this problem by combining traditional mining techniques along with some heuristics based on the XML semantics.

Aggarwal et al. (2007) propose *XProj*, a partition-based clustering algorithm which works with frequent substructures of the underlying XML documents. During the clustering, instead of using individual XML documents as representatives for partitions, the algorithm uses *sets* of substructures of the documents as possible representatives. A set $S$ of substructures is said to be a representative of a given collection if each structure within it appears as a frequent substructure in that collection.

A substructure $s$ of a rooted, ordered, labeled tree $T$ is defined as an undirected connected, labeled, acyclic graph, whose vertices and edges can be one-to-one mapped to a subset of vertices and edges of $T$ that preserves the vertex labels and ancestor-descendant relationships among the corresponding vertices. Such a substructure $s$ is defined to be frequent in the collection $D$ of XML documents at a user defined minimum support, *minsup*, if it occurs as a substructure of at least *minsup* fraction of the documents in the collection $D$. A mapping between a substructure $s$ and a tree $T$ is called *alignment* and is defined to be a correspondence from each node in $s$ to a node in $T$. If there is no alignment that matches the node $x$ of $T$ with a node in $s$, then $x$ is said to be uncovered by $s$.

Based on the above definitions, the authors define the structural similarity $\delta(T, S)$ between an XML document $T$ and a structural collection $S = \{s_1, \ldots, s_k\}$ to be the fraction of nodes in $T$ which are covered by some structure in $S$. Similarly, the structural similarity $\Delta(\mathbf{T}, S)$ between a set of XML document trees $\mathbf{T}$ and a structural collection $S = \{s_1, \ldots, s_k\}$ is defined as the average structural similarity over the different documents in $\mathbf{T}$ to $S$.

Finally, for a given level of user defined minimum support, the *frequent substructural self-similarity* of a document collection $D$ at level

$l$ is defined as the structural similarity $\Delta(D, S_l)$, where $S_l$ is the set of frequent substructures of $D$ with $l$ nodes. Note that the frequent substructural self-similarity of a document collection provides a good understanding of the level of homogeneity in the document collection from a substructural point of view. When a collection contains noisy and random documents, it will not be possible to mine frequent structures which cover a significant fraction of nodes in the collection. Consequently, the self-structural similarity index is also likely to be low. On the other hand, for a homogeneous collection, a very high percentage of nodes are likely to be covered by frequent structures. Therefore, the frequent substructural self-similarity can be used as a surrogate for the self-similarity behavior of collection at the structural level.

As previously mentioned, the problem of actually indentifying the frequent substructures of an XML document collection is not trivial. Aggarwal et al. (2007) proposes an approximate substructure mining technique based on the sequence of a pre-order depth-first traversal of the tree edges, where an edge is denoted by a pair of node labels. The advantage of the edge sequence representation is that it preserves both the parent-child relationship and the ordering among the sibling nodes. Due to that, if a tree $T$ is contained in a tree $T'$, then the edge sequence representation of $T$ is a subsequence of the edge sequence representation of $T'$. Thus, the problem of frequent substructures mining can be reduced to that of frequent sub-sequence mining. The authors utilize a revised version of BIDE (Wang & Han, 2004), a sequential pattern mining algorithm, to mine sequences of a specific size on a collection of XML documents.

The XProj algorithm is a traditional partition-based clustering algorithm that takes as input the collection of the XML documents and the number of clusters $k$ to be formed. A sketch of the algorithm is displayed in Figure 5. The idea is to use a substructural modification of a partition-based approach in which the clusters of documents are built around groups of representative substructures. Thus, instead of a single representative of a partition-based algorithm, the authors use a substructural set representative for the structural clustering algorithm. Initially, the document set $D$ is randomly divided into $k$ partitions with equal size, and the sets of substructure representatives are generated by mining frequent substructures of size $l$ from these partitions. Similarly, in each iteration, the substructural representatives (of a particular size and a particular support level) of a given partition are the frequent structures from that partition. These structural representatives are used to partition the document collection and vice-versa. Once the partitions have been computed, they are utilized to re-compute the representative sets. These re-computed representative sets are

*Figure 5. Sketch of the XProj clustering algorithm*

**Algorithm: XProj**

**Input:** collection of documents $D$, minimum support *minsup*, structural size $l$, and number of desired clusters $k$
**Output:** a partition of $D$ in $k$ clusters

1: Initialize representative sets $S_1, \ldots, S_k$
2: **while** (!*convergence_criterion*) **do**
3: Assign each document $T \in D$ to one of the sets in $\{S_1, \ldots, S_k\}$ using coverage-based similarity criterion
4: Compute the frequent substructures of size $l$ from each partition $M_i$ using sequential transformation paradigm
5: **if** ($|M_i| \times minsup) \geq 1$ **then**
6: $S_i \leftarrow$ frequent substructures of size $l$ from $M_i$
7: **endWhile**

defined as the frequent substructures of size $l$ from each partition.

## Algorithms Based on Node/Edge Summaries

Algorithms in this category try to reduce the complexity due to the large size of XML documents by introducing compact representations of each document, based on node/edge summarization. Those representations are then used to actually define the distance between the corresponding documents and finally cluster the documents into groups. The complexity of these algorithms is lower than the algorithms of the previous categories, thanks to the more compact and simplified representations utilized for each XML document.

Lian, Cheung, Mamoulis, and Yiu (2004) propose S-GRACE, a structure-based XML clustering algorithm. S-GRACE utilizes a compact representation of a collection of XML documents, called *structured graph* (or *s-graph*). Given a set $C$ of XML documents, the s-graph $sg(C) = (N, E)$ is a directed graph such that $N$ is the set of all the elements and attributes in the documents in $C$ and $(a, b) \in E$ if and only if $a$ is a parent element of element $b$ or $b$ is an attribute of element $a$ in some document in $C$. The construction of $sg(C)$ can be done efficiently by a single scan of the documents in $C$, provided that each document fits into memory.

Single XML documents are also represented by a structured graph, which is more compact than the real XML document as repeated edges in the document appear only once in its corresponding structured graph. The structural distance between two XML documents $T_1$ and $T_2$ is defined as follows:

$$dist\left(T_1, T_2\right) = 1 - \frac{\left|sg\left(T_1\right) \cap sg\left(T_2\right)\right|}{\max\left\{\left|sg\left(T_1\right)\right|, \left|sg\left(T_2\right)\right|\right\}}$$

The proposed distance proposed in (Lian et al., 2004) has a nice characteristic. It prevents an s-graph which is a subgraph of another s-graph from being "swallowed," if they should form two clusters. In Figure 6, we have three s-graphs such that $dist(g_2, g_3) = 0.25$ and $dist(g_1, g_2) = dist(g_1, g_3) = 0.6$. A clustering algorithm with this metric can separate the documents associated with $g_2$ and $g_3$ from those with $g_1$, even though both $g_2$ and $g_3$ are subgraphs of $g_1$. Following the same reason, outliers with large s-graphs would be prevented from wrongly swallowed non-outliers whose s-graphs are subgraphs of the outliers' s-graphs.

The S-GRACE algorithm is a hierarchical clustering algorithm that applies ROCK (Guha, Rastogi, & Shim, 1999) on the s-graphs extracted from the documents. As pointed out in (Guha et al., 1999), pure distance-based clustering algorithms may not be effective on categorical or binary data. ROCK tries to handle the case that, even though some data points may not be close enough in distance but they share a large number of common neighbors, it would be beneficial to consider them belonging to the same cluster. This observation would help to cluster s-graphs which a share large number of common neighbors.

*Figure 6. Example s-graphs used in the S-GRACE clustering algorithm*

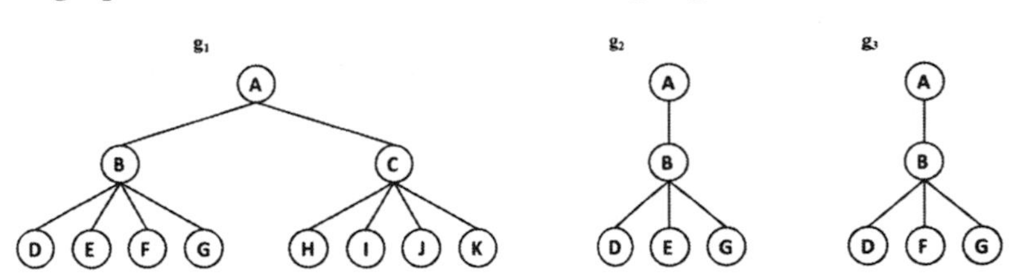

A family of recently developed XML clustering algorithms that utilize simplified representations of XML documents is represented by (Nayak & Xu, 2006) and (Antonellis et al., 2008). These two algorithms summarizing either the nodes or the edges at each level of the document. Nayak and Xu (2006) introduce *LevelStructure*, a compact structure that summarizes the distinct nodes at each level of an XML document, whereas Antonellis et al. (2008) introduce *LevelEdge*, a structure that summarizes the distinct edges at each level of an XML document. An example of LevelStructure and LevelEdge are presented in Figure 7.

Both LevelStructure and LevelEdge are organized as a vector of levels, where each level contains a list of distinct nodes (edges resp.). Although compact and small in size, LevelStructure has a main drawback which can result in totally erroneous results during the clustering process of a set of XML documents represented by their LevelStructures: it misses information about the structural relationships (parent/child, ancestor/descendant) between nodes. The only structural information contained in LevelStructure is which nodes are presented in each level of the XML document, while the relationships between nodes of different levels are missing.

The main advantage of the LevelEdge representation of an XML document in relation to the LevelStructure representation is the preservation of the structural relationships between nodes of consecutive levels of the XML documents in the form of edges. Each edge represents a parent/child relationship between the nodes corresponding to its two points. Thus, the LevelEdge representation summarizes all distinct parent/child relationships in each level of the XML document, instead of simply summarizing the distinct nodes as LevelStructure does. As a result, in all cases of real XML documents, either heterogeneous or homogeneous, the summarized edge information for each level can effectively distinguish between semantically and structurally different XML documents.

Consider for example a set of heterogeneous XML documents derived from different DTDs which do not share the same node tags. In such a case, both the LevelEdge and LevelStructure representations can be utilized in order to distinguish between two different XML documents. However, there is a possibility that some of the documents in the set share a subset of the same node tags but contain different parent/child relationships between such nodes. The LevelEdge representations of two such documents will be very different because they encode edges, instead of nodes. On

*Figure 7. Example of LevelStructure and LevelEdge: (a) sample XML document, (b) LevelStructure, and (c) LevelEdge*

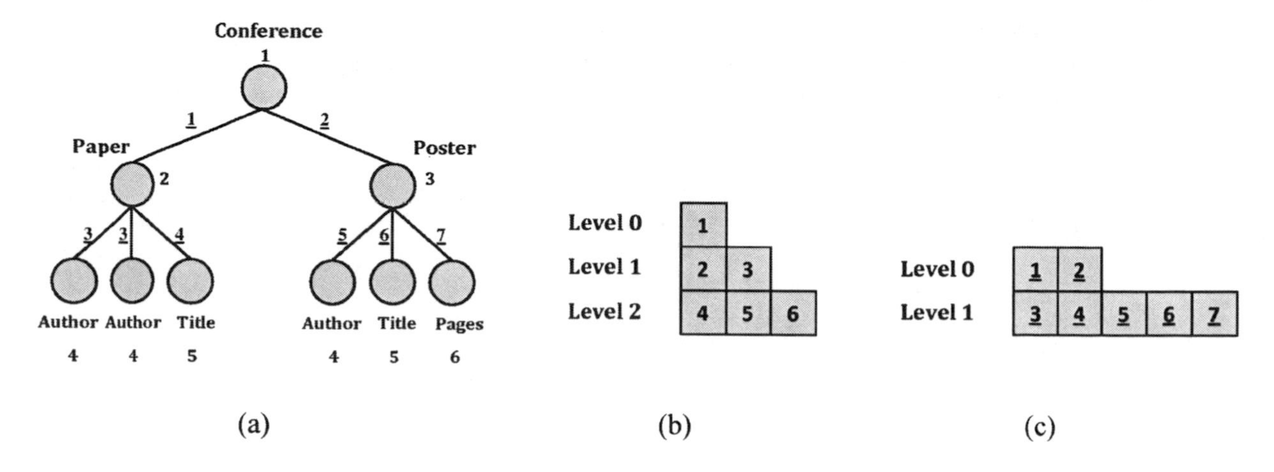

the other hand, the corresponding LevelStructure representations of the two documents may be similar enough to be considered as homogeneous XML documents. Regarding a set of homogeneous XML documents, the LevelStructure representation totally fails to distinguish between two XML documents derived from different sub-DTDs as they share the same set of node tags in each level. By contrast, the LevelEdge structure can distinguish between two such documents, as they usually differ in the absence or existence of extra edges in some levels (e.g., optional attributes and/or optional children nodes).

Based on the LevelStructure and LevelEdge representation of an XML document, the authors define an appropriate structural similarity between a pair of XML documents which counts the portion of the common nodes (edges resp.) at each level of the documents.

Consider two LevelEdge representations $L_1$ and $L_2$ with $N_1$ and $N_2$ levels, respectively, and a positive integer $a > 0$. Let $m = \min(N_1, N_2)$ and $M = \max(N_1, N_2)$. The similarity measure between $L_1$ and $L_2$ is defined as follows:

$$sim\left(L_1, L_2\right) = \frac{\sum_{i=0}^{m-1} c_i \times a^{m-i-1}}{\sum_{j=0}^{M-1} t_j \times a^{M-j-1}}$$

where $c_i$ denotes the number of common distinct edges in the level $i$ of $L_1$ and $L_2$, while $t_j$ denotes the total number of distinct edges in the level $j$ of both $L_1$ and $L_2$. The integer $a$ is a user-defined weight factor which is used to indicate that higher level edges are semantically more important in XML documents. The denominator in the above formula denotes the total weight of all distinct edges in both trees, while the numerator denotes the total weight of the common edges in levels of $L_1$ and $L_2$. Thus, the more common edges in high levels the two LevelEdge representations have, the more similar they are. The intuition behind weighting the number of common edges accordingly to the corresponding level is that edges in higher levels of the XML document contribute in the semantics of the XML document more than edges in lower levels. A similar measure is also proposed in case of the LevelStructure representation.

Based on the defined similarity measure, Antonellis et al. (2008) propose *XEdge*, a k-Means-like clustering algorithm (Jain & Dubes, 1988) that groups XML documents into clusters. Each cluster is also represented by a LevelEdge which summarizes the distinct edges of all the XML documents assigned to the corresponding cluster. An overview of the proposed clustering scheme is described in Figure 8.

The main advantage of the above discussed algorithms is their speed and scaling in case of a large collection of XML documents. Real XML

*Figure 8. Sketch of the XEdge clustering algorithm*

**Algorithm: XEDGE**

**Input:** set of LevelEdge representations $\{L_1, \ldots, L_m\}$, number of desired clusters *k*
**Output:** a set of *k* clusters

1: Initialize *k* empty clusters
2: Calculate the initial centroid for each cluster
using the method described in (Bradley & Fayyad, 1998)
3: **repeat**
4: Assign each LevelEdge representation to the closest cluster
5: When all the LevelEdge representations have been assigned,
re-calculate the new cluster representatives
6: **until** no cluster representative is changed

documents tend to have lots of repeated nodes/edges, thus their corresponding LevelStructure/LevelEdge representations are much smaller and less complex. Note that instead of a k-Means like clustering algorithm, hierarchical clustering algorithms could also be applied as well.

## CONTENT-BASED AND HYBRID XML CLUSTERING

Content-based clustering of XML documents ignores the structural information of the documents and focus only on their content features. It is usually applied in cases where we need to cluster the documents only accordingly to their text information or in cases where we know a-priori that all the documents share similar structure, so structure-based clustering would not lead to meaningful results. If we leave out the structural hierarchy of an XML document, then the problem of document clustering becomes very similar to the well-studied problem of clustering flat documents. In fact, content-based XML clustering algorithms usually resort to traditional text clustering algorithms. In this context, the *Vector Space Model* is widely used to represent each XML document as a vector of terms, which are extracted from the text contained in the attributes as well as in leaf nodes. The relevance weight of terms is usually either binary or based on the popular *tf-idf* weighting scheme (Salton, Wong, & Yang, 1975). Then the cosine similarity measure is preferably utilized to calculate the actual similarity between two vector representations of XML documents.

The *hybrid* XML clustering algorithms go beyond the content information within the documents and combine the content clustering with some type of structural clustering, in order to achieve better results.

(Yoon, Raghavan, Chakilam, & Kerschberg, 2001) propose *BitCube*, a scheme for indexing XML documents. The proposed bit-index is a 3-dimension index which stores information about documents, root-to-leaf paths (called *Epaths*) and text words. The *ijk* bit in BitCube is set to 1 only if the *i*-th document contains the *j*-th path and this path ends with the *k*-th word (in the corresponding document). A major drawback of BitCube is its size, which is equal to the product of the number of documents, the number of paths, and the number of words. Thus, dimension reduction is necessary by grouping common tags together or removing stop words. The similarity for any pair of XML documents is then calculated based on the common bits on the BitCube. This similarity measure can be utilized by any common clustering algorithm to group the input document collection into clusters. The proposed index can also be used to efficiently retrieve information about the indexed XML documents and XML paths. The authors show that BitCube creation time scales good in most cases while the retrieval time remains constant in all cases.

The first algorithm for clustering XML documents by content based on a simple Vector Space Model is that proposed in (Doucet & Ahonen, 2002). Instead of simply using the text terms, this algorithm also extracts the distinct tags as terms as well. That way, the vector representation of each XML document integrates both the content information and a subset of the structural information (tag names) of the original XML document. Its main drawback is the increased number of dimensions (distinct tags plus distinct words), which may lead to low efficiency when applied to real-world cases.

(Vercoustre, Fegas, Gul, & Lechevallier (2005) represent each XML document as a set of distinct root-to-leaf paths. Such paths can be purely structural or hybrid (i.e., they also contain the text of the leaf nodes). In order to efficiently cluster the resulting representations, the authors propose two techniques for reducing the number of distinct paths, thus reducing the number of dimensions used to represent each XML document: *structure reduction* and *text reduction*. Structure reduction tries to re-group some tags in more semantic categories, using the knowledge of the schema or the collections. For example, different tags with the same semantics can be replaced by a single tag, thus reducing the number of paths. Text reduction tries to remove words that do not add to the semantics of the XML documents, such as stop words and short terms (e.g., words shorter than 4 characters). After the reduction of distinct paths, the frequency of each path inside a document is calculated using the *tf-idf* term relevance weighting function and each XML document is represented using the Vector Space Model. Based on the calculated representation vectors, the authors utilize a k-Means-based clustering algorithm to partition the XML document collection into meaningful clusters. The overview of the algorithm proposed in (Vercoustre et al., 2005) is shown in Figure 9.

Another hybrid clustering algorithm is proposed in (Doucet & Lehtonen, 2006), which exploits both the semantics of the text and its structure markup contained in XML documents. The algorithm builds two separate feature sets for each XML document: one based only on the text and one based only on the tags (structure). Both feature sets are represented using the Vector Space Model. The algorithm, instead of simply combining the two feature sets into a single vector representation, works in two steps. In the first step, only the structural features are used to create $n$ clusters, where $n$ is the number of desired clusters. The resulted clusters are checked for their internal similarity based on a user-specified threshold and only $m$ ($m < n$) clusters that satisfy the threshold are kept. In the next step, the k-Means algorithm is applied on the text features with $k = n - m$. Finally, the algorithm combines the clusters formed by the two steps to create $n$ clusters. The overview of the algorithm proposed in (Doucet & Lehtonen, 2006) is shown in Figure 10.

The hybrid clustering algorithm in (Tran, Nayak, & Bruza, 2008) defines a similarity measure based both on the structural and content features of the corresponding XML documents. The content features are encoded as a vector of terms, where the weight of each term is its frequency inside the document. On the other hand, the structural features are encoded as a vector of distinct root-to-leaf paths, where the weight of each path is the number of occurrences inside the document. The similarity between a pair of documents is calculated as the weighted average of the content similarity and the structural similarity of the documents. The algorithm creates a similarity matrix for the input set of XML documents and then utilizes this matrix for clustering the documents. The authors do not propose a specific clustering algorithm, as any of the exist-

*Figure 9. Sketch of the clustering algorithm proposed in (Vercoustre, Fegas, Gul, & Lechevallier, 2005)*

**Algorithm:** *(Vercoustre, Fegas, Gul, & Lechevallier, 2005)*

**Input:** collection of documents *D*, number of desired clusters *k*
**Output:** a partition of D in *k* clusters

*//Step 1: path extraction*
1: Find the distinct structural and text paths for each document
*//Step 2: path reduction and content preprocessing*
2: Group similar tags together
3: Remove stop words and short terms
4: Calculate the vector representation of each document
*//Step 3: document clustering*
5: Perform k-Means on the document vector representations

*Figure 10. Sketch of the clustering algorithm proposed in (Doucet & Lehtonen, 2006)*

**Algorithm:** *(Doucet & Lehtonen, 2006)*
**Input:** collection of documents *D*, number of desired clusters *n*, similarity threshold *s*
**Output:** a partition of D in *n* clusters

*//Step 1: tag-based clustering*
1: Based on tag-features only, perform k-Means with $k = n$
2: Keep the *m* clusters with an internal similarity higher than *s*
*//Step 2: text-based clustering*
3: Based on text-features only, perform k-Means with $k = n - m$
*//Step 3: final clustering*
4: The *m* tag-based clusters and the $(n - m)$ text-based clusters are combined to form the final *n*-clustering

ing, such as k-Means, can be used. Figure 11 presents a sketch of this algorithm.

## SEMANTIC XML CLUSTERING

The increase in volume of XML-based application scenarios makes data sources utilize not only different structural and content features but also different ways to semantically annotate the data. As a consequence, different XML documents may represent semantically related data even if they use different markup tags which refer to different schemas. In addition, the content of two XML documents may be related even if they do not use exactly the same text terms to represent it. In such cases, a semantic approach to XML clustering is needed to resolve any ambiguity between the utilized markup tags or text terms on the XML documents. This problem has recently gained focus and various approaches (Tagarelli & Greco, 2004; Nayak, 2006; Tagarelli & Greco, 2010) have been proposed to address it. Any semantic approach to XML clustering should be applied in both the structural markup tags and the textual elements (text stored in leaf nodes and attribute nodes), hence semantic XML clustering can be considered as an improvement to both structural-based and content-based XML clustering.

The authors in (Tagarelli & Greco, 2010) propose the *SemXClust* framework to semantic XML clustering that tries to address semantic measures for both structural and content features of the XML documents. The proposed algorithm investigates

*Figure 11. Sketch of the clustering algorithm proposed in (Tran, Nayak, & Bruza, 2008)*

**Algorithm:** *(Tran, Nayak, & Bruza, 2008)*
**Input:** collection of documents *D*, weight factor *l*
**Output:** a clustering of the documents in *D*

*//Step 1: preprocessing*
1: Extract the distinct text terms of each document (remove stop words)
2: Extract the distinct root-to-leaf paths of each document
3: Calculate the content representation of documents based on the Vector Space Model
4: Calculate the structure representation of documents based on the Vector Space Model
*//Step 2: similarity matrix computation*
5: **for** each pair of documents **do**
6: Calculate the content similarity
7: Calculate the structural similarity
8: Calculate the combined similarity using the weight factor *l*
9: **endFor**
*//Step 3: final clustering*
10: Apply any clustering algorithm based on the similarity matrix

the semantic relatedness of XML documents by analyzing structure as well as content information and generating XML features with the support of a lexical ontology knowledge.

Structure analysis is applied to XML tag paths and is utilized to address the inherent ambiguity of the meaning of tag names, which is typically expressed in synonymies. The algorithm selects the most appropriate sense for each tag name by performing a word sense disambiguation (WSD) task tailored to XML data. Content analysis is applied to textual elements and combines methods that are conceived to compute term relevance from both syntactic and semantic viewpoints. WordNet (Fellbaum, 1998) is used as lexical ontology to enable a dictionary-based WSD that is applied to both structure and content features of the XML documents. In dictionary-based WSD the assumption is that the most plausible sense to assign to multiple co-occurring words is the one that maximizes the relatedness among the chosen senses.

In order to capture different ways of associating XML content with structure information, an XML document is represented in terms of smaller documents that are cohesive according to the underlying semantics of the original document. More precisely, XML documents are decomposed according to the notion of *tree tuple*. Intuitively, a tree tuple is a tree-based representation of a maximal set of distinct values that are correlated according to the structural semantics of the original document tree. Given an XML tree $T$, an XML *tree tuple* $t$ derived from $T$ is a maximal subtree of $T$ such that, for each path $p$ in $T$, the size of the answer of $p$ on $t$ is not greater than 1. The set of complete paths in $t$ is denoted as $P_t$.

Each XML document is modeled as a set of transactions, each of which corresponds to a tree tuple that has been derived from that document and decomposed into its distinct paths and respective answers. In this way, the item domain is built over the leaf elements of the tree tuples in the collection, so that each item represents a distinct pair path-answer. More formally, given an XML tree tuple $t$ and a path $p \in P_t$, an XML *tree tuple item* in $t$ is a pair $(p, A_t(p))$, where $A_t(p)$ denotes the answer of $p$ on $t$. The XML *transaction* corresponding to $t$ is the set of XML tree tuple items of $t$, which is $I_t = \{(p, A_t(p)) \mid p \in P_t\}$.

The extracted tree tuple items are the basis to generate the structure and content features of the XML documents, which is summarized as follows:

- **Structure features.** Tag paths are considered for extracting structure features from XML data. For any given path $p$, the algorithm tries to provide each tag in $p$ with a unique sense chosen from the reference lexical ontology. Since selected senses should be appropriate contextually to $p$, they use a *path context*, i.e., the series of node tags of $p$, by building a *synset graph SG(p)* and utilizing it for the disambiguation of all the tag names in $p$. A synset graph is a directed graph of layered form, such that each layer consists of all the possible senses of any given tag in the path, and the layers are connected according to the order of the tags in the path.
- **Content features.** Content features are generated from the text content units (TCUs) associated to XML tree tuple items. A TCU is either the text assigned to a leaf node or an attribute node. The authors introduce two weighting functions in order to measure syntactic and semantic relevance of terms.
    - *Syntactic relevance* of terms is calculated using a new term relevance weighting function, called *ttf.itf*. The relevance of a term increases with the term frequency within the local TCU, with the term popularity across the TCUs of the local tree tuple (transaction) and the TCUs of the local document tree, and with the term rarity across the whole collection of TCUs.

- *Semantic relevance*. The authors use the degree of polysemy to calculate the semantic relevance between terms. The key idea is to weight the semantic relevance of a term with respect to a notion of semantic rarity, in such a way that the higher the number of meanings of the term, the lower its rarity, thus its relevance.

In order to cluster the XML transactions, the authors introduce a similarity measure between a pair of tree tuple items $e_i$, $e_j$ as follows:

$$sim(e_i, e_j) = f \times sim_S(e_i, e_j) + (1\text{-}f) \times sim_C(e_i, e_j)$$

where $sim_S(e_i, e_j)$ (resp. $sim_C(e_i, e_j)$) is the structural (resp. content) similarity between $e_i$, $e_j$ and $f \in [0..1]$ controls the contribution of the structural part to the overall similarity.

The structural similarity between $e_i$, $e_j$ is defined as:

$$sim_s\left(e_i, e_j\right) = \frac{1}{n+m}\left(\sum_{tg \in p_i} sim(tg, p_j) + \sum_{tg \in p_j} sim(tg, p_i)\right)$$

where $tg$ is a tag path. The similarity between a tag $tg$ and a path $p$ is defined as the average *tag sense* similarity of the $tg$ with the tags of $p$. The tag sense similarity between two tag names is calculated based on the similarity between the senses assigned to the corresponding tags.

The content similarity between $e_i$, $e_j$ is measured by comparing their respective TCUs. Given a collection of XML tree tuples $T$, any TCU $u_i$ is modeled using a vector, whose $j$-th component corresponds to an index term, $w_j$, and contains value that expresses the relevance of term $w_j$ with respect to the TCU $u_i$. The size of each TCU vector is equal to the size of the collection vocabulary, i.e., the set of index terms extracted from all TCUs in $T$. The well-known *cosine similarity* is used to measure the similarity between TCU vectors.

The proposed similarity between a pair of tree tuple items can be combined with any traditional clustering algorithm in order to group the XML transactions according to their tree tuple item based similarity. The authors propose two such clustering algorithms: *XKMeans*, based on the k-Means algorithm, and *XFIHC*, which is based on frequent itemset mining. The experimental results have shown that XKMeans usually achieves better results than XFIHC. On the other hand, XFIHC is designed to form a cluster hierarchy, which is more useful for browsing and it generally provides meaningful cluster descriptions that exploit frequent itemsets.

## APPLICATION DOMAINS

Since the XML language can encode and represent various kinds of hierarchical data, clustering XML documents is useful in any application domain that needs management and processing of hierarchical data. Some significant examples are discussed in the following.

- **Automatic extraction of DTDs or XML Schemas.** XML documents may optionally conform to a DTD (Document Type Definition) or XML Schema. An available schema enables the exchange of documents through common vocabulary of tags and can be used to generate relational schemas to efficiently store and query XML documents in relational database systems. In case of massive construction of XML documents from various external data sources, the schema may be omitted. Identifying groups (clusters) of XML documents that share a similar structure can help schema extraction systems to build meaningful DTDs or XML Schemas for each discovered cluster of XML documents.
- **Web service discovery.** The wide use of the Web for everyday tasks is mak-

ing Web services an essential part of the Internet customer's daily life. Users query the Internet for a required Web service and get back a set of Web services that may or may not satisfy their request. To get the most relevant Web services that satisfy the user's request, the user has to construct the request using the keywords that best describe the user's objective and match correctly with the Web service name or location. Clustering Web services according to the similarity between their functions can greatly boost the ability of Web service search engines to retrieve the most relevant Web services. Each Web service can be described using the Web Service Description Language (WSDL), which is an XML language. XML clustering can hence be performed on a collection of WSDL documents to cluster them into functionally similar Web service groups. Due to the common shared structure of all the WSDL documents, applying a content-only or hybrid XML clustering algorithm would lead to better results in this case.

- **Native XML databases.** With the rapid growth of XML technologies, traditional relational databases are often replaced by native XML databases, which store information directly into XML data. Query execution planes can be greatly boosted by forwarding the queries only to related groups of XML documents. Thus, a preprocessing step for grouping the XML document collection into clusters, based on their content and structural similarity, may increase the efficiency of the query processing mechanism. In case only content queries are supported, then in order to achieve better results, only content clustering should be applied.
- **Spatial data management.** Spatial data are often hierarchically organized in data model catalogs expressed in a XML format. For example, areas that include forests with lakes, rivers and farms can be represented as tree-like structures using XML documents. Clustering by structure can identify spatial entities with similar structure, e.g., entities with areas that include forests with lakes. This is an example where content clustering may not be needed, thus only a structure-based approach should be utilized.
- **Bioinformatics.** XML is well-suited and provides an excellent standard for capturing and expressing complex biological information (Direen & Jones, 2003). The discovery of structural similar macromolecular tree patterns, encoded as XML documents, is a useful task in bioinformatics. The detection of homologous protein structures encoded as XML documents (i.e., sets of protein structures sharing a similar structure) is such an example.
- **Personalization & recommendation systems.** Modern websites and e-shops utilize complex techniques to provide personalized content to their users and recommend additional products or links that the current user may be interested in. XML is widely used for representing the user profiles by storing information about their clickstream and buying history. The detection of customer groups with similar profiles is crucial in order to provide the appropriate personalized services.
- **Selective dissemination of information.** Information filtering systems constitute a critical component in modern information seeking applications. As the number of users grows and the information available becomes even bigger, it is imperative to employ scalable and efficient representation and filtering techniques. Typically, the use of XML representation entails the profile representation with the use of the XPath query language and the employ-

ment of efficient heuristic techniques for constraining the complexity of the filtering mechanism. XML clustering can be applied on the stored user profiles to create groups of common profiles and create a descriptor profile for every cluster: a profile that summarizes all the user profiles inside that cluster. The system then can utilize those clusters in order to boost the filtering procedure. An incoming document is first filtered against every cluster descriptor and if it is matched, then it is filtered against the user profiles inside this cluster. This way, the document is not filtered against user profiles belonging to non-matched clusters, thus greatly improving the efficiency of the filtering mechanism.

## CONCLUSION

In this chapter we presented the special challenges introduced by the problem of efficiently clustering a set of XML documents, and overviewed the most prominent algorithms for clustering XML documents. Existing algorithms can be categorized according to which features (structure and/or content) of the underlying XML documents are considered when defining the distance/similarity measure for XML documents. In addition, due to the heterogeneity of XML data sources, a semantic analysis is also needed to disambiguate the sense of tag names and text terms used in the XML documents. Our overview hence covered both structure-based, content-based and semantic XML document clustering, and provided algorithmic details of the discussed clustering methods. Finally, we briefly discussed a list of real-world applications that require an efficient and scalable solution to the problem of XML clustering due to their nature.

## REFERENCES


Aggarwal, C., Feng, J., Ta, N., & Zaki, M. (2007). XProj: A framework for projected structural clustering of XML documents. In P. Berkhin, R. Caruana, & X. Wu (Eds.), *Proceedings of the 13th ACM SIGKDD International Conference on Knowledge Discovery and Data Mining (KDD)*, (pp. 46-55). ACM.

Antonellis, P., Makris, C., & Tsirakis, N. (2008). XEdge: Clustering homogeneous and heterogeneous XML documents using edge summaries. In R. L. Wainwright & H. Haddad (Eds.), *Proceedings of the 2008 ACM Symposium on Applied Computing (SAC)*, (pp. 1081-1088). ACM.

Bradley, P. S., & Fayyad, U. M. (1998). Refining initial points for k-means clustering. In J. W. Shavlik (Ed.), *Proceedings of the Fifteenth International Conference on Machine Learning (ICM)*, (pp. 91-99). Morgan Kaufmann.

Chawathe, S. (1999). Comparing hierarchical data in external memory. In M. P. Atkinson, M. E. Orlowska, P. Valduriez, S. B. Zdonik, & M. L. Brodie (Eds.), *Proceedings of 25th International Conference on Very Large Data Bases (VLDB)*, (pp. 90-101). Morgan Kaufmann.

Chawathe, S., & Molina, H. G. (1997). Meaningful change detection in structured data. In J. Peckham (Ed.), *Proceedings ACM SIGMOD International Conference on Management of Data (SIGMOD)*, (pp. 26-37). ACM.

Dalamagas, T., Cheng, T., Winkel, K., & Sellis, T. K. (2006). A methodology for clustering XML documents by structure. *Information Systems, 31*(3), 187–228. doi:10.1016/j.is.2004.11.009

Direen, H. G., & Jones, M. S. (2003). Knowledge management in bioinformatics. In Chaudhri, A. B., Rashid, A., & Zicari, R. (Eds.), *XML data management: Native XML and XML-enabled database systems* (pp. 291–319). Addison-Wesley.

Doucet, A., & Ahonen-Myka, H. (2002). Naïve clustering of a large XML document collection. In N. Fuhr, N. Gövert, G. Kazai, & M. Lalmas (Eds.) *Proceedings of the First Workshop of the Initiative for the Evaluation of XML Retrieval (INEX)*, (pp. 81-87).

Doucet, A., & Lehtonen, M. (2006). Unsupervised classification of text-centric XML document collections. In N. Fuhr, M. Lalmas, & A. Trotman (Eds.), *Comparative Evaluation of XML Information Retrieval Systems, 5th International Workshop of the Initiative for the Evaluation of XML Retrieval (INEX) Lecture Notes in Computer Science: Vol. 4518* (pp. 497-509). Springer.

Fellbaum, C. (Ed.). (1998). *WordNet: An electronic lexical database*. Massachusetts, USA: MIT Press.

Guha, S., Rastogi, R., & Shim, K. (1999). ROCK: A robust clustering algorithm for categorical attributes. *Proceedings of the 15th International Conference on Data Engineering (ICDE)*, (pp. 512-521). IEEE Computer Society Press.

Hubert, L. J., & Levin, J. R. (1976). A general statistical framework for accessing categorical clustering in free recall. *Psychological Bulletin, 83*(6), 1072–1082. doi:10.1037/0033-2909.83.6.1072

Jain, A. K., & Dubes, R. C. (1988). *Algorithms for clustering data*. New Jersey: Prentice-Hall.

Kutty, S., Tran, T., Nayak, R., & Li, Y. (2007). Clustering XML documents using closed frequent subtrees: A structural similarity approach. In N. Fuhr, J., Kamps, M. Lalmas, & A. Trotman (Eds.), *Focused Access to XML Documents, 6th International Workshop of the Initiative for the Evaluation of XML Retrieval (INEX) Lecture Notes in Computer Science: Vol. 4862* (pp. 183-194). Springer.

Lian, W., Cheung, D. W., Mamoulis, N., & Yiu, S.-M. (2004). An efficient and scalable algorithm for clustering XML documents by structure. *IEEE Transactions on Knowledge and Data Engineering, 16*(1), 82–96. doi:10.1109/TKDE.2004.1264824

Nayak, R. (2006). Investigating semantic measures in XML clustering. *International Conference on Web Intelligence,* (pp. 1042-1045). IEEE Computer Society Press.

Nayak, R., & Xu, S. (2006). XCLS: A fast and effective clustering algorithm for heterogeneous XML documents. In W. K. Ng, M. Kitsuregawa, J. Li, & K. Chang (Eds.), *Advances in Knowledge Discovery and Data Mining, 10th Pacific-Asia Conference (PAKDD) Lecture Notes in Computer Science: Vol. 3918*. (pp. 292-302). Springer.

Nierman, A., & Jagadish, H. V. (2002). Evaluating structural similarity in XML documents. In M. F. Fernandez & Y. Papakonstantinou (Eds.), *Proceedings of the Fifth International Workshop on the Web and Databases (WebDB),* (pp. 61-66).

Salton, G., Wong, A., & Yang, C. S. (1975). A vector space model for automatic indexing. *Communications of the ACM, 18*(11), 613–620. doi:10.1145/361219.361220

Selkow, S. M. (1977). The tree-to-tree editing problem. *Information Processing Letters, 6*(6), 184–186. doi:10.1016/0020-0190(77)90064-3

Shasha, D., & Zhang, K. (1997). Approximate tree pattern matching. In Apostolico, A., & Galil, Z. (Eds.), *Pattern matching in strings, trees and arrays* (pp. 341–371). Oxford University Press.

Tagarelli, A., & Greco, S. (2004). Clustering transactional XML data with semantically-enriched content and structural features. In X. Zhou, S. Y. W. Su, M. P. Papazoglou, M. E. Orlowska, & K. G. Jeffery (Eds.), *Web Information Systems, 5th International Conference on Web Information Systems Engineering (WISE) Lecture Notes in Computer Science: Vol. 3306* (pp. 266-278). Springer.

Tagarelli, A., & Greco, S. (2010). Semantic clustering of XML documents. *ACM Transactions on Information Systems, 28*(1), 1–56. doi:10.1145/1658377.1658380

Tran, T., Nayak, R., & Bruza, P. (2008). Combining structure and content similarities for XML document clustering. In J. F. Roddick, J. Li, P. Christen, & P. J. Kennedy (Eds.), *Data Mining and Analytics 2008, Proceedings of the Seventh Australasian Data Mining Conference (AusDM) Conferences in Research and Practice in Information Technology: Vol. 87.* (pp. 219-226). Australian Computer Society.

Vercoustre, A. M., Fegas, M., Gul, S., & Lechevallier, Y. (2005). A flexible structured-based representation for XML document mining. In N. Fuhr, M. Lalmas, S. Malik, & G. Kazai (Eds.), *Advances in XML Information Retrieval and Evaluation, 4th International Workshop of the Initiative for the Evaluation of XML Retrieval (INEX) Lecture Notes in Computer Science: Vol. 3977* (pp. 443–457). Springer.

Wang, J., & Han, J. (2004). BIDE: Efficient mining of frequent closed sequences. *Proceedings 20th International Conference on Data Engineering (ICDE),* (pp. 79-90). IEEE Computer Society Press.

Yoon, J., Raghavan, V., Chakilam, V., & Kerschberg, L. (2001). BitCube: A three-dimensional bitmap indexing for XML documents. *Journal of Intelligent Information Systems, 17*(2-3), 241–252. doi:10.1023/A:1012861931139

# Chapter 8
# Fuzzy Approaches to Clustering XML Structures

**Michal Kozielski**
*Silesian University of Technology, Poland*

## ABSTRACT

*Information on the hierarchical nature of XML data is essential in tasks of learning from XML document structures. Within this view, XML documents can be regarded as multi-represented data, which is the case when multiple representations of the document correspond to the generation of features at each structure level of the document separately. This chapter raises the importance of using fuzzy approaches to clustering XML document structures, since these approaches are shown to be effective in combining the information coming from different document representations that correspond to different hierarchy levels. For this purpose, we overview fuzzy encoding and similarity methods and present fuzzy clustering approaches which are particularly suited for being extended to handle XML document structures. We propose two different scenarios of fuzzy clustering of XML structures, which aim to either encode the document structure hierarchy using a fuzzy bag model or to specifically handle the multi-representation of the documents.*

## INTRODUCTION

XML documents are complex data objects having hierarchical structure. Therefore, it is not possible to apply conventional similarity measures directly to the analysis of XML document structures. One approach to address this issue is to analyse the structural similarity of XML documents by means of dedicated (tree-based) similarity measures (Nayak, 2008; Dalamagas, Cheng, Winkel, & Sellis, 2004; Nierman & Jagadish, 2002). Another approach consists in encoding the XML structure predominantly into the form of a feature vector and then analysing these feature vectors by means of

DOI: 10.4018/978-1-61350-356-0.ch008

a conventional similarity measure. This approach includes such encoding methods as bit encoding (Lian, Cheung, Mamoulis, & Yiu, 2004; Yoon, Raghavan, Chakilam, & Kerschberg, 2001), signal encoding (Flesca, Manco, Masciari, & Pugliese, 2005), and fuzzy encoding (Ceravolo, Nocerino, & Viviani, 2004). Some of the encoding methods here mentioned will be described in detail in this chapter. Moreover, since the focus of this chapter is not to review existing clustering approaches and methods for XML clustering (the interested reader can refer to Chapter "The Role of Schema and Document Matchings in XML Source Clustering" and Chapter "XML Document Clustering: An Algorithmic Perspective"), we make just a mention here of some of those methods by distinguishing them from a clustering strategy viewpoint. In this respect, existing XML clustering methods have been developed based on the following main approaches: agglomerative hierarchical (Nayak, 2008; Nayak & Tran, 2007; Dalamagas, Cheng, Winkel, & Sellis, 2006; Nayak & Iryadi, 2006; Costa, Manco, Ortale, & Tagarelli, 2004; Nierman & Jagadish, 2002), frequent-itemset-based hierarchical (Tagarelli & Greco, 2010), partitional (Tagarelli & Greco, 2010, 2006; Antonellis, Makris, & Tsirakis, 2008; Wang, Liu, & Wang, 2005), tree-partitioning (Bordawekar & Shmueli, 2004), and self-organizing maps (Hagenbuchner, Sperduti, Tsoi, Trentini, Scarselli, & Gori, 2006), and fuzzy (Kozielski, 2007).

XML documents can be regarded as multi-represented data because each document can have several representations when we consider features at each structure level separately. To cluster multi-represented data, information having different representations may be combined at the level of similarity matrices by means of some arithmetic operations or fuzzy aggregation operations. The resulting partition (clustering solution) can also be determined as a particular combination of the partitions derived for each representation separately.

Essentially, multi-represented data clustering consists in combining different types of information during the clustering process. One algorithm of this type is the density-based method DBSCAN that was modified in order to handle the multi-represented nature of the data (Kailing, Kriegel, Pryakhin, & Schubert, 2004). Union and intersection operations were introduced into the algorithm in order to verify if the chosen data objects are dense in any or all the representations that are analysed. This method was also used in the OPTICS algorithm (Achtert, Kriegel, Pryakhin, & Schubert, 2005), which is based on the DBSCAN algorithm but is less sensitive to the values of the parameters required by the method.

There are also examples of fuzzy algorithms combining different types of information during the clustering process. *Collaborative fuzzy clustering* (Pedrycz, 2002), which is based on the Fuzzy C-Means algorithm was introduced in order to cluster data in a distributed environment. Another method is the *Proximity-based Fuzzy Clustering* (Pedrycz, Loia, & Senatore, 2004), which introduces additional information (e.g., expert knowledge) to the clustering process. Both methods were further developed to the form of *Proximity-based Collaborative Clustering* (Loia, Pedrycz, & Senatore, 2007; Pedrycz & Rai, 2008).

There is however an inherent difficulty in directly applying the aforementioned methods to XML data. XML structures are hierarchical and the representations of their different structure levels should not be considered as equally significant.

The structure of XML documents is usually modelled by a rooted labelled tree where parent-child relationships between the elements define a document hierarchy. It is a common assumption that the most general and therefore important information is enclosed nearby the root element concerning the structure of an XML document. The features which are placed on the levels neighbouring a root element should have a greater influence on the analysis results than the deeply nested leaf nodes. For example, if two XML documents have different root elements then all the paths starting from the root element will be different for each document. It may also be assumed that the root element content is different and that compared structures are significantly (if not completely) different in that case. By contrast, differences in the structure at a leaf level should be much less important and influencing. This assumption holds in several studies concerning XML structure clustering, such as, e.g., (Ceravolo, Nocerino, & Viviani, 2004; Nayak, 2008; Kozielski, 2007). Hence, it will also influence further considerations in this chapter and determine our methods for XML structure clustering.

Computing similarity of XML tree-like structures and clustering these structures as multi-represented data are the problems where fuzzy methods can be applied with success. Fuzzy approaches are in fact able to represent and process the hierarchical structure of XML documents taking under consideration the differences in the significance of hierarchical information. Fuzzy clustering methods are also able to combine intuitively the information coming from different data representations corresponding to different hierarchy levels. These two facts motivate the application of fuzzy methods to XML structures analysis. In this respect, we present the fuzzy methods and two different scenarios that use different fuzzy approaches to clustering XML structures considering the node hierarchy. In particular, we will focus on fuzzy structure encoding (Ceravolo et al., 2004) and the fuzzy clustering algorithms Conditional Fuzzy C-Means (Pedrycz, 1996) and Proximity-based Fuzzy Clustering (Pedrycz et al., 2004) implemented into an XML-enabled method called *Multilevel* (Kozielski, 2007).

The structure of this chapter is as follows. First, some basic definitions related to the area of this chapter and the two scenarios of analysis are presented. Next, a thorough description of the methods applied to the considered scenarios is provided. Finally, the scenarios analysed are described and discussed.

## BACKGROUND

This section provides an introduction to the basic notions of this chapter, namely fuzzy sets and the modelling of XML structures as multi-represented data. Different scenarios of clustering XML structures by means of fuzzy methods are also discussed.

In regard to the basic notation that will be used across this chapter, sets are represented by capital letters (e.g., $X$), vectors are represented by letters in bold type (e.g., $\mathbf{x}$), matrices are represented by capital letters in bold type (e.g., $\mathbf{U}$), and XML documents are represented as either sets or vectors depending on the method of analysis being considered.

### Fuzzy Sets

Fuzzy sets were introduced and defined by Zadeh (1965). The natural application of fuzzy sets are complex phenomena that are difficult to be described in a precise way. Imprecise (fuzzy) way of thinking and analysis is also typical for humans. It helps us, for instance, to recognise faces and voice.

The theory of classical (crisp) sets states that an object $x$ from a universe $H$ can belong ($x \in A$) or not belong ($x \notin A$) to a given set $A$. This can be presented in the form of characteristic function:

$$\chi_A : H \rightarrow \{0,1\}$$

where the value of the characteristic function depends on whether object $x$ belongs to set $A$ or not, i.e., $\chi_A(x) = 1$ if $x \in A$, and $\chi_A(x) = 0$ if $x \notin A$.

The theory of fuzzy sets states that an object can belong to a set partially, which is described by a membership function:

$$\mu_A : H \rightarrow [0,1]$$

There are several forms of fuzzy set representation. Zadeh introduced a representation in which a fuzzy set $A$ is defined as:

$$A = \sum_{x \in H} \mu_A(x) / x$$

where $\Sigma$ is not an arithmetical sum but denotes a sum of the set elements, and / is a separator. Fuzzy sets may also be defined as ordered pair:

$$A = \{(x, \mu_A(x)) \mid x \in X, \mu_A(x) \in [0,1]\}$$

Another representation that will be used in this chapter with regard for the clarity has a form:

$$A = \{\mu_A(x) / x \mid x \in X, \mu_A(x) \in [0,1]\}$$

The representations presented above can be clarified by the following examples. Considering a universe of temperature definitions $H = \{cold, warm, hot\}$, the fuzzy set $A$ of the temperature felt currently by a person can be presented in the following way:

$A = 0.1/cold + 0.9/warm + 0.4/hot$

or

$A = \{(cold, 0.1), (warm, 0.9), (hot, 0.4)\}$

or

$A = \{0.1/cold, 0.9/warm, 0.4/hot\}$

One of the first applications of fuzzy sets was *fuzzy clustering*. Fuzzy clustering methods define the partition of a set of data objects into groups where each object belongs to each group with a certain membership value ($\mu$) calculated during the clustering process. This is contrast with crisp (hard) partitioning where, if a data object belongs to one group, it cannot belong to any other group. Fuzzy partition matrix shows that an object can belong to several groups with a different degree, which is expressed by means of membership values.

The basic and most popular fuzzy clustering algorithm is the *Fuzzy C-Means* (FCM) method. Many other fuzzy clustering methods present their own specific features which are based on this algorithm. The *Conditional Fuzzy C-Means* (CFCM) algorithm (Pedrycz, 1996) is a method that enables changes of significance of the analysed data objects according to the condition parameter provided by the user. Another important method is the *Proximity-based Fuzzy C-Means* (PFCM) algorithm (Pedrycz, 2004), which enables the introduction of additional information into the clustering process. These methods will be presented in detail in the following sections because they have been applied (Kozielski, 2007) or can be applied to clustering XML structures.

## XML as Multi-Represented Data

Data can be regarded as multi-represented when it is possible to describe a data object by means of different sets of disjoint features or, in general, by means of representations coming from different domains, e.g., numerical data and ontology. A data object having multiple representations can be seen differently in each of these representations (as illustrated in Figure 1) and the similarities between the data objects in each representation can be different.

XML documents, which are data objects having complex structure, can also be regarded as multi-represented data. The two intuitive representations of XML documents are indeed its structure and its content. However, when only structure is taken under consideration then the features identified at each structure level can be seen as separate representations of a document. The documents can be represented therefore as a hierarchy of representations corresponding to different structure levels.

*Figure 1. Multi-represented data as seen differently in each representation*

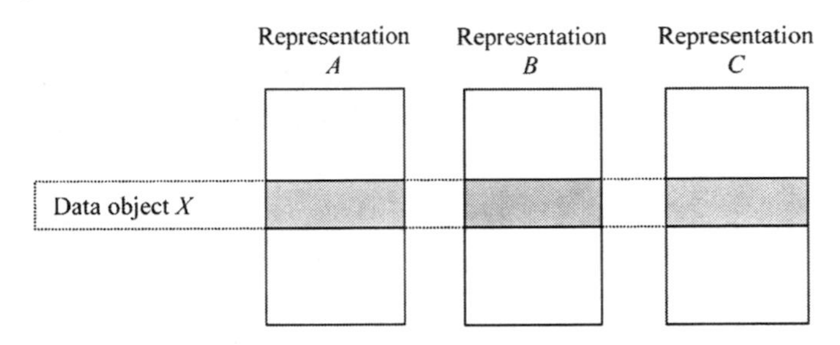


*Figure 2. Examples of XML documents and their structure*

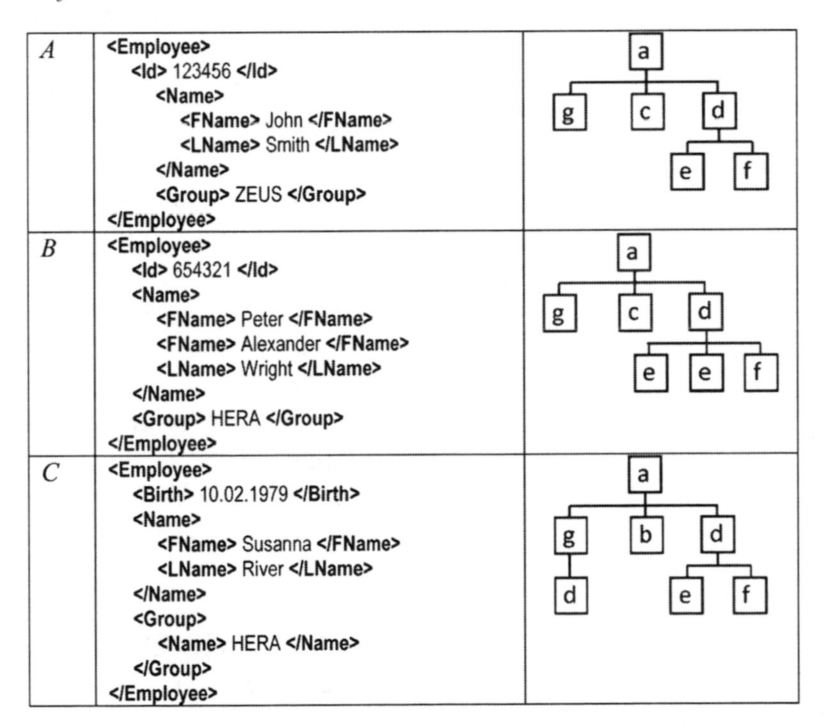


Suppose to apply the multi-representation idea to the example XML documents presented in Figure 2 (where the tree structure representation uses the abbreviations of tag names presented in Table 1). The document *A* can be represented by its root element which carries the most important information about the document and it can be represented by the elements present at the second and the third level as it is illustrated in Figure 3.

In the following, we will describe how clustering of XML documents regarded as multi-represented data with a hierarchy of representations can be performed by the fuzzy clustering methods suitably adapted to a multi-represented XML domain.

## Fuzzy Approaches to Clustering XML Structures

This section will show two scenarios enabling the cluster analysis of XML documents structures and taking under consideration the hierarchical nature

*Table 1. Tag names and their symbols used in Figure 2*

| Tag name | Symbol |
|---|---|
| Employee | a |
| Birth | b |
| Id | c |
| Name | d |
| FName | e |
| LName | f |
| Group | g |

of these structures. These scenarios are based on the fuzzy methods previously mentioned which will be presented in detail in the following sections.

When considering methods that encode XML structure into the form of a feature vector, two types of approaches can be distinguished:

- *flat structure encoding*, which includes methods that encode only occurrences of elements and attributes but do not encode their position in a document tree;
- *hierarchical structure encoding*, which includes methods that encode the occurrences of elements and attributes and also their position (level) in a document tree.

Flat structure encoding methods such as, e.g., *bit encoding*, produce feature vectors that do not contain information about XML structure hierarchy. It is however possible to calculate during the encoding process a hierarchy level of a feature as an additional explicit information used further by a clustering algorithm.

*Fuzzy encoding* can be regarded as an example of hierarchical structure encoding. Fuzzy encoding defines the structure of an XML document as a fuzzy bag. Each feature is represented by its cardinality and a membership value calculated on the basis of the feature's level in the XML document structure.

Within this view, a *multilevel* approach, by enabling the clustering on consecutive levels of the XML document feature space, contrasts with traditional algorithms that do not take into account additional explicit information about the feature location in the hierarchical structure and that cluster feature vectors by analysing the whole feature space. On the other hand, with respect to clustering approaches that aim to exploit the hierarchical XML structures, clustering XML documents can be performed on feature vectors that are either the result of a hierarchical structure encoding method or the result of a flat structure encoding method. In the first case, fuzzy XML structure encoding and traditional clustering algorithms can be applied, whereas the latter case refers to flat encoding combined with a multilevel clustering approach.

## STRUCTURE ENCODING AND SIMILARITY

In this section, we present two encoding approaches that enable XML structure similarity and

*Figure 3. XML document structures regarded as multi-represented data*

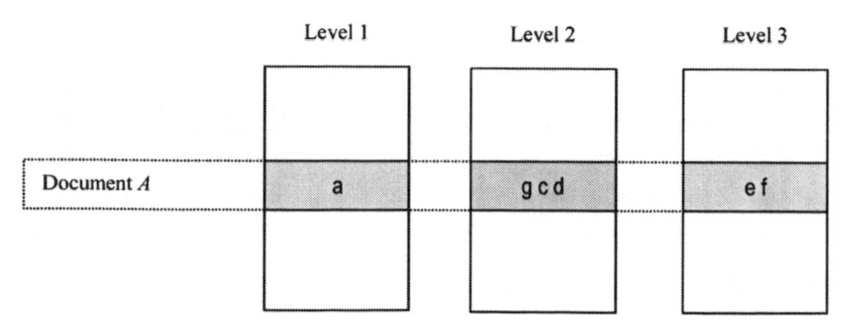

that are well-suited for the clustering scenarios defined in the previous section.

## Flat Feature Vector Representation

Bit encoding (Lian et al., 2004; Yoon et al., 2001) is a particular case of flat structure encoding. Bit encoding defines the structure of an XML document as a string of bits. Each bit in a feature vector denotes occurrence or lack of occurrence of a chosen part of XML structure in the analysed document. For instance, a pair of nodes (Lian et al., 2004) connected in a parent-child relation or a path (Yoon et al., 2001) starting from the root element and leading to a specific node may be taken as a part of the structure.

The formal definition of bit encoding can be presented as follows. Let us denote a set of XML documents as $D$. The set of features for the documents in $D$ is denoted as $\Gamma$ and called dictionary of the features. Bit encoding models the structure of each XML document as a feature vector $\mathbf{x}_k = [x_{ki}]$, with $i = 1, \ldots, n$ and $k = 1, \ldots, N$, where $n = \text{Card}(\Gamma)$ is the number of features, $N$ is the number of documents and $x_{ki} \in \{0,1\}$.

The process of bit encoding can be explained as in Table 2, where pairs of nodes are encoded and the resulting feature vectors are shown for each of the three simple XML documents presented in Table 1.

*Table 2. Example of XML structure bit encoding*

| | Document | | |
|---|---|---|---|
| **Dictionary of features** | *A* | *B* | *C* |
| Employee – Id | 1 | 1 | 0 |
| Employee - Birth | 0 | 0 | 1 |
| Employee - Name | 1 | 1 | 1 |
| Employee - Group | 1 | 1 | 1 |
| Name – FName | 1 | 1 | 1 |
| Name – LName | 1 | 1 | 1 |
| Group – Name | 0 | 0 | 1 |

Differences in the structures of the example documents are reflected in the feature vectors created in encoding process. The similarity of XML documents encoded in this way can be calculated by one of the methods defined for categorical data, such as the Jaccard coefficient, Czekanowski similarity, and Sokal-Michener similarity (Doreian, Batagelj, Ferligoj, 2005; Han & Kamber, 2001).

For instance, the similarity between two bit vectors calculated by using the Jaccard coefficient can be defined as:

$$s(\mathbf{x}_k, \mathbf{x}_m) = \frac{|and(\mathbf{x}_k, \mathbf{x}_m)|}{|or(\mathbf{x}_k, \mathbf{x}_m)|}$$

where $|and(\mathbf{x}_k, \mathbf{x}_m)|$ denotes the number of features having value 1 for both feature vectors $\mathbf{x}_k$ and $\mathbf{x}_m$, $|or(\mathbf{x}_k, \mathbf{x}_m)|$ denotes the number of features having value 1 for any of the feature vectors $\mathbf{x}_k$ or $\mathbf{x}_m$, and $n$ is the number of features creating the feature vector. As another example, the dissimilarity between two bit vectors by using the Hamming distance is as:

$$d(\mathbf{x}_k, \mathbf{x}_m) = \frac{|xor(\mathbf{x}_k, \mathbf{x}_m)|}{n}$$

where $|xor(\mathbf{x}_k, \mathbf{x}_m)|$ denotes the number of features having different values for both feature vectors $\mathbf{x}_k$ and $\mathbf{x}_m$.

In the XML context, an example is given in (Yoon et al., 2001), where the distance between two XML structures is calculated according to the following formula:

$$d(\mathbf{x}_k, \mathbf{x}_m) = \frac{|xor(\mathbf{x}_k, \mathbf{x}_m)|}{\max(|\mathbf{x}_k|, |\mathbf{x}_m|)}$$

where $|\mathbf{x}_k|$ and $|\mathbf{x}_m|$ denote the number of "ones" present in feature vector $\mathbf{x}_k$ and $\mathbf{x}_m$, respectively.

Another example can be found in (Lian et al., 2004), where the distance between two XML structures is computed as:

$$d(\mathbf{x}_k, \mathbf{x}_m) = 1 - \frac{|and(\mathbf{x}_k, \mathbf{x}_m)|}{\max(|\mathbf{x}_k|, |\mathbf{x}_m|)}$$

Consider again the example documents $A$, $B$ and $C$ in Figure 1. By using the Hamming distance, the distance values $d(\mathbf{x}_A, \mathbf{x}_B)$ and $d(\mathbf{x}_A, \mathbf{x}_C)$ are computed as $d(\mathbf{x}_A, \mathbf{x}_B) = 0/7 = 0$, and $d(\mathbf{x}_A, \mathbf{x}_C) = 3/7 \approx 0.43$. Alternatively, in terms of similarity based on Hamming distance, i.e.,:

$$s(\mathbf{x}_A, \mathbf{x}_B) = 1 - d(\mathbf{x}_A, \mathbf{x}_B)$$

the XML document structure similarity values are: $s(\mathbf{x}_A, \mathbf{x}_B) = 1$, and $s(\mathbf{x}_A, \mathbf{x}_C) \approx 0.57$.

The values calculated reflect the structural difference between the documents $A$ and $C$. However, the different cardinality of elements in documents $A$ and $B$ was not recognised since bit encoding does not encode element cardinalities.

Bit encoding is a very simple method producing as a result feature vectors of high clarity that can be easily compared. The main drawback of this method is related to the very large number of features creating feature vectors.

When the number of occurrences of XML structure parts is important, it is possible to modify the bit encoding and use natural numbers instead of $\{0,1\}$. This type of method is called *cardinality encoding*. Distance for XML structures encoded in this way can be calculated by means of, e.g., the well-known Euclidean distance:

$$d(\mathbf{x}_k, \mathbf{x}_m) = \sqrt{\sum_{i=1}^{n} (x_{ki} - x_{mi})^2}$$

Cardinality and bit encoding do not encode a level on which a given feature is placed in a document. For this reason, it is advisable to consider the feature's level information during the encoding process and use it later during the clustering process.

## Fuzzy Encoding

Fuzzy encoding (Ceravolo & Damiani, 2005; Ceravolo et al., 2004; Damiani et al., 2004) is a particular case of hierarchical structure encoding. As said before, fuzzy encoding defines the structure of XML document as a fuzzy bag (Rocacher, 2003), where each feature is represented by its cardinality and a membership value calculated on the basis of the feature's level in XML document structure. The membership value can be calculated in a very simple way (Damiani et al., 2004):

$$\mu = \frac{1}{L}$$

or according to a more complex formula (Ceravolo et al., 2004):

$$\mu = \frac{\sum_{l=0}^{L-1} l!\xi_{l+1}}{L!},$$

where $L$ is the level in the XML document structure where a given node is placed, and $\xi \in [0, 1]$ is a node importance value which can be provided by an expert.

The membership value calculated by means of the above two formulas shows the significance of a given node in the document structure. The closer to the document's root element the feature is placed, the larger its significance represented by means of membership value is.

As a result of XML document fuzzy encoding, the fuzzy bag $X$ of the following form is calculated:

$$X = \left\{ < \mu_X^1(x), \ldots, \mu_X^n(x) > /x \mid x \in \mathrm{H}, \mu_X^k(x) \in [0,1] \right\}$$

where $n$ is the cardinality of a feature $x$, $H$ is the universe of features.

A fuzzy bag can be represented in terms of fuzzy cardinality $\Omega$ (Rocacher, 2003), which results in the following form of encoding of XML document structure:

$$X = \left\{ \Omega_X(x) * x, | \; x \in \mathrm{H} \right\}$$

where fuzzy set $X$ has values from universe $H$, * is a separator, $\Omega X(x)$ is the fuzzy cardinality defined as:

$$\Omega_X(x) = \left\{ \mu(k) \,/\, k \mid k = 0, \ldots, n \right\}$$

where $n$ is the cardinality of a feature $x$ and

$$\mu(k) = \sup\{\alpha : Card(X(x)_{\alpha}) \geq k\}$$

The fuzzy encoding process can be explained by the example XML documents in Figure 1. Fuzzy encoding of documents $A$, $B$ and $C$ will produce the following result when simple encoding (Damiani et al., 2004) is used for the membership definition:

```
A = {<1>/a, <0.5>/c, <0.5>/d,
<0.33>/e, <0.33>/f, <0.5>/g}
B = {<1>/a, <0.5>/c, <0.5>/d, <0.33,
0.33>/e, <0.33>/f, <0.5>/g}
C = {<1>/a, <0.5>/b, <0.5, 0.33>/d,
<0.33>/e, <0.33>/f, <0.5>/g}
```

The fuzzy cardinality representations of the examples presented above have the following form:

```
A = {{1/0, 1/1}*a, {1/0, 0.5/1}*c,
{1/0, 0.5/1}*d, {1/0, 0.33/1}*e,
{1/0, 0.33/1}*f, {1/0, 0.5/1}*g}
B = {{1/0, 1/1}*a, {1/0, 0.5/1}*c,
{1/0, 0.5/1}*d, {1/0, 0.33/1,
0.33/2}*e, {1/0, 0.33/1}*f, {1/0,
0.5/1}*g}
C = {{1/0, 1/1}*a, {1/0, 0.5/1}*b,
{1/0, 0.5/1, 0.33/2}*d, {1/0,
0.33/1}*e, {1/0, 0.33/1}*f, {1/0,
0.5/1}*g}
```

Similarity of the fuzzy sets $X_k$ and $X_m$ can be calculated according to the following formula (Bouchon-Meunier, Rifqi, Bothorel, 1996):

$$s\left(X_k, X_m\right) = \frac{M\left(X_k \cap X_m\right)}{M\left(X_k \cup X_m\right)}$$

where the fuzzy measure $M$ on a fuzzy set $X$ having values from a universe $H$ is defined as (Bouchon-Meunier et al., 1996):

$$M\left(X\right) = \sum_{x \in \mathrm{H}} \mu_X\left(x\right)$$

The extension principle enables the application of the above formula to fuzzy bags obtained by means of fuzzy encoding. In this case, fuzzy cardinality representation of fuzzy bag (Rocacher, 2003) is used, therefore it is needed to calculate:

$$\Omega_{X_k \cap X_m}(x) = \min\left(\Omega_{X_k}(x), \Omega_{X_m}(x)\right)$$
$$\Omega_{X_k \cup X_m}(x) = \max\left(\Omega_{X_k}(x), \Omega_{X_m}(x)\right)$$

Membership values for the operations on fuzzy bags are calculated in the following way:

$$\mu_{\Omega_{X_k \cap X_m}}(z) = \sup_{z = \min(t,v)} \min\left(\mu_{\Omega_{X_k}}(t), \mu_{\Omega_{X_m}}(v)\right)$$
$$\mu_{\Omega_{X_k \cap X_m}}(z) = \sup_{z = \max(t,v)} \min\left(\mu_{\Omega_{X_k}}(t), \mu_{\Omega_{X_m}}(v)\right)$$

The similarity between two XML document structures encoded into the form of fuzzy bags is then computed as follows. Initially, intersection and sum of the fuzzy bag encoding documents $A$ and $B$, and $A$ and $C$ are calculated:

```
A ∩ B = {{1/0, 1/1}*a, {1/0,
0.5/1}*c, {1/0, 0.5/1}*d, {1/0,
0.33/1}*e, {1/0, 0.33/1}*f, {1/0,
0.5/1}*g}
A ∪ B = {{1/0, 1/1}*a, {1/0,
0.5/1}*c, {1/0, 0.5/1}*d, {1/0,
0.33/1, 0.33/2}*e, {1/0, 0.33/1}*f,
{1/0, 0.5/1}*g}
A ∩ C = {{1/0, 1/1}*a, {1/0,
0.5/1}*d, {1/0, 0.33/1}*e, {1/0,
0.33/1}*f, {1/0, 0.5/1}*g}
A ∪ C = {1/0, 1/1}*a, {1/0, 0.5/1}*b,
{1/0, 0.5/1}*c, {1/0, 0.5/1,
0.33/2}*d, {1/0, 0.33/1}*e, {1/0,
0.33/1}*f, {1/0, 0.5/1}*g}
```

Next, the fuzzy measure $M$ is applied on the fuzzy bags resulting from the operations above:

```
M(A ∩ B) = 1 + 0.5 + 0.5 + 0.33 +
0.33 + 0.5 = 3.11
M(A ∪ B) = 1 + 0.5 + 0.5 + 0.33 +
0.33 + 0.33 + 0.5 = 3.44
M(A ∩ C) = 1 + 0.5 + 0.33 + 0.33 +
0.5 = 2.66
M(A ∪ C) = 1 + 0.5 + 0.5 + 0.5 + 0.33
+ 0.33 + 0.33 + 0.5 = 3.99
```

Finally, a quotient of the appropriate values is calculated:

```
s(A,B) = 3.11/3.44 ≈ 0.90
s(A,C) = 2.66/3.99 ≈ 0.67
```

This result reflects the differences existing in the structures of the analysed documents. Cardinality of the element FName creates a difference between documents $A$ and $B$. Slightly larger differences, like different elements Id and Birth, and one additional element Name, also exist between documents $A$ and $C$. These structural differences result as similarity values $s(A,B)$ and $s(A,C)$ smaller then 1. Moreover, the extent of such differences is reflected by the inequality $s(A,B) > s(A,C)$.

Fuzzy encoding is a more complex method comparing to bit or cardinality encoding but it encodes a structure level hierarchy into a "feature vector" produced. However, a drawback of this method can be found in that it does not consider parent-child relations during the encoding process.

## FUZZY CLUSTERING ALGORITHMS

This section presents clustering algorithms that will be then applied to one of the scenarios of XML structure analysis. The fuzzy clustering algorithms here considered are based on the popular *Fuzzy C-Means* (FCM) algorithm. Therefore, the FCM method will first be briefly recalled as an introduction to the further methods.

The FCM algorithm is a partitional clustering method that iteratively minimises a given criterion function in order to calculate a partition of the input data set. As a result of the algorithm, a fuzzy partition into $c$ groups is calculated, therefore it is required to provide as a parameter the number of groups $c$ that are expected to be discovered. The FCM algorithm minimises the criterion function in the iteratively performed steps presented as follows:

1. select $c$ cluster prototypes;
2. calculate the cluster membership value of each data object (on the basis of the data object-prototype distances);
3. calculate the new cluster prototypes (on the basis of the data object membership values);
4. return to step 2 if a stop condition is not met, otherwise the algorithm stops.

The criterion function that is minimised in the FCM clustering process is defined as:

$$Q = \sum_{i=1}^{c} \sum_{k=1}^{N} u_{ik}^{m} \left\| \mathbf{x}_k - \mathbf{v}_i \right\|^2$$

where $||\mathbf{x}_k - \mathbf{v}_i||$ denotes the distance between a data object $\mathbf{x}_k$ and a cluster prototype $\mathbf{v}_i$, $m > 1$ is a parameter influencing the fuzziness of the clusters.

The result of the algorithm are a fuzzy partition matrix $\mathbf{U}=[u_{ik}]$ and a prototype matrix $\mathbf{V}=[\mathbf{v}_i]$. The set of all possible fuzzy partitions of $N$ data objects into $c$ clusters is defined as:

$$\tilde{U} = \left\{ u_{ik} \in [0,1] \middle| \; \sum_{i=1}^{c} u_{ik} = 1, \forall k, \; 0 < \sum_{k=1}^{N} u_{ik} < N, \forall i \right\}$$

The partition matrix $\mathbf{U} \in \tilde{U}$ is defined as:

$$u_{ik} = \sum_{j=1}^{c} \left( \frac{\left\| \mathbf{x}_k - \mathbf{v}_i \right\|}{\left\| \mathbf{x}_k - \mathbf{v}_j \right\|} \right)^{\frac{-2}{m-1}}$$

The cluster prototypes are calculated according to the following formula:

$$\mathbf{v}_i = \frac{\sum_{k=1}^{N} \left( u_{ik} \right)^m \mathbf{x}_k}{\sum_{k=1}^{N} \left( u_{ik} \right)^m}$$

## Conditional Fuzzy C-Means

An interesting modification of the FCM algorithm is the *Conditional Fuzzy C-Means* (CFCM) algorithm presented in (Pedrycz, 1996) and generalised in (Łęski, 2003). The CFCM algorithm assumes that different data objects may have different impact on the resulting partition. This impact is determined by a condition $f_k$ connected with each data object $\mathbf{x}_k$. It is therefore possible to restrict the overall membership values of the data objects by means of condition $f_k$. In this case, all the possible partition matrices which may be calculated for $N$ data objects clustered into $c$ clusters can be defined as:

$$\tilde{U} = \left\{ u_{ik} \in [0,1] \middle| \; \sum_{i=1}^{c} u_{ik} = f_k, \forall k, \; 0 < \sum_{k=1}^{N} u_{ik} < N, \forall i \right\}$$

A partition matrix $\mathbf{U} \in \tilde{U}$ resulting from the CFCM algorithm is defined as:

$$u_{ik} = f_k \sum_{j=1}^{c} \left( \frac{\left\| \mathbf{x}_k - \mathbf{v}_i \right\|}{\left\| \mathbf{x}_k - \mathbf{v}_j \right\|} \right)^{\frac{-2}{m-1}}$$

The cluster prototypes are computed as in the case of the FCM algorithm.

## Proximity-Based Fuzzy C-Means

The *Proximity-based Fuzzy C-Means* (PFCM) algorithm (Pedrycz et al., 2004; Loia et al., 2003) extends the functionality of the FCM method by enabling the incorporation of additional information into the analysis. Such additional information can be exemplified as, e.g., expert knowledge or generally any other data representation different from the one determined as the basis of the analysis. This additional information can be represented in the form of proximity matrix. It is worth recalling that any proximity measure satisfies the conditions of symmetry and reflexivity. Proximity is hence a more general concept than similarity, which needs an additional condition – transitivity – to be defined.

Proximity of the data objects is calculated on the basis of the partition matrix determined by the FCM algorithm by means of the expression:

$$\mathbf{p}\left[k_1, k_2\right] = \sum_{i=1}^{c} \left( \min\left( u_{ik_1}, u_{ik_2} \right) \right)$$

The PFCM algorithm consists of two iteratively performed steps:

1. data-driven partition calculation,
2. additional information-driven partition calculation.

The first step is performed by means of the FCM algorithm. The introduction of the additional proximity based information into the clustering algorithm is performed by a phase of gradient optimisation. FCM provides a frame for the whole algorithm which contains the gradient optimisation process performed in an internal loop as shown in Figure 4.

The criterion that is optimised in the consecutive iterations of the algorithm has the following form:

$$Q = \sum_{k_1=1}^{N}\sum_{k_2=1}^{N}\left(\hat{\mathbf{p}}\left[k_1,k_2\right] - \mathbf{p}\left[k_1,k_2\right]\right)^2 \mathbf{b}\left[k_1,k_2\right]\mathbf{d}\left[k_1,k_2\right]$$

where $\hat{\mathbf{p}}\left[k_1,k_2\right]$ is the proximity calculated on the basis of the partition matrix derived in the FCM step, $\mathbf{p}\left[k_1,k_2\right]$ is the proximity representing additional user-provided information, $\mathbf{b}\left[k_1,k_2\right]$ is a binary matrix that denotes presence (1) or lack of (0) proximity values for a given pair of data objects, $\mathbf{d}\left[k_1,k_2\right]$ is the distance between two data objects. The membership values of the partition matrix are calculated in a gradient optimisation process according to the following formula:

$$u_{st}\left(r+1\right) = \left[u_{st}\left(r\right) - \alpha\frac{\partial Q}{\partial u_{st}\left(r\right)}\right]_{0,1} \qquad s = 1, \ldots, c, t = 1, \ldots, N$$

where $r$ denotes the current iteration, $\alpha$ is a positive learning rate, $[]_{0,1}$ indicates that the results are clipped to a unit interval.

The derivative presented in the formula above can be explicated as follows:

$$\frac{\partial Q}{\partial u_{st}\left(r\right)} = \sum_{k_1=1}^{N}\sum_{k_2=1}^{N}\frac{\partial}{\partial u_{st}}\left(\sum_{i=1}^{c}\left(u_{ik_1}\wedge u_{ik_2}\right) - \mathbf{p}\left[k_1,k_2\right]\right)^2$$
$$= 2\sum_{k_1=1}^{N}\sum_{k_2=1}^{N}\left(\sum_{i=1}^{c}\left(u_{ik_1}\wedge u_{ik_2}\right) - \mathbf{p}\left[k_1,k_2\right]\right)\frac{\partial}{\partial u_{st}}\sum_{i=1}^{c}\left(u_{ik_1}\wedge u_{ik_2}\right)$$

Finally, the derivative computed results in binary values depending on the following condition:

$$\frac{\partial}{\partial u_{st}}\sum_{i=1}^{c}\left(u_{ik_1}\wedge u_{ik_2}\right) = \begin{cases} 1 & \text{if} \quad t = k_1 \quad \text{and} \quad u_{sk_1} \leq u_{sk_2} \\ 1 & \text{if} \quad t = k_2 \quad \text{and} \quad u_{sk_2} \leq u_{sk_1} \\ 0 & \text{otherwise} \end{cases}$$

*Figure 4. Schematic diagram of the PFCM algorithm*

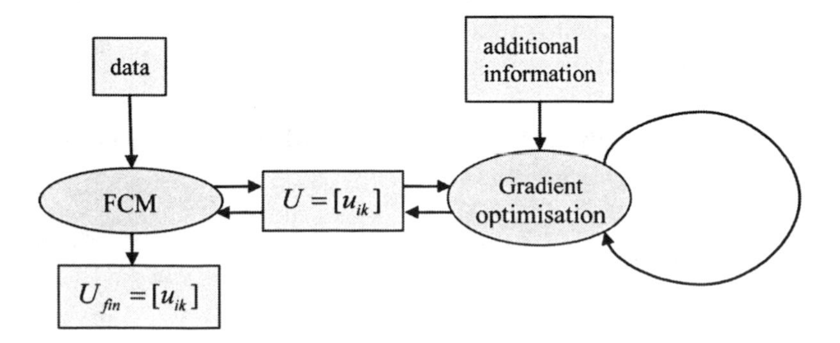

## FUZZY CLUSTERING OF XML STRUCTURES

This section presents in detail two different scenarios of fuzzy clustering of XML structures. It also introduces a *Multilevel* clustering approach dedicated to XML structure analysis and utilized by one of the scenarios.

As previously mentioned, we consider two approaches to clustering XML structures. Both of them correspond to the observation that XML nodes have different significance depending on their level in a structure hierarchy.

The first approach makes use of the encoding method that produces the feature vectors retaining the information about the XML hierarchy. Fuzzy encoding is an example of such method. The membership value of each node calculated by means of this method depends on its level in a document hierarchy. Therefore, the differences of position of the nodes are taken under consideration when similarity of the document structures is calculated. The similarity matrix calculated on the basis of fuzzy encoded XML documents can be further utilized by such clustering algorithms as the agglomerative hierarchical methods (e.g., complete link hierarchical clustering) or the density-based methods (e.g., DBSCAN).

The second approach needs a special type of clustering method that is able to use information about the structure levels of the analysed XML nodes. In this approach, simple encoding methods like bit or cardinality encoding methods can be applied. Bit and cardinality encoding methods are not able to enclose hierarchical information into a feature vector. The structure level of each XML node can be however easily recorded during the encoding process and used within the clustering algorithm. A clustering algorithm able to make use of such information is *Multilevel clustering of XML documents* (Kozielski, 2007). In order to illustrate and compare the above two approaches, the characteristics of these scenarios are presented in Table 3.

*Multilevel clustering of XML documents* (ML) (Kozielski, 2007; Kozielski, 2008) starts clustering at a root level and continues the process at the following levels. In this way it differentiates features treating the elements placed in the neighbourhood of a root element as more significant. It is possible to stop the algorithm at a certain level of the document structure tree reducing a number of features which are processed. Clustering on each level can be performed by means of any clustering algorithm. The general pseudo-code description of the ML method is presented next, while an illustrative scheme of how the algorithm is performed (how the document features are analysed) is presented in Figure 5:

1. start at the document root level ($l$=1);
2. for each consecutive level $l$+1 in a document structure:
   a. calculate the impact of the partition derived at the previous level $l$;

*Table 3. Comparison of the two scenarios of fuzzy clustering XML structures*

| | | Approach *A* | Approach *B* |
|---|---|---|---|
| **Encoding process** | *method* | Hierarchical encoding<br>(e.g., fuzzy encoding) | Flat encoding<br>(e.g., bit encoding) |
| | *result* | feature vectors representing hierarchical structure | • feature vectors representing flat structure<br>• information about the hierarchy of features |
| **Clustering process** | *method* | "Traditional" clustering algorithm<br>(e.g., complete link hierarchical clustering) | Hierarchy aware clustering algorithm<br>(e.g., Multilevel clustering) |
| | *result* | Partition taking under consideration hierarchical nature of data | |

Figure 5. Example steps of the multilevel clustering

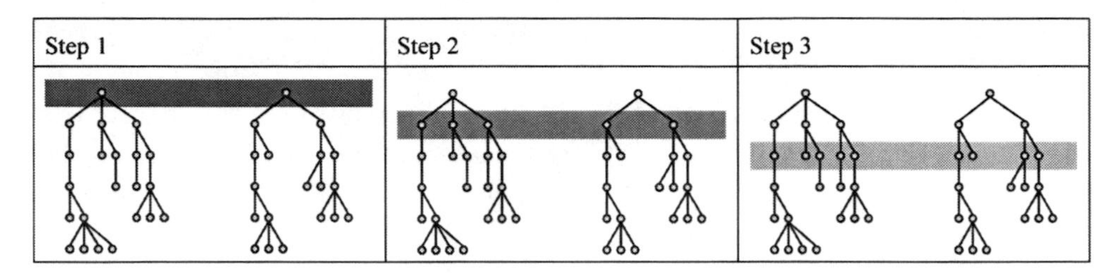


b. create new partition into $c_{l+1}$ groups based on the information at the previous level $l$;

3. if the total number of clusters $c$ is reached or the maximal structure level $L$ is reached, the algorithm stops.

Figure 6 illustrates an example of results obtained by hard clustering applied to the ML method. In Figure 6(a), the feature space of a set of XML documents is represented with respect to three levels of XML document structures. Documents are placed on the horizontal axis, structure levels are placed on the vertical axis, and the existing clusters relevant to different feature values are depicted by different colours. The result of applying hard ML (Figure 6(b)) is marked by thick black lines separating the clusters, where the final number of clusters was set to three. The example shown in this figure also illustrates a problem which may be encountered when applying hard clustering (e.g., *k*-means algorithm) to the ML method. The hard partitioning on the second level of the document trees is directly transferred to the next iteration and determines the clusters on the third level making one of them inconsistent. In order to solve the presented problem, it is needed to introduce an algorithm that can affect the clustering on level $l+1$ by the results of the clustering performed on level $l$ without determining them in a hard way.

The fuzzy partition matrix calculated in a fuzzy clustering algorithm shows us that there are data objects that belong very clearly to one group only (the membership value is remarkably the highest for this group). Moreover, there can be some data objects almost equally belonging to two different groups. Therefore, application of fuzzy clustering algorithm to the ML method at level $l$ will suggest (but not strictly determine) the direction of clustering at level $l+1$ by means of a fuzzy partition. The "suggestions" in the form of fuzzy partition matrix calculated at level $l$ have to be provided as a parameter to the clustering method executed at level $l+1$.

The application of fuzzy clustering algorithm to the ML approach is illustrated in Figure 7, analogously to Figure 6. The curves in Figure 7(b) represent the fuzzy membership values of the documents, and Figure 7(c) shows the final hard result of the clustering performed by means of fuzzy ML method, which overcomes the problem identified in Figure 6(b).

Figure 6. Illustration of (a) feature space of a set of XML documents and (b) the partition created by hard Multilevel clustering of XML documents

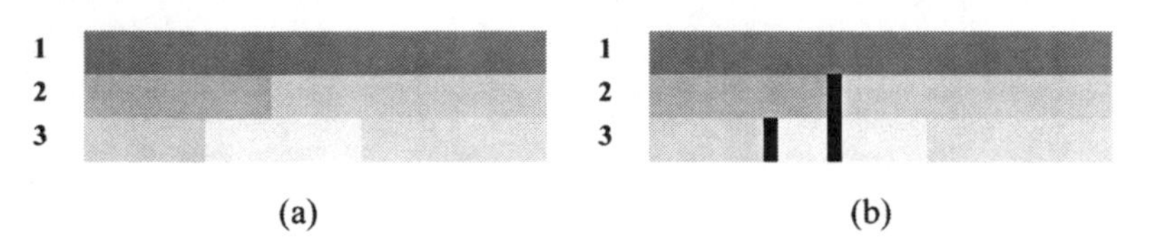

*Figure 7. Illustration of (a) feature space of a set of XML documents, (b) the partition created by fuzzy Multilevel clustering of XML documents, and (c) the resulting hard partition*

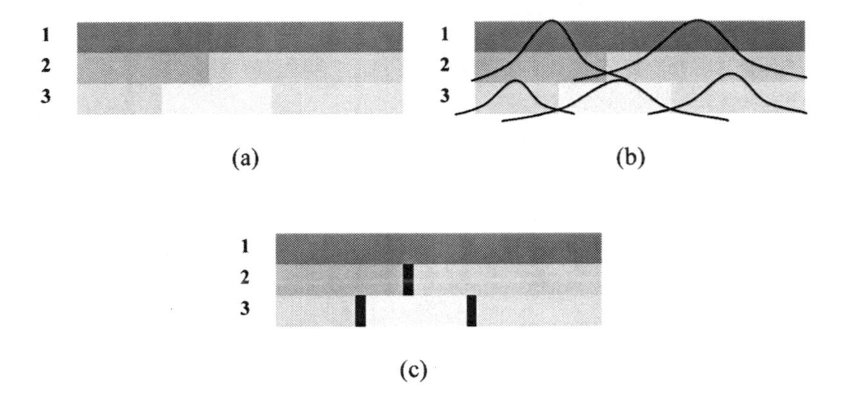


## The MLCFCM Algorithm

In the following, we describe as two types of fuzzy clustering algorithms are applied to the ML approach. The *Conditional Fuzzy C-Means* (CFCM) algorithm (Pedrycz, 1996) is one of these algorithms (Kozielski, 2007). The ML method utilizing the CFCM algorithm will be hereinafter referred to as MLCFCM.

CFCM can use a condition $f_k$ influencing the resulting partition calculated by means of this algorithm. The partition matrix $\mathbf{U}^l$ to be calculated by MLCFCM at a current level $l$ of the document structure trees becomes the base for condition matrix $\mathbf{F}^l = [f_{ki}]$ (where $i = 1, \ldots, c$) which contains the values of the condition parameter used in CFCM. In this way, we do not apply a single condition value to each document but a vector of values ($\mathbf{f}_k$) that modify the impact of this document on each cluster. Condition parameters impact on a new fuzzy partition $\mathbf{U}^{l+1}$ on a level $l+1$. The final partition $\mathbf{U}^L$, where $L$ being a maximal analysed structure level is a stop condition provided by a user, can be made as binary giving a hard partition and a set of disjoint clusters. The clustering process performed by the MLCFCM algorithm is illustrated in Figure 8.

There are some issues connected with the MLCFCM clustering. In fact, the following parameters have to be provided to the algorithm:

- information about the level of each feature in the form of a feature vector containing integer values,
- the total number of groups $c$,

*Figure 8. Illustration of the MLCFCM algorithm*

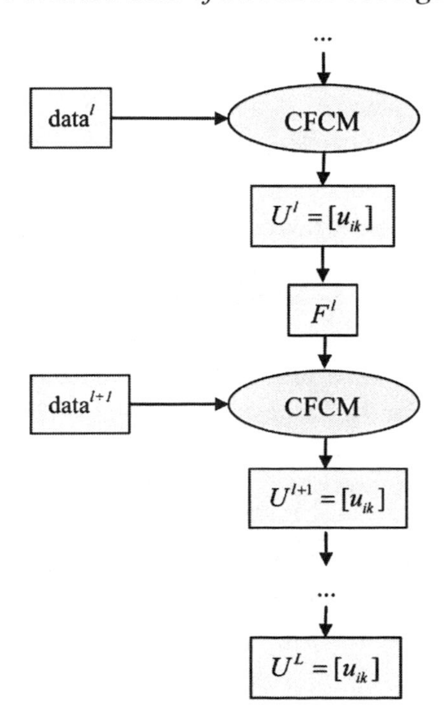

- the number of groups that are to be created on each consecutive structure level.

Evaluating a number of groups is a known problem discussed thoroughly in literature. It will not be therefore analysed in this place. However, it must be taken under consideration that additional analysis is needed in order to define the number of groups on each XML document structure level.

Another issue that must be taken under consideration is the transfer of information between clustering at level $l$ and $l$+1. This inter-level information transfer is preformed in case of the MLCFCM method by transforming the resulting fuzzy partition into the condition matrix. The process consists of two types of transformations:

change of the partition matrix dimensionality enabling the impact of the given partitioning on each cluster created at the next level $l$+1:

$$\hat{\mathbf{U}}^{l+1}_{(c_{l+1}\times N)} = \delta\left(\mathbf{U}^{l}_{(c_l\times N)}\right),$$

modification of the partition matrix values giving the expected impact of the condition parameters:

$$\mathbf{F}^{l+1} = g(\hat{\mathbf{U}}^{l+1}).$$

The result of the algorithm is a fuzzy partition matrix containing the membership values of each document to each cluster. The matrix can be further processed in order to point the noise documents in the analysed collection. The documents that do not create coherent clusters can be defined as noise data. We can recognise such data looking for the documents having equal or nearly equal membership values. Two examples of such documents are:

- a document that is equally similar to two or more groups (e.g., combining two types of structures),
- a document that is very different from each of the structure types creating the clusters and therefore it is equally very distant to all the groups.

If the coherent clusters are needed as a result of the analysis then the resulting partition should be reduced by rejecting all the documents having insufficient variance of cluster membership values.

If a crisp clustering result is needed then the final fuzzy partition matrix $\mathbf{U}^L = [u_{ik}]$ can be binarised according to the following formula:

$$u_{ik} = \begin{cases} 1, & if\ u_{ik} = \max_{j=1..c_l}(u_{jk}) \\ 0, & if\ u_{ik} \neq \max_{j=1..c_l}(u_{jk}) \end{cases}$$

The implementation of the MLCFCM algorithm in (Kozielski, 2007) shows that this method is able to correctly detect groups in the hierarchical structure of XML documents. The structures analysed were artificially generated in order to reflect the example presented in Figure 7. The algorithm was also tested on real-life data (Kozielski, 2008). The application of the ML clustering algorithm in order to speed up the execution of qualitative and quantitative selective queries on a collection of XML documents was assessed in the experiments. Results showed that the quality of clustering depends on the complexity of the XML document structures.

The MLCFCM method proved to be able to perform better comparing to "traditional" hard clustering methods making use of the hierarchical XML structure encoding (approach *A* in Table 3). The experiments showed that the structure type of the XML documents that are clustered is an important factor influencing the results of the analysis. The MLCFCM method gives better results comparing to hard clustering methods in the case of text-centric XML documents. This result can be explained by a feature space reduction when the ML method is applied. When data-centric and text-centric XML documents are analysed by means of "traditional" clustering algorithms, it can be seen that the necessity of the full feature space analysis strongly reduces the quality of results in case of the latter structure type. By contrast, the characteristics of the MLCFCM method make the quality of results more stable and independent of the clustered documents structures.

## The MLPFCM Algorithm

The *Proximity-based Fuzzy C-Means* (PFCM) algorithm (Pedrycz et al., 2004) is the second approach that can be implemented following the ML method, and will be called MLPFCM. As previously mentioned, the PFCM algorithm can in fact utilize additional information provided in the form of a proximity matrix which is calculated on the basis of the FCM fuzzy partition matrix. The basic data that are analysed by means of the MLPFCM method refers to the XML documents described by the features existing at a given structure level $l+1$. The additional information influencing the clustering results is the partition matrix calculated on the level $l$ and transformed to obtain the form of a proximity matrix. The clustering process performed by the MLPFCM algorithm is illustrated in Figure 9.

The approaches previously presented ensure that clustering on a level closer to the root element will influence the partitioning of the features that are placed further in the XML document tree. At the same time, a direct transfer of cluster borders (which is performed when hard clustering is used) is avoided, which enables the algorithm to produce a correct result for the case presented in Figure 7. It is also possible to stop the algorithm at a certain level of the document structure tree reducing the number of features that are processed.

## FUTURE RESEARCH DIRECTIONS

The methods presented in this chapter have shown the possible application of fuzzy clustering to XML structure analysis. The two possible scenarios and the applications of the methods presented do not exhaust however the domain of fuzzy analysis of XML documents. There are still several open issues to be solved.

One of the possible future research is application of another clustering algorithm to the

*Figure 9. Illustration of the MLPFCM algorithm*

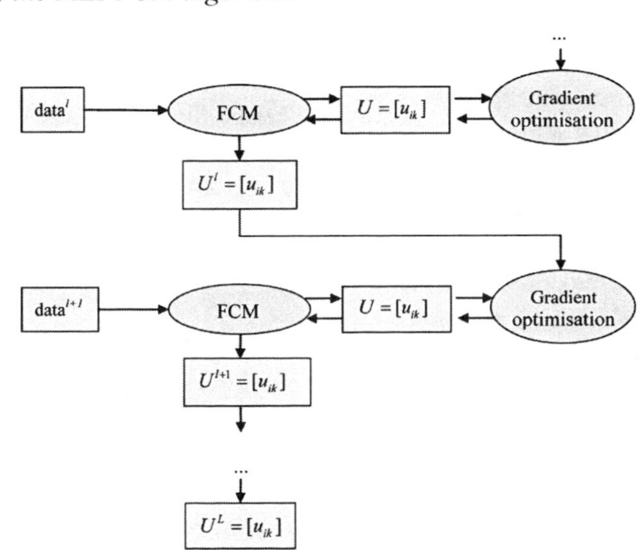

ML approach. The methods based on the FCM algorithm presented in the previous sections require a parameter pointing a number of clusters that have to be revealed in data. This task is not trivial especially when complex data like XML documents are considered. The ML method performs clustering on each structure level which introduces additional complexity connected with the number of clusters. It is interesting therefore to analyse other clustering algorithms, like e.g., density-based methods, that do not require to apply this parameter.

Further analysis including comparison of the two scenarios of fuzzy clustering XML structures and development of these scenarios would also be valuable. The ML method has shown to be useful when the analysis of XML documents having complex structure is performed (Kozielski, 2008). The modelling of a collection of complex XML documents (e.g., text-centric XML documents) by means of bit encoding may produce very large feature vectors. In this case, it may be profitable to apply the ML method that stops at a chosen structure level and reduces the complexity of the analysis. For instance, we may prefer to generalise the structure information by analysing only the first *k* levels instead of taking under consideration all the details represented by leaf nodes. Further analysis of this issue considering different applications of the methods could give a new interesting insight into the topic at hand.

Another interesting future direction refers to the combination of text and structure analysis in our fuzzy approach, as XML documents contain text data on different structure levels and it is usual to analyse text in the context of a document structure. The ML method makes it possible to combine information from different sources.

## CONCLUSION

This chapter presented and discussed application of fuzzy methods to clustering XML document structures. The observation that the importance of XML nodes depends on their position in a document structure was laid as a base point of the presented analysis. Application of fuzzy approaches enables proper modelling of this observation which makes the presented methods interesting.

Two different scenarios of the analysis were presented in the chapter. The first one encodes the hierarchy of the document structure into a fuzzy bag. The latter scenario utilizes hierarchical information in the *Multilevel* clustering algorithm.

Other different implementations are possible for the above scenarios. The chapter also discussed some future directions of research that could be conducted in the context of fuzzy clustering of XML documents. Several open areas indeed would need to be explored.

## REFERENCES

Achtert, E., Kriegel, H. P., Pryakhin, A., & Schubert, M. (2005). Hierarchical density-based clustering for multi-represented objects. In Z. W. Ras, S. Tsumoto, & D. A. Zighed (Eds.), *IEEE Workshop on Mining Complex Data (MCD 2005), 5th International Conference on Data Mining (ICDM)*, (pp. 9-16).

Ankerst, M., Breunig, M., Kriegel, H. P., & Sander, J. (1999). OPTICS: Ordering points to identify the clustering structure. *SIGMOD Record*, *28*(2), 49–60. doi:10.1145/304181.304187

Antonellis, P., Makris, C., & Tsirakis, N. (2008). XEdge: Clustering homogeneous and heterogeneous XML documents using edge summaries. In R. L. Wainwright, & H. Haddad (Eds.), *Proceedings of the 2008 ACM Symposium on Applied Computing (SAC)*, (pp. 1081-1088), ACM.

Bordawekar, R., & Shmueli, O. (2004). Flexible workload-aware clustering of XML documents. In Z. Bellahsene, T. Milo, M. Rys, D. Suciu, & R. Unland (Eds.), *Proceedings of the Second International XML Database Symposium (XSym) Lecture Notes in Computer Science: Vol. 3186* (pp. 204–218). Springer.

Bouchon-Meunier, B., Rifqi, M., & Bothorel, S. (1996). Towards general measures of comparison of objects. *Fuzzy Sets and Systems*, *84*(2), 143–153. doi:10.1016/0165-0114(96)00067-X

Ceravolo, P., & Damiani, E. (2005). Mining class hierarchies from XML data: Representation techniques. In B. Reusch (Ed.), *Computational intelligence, theory and applications (fuzzy days): Vol. 33. Advances in soft computing* (pp. 385-396). Springer.

Ceravolo, P., Nocerino, M. C., & Viviani, M. (2004). Knowledge extraction from semi-structured data based on fuzzy techniques. In Negoita, M. G., Howlett, R. J., & Jain, L. C. (Eds.), *Knowledge-Based Intelligent Information & Engineering Systems (KES) Lecture Notes in Computer Science* (*Vol. 3215*, pp. 328–334). Springer. doi:10.1007/978-3-540-30134-9_44

Costa, G., Manco, G., Ortale, R., & Tagarelli, A. (2004). A tree-based approach to clustering XML documents by structure. In J.-F. Boulicaut, et al. (Eds.), *Eighth European Conference on Principles and Practice of Knowledge Discovery in Databases (PKDD) Lecture Notes in Computer Science: Vol. 3202* (pp. 137-148), Springer.

Dalamagas, T., Cheng, T., Winkel, K., & Sellis, T. (2004). Clustering XML documents using structural summaries. In Lindner, W., Mesiti, M., Türker, C., Tzitzikas, Y., & Vakali, A. (Eds.), *Workshops on Current Trends in Database Technology (EDBT) Lecture Notes in Computer Science* (*Vol. 3268*, pp. 547–556). Springer. doi:10.1007/978-3-540-30192-9_54

Dalamagas, T., Cheng, T., Winkel, K. J., & Sellis, T. (2006). A methodology for clustering XML documents by structure. *Information Systems*, *31*(3), 187–228. doi:10.1016/j.is.2004.11.009

Damiani, E., Nocerino, M. C., & Viviani, M. (2004). Knowledge extraction from an XML data flow: Building a taxonomy based on clustering technique. *Eighth Meeting EURO Working Group on Fuzzy Sets (EUROFUSE 2004)*, (pp. 133-142)

Ester, M., Kriegel, H., Sander, J., & Xu, X. (1996). A density-based algorithm for discovering clusters in large spatial databases with noise. In *International Conference on Knowledge Discovery in Databases and Data Mining (KDD)*, (pp. 226-231).

Flesca, S., Manco, G., Masciari, E., Pontieri, L., & Pugliese, A. (2005). Fast detection of XML structural similarity. *IEEE Transactions on Knowledge and Data Engineering*, *17*(2), 160–175. doi:10.1109/TKDE.2005.27

Guha, S., Rastogi, R., & Shim, K. (1999). ROCK: A robust clustering algorithm for categorical attributes. *Proceedings of the 15th International Conference on Data Engineering (ICDE)*, (pp. 512-521). IEEE Computer Society Press.

Hagenbuchner, M., Sperduti, A., Tsoi, A. C., Trentini, F., Scarselli, F., & Gori, M. (2006). Clustering XML documents using self-organizing maps for structures. In N. Fuhr, M. Lalmas, S. Malik, & G. Kazai (Eds.), *4th International Workshop of the Initiative for the Evaluation of XML Retrieval (INEX): Vol. 3977. Lecture Notes in Computer Science* (pp. 481–496). Springer.

Han, J., & Kamber, M. (2001). *Data mining: Concepts and techniques*. San Francisco, CA: Morgan Kaufmann.

Kailing, K., Kriegel, H. P., Pryakhin, A., & Schubert, M. (2004). Clustering multi-represented objects with noise. In H. Dai, R. Srikant, & C. Zhang (Eds.), *Advances in Knowledge Discovery and Data Mining, 8th Pacific-Asia Conference (PAKDD) Lecture Notes in Computer Science: Vol. 3056* (pp. 394-403). Springer.

Kozielski, M. (2007). Multilevel conditional fuzzy c-means clustering of XML documents. In J. N. Kok, J. Koronacki, R. L. de Màntaras, S. Matwin, D. Mladenic, & A. Skowron (Eds.), 11th *European Conference on Principles and Practice of Knowledge Discovery in Databases (PKDD) Lecture Notes in Computer Science: Vol. 4702*. (pp. 532–539). Springer.

Kozielski, M. (2008). *Grupowanie dokumentów XML względem ich struktury (in Polish)*. Ph.D. dissertation, Silesian University of Technology, Gliwice, Poland.

Łęski, J. (2003). Generalized weighted conditional fuzzy clustering. *IEEE Transactions on Fuzzy Systems, 11*(6), 709–715. doi:10.1109/TFUZZ.2003.819844

Lian, W., Cheung, D. W., Mamoulis, N., & Yiu, A. M. (2004). An efficient and scalable algorithm for clustering XML documents by structure. *IEEE Transactions on Knowledge and Data Engineering, 16*(1), 82–96. doi:10.1109/TKDE.2004.1264824

Loia, V., Pedrycz, W., & Senatore, S. (2003). P-FCM: A proximity-based fuzzy clustering for user-centered web applications. *International Journal of Approximate Reasoning, 34*(2-3), 121–144. doi:10.1016/j.ijar.2003.07.004

Loia, V., Pedrycz, W., & Senatore, S. (2007). Semantic Web content analysis: A study in proximity-based collaborative clustering. *IEEE Transactions on Fuzzy Systems, 15*(6), 1294–1312. doi:10.1109/TFUZZ.2006.889970

Nayak, R. (2008). Fast and effective clustering of XML data utilizing their structural information. *Knowledge and Information Systems, 14*(2), 197–215. doi:10.1007/s10115-007-0080-8

Nayak, R., & Iryadi, I. (2006). XMine: A methodology for mining XML structure. In X. Zhou, J. Li, H. T. Shen, M. Kitsuregawa, & Y. Zhang (Eds.), *The 8th Asia Pacific Web Conference (APWeb) Lecture Notes in Computer Science: Vol. 3841*, (pp. 786–792). Springer.

Nayak, R., & Tran, T. (2007). A progressive clustering algorithm to group the XML data by structural and semantic similarity. *International Journal of Pattern Recognition and Artificial Intelligence, 21*(4), 723–743. doi:10.1142/S0218001407005648

Nierman, A., & Jagadish, H. V. (2002). Evaluating structural similarity in XML documents. In *Proceedings of the 5th International Workshop on the Web and Databases (WebDB)*, (pp. 61-66).

Pedrycz, W. (1996). Conditional fuzzy c-means. *Pattern Recognition Letters, 17*(6), 625–631. doi:10.1016/0167-8655(96)00027-X

Pedrycz, W. (2002). Collaborative fuzzy clustering. *Pattern Recognition Letters, 23*(14), 1675–1686. doi:10.1016/S0167-8655(02)00130-7

Pedrycz, W., Loia, V., & Senatore, S. (2004). P-FCM: A proximity-based fuzzy clustering. *Fuzzy Sets and Systems, 148*(1), 21–41. doi:10.1016/j.fss.2004.03.004

Pedrycz, W., & Rai, P. (2008). Collaborative clustering with the use of fuzzy c-means and its quantification. *Fuzzy Sets and Systems, 159*(18), 2399–2427. doi:10.1016/j.fss.2007.12.030

Rocacher, D. (2003). On fuzzy bags and their application to flexible querying. *Fuzzy Sets and Systems, 140*(1), 93–110. doi:10.1016/S0165-0114(03)00029-0

Strehl, A., & Ghosh, J. (2002). Cluster ensembles – A knowledge reuse framework for combining multiple partitions. *Journal of Machine Learning Research, 3*, 583–617.

Tagarelli, A., & Greco, S. (2006). Toward semantic XML clustering. In J. Ghosh, D. Lambert, D. B. Skillicorn, & J. Srivastava (Eds.), *Proceedings of the 6th SIAM International Conference on Data Mining (SDM)*, (pp. 188-199). SIAM.

Tagarelli, A., & Greco, S. (2010). Semantic clustering of XML documents. *ACM Transactions on Information Systems*, *28*(1). doi:10.1145/1658377.1658380

Wang, J. T. L., Liu, J., & Wang, J. (2005). XML clustering and retrieval through principal component analysis. *International Journal of Artificial Intelligence Tools*, *14*(4), 683–699. doi:10.1142/S0218213005002326

Yoon, J. P., Raghavan, V., Chakilam, V., & Kerschberg, L. (2001). BitCube: A three-dimensional bitmap indexing for XML documents. *Journal of Intelligent Information Systems*, *17*(2-3), 241–254. doi:10.1023/A:1012861931139

Zadeh, L. A. (1965). Fuzzy sets. *Information and Control*, *8*(3), 338–353. doi:10.1016/S0019-9958(65)90241-X

## ADDITIONAL READING

Additional reading on clustering: a review: (Jain et al., 1999), validation techniques: (Halkidi et al., 2001)

Additional reading on complex multi-represented data clustering: information combination at the level of similarity matrices: (Kustra & Zagdanski, 2006), (Havens et al., 2008), cluster ensemble approaches: (Johnson & Kargupta, 1999; Strehl & Ghosh, 2002; Topchy et al., 2005), application of fuzzy methods: (Gruca et al., 2009).

Additional reading on fuzzy clustering: approaches different than c-means method – relational clustering – fuzzy c-medoids: (Krishnapuram et al., 2001)

Additional reading on fuzzy sets: introduction to the topic: (Pedrycz & Gomide, 1998) and a very exhaustive work (Łęski, 2008) covering the topics of fuzzy sets, neuro-fuzzy systems and also fuzzy clustering methods; unfortunately only in Polish.

Gruca, A., Kozielski, M., & Sikora, M. (2009). Fuzzy Clustering and Gene Ontology Based Decision Rules for Identification and Description of Gene Groups, *International Conference on Man-Machine Interaction (ICMMI): Vol. 59. Advances in Soft Computing* (pp. 141–149). Springer.

Halkidi, M., Batistakis, Y., & Vazirgiannis, M. (2001). On Clustering Validation Techniques. *Journal of Intelligent Information Systems*, *17*(2-3), 107–145. doi:10.1023/A:1012801612483

Havens, T. C., Keller, J. M., MacNeal Rehrig, E., Appel, H. M., Popescu, M., Schultz, J. C., & Bezdek, J. C. (2008). Fuzzy Custer Analysis of Bioinformatics Data Composed of Microarray Expression Data and Gene Ontology Annotations. In *North American Fuzzy Information Processing Society (NAFIPS)*, (pp. 1-6). IEEE Computer Society.

Jain, A. K., Murty, M. N., & Flynn, P. J. (1999). Data Clustering: A Review. *ACM Computing Surveys*, *31*(3), 264–323. doi:10.1145/331499.331504

Johnson, E. L., & Kargupta, H. (1999). Collective Hierarchical Clustering from Distributed, Heterogeneous Data. In M. J. Zaki, and C. T. Ho (Eds.), *Large-Scale Parallel Data Mining: Vol. 1759. Lecture Notes in Computer Science* (pp. 221-244). Springer.

Krishnapuram, R., Joshi, A., Nasraoui, O., & Yi, L. (2001). Low-Complexity Fuzzy Relational Clustering Algorithms for Web Mining. *IEEE Transactions on Fuzzy Systems*, *9*(4), 595–607. doi:10.1109/91.940971

Kustra, R., & Zagdanski, A. (2006). Incorporating Gene Ontology in Clustering Gene Expression Data. In *Proceedings of the 19th IEEE Symposium on Computer-Based Medical Systems*, (pp. 555-563). IEEE Computer Society.

Łęski, J. (2008). *Systemy neuronowo-rozmyte*. Warszawa: WNT. (in Polish)

Pedrycz, W., & Gomide, F. (1998). *An Introduction to Fuzzy Sets; Analysis and Design*. MIT Press.

Topchy, A., Jain, K., & Punch, W. (2005). Clustering Ensembles: Models of Consensus and Weak Partitions. *IEEE Transactions on Pattern Analysis and Machine Intelligence*, *27*(12), 1866–1881. doi:10.1109/TPAMI.2005.237

# Chapter 9
# XML Tree Classification on Evolving Data Streams[1]

**Albert Bifet**
*University of Waikato, New Zealand*

**Ricard Gavaldà**
*UPC Barcelona Tech, Spain*

## ABSTRACT

*Nowadays, advanced analysis of data streams is quickly becoming a key area of data mining research, as the number of applications demanding such processing increases. Online mining when such data streams evolve over time, that is, when concepts drift or change completely, is becoming one of the core issues. At the same time, closure-based mining on relational data has recently provided some interesting algorithmic developments as well as practical uses. In this chapter we show how to use closure-based mining to reduce drastically the number of attributes in XML tree classification tasks. Moreover, using maximal frequent trees, we reduce even more the number of attributes needed in tree classification, in many cases without losing accuracy. We show a general framework to classify XML trees using subtree occurrence, composing a Tree XML Closed Frequent Miner with a classifier algorithm. We present specific methods that can adaptively mining closed patterns from data streams that change over time.*

## INTRODUCTION

Pattern classification and frequent pattern discovery have possibly become the most important data mining tasks over the last decade. Nowadays, they are becoming harder, as the size of the pattern datasets is increasing, data often comes from sequential, streaming sources, and we cannot assume that data has been generated from a static distribution. If we want accuracy in the results of our algorithms, we have to consider that the distribution that generates data may vary over time, often in an unpredictable and drastic way.

DOI: 10.4018/978-1-61350-356-0.ch009

Tree Mining is becoming an important field of research due, among others, to the fact that XML patterns are tree patterns and that XML has become a standard for information representation and exchange over the Internet. XML data is growing and it will soon constitute one of the largest collection of human knowledge. Other applications of tree mining appear in chemical informatics, computer vision, text retrieval, bioinformatics, and Web analysis (Nayak et al., 2009, Denoyer, Gallinari, & Vercoustre, 2006). XML tree classification (Denoyer & Gallinari, 2004) has been done traditionally using information retrieval techniques considering the labels of nodes as bags of words (Campos, Fernandez-Luna, Huete, & Romero, 2008, Yang & Zhang, 2008) without taking into account the structure of the trees (Ceci & Appice, 2006). With the development of frequent tree miners, classification methods using frequent trees appeared (Zaki & Aggarwal, 2003, Kudo & Matsumoto, 2004, Collins & Duffy, 2001, Kashima & Koyanagi, 2002). Recently, closed frequent miners were proposed (Chi, Xia, Yang, & Muntz, 2005, Termier et al., 2008, Arimura & Uno, 2005), and using them for classification tasks is the next natural step (Kutty, Tran, Nayak, & Li, 2008, Candillier et al., 2007).

The main advantage of using closed patterns is that they still contain the essential information about frequent patterns while eliminating redundant one. In this chapter we show how closure-based mining can be used to reduce drastically the number of attributes in tree classification tasks. Also, we show how to use maximal frequent trees to reduce even more the number of attributes needed in tree classification, in many cases without loosing accuracy.

We study and show a general framework to classify XML trees based on subtree occurrence. It is formed by the composition of a *tree XML closed frequent miner* with a *classification algorithm*. We discuss specific methods for adaptively dealing with the problem on data streams that vary over time.

The rest of the chapter is organized as follows. We discuss the data stream setting and mention briefly some previous XML classification methods in Section "Background". Sections "Frequent Pattern Compression" and "Classification using Compressed Frequent Patterns" introduce a tree closure operator and its properties needed for XML classification. Section "XML Tree Classification framework on data streams" shows the tree classification framework and introduces an adaptive closed frequent mining method. Experimental results are discussed in Section "Experimental Evaluation". Finally, Section "Conclusions and Future Works" concludes this chapter.

## BACKGROUND

### Data Streams

Conventional knowledge discovery tools assume that the volume of data is such that we can store all data in memory or local secondary storage, and there is no limitation on processing time. In the *data stream* model, data is not all available at once, but arrives in sequence and results must be given at all times with respect to the data seen so far. Additionally, not all data can be stored for future revisiting, and results must be computed essentially in real time; that is, we have memory and time restrictions. Examples of data streams are sensor streams, video streams, network event logs, telephone call records, credit card transactional flows, etc. An important fact is that the nature or distribution of data may be evolving over time, so we need methods that adapt automatically.

The following constraints apply in data streams:

1. Data arrives as a potentially infinite sequence. Thus, it is impossible to store it all. Only a small summary can be computed and stored.

2. The speed of arrival is fast, so that each particular element has to be processed essentially in real time, and then discarded.
3. The distribution generating the items may change over time. Thus, data from the past may become irrelevant (or even harmful) for the current prediction.

Under the constraints of the data stream model, the main properties of an ideal learning method are the following: high accuracy, fast adaption to change, low computational cost in both space and time, and minimal number of parameters to be provided by the user. Theoretical guarantees of performance are very desirable features too.

These properties may be interdependent: adjusting the time and space used by an algorithm can influence performance. By storing more precomputed information, such as look up tables, an algorithm can run faster at the expense of space. An algorithm can also run faster by processing less information, either by stopping early or storing less, thus having less data to process. The more time an algorithm has, the more likely it is that performance can be increased.

The state-of-the-art methods for classification of evolving data streams are learners based on decision trees (Mitchell, 1997). A *Hoeffding tree* (Domingos & Hulten, 2000) is an incremental, anytime decision tree induction algorithm that is capable of learning from massive data streams, assuming that the distribution generating examples does not change over time. Hoeffding trees exploit the fact that a small sample can often be enough to choose an optimal splitting attribute. This idea is supported mathematically by the Hoeffding bound, which quantifies the number of observations (in our case, examples) needed to estimate some statistics within a prescribed precision (in our case, the information gain of an attribute). More precisely, the Hoeffding bound states that with probability $1-\delta$, the true mean of a random variable of range $R$ will not differ from the estimated mean after $n$ independent observations by more than:

$$\epsilon = \sqrt{\frac{R^2 \ln(1/\delta)}{2n}}.$$

A theoretically appealing feature of Hoeffding Trees is that one can show that the output of a Hoeffding tree is asymptotically nearly identical to that of a non-incremental learner using infinitely many examples.

Bagging and boosting (Mitchell, 1997) are ensemble methods used to improve the accuracy of classifier methods. Non-streaming bagging builds a set of $M$ base models, training each model with a bootstrap sample of size $N$ created by drawing random samples with replacement from the original training set. Each base model's training set contains each of the original training example $K$ times where $P(K=k)$ follows a binomial distribution. This binomial distribution for large values of $N$ tends to a Poisson(1) distribution, where Poisson(1)=exp(−1)/$k$!. Using this fact, Oza and Russell (2001, 2001) proposed *Online Bagging*, an online method that instead of sampling with replacement, gives each example a weight according to Poisson(1). In (Bifet, Holmes, Pfahringer, Kirkby, & Gavaldà, 2009) two new state-of-the-art bagging methods were presented: ASHT Bagging using trees of different sizes, and ADWIN Bagging using a change detector to decide when to discard underperforming ensemble members.

Boosting algorithms combine multiple base models to obtain a small generalization error. Non-streaming boosting builds a set of models sequentially, with the construction of each new model depending on the performance of the previously constructed models. The intuitive idea of boosting is to give more weight to misclassified examples, and reduce the weight of the correctly classified ones.

From studies appearing in the literature (N. C. Oza & Russell, 2001, N. Oza & Russell, 2001, Bifet et al., 2009), the Online Bagging method seems to perform better than online boosting methods.

## XML Tree Classification

In the past years, several methods have been proposed for XML tree classification. Zaki and Aggarwal presented XRules in (Zaki & Aggarwal, 2003). Their classification method mines frequent trees in order to create classification rules. They do not use closed frequent trees, only frequent trees. XRules is cost-sensitive and uses Bayesian rule based class decision making. They also proposed methods for effective rule prioritization and testing.

Kudo and Matsumoto presented a boosting method for tree classification in (Kudo & Matsumoto, 2004), which consists of decision stumps that use significant frequent subtrees as features and a boosting algorithm which employs the subtree-based decision stumps as weak learners. With Maeda they extended this classification method to graphs in (Kudo, Maeda, & Matsumoto, 2004).

Other works use SVMs defining tree kernels (Collins & Duffy, 2001, Kashima & Koyanagi, 2002). Tree kernel is one of the convolutions kernels, and maps the example represented in a labeled ordered tree into all subtree spaces. The feature space uses frequent trees rather than closed trees.

Chi et al. proposed CMTreeMiner (2005), the first algorithm to discover all closed and maximal frequent labeled induced subtrees without first discovering all frequent subtrees. CMTreeMiner shares many features with CloseGraph (Yan & Han, 2003). Termier et al. proposed DryadeParent (2008), based on the hooking principle first introduced in Dryade. They claim that the branching factor and depth of the frequent patterns to find are key factors in the complexity of tree mining algorithm and that DryadeParent outperforms CMTreeMiner, on datasets where the frequent patterns have a high branching factor.

## Frequent Pattern Compression

In this section we describe the mathematical framework that forms the basis of our tree mining methods. It was essentially proposed in (Balcázar, Bifet, & Lozano, 2010, Bifet & Gavaldà, 2008, 2009).

*Formal concept analysis* (Ganter & Wille, 1999) is a mathematical theory of data analysis which identifies conceptual structures among data sets. It is interested in (possibly infinite) sets endowed with a partial order relation $\preceq$. Elements of these sets are generically called *patterns*. The set of all patterns will be denoted with $T$, but actually all our developments will proceed in some finite subset of $T$ which will act as our universe of discourse.

Given two patterns $t$ and $t'$, we say that $t$ is a *subpattern* of $t'$, or $t'$ is a *super-pattern* of $t$, if $t \preceq t'$. Two patterns $t$, $t'$ are said to be *comparable* if $t \preceq t'$ or $t' \preceq t$. Otherwise, they are incomparable. Also we write $\prec$ if $t$ is a proper subpattern of $t'$(that is $t \preceq t'$ and $t \neq t'$).

The input to our data mining process is a dataset $D$ of transactions, where each transaction $s \in D$ consists of a transaction identifier, *tid*, and a transaction pattern. The dataset is a finite set in the standard setting, and a potentially infinite sequence in the data stream setting. Tids are supposed to run sequentially from 1 to the size of $D$. From that dataset, our universe of discourse $U$ is the set of all patterns that appear as subpatterns of some pattern in $D$. Figure 1 shows a finite dataset example of trees.

As is standard, we say that a transaction $s$ *supports* a pattern $t$ if $t$ is a subpattern of the patterns in transaction $s$. The number of transactions in the dataset $D$ that support $t$ is called the *support* of the pattern $t$. A subpattern $t$ is called *frequent* if its support is greater than or equal to a given threshold *min_sup*. The frequent subpattern mining problem is to find all frequent subpatterns in a given dataset. Any subpattern of a frequent pattern is also frequent and, therefore, any superpat-

*Figure 1. A dataset example of 4 tree transactions*

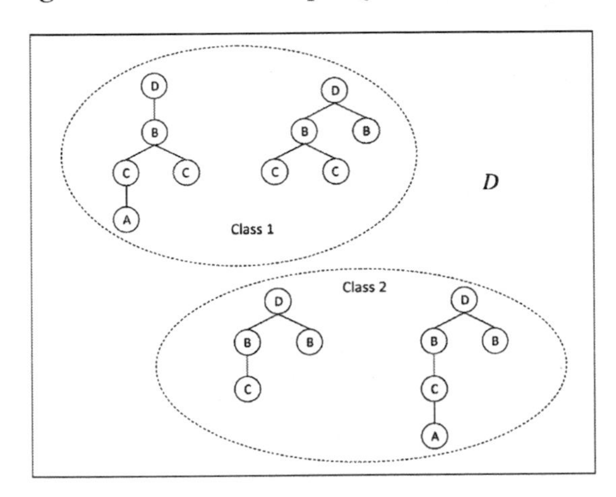


tern of a nonfrequent pattern is also nonfrequent (the *antimonotonicity* property).

We define a frequent pattern $t$ to be *closed* if none of its proper superpatterns has the same support as it has. Generally, there are much fewer closed patterns than frequent ones. In fact, we can obtain all frequent subpatterns with their support from the set of frequent closed subpatterns with their supports. So, the set of frequent closed subpatterns maintains the same information as the set of all frequent subpatterns.

We define a frequent pattern $t$ to be *maximal* if none of $t$'s proper superpatterns is frequent. All maximal patterns are closed, but not all closed patterns are maximal, so there are more closed patterns than maximal.

Note that we can obtain all frequent subpatterns from the set of maximal frequent subpatterns, although not their support. So, the set of maximal frequent subpatterns is an approximation, sufficient for many purposes, of the information in the set of all frequent subpatterns.

## Classification Using Compressed Frequent Patterns

The pattern classification problem is defined as follows. A set of examples of the form $(t, y)$ is given, where $y$ is a discrete class label and $t$ is a pattern. The goal is to produce from these examples a model $\hat{y} = f(t)$ that will predict the classes $y$ of future pattern examples.

Most standard classification methods can only deal with vector data, which is only one of many possible pattern structures. To apply them to other types of patterns, such as trees, we can use the following approach: we convert the pattern classification problem into a vector classification learning task, transforming patterns into vectors of attributes. Each attribute denotes the presence or absence of a particular subpattern, and we will create attributes for all frequent subpatterns, or for a subset of these. More precisely, suppose $D$ has $d$ frequent subpatterns denoted by $t_1, \ldots, t_d$. We map any pattern $t$ to a vector $x$ of $d$ attributes: $x = (x_1, \ldots, x_d)$ such that for each attribute $i$, $x_i = 1$ if $t_i \preceq t$ or $x_i = 0$ otherwise.

As the number of frequent subpatterns may be huge, we perform a feature selection process, selecting a subset of these frequent subpatterns, maintaining exactly or approximately the same information. Figures 2 and 3 show frequent trees and its conversion to vectors of attributes. Note that closed trees have the same information as frequent trees, but maximal trees loose some information about supports, as mentioned in the previous section.

## Closed Frequent Patterns

The Galois connection is a central notion used in formal concept analysis (Ganter & Wille, 1999, Priss, 2006). It is a duality between two types of items that relate to each other, such as objects and attributes, or documents and terms. A pair of a set of formal objects and a set of formal attributes that are closed is called a *formal concept*. The Galois connections and the sets of formal concepts can be visualized using concept lattices or Galois lattices. The nodes in a Galois lattice represent formal concepts. The closed trees for the dataset of Figure 1 are shown in the Galois lattice of Figure

*Figure 2. Frequent trees from the dataset example (min_sup = 30%), and their corresponding attribute vectors*

| | closed | frequent non-closed | transaction 1 2 3 4 |
|---|---|---|---|
| $c_1$ | D–B–(C, C) | B–(C, C) | 1 0 1 0 |
| $c_2$ | D–B–C–A | B–C–A; C–A; A | 1 0 0 1 |
| $c_3$ | D–(B–C, B) | D–(B, B) | 0 1 1 1 |
| $c_4$ | D–B–C | D–B; D; B–C; B; C | 1 1 1 1 |

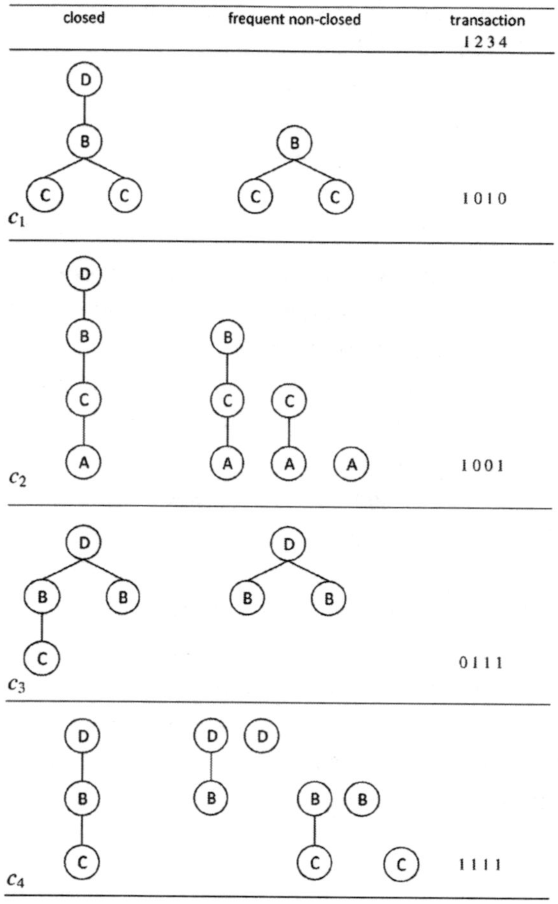

4. Nodes represent formal concepts consisting of closed trees and *tid* transactions.

Recall that if $X$ is a set with a partial order $\leq$, a *closure operator* on $X$ is a function $C: X \rightarrow X$ that satisfies the following for all $x$ in $X$: $x \leq C(x)$, $C(x) = C(C(x))$, for all $y \in X$, $x \leq y$ implies $C(x) \leq C(y)$. A Galois connection is provided by two functions, relating two lattices in a certain way. Here our lattices are not only plane power sets of the transactions but also plain power sets of the corresponding solutions. On the basis of the binary relation $t \preceq t'$, the following definition and proposition are rather standard.

**Definition 1.** *The Galois connection pair is defined by:*

- *For finite* $A \subseteq D$, $\sigma(A) = \{t \in T \mid \forall t' \in A(t \preceq t')\}$
- *For finite* $B \subset T$, *not necessarily in D,* $\tau_D(B) = \{t' \in D \mid \forall t \in B(t \preceq t')\}$

**Proposition 1.** *The composition* $\Gamma_D = \sigma \circ \tau_D$ *is a closure operator on the subsets of D.*

**Theorem 1.** *A pattern t is closed for D if and only if it is maximal in* $\Gamma_D(\{t\})$.

*Figure 3. Closed and maximal frequent trees from the dataset example (min_sup = 30%), and their corresponding attribute vectors*

| | Frequent Trees | | | | | | | | | | | | | | |
|---|---|---|---|---|---|---|---|---|---|---|---|---|---|---|---|
| | $c_1$ | | $c_2$ | | | | $c_3$ | | $c_4$ | | | | | | |
| **Id** | $c_1$ | $f_1^1$ | $c_2$ | $f_2^1$ | $f_2^2$ | $f_2^3$ | $c_3$ | $f_3^1$ | $c_4$ | $f_4^1$ | $f_4^2$ | $f_4^3$ | $f_4^4$ | $f_4^5$ |
| **1** | 1 | 1 | 1 | 1 | 1 | 1 | 0 | 0 | 1 | 1 | 1 | 1 | 1 | 1 |
| **2** | 0 | 0 | 0 | 0 | 0 | 0 | 1 | 1 | 1 | 1 | 1 | 1 | 1 | 1 |
| **3** | 1 | 1 | 0 | 0 | 0 | 0 | 1 | 1 | 1 | 1 | 1 | 1 | 1 | 1 |
| **4** | 0 | 0 | 1 | 1 | 1 | 1 | 1 | 1 | 1 | 1 | 1 | 1 | 1 | 1 |

| | Closed Trees | | | | Maximal Trees | | | |
|---|---|---|---|---|---|---|---|---|
| **Id** | $c_1$ | $c_2$ | $c_3$ | $c_4$ | $c_1$ | $c_2$ | $c_3$ | **Class** |
| **1** | 1 | 1 | 0 | 1 | 1 | 1 | 0 | **1** |
| **2** | 0 | 0 | 1 | 1 | 0 | 0 | 1 | **2** |
| **3** | 1 | 0 | 1 | 1 | 1 | 0 | 1 | **1** |
| **4** | 0 | 1 | 1 | 1 | 0 | 1 | 1 | **2** |

*Figure 4. Example of Galois Lattice of closed trees. Nodes represent formal concepts consisting of closed trees and tid transactions*

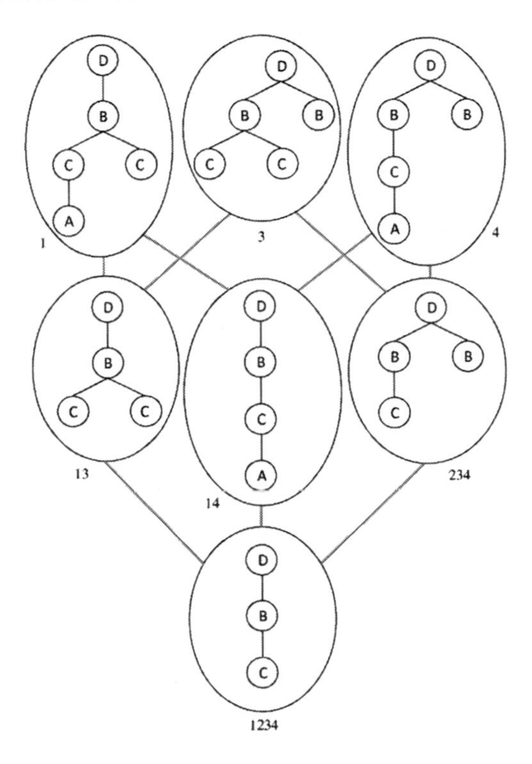


In other words, Theorem 1 states that each closed set is uniquely defined through its maximal elements. On this basis, our algorithms can avoid duplicating calculations and redundant information by just storing the maximal patterns of each closed set. We denote $\Delta(t)$ as the set of maximal patterns of each closed set of $\Gamma_D(\{t\})$. We can relate the closure operator to the notion of closure based on support, as previously defined, as follows: $t$ is closed for $D$ if and only if $\Delta_D(\{t\})=\{t\}$.

Following the standard usage on Galois lattices, we consider now implications of the form $A \rightarrow B$ for sets of patterns $A$ and $B$ from $U$. Specifically, we consider the following set of rules: $A \Rightarrow \Gamma_D(A)$. Alternatively, we can split the consequents into $\{A \rightarrow t \mid t \in \Gamma_D(A)\}$.

It is easy to see that $D$ obeys all these rules: for each $A$, any pattern of $D$ that has as subpatterns all the patterns of $A$ has also as subpatterns all the patterns of $\Gamma_D(A)$.

**Proposition 2.** *Let $t_i$ be a frequent pattern for D. A transaction pattern t satisfies $t_i \preceq t$, if and only if it satisfies $\Delta_D(t_i) \preceq t$.*

We can use Proposition 2 to reduce the number of attributes on our classification task, using only closed frequent patterns, as they keep the same information. The attribute vector of a frequent pattern will be the same as its closed pattern attribute vector. Figure 3 shows the attribute vectors for the dataset of Figure 1.

## Maximal Frequent Patterns

Maximal patterns are patterns that do not have any frequent superpattern. All maximal patterns are closed patterns. If *min_sup* is zero, then maximal patterns are transaction patterns. We denote by $M_1(t), \ldots, M_m(t)$ the maximal superpatterns of a pattern $t$. We are interested in the implications of the form $t_c \Rightarrow (M_1(t) \vee \ldots \vee M_m(t))$ where $t_c$ is a closed pattern.

**Proposition 3.** *Let $t_c$ be a closed non-maximal frequent pattern for D. Let $M_1(t_c), \ldots, M_m(t_c)$ be the maximal superpatterns of pattern $t_c$. A transaction pattern t satisfies $t_c \prec t$, if and only if at least one of the maximals superpattern $M_i(t_c)$ of pattern $t_c$ satisfies $M_i(t_c) \preceq t$.*

***Proof.*** *Suppose that pattern $t_c$ satisfies $t_c \prec t$ but no maximal superpattern $M_i(t_c)$ satisfies $M_i(t_c) \preceq t$. Then, pattern $t_c$ has no frequent superpattern. Therefore, it is maximal, contradicting the assumption. Suppose, for the other direction, that a maximal superpattern $M_i(t_c)$ of $t_c$ satisfies $M_i(t_c) \preceq t$. Then, as $t_c$ is a $M_i(t_c)$ subpattern, $t_c \preceq M_i(t_c)$, and it holds that $t_c \preceq M_i(t_c) \preceq t$.* □

In the example of Figure 3, $c_4$ is a non-maximal frequent pattern, and $c_1$, $c_2$, $c_3$ are its maximal superpatterns. We see in this example that $c_4 \rightarrow c_1 \vee c_2 \vee c_3$.

For non-maximal closed patterns, the following set of rules holds if $t_c$ is not a transaction pattern: $t_c \Rightarrow \vee M_i(t_c)$

Note that for a transaction pattern $t_c$ that it is closed and non-maximal, there is no maximal superpattern $M_i(t_c)$ of pattern $t_c$ that satisfies $M_i(t_c) \preceq t_c$.

If there are no closed non-maximal transaction patterns, we do not need to use all closed patterns as attributes, since non-maximal closed patterns may be derived from maximal patterns. Using Proposition 3, we may reduce the number of attributes on our classification task, using only maximal frequent patterns, as they keep much of the information as closed frequent patterns.

## XML TREE CLASSIFICATION FRAMEWORK ON DATA STREAMS

In this section we specialize the previous approach to the case of labeled trees, such as XML trees.

*Trees* are connected acyclic graphs, *rooted trees* are trees with a vertex singled out as the root, and *unranked* trees are trees with unbounded arity. We say that $t_1, \ldots, t_k$ are the *components* of tree $t$ if $t$ is comprised of a node (the root) joined to the roots of all the $t_i$'s. We can distinguish between the cases where the components at each node form a sequence (*ordered trees*) or just a set (*unordered trees*). We will deal with rooted, unranked trees. We assume the presence of labels on the nodes.

An *induced subtree* of a tree $t$ is any connected subgraph rooted at some node $v$ of $t$ such that its vertices and edges are subsets of those of $t$. An *embedded subtree* of a tree $t$ is any connected subgraph rooted at some node $v$ of $t$ that does not break the ancestor-descendant relationship among the vertices of $t$. We are interested in induced subtrees. Formally, let $s$ be a rooted tree with vertex set $V'$ and edge set $E'$, and $t$ a rooted tree $t$ with vertex set $V$ and edge set $E$. Tree $s$ is an *induced subtree* (or simply a *subtree*) of $t$ (written $t' \preceq t$) if and only if 1) $V' \subseteq V$, 2) $E' \subseteq E$, and 3) the labeling of $V'$ is preserved in $t$. This notation can be extended to sets of trees $A \preceq B$: for all $t \in A$, there is some $t' \in B$ for which $t \preceq t'$.

Our XML tree classification framework has the following components (Figure 5):

- An XML closed frequent tree miner, for which we could use any incremental algorithm that maintains a set of closed frequent trees.
- A converter of trees into attribute vectors.
- A data stream classifier, which we will feed with tuples to be classified online. Attributes in these tuples represent the occurrence of the current closed trees in the originating tree, although the classifier algorithm needs not be aware of this.

In the following we describe the two main components of the framework, the XML closed frequent tree miner and the data stream classifier.

### Adaptive Tree Mining on Evolving Data Streams

We show three closed tree mining algorithms that may be used in the first component of the framework: an incremental method, a sliding window algorithm and an adaptive one. This is basically an adaptation of the theoretical framework developed in (Bifet & Gavaldà, 2008), which deals with a quite general notion of pattern and subpattern, to the case of labeled rooted trees.

*Figure 5. The XML data stream classification framework*

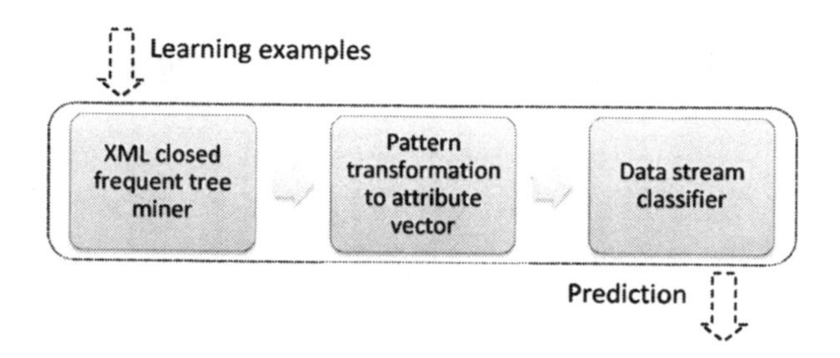

Let $D_1$ be the transaction set seen so far, whose set of closed patterns $T_1$ we have computed already. Suppose that a new batch of patterns $D_2$ arrives. The method computes its set of closed patterns, $T_2$, and then it updates the closed pattern set to that of $D_1 \cup D_2$ using procedure CLOSED_SUBPATTERN_MINING_ADD, which is shown in Figure 6.

Figure 7 shows the pseucodode of CLOSED_SUBPATTERN_MINING_DELETE. The method checks for every *t* pattern in $T_2$ in ascending order whether its subpatterns are still closed or not after deleting some transactions. It does this by looking for a closed superpattern with the same support.

For maximal frequent trees, the following properties hold:

- adding a tree transaction to a dataset of trees *D*, may increase or decrease the number of maximal trees for *D*;
- adding a transaction with a closed tree to a dataset of trees *D*, may modify the number of maximal trees for *D*;
- deleting a tree transaction from a dataset of trees *D*, may increase or decrease the number of maximal trees for *D*;
- deleting a tree transaction that is repeated in a dataset of trees *D* from it, may modify the number of maximal trees for *D*;
- a non-maximal closed tree may become maximal if
- it was not frequent and now its support increases to a value higher or equal to *min_sup*,
- all of its maximal supertrees become non-frequent;
- a maximal tree may become a non maximal tree if
- its support decreases below *min_sup*,

*Figure 6. The CLOSED_SUBPATTERN_MINING_ADD algorithm*

**Algorithm: CLOSED_SUBPATTERN_MINING_ADD**
**Input:** pattern sets $T_1$ and $T_2$ (frequent closed patterns of datasets $D_1$ and $D_2$), minimum support *min_sup*
**Output:** the set *T* of frequent closed patterns of dataset $D_1 \cup D_2$

```
1: T ← T1
2: for each t in T2 in size-ascending order do
3:    if t is closed in T1 then
4:       supportT(t) = supportT(t) + supportT2(t)
5:       for each subpattern t' of t do
6:          if t' is in T1 then
7:             if t' support is not updated then
8:                insert t' into T
9:                supportT(t') = supportT(t') + supportT2(t')
10:         else skip processing t' and all its subpatterns
11:   else
12:      insert t into T
13:      for each subpattern t' of t do
14:         if t' support is not updated then
15:            if t' is in T1 then
16:               supportT(t') = supportT(t') + supportT2(t')
17:            if t' is closed then
18:               insert t' into T
19:               supportT(t') = supportT(t') + supportT2(t')
20:         else skip processing t' and all its subpatterns
21: delete from T patterns with support below min_sup
22: return T
```

*Figure 7. The CLOSED_SUBPATTERN_MINING_DELETE algorithm*

```
Algorithm: CLOSED_SUBPATTERN_MINING_DELETE
Input: pattern sets T1 and T2 (frequent closed patterns of datasets D1 and D2),
       minimum support min_sup
Output: the set T of frequent closed patterns of dataset D1 ∪ D2

 1: T ← T1
 2: for each t in T2 in size-ascending order do
 3:     for each t' that can be obtained deleting nodes from t do
 4:         if t' support is not updated then
 5:             if t' is in T1 then
 6:                 if t' is not closed then
 7:                     delete t' from T
 8:                 else supportT(t') = supportT(t') – supportT2(t')
 9:             else skip processing t' and all its subpatterns
10: delete from T patterns with support below min_sup
11: return T
```

- a non-frequent closed supertree becomes frequent.

We can check if a closed tree becomes maximal when removing closed trees because they do not have enough support, adding a new closed tree to the dataset, or deleting a closed tree from the dataset.

The batches are processed using TREENAT, a non-incremental algorithm explained in (Balcázar et al., 2010). In this algorithm, subtrees are represented to be checked as frequent and closed on the dataset in such a way that extending them by one single node, in all possible ways, corresponds to a clear and simple operation on the representation. The completeness of the procedure is assured, that is, all trees can be obtained in this way. This allows not having to extend trees that are found to be already nonfrequent.

The pseudocode of this method, TREENAT is presented in Figures 8 and 9. Note that the first line of the algorithm is a canonical representative checking, which is a check frequently used in tree mining literature. In (Balcázar et al., 2010) the authors selected one of the ordered trees corresponding to a given unordered tree to act as a canonical representative: by convention, this canonical representative has larger trees always to the left of smaller ones.

The main difference of TREENAT with CMTreeMiner is that CMTreeMiner needs to store all occurrences of subtrees in the tree dataset to use its pruning methods, whereas TREENAT does not. The number of occurrences is high if the trees are

*Figure 8. The TREENAT mining algorithm*

```
Algorithm: TREENAT
Input: tree dataset D, minimum support min_sup
Output: the frequent closed tree set T of D

1: t ← •
2: T ← ∅
3: T ← CLOSED_SUBTREE_MINING(t, D, min_sup, T)
4: return T
```

*Figure 9. The CLOSED_SUBTREE_MINING algorithm*

```
Algorithm: CLOSED_SUBTREE_MINING
Input: tree representation t, tree dataset D, minimum support min_sup
Output: the frequent closed tree set T of D

 1: if t ≠ CANONICAL_REPRESENTATIVE(t) then
 2:     return T
 3: for each t' that can be extended from t in one step do
 4:     if support(t') ≥ min_sup then
 5:         T ← CLOSED_SUBTREE_MINING(t', D, min_sup, T)
 6:     if support(t') = support(t) then
 7:         t is not closed
 8: if t is closed then
 9:     insert t into T
10: return T
```

big, or the number of labels is small. In this case, CMTreeMiner needs more memory and time to process them. Otherwise, if the size of the trees is small, or the number of labels is high then CMTreeMiner outperforms TREENAT, since it can use the power of its pruning methods.

Our framework can use one of the following three tree mining algorithms, adapting the general framework for patterns presented in (Bifet & Gavaldà, 2008):

- INCTREEMINER, an incremental closed tree mining algorithm. Every time a new batch of instances arrives, the method computes the new closed trees using TREENAT and adds them using CLOSED_SUBPATTERN_MINING_ADD.
- WINTREEMINER, a sliding window closed tree mining algorithm. Every time a new batch of instances arrives, the method computes the new closed trees using TREENAT, adds them using CLOSED_SUBPATTERN_MINING_ADD, and removes the old closed trees using CLOSED_SUBPATTERN_MINING_DELETE if needed.
- ADATREEMINER, an adaptive closed tree mining algorithm that, like INCTREEMINER, uses CLOSED_SUBPATTERN_MINING_ADD to add the closed trees, but has an additional adaptive mechanism to remove the old frequent closed without needing a sliding window size parameter as in WINTREEMINER. We describe it in more detail next.

ADATREEMINER is a new tree mining method for dealing with concept drift, using ADWIN (Bifet & Gavaldà, 2007), an algorithm for detecting change and dynamically adjusting the length of a data window. ADWIN solves in a well-specified way the problem of tracking the average of a stream of bits or real-valued numbers. ADWIN keeps a variable-length window of recently seen items, with the property that the window has the maximal length statistically consistent with the hypothesis "there has been no change in the average value inside the window".

More precisely, an older fragment of the window is dropped if and only if there is enough evidence that its average value differs from that of the rest of the window. This has two consequences: one, that change reliably declared whenever the window shrinks; and two, that at any time the average over the existing window can be reliably taken as an estimation of the current average in the stream (barring a very small or very recent change that is still not statistically visible). A formal and quantitative statement of these two points (a theorem) can be found in (Bifet & Gavaldà, 2007).

ADWIN is parameter- and assumption-free in the sense that it automatically detects and adapts to the current rate of change. Its only parameter is a confidence bound $\delta$, indicating how confident we want to be in the algorithm's output, inherent to all algorithms dealing with random processes.

Also important for our purposes, ADWIN does not maintain the window explicitly, but compresses it using a variant of the exponential histogram technique in (Datar, Gionis, Indyk, & Motwani, 2002). This means that it keeps a window of length $W$ using only $O(\log W)$ memory and $O(\log W)$ processing time per item, rather than the $O(W)$ one expects from a naïve implementation. When windows tend to be large, this usually results in substantial memory savings.

We propose two strategies to deal with concept drift:

- **AdaTreeMiner1:** Using a sliding window, with an ADWIN estimator deciding the size of the window.
- **AdaTreeMiner2:** Maintaining an ADWIN estimator for each closed set in the lattice structure.

In the second strategy, we do not delete transactions. Instead, each ADWIN monitors the support of a closed pattern. When it detects a change, we can conclude reliably that the support of this pattern seems to be changing in the data stream in recent times.

## Data Stream Classifier

The second component of the framework is based on MOA. Massive Online Analysis (MOA) (Bifet, Holmes, Kirkby, & Pfahringer, 2010, Bifet et al., 2009) is a framework for online learning from continuous supplies of examples, such as data streams. It is closely related to the well-known WEKA project (Hall et al., 2009), and it includes a collection of offline and online as well as tools for evaluation. In particular, it implements boosting, bagging, and Hoeffding Trees, both with and without Naïve Bayes classifiers at the leaves. It uses MOA bagging and boosting of decision trees, because these ensemble methods are considered the state-of-the-art classification methods.

An important issue in streaming classification is the evaluation methodology. In traditional batch learning the problem of limited data is overcome by analyzing and averaging multiple models produced with different random arrangements of training and test data. In the stream setting the problem of (effectively) unlimited data poses different challenges. One solution involves taking snapshots at different times during the induction of a model to see how much the model improves.

The evaluation procedure of a learning algorithm determines which examples are used for training the algorithm, and which are used to test the model output by the algorithm. When considering what procedure to use in the data stream setting, one of the unique concerns is how to build a picture of accuracy over time. Two main approaches arise:

- **Holdout:** When traditional batch learning reaches a scale where cross-validation is too time-consuming, it is often accepted to instead measure performance on a single holdout set. This is most useful when the division between train and test sets has been pre-defined, so that results from different studies can be directly compared.
- **Interleaved Test-Then-Train or Prequential:** Each individual example can be used to test the model before it is used for training, and then the accuracy can be incrementally updated. When intentionally performed in this order, the model is always being tested on examples it has not seen. This scheme has the advantage that no holdout set is needed for testing, making maximum use of the available data.

It also ensures a smooth plot of accuracy over time, as each individual example will become increasingly less significant to the overall average (Gama, Sebastião, & Rodrigues, 2009).

As a word of caution, let us note that data stream classification is a relatively new field, and therefore these evaluation practices are not nearly as well researched and established as they are in the traditional batch setting.

## EXPERIMENTAL EVALUATION

The main goals of this section are demonstrating the performance of the proposed XML classification methods using a streaming evaluation, and illustrating the scalability of the proposed closed frequent tree miners to large datasets.

We discuss in this section the results of running these algorithms on synthetic and real data. All experiments were performed on a 2.0 GHz Intel Core Duo PC machine with 2 Gigabyte main memory, running Ubuntu 8.10.

### Tree Classification

To create synthetic datasets, we use the tree generation program of Zaki (2002), available from his web page. We generate two mother trees, one for each class. The first mother tree is generated with the following parameters: the number of distinct node labels $N = 200$, the total number of nodes in the tree $M = 1{,}000$, the maximal depth of the tree $D = 10$ and the maximum fanout $F = 10$. The second one has the following parameters: the number of distinct node labels $N = 5$, the total number of nodes in the tree $M = 100$, the maximal depth of the tree $D = 10$ and the maximum fanout $F = 10$.

A stream is generated by mixing the subtrees created from these mother trees. In our experiments, we set the total number of trees in the dataset to be $T = 1{,}000{,}000$. We added artificial drift changing labels of the trees every 250,000 samples, so closed and maximal frequent trees evolve over time. We use prequential evaluation and bagging of 10 Hoeffding Trees enhanced with adaptive Naïve Bayes leaf predictions, as classification method. This adaptive Naïve Bayes prediction method monitors the error rate of majority class and Naïve Bayes decisions in every leaf, and chooses to employ Naïve Bayes decisions only where they have been more accurate in past cases. Table 1 shows classification results. We observe that AdaTreeMiner1 is the most accurate method, and that the accuracy of WinTreeMiner depends on the size of the window.

As real datasets, we use the Log Markup Language (LOGML) dataset from (Punin, Krishnamoorthy, & Zaki, 2001, Zaki & Aggarwal, 2003), that describes log reports at their CS department website. LOGML provides a XML vocabulary to structurally express the contents of the log file information in a compact manner. Each user session is expressed in LOGML as a graph, and includes both structure and content.

The real CSLOG data set spans 3 weeks worth of such XML user-sessions. To convert this into

*Table 1. Comparison of classification algorithms. Memory is measured in MB. The best individual accuracy is indicated in boldface*

| Bagging | Time | Acc. | Mem. |
|---|---|---|---|
| AdaTreeMiner1 | 161.61 | **80.06** | 4.93 |
| AdaTreeMiner2 | 212.57 | 65.78 | 4.42 |
| WinTreeMiner W=100,000 | 192.01 | 72.61 | 6.53 |
| WinTreeMiner W=50,000 | 212.09 | 66.23 | 11.68 |
| IncTreeMiner | 212.75 | 65.73 | 4.4 |
| | | | |
| **Boosting** | **Time** | **Acc.** | **Mem.** |
| AdaTreeMiner1 | 236.31 | **79.83** | 4.8 |
| AdaTreeMiner2 | 326.8 | 65.43 | 4.25 |
| WinTreeMiner W=100,000 | 286.02 | 70.15 | 5.8 |
| WinTreeMiner W=50,000 | 318.9 | 63.94 | 9.87 |
| IncTreeMiner | 317.95 | 65.55 | 4.25 |

a classification data set, each user-session is categorized into one of two class labels: *edu* corresponds to users from an "edu" domain, while the other class corresponds to all users visiting the CS department from any other domain. Each week's logs are separated into a different data set (CSLOGx, where x stands for the week; CSLOG12 is the combined data for weeks 1 and 2). Notice that the *edu* class has much lower frequency rate than the other.

Table 2 shows the results on bagging and boosting using 10 Hoeffding Trees enhanced with adaptive Naïve Bayes leaf predictions. The results are very similar for the two ensemble learning methods. Using maximal and closed frequent trees, we obtain results similar to (Zaki, 2002). Comparing maximal trees with closed trees, we see that maximal trees use 1/4 to 1/3rd of attributes, 1/3 of memory, and they perform better in terms of accuracy. While the reduction in number of attributes and memory is totally expected, the fact that maximal trees allow for more accurate classification is an unexpected plus.

## Closed Frequent Labeled Tree Mining

As previously mentioned, CMTreeMiner is the state-of-the-art method for closed frequent tree mining. It shares many features with CloseGraph (Yan & Han, 2003), and uses two pruning techniques: the *left-blanket* and *right-blanket* pruning. The *blanket* of a tree is defined as the set of immediate supertrees that are frequent, where an *immediate supertree* of a tree $t$ is a tree that has one more vertex than $t$. The *left-blanket* of a tree $t$ is the blanket where the vertex added is not in the right-most path of $t$ (the path from the root to the right-most vertex of $t$). The *right-blanket* of a tree $t$ is the blanket where the vertex added is in the right-most path of $t$. The method is as follows: it computes, for each candidate tree, the set of trees that are occurrence-matched with its blanket's trees. If this set is not empty, two pruning techniques are applied using the left-blanket and right-blanket. If it is empty, then it is checked if the set of trees that are transaction-matched but not occurrence matched with its blanket's trees is also empty. If this is the case, there is no supertree

*Table 2. Comparison of tree classification algorithms. Memory is measured in MB. The best individual accuracies are indicated in boldface (one per row)*

| BAGGING | | Maximal | | | | | | Closed | | | | | |
|---|---|---|---|---|---|---|---|---|---|---|---|---|---|
| | | Unordered | | | Ordered | | | Unordered | | | Ordered | | |
| | #Trees | Att. | Acc. | Mem. | Att. | Acc. | Mem. | Att. | Acc. | Mem. | Att. | Acc. | Mem. |
| **CSLOG12** | 15483 | 84 | **79.64** | 1.2 | 77 | 79.63 | 1.1 | 228 | 78.12 | 2.54 | 183 | 78.12 | 2.03 |
| **CSLOG23** | 15037 | 88 | **79.81** | 1.21 | 80 | 79.8 | 1.09 | 243 | 78.77 | 2.75 | 196 | 78.89 | 2.21 |
| **CSLOG31** | 15702 | 86 | **79.94** | 1.25 | 80 | 79.87 | 1.17 | 243 | 77.6 | 2.73 | 196 | 77.59 | 2.10 |
| **CSLOG123** | 23111 | 84 | **80.02** | 1.7 | 78 | 79.97 | 1.58 | 228 | 78.91 | 4.18 | 181 | 78.91 | 3.31 |
| **BAGGING** | | **Maximal** | | | | | | **Closed** | | | | | |
| | | **Unordered** | | | **Ordered** | | | **Unordered** | | | **Ordered** | | |
| | **#Trees** | **Att.** | **Acc.** | **Mem.** | **Att.** | **Acc.** | **Mem.** | **Att.** | **Acc.** | **Mem.** | **Att.** | **Acc.** | **Mem.** |
| **CSLOG12** | 15483 | 84 | **79.46** | 1.21 | 77 | 79.83 | 1.11 | 228 | 75.84 | 2.97 | 183 | 77.28 | 2.37 |
| **CSLOG23** | 15037 | 88 | 79.91 | 1.23 | 80 | **80.24** | 1.14 | 243 | 77.24 | 2.96 | 196 | 78.99 | 2.38 |
| **CSLOG31** | 15702 | 86 | **79.77** | 1.25 | 80 | 79.69 | 1.17 | 243 | 76.25 | 3.29 | 196 | 77.63 | 2.62 |
| **CSLOG123** | 23111 | 84 | 79.73 | 1.69 | 78 | **80.03** | 1.56 | 228 | 76.92 | 4.25 | 181 | 76.43 | 3.45 |

with the same support and then the tree is closed. CMTreeMiner is a labeled tree method and it was not designed for unlabeled trees.

The main difference with our work is that CMTreeMiner is not incremental and only works with bottom-up subtrees, while our new method works is fully incremental (in fact, streaming) and works with both bottom-up and top-down subtrees.

As synthetic data, we use the same dataset as in (Chi et al., 2005) and (Zaki, 2002) for rooted ordered trees. The synthetic dataset T8M is generated by the tree generation program of Zaki (2002), used also for our evaluation on tree classification. In brief, a mother tree is generated first with the following parameters: the number of distinct node labels $N = 100$, the total number of nodes in the tree $M = 10{,}000$, the maximal depth of the tree $D = 10$ and the maximum fanout $F = 10$. The dataset is then generated by creating subtrees of the mother tree. In our experiments, we set the total number of trees in the dataset to be from $T = 0$ to $T = 8{,}000{,}000$.

The results of the experiments on synthetic data are shown in Figures 10-13. We observe that

*Figure 10. Time used on ordered trees, T8M dataset*

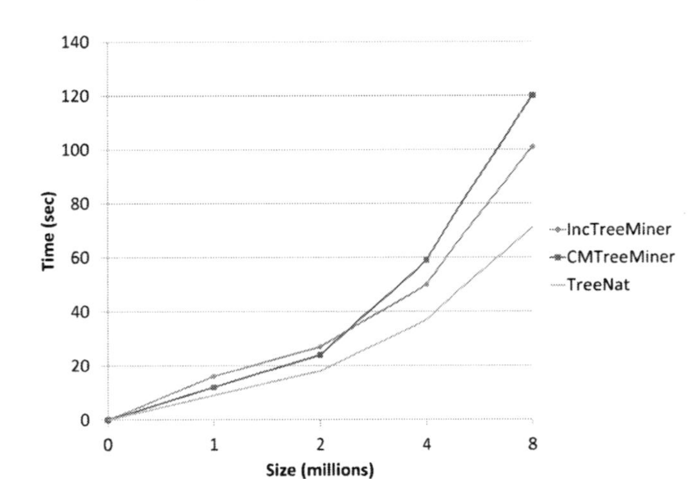


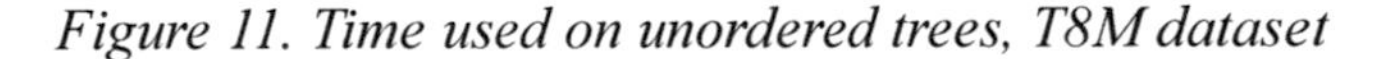

*Figure 11. Time used on unordered trees, T8M dataset*

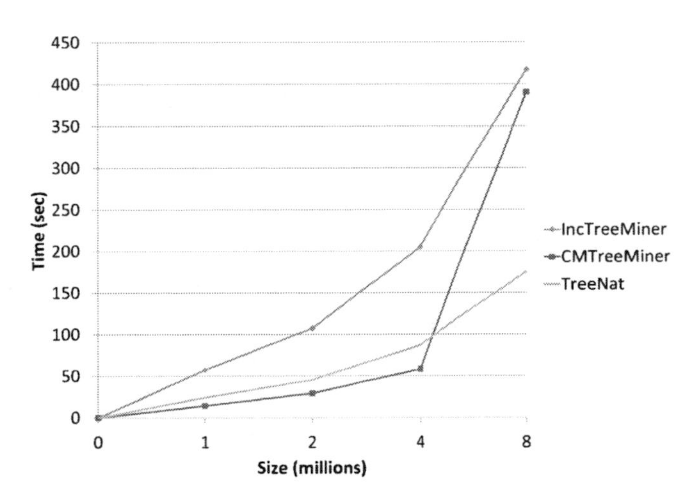

*Figure 12. Memory used on ordered trees, T8M dataset*

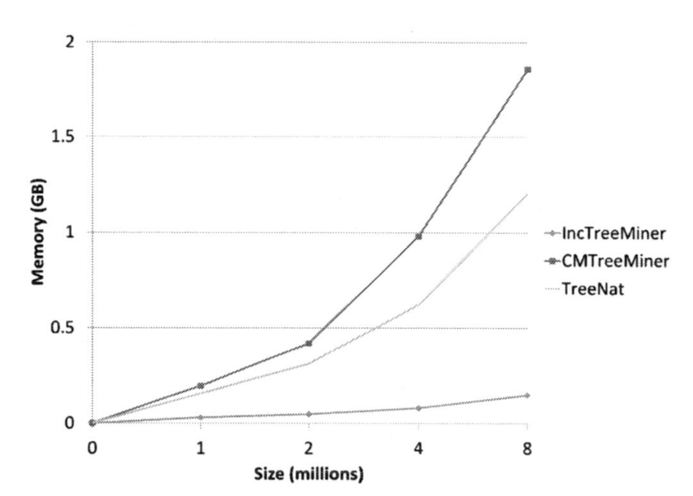


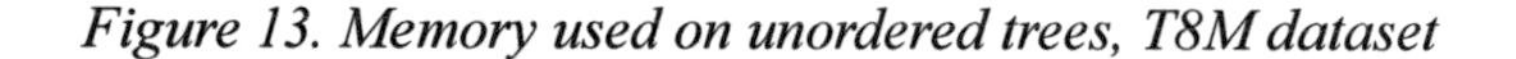

*Figure 13. Memory used on unordered trees, T8M dataset*

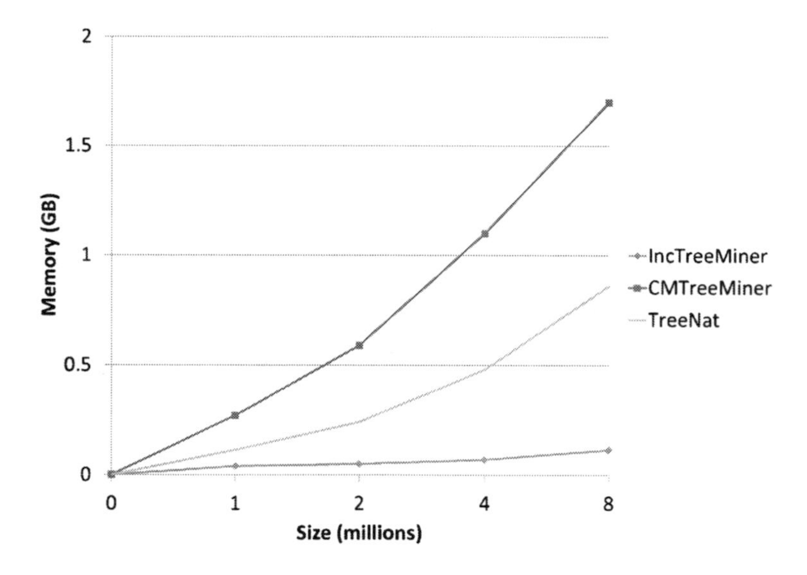


as the data size increases, the running times of IncTreeMiner and CMTreeMiner become closer, and that IncTreeMiner uses much less memory than CMTreeMiner. CMTreeMiner failed in our experiments when dataset size reached 8 million trees: not being an incremental method, it must store the whole dataset in memory all the time in addition to the lattice structure, in contrast with our algorithms.

In Figure 14 we also compare WinTreeMiner with different window sizes to AdaTreeMiner on T8M dataset. We observe that the two versions of AdaTreeMiner outperform WinTreeMiner for all window sizes.

## CONCLUSION AND FUTURE WORK

The scheme for classification based on these new methods, efficiently selects a reduced number of attributes, and achieves higher accuracy (even more in the more selective case in which we keep only

*Figure 14. Time used on ordered trees on T8M dataset, varying window size*

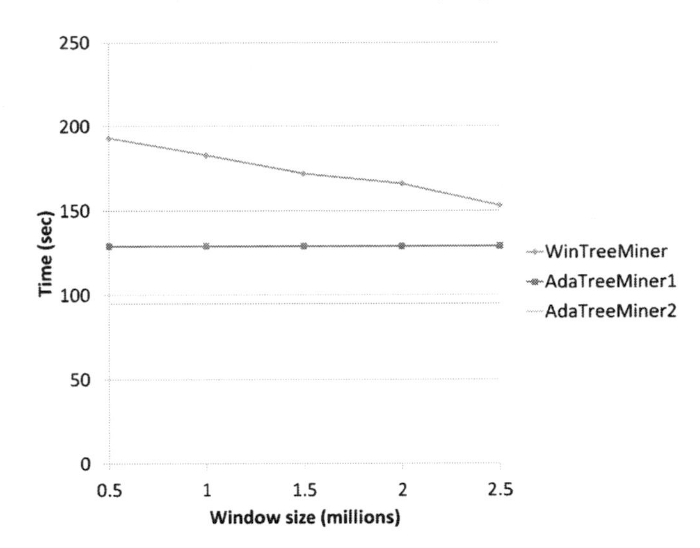


attributes corresponding to maximal trees). This new approach to tree mining outperforms CMTreeMiner in time and memory consumption when the number of trees is huge, because CMTreeMiner is not an incremental method and it must store the whole dataset in memory all the time.

Song et al. (2007) introduced the concept of relaxed frequent itemset using the notion of relaxed support. We can see relaxed support as a mapping from all possible dataset supports to a set of relaxed intervals. Relaxed closed mining is a powerful notion that reduces the number of closed subpatterns. The concept of logarithmic relaxed frequent pattern was introduced in (Bifet & Gavaldà, 2008). It would be interesting to apply this notion to this new classification method by introducing an attribute for each relaxed frequent closed pattern, instead of one for each closed frequent pattern.

Another interesting extension to the work presented in this chapter is to use generators (Li, Li, Wong, Pei, & Dong, 2006). In (Balcázar, Bifet, & Lozano, 2008) the authors were interested in implications of trees of the form $G \rightarrow Z$, where $G$ is a generator of $Z$. When $\Gamma(G) = Z$ for a set of trees $G \neq Z$ and $G$ is minimal among all the candidates with closure equal to $Z$, we say that $G$ is a generator of $Z$. Generator based representations contain the same information as the frequent closed ones.

## ACKNOWLEDGMENT

R. Gavaldà is partially supported by the EU Network of Excellence PASCAL, by the Spanish Ministry of Science and Technology contract TIN-2008-06582-C03-01 (SESAAME). by the Generalitat de Catalunya 2009-SGR-1428 (LARCA), and by the EU PASCAL2 Network of Excellence (FP7-ICT- 216886).

## ADDITIONAL READING

Classic references to Formal Concept Analysis are (Ganter & Wille, 1999, Priss, 2006). Recent references to data stream mining are (Domingos & Hulten, 2000, N. C. Oza & Russell, 2001, N. Oza & Russell, 2001, Bifet et al., 2009). XML classification methods using frequent trees appeared in (Zaki & Aggarwal, 2003, Kudo & Matsumoto, 2004, Collins & Duffy, 2001, Kashima & Koyanagi, 2002). Closed frequent miners were proposed (Chi et al., 2005, Termier et al., 2008, Arimura & Uno, 2005). And for recent XML classification works, see (Nayak et al., 2009, Denoyer et al., 2006, Kutty et al., 2008, Campos et al., 2008, Yang & Zhang, 2008, Denoyer & Gallinari, 2004, Candillier et al., 2007).

## REFERENCES

Arimura, H., & Uno, T. (2005). An output-polynomial time algorithm for mining frequent closed attribute trees. In S. Kramer, & B. Pfahringer (Eds.), *Proceedings of the 15th International Conference Inductive Logic Programming (ILP) Lecture Notes in Computer Science: Vol. 3625* (pp. 1-19). Springer.

Balcázar, J. L., Bifet, A., & Lozano, A. (2008). Mining implications from lattices of closed trees. In Guillet, F., & Trousse, B. (Eds.), *Extraction et gestion des connaissances* (pp. 373–384). EGC.

Balcázar, J. L., Bifet, A., & Lozano, A. (2010). Mining frequent closed rooted trees. *Machine Learning, 78*(1-2), 1–33. doi:10.1007/s10994-009-5123-9

Bifet, A., & Gavaldà, R. (2007). Learning from time-changing data with adaptive windowing. In *Proceedings of the SIAM International Conference on Data Mining (SDM)*. SIAM.

Bifet, A., & Gavaldà, R. (2008). Mining adaptively frequent closed unlabeled rooted trees in data streams. In *Proceedings of the 14th ACM International Conference on Knowledge Discovery and Data Mining (KDD),* (pp. 34-42). ACM.

Bifet, A., & Gavaldà, R. (2009). Adaptive XML tree classification on evolving data streams. In *Proceedings of the European Conference Machine Learning and Knowledge Discovery in Databases (ECML/PKDD)* [Springer.]. *Lecture Notes in Computer Science, 5781*, 147–162. doi:10.1007/978-3-642-04180-8_27

Bifet, A., Holmes, G., Kirkby, R., & Pfahringer, B. (2010). MOA: Massive online analysis. *Journal of Machine Learning Research, 11*, 1601–1604. Retrieved from http://moa.cs.waikato.ac.nz/.

Bifet, A., Holmes, G., Pfahringer, B., Kirkby, R., & Gavaldà, R. (2009). New ensemble methods for evolving data streams. *In Proceedings of the 15th ACM International Conference on Knowledge Discovery and Data Mining (KDD),* (pp. 139-148). ACM.

Candillier, L., Denoyer, L., Gallinari, P., Rousset, M. C., Termier, A., & Vercoustre, A. M. (2007). Mining XML documents. In Poncelet, M. T. P., Masseglia, F., & Teisseire, M. (Eds.), *Data mining patterns: New methods and applications* (pp. 198–219). Information Science Reference. doi:10.4018/978-1-59904-162-9.ch009

Ceci, M., & Appice, A. (2006). Spatial associative classification: Propositional vs structural approach. *Journal of Intelligent Information Systems, 27*(3), 191–213. doi:10.1007/s10844-006-9950-x

Chi, Y., Xia, Y., Yang, Y., & Muntz, R. R. (2005). Mining closed and maximal frequent subtrees from databases of labeled rooted trees. *IEEE Transactions on Knowledge and Data Engineering, 17*(2), 190–202. doi:10.1109/TKDE.2005.30

Collins, M., & Duffy, N. (2001). New ranking algorithms for parsing and tagging: kernels over discrete structures, and the voted perceptron. In *Proceedings of the 40th Annual Meeting on Association for Computational Linguistics (ACL),* (pp. 263-270).

Datar, M., Gionis, A., Indyk, P., & Motwani, R. (2002). Maintaining stream statistics over sliding windows. *SIAM Journal on Computing, 31*(6), 1794–1813. doi:10.1137/S0097539701398363

de Campos, L., Fernandez-Luna, J., Huete, J., & Romero, A. (2008). Probabilistic methods for structured document classification at INEX'07. In N. Fuhr, J. Kamps, M. Lalmas, & A. Trotman (Eds.), *Focused Access to XML Documents: 6th International Workshop of the Initiative for the Evaluation of XML Retrieval (INEX) Lecture Notes in Computer Science: Vol. 4862* (pp. 195-206). Springer.

Denoyer, L., & Gallinari, P. (2004). Bayesian network model for semi-structured document classification. *Information Processing and Management, 40*(5), 807.827.

Denoyer, L., Gallinari, P., & Vercoustre, A.-M. (2006). Report on the XML mining track at INEX 2005 and INEX 2006. In *Comparative Evaluation of XML Information Retrieval Systems, 5th International Workshop of the Initiative for the Evaluation of XML Retrieval (INEX)* [Springer.]. *Lecture Notes in Computer Science, 4518*, 432–443. doi:10.1007/978-3-540-73888-6_41

Domingos, P., & Hulten, G. (2000). Mining high-speed data streams. In *Proceedings of the ACM International Conference on Knowledge Discovery and Data Mining (KDD),* (pp. 71-80). ACM.

Gama, J., Sebastião, R., & Rodrigues, P. P. (2009). Issues in evaluation of stream learning algorithms. In *Proceedings of the 15th ACM International Conference on Knowledge Discovery and Data Mining (KDD),* (pp. 329-338). ACM.

Ganter, B., & Wille, R. (1999). *Formal concept analysis: Mathematical foundations*. Springer.

Hall, M., Frank, E., Holmes, G., Pfahringer, B., Reutemann, P., & Witten, I. H. (2009). The WEKA data mining software: An update. *SIGKDD Explorations, 11*(1), 10–18. doi:10.1145/1656274.1656278

Kashima, H., & Koyanagi, T. (2002). Kernels for semi-structured data. In *Proceedings of the Nineteenth International Conference Machine Learning (ICML),* (pp. 291-298). Morgan Kaufmann.

Kudo, T., Maeda, E., & Matsumoto, Y. (2004). An application of boosting to graph classification. In *Advances in Neural Information Processing Systems, 17*. NIPS.

Kudo, T., & Matsumoto, Y. (2004). A boosting algorithm for classification of semi-structured text. In *Proceedings of the 2004 Conference on Empirical Methods in Natural Language Processing (EMNLP),* (pp. 301-308). ACL.

Kutty, S., Tran, T., Nayak, R., & Li, Y. (2008). Clustering XML documents using closed frequent subtrees: A structural similarity approach. In N. Fuhr, J. Kamps, M. Lalmas, & A. Trotman (Eds.), *Focused Access to XML Documents, 6th International Workshop of the Initiative for the Evaluation of XML Retrieval (INEX) Lecture Notes in Computer Science: Vol. 4862* (pp. 183-194). Springer.

Li, J., Li, H., Wong, L., Pei, J., & Dong, G. (2006). Minimum description length principle: Generators are preferable to closed patterns. In *Proceedings of the AAAI Conference on Artificial Intelligence (AAAI).*

Mitchell, T. (1997). *Machine learning. McGraw-Hill Education*. ISE Editions.

Nayak, R., De Vries, C. M., Kutty, S., Geva, S., Denoyer, L., & Gallinari, P. (2009). Overview of the INEX 2009 XML mining track: Clustering and classification of XML documents. In *Focused Retrieval and Evaluation, 8th International Workshop of the Initiative for the Evaluation of XML Retrieval (INEX)* [Springer.]. *Lecture Notes in Computer Science, 6203*, 366–378. doi:10.1007/978-3-642-14556-8_36

Oza, N. C., & Russell, S. (2001). Online bagging and boosting. In *Artificial Intelligence and Statistics* (pp. 105-112).

Oza, N. C., & Russell, S. J. (2001). Experimental comparisons of online and batch versions of bagging and boosting. In *Proceedings of the ACM International Conference on Knowledge Discovery and Data Mining (KDD)*, (pp. 359-364). ACM.

Priss, U. (2006). Formal concept analysis in information science. *Annual Review of Information Science & Technology*, *40*(1), 521–543. doi:10.1002/aris.1440400120

Punin, J. R., Krishnamoorthy, M. S., & Zaki, M. J. (2001). LOGML: Log markup language for Web usage mining. In *WEBKDD 2001 - 3rd International Workshop on Mining Web Log Data Across All Customers Touch Points: Vol. 2356. Lecture Notes in Computer Science* (pp. 88-112). Springer.

Song, G., Yang, D., Cui, B., Zheng, B., Liu, Y., & Xie, K. (2007). CLAIM: An efficient method for relaxed frequent closed itemsets mining over stream data. In *Proceedings of the DASFAA 12th International Conference on Database Systems for Advanced Applications (DASFAA)* [Springer.]. *Lecture Notes in Computer Science*, *4443*, 664–675. doi:10.1007/978-3-540-71703-4_56

Termier, A., Rousset, M.-C., Sebag, M., Ohara, K., Washio, T., & Motoda, H. (2008). DryadeParent, an efficient and robust closed attribute tree mining algorithm. *IEEE Transactions on Knowledge and Data Engineering*, *20*(3), 300–320. doi:10.1109/TKDE.2007.190695

Yan, X., & Han, J. (2003). CloseGraph: Mining closed frequent graph patterns. In *Proceedings of the ACM International Conference on Knowledge Discovery and Data Mining (KDD),* (pp. 286-295). ACM.

Yang, J., & Zhang, F. (2008). XML document classification using extended VSM. In N. Fuhr, J. Kamps, M. Lalmas, & A. Trotman (Eds.), *Focused Access to XML Documents, 6th International Workshop of the Initiative for the Evaluation of XML Retrieval (INEX) Lecture Notes in Computer Science: Vol. 4862.* (pp. 234-244). Springer.

Zaki, M. J. (2002). Efficiently mining frequent trees in a forest. In *Proceedings of the ACM International Conference on Knowledge Discovery and Data Mining (KDD),* (pp. 71-80). ACM.

Zaki, M. J., & Aggarwal, C. C. (2003). XRules: An effective structural classifier for XML Data. In L. Getoor, T. E. Senator, P. Domingos, & C. Faloutsos (Eds.), *Proceedings of the ACM International Conference on Knowledge Discovery and Data Mining (KDD),* (pp. 316–325). ACM.

## ENDNOTE

1. A preliminary version of this work was presented at the ECML PKDD 2009 conference

# Chapter 10
# Data Driven Encoding of Structures and Link Predictions in Large XML Document Collections

**Markus Hagenbuchner**
*University of Wollongong, Australia*

**Chung Tsoi**
*Macau University of Science and Technology, China*

**Shu Jia Zhang**
*University of Wollongong, Australia*

**Milly Kc**
*University of Wollongong, Australia*

## ABSTRACT

*In recent years there have been some significant research towards the ability of processing related data, particularly the relatedness among atomic elements in a structure with those in another structure. A number of approaches have been developed with various degrees of success. This chapter provides an overview of machine learning approaches for the encoding of related atomic elements in one structure with those in other structures. The chapter briefly reviews a number of unsupervised approaches for such data structures which can be used for solving generic classification, regression, and clustering problems. We will apply this approach to a particularly interesting and challenging problem: The prediction of both the number and their locations of the in-links and out-links of a set of XML documents. In this problem, we are given a set of XML pages, which may represent web pages on the Internet, with in-links and out-links. Based on this training dataset, we wish to predict the number and locations of in-links and out-links of a set of XML documents, which are as yet not linked to other existing XML documents. To the best of our knowledge, this is the only known data driven unsupervised machine learning approach for the prediction of in-links and out-links of XML documents.*

DOI: 10.4018/978-1-61350-356-0.ch010

## INTRODUCTION

The traditional approach to processing data is by using numeric vectors of some fixed dimension as a means of representing the data, where the vector elements describe features of an associated data item (Haykin, 1994). Such representation is suitable when the data items are independent or when any existing dependencies are not relevant for the solving of a given problem. A common situation in which data items are dependent is in time series information processing (Haykin, 1994). In this case, a data entry may depend on another data entry which occurred in a prior time instance, and such dependency may be relevant for a given problem (Haykin, 1994). Data items which are sequentially organized are referred to as *sequences*. For example, in financial forecasting or in speech recognition, it is important that such dependency can be represented and encoded (Haykin, 1994). Note that unlike data vectors which are often of the same dimension, in the cases where they are not of the same dimension, then the technique of "zero padding" is used to ensure that all data vectors are of the same dimension (Haykin, 1994), there is not normally a restriction to the length of sequences. When data items are "related" to several other data items, then such dependencies are popularly described by a *graph*, hence such instances are referred to as *graph data structures*. Note that here, the data items are "related" in that the data objects, represented by nodes of a graph, are connected by links, directed or un-directed, cyclic, or acyclic, which express the relationships among the data objects. A very large number of practical problems can be represented as a graph data structure. For example, problems in molecular chemistry, image processing, computer security systems, weather forecasting, etc. can be addressed by processing the dependencies which are represented in graph structured data. Since sequences are a special case of graphs (graphs with an out-degree of 1), and since vectors are also a special case of graphs (a graph with a single node), graph data structures provide the most generic means for data representation. Any approach capable of encoding graphs can also solve time series problems and problems in which the data can be represented in vector spaces.

Simple graphs consist of two basic elements, namely, *nodes* and the binary relations called *links*. The nodes represent atomic entities of a domain. For example, a document may be represented by a node. A node may be labeled to describe the associated entity. For example, a node label may contain descriptive features of the associated document. These features could be the number of words in the document, the occurrence of certain words in the document, the frequency with which certain words occurred in the document, etc. A link exists between any two nodes if these nodes are "related" in some way. For example, a document may contain a hyperlink to another document. In this case, there is a directed link from the node representing the source document to the node which represents the target document of the hyperlink. A link may also be labeled in order to describe its properties. For example, a label associated with a link may indicate the strength of a link. Links may be directed (such as in the hyperlink case) or undirected (such as the links indicating atomic bindings of a molecule). The total number of all outgoing links of a node is called the *outdegree* of the node, while the total number of all incoming links is called the *indegree* of a node. In the case of undirected links, this is referred to as the *degree* of a node. The size of a graph $G$ is the total number of nodes in $G$ and is denoted by $n=|G|$. If there exists a path along the links in $G$ from one node to another then these nodes are said to be *connected*, otherwise they are *disconnected*. The shortest path along the link structure between a pair of nodes in $G$ is called the *distance* between these nodes.[1]

The importance of an ability to process graph structured information is highlighted by the fact that most documents are created electronically nowadays. The content of a document is stored as normal text whereas the layout, appearance, and structure of the text is described by a machine readable annotating text. In this context, the Extensible Markup Language (XML) has established itself as one of the most important mechanisms for describing layout, appearance, and structure of an electronic document. The increasing popularity of XML is due to its simplicity and generality. Since XML documents are becoming more and more widespread and thus the development of tools capable of dealing with XML documents is more and more important. An important observation is that XML imposes a logical tree-like structure on a document meaning that XML provides a means to represent documents naturally as a data tree. Since XML describes the structure and appearance of a document, hence the associated tree representation suitably represents the structure and appearance of a document. Moreover, XML allows the linking of documents via the so called *hyperlinks*. This means that it is possible to represent a collection of documents by means of a set of interlinked trees. This chapter addresses possible machine learning approaches to dealing with such types of data, and proposes a means to predict inter-document links.

A number of data mining techniques, e.g., syntactical grammar (Fu, 1977), have been developed to deal with these types of input data structures. This chapter will focus on machine learning techniques. The traditional approach to processing data vectors in machine learning is through Multi-Layer Perceptron Neural networks (MLP) (Haykin, 1994), and Self-Organizing Maps (SOMs) (Haykin, 1994), whereas the traditional approach to processing sequences is by using Elman Networks (Elman, 1990; Kohonen, 1990; D. E. Rumelhart et al., 1986). Machine learning approaches for the processing of graphs have only recently been introduced (Hagenbuchner et al., 2003; Kc et al., 2010; Scarselli et al., 2009a), and have already been very successful in solving several benchmark problems (Hagenbuchner et al., 2006; Kc et al., 2007; Zhang et al., 2009).

This chapter describes a general framework in which graph structured information can be encoded for machine learning applications. The organization of this chapter is such that it will first give a detailed view of one particular class of machine learning methods which, as we will find, is particularly suitable for solving the challenging task of predicting links in an interlinked domain. Then, an explicit description of such an application domain is provided. A practical deployment and associated experimental findings to a benchmark problem, viz., the prediction of the number and locations of in-links and out-links of a set of XML documents are then to demonstrate the capabilities of the deployed machine learning methods. Finally, a summary of this chapter and some future directions are provided.

## Encoding Structures in Machine Learning

The general approach to encoding structured information in machine learning is by encoding individual nodes of a given graph one at a time. When processing a particular node, the node's direct neighbors are taken into account by using an internal representation of these neighbors as an additional input to the current node. The repeated recursive processing of the nodes in a graph ensures that information is eventually passed from any node to any other node in the graph. The main difference between the various machine learning methods is in the way by which such internal representation is produced. In the following, we will refer to the internal representation of a node as the *state* of the node. The nomenclature is derived from the fact that the internal representation of a node is the network's response to a given set of inputs to the node together with its neighbors. In other words, it reflects the network's *state* in response to a given set of input nodes linked to the node.

The key idea in our work is to represent each node using a neural network. While the same neural network is used to encode all the nodes in a dataset, it is the network's *activation* that is used to represent each node. Then, this node's response (the state of the node) is obtained through the inputs which are derived by nodes which are linked to the current node. Each of the nodes connected via a link to the current node is in turn represented by a response (state) which is the result of nodes which are incident on it. Thus, by processing each node of a graph in turn, it is possible to recursively process the nodes in the graph, and eventually, all nodes will be considered.

There are two main types of neural networks, namely, supervised neural networks and unsupervised neural networks. Supervised neural networks are deployed when a teacher (target) signal is available for a given set of data (the training dataset consists of a set of graphs together with an associated teacher signal at an output node, or a set of teacher signals in a set of output nodes). The teacher signal is utilized as the target information for supervised neural networks. Unsupervised neural networks are deployed if no supervising (teacher) signal exists. In this case the training dataset simply consists of a set of graphs, but there is no teacher signal associated with any of the nodes. The training procedures (the learning of the unknown parameters by the processing of the training dataset) of these two types of neural networks differ significantly.

## Supervised Learning of Structured Data

The availability of ground truth information (teacher signals) for a given set of nodes allows for the learning of neural networks with specific targets. MLP based systems are parameterized systems which can be trained if the target information is available (Haykin, 1994). This is performed by comparing the desired target value with the actual output produced by an MLP to form an error signal. A gradient descent method is adopted to minimize the sum of error signals through the entire training dataset during the training process. Formal proofs exist which show that such methods can produce optimal results under some conditions (Hornik et al., 1989).

The supervised encoding of graph structured data is achieved by extending an MLP by a recursive element (Scarselli et al., 2009b). The error is computed as in the MLP case, and the gradients are propagated back through the recursive structure of the neural network (Scarselli et al., 2009b).

Since in this chapter we will not be using supervised approaches, hence we will not consider this approach further, except to indicate that there are developments in supervised approaches to graph structured input data (Bianucci et al., 1998; Scarselli et al., 2009b), which had been proved to be very successful in processing graph structured data (Scarselli et al., 2009a).

## Unsupervised Learning of Structured Data

Target information may not exist in many real-world problems. This is particularly the case for data mining problems. This rules out the application of supervised machine learning approaches. Unsupervised machine learning algorithms exist when there is a set of vectors **u** for which there is no associated target. One of the most popular and most widely adopted algorithms is the Self-Organizing Map (SOM) (Kohonen, 1990). A SOM performs a mapping from a high dimensional input space to a low dimensional display space in such a way that input data which are close to one another in the input space are mapped near to each other on the display space (Kohonen, 1990). Hence, a SOM can be used for the clustering or dimension reduction of a set of input data. One of the most appealing properties of the SOM is that the algorithm is computationally very efficient, hence a SOM can be easily applied to large scale applications (Kohonen, 1997). Moreover, the training algorithm of a SOM does not rely on the computation of a gradient, therefore the SOM does not suffer from any long term dependency problems that afflict gradient descent learning methods (Bengio et al., 1994).

The usefulness of SOM can be observed through its widespread adoption by practitioners, however, the representation of the input data in the form of disjointed sets limits its ability to effectively encode complex or structured data. As such, various extensions of the standard SOM were created, one of which is the extension which allows the encoding of graph structured information (Hagenbuchner et al., 2003). This is an interesting aspect since this allows the mapping of graphs onto a fixed dimensional display space. One approach uses the edit distance to define similarity in the competitive step of the training algorithm (Bunke, 1990). However, the approach is computationally extremely expensive, therefore it is restricted to solving very small toy problems only. The approaches (Hagenbuchner et al., 2003, 2001) described in this chapter are much more scalable and have already been applied to a variety of data-mining problems. But more importantly, the SOM based methods described in this chapter are not only capable of encoding relatedness that may exist between vectors and graphs but also they are capable of predicting the number and location of links.

## SELF-ORGANIZING MAP FOR STRUCTURES

The basic SOM defines a mapping from an input data space onto a regular $q$-dimensional array of the so called *neurons* (Kohonen, 1995), alternatively known as a display space of $q$-dimensions. It is very common that $q$=2. Every neuron $i$ of the map is associated with an $n$-dimensional codebook vector $\mathbf{m}_i = (\mathbf{m}_{i1}, \ldots, \mathbf{m}_{in})^T$, where $\mathbf{m}_i$ is said to be a weight vector and its elements are said to be weights, and $T$ denotes the transpose of a vector. The neurons of the map are connected to adjacent neurons by a neighborhood relation where rectangular and hexagonal are the most common ones (Kohonen, 1995).

Adjacent neurons belong to the neighborhood $N_i$ of a neuron $i$. Neurons belonging to $N_i$ are updated according to a neighborhood function $f(\cdot)$, where the *Gaussian-bell* shape function is most commonly used (Kohonen, 1995). The number of neurons determines the granularity of the mapping, which has an effect on the accuracy and generalization capability of the SOM (Kohonen, 1995).

The training algorithm of the weights associated with each neuron is performed in two steps:

**Competitive step:** One sample vector $\boldsymbol{u}$ is randomly drawn from the input data set and its similarity to the codebook vectors is computed. The minimum Euclidean distance is typically used for this purpose. A winning neuron is then computed through the following operation:

$$r = \arg\min_i \|\mathbf{u} - \mathbf{m}_i\| \quad (1)$$

**Cooperative step:** The best matching codebook $\mathbf{m}_r$ as well as its topological neighbors are moved closer to the input vector in the input space. The magnitude of the attraction is governed by the learning rate $\alpha$ and by a neighborhood function $f(\Delta_{ir})$, where $\Delta_{ir}$ is the topological distance between $\mathbf{m}_r$ and $\mathbf{m}_i$. The updating algorithm is given by:

$$\Delta\mathbf{m}_i = \alpha(t) f(\Delta_{ir})(\mathbf{m}_i - \mathbf{u}) \quad (2)$$

where $\alpha$ is a learning coefficient, and $f(\cdot)$ is the neighborhood function which controls the amount which the weights of the neighboring neurons are updated. The neighborhood function $f(\cdot)$ can take the form of a Gaussian function:

$$f(\Delta_{ir}) = \exp\left(-\frac{\|\mathbf{l}_i - \mathbf{l}_r\|^2}{2\sigma^2}\right) \quad (3)$$

where $\sigma$ is the spread, and $\mathbf{l}_r$ is the location of the winning neuron, and $\mathbf{l}_i$ is the location of the $i$-th neuron in the lattice. Other neighborhood functions are possible (Kohonen, 1990).

The two steps together constitute a single training step and they are repeated until the training ends. As the learning proceeds and new input vectors are input to the map, the learning rate $\alpha(t)$ gradually decreases to zero according to a specified learning rate function type. Along with the learning rate, the neighborhood radius decreases as well. This means that the number of training steps must be fixed prior to training the SOM because the rate of convergence in the neighborhood function and the learning rate are calculated accordingly.

## The Self Organizing Map for Structured Data

The Self-Organizing Map for Structured Data (SOM-SD) extends the SOM algorithm so as to allow the encoding of causal relations that may exist between a set of input vectors. The basic idea is analogous to the supervised machine learning approach: Take the network's response to directly related vectors as an additional input. The main difference lies in the form by which a SOM produces a response. The response of a SOM to a given input is produced by Equation 1. The SOM-SD uses the 2-dimensional coordinates of the winning neuron as the state information for an associated input vector, and the input vectors are formed by concatenating the $j$-th node's label $\mathbf{u}_j$ with the state of the node's neighbors $\mathbf{c}_{ne[j]}$ forming an input vector $\mathbf{x} = [\boldsymbol{u}_j, \boldsymbol{c}_{ch[j]}]$, where $\boldsymbol{c}_{ch[j]}$ are the concatenated coordinates of the winning neurons of the children of node $j$. The newly formed input vectors $\mathbf{x}$ are of dimension $n = p + 2o$, where $p = |\mathbf{u}|$, and $o$ is the maximum out-degree of a graph $G$. The codebook vectors $\mathbf{m}$ are of the same dimension.

Training a SOM-SD is analogous to the training of the SOM where Equation 1 is modified as follows:

$$r = \arg\min_i \|(\boldsymbol{x} - \mathbf{m}_i)\,\Lambda\| \tag{4}$$

where $\Lambda$ is a $n \times n$ dimensional diagonal matrix. Its diagonal elements $\lambda_{11}, \ldots, \lambda_{pp}$ are set to $\mu$, all remaining diagonal elements are set to $1-\mu$. The constant $\mu$ influences the contribution of the data label component to the Euclidean distance, and $1-\mu$ controls the influence of the children's coordinates to the Euclidean distance. Equation 2 in this case is modified as follows:

$$\Delta\mathbf{m}_i = \alpha(t)\, f(\Delta_{ir})(\mathbf{m}_i - \boldsymbol{x}) \tag{5}$$

Since the order of the state vector elements in $\boldsymbol{x}$ matters, and since a SOM-SD can only take the state information of offsprings, hence a SOM-SD can encode causal relationships in ordered tree structured data only. Many problems can be solved using directed ordered trees. This is because objects in computer science are popularly described by various types of parsing trees (Fu, 1977). The SOM-SD has been very successful in a range of application domains and has set the state-of-the-art performances (Hagenbuchner et al., 2006; Kc et al., 2007) in this type of problems.

## The Contextual SOM-SD

A SOM-SD can only encode causal relationships in a directed acyclic graph. This means that the mappings produced by the SOM-SD are independent of a node's relationship with any parent node. The ability of encoding contextual information in which not only the information about child nodes is available, but also the information on the parents of the current node is of relevance in a number of application domains. For example, in recommender systems (Takács et al., 2009), it is important to be able to encode the context within which a causal relationship occurred. The Contextual SOM-SD (CSOM-SD) (Hagenbuchner et al., 2005) extends the SOM-SD algorithm in order to encode contextual relationships in directed ordered tree structured learning problems. This is achieved by concatenating the state information of a node's offsprings as well as the state information of a node's parents such that an input vector becomes $\mathbf{x} = [\mathbf{u}, \mathbf{c}_{ch[i]}, \mathbf{c}_{pa[i]}]$, where $\mathbf{c}_{pa[i]}$ are the coordinates of the winning neurons of the parents of node $i$, and $\mathbf{c}_{ch[i]}$ is as before. The input vectors are made constant in size by padding with an illegal coordinate (such as $(-1,-1)$) for nodes with an outdegree or indegree smaller than the maximum outdegree or smaller indegree respectively. The training algorithm remains unchanged; it is the same as the one used for SOM-SD with the exception that $\Lambda$ in Equation 4 is now a $m \times m$ dimensional diagonal matrix. Its diagonal elements $\lambda_{11}, \ldots, \lambda_{pp}$ are set to $\mu_1$, a constant, the elements $\lambda_{p+1p+1}, \ldots, \lambda_{nn}$ are set to $\mu_2$, another constant, and all remaining diagonal elements are set to $1-\mu_1-\mu_2$.

## The Probability Mapping Graph SOM

The most advanced unsupervised machine learning approach to encoding structures is the Probability Measure Graph SOM (PMGraphSOM). The PMGraphSOM is capable of encoding general graphs which may feature directed or undirected links (or a mixture of both), have an arbitrary degree, and may contain cyclic dependencies (Hagenbuchner et al., 2009; Kc et al., 2010).

The PMGraphSOM achieves this through a two-fold modification of the SOM-SD algorithm. First, the PMGraphSOM modifies the interpretation of the *state* vector. Instead of concatenating the coordinates (the *state*) associated with the winning neuron of each child, parent, or neighbor, the PMGraphSOM consolidates the mappings of all a node's neighbors by considering the mappings produced by all neighbors in the display map $\boldsymbol{M}$. The map $\boldsymbol{M}$ consists of elements (the neurons) which can be active if a node is mapped to a location. Thus, the PMGraphSOM forms input vectors by concatenating the node label with the activation of the map when mapping all the node's neighbors. Since the size of $\boldsymbol{M}$ is fixed, hence the input dimension is fixed and independent of the degree of any node in a set of data.

The similarity measure in the competitive step in Equation 4 does not work as desired when using the activations of $\boldsymbol{M}$ instead of the coordinate values as with SOM-SD or CSOM-SD. The problem is that the Euclidean distance measure used in Equation 4 does not make a distinction as whether any change of a mapping during the cooperative step has been mapped to a nearby location or to a location far away on the map. A *soft coding* of the mappings is applied to account for the likelihood of any changes in the mapping of nodes in subsequent iterations (Hagenbuchner et al., 2009). In other words, instead of *hard coding* the mappings of nodes to be either 1 if there is a mapping at a given location, or 0 if there is no mapping at a given location, the likelihood of a mapping in a subsequent iteration is encoded by a probability value. It is known that due to the effects of the training algorithm it is most likely that the mapping of a node will be unchanged in the next iteration. But since all vectors associated with the grid points in the display map are updated, and since those vectors which are close to a winning entry (as measured by the Euclidean distance) are updated more strongly (controlled by the Gaussian function), hence it is more likely that any change of a mapping will be to a nearby location rather than to a location far away from the last update. These likelihoods are directly influenced by the neighborhood function and its spread. The PMGraphSOM incorporates the likelihood of a mapping as follows:

$$M_i = \frac{e^{-\frac{\{i_1, j_1\} - \{i_k, j_k\}^{2}}{2\sigma(t)^2}}}{\sqrt{2\pi}\sigma(t)} \quad (6)$$

where $M_i$ refers to the $i$-th element of the map, $\sigma(t)$ decreases with time $t$ towards zero, and $\{i_k, j_k\}$ are the coordinates of the winning vector, while $\{i_1, j_1\}$ are the coordinates of the vector in the display space. The computation is cumulative for all the $i$-th node's neighbors. The term at the denominator in Equation 6 normalizes the states such that the sum of terms $M_i$ is approximately equal to 1.0. It can be observed that this approach accounts for the fact that during the early stages of the training process it is likely that mappings can change significantly, whereas towards the end of the training process, as $\sigma(t) \rightarrow 0$, the state vectors become more and more similar to the hard coding method. It was shown that this approach helps to significantly improve the stability of the GraphSOM,[2] and allows the setting of large learning rates while providing an overall improvement in the clustering performance (Hagenbuchner et al., 2009).

Figure 1 illustrates the general idea underlining the encoding of hyperlinked XML documents by a SOM. The figure illustrates that a set of hyperlinked XML documents can be readily represented as a graph. Each node of the graph represents a document. Attached to a node is a label which describes the content of properties of the associated XML document. Note that the dimension of a node label can be arbitrary. This means that it is possible to describe any XML document to any arbitrary detail. Sometimes it can be useful to set the dimension of the node label to zero in cases where only the hyperlink structure is of relevance for a given task.

Each node in the graph is then processed by a SOM by concatenating the label of the node with the state of the node's neighbors. As an example, let us assume that node 2 and node 3 (the Figure has labeled the nodes by a unique value for ease of reference) have already been processed. Let us further assume that node 2 was mapped to location $\mathbf{l}_3$ and node 3 was mapped to location $\mathbf{l}_5$ of the map, then when processing node 1 in the case of SOM-SD the input vector would be $\mathbf{u}_1 = (12, 4.12, 7.2, 1, 4, 2, 1)$. Thus, it can be observed that the network input is simply the concatenation of the node label with the network's response (in the SOM-SD's case the coordinates of the codebooks activated by the node's offsprings). Step 2 of the training algorithm updates the codebooks so as to make them more similar to the input. This means that the codebook encodes both the data

*Figure 1. A set of 3 hyperlinked XML documents with the associated graph representation (top), and a SOM of size 5×2 (bottom)*

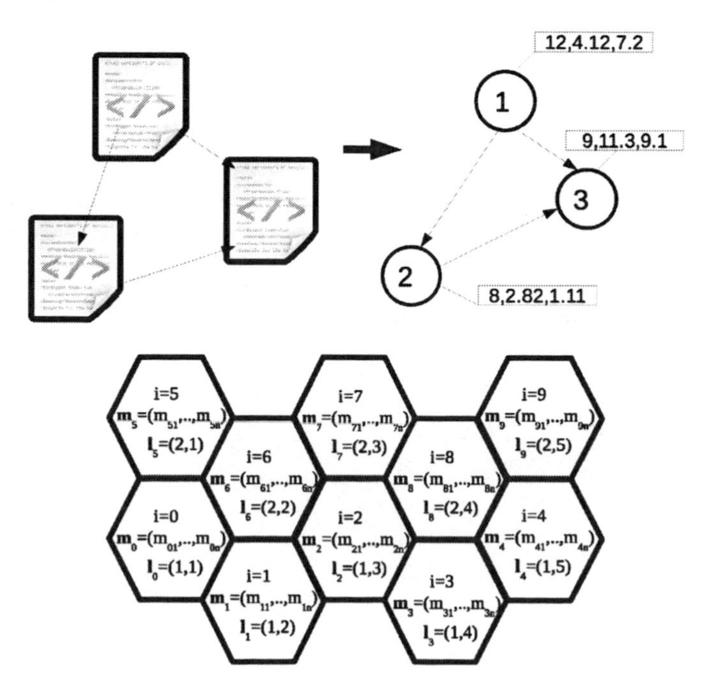

label and context of a node. Thus, if we know the activation of a node without explicit knowledge of the node's context, then we can extract the context from the state vector component of the codebook vector (in the previous example, the last 4 elements of the codebook vector hold information on up to two offsprings of a node). This property is important later in this chapter when describing an approach to link prediction. Given the same scenario described before, the input for a PMGraphSOM when processing node 1 would be $\mathbf{u}_1 = (12, 4.12, 7.2, m_0, m_1, m_2, m_3, m_4, m_5, m_6, m_7, m_8, m_9)$, where the $m_i$ are computed according to Equation 6 and by using the coordinates of the winners. Again, it can be observed that the state vector component of the codebook vectors, once trained, would encode the context of a given node.

## INCOMING AND OUTGOING LINK PREDICTION IN XML DOCUMENTS

While the SOMs described in this chapter are popularly applied to learning problems requiring the clustering or dimension reduction of related data vectors, we will show that it is also possible to predict incoming or outgoing links (in the case of a domain containing directed links) or links to neighbors (in the case of domains containing undirected links).

The input vectors of a SOM-SD contain hybrid information consisting of a data label element and a state vector element. Equation 4 determines the codebook vector which is most similar to an input vector, and Equation 5 reinforces the similarity by adjusting the elements of the codebook vector accordingly. This means that the codebook vectors become more and more similar to the input vectors. Ideally, at the end of the training process there would be one codebook vector for each distinct input vector and the value of the codebook vector would be identical to the associated input vector. This means that the codebook vectors encode the data label components as well as the state information about a node's neighbors. Since the state information refers to a coordinate value of the map, it is possible to consider the codebook vectors located at such coordinates in order to determine the properties of the child nodes. Recursively applied, it becomes possible to start from a codebook entry at a given coordinate value and then to unfold the associated structural information. Now, the interesting aspect is as follows: assume there is a new node $n_k$ for which the relationship with other nodes in a graph is unknown, then it is possible to compute the location of the best matching neuron (using Equation 4) and then to investigate the state component of the associated codebook vector. The procedure will reveal how $n_k$ is related to other nodes in the training dataset. We refer to this as *codebook-based link inference*.

A second approach to link prediction has been proposed (Kc et al., 2010): It is known that during training a best matching codebook has been obtained for each of the nodes in a graph. Since each codebook may be activated by a number of nodes, these codebooks are said to be a *representation* of these nodes. Due to the topology preserving ability of the SOMs, it can be said that all nodes which activate the same (or nearby) codebook are most closely related to each other in terms of content and topology. This means that a node mapped at a neuron location is likely to exhibit the same links and link structure as other nodes which are mapped to the same neuron. This gives rise to the possibility of mapping a new node $n_k$ for which the relationship with other nodes in a graph is unknown and then to select a candidate from the training dataset which was mapped to the same location. This candidate can then be expected to exhibit a close resemblance to the features of $n_k$, and will provide complementary information about the (proposed) topology of $n_k$. This approach is called a *content-based link inference*.

We note that both approaches can only work if the nodes are labeled by a vector whose dimension is non-zero. Moreover, the former approach is computationally more demanding since a recursive unfolding of the codebook vectors is required in order to obtain the complete view of a graph, whereas the latter approach requires considerably more storage since the mapping of all nodes and all graphs in a training dataset needs to be remembered.

Both approaches can also be applied to the CSOM-SD and the PMGraphSOM. In the case of the CSOM-SD, the codebooks of a trained CSOM-SD contain an encoding of the structural relationships with the parents as well as the children of a node, while in the PMGraphSOM the codebooks contain information about the structural relationships with all the neighbors of a given node.

## EXPERIMENTAL RESULTS

Processing and encoding structural information remains a challenging problem and a very dynamic research area. There exist several initiatives which organize annual international competitions on data mining tasks requiring the processing of structured and/or semistructured information. For example, the Text Analysis Conference (TAC) issues annual challenges on the clustering, classification, or summarization of XML structured document collections. Moreover, the Initiative for the Evaluation of XML Retrieval (INEX) organizes annual competitions on the clustering, classification, as well as on the link prediction tasks in large scale XML document collections. The advantage of such challenges is that they provide an open platform where anyone can participate so that a multitude of comparative results are available. They provide interested researchers with a summary of available approaches, and an overview of the state-of-the-art approaches and their results.

In this chapter we will be using a large dataset provided by the INEX 2009 competition in order to demonstrate the capability of the SOMs to perform in link prediction tasks. Here, the prediction will focus on the links between documents within the provided dataset.

### Dataset Characteristics

The dataset used for the experiments in this chapter is that provided for the INEX 2009 Link-the-wiki challenge. The collection consists of a data dump of the Wikipedia web site taken on 8 October 2008; it contains 2,666,190 articles, is compressed to 50.7GB in size, and is annotated with the 2008-w40-2 version of YAGO, which is a knowledge base developed at the Max-Planck-Institute Saarbrucken. The knowledge base contains information harvested from Wikipedia and linked to Wordnet. YAGO contains more than 2 million entities (like persons, organizations, cities, etc.), and contains 20 million facts about these entities. YAGO has a manually confirmed accuracy of 95%. It can be queried online. The documents are formatted in XML.

### Encoding and Prediction of Inter-Document Links

Given a new Wikipedia document, the aim of this experiment is to extract and analyze the document content, and recommend a set of incoming and outgoing links from the particular document to other documents in the collection. A set of 5,000 Wikipedia documents was said to have been randomly selected from the collection for the purpose of serving as the testing dataset for the experiment on inter-document link discovery.

Since these selected documents are not truly orphaned documents (as there are orphaned documents which contain no incoming or outgoing links, a situation similar to the newly introduced documents onto the Web), we removed these orphaned documents and their hyperlinks from the collection to simulate the situation of genuinely introducing new documents into the Web. This results in a training dataset consisting of 2,661,190 documents, all of which do not contain any link information about the 5,000 documents in the testing dataset.

The training dataset is represented as a directed graph where each node is a web page. Each page is then represented by a state vector encoding both its contextual and link structural information. Before the data can be trained by PMGraphSOM, decisions need to be taken regarding the selection of features to be used to describe each document in the form of node labels. It was important to select a feature which could represent each document, but such features cannot contain any link information, as otherwise the testing process would not be able to use the same feature as node labels to represent the test data.

Some analysis revealed that the category information associated with Wikipedia documents could be used as a representative feature. The category extraction process identified 8,918,924 categories in total, which could be consolidated to 362,251 unique categories. The maximum number of categories to which a single document belonged is 2,022, whereas there are 118,209 documents with no associated category information at all. If the category information is to be used without any processing, the large dimension would prevent the training process from completing within a reasonable amount of time. The experiments were carried out on machines fitted with 2.3GHz AMD Opteron CPUs. We considered 36 hours reasonable for training a network (A faster CPU or the parallelization of the implementation would significantly reduce the training times, and hence, would help to avoid the dimension reduction step used here); therefore, we decided to perform some dimension reduction first.

Singular Value Decomposition (SVD) was considered for a dimension reduction step (Golub & Kahan, 1965). However, SVD would require the building of a 2,661,190×362,251 matrix which is far too large for the capacity of computers which we had available for this project. Hence, another approach to dimension reduction was taken. This second approach utilizes a well known Multi-Layer Perceptron (MLP) algorithm (Haykin, 1994) to assist in dimension reduction. The MLP algorithm is generally applied to neural network architectures which consist of an input layer, followed by one or more hidden layers of neurons, and then an output layer of neurons, where all neurons in a layer are fully connected to all neurons in the next layer (Haykin, 1994). To utilize MLP for dimension reduction we use an architecture known as the "Auto-Associative Memory" (AAM) architecture (D. Rumelhart & McClelland, 1986). In an AAM, both the input and output dimensions are the number of unique categories (362,251), and the dimension of the single hidden layer will be the dimension with which we would like to reduce it to. Using this configuration, the number of neurons (dimensions) in the hidden layer is less than the dimension of the input layer or the output layer, so the encoding process in the hidden layer is a compression of information from the input. Then the connection between the single hidden layer neurons and the output layer neurons can be seen as un-compressing the information back to the original dimension.

For training purposes, the input data is also used as the target, so that the MLP can learn a mapping which loses the least amount of information through the compression (hidden) layer of an auto-associative memory. It is known that an MLP trained in this fashion results in a dimension reduction which is qualitatively equivalent to those obtained by using a SVD algorithm but without the need of having to store a large matrix in memory.

After the node labels are reduced to a more manageable dimension (here we use 16) using the MLP technique as indicated, attention was shifted to the incorporation of link structures within the training dataset. PMGraphSOM is capable of incorporating link information to assist in the training process, therefore the link structure of the training dataset could be used for training purposes without further processing. However, some analysis on the links within the dataset revealed that the total number of links is 136,304,216; this equates to a mean of approximately 51.22 links

*Table 1. Statistics of the link structure of the training dataset*

| | Max | Min | Standard deviation | Num. of documents without links |
|---|---|---|---|---|
| Out-degree | 5295 | 0 | 92.96 | 36,978 |
| In-degree | 549,658 | 0 | 476.18 | 304,518 |

per page. These links are unlikely to be distributed equally, therefore, separate analysis of the out-links and in-links were also conducted. The statistical results can be found in Table 1. The standard deviation indicates that the number of in-links varies much more than the number of out-links. This property is important since it implies that the dataset is unbalanced with respect to the incoming and outgoing links.

Such imbalances in the training dataset are known to potentially cause problems with any machine learning approach.

Although the link structure of the testing dataset will not be used during training, some analyses were carried out to ascertain if the testing dataset and the training dataset are comparable. This is especially important in machine learning, as a training dataset, which is representative of the testing dataset, will be able to provide more accurate results for the documents the network has not encountered previously. The statistics of the link structure for the testing dataset are included in Table 2.

As can be observed from comparing the statistical information of the link structure, the training dataset and the testing dataset have a number of significant differences.

- **The number of documents with no links:** It can be observed that a little more than 1% of documents in the training dataset have no out-links. Based on this ratio, approximately 50 documents in the testing dataset are expected to have no out-links, but the testing dataset contains no such type of documents. The in-link also has a similar problem: with the training dataset containing approximately 11% of documents with no links, in comparison with 7% in the testing dataset.
- **A higher number of links in the testing dataset:** The average number of out-links and in-links per document in the testing dataset are consistently higher than the 51.22 links per page average in the training dataset.

These differences suggest that the testing dataset is not a random sampling from the problem domain, but rather a subset selected by some (unknown) criteria. Again, this can impose some added challenges to a machine learning approach.

*Learning for link discovery.* We learn patterns of the Wikipedia links by feeding the training dataset to a PMGraphSOM. After training, all Wikipedia pages will be mapped onto a 2-dimensional display space where pages with similar contextual content and link structure will ideally be mapped onto the same codebook or onto nearby codebooks. Based on this property of the SOM

*Table 2. Statistics of the link structure of the test dataset*

| | Total | Max | Min | Mean | Std. dev. | Num. of docs. without links |
|---|---|---|---|---|---|---|
| Out-degree | 461,741 | 245 | 1 | 92.35 | 46.05 | 0 |
| In-degree | 311,423 | 3095 | 0 | 62.28 | 131.50 | 372 |

training algorithm, we are able to discover links for the 5,000 testing pages by inferring from the codebooks of a trained map.

We used two approaches to infer from the trained map, which are the codebook-based and the content-based link inference approaches previously described. Each of these two approaches can produce an arbitrary number of links which is only limited by the size of the map (for the codebook-based approach), or by the existing link structure of the training dataset (for the content-based approach). These inferred links are then to be ranked in descending order from the most likely link to the least likely link. Then we will truncate the list of links to the maximum allowable 250 for both the in-links as well as the out-links. Note that the computed rank values will also play an important role in the evaluation of the results.

Three ranking algorithms were considered for this task.

1. The first is based on the energy flow of a page (Page et al., 1999). This is calculated by accumulating scores when a page receives in-links, but distributing scores when a page contains out-links. The list of proposed out-links for each of the documents in the test dataset are ordered according to their associated scores. The inverse of accumulating scores from the out-links, and distributing scores to the in-links, is used to order the list of proposed in-links for each test document.
2. The second ranking algorithm is based on frequency. For example, if many of the training documents indicate that a link is a likely in-link or out-link, then it has a higher likelihood of being proposed, and therefore will be ranked higher.
3. The third ranking algorithm is based on the Euclidean distance of the test document and the training documents. This ensures that the training documents with more contextual feature similarity are ranked higher.

We obtained results for each of the two link inference approaches, and investigated the impact of the three ranking mechanisms. Unless specified otherwise, the training of the PMGraphSOM used the training parameters of 3 iterations, a radius of 10, an initial learning rate of 0.9 and a seed number of 7. Other parameters such as the size of the map, and the weight $\mu$ were varied as indicated later in this chapter.

From the above list of training parameters, the number of iterations refers to the number of times the entire training dataset was processed during training. Due to the large number of training data, and due to the fact that a PMGraphSOM is updated on every node of an input graph, and hence, within each of the training iteration, the PMGraphSOM is updated 2,661,190 times. Since the dataset contains a large degree of redundant (or very similar) information, it suffices to train the map for a relatively small number of iterations. The radius refers to the distance from the winning neuron within which update will take place. Moreover, since the mapping is expected to be more randomized in the early phase of training, and then become more stable and more representative as training progresses, the number of codebooks around the winning neuron which need updating is also expected to decrease. This is in fact implemented in practice by decreasing the radius as training progresses, therefore, the specified radius value only refers to the initial radius, and subsequent radius values are calculated based on the training progress until it approaches a value of 1. Learning rate governs how much update should take place, and uses a similar approach as radius, in terms of its strength as training progresses, so the learning rate specified is the initial learning rate. Through the training iteration, learning rate will approach 0; this is commonly done with SOM based algorithms to aid convergence. The grouping concept was introduced with the PMGraphSOM approach. The grouping of codebooks allows the granularity of the map to be altered for training, and improves training efficiency as this reduces the dimension of the codebook vector. Training with groupings were attempted, but they did not produce improvements for the testing dataset, therefore for the experiments conducted, no grouping was used. The seed value was used to simply allow the purpose of being able to reproduce the results, as if it was not specified, a random seed value would have been used every time the algorithm is applied. The seed influences the initial condition of the network.

Fixing the above mentioned training parameters allows other parameters to be varied and tested. The parameters under investigation here are the map size and the weights μ. We attempted a large number of combinations of map sizes and weights, the resulting trained maps were analyzed on the testing dataset. We selected the five most representative results submitted by us to the INEX LinkTheWiki track for the purpose of visualizing the results in this chapter. The map size and weights for corresponding submissions are indicated in Table 3. These submitted training tasks were the only results produced from unsupervised machine learning approaches amongst the approaches attempted by other researchers (He & de Rijke, 2010; Itakura & Clarke, 2010).

The first submission does not have any associated information about the training process, because it was not trained, but merely ranked. PMgraphSOMs were trained for submission associated with the IDs 02 to 05. The map size refers to the horizontal and vertical extent of the 2-dimensional map ***M***. The parameters $\mu_1$, $\mu_2$, and $\mu_3$ are weights, such that their sum is equal to 1; precisely, $\mu_1$ is the weight associated with the node labels, $\mu_2$ is the weight associated with the out-links (the vectors associated with the out-links), and $\mu_3$ is the weight associated with the in-links (the vectors associated with the in-links). In other words, we use the state of ***M*** for the children of a node, and a second state of ***M*** for the parents of a node. This is because otherwise the PMGraph-SOM considers the links as being undirected whereas the task is to detect both, in-links and out-links rather than all the neighbors of a node. A large variation of the weights were attempted during training, and it was observed that the weights associated with the links are generally significantly smaller than the weights assigned to node labels; this could be attributed to the differences in the dimensions, and the magnitude of the vectorial elements. For example, in this experimental set up, a 16 dimensional vector is used to represent the node labels, whereas the information about the links (both in-links and out-links) are represented by much larger vectors that are dependent on the map size. It should be noted that submissions 04 and 05 are based on the same trained map, but different ranking algorithms were applied to produce different sets of results.

The frequency of activation of each codebook after the training process (the trained map) can be observed in Figure 2, Figure 3 and Figure 4 respectively. In these figures, the number in each cell (codebook) indicates the number of activation, and to provide a better overview of the maps, the cells are coloured in grey scale with darker cells indicating higher activation. A group of adjacent

*Table 3. Statistics of the test set's link structure*

| Submission ID | Map size | $\mu_1$ | $\mu_2$ | $\mu_3$ | Trained map |
|---|---|---|---|---|---|
| 01 | - | - | - | - | - |
| 02 | 20x40 | 0.999 | 0.0005 | 0.0005 | Fig. 2 |
| 03 | 10x30 | 1.0 | 0.0 | 0.0 | Fig. 3 |
| 04 | 20x40 | 0.991 | 0.0045 | 0.0045 | Fig. 4 |
| 05 | 20x40 | 0.991 | 0.0045 | 0.0045 | Fig. 4 |

dark cells surrounded by light-coloured cells indicates a cluster. Some clusters seem to have clear boundaries, such as the cluster in the lower-right quadrant in Figure 3, while some clusters may appear to overlap with another cluster, such as the clusters stretching horizontally across the centre towards the right-hand side of the map in Figure 3. The ideal map would be one with several distinct clusters formed by similar documents mapped in the same or in neighboring cells, while a poorly trained map would show a more random activation, which often makes the identification of clusters difficult. The trained maps illustrated here show reasonable clustering on all maps, exhibiting some distinct clusters.

## Results and Evaluation

The performance measure for participating in the challenge includes Precision, Recall, Mean Average Precision (MAP) and interpolated precision (Precision @R). The evaluation mechanism used to compare the results across the participating groups is the interpolated precision. Therefore the evaluation mechanism used for this task is also based on the interpolated precision.

Interpolated precision is precision evaluated on different granularities to observe the performance achievable when varying the number of top ranked links considered. If precision and recall are defined as $|t \cup r|/|r|$ and $|t \cup r|/|t|$, where $t$ refers to the actual links contained in the test set and $r$ the links proposed by us, calculating precision for the top $n$ links for each page would be calculated by restricting the size of $t$ to a maximum of $n$. This is expected to reveal the effectiveness of the ranking algorithms used.

The performance measured using interpolated precision and recall for the 5 submissions are included in Table 4. Each of the submissions use a different combination of training configuration and ranking algorithm. Although the results may appear generally low, with the Precision@250 ranging from 0.00002 to 0.01817, however, this marks a vast improvement over the results obtained by using a random process. The accuracy

*Figure 2. The trained map corresponding to submission 02. Larger maps generally produced a refined clustering*

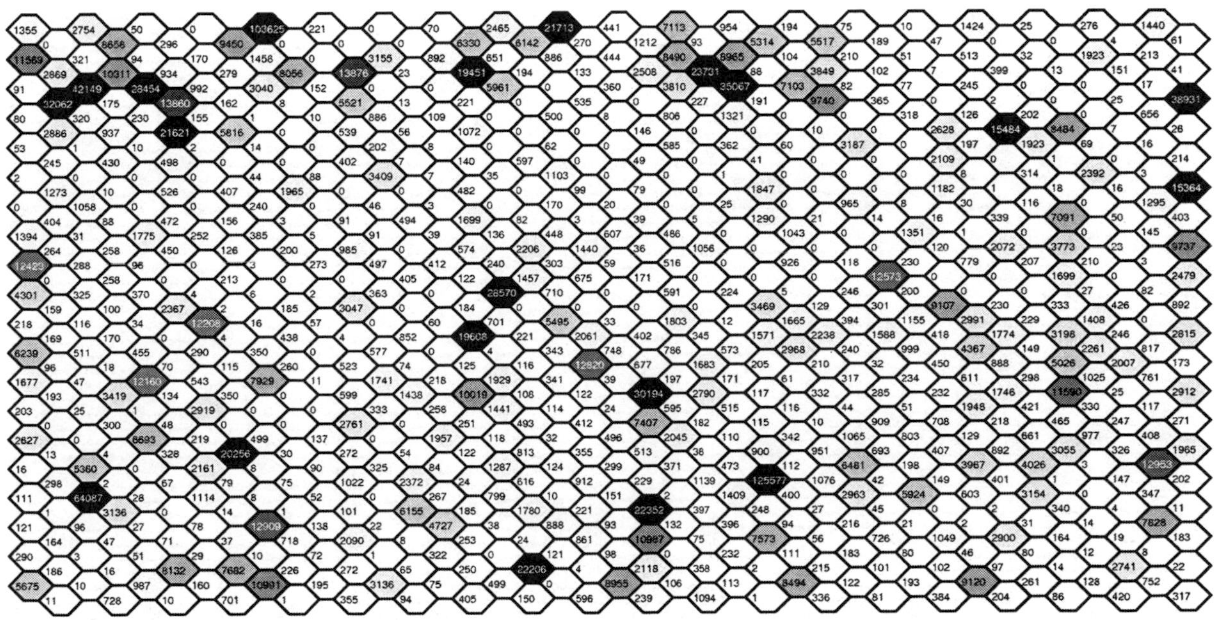

*Figure 3. The trained map corresponding to submission 03*

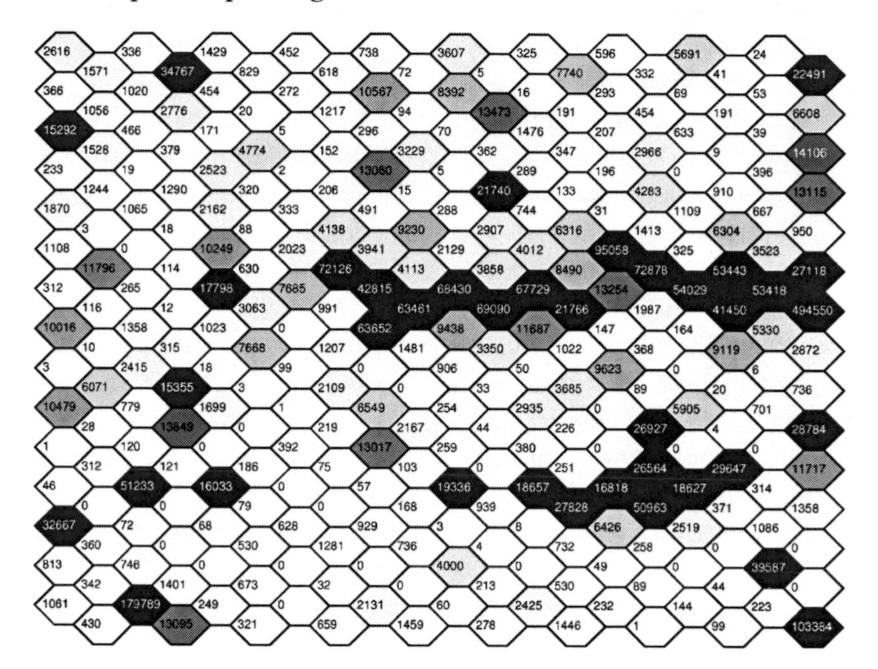

of a random process is less than 0.00001 on an average, hence the proposed approach performs by 3 to 5 orders of magnitude better. It is important to note that these results were obtained using an unsupervised machine learning approach, so it cannot be expected to perform as well as supervised approaches that utilize teacher signals for guidance and correction during training.

*Figure 4. Visualization of the mappings on the trained map corresponding to submissions 04 and submission 05*

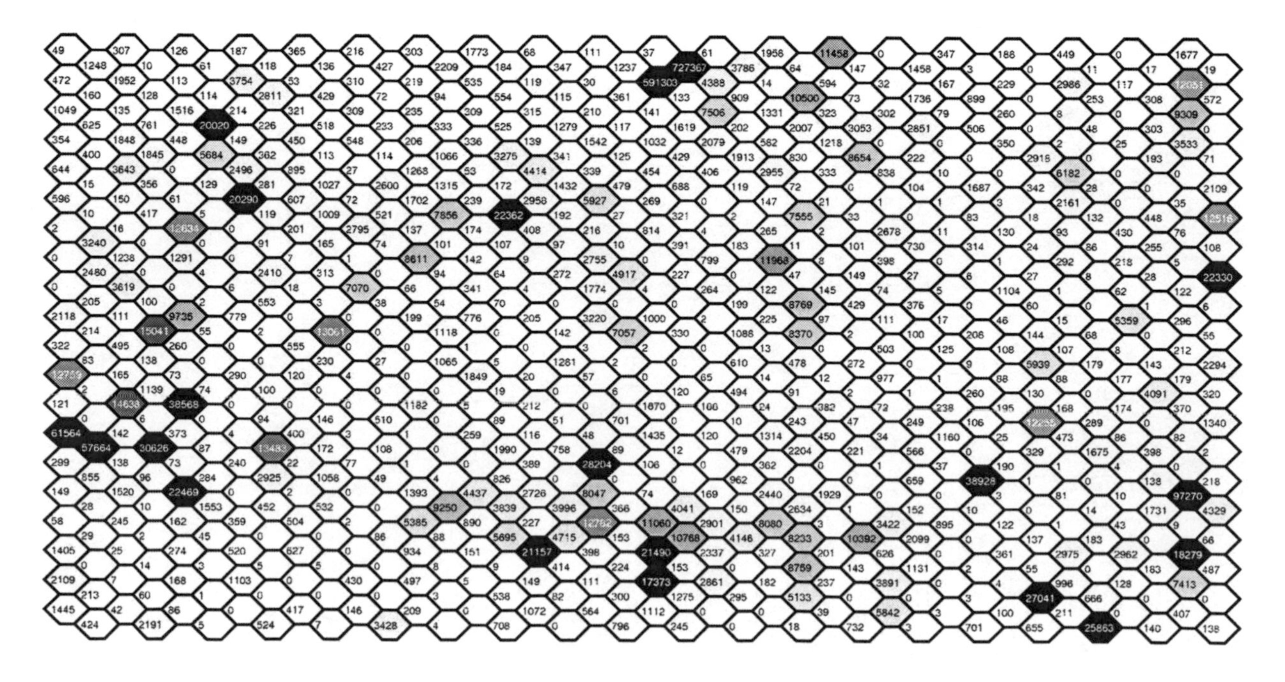

*Table 4. The performance of proposed links as predicted by our algorithms*

| Submission ID | 01 | 02 | 03 | 04 | 05 |
|---|---|---|---|---|---|
| Link inference method | Consider all | Content-based | Content-based | Codebook-based | Content-based |
| Ranking algorithm | Energy flow | Link frequency | Link frequency | Euclid. distance | Euclid. distance |
| Recall for out-links | 0.00377 | 0.02942 | 0.03202 | 0.00070 | 0.00448 |
| Precision@250 out-links | 0.00136 | 0.01057 | 0.01817 | 0.00025 | 0.00161 |
| Precision@100 out-links | 0.00168 | 0.01795 | 0.02162 | 0.00002 | 0.00147 |
| Precision@20 out-links | 0.00040 | 0.03941 | 0.04489 | 0.00003 | 0.00268 |
| Recall for in-links | 0.00032 | 0.00050 | 0.00095 | 0.00010 | 0.00029 |
| Precision@250 in-links | 0.00008 | 0.00012 | 0.00025 | 0.00002 | 0.00007 |
| Precision@100 in-links | 0.00007 | 0.00008 | 0.00037 | 0.00003 | 0.00008 |
| Precision@20 in-links | 0.00007 | 0.00018 | 0.00107 | 0.00001 | 0.00008 |

Submission 01 is the best result achievable without using a trained map, but instead, simply apply the ranking algorithm over the entire dataset, and identify the top few ranked pages. As may be observed from Table 4, this simple procedure produces one of the worst results when compared with those obtained using the training process. Although most of the results from a trained map out-performed the un-trained result, the best performance using the trained data, is obtained from submission 03, which uses content-based link inference approach, and is ranked by link frequency. The associated map is visualized in Figure 2. The visualization indicates that the increased size of the display space allows for a more sharply defined clustering of the nodes. When training the same size of a map by strengthening the weight $\mu_2$ and $\mu_3$ (the influence of the state vectors) this produced a mapping as shown in Figure 4. The effect is a reduction in the number of clusters while strengthening the remaining clusters (the number of activations within a cluster increased sharply) causing an overall reduction in the accuracy of the predicted links. This indicates the importance of the information provided by the data label (weighted by $\mu_1$) in link prediction tasks. The main reason for this is that the test data does not contain any link information, hence the similarity with codebook values is based solely on the content based similarity provided through the data label component.

These representative results show that the content-based link inference approach produces better performance than the codebook- based link inference approach, and that the ranking by link frequency produces better results than ranking by Euclidean distance. Another observation from Table 4 is that no matter which inference method or ranking algorithm is used, the in-links proposed are less accurate than the out-links proposed. These results and observations allow us to draw the conclusion that encoding the link structure and incorporating textual information about the documents in the training process is able to achieve a significantly improved performance; provided that the link inference approach and ranking approach are appropriately chosen. It was also shown that by increasing the size of the SOM, this will enhance the precision of the prediction at the cost of additional computational time. Thus, the precision of the SOM for link prediction tasks is constrained by the discrete nature of the mapping space.

We note that the approach described in this chapter is *unsupervised*. To the best of our knowledge, there exists no other unsupervised machine learning approach to link prediction at this time. The dataset used is a benchmark problem which has been used by a number of others. The state-of-the-art performance for this benchmark problem is, when $R$=250, an interpolated precision of approximately 0.05. This was achieved by a supervised approach (Huang et al., 2010).

The experiments in this chapter have demonstrated that extensions of SOM for encoding structured data, in particular PMGraphSOM, is capable of encoding and predicting inter-document links in a dataset, given the appropriate features, inference approaches and ranking methods. This has implications on its potential to solve other real-word problems, as there could be two directions to the link prediction problem: the prediction of inter-document links such as hyperlinks as was presented in this chapter, and the prediction of intra-document links such as the relationship between elements of a single document. It is also possible to predict both types of links at the same time. The latter requires what is known as the Graph-of-graph (GoG) concept (Zhang et al., 2010) though the GoG is yet to be explored for the unsupervised case. The GoG concept recognizes that intra-document links depict the relationships among the nodes of a document. These nodes can be words, or paragraphs in the document. Whereas for inter-document links, they express the relationship between documents. For example, one document may be dependent on another document (it makes a reference to this other document). This other document may in turn be dependent on yet another document (it makes a reference to this other document). If each document is modeled by a graph structure consisting of nodes and links (intra-document links), then the dependency between documents can be represented as a directed link from one document to another. Thus, this creates a model in which one graph is related to another graph, and this other graph is in turn related to yet another graph. This is what we called a GoG situation. This is quite common in XML documents or web pages in which there are references to other documents or web sites. As indicated, we have yet applied to this case. In this chapter we have not considered the GoG models. In other words, each document is considered by itself, without dependency except the number of links and the locations in which they arrive from other XML documents, or going to other XML documents. However, it can be observed that the GoG model can be achieved through extensions to the PMGraphSOM. The main challenge with this is how such an extended PMGraphSOM can be trained in a scalable fashion.

Time complexity of the presented approach has been addressed in another publication (Hagenbuchner et al., 2003). In summary, the computational time complexity of the presented approach grows linearly with the number of nodes in a dataset (Hagenbuchner et al., 2003). This behaviour is analogous to the time complexity of the standard SOM approach (which grows linearly with the size of the training set). Thus, the approach presented in this paper is suitable for large scale data mining tasks.

## FUTURE RESEARCH DIRECTIONS

Graph mining, link analysis, and link prediction are hot research topics. Numerous directions are currently being explored. Future research directions as are relevant to the materials presented in this chapter would be as follows:

- **Continuous mapping spaces:** Self-Organizing Map approach consists of a set of codebook vectors arranged on a regular grid. This means that the number of codebook vectors is limited, and that the layout of the grid discretizes the mapping of the display space. The aim of a future research project could be to introduce a mapping space that is continuous. One possibility would be to expand on the "probability measure" idea expressed in this chapter by describing a mapping by a Gaussian function rather than by coordinate values. In other words, each codebook could be interpreted as the representative of a multivariate Gaussian function. The median of the Gaussian would be fixed at a given location, but the description of a mapping would be continuous. The details to how this can be achieved are yet to be explored.

- **Convergence theorem and proof:** There exists no proof of convergence for any of the many Self-Organizing Map approaches. This is mostly due to the absence of an error function in the training algorithms for a SOM. If one could introduce some form of a continuously differentiable error function to the SOM training algorithm, then it should be possible to formally analyse the convergence properties of a SOM.
- **Supervised link prediction approaches:** Supervised machine learning approaches could be expected to outperform most unsupervised approaches. There is currently no known supervised machine learning approach suitable for link prediction tasks. The main problem is that existing supervised machine learning methods are unable to reverse the information stream through a given model (to conclude from a given output what the associated input would have looked like). It may be possible to explicitly train a supervised machine learning method by adopting an auto-association approach (i.e., by extending the model by a second component which is trained to reconstruct the input from a given output). This approach remains to be explored in details.
- **Extension to hypergraphs:** Hypergraphs are a generalization of graph data structures in that its links can represent a one-to-many relationship. This means that hypergraphs allow nodes to be connected to several other nodes by a single link. Hypergraphs are suitable to encode relationships as they occur in several applications such as, for example, electrical circuits, molecular chemistry. There is currently no known machine learning approach capable of encoding hypergraphs. A possibility may be to represent each link by a neural network. This would be in addition to encoding each node by a neural network as was described in this chapter. Effectively, this could mean that a hypergraph could be encoded by training two maps concurrently; one for the encoding of the nodes, and a second one for encoding the links of a hypergraph. A suitable training algorithm would need to be developed.

## CONCLUSION

The work presented in this chapter is the latest in the area of unsupervised machine learning in the domain of graph structured information. The approach presented in this chapter is the only known unsupervised machine learning approach that can encode graph data structures and, once trained, can be used to reconstruct the original structure by starting from a single node. The simplicity and scalability of the algorithm are some of the properties which make its application to very large learning problems on link prediction a possibility. While the accuracy of the methods improves the prediction of links by three orders of magnitude when compared with those obtained by using random selections, it was also shown that the cardinality of the Self-Organizing Map can be an inhibiting factor on the accuracy of a predicted link. The avoidance of this cardinality problem, and the development of supervised approaches to link prediction remain open problems yet to be solved. These would pose as challenges for future research.

The approach presented in this paper is also beneficial for tasks requiring the clustering of structured information. For example, the SOM-SD holds the state-of-the-art performance for several benchmark problems (e.g., provided by INEX) on the clustering of relatively large sets of XML documents (Hagenbuchner et al., 2006; Kc et al., 2007), and has been successfully used as a filter on a spam detection task in hyper-linked domain (Di Noi et al., 2010). The versatility of the method underlines the benefits of data driven approaches, and shows that SOM based methods continue to be beneficial for solving real world data mining problems.

## ACKNOWLEDGMENT

The authors wish to acknowledge partial financial support from an Australian Research Council Discovery Project grant DP077148 (2007 - 2009) for the work which is reported in this chapter.

## REFERENCES

Bengio, Y., Frasconi, P., & Simard, P. (1994). Learning long-term dependencies with gradient descent is difficult. *IEEE Transactions on Neural Networks*, *5*(5), 157–166. doi:10.1109/72.279181

Bianucci, A., Micheli, A., Sperduti, A., & Starita, A. (1998). Quantitative structure-activity relationships of benzodiazepines by recursive cascade correlation. In *Proceedings of the 1998 IEEE International Joint Conference on Neural Networks. IEEE World Congress on Computational Intelligence (IJCNN)*, (p. 117). IEEE Computer Society.

Bunke, H. (1990). String grammars for syntactic pattern recognition. In Bunke, H., & Sanfeliu, A. (Eds.), *Syntactic and structural pattern recognition, theory and applications* (pp. 29–55). World Scientific Pubblishing.

Di Noi, L., Hagenbuchner, M., Scarselli, F., & Tsoi, A. (2010). Web Spam detection by probability mapping graphsoms and graph neural networks. In K. Diamantaras, W. Duch, & L. Iliadis (Eds.), *Proceedings of the 20th International Conference on Artificial Neural Networks (ICANN) Lecture Notes in Computer Science: Vol. 6353.* (pp. 372-381). Springer.

Elman, J. L. (1990). Finding structure in time. *Cognitive Science*, *14*(2), 179–211. doi:10.1207/s15516709cog1402_1

Fu, K. (1977). Tree languages and syntactic pattern recognition. In Chen, C. (Ed.), *Pattern recognition and artificial intelligence* (pp. 257–291). Academic Press.

Golub, G. H., & Kahan, W. (1965). Calculating the singular values and pseudo-inverse of a matrix. *Journal of the Society for Industrial and Applied Mathematics: Series B. Numerical Analysis*, *2*(2), 205–224.

Hagenbuchner, M., Sperduti, A., & Tsoi, A. (2003). A self-organizing map for adaptive processing of structured data. *IEEE Transactions on Neural Networks*, *14*(3), 491–505. doi:10.1109/TNN.2003.810735

Hagenbuchner, M., Sperduti, A., & Tsoi, A. (2005). *Contextual self-organizing maps for structured domains*. In Workshop on Relational Machine Learning.

Hagenbuchner, M., Sperduti, A., Tsoi, A., Trentini, F., Scarselli, F., & Gori, M. (2006). Clustering XML documents using self-organizing maps for structures. In N. Fuhr, M. Lalmas, S. Malik, & G. Kazai (Eds.), *Advances in XML Information Retrieval and Evaluation, 4th International Workshop of the Initiative for the Evaluation of XML Retrieval (INEX) Lecture Notes in Computer Science: Vol. 3977.* (pp. 481-496). Springer.

Hagenbuchner, M., Tsoi, A., & Sperduti, A. (2001). A supervised self-organising map for structured data. In Allison, N., Yin, H., Allison, L., & Slack, J. (Eds.), *WSOM2001 - Advances in Self-Organising Maps* (pp. 21–28). Springer. doi:10.1007/978-1-4471-0715-6_4

Hagenbuchner, M., Zhang, S., Tsoi, A., & Sperduti, A. (2009). Projection of undirected and non-positional graphs using self organizing maps. In *Proceedings of the European Symposium on Artificial Neural Networks - Advances in Computational Intelligence and Learning (ESANN)*, (pp. 559-564).

Haykin, S. (1994). *Neural networks, a comprehensive foundation*. Macmillan College Publishing Company, Inc.

He, J., & de Rijke, M. (2010). An exploration of learning to link with Wikipedia: Features, methods and training collection. In S. Geva, J. Kamps, & A. Trotman (Eds.), *Focused Retrieval and Evaluation, 8th International Workshop of the Initiative for the Evaluation of XML Retrieval (INEX) Lecture Notes in Computer Science: Vol. 6203*. (pp. 324-330). Springer.

Hornik, K., Stinchcombe, M. B., & White, H. (1989). Multilayer feedforward networks are universal approximators. *Neural Networks, 2*(5), 359–366. doi:10.1016/0893-6080(89)90020-8

Huang, W., Geva, S., & Trotman, A. (2010). Overview of the INEX 2009 link: The Wiki track. In S. Geva, J. Kamps, & A. Trotman (Eds.), *Focused Retrieval and Evaluation, 8th International Workshop of the Initiative for the Evaluation of XML Retrieval (INEX) Lecture Notes in Computer Science: Vol. 6203*. (pp. 312-323). Springer.

Itakura, K., & Clarke, C. (2010). University of Waterloo at INEX 2009: Ad hoc, book, entity ranking, and link-the-wiki tracks. In S. Geva, J. Kamps, and A. Trotman (Eds.), *Focused Retrieval and Evaluation, 8th International Workshop of the Initiative for the Evaluation of XML Retrieval (INEX) Lecture Notes in Computer Science: Vol. 6203*. (pp. 331-341). Springer.

Kc, M., Chau, R., Hagenbuchner, M., Tsoi, A., & Lee, V. C. S. (2010). A machine learning approach to link prediction for interlinked documents. In S. Geva, J. Kamps, & A. Trotman (Eds.), *Focused Retrieval and Evaluation, 8th International Workshop of the Initiative for the Evaluation of XML Retrieval (INEX) Lecture Notes in Computer Science: Vol. 6203*. (pp. 342-354). Springer.

Kc, M., Hagenbuchner, M., Tsoi, A., Scarselli, F., Gori, M., & Sperduti, A. (2007). XML document mining using contextual self-organizing maps for structures. In N. Fuhr, M. Lalmas, & A. Trotman (Eds.), *Comparative Evaluation of XML Information Retrieval Systems, 5th International Workshop of the Initiative for the Evaluation of XML Retrieval (INEX) Lecture Notes in Computer Science: Vol. 4518*. (pp. 510-524). Springer.

Kohonen, T. (1990). *Self-organisation and associative memory* (3rd ed.). Springer.

Kohonen, T. (1995). *Self-organizing maps* (*Vol. 30*). Springer.

Kohonen, T. (1997). Exploration of very large databases by self-organizing maps. In *Proceedings of the IEEE International Conference on Neural Networks* (pp. 1-6). IEEE Computer Society.

Page, L., Brin, S., Motwani, R., & Winograd, T. (1999). *The Pagerank citation ranking: Bringing order to the Web*. Stanford InfoLab.

Rumelhart, D. E., Hinton, G. E., & Williams, R. J. (1986). Learning internal representations by error propagation. In D. E. Rumelhart, & J. L. McClelland (Eds.), *Parallel distributed processing: Explorations in the microstructure of cognition, vol. 1: Foundations* (pp. 318-362). MIT Press.

Rumelhart, D. E., & McClelland, J. L. (1986). *Parallel distributed processing* (*Vol. 1*). MIT Press.

Scarselli, F., Gori, M., Tsoi, A., Hagenbuchner, M., & Monfardini, G. (2009a). Computational capabilities of graph neural networks. *IEEE Transactions on Neural Networks, 20*(1), 81–102. doi:10.1109/TNN.2008.2005141

Scarselli, F., Gori, M., Tsoi, A., Hagenbuchner, M., & Monfardini, G. (2009b). The graph neural network model. *IEEE Transactions on Neural Networks, 20*(1), 61–80. doi:10.1109/TNN.2008.2005605

Takács, G., Pilászy, I., Németh, B., & Tikk, D. (2009). Scalable collaborative filtering approaches for large recommender systems. *Journal of Machine Learning Research, 10*, 623–656.

Zhang, S., Hagenbuchner, M., Scarselli, F., & Tsoi, A. (2010). Supervised encoding of graph-of-graphs for classification and regression problems. In S. Geva, J. Kamps, & A. Trotman (Eds.), *Focused Retrieval and Evaluation, 8th International Workshop of the Initiative for the Evaluation of XML Retrieval (INEX) Lecture Notes in Computer Science: Vol. 6203* (pp. 449-461). Springer.

Zhang, S., Hagenbuchner, M., Tsoi, A., & Sperduti, A. (2009). Self organizing maps for the clustering of large sets of labeled graphs. In S. Geva, J. Kamps, & A. Trotman (Eds.), *Advances in Focused Retrieval, 7th International Workshop of the Initiative for the Evaluation of XML Retrieval (INEX) Lecture Notes in Computer Science: Vol. 5631.* (pp. 207-221). Springer.

## ADDITIONAL READING

Aho, A. & Ullman, J. (1992). *Foundations of Computer Science.*

Bellman, R. E. (1961). *Adaptive Control Processes: A Guided Tour.* Princeton University Press.

Erwin, E., Obermayer, K., & Schulten, K. (1992). Self-organizing Maps: Ordering, Convergence Properties and Energy Functions. *Biological Cybernetics, 67*(1), 47–55. doi:10.1007/BF00201801

Frasconi, P., Gori, M., & Sperduti, A. (1998). A General Framework for Adaptive Processing of Data Structures. *IEEE Transactions on Neural Networks, 9*(5), 768–785. doi:10.1109/72.712151

Gonzalez, A. I., Graña, M., D'Anjou, A., Albizuri, F. X., & Cottrell, M. (1997). A Sensitivity Analysis of the Self Organizing Map as an Adaptive One-pass Non-stationary Clustering Algorithm: The Case of Color Quantization of Image Sequences. *Neural Processing Letters, 6*(3), 77–89. doi:10.1023/A:1009663723152

Hagenbuchner, M. (2002). *Adaptive Processing of Structured Information using Artificial Neural Networks.* PhD thesis, University of Wollongong.

Hagenbuchner, M., Gori, M., Tsoi, A., Bunke, H., & Irniger, C. (2002). Using Attributed Plex Grammars for the Generation of Image and Graph Databases. *Pattern Recognition Letters, 24*(8), 1081–1087. doi:10.1016/S0167-8655(02)00254-4

Hammer, B., Micheli, A., Sperduti, A., & Strickert, M. (2004). A General Framework for Unsupervised Processing of Structured Data. *Neurocomputing, 57*, 3–35. doi:10.1016/j.neucom.2004.01.008

Hammer, B., & Sperschneider, V. (1997). Neural Networks Can Approximate Mappings on Structured Objects. In *Proceedings of the 2nd International Conference on Computational Intelligence and Neuroscience (ICCIN)*, (pp. 211-214).

Hartigan, J. A. (1975). *Clustering Algorithms.* John Wiley & Sons Inc.

Hassoun, M. H. (1995). *Fundamentals of Artificial Neural Networks.* MIT Press.

Papadimitriou, C. H. (1994). *Computational Complexity.* Addison Wesley.

Pollack, J. B. (1989). Implications of Recursive Distributed Representations. In Touretzky, D. S. (Ed.), *Advances in Neural Information Processing Systems* (pp. 527–536). Morgan Kaufman.

Rojas, R., & Feldman, J. (1996). *Neural Networks: A Systematic Introduction*. Springer.

Tan, P.-N., Steinbach, M., Tan, V. K., & Pang-Ning (Eds.). (2005). *Introduction to Data Mining*. Pearson Addison Wesley.

Yin, H., & Allinson, N. (1995). On the Distribution and Convergence of Feature Space in Self-organizing Maps. *Neural Computation*, *7*(6), 1178–1187. doi:10.1162/neco.1995.7.6.1178

## ENDNOTES

1. In this chapter, we are not dealing with hypergraphs, in which a link may connect to more than one node in a graph.
2. GraphSOM is an earlier version of SOM specifically designed to handle graph inputs through the *state* representation of the winning nodes in the map *M*. This was before we used the probability mapping idea as indicated in this chapter.

# Section 3
# Association Mining

# Chapter 11
# Frequent Pattern Discovery and Association Rule Mining of XML Data

**Qin Ding**
*East Carolina University, USA*

**Gnanasekaran Sundarraj**
*Pennsylvania State University, USA*

## ABSTRACT

*Finding frequent patterns and association rules in large data has become a very important task in data mining. Various algorithms have been proposed to solve such problems, but most algorithms are only applicable to relational data. With the increasing use and popularity of XML representation, it is of importance yet challenging to find solutions to frequent pattern discovery and association rule mining of XML data. The challenge comes from the complexity of the structure in XML data. In this chapter, we provide an overview of the state-of-the-art research in content-based and structure-based mining of frequent patterns and association rules from XML data. We also discuss the challenges and issues, and provide our insight for solutions and future research directions.*

## INTRODUCTION

Association rule mining and frequent pattern mining are important problems in data mining (Agrawal, Mannila, Srikant, Toivonen, & Verkamo, 1996; Han & Kamber, 2006; Tan, Steinbach, & Kumar, 2006). These two problems are closely related and they aim to discover patterns that occur frequently in large datasets. The problems were originally proposed for market basket transaction data regarding store items purchased on a per-transaction basis. An example is that by analyzing the customer transaction data at Amazon.com, we found that most customers who bought book "A" also bought books "B" and "C". Discovering such customer purchase behaviors can be very useful

DOI: 10.4018/978-1-61350-356-0.ch011

in decision making and other business-related applications. Many algorithms have been proposed to discover association rules and frequent patterns, such as Apriori (Agrawal & Srikant, 1994) and FP-growth (Han, Pei, & Yin, 2000; Han, Pei, Yin, & Mao, 2004). However, most of such algorithms are only applicable to relational data.

In the past decade, XML has become a standard for representing and exchanging information. With the increasing popularity of XML representation and the large amount of XML data available, it becomes important and necessary for researchers to study how to extend association rule mining and frequent pattern mining to XML data so that interesting patterns can be discovered from XML documents. This is a very interesting yet challenging field. The problem was first proposed in 2002 and since then it has gained more attention from an increasing number of researchers.

A simple approach to mining association rules and frequent patterns on XML data is to convert XML data into relational format, and then use the traditional algorithms to perform association rule mining and frequent pattern mining. However, by doing so, the structure information in XML data is mostly lost. As XQuery (W3C XML Query) becomes a standard query language for XML data, researchers have also attempted to use XQuery or extend the features in XQuery to support frequent pattern mining on XML data (Braga, Campi, Ceri, Klemettinen, & Lanzi, 2002a, 2002b; Wan & Dobbie, 2003; Romei & Turini, 2010). The existing or extended features of the XQuery language facilitate the computation needed for mining XML association rules and frequent patterns. However, it also adds an extra layer which in turn brings additional overhead; more importantly, this kind of language-dependent approach lacks flexibility since XQuery is a query language and was not designed for data mining. Therefore it is desired to develop non-XQuery-based approach for frequent pattern discovery on XML data.

Most early work on XML association rule mining and frequent pattern mining focused on mining the content of XML documents (Braga et al., 2002a, 2002b; Wan & Dobbie, 2003; Meo & Psaila, 2002). Besides mining the content in XML documents, it is also interesting in mining the structure (Cong, Yi, Liu, Wang, 2002). For example, frameworks and algorithms have been proposed to discover dynamic structural changes over a collection of historical XML documents (Zhao, Bhowmick, Mohania, & Kambayashi, 2004; Zhao, Bhowmick, & Mohania, 2004; Zhao, Bhowmick, & Gruenwald, 2005; Zhao & Bhowmick, 2005; Zhao, Chen, Bhowmick, & Madria, 2005; Zhao, Bhowmick, & Madria, 2006; Leonardi, Bhowmick, & Madria, 2005; Leonardi, Hoai, Bhowmick, & Madria, 2006, 2007; Leonardi & Bhowmick, 2006a, 2006b, 2007; Leonardi, Budiman, & Bhowmick, 2005; Chen, Bhowmick, & Chia, 2004a, 2004b; Cobena, Abiteboul, & Marian, 2002). Another type of structure-based XML mining is to discover frequent XML query patterns to improve query response time (Yang, Lee, Hsu, & Acharya, 2003; Yang, Lee, & Hsu, 2003; Yang, Lee, Hsu, & Guo, 2004; Yang, Lee, & Hsu, 2004a, 2004b; Yang, Lee, Hsu, Huang, & Wang, 2008; Hua, Zhao, & Chen, 2007; Li, Feng, Wang, Zhang, & Zhou, 2006; Li, Feng, Wang, & Zhou, 2009; Feng, Qian, Wang, & Zhou, 2006; Chen, Yang, & Wang, 2004). Overall, both content-based and structure-based frequent pattern mining on XML data are still at their preliminary stage with many open questions and solutions to be tackled.

The objective of this chapter is to provide an overview of research on content-based and structure-based association rule mining and frequent pattern discovery on XML data. We will discuss various approaches with its advantages, limitations, and issues. We will also provide our insight for future direction in this research field. The remainder of this chapter is organized as follows. In next section, we introduce the background on association rule mining and frequent pattern mining in general, followed by the problem on XML data. Section "Mining frequent patterns and association rules on XML data" details the current state-of-the-art research on association rule mining on XML data, in particular, the content-based mining and structure-based mining. We provide our insight about future directions in Section "Future research directions" and finally summarize the chapter.

## BACKGROUND

The problems of association rule mining and frequent pattern mining were first proposed in 1993 by Agrawal and his colleagues (Agrawal, Imielinski, & Swami, 1993). Various algorithms have been proposed, such as Apriori (Agrawal & Srikant, 1994), DHP (Park, Chen, & Yu, 1995), DIC (Brin, Motwani, Ullman, & Tsur, 1997), Partition (Savasere, Omiecinski, & Navathe, 1995), and FP-growth (Han et al., 2000; Han et al., 2004), among which Apriori is the basic and the most commonly used algorithm.

A formal definition of association rules (Agrawal & Srikant, 1994) is as follows. Let $I = \{i_1, i_2, ..., i_m\}$ be a set of literals, called *items*. Let $D$ be a set of *transactions*, where each transaction $T$ is a set of items such that $T \subseteq I$. Associated with each transaction is a unique identifier, called its TID. We say that a transaction $T$ contains $X$, a set of some items in $I$, if $X \subseteq T$. An *association rule* is an implication of the form $X \rightarrow Y$, where $X \subset I$, $Y \subset I$, and $X \cap Y = \emptyset$ in $I$. $X$ is called the antecedent while $Y$ is called the consequence of the rule. There are two primary measures for each rule, namely *support* and *confidence*. The rule $X \rightarrow Y$ has support $s$% in the transaction set $D$ if $s$% of transactions in $D$ contain both $X$ and $Y$. The rule has confidence $c$% if $c$% of transactions in $D$ that contain $X$ also contain $Y$. The formal definition of support and confidence are given as follows:

$$support(X \rightarrow Y) = support(X \cup Y)$$

$$confidence(X \rightarrow Y) = \frac{support(X \cup Y)}{support(X)}$$

The support of $X \rightarrow Y$ indicates how frequently $X$ and $Y$ occur together, while the confidence indicates how frequently $Y$ occurs given that $X$ occurs. The higher the support and the confidence, the more interesting the rule is. Support and confidence are commonly used to measure the interestingness of association rules, but other measurements, such as *lift* (also called interest) and *conviction*, have also been proposed as alternative measurements (Brin et al., 1997). Lift and conviction are defined below:

$$lift(X \rightarrow Y) = \frac{support(X \cup Y)}{support(X) \times support(Y)}$$

$$convinction(X \rightarrow Y) = \frac{1 - support(Y)}{1 - confidence(X \rightarrow Y)}$$

Lift is a ratio between the observed support of $X \cup Y$ and its expected support under the assumption that $X$ and $Y$ are independent. As can be seen from the definition, $lift(X \rightarrow Y) = lift(Y \rightarrow X)$, but the conviction may be different for $X \rightarrow Y$ and $Y \rightarrow X$. If the lift or conviction of $X \rightarrow Y$ is close to 1, it means that $X$ and $Y$ are independent and the rule is not interesting.

Most association rule mining algorithms use support and confidence to measure the rule interestingness. For a user-specified minimum support *s_min* and minimum confidence *c_min*, the task of association rule mining is to extract, from the given data set $D$, the association rules that have support and confidence greater than or equal to the user-specified values.

The task of association rule mining is typically divided into two phases. The first phase is to find a list of items (i.e., itemsets), which occur frequently. These itemsets are called *frequent itemsets* (or *large itemsets*) and their support exceeds the minimum support threshold. The second phase is to derive all the rules from frequent itemsets so that the confidence for each rule satisfies the minimum confidence requirement. Since the second phase is straightforward, most algorithms only deal with the first step, which is also referred as "frequent pattern mining" or "frequent pattern discovery".

Most algorithms, such as Apriori, use an iterative approach to find all the frequent itemsets based on the principle that a subset of a frequent itemset is also frequent. The Apriori-like approaches use the candidate generation and verification framework to generate the potentially frequent itemsets and then perform the actual counting on them.

Figure 1 shows the step-wise procedure for the Apriori algorithm. It generates the candidate itemsets to be counted in the current pass by using only the itemsets found frequently in the previous pass. The key idea of the Apriori algorithm lies in the "downward-closed" property (also called "Apriori property" or "Apriori Principle") of the support, namely, if an itemset has minimum support, then all its subsets also have minimum support. Based on this property, we know that any subset of a frequent itemset must also be frequent; in other words, any superset of an infrequent itemset must also be infrequent. This observation motivates the step-wise idea to first generate frequent itemsets with only one item (called frequent 1-itemsets), then frequent 2-itemsets, and so forth. During each iteration only candidates found to be frequent in the previous iteration are used to generate a new candidate set during the next iteration. The candidate itemsets having *k* items (called candidate *k*-itemset, i.e., $C_k$) can be generated by joining frequent itemsets having *k*-1 items (i.e., $L_{k-1}$) and pruning those itemsets that contain any subset being infrequent. The algorithm terminates when no frequent itemsets can be further generated.

Unlike Apriori and Apriori-like approaches, FP-growth does not use a candidate generation step (Han et al., 2000; Han et al., 2004; Han & Kamber, 2006). In the FP-growth algorithm, a structure called Frequent Pattern tree (FP-tree) is used to store the compressed and important information about frequent patterns. FP-Growth algorithm adopts divide-and-conquer strategy by transforming the problem of discovering long frequent patterns to looking for shorter ones recursively. First it computes the frequent items and represents the frequent items as a compressed database in FP-tree format. The rule mining is then performed on this tree. This means that the dataset *D* needs to be scanned only once. In addition, this algorithm does not require the candidate itemset generation. There are two advantages of the FP-growth algorithm: (1) The FP-tree is usually smaller than the original database and, thus, saves the costly database scans in the mining process. (2) It applies a pattern growth method that avoids candidate generation. FP-growth runs faster than the Apriori algorithm when the data-

*Figure 1. The Apriori algorithm*

**Algorithm: APRIORI**

**Input:** transactional dataset *D*, minimum support *min_sup*
**Output:** set *L* of frequent itemsets in *D*

```
1: L1 ← findFrequent1-Itemsets(D, min_sup)
2: for (k = 2; Lk-1 ≠ ∅; k++)
3:    Ck ← joinAndPrune(Lk-1, min_sup)   //generate new candidates
4:    for each transaction t ∈ D
5:       Ct ← candidateSubset(Ck, t)      //candidates contained in t
6:       for each c ∈ Ct
7:          increment(c.count)
8:    Lk ← {c ∈ Ck | c.count ≥ min_sup}
9: return L ← ∪k Lk
```

set is relatively small. However, when the dataset is large, the constructed FP-tree cannot fit in main memory, and there is significant downgrade in the FP-growth performance.

Figure 2 shows an example of a small transaction dataset and its FP-tree (Han et al., 2000). The frequent size-1 items are sorted in their frequency order in the header table. Each entry in the header table will contain the frequent item and a link to a node in the FP-tree that has the same item name. Following this link from the header table, one can reach all nodes in the tree having the same item name. Each node in the FP-tree, other than the root node, will contain the item name, support count, and a pointer to link to another node in the tree that has the same item name. Once FP-tree is constructed, frequent patterns will be mined from FP-tree by using the divide-and-conquer strategy.

Besides the Apriori and FP-growth algorithms, other algorithms have been proposed to improve the efficiency for association rule mining. For example, Park et al. (1995) proposed a hash-based algorithm to reduce the size and number of candidate *k*-itemsets, especially candidate 2-itemsets. Brin et al. (1997) proposed the Dynamic Itemset Counting (DIC) algorithm to reduce the number of database scans by generating candidate itemsets at dynamic time points rather than waiting for a round of database scan is completed. A candidate itemset is generated when all of its subsets are estimated to be frequent; by doing so, the counting for such candidate itemsets can start earlier. Savasere et al. (1995) proposed the Partition algorithm which divides the data into multiple non-overlapping partitions so that each partition can fit in main memory. It first discovers local frequent itemsets in each partition and then forms global frequent itemsets based on the principle that an itemset is potentially frequent globally only if it is locally frequent in at least one partition. The partition algorithm only requires two database scans. All these algorithms aim to reduce the number of database scans in the mining process.

The problem of mining frequent itemsets can also be extended to mine *closed* frequent itemsets and *maximal* frequent itemsets. An itemset is closed if none of its immediate supersets has

*Figure 2. An example of (a) transactional dataset and (b) its Frequent-Pattern tree (FP-tree)*

| TID | Items | Ordered frequent Items |
|---|---|---|
| 1 | {*f, a, c, d, g, i, m, p*} | {*f, c, a, m, p*} |
| 3 | {*a, b, c, f, l, m, o*} | {*f, c, a, b, m*} |
| 4 | {*b, f, h, j, o, w*} | {*f, b*} |
| 5 | {*b, c, k, s, p*} | {*c, b, p*} |
| 6 | {*a, f, c, e, l, p, m, n*} | {*f, c, a, m, p*} |

(a)

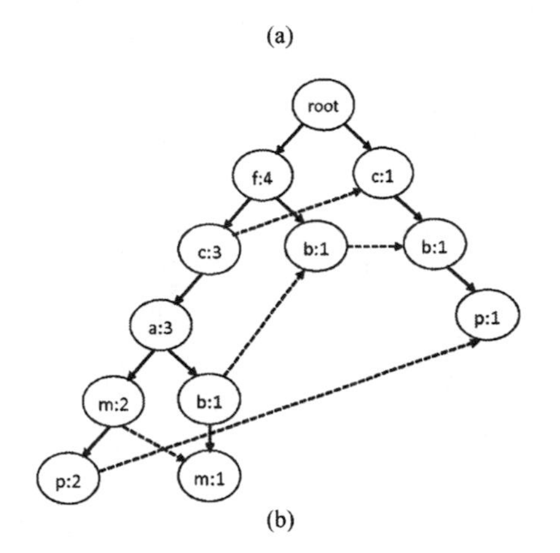


(b)

exactly the same support (Tan et al., 2006). A maximal frequent itemset is a frequent itemset of which none of its superset is frequent.

Several survey papers have been published for association rule mining and frequent pattern mining (Ceglar & Roddick, 2006; Chi, Muntz, Nijssen, & Kok, 2005; Han, Cheng, Xin, & Yan, 2007). Most algorithms mentioned above for association rule mining and frequent itemset mining, including Apriori and FP-growth, are designed for relational data only. With XML data, the task of association rule mining and frequent pattern mining is much more difficult. A naïve approach is to convert the XML data into relational data, and then apply the traditional algorithms. But by doing so, the structure information in XML data is also lost. Therefore, developing new approaches and algorithms to perform association rule mining and frequent pattern mining on XML data becomes necessary.

Since the problem of frequent pattern mining from XML data was first introduced in 2002, it has continuously attracted attentions from researchers around the world. In (Braga et al., 2002a, 2002b; Braga, Campi, Ceri, Klemettinen, & Lanzi, 2003) an operator called "XMINE" is proposed to extract association rules from native XML documents. Wan and Dobbie (2003) proposed an XQuery-based Apriori-like approach to mining association rules from XML data. Termier, Rousset, and Sebag (2002) proposed an algorithm called TreeFinder to search frequent trees from a collection of tree-structured XML data, which extends the concept of "frequent itemset" to "frequent tree structure". Feng and Dillon (2004) proposed a template-guided framework for association rule mining on XML data. Ding and Sundarraj (2006) adapted the Apriori and FP-growth algorithms to perform general association rule mining on XML data in a more efficient way. In recent years, frameworks and algorithms have also been proposed for mining structure-related frequent patterns on XML data (Zhao et al., 2006; Yang et al., 2008).

Research on XML frequent pattern mining is still at its infant stage and existing approaches are far from mature. For example, most proposed approaches can only derive specific rules or a subset of rules rather than the complete set of rules. The XQuery-based approach is promising, but not very efficient. Up to date, there are still many open problems in this research field. The big challenge is how to deal with the complexity of the structure in XML data.

## MINING FREQUENT PATTERNS AND ASSOCIATION RULES ON XML DATA

In this section, we will focus on two types of association rule mining on XML data, i.e., content-based mining and structure-based mining.

### Content-Based Mining of XML Data

To perform content-based mining on XML data, we assume that the XML documents are static. The mining task can be performed on a single XML document or a collection of XML documents.

**Problem Definition.** *In content-based XML association rule mining, an item is a node in an XML tree structure which can be represented by an XPath (W3C XML Path Language) expression, since XPath is a language for navigating in XML documents and can be used to address portions of an XML document. Given a minimum support threshold and a minimum confidence threshold, an association rule indicates certain itemsets that occur frequently together.*

For example, from the XML document shown in Figure 3, we might be able to discover such patterns as "*researchers who published about XPath also published something related to XQuery*" where "*XPath*" and "*XQuery*" are keywords of the publications. This interesting pattern can be represented as an association rule in the format of "*XPath → XQuery*". Minimum support and minimum confidence thresholds are specified by users and an association rule should have support and confidence above the user specified thresholds. Typically output of association rule mining is also represented in XML format. Below is the formal definition of the problem:

- **Input:** A single or a collection of XML documents, mining context (such as XPath expression for transaction, item, itemset), minimum support threshold $s_{min}$, and minimum confidence $c_{min}$.
- **Output:** Association rules of the form $A \rightarrow B$ with support $s$ and confidence $c$, where $A$ and $B$ are distinct itemsets and $s \geq s_{min}$, and $c \geq c_{min}$.

The approaches used in content-based XML mining can be divided into two categories, XQuery-based mining and non-XQuery-based mining. XQuery-based approach utilizes or extends the facilities provided in XQuery to perform the mining task, whereas non-XQuery-based approach does not rely on XQuery to perform the computation needed in XML data mining.

## XQuery-Based Content Mining

XQuery is a query language for XML data, just like the SQL query language for relational databases. XQuery provides a flexible way to extract XML data from XML documents.

Preliminary research on XML association rule mining indicates that the XQuery language provides certain expression power to perform the computation needed in some data mining tasks, such as association rule mining. Wan and Dobbie used XQuery to implement the Apriori algorithm (Wan & Dobbie, 2003). By using XQuery, no pre-processing and post-processing are needed to transform XML data into relational format, or vice versa. Their algorithm can mine any set of items that can be written in an XPath expression. However, the XQuery implementation of the Apriori algorithm is not efficient enough and the performance largely depends on the number of frequent itemsets and the dataset size. The proposed XQuery-based approach is more suitable for small datasets, but not very efficient for very large datasets. Another limitation of the work is that it cannot handle XML data with very complex and irregular structure.

Braga et al. (2002a, 2002b, 2003) introduced an XQuery-like operator to perform association

*Figure 3. A sample XML document fragment for association rule mining*

```
<ResearchGroup>
  <Researcher>
    <Publications>
      <Book year="2005" name="XML Query Languages">
        <Publisher> Springer </Publisher>
        <Keyword>XML</Keyword>
        <Keyword>XQuery</Keyword>
      </Book>
      <Journal year="2002" name="TKDE" vol="32" issue = "2" Publisher="IEEE">
        <Title> XML Indexing </Title>
        <Keyword>XPath</Keyword>
        <Keyword>XML</Keyword>
      </Journal>
    </Publications>
  </Researcher>
  ........
</ResearchGroup>
```

rule mining on native XML documents. The problem can be described as follows. Given a generic XML document, the problem is to discover a set of association rules that captures interesting relationships among fragments of the XML document. The XQuery-like mining operator specifies the mining context, the head and body of the rule, and other constraints. The output is also represented in the XML format. XPath expressions are used to specify the mining context.

Romei and Turini (2010) designed an XQuery-like language, called XQuake (standing for XQuery-based Applications for Knowledge Extraction), to support XML data mining. The language is used to specify domain knowledge, operation parameters, and complex queries. A mining query includes a set of XQuery functions, variable declarations, and XQuake operator to specify the mining algorithm. For example, to discover frequent itemsets, the user needs to specify the input sources including itemsets, transactions, and items, as well as the mining operator. The XQuake language allows user to specify either a mining algorithm in XQuery or using external functions. The authors noted that the optimization of XQuery expressions can have a great impact on the performance.

## Non-XQuery-Based Content Mining

Ding and Sundarraj (2006) provided a Java-based implementation of Apriori and FP-growth algorithms for XML data. They used the Document Object Model (DOM) to implement the Apriori algorithm, and Simple API for XML (SAX) to implement the FP-growth algorithm. Similar to XQuery-based approaches, a configuration file is needed for users to specify transactions, items, etc. The generated rules are presented in XML format. In their implementation, the FP-trees are also stored in XML format, which allows XPath expressions to be used to efficiently query a node in a FP-tree. Without the extra XQuery layer, such non-XQuery-based approach demonstrates higher flexibility and efficiency.

Ding and Sundarraj's non-XQuery approach proves to be faster than the XQuery-based approach because the XQuery-based approach has higher overhead. Figure 4 shows the performance comparison between XQuery-based Apriori and non-XQuery based Apriori approach. Their experimental results also show that the FP-growth algorithm performs better than Apriori on XML data. The test datasets were synthetic XML transaction datasets that had similar format to those used in (Wan & Dobbie, 2003). If the input XML document has very complicated structure, it will need to be preprocessed first. The output lists multiple association rules along with their support and confidence measurement.

(Shin, Paik, & Kim, 2006; Paik, Youn, & Kim, 2005) describe an approach to mining association rules from a collection of XML documents by using a data structure called HILOP (Hierarchical layered structure of PairSet) and the cross filtering algorithm. Each of the XML documents corresponds to a database record. The mining process consists of three steps. The first step is to convert tree-structured data into hierarchical structure PairSets. The second step is to manipulate the data stored in PairSets. The third step is to mine association rules from PairSets. The HILOP data structure can significantly reduce the number of iterations for candidate-tree-item-pruning and can simplify each iteration without time-consuming tree item join operation, while the cross filtering algorithm reduces the number of candidate sets.

## Structure-Based Mining on XML Data

Apart from the content, the structure of the XML document and the changes the structure undergoes can also often yield very useful information. In the following, we look at two structural data mining techniques that have wide variety of practical applications.

*Figure 4. Non-XQuery-based vs. XQuery-based Apriori performance on XML test dataset*

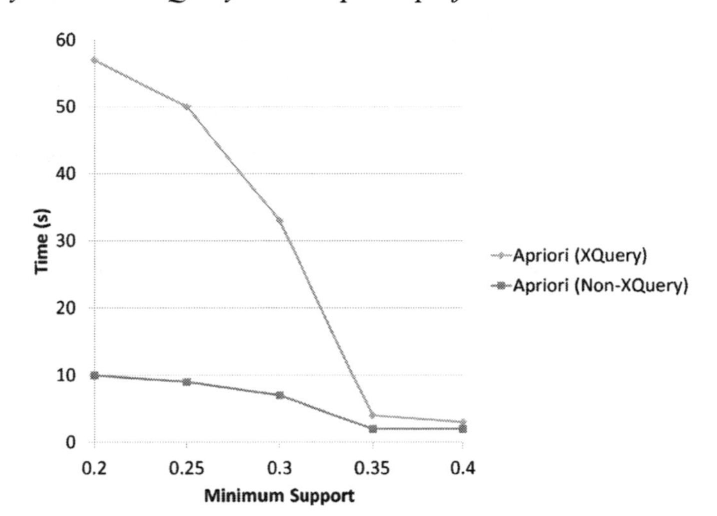


## Frequent Pattern Mining

In this task, structural patterns that occur frequently (frequent patterns) in a given set of XML documents are identified (Zaki, 2005). Compared to frequent itemset mining, frequent pattern mining is more difficult to solve, and borrows many ideas from content-based mining algorithms.

In order to study structured relational data, graphs are often used to formalize the problem. From the complexity analysis, the problem of finding frequent subgraphs is not solvable efficiently. Fortunately, in most of the real world applications, XML documents have tree structure, and even if an XML document does not have a tree structure, we can utilize the node splitting method (Ozu et al., 2002) to convert it into a tree. Here we will review various approaches for the frequent pattern mining problem on labeled trees.

This problem has a wide variety of applications including bioinformatics, structural rule mining, classification, and web mining, to name a few. In addition, this tree mining approach can also be used as a first step towards efficient graph mining (Nijssen & Kok, 2004). Let us consider the Web Usage Mining problem (Cooley, Mobasher, & Srivastava, 1997). Companies collect large amounts of data about the usage of their Web sites in the logs generated by the servers. These logs contain the link information that the user followed to get to a particular Web page. These link information offer valuable insights that can be utilized in many different ways. For example, this data sheds light into how to organize these Web pages to create better user experience. Knowing the most frequently accessed Web pages enables better targeting of advertisements. This information can also be used to classify users by their access patterns. Zaki and Aggarwal (2003) proposed algorithms for classifying XML documents based on their subtree structures.

In bioinformatics, RNA structures are essentially trees, and it is often desired to find the common patterns in the catalogued RNA sequences. Also, this problem has direct application in structural rule mining and classification (Deshpande, Kuramochi, & Karypis, 2003; Huan et al., 2004; Zaki & Aggarwal, 2003).

Knowledge about the frequent subtrees from a database of labeled trees can help us with building efficient indexes on these databases so that queries against them can be served quickly. This is another important area of application for frequent pattern mining problem, and it has gained much attention (Yang et al., 2003; Yang et al., 2004; Yang et al.,

2004a, 2004b; Yang et al., 2008; Hua et al., 2007; Li et al., 2006; Feng et al., 2006; Li et al., 2009)

We now provide an overview of various approaches to the frequent pattern mining problem, and discuss the differences between them.

**Problem Definition.** *For the purpose of structure mining, an XML document can be considered as a labeled rooted tree. As we mentioned before, even if an XML document does not have tree structure, we can utilize the node splitting method to convert it into a tree.*

Let $T = (V, E)$ be a labeled rooted tree, where $V$ is set of labeled nodes and $E$ is the set of branches. The label of each node in $T$ is taken from a set of labels, $L = \{L_0, L_1, L_2, \ldots, L_{m-1}\}$. A tree $R = (V_r, E_r)$ is regarded as an *induced* subtree of $T = (V, E)$ if $V_r \subseteq V$ and each branch $e_r \in E_r$ is also a branch in E, i.e., $e_r \in E$. On the other hand, a tree $S = (V_s, E_s)$ is regarded as an *embedded* subtree of $T = (V, E)$ if $V_s \subseteq V$ and for each branch $e_s = (v_x, v_y) \in E_s$, if $v_x$ is an ancestor of $v_y$ in $T$. So, it can be noted that induced subtree is a special case of embedded subtree. Since embedded subtree is more expressive than induced subtree, many algorithms adopt embedded subtree.

Figure 5(a) shows a tree, say $T$, with nodes labeled $A$ through $G$. The trees shown in Figure 5(b) and Figure 5(c) are subtrees of $T$, where the subtree shown in Figure 5(b) is an induced subtree of $T$, and the one shown in Figure 5(c) is an embedded subtree of $T$.

Let $D$ denote a set of trees, and let $n$ denote the number of trees in $D$. A tree is called frequent if it is an embedded subtree in at least $n \times s_{min}$ trees in $D$, where $s_{min}$ is the user-specified minimum support. We now formally define the frequent pattern mining problem as follows:

- **Input:** a set $D$ of trees and a minimum support $s_{min}$.
- **Output:** a set of trees, where each tree $S$ is an embedded subtree in at least $n \times s_{min}$ trees in $D$.

This problem has close relation to association rule mining (Agrawal et al., 2003; Agrawal et al., 1996) and structural rule mining (Agrawal & Srikant, 1995). It is also related to the more general *graph isomorphism* problem (Shamir & Tsur, 1999), *tree pattern* problem (Cole, Hariharan, & Indyk, 1999), and *tree inclusion* problem (Kilpelalnen & Mannila, 1995). These first two problems deal with induced subtrees, whereas the last one deals with embedded subgraphs, just as the frequent pattern matching.

Several recent methods for frequent pattern matching have been proposed. Asai et al. (2002) presented an Apriori-like level-wise candidate generation and pattern matching-based counting approach. Another approach similar to this has been proposed in (Wang & Liu, 1998; Wang & Liu, 2000), but this algorithm deals with induced subtrees only. Chen et al. (2001) proposed a problem of estimating the number of matches accurately, but their approach also handles induced subtrees

*Figure 5. An example tree with its subtrees*

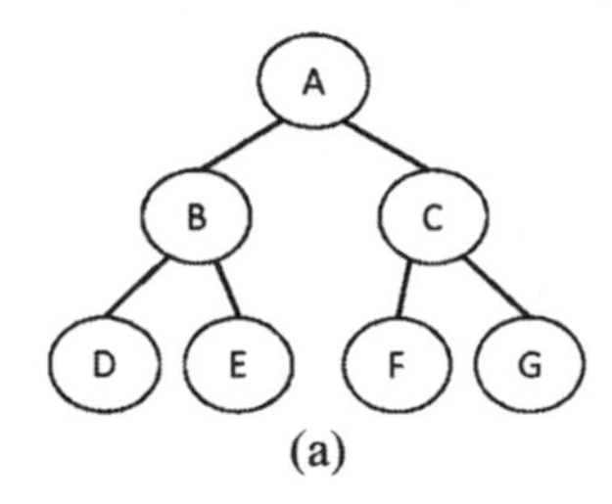


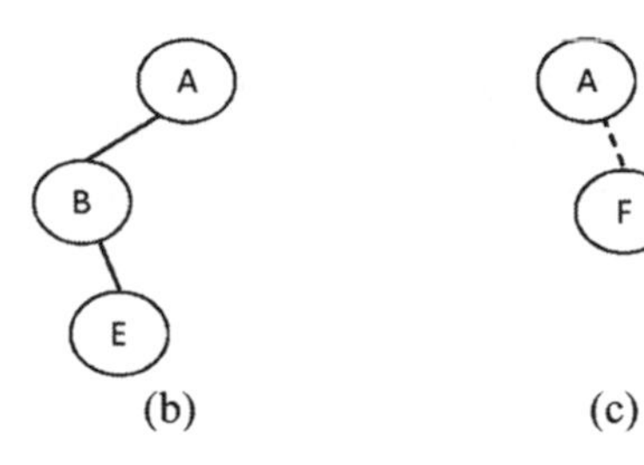

only. In the context of XML, this problem has similarity to the *frequent query pattern* problem, which studies the indexing and querying patterns of XML documents (Li & Moon, 2001; Zhang, Naughton, Dewitt, Luo, & Lohman, 2001; Abiteboul & Vianu, 1997; Fernandez & Suciu, 1998; Yang et al., 2008; Li et al., 2009). The major difference between these works and the frequent pattern mining problem is that the former uses user-specified queries whereas the later attempts to find all frequent tree patterns. Yang et al. (2003, 2008) proposed the FastXMiner and later the 2PXMiner algorithms for mining frequent XML query patterns. The AGM algorithm (Inokuchi, Washio, & Motoda, 2000) and FSM (Kuramochi & Karypis, 2001; Kuramochi & Karypis, 2004; Kuramochi & Karypis, 2005) algorithms tackle the frequent graph pattern problem using an Apriori-style depth first approach. The SUBDUE algorithm (Cook & Holder, 1994, 2000) also discovers frequent graph patterns using a minimum description length approach. A beam search-based approach was described in (Yoshida & Motoda, 1995) for the frequent graph pattern problem. The Inductive Logic Programming approach, called TreeFinder (Termier et al., 2002), is not a complete method, i.e, it can miss many frequent subtrees, especially when the support is lowered or when the different trees in the database have common node labels. Zaki (2005) proposed a depth-first approach, called TreeMiner for fast subtree support counting algorithm to this problem. TreeMiner is a complete method and outperforms breadth-first approaches like FREQT (Asai et al., 2002).

The Unot algorithm (Asai, Arimura, Uno, & Nakano, 2003) and the uFreqt algorithm (Nijssen & Kok, 2003) extend FREQT to mine induced subtrees. Chi, Yang, and Muntz (2004) proposed an algorithm called HybridTreeMiner that uses the combined depth-first/breadth-first traversal approach and generates candidates using both joins and extensions. Wang and Liu (1998) and later Xiao, Yao, Li, & Dunham (2003) proposed a different approach to this problem. Their PathJoin algorithm mines frequent subtrees by joining root paths of other trees.

In FreeTreeMiner (Chi, Yang, & Muntz, 2003) the breadth-first traversal idea is adopted to discover all frequent induced subtrees from a database of labeled trees. Like Apriori, this algorithm finds all frequent 1-subtrees (frequent subtrees with a single vertex), then repeatedly, all candidate $(k+1)$-subtrees are generated by joining pairs of frequent $k$-subtrees. The Gaston algorithm (Nijssen & Kok, 2004) is another approach to this problem, and it extends from the depth-first/breadth-first approach of the HybridTreeMiner. Ruckert and Kramer (2004) proposed a form of FreeTreeMiner that searches for frequent trees in a database of graphs.

All these algorithms mine frequent induced subtrees and frequent embedded subtrees from a database of labeled trees. Often, the number of such frequent trees can grow exponentially large and the end-users would be overwhelmed by the output. They are often considered noise, and seldom provide insight into the data that the user is analyzing. Also, from the complexity point of view, the exponential number of trees can make the problem intractable. To address this, Wang and Liu (1998) and Xiao et al. (2003) proposed a concept called Maximal Frequent Subtrees. If a frequent subtree has no frequent proper supertrees, then it is called maximal frequent subtrees. Even though maximal frequent subtrees offer the much needed insight about the problem domain, they are still intractable. In this repsect, Chi, Yang, Xia, and Muntz (2004) presented the first algorithm, CMTreeMiner, to discover all closed frequent subtrees and maximal frequent subtrees.

Termier, Rousset, and Sebag (2004) proposed an algorithm, called DRYADE, to the frequent closed tree mining problem, and this algorithm allows for mining from highly heterogeneous databases. The authors also introduced the concept of patterns, where trees do not contain two siblings with the same label. Termier et al. (2008) later improved this algorithm, and presented DRY-

ADEPARENT algorithm, which outperforms the CMTreeMiner algorithm. Jiménez, Berzal, and Talavera (2010) proposed a highly scalable and parallelizable algorithm, called POTMiner, for frequent induced subtree and embedded subtree mining. This algorithm handles partially-ordered trees well.

## Structural Rule Mining

In content-based rule mining, a set of XML documents is processed to extract association rules based on the content in the documents. By contrast, in structural rule mining a sequence of historical versions of a document is analyzed for association rules based on the structure of the document as it goes through changes over time. For this reason, the content-based rule mining is often referred as *snapshot rule mining*, as it takes a snapshot of all documents at a particular instance in time, and performs rule mining across all these documents.

Often in many real-world applications, the structure of an XML document undergoes changes over time, and this is due to addition of new nodes and/or deletion of existing nodes. This dynamic nature of XML gives rise to the problem of discovering hidden but useful knowledge about the structural changes. This knowledge has practical applications in XML change detection (Wang, DeWitt, & Cai, 2003; Cobena et al., 2002; Leonardi et al., 2005; Leonardi et al., 2007; Leonardi & Bhowmick, 2007), dynamic XML indexing, and semantic meaning extraction (Zhao et al., 2006).

**Problem Definition.** *In structural rule mining, addition and deletion of nodes is being studied over a sequence of historical versions of an XML document. Note that this is different from the content-based rule mining in which a set of XML documents collected at a certain point in time is analyzed to extract association rules. In structural rule mining, the sequence of historical versions of an XML document is analyzed for interesting association rules.*

Let $<t_i, t_{i+1}>$ be two versions of a subtree $t$ in $T$, where $T$ represents the entire XML document. The objective of structural rule mining is to extract association rules of the form $\Delta X \Rightarrow \Delta Y$, where $X = (V_x, E_x)$ and $Y = (V_y, E_y)$ are induced subtrees in $T$, $V_x \cap V_y = \emptyset$, and support and confidence for the rule are greater than or equal to the user-specified $s_{min}$ and $c_{min}$, respectively. Here $\Delta X$ indicates a change in the subtree $X$. We now formally define the frequent pattern mining problem as follows:

- **Input:** a set of trees that represent the historical versions of an XML document $T$, a minimum support $s_{min}$, and minimum confidence $c_{min}$.
- **Output:** association rules of the form $A$: $\Delta X \rightarrow \Delta Y$, where $X = (V_x, E_x)$ and $Y = (V_y, E_y)$ are induced subtrees in the versions of $T$, $V_x \cap V_y = \emptyset$, $s_A \geq s_{min}$, and $c_A \geq c_{min}$. Here $\Delta X$ indicates a change in the subtree $X$.

The first step in structure-based rule mining is to extract the structural changes between the historical versions. Several techniques for detecting changes to XML documents have been proposed. Some of the notable ones include TreeDiff (Curbera & Epstein, 1999), XyDiff (Cobena et al., 2002), and XDiff (Wang et al., 2003). TreeDiff uses hash values of the XML nodes to detect the changes in the XML documents. However, the results generated by TreeDiff may not be optimal. XyDiff uses both the hash values and the subtree size at each node in a bottom-up fashion. Like TreeDiff, XyDiff is also not guaranteed to generate optimal results. On the other hand, XDiff produces more accurate results compared to XyDiff and is also more efficient in terms of runtime complexity. The downside of XDiff is that it cannot handle very large XML documents. Leonardi, Bhowmick, Dharma, and Madria (2004) proposed a more scalable change detection system without having to keep the entire XML documents in memory. Their approach uses set of XML queries against XML documents stored in database systems. Based on their experimental results, this approach has better scalability, running time, and comparable result quality compared with XDiff.

Once the structural deltas are collected from the historical version, the next step is to mine association rules from them. These rules, for example, will be of the form "whenever the structure of the *Products* subtree changed, the structure of the *Training* subtree changed as well." Even though several algorithms exist for structural change detection, the problem of mining association rules from the structural deltas is still at its very early stage. Chen et al. (2004) proposed an FP-Growth based algorithm, called Weighted-FPgrowth, for this problem, where both the frequency and the degree of changes to XML structure are considered. The weights are used to measure how significantly subtrees in a set usually change. The authors also proposed an optimized version of the algorithm.

## FUTURE RESEARCH DIRECTIONS

The open issue in XML association rule mining and frequent pattern discovery is how to deal with the complexity of the structure of XML data. Since the structure of XML data can be very complex and irregular, identifying the mining context on such XML data may become very difficult.

In content-based mining, it is expected that there will be continuous research on either extending XQuery or developing new languages to support XML data mining. However, data mining is far more challenging than database querying; therefore, due to the lack of flexibility and limited expression power of XQuery plus additional overhead, more focus is expected to be given to non-Query-based approaches and algorithms to mine frequent patterns and association rules from XML data. Another direction in content-based mining is to extend from mining specific rules to the complete set of rules on XML data.

In structure-based mining, the problem of mining frequent patterns has been studied relatively well due to its enormous real-world applications, but the structural rule mining has not attracted that much research. It is expected to see more research efforts on structure rule mining. For the problem of mining frequent query patterns, one future research direction is to develop better pruning techniques to reduce the number of candidate trees at early stages. The other direction is to develop approaches for incremental mining of frequent query patterns. It is also interesting to discover co-occurring patterns. It is expected to apply the patterns discovered in XML mining toward improving XML query efficiency, especially for very large XML documents. The work in (Baralis, Garza, Quintarelli, & Tanca, 2007) on answering XML queries by means of data summaries is an example of research in this direction.

It is also desirable to develop approaches that integrate content-based mining and structure-based mining on XML data. Such approaches can discover frequent patterns from both content and structure of XML data. Mazuran, Quintarelli, and Tanca (2007) proposed an approach to extract tree-based association rules from XML documents, which involves both the content and structure information of the documents. More work is expected to be done along this line.

Other research directions in XML association rule mining and frequent pattern discovery may include developing efficient and scalable mining algorithms for very large XML data, facilitating incorporation of domain knowledge, utilizing XML indexing and caching for mining, advancing pre-processing techniques for XML data, developing online and incremental mining algorithms on dynamic XML data, combining XML association rule and frequent pattern mining with other data mining techniques such as clustering and classification, developing parallel and distributed algorithms to mine XML association rules and frequent patterns, integrating constraint-based mining and pruning techniques on XML data, exploring a general framework to support content and structure based mining, integrating XML mining with web mining, spatial data mining, and data mining on bioinformatics field, as well as developing new applications in XML association rule mining. It is also anticipated that some XML benchmark data be developed for XML association rule mining and frequent pattern mining as well as for other XML mining tasks.

## CONCLUSION

Data mining on XML data has become an increasingly important and demanding yet challenging task. In this chapter, we provided an overview of association rule mining and frequent pattern mining on XML data as well as our insights for future research directions. We discussed both content-based mining and structure-based mining. In particular, we discussed the XQuery-based approach and non-XQuery-based approach for content-based mining. As for structure-based mining, we focused on frequent pattern mining and structural rule mining on XML data.

The research on mining association rules and frequent patterns on XML data is still at its preliminary stage and many questions remain open. As the techniques to support XML semi-structured data are further developed and more XML data become available in many application domains, we expect to see more research efforts to be made on association rule mining and frequent pattern discovery on XML data.

## REFERENCES

W3C. (n.d.). *XML path language* (XPath). Retrieved from http://www.w3.org/TR/xpath/

W3C. (n.d.). *XML query* (XQuery). Retrieved from http://www.w3.org/XML/Query/

Abiteboul, S., & Vianu, V. (1997). Regular path expressions with constraints. In *Proceedings of the 16th ACM International Conference on Principles of Database Systems (PODS)*, (pp. 122-133).

Agrawal, R., Imielinski, T., & Swami, A. (1993). Mining association rules between sets of items in large database. In P. Buneman, & S. Jajodia (Eds.), *Proceedings of the ACM International Conference on Management of Data (SIGMOD)*, (pp. 207-216). ACM.

Agrawal, R., Mannila, H., Srikant, R., Toivonen, H., & Verkamo, A. I. (1996). Fast discovery of association rules. In Fayyad, U., Piatetsky-Shapiro, G., Smyth, P., & Uthurusamy, R. (Eds.), *Advances in knowledge discovery and data mining* (pp. 307–328). AAAI Press.

Agrawal, R., & Srikant, R. (1994). Fast algorithms for mining association rules in large databases. In J. B. Bocca, M. Jarke, & C. Zaniolo (Eds.), *Proceedings of the 20th International Conference on Very Large Data Bases (VLDB)*, (pp. 487-499). Morgan Kaufmann.

Agrawal, R., & Srikant, R. (1995). Mining Sequential Patterns. In P. S. Yu, & A. L. P. Chen (Eds.), *Proceedings of the 11th IEEE International Conference on Data Engineering (ICDE)*, (pp. 3-14). IEEE Computer Society.

Asai, T., Abe, K., Kawasoe, S., Arimura, H., Satamoto, H., & Arikawa, S. (2002). Efficient substructure discovery from large semi-structured data. In R. L. Grossman, J. Han, V. Kumar, H. Mannila, & R. Motwani (Eds.), *Proceedings of the SIAM International Conference on Data Mining (SDM)*, (pp. 158-174).

Asai, T., Arimura, H., Uno, T., & Nakano, S. (2003). Discovering frequent substructures in large unordered trees. In *Proceedings of the 6th International Conference on Discovery Science* [Springer.]. *Lecture Notes in Computer Science*, *2843*, 47–61. doi:10.1007/978-3-540-39644-4_6

Baralis, E., Garza, P., Quintarelli, E., & Tanca, L. (2007). Answering XML queries by means of data summaries. *ACM Transactions on Information Systems, 25*(3), 1–33. doi:10.1145/1247715.1247716

Braga, D., Campi, A., Ceri, S., Klemettinen, M., & Lanzi, P. L. (2002a). A tool for extracting XML association rules. In *Proceedings of the 14th IEEE International Conference on Tools with Artificial Intelligence (ICTAI)*, (pp. 57-65). IEEE Computer Society.

Braga, D., Campi, A., Ceri, S., Klemettinen, M., & Lanzi, P. L. (2002b). Mining association rules from XML data. In Y. Kambayashi, W. Winiwarter, & M. Arikawa (Eds.), *Proceedings of the 4th International Conference on Data Warehousing and Knowledge Discovery (DaWaK) Lecture Notes in Computer Science: Vol. 2454* (pp. 21-30). Springer.

Braga, D., Campi, A., Ceri, S., Klemettinen, M., & Lanzi, P. L. (2003). Discovering interesting information in XML data with association rules. In *Proceedings of the 18th ACM Symposium on Applied Computing (SAC)*, (pp. 450-454). ACM.

Brin, S., Motwani, R., Ullman, J. D., & Tsur, S. (1997). Dynamic itemset counting and implication rules for market basket data. In J. Peckham (Ed.), *Proceedings of the ACM International Conference on Management of Data (SIGMOD)*, (pp. 255-264). ACM.

Ceglar, A., & Roddick, J. F. (2006). Association mining. *ACM Computing Surveys, 38*(2), 1–42. doi:10.1145/1132956.1132958

Chen, L., Bhowmick, S. S., & Chia, C. (2004a). Mining association rules from structural deltas of historical XML documents. In H. Dai, R. Srikant, & C. Zhang (Eds.), *Proceedings of the 8th Pacific-Asia Conference on Knowledge Discovery and Data Mining (PAKDD)*, (pp. 452-457).

Chen, L., Bhowmick, S. S., & Chia, L.-T. (2004b). Mining maximal frequently changing subtree pattern from XML documents. In *Proceedings of the 6th International Conference on Data Warehousing and Knowledge Discovery (DaWaK)* [Springer.]. *Lecture Notes in Computer Science, 3181*, 68–76. doi:10.1007/978-3-540-30076-2_7

Chen, Y., Yang, L. H., & Wang, Y. G. (2004). Incremental mining of frequent XML query patterns. In *Proceedings of the 4th IEEE International Conference on Data Mining (ICDM)*, (pp. 343-346). IEEE Computer Society.

Chen, Z., Jagadish, H. V., Korn, F., Koudas, N., Muthukrishnan, S., Ng, R. T., & Srivastava, D. (2001). Counting twig matches in a tree. In *Proceedings of the 17th International Conference on Data Engineering (ICDE)*, (pp. 595-606). IEEE Computer Society.

Chi, Y., Muntz, R. R., Nijssen, S., & Kok, J. N. (2005). Frequent subtree mining - An overview. *Fundamenta Informaticae, 66*(1-2), 161–198.

Chi, Y., Yang, Y., & Muntz, R. R. (2003). Indexing and mining free trees. In *Proceedings of the 3rd IEEE International Conference on Data Mining (ICDM)*, (pp. 509-512). IEEE Computer Society.

Chi, Y., Yang, Y., & Muntz, R. R. (2004). HybridTreeMiner: An efficient algorithm for mining frequent rooted trees and free trees using canonical forms. In *Proceedings of the 16th International Conference on Scientific and Statistical Database Management (SSDBM)*, (pp. 11-20). IEEE Computer Society.

Chi, Y., Yang, Y., Xia, Y., & Muntz, R. R. (2004). CMTreeMiner: Mining both closed and maximal frequent subtrees. In H. Dai, R. Srikant, & C. Zhang (Eds.), *Proceedings of the 8th Pacific Asia Conference on Knowledge Discovery and Data Mining (PAKDD) Lecture Notes in Computer Science: Vol. 3056* (pp. 63-73). Springer.

Cobena, G., Abiteboul, S., & Marian, A. (2002). Detecting changes in XML documents. In *Proceedings of the 18th IEEE International Conference on Data Engineering (ICDE),* (pp. 41-52). IEEE Computer Society.

Cole, R., Hariharan, R., & Indyk, P. (1999). Tree pattern matching and subset matching in deterministic o(n log 3 n)-time. In *Proceedings of ACM-SIAM Symposium on Discrete Algorithms (SODA),* (pp. 245-254). ACM.

Cong, G., Yi, L., Liu, B., & Wang, K. (2002). Discovering frequent substructures from hierarchical semi-structured data. In R. L. Grossman, J. Han, V. Kumar, H. Mannila, & R. Motwan (Eds.), *Proceedings of the 2nd SIAM International Conference on Data Mining (SDM),* (pp. 175-192). SIAM.

Cook, D. J., & Holder, L. B. (1994). Substructure discovery using minimum description length and background knowledge. *Journal of Artificial Intelligence Research, 1*, 231–255.

Cook, D. J., & Holder, L. B. (2000). Graph-based data mining. *IEEE Intelligent Systems, 15*(2), 32–41. doi:10.1109/5254.850825

Cooley, R., Mobasher, B., & Srivastava, J. (1997). Web mining: Information and pattern discovery on the World Wide Web. In *Proceedings of the 9th IEEE International Conference on Tools with Artificial Intelligence (ICTAI),* (pp. 558-567). IEEE Computer Society.

Curbera, F. P., & Epstein, D. A. (1999). Fast difference and update of XML documents. In *Proceedings of XTech.*

Deshpande, M., Kuramochi, M., & Karypis, G. (2003). Frequent sub-structure-based approaches for classifying chemical compounds. In *Proceedings of the 3rd IEEE International Conference on Data Mining (ICDM),* (pp. 35-42). IEEE Computer Society.

Ding, Q., & Sundarraj, G. (2006). Association rule mining from XML data. In S. F. Crone, S. Lessmann, & R. Stahlbock (Eds.), *Proceedings of International Conference on Data Mining (DMIN),* (pp. 144-150). CSREA Press.

Feng, J., Qian, Q., Wang, J., & Zhou, L. (2006). Exploit sequencing to accelerate hot XML query pattern mining. In H. Haddad (Ed.), *Proceedings of ACM Symposium of Applied Computing (SAC),* (pp. 517-524). ACM.

Feng, L., & Dillon, T. S. (2004). Mining XML-enabled association rules with templates. In B. Goethals, and A. Siebes (Eds.), *Proceedings of the 3rd Workshop on Knowledge Discovery in Inductive Databases (KDID) Lecture Notes in Computer Science: Vol. 3377.* (pp. 66-88). Springer.

Fernandez, M. F., & Suciu, D. (1998). Optimizing regular path expressions using graph schemas. In *Proceedings of the 14th IEEE International Conference on Data Engineering (ICDE),* (pp. 14-23). IEEE Computer Society.

Han, J., Cheng, H., Xin, D., & Yan, X. (2007). Frequent pattern mining: Current status and future directions. *Data Mining and Knowledge Discovery, 15*(1), 55–86. doi:10.1007/s10618-006-0059-1

Han, J., & Kamber, M. (2006). *Data mining concepts and techniques*. Morgan Kaufmann.

Han, J., Pei, J., & Yin, Y. (2000). Mining frequent patterns without candidate generation. In W. Chen, J. F. Naughton, & P. A. Bernstein (Eds.), *Proceedings of the ACM International Conference on Management of Data (SIGMOD),* (pp. 1-12). ACM.

Han, J., Pei, J., Yin, Y., & Mao, R. (2004). Mining frequent patterns without candidate generation: A frequent pattern tree approach. *Data Mining and Knowledge Discovery, 8*(1), 53–87. doi:10.1023/B:DAMI.0000005258.31418.83

Hua, C., Zhao, H., & Chen, Y. (2007). Mining XML frequent query patterns. In W. Wang, Y. Li, Z. Duan, L. Yan, H. Li, & X. Yang (Eds.), *7th International Conference on e-Business, e-Services, and e-Society (I3E (1)): Vol. 251. International Federation for Information Processing* (pp. 26-34). Springer.

Huan, J., Wang, W., Washington, A., Prins, J., Shah, R., & Tropshas, A. (2004). Accurate classification of protein structural families using coherent sub-graph analysis. In *Proceedings of the Pacific Symposium on Biocomputing (PSB)*, (pp. 411-422).

Inokuchi, A., Washio, T., & Motoda, H. (2000). An Apriori-based algorithm for mining frequent substructures from graph data. In D. A. Zighed, H. J. Komorowski, & J. M. Zytkow (Eds.), *Proceedings of the 4th European Conference on Principles of Knowledge Discovery and Data Mining (PKDD) Lecture Notes in Computer Science: Vol. 1910* (pp. 13-23).

Jiménez, A., Berzal, F., & Talavera, J. C. C. (2010). POTMiner: Mining ordered, unordered, and partially-ordered trees. *Knowledge and Information Systems*, *23*(2), 199–224. doi:10.1007/s10115-009-0213-3

Kilpelalnen, P., & Mannila, H. (1995). Ordered and unordered tree inclusion. *SIAM Journal on Computing*, *24*(2), 340–356. doi:10.1137/S0097539791218202

Kuramochi, M., & Karypis, G. (2001). Frequent subgraph discovery. In N. Cercone, T. Y. Lin, & X. Wu (Eds.), *Proceedings of the 1st IEEE International Conference on Data Mining (ICDM)*, (pp. 313-320). IEEE Computer Society.

Kuramochi, M., & Karypis, G. (2004). Finding frequent patterns in a large sparse graph. In M. W. Berry, U. Dayal, C. Kamath, & D. B. Skillicorn (Eds.), *Proceedings of the 4th SIAM International Conference on Data Mining (SDM)*, (pp. 345-356). SIAM.

Kuramochi, M., & Karypis, G. (2005). Finding frequent patterns in a large sparse graph. *Data Mining and Knowledge Discovery*, *11*(2), 243–271. doi:10.1007/s10618-005-0003-9

Leonardi, E., & Bhowmick, S. S. (2005). Detecting changes on unordered XML documents using relational databases: A schema-conscious approach. In O. Herzog, H.-J. Schek, N. Fuhr, A. Chowdhury, & W. Teiken (Eds.), *Proceedings of the ACM International Conference on Information and Knowledge Management (CIKM)*, (pp. 509-516). ACM.

Leonardi, E., & Bhowmick, S. S. (2006a). Oxone: A scalable solution for detecting superior quality deltas on ordered large XML documents. In D. W. Embley, A. Olivé, & S. Ram (Eds.), *Proceedings of the 25th International Conference on Conceptual Modeling (ER) Lecture Notes in Computer Science: Vol. 4215*. (pp. 196-211). Springer.

Leonardi, E., & Bhowmick, S. S. (2006b). Xandy: A scalable change detection technique for ordered XML documents using relational databases. *Data & Knowledge Engineering*, *59*(2), 476–507. doi:10.1016/j.datak.2005.06.006

Leonardi, E., & Bhowmick, S. S. (2007). XANADUE: A system for detecting changes to XML data in tree-unaware relational databases. In C. Y. Chan, B. C. Ooi, & A. Zhou (Eds.), *Proceedings of the ACM International Conference on Management of Data* (SIGMOD), (pp. 1137-1140). ACM.

Leonardi, E., Bhowmick, S. S., Dharma, T. S., & Madria, S. K. (2004). Detecting content changes on ordered XML documents using relational databases. In F. Galindo, M. Takizawa, & R. Traunmüller (Eds.), *Proceedings of the 15th International Conference on Database and Expert Systems Applications (DEXA) Lecture Notes in Computer Science: Vol. 3180* (pp. 580-590). Springer.

Leonardi, E., Bhowmick, S. S., & Madria, S. K. (2005). Xandy: Detecting changes on large unordered XML documents using relational databases. In L. Zhou, B. C. Ooi, & X. Meng (Eds.), *Proceedings of the 10th International Conference on Database Systems for Advanced Applications (DASFAA) Lecture Notes in Computer Science: Vol. 3453.* (pp. 711-723). Springer.

Leonardi, E., Budiman, S. L., & Bhowmick, S. S. (2005). Detecting changes to hybrid XML documents using relational databases. In K. V. Andersen, J. K. Debenham, & R. Wagner (Eds.), *Proceedings of the 15th International Conference on Database and Expert Systems Applications (DEXA) Lecture Notes in Computer Science: 3588.* (pp. 482-492). Springer.

Leonardi, E., Hoai, T. T., Bhowmick, S. S., & Madria, S. K. (2006). DTD-Diff: A change detection algorithm for DTDs. In M.-L. Lee, K.-L. Tan, & V. Wuwongse (Eds.), *Proceedings of 11th International Conference on Database Systems for Advanced Applications (DASFAA) Lecture Notes in Computer Science: Vol. 3882.* (pp. 817-827). Springer.

Leonardi, E., Hoai, T. T., Bhowmick, S. S., & Madria, S. K. (2007). DTD-Diff: A change detection algorithm for DTDs. *Data & Knowledge Engineering, 61*(2), 384–402. doi:10.1016/j.datak.2006.06.003

Li, G., Feng, J., Wang, J., Zhang, Y., & Zhou, L. (2006). Incremental mining of frequent query patterns from XML queries for caching. In *Proceedings of the 6th IEEE International Conference on Data Mining (ICDM),* (pp. 350-361). IEEE Computer Society.

Li, G., Feng, J., Wang, J., & Zhou, L. (2009). Incremental sequence-based frequent query pattern mining from XML queries. *Data Mining and Knowledge Discovery, 18*(3), 472–516. doi:10.1007/s10618-009-0126-5

Li, Q., & Moon, B. (2001). Indexing and querying XML data for regular path expressions. In P. M. G. Apers, P. Atzeni, S. Ceri, S. Paraboschi, K. Ramamohanarao, & R. T. Snodgrass (Eds.), *Proceedings of the 27th International Conference on Very Large Data Bases (VLDB),* (pp. 361-370). Morgan Kaufmann.

Mazuran, M., Quintarelli, E., & Tanca, L. (2007). Mining tree-based frequent patterns from XML. In T. Andreasen, R. R. Yager, H. Bulskov, H. Christiansen, & H. L. Larsen (Eds.), *Proceedings of the 8th International Conference on Flexible Query Answering Systems (FQAS) Lecture Notes in Computer Science: Vol. 5822.* (pp. 287-299). Springer.

Meo, R., & Psaila, G. (2002). Toward XML-based knowledge discovery systems. In *Proceedings of the 2nd IEEE International Conference on Data Mining (ICDM)*, (pp. 665-668). IEEE Computer Society.

Nijssen, S., & Kok, J. N. (2003). Efficient discovery of frequent unordered trees. In *Proceedings of the 1st International Workshop on Mining Graphs, Trees and Sequences,* (pp. 55-64).

Nijssen, S., & Kok, J. N. (2004). A quick start in frequent structure mining can make a difference. In *Proceedings of the ACM SIGKDD International Conference on Knowledge Discovery and Data Mining (KDD)*, (pp. 647-652). ACM.

Ozu, N., Anderson, R., Duckett, J., Watt, A., Mohr, S., Williams, K., … Visco, K. (2002). *Professional XML.* Wrox Press Ltd.

Paik, J., Youn, H. Y., & Kim, U. (2005). A new method for mining association rules from a collection of XML documents. In O. Gervasi, M. L. Gavrilova, V. Kumar, A. Laganà, H. P. Lee, Y. Mun, D. Taniar, & C. J. K. Tan (Eds.), *International Conference on Computational Science and Its Applications (ICCSA (2)) Lecture Notes in Computer Science: Vol. 3481.* (pp. 936-945). Springer.

Park, J. S., Chen, M.-S., & Yu, P. S. (1995). An effective hash-based algorithm for mining association rules. In M. J. Carey, & D. A. Schneider (Eds.), *Proceedings of the ACM International Conference on Management of Data (SIGMOD),* (pp. 175-186). ACM.

Romei, A., & Turini, F. (2010). XML data mining. *Software, Practice & Experience, 40*(2), 101–130. doi:10.1002/spe.944

Ruckert, U., & Kramer, S. (2004). Frequent free tree discovery in graph data. In H. Haddad, A. Omicini, R. L. Wainwright, & L. M. Liebrock (Eds.), *Proceedings of the ACM Symposium on Applied Computing (SAC)*, (pp. 564-570). ACM.

Savasere, A., Omiecinski, E., & Navathe, S. (1995). An efficient algorithm for mining association rules in large databases. In U. Dayal, P. M. D. Gray, & S. Nishio (Eds.), *Proceedings of the 21st International Conference on Very Large Data Base (VLDB)*, (pp. 432-444). Morgan Kaufmann.

Shamir, R., & Tsur, D. (1999). Faster subtree isomorphism. *Journal of Algorithms, 33*(2), 267–280. doi:10.1006/jagm.1999.1044

Shin, J., Paik, J., & Kim, U. (2006). Mining association rules from a collection of XML documents using cross filtering algorithm. In *Proceedings of International Conference on Hybrid Information Technology (ICHIT)*, (pp. 120-126). IEEE Computer Society.

Tan, P.-N., Steinbach, M., & Kumar, V. (2006). *Introduction to data mining*. Addison Wesley.

Termier, A., Rousset, M.-C., & Sebag, M. (2002). TreeFinder: A first step towards XML data mining. In *Proceedings of the 2nd IEEE International Conference on Data Mining (ICDM)*, (pp. 450-457). IEEE Computer Society.

Termier, A., Rousset, M.-C., & Sebag, M. (2004). Dryade: A new approach for discovering closed frequent trees in heterogeneous tree databases. In *Proceedings of the IEEE International Conference on Data Mining (ICDM),* (pp. 543-546). IEEE Computer Society.

Termier, A., Rousset, M.-C., Sebag, M., Ohara, K., Washio, T., & Motoda, H. (2008). DryadeParent: An efficient and robust closed attribute tree mining algorithm. *IEEE Transactions on Knowledge and Data Engineering, 20*(2), 300–320. doi:10.1109/TKDE.2007.190695

Wan, J. W. W., & Dobbie, G. (2003). Extracting association rules from XML documents using XQuery. In *Proceedings of the ACM International Workshop on Web Information and Data Management (WIDM)*, (pp. 94-97). ACM.

Wang, K., & Liu, H. (2000). Discovering structural association of semistructured data. *IEEE Transactions on Knowledge and Data Engineering, 12*(3), 353–371. doi:10.1109/69.846290

Wang, K., & Liu, H. Q. (1998). Discovering typical structures of documents: A road map approach. In *Proceedings of the 21st ACM SIGIR Conference on Research and Development in Information Retrieval (SIGIR),* (pp. 146-154). ACM.

Wang, Y., DeWitt, D. J., & Cai, J.-Y. (2003). X-Diff: An effective change detection algorithm for XML documents. In U. Dayal, K. Ramamritham, & T. M. Vijayaraman (Eds.), *Proceedings of the 19th IEEE International Conference on Data Engineering (ICDE),* (pp. 519-530). IEEE Computer Society.

Xiao, Y., Yao, J. F., Li, Z., & Dunham, M. (2003). Efficient data mining for maximal frequent subtrees. In *Proceedings of the 3rd IEEE International Conference on Data Mining (ICDM),* (pp. 379-386). IEEE Computer Society.

Yang, L. H., Lee, M. L., & Hsu, W. (2003). Efficient mining of XML query patterns for caching. In *Proceedings of the 29th International Conference on Very Large Data Bases (VLDB),* (pp. 69-80). Morgan Kaufmann.

Yang, L. H., Lee, M. L., & Hsu, W. (2004a). Approximate counting of frequent query patterns over XQuery stream. In Y.-J. Lee, J. Li, K.-Y. Whang, & D. Lee (Eds.), *Proceedings of 9th International Conference on Database Systems for Advances Applications (DASFAA) Lecture Notes in Computer Science: Vol. 2973* (pp. 75-87). Springer.

Yang, L. H., Lee, M. L., & Hsu, W. (2004b). Finding hot query patterns over an XQuery stream. *The VLDB Journal, 13*(4), 318–332. doi:10.1007/s00778-004-0134-4

Yang, L. H., Lee, M. L., Hsu, W., & Acharya, S. (2003). Mining frequent query patterns from XML queries. In *Proceedings of the 8th International Conference on Database Systems for Advanced Applications (DASFAA)*, (pp. 355-362). IEEE Computer Society.

Yang, L. H., Lee, M. L., Hsu, W., & Guo, X. (2004). 2PXMiner: An efficient two pass mining of frequent XML query patterns. In W. Kim, R. Kohavi, J. Gehrke, & W. DuMouchel (Eds.), *Proceedings of the 10th ACM SIGKDD International Conference on Knowledge Discovery and Data Mining (KDD),* (pp. 731-736). ACM.

Yang, L. H., Lee, M. L., Hsu, W., Huang, D., & Wang, L. (2008). Efficient mining of frequent XML query patterns with repeating-siblings. *Information and Software Technology, 50*(5), 375–389. doi:10.1016/j.infsof.2007.02.019

Yoshida, K., & Motoda, H. (1995). CLIP: Concept learning from inference patterns. *Artificial Intelligence, 75*(1), 63–92. doi:10.1016/0004-3702(94)00066-A

Zaki, M. J. (2005). Efficiently mining frequent trees in a forest: Algorithms and applications. *IEEE Transactions on Knowledge and Data Engineering, 17*(8), 1021–1035. doi:10.1109/TKDE.2005.125

Zaki, M. J., & Aggarwal, C. (2003). XRULES: An effective structural classifier for XML data. In L. Getoor, T. E. Senator, P. Domingos, & C. Faloutsos (Eds.), *Proceedings of the 9th ACM SIGKDD International Conference on Knowledge Discovery and Data Mining (KDD),* (pp. 316-325). ACM.

Zhang, C., Naughton, J., Dewitt, D., Luo, Q., & Lohman, G. (2001). On supporting containment queries in relational database management systems. In *Proceedings of the ACM International Conference on Management of Data (SIGMOD),* (pp. 425-436). ACM.

Zhao, Q. Bhowmick, S. S., & Madria S. (2006). Research issues in web structural delta mining. In T. Y. Lin, S. Ohsuga, C.-J. Liau & X. Hu (Eds.), *Foundations and novel approaches in data mining: Vol. 9. Studies in computational intelligence* (pp. 272-289). Springer.

Zhao, Q., & Bhowmick, S. S. (2005). FASST mining: Discovering frequently changing semantic structure from versions of unordered XML documents. In L. Zhou, B. C. Ooi, & X. Men (Eds.), *Proceedings of the 10th International Conference on Database Systems for Advanced Applications (DASFAA) Lecture Notes in Computer Science: Vol. 3453* (pp. 724-735). Springer.

Zhao, Q., Bhowmick, S. S., & Gruenwald, L. (2005). Mining conserved XML query paths for dynamic-conscious caching. In O. Herzog, H.-J. Schek, N. Fuhr, A. Chowdhury, & W. Teiken (Eds.), *Proceedings of the 14th ACM International Conference on Information and Knowledge Management (CIKM),* (pp. 219-220). ACM.

Zhao, Q., Bhowmick, S. S., & Mohania, M. (2004). Discovering pattern-based dynamic structures from versions of unordered XML documents. In Y. Kambayashi, M. K. Mohania, & W. Wöß (Eds.), *Proceedings of the 6th International Conference on Data Warehousing and Knowledge Discovery (DaWaK) Lecture Notes in Computer Science: Vol. 3181.* (pp. 77-86). Springer.

Zhao, Q., Bhowmick, S. S., Mohania, M. K., & Kambayashi, Y. (2004). Discovering frequently changing structures from historical structural deltas of unordered XML. In D. A. Grossman, L. Gravano, C. Zhai, O. Herzog, & D. A. Evans (Eds.), *Proceedings of the 13th ACM International Conference on Information and Knowledge Management (CIKM)*, (pp. 188-197). ACM.

Zhao, Q., Chen, L., Bhowmick, S. S., & Madria, S. (2006). XML structural delta mining: Issues and challenges. *Data & Knowledge Engineering, 59*(3), 627–651. doi:10.1016/j.datak.2005.10.002

# Chapter 12
# A Framework for Mining and Querying Summarized XML Data through Tree-Based Association Rules

**Mirjana Mazuran**
*Politecnico di Milano, Italy*

**Elisa Quintarelli**
*Politecnico di Milano, Italy*

**Angelo Rauseo**
*Politecnico di Milano, Italy*

**Letizia Tanca**
*Politecnico di Milano, Italy*

## ABSTRACT

*The massive amount of datasets expressed in different formats, such as relational, XML, and RDF, available in several real applications, may cause some difficulties to non-expert users trying to access these datasets without having sufficient knowledge on their content and structure. Moreover, the processes of query composition, especially in the absence of a schema, and interpretation of the obtained answers may be non-trivial. Data mining techniques, already widely applied to extract frequent correlations of values from both structured and semistructured datasets, provide several interesting solutions for knowledge elicitation. However, the mining process is often guided by the designer, who determines the portion of a dataset where useful patterns can be extracted based on his/her deep knowledge of the application scenario. In our opinion, a research challenge is to mine hidden information from huge datasets, and then use it order to gain useful knowledge.*

DOI: 10.4018/978-1-61350-356-0.ch012

*In this work we describe the TreeRuler tool, which makes it possible for inexperienced users to access huge XML (or relational) datasets. TreeRuler encompasses two main features: (1) it mines all the frequent association rules from input documents without any a-priori specification of the desired results, and (2) it provides quick, summarized, thus often approximate answers to user's queries, by using the previously mined knowledge. TreeRuler has been developed in the scenario of the Odyssey EU project dealing with information about crimes, both for the relational and XML data model. In this chapter we mainly focus on the objectives, strategies, and difficulties encountered in the XML context.*

## INTRODUCTION

One of the trickiest problems of finding information in the context of large datasets is reaching fast and concise answering capabilities. This is a consequence of the enormous amount of available data: useful information resides behind a thick and matt wall, which is the "noise" generated by all the uninteresting data around it.

An experienced user, with a good understanding of the document structure, can obtain what s/he seeks by means of a careful selection of the dataset content. Instead, inexperienced users need the support of a knowledge discovery system able to search, retrieve and "highlight" information starting from simple inputs.

Data mining techniques can be successfully applied to face the challenges of this scenario. They offer a privileged way to deal with the information overload problem by extracting frequent patterns and providing intensional, often approximate, information both about the content and the structure of a document. An intensional representation of a dataset is a set of patterns (e.g., association rules, clusters, etc.) describing the most relevant properties of the dataset. Intensional information is thus a *summarized representation* of the original document, which means that *less space is required to store it* and *less time is required to query it*.

The extraction of intensional information through the use of data mining techniques has been proposed in the literature, both with respect to the relational model (Agrawal, Imieliński, & Swami, 1993; Agrawal & Srikant, 1995) and to the XML format (Braga, Campi, Klemettinen, & Lanzi, 2002; Oliboni, Combi, & Rossato, 2005; Youn, Paik, & Kim, 2005; Weigand, Feng, Dillon, & Chang, 2003; Liu & Zeleznikow, 2005; Wan & Dobbie, 2005; Wang & Liu, 2000). However, while in the relational context a lot of algorithms (downloadable from Goethals & Zaki, 2004), and tools (e.g., Weka[1]) have been proposed, the literature about this topic is not as rich in the XML context. Major difficulties consist in the fact that XML is more expressive than the relational format and allows to represent both the structure and content of information in a different (i.e., hierarchical) way. Such novelty has made it difficult to give a generally accepted definition of how an association rule or a cluster should look like in the XML context.

Nevertheless, given the tree-based nature of XML documents, there have been a number of attempts to use data mining to extract frequent *tree-shaped XML patterns* (Li, Xiao, Yao, & Dunham, 2003; Berzal, Jiménez, & Cubero, 2008; Termier, Rousset, & Sebag, 2004; Kawasoe, Arimura, Sakamoto, Asai, Abe, & Arikawa, 2002; Yang, Xia, Chi, & Muntz, 2004; Zaki, 2005). More information about frequent subtree mining can be found in (Chi, Muntz, Nijssen, & Kok, 2004); see also Chapter "Frequent Pattern Discovery and Association Rule Mining of XML Data". Moreover, the Background Section highlights the differences of our approach w.r.t. the literature.

The research presented in the chapter addresses the problems of: (1) extracting intensional information from XML datasets without guiding the mining process, (2) representing it by means of appropriate association rules, and (3) allowing users to use such information in the query-answering process.

We describe the TreeRuler tool, which supports casual (or possibly inexperienced) users to easily manage huge amounts of XML data. Our main objectives are:

1. applying efficient data mining techniques to extract a summarized view of both the content and the structure of huge XML documents;
2. using the extracted information to provide users with *intensional query-answering* capabilities, that is the possibility to query the extracted knowledge rather than the original dataset.

The intensional knowledge extracted in Step 1 is more concise than the original XML document because it represents it in terms of a set of its most frequent properties. These properties can be exploited to obtain fast and concise answers, though potentially partial and approximate.

TreeRuler has been developed in the scenario of the *Odyssey EU project*[2] which aims at allowing police organizations to share information about crimes across the European Union. Main goal of the project is to provide automated intelligence for data analysis to speed up police response times. Enormous amounts of data is shared and managed by users, such as police officers and detectives, who thus need an intuitive and easy way to take advantage of it; the main aim of TreeRuler is to ease the access to shared and huge datasets containing information about crimes in an effective and efficient way.

The Odyssey dataset contains different kinds of data expressed both in the relational and XML models. We mainly focus on the ballistic elements, which are strictly connected to other elements useful to the investigations, such as data about the incidents in which the ballistic items were involved, persons related to the investigations, vehicles and locations. All these data will be analyzed and processed to effectively support the investigation activities.

As an example of use-case, think of a senior investigating officer who is looking for information about international crimes and wants to know the number of crimes involving the same weapons in each state. The proposed framework can efficiently support this kind of requests by looking - into the association rules previously mined by TreeRuler on the current datasets - for any correlation involving the same weapon(s) in different locations in Europe. The summarized answers from the system might point at the most affected cities, which can be then used to retrieve the complete crime information in a next step. Therefore, besides the summarized information itself, the system can provide suggestions for formulating a more precise query over the extensional information.

Based on the described scenario, the main contribution of this chapter is the proposal of a novel tool, TreeRuler, for intensional knowledge extraction and usage mainly in the XML context. As explained, though data mining techniques have been widely applied to extract implicit knowledge from huge sources of information, their application to the XML context is still poor or missing, the main reason being the lack of a universally agreed-upon definition of association rule for documents that are characterized by a tree structure which conveys part of the semantics and may be irregular or partial. Therefore, while tools like Weka have success for relational data, to the best of our knowledge similar tools have not yet been proposed in the XML context.

With Tree Ruler, during the extraction process, data mining is applied to output a set of Tree-based Association Rules (TARs) (Mazuran, Quintarelli, & Tanca, 2009), that is, a set of properties characterizing the document. The novelty of TARs is that they preserve the structure of the extracted information by showing the structural dependencies among different nodes in the dataset. For example, a TAR may state that, given an XML document and a node n labeled Incident, in 75% of the cases,

```
if n/Incident_Type=''violent crime''
then
n/Ballistic_Items/Ballistic_Item/
Item_Type/Bullet=''9mm''.
```

That is, 75% of violent crimes were performed with a bullet with diameter of 9mm. Notice that this simple rule describes the co-relation between two trees, thus, it contains information both on frequent content values and on the exact structure (i.e., the paths) of these values inside the mined document. Note that it is also possible to mine TARs that describe only structural information (i.e., without PCDATA).

Therefore, mined TARs offer a summarized, approximate view of the content as well as the structure of the original XML document. Once TARs have been mined and stored, TreeRuler accepts user queries, directed to the original document, which are automatically translated into queries that can be executed over the extracted TARs. The intensional answer provided by TreeRuler is *the set of TARs satisfying the user request.*

We have applied the proposed methodology to XML as well as to relational data, and have faced different problems due to the underlying data models. In the following we will explain in detail the tool for XML data, also reporting the different challenges and difficulties that arise with the relational data model.

## BACKGROUND

XML was originally proposed as a standard to represent, exchange, and publish information on the Web but its usage has widely spread to many other application fields, leading to the creation of a huge quantity of XML datasets. Since XML is a rather verbose representation of data, such datasets usually require a lot of space to be stored and of time to be queried. Therefore, in the past years the database research community has put a lot of effort in designing efficient methods and both expressive and intuitive languages to manage and query XML data (e.g., XPath (World Wide Web Consortium, 1999) and XQuery (World Wide Web Consortium, 2002)). At the same time, graphical, visual interfaces, such as XQBE (Braga, Campi, & Ceri, 2005) were proposed, with the main aim to be intuitive for naive users.

The rapid spread of XML documents also motivated the application of notions coming from the Knowledge Discovery in Databases (KDD), whose aim is to extract interesting knowledge from datasets, such as clusters, decision rules, and association rules. In particular, association rules have proved to be effective in representing interesting relations in huge datasets, thus the notion of association rule originally introduced in the context of Relational Databases (RDB) has been adapted to XML in recent years.

To generate association rules in the RDB field (e.g., for the classic market-basket analysis), the analysis starts with the construction of sets of data items (itemsets) that frequently appear together in transactions or records (Agrawal & Srikant, 1994); then, regularities among the itemsets describing different transactions are searched for. By contrast, looking into an XML dataset requires some attention also to the structure of the data: rather than a simple set to analyze, there is a more complex tree structure, which brings much more information than the simple content values of a relational dataset, and which has to be taken into consideration to fully understand the meaning of the data itself.

In general, association rules describe the co-occurrence of data items in a large amount of collected data (Agrawal & Srikant, 1994). They are extracted from frequent itemsets and are represented as implications of the form $X \Rightarrow Y$, where $X$ and $Y$ are two arbitrary disjoint sets of data items. The quality of an association rule is usually measured by means of *support* and *confidence*. Support ($supp(X \Rightarrow Y)$) corresponds to the frequency of the set $X \cup Y$ in the dataset, while confidence ($conf(X \Rightarrow Y)$) corresponds to the conditional probability of finding $Y$, given $X$, which is defined as the support of $X \cup Y$ divided by the support of $Y$.

In the relational context, association rules are extracted from the history of the transactions on the database, therefore both $X$ and $Y$ are items (that is, values of attributes) contained in some transaction. In the XML context, association rules have to be extracted from a tree-based representation of data. Different approaches have been proposed in the literature to face this challenge. In (Wan & Dobbie, 2003), a set of XQuery functions implementing the Apriori algorithm is proposed, while (Braga, Campi, Klemettinen, & Lanzi, 2002) introduces a new specific operator that deals with XML data. However, both approaches require the structure of the rule to be defined in advance, thus forcing the designer to have some knowledge about the structure of the XML document.

The aim of this chapter is to provide a more general approach to the problem of mining association rules from XML documents, which is mining all frequent rules without constraints on their structure. (Youn, Paik, & Kim, 2005) proposes a similar approach based on extracting association rules between tree fragments in a forest of XML documents. However, this approach (1) requires the document fragments to be disjoint, thus not showing the relationships among them; (2) represents fragments as *embedded subtrees* (see the definition below), thus they do not always show the real structure data has in the document; (3) does not support mining within a single XML document. To overcome these limitations, (Mazuran, Quintarelli, & Tanca, 2009) proposed *Tree-based Association Rules* (TARs), which are general association rules representing implications between trees within a single XML document.

Following the Infoset convention (World Wide Web Consortium, 2004), an XML document is represented as a tree $T = (N, E, r, l)$, where $N$ is the set of nodes, $r \in N$ is the root of the tree, $E$ is the set of edges and $l: N \rightarrow L$ is the label function which returns the tags (the names) of the nodes, (with $L$ the domain of all tags).

At the basis of the tree analysis lies the concept of *frequent subtree,* similar to that of *frequent itemset* referred in the classic problem definition (Agrawal & Srikant, 1994). Figure 1 shows an example of an XML document, its tree-based representation, and three *induced subtrees* extracted from the document. Given a tree $T$, the induced subtrees of $T$ are subtrees that preserve the original parent-child relationships of $T$. On the other hand, *embedded subtrees* only maintain the ancestor relationship between nodes.

*Figure 1. (from left to right) an example of XML document, its tree-based representation, and three induced subtrees of the document tree*

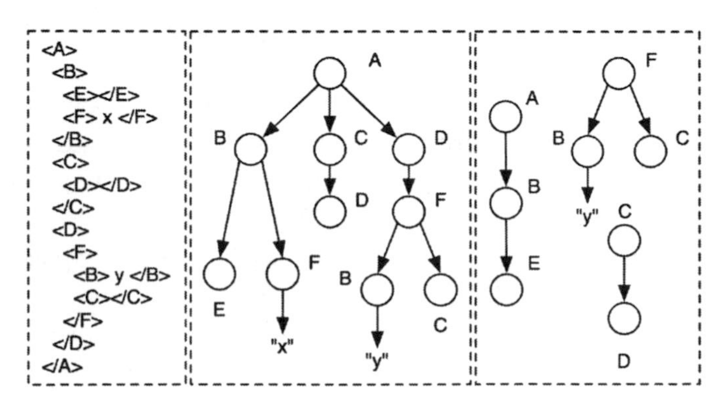

Given any subtree $t = (N_t, E_t, r_t, l_t)$ of an XML document tree and a user-fixed support threshold $S_{min}$: (1) $t$ is *frequent* if its support is greater or at least equal to $S_{min}$ (2) $t$ is *maximal* if it is frequent and none of its proper super-trees is frequent; (3) $t$ is *closed* if it is frequent and none of its super-trees has the same support as $t$. Moreover, the considered trees can be either ordered (i.e., the children of each node are ordered) or unordered.

Tree-based Association Rules (TARs) (Mazuran, Quintarelli, & Tanca, 2009) extend the classical association rule notion in order to take into account information about the structure of the original XML dataset while producing a synthesis of it. A TAR is a tuple of the form $(S_B, S_H, s, c)$, where $S_B = (N_B, E_B, r_B, l_B)$ and $S_H = (N_H, E_H, r_H, l_H)$ are trees, and $s$ and $c$ are real numbers representing the support and confidence of the rule, respectively. Furthermore, $S_B$ is an induced subtree of $S_H$. For the sake of readability, we shall often use the short notation $S_B \Rightarrow S_H$ ($S_B$ is the *body* or *antecedent*, while $S_H$ is the *head* or *consequent* of the rule).

If we denote with $count(S, D)$ the number of occurrences of a subtree $S$ in the tree $D$, and with $|D|$ the number of nodes of $D$, the support of a TAR $S_B \Rightarrow S_H$ is defined as $count(S_H, D) / |D|$, and the confidence is defined as $count(S_H, D) / count(S_B, D)$.

Several structural and value-indexing techniques to improve XML query execution time have been proposed in the literature (Boncz et al., 2006; Chung, Min, & Shim, 2002; He & Yang, 2004; Kay, 2008; Chen, Lim, & Ong, 2003). In these approaches, "path-indices" are constructed at design time based on the expected frequent queries, in order to single out relevant nodes that can be extracted during query processing. In our approach, the information that is queried is not the original document, but the extracted rules; we will see in the following that TreeRuler also provides indices, but these are used for indexing the TARs themselves.

Another related field is the pre-computation of materialized views for data warehouses (Harinarayan, Rajaraman, & Ullman, 1996), in order to use these views to speed-up OLAP query computation. Similarly to our case, such representation yields a general-purpose, portable, and condensed representation of XML documents which still maintains the XML nature and so can be easily exploited by any XML query engine. However, differently from materialized views, our summarized representation may leave out some (less frequent) information, but on the other hand it highlights important elements in the data and their structure, even if they are implicit in the original schema definition, thus helping the user to refine subsequent searches.

Consider the XML document in Figure 2 which is a portion of the Odyssey XML dataset whose DTD is presented in Figure 3; it is possible to extract two types of TARs:

- *instance TARs* (iTARs), which are association rules providing information both on the structure and on the PCDATA values contained in a target XML document (see Figure 4A and Figure 4B).
- *structure TARs* (sTARs), which are association rules on the structure of the XML document, i.e., no PCDATA is present in an sTAR (see Figure 4).

Figure 4 shows some examples of iTARs and sTARs corresponding to the XML document in Figure 2. Rule (A) states that, if there is a node labeled Incident in the document, it probably has a child labeled Incident_Type whose value is violent crime. Rule (B) states that, if there is a path composed by the following sequence of nodes: Incident/Incident_Type, and the content of Incident_Type is violent crime, then path Incident/Crime_Details probably has another child labeled Injury_Sustained whose content is yes. Finally, rule (C) states that, if there is a node Incident, then that node probably has three other children

*Figure 2. A portion of the Odyssey XML document tree*

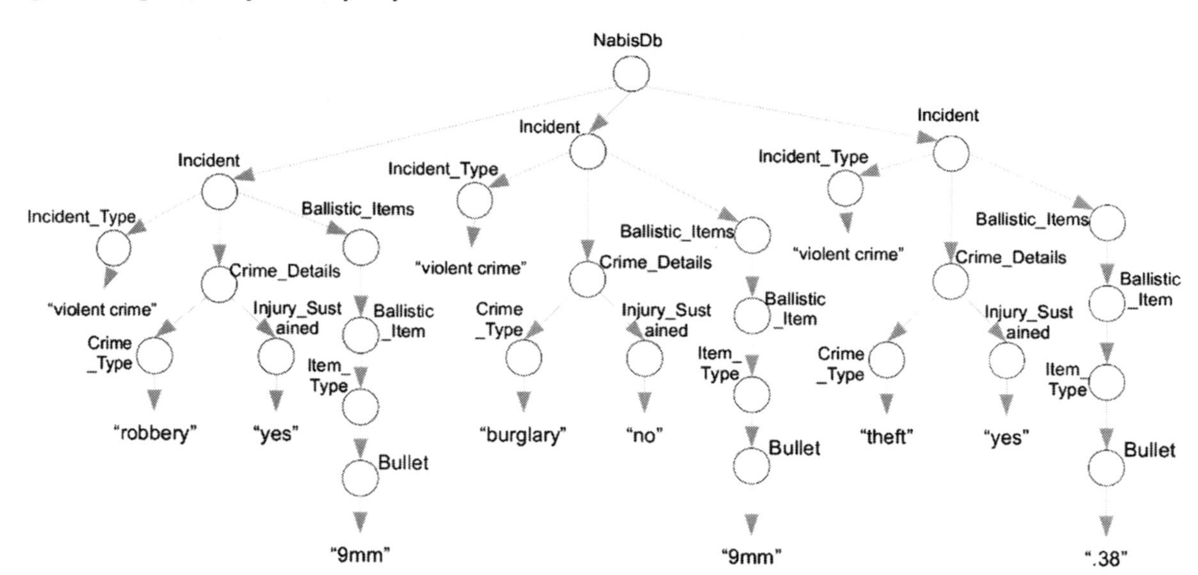


*Figure 3. A simplified version of the Odyssey DTD structure*

```
<!ELEMENT NabisDb (Incident*)>
<!ELEMENT Incident (Incident_Type, Crime_Details, Ballistic_Items*)>
<!ATTLIST Incident Incident_ID CDATA #REQUIRED >
<!ELEMENT Incident_Type (#PCDATA)>
<!ELEMENT Crime_Details (Crime_Type, Injury_Sustained*) >
<!ATTLIST Crime_Details Crime_Code CDATA #REQUIRED >
<!ELEMENT Crime_Type (#PCDATA)>
<!ELEMENT Injury_Sustained (#PCDATA)>
<!ELEMENT Ballistic_Items (Ballistic_Item+) >
<!ELEMENT Ballistic_Item (Item_Type)>
<!ATTLIST Ballistic_Item Item_Code CDATA #REQUIRED >
<!ELEMENT Item_Type (Bullet|Firearm)>
<!ELEMENT Bullet (#PCDATA) >
<!ELEMENT Firearm (#PCDATA) >
```

labeled Incident_Type, Crime_Details, with its own children Crime_Type and Injury_Sustained, and Ballistic_Item. All these examples show the interest in rules with the antecedent that is an induced subtree of the consequent, because we want to find how the tree $S_B$ is structurally related to the tree $S_H$.

Table 1 shows, for each one of these rules, its support and confidence. The TARs are *approximate* when their confidence is lower than 1; on the contrary, they are *exact* if their confidence is equal to 1, and thus in this case the conveyed information is precise. Notice again that TARs are more expressive than classic association rules because they provide structural information besides the content-related one; moreover, they are more expressive than XML association rules (Youn, Paik, & Kim, 2005) because the latter describe co-occurrences of paths and do not show how these paths are related one to the other.

In TreeRuler, we exploit TARs to provide intensional query answering, that is, answering to a query with a set of properties rather than with the actual data.

*Figure 4. Examples of iTARs (A and B) and sTARs (C)*

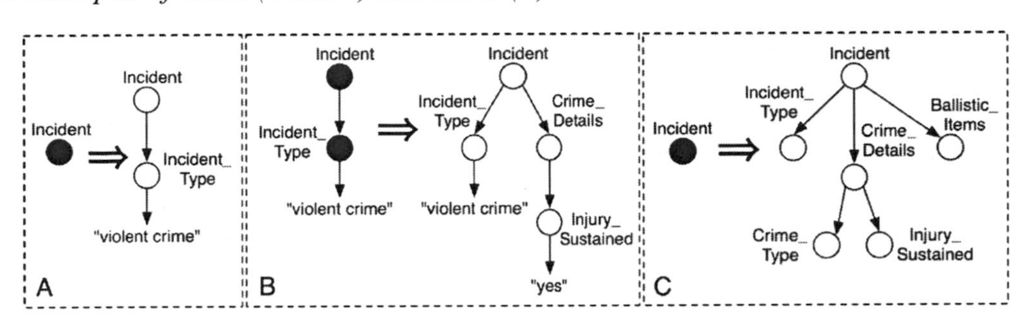


*Table 1. Support and confidence of rules in Figure 4*

| Rule | Rule support | Body support | Rule confidence |
|---|---|---|---|
| A | 3/25 = 0.12 | 3/25 = 0.12 | 0.12/0.12 = 1 |
| B | 2/25 = 0.08 | 3/25 = 0.12 | 0.08/0.12 = 0.67 |
| C | 3/25 = 0.12 | 3/25 = 0.12 | 0.12/0.12 = 1 |

The use of TARs to provide intensional answers is particularly interesting for certain classes of queries, typically queries that impose filters on the contents of the dataset (i.e., "*Find all the incidents in which a bullet was collected*" or "*Find all the incidents in which someone suffered injuries*"). Potentially any query containing filtering patterns over the data could be answered by the rules containing the same matching filters. Counting queries are also interesting targets for TARs, because when a mined rule that matches the original query is found, a faster and exact answer can be obtained. Indeed, it is sufficient to invert the ratio that defines the support of TAR to obtain the number of the trees with the "shape" of the consequent of the rule, from which the antecedent was induced (i.e., "*Count all the violent crimes*" will match the TAR represented in Figure 4B and result in 0.25*8 = 2).

## MANAGING TREE-BASED ASSOCIATION RULES

The main goal of our framework is the efficient exploitation of the knowledge contained (and often sunk) into large XML datasets, and the first step we propose to accomplish such objective is to mine complex and informative association rules from these datasets. Rather than proposing yet another algorithm to extract frequent subtrees from an XML dataset, we extend an efficient tree-mining algorithm proposed in the literature, to efficiently obtain the interesting TARs. The second step is to allow users to redirect to the extracted TARs the query which was posed on the original XML dataset. In the following we will first explain the algorithm for frequent subtree mining we start from, which has been selected thanks to its expected efficiency, and we will show how to obtain the TARs starting from the outputs of such algorithm. Then we will present how the extracted TARs can be stored and queried to obtain faster, though often partial and approximate intensional answers to user queries.

In our mining process, an appropriate selection of support and confidence thresholds is fundamental in order to infer a set of TARS that represent a "good intensional description" of a wide portion of the original data. However, the complete coverage of the original dataset and the substitution of the traditional querying process is not our goal. Indeed, our aim is to provide a data coverage sufficient to obtain frequent and interesting information to be brought to the user attention and to help him/her in subsequent query reformulation or refinement.

The choice of the support threshold is tightly linked to the frequency of the data; in fact, a high support threshold could lead to low data coverage, so it should be tuned with respect to the data quality, while confidence, which provides a reliability index related to the data, can be used to define the required level of certainty and thus a relatively high value should be set to obtain certain information. The process of defining good support and confidence thresholds is, indeed, task-dependent and a universal strategy is not advisable.

## Extracting TARs

Mining TARs is a process composed by two steps: (1) mining frequent subtrees from the XML document, and (2) computing interesting rules for each of the previously mined frequent subtree. The problem of computing interesting rules from frequent subtrees can be compared to the problem of extracting classic association rules from large sets of elements, originally introduced in (Agrawal & Srikant, 1994). In our work, rules are mined starting from the maximal frequent subtrees of the tree-based representation of an XML document. We consider ordered or unordered XML trees, and we use the CMTreeMiner algorithm (Chi, Yang, Xia, & Muntz, 2004) to extract frequent subtrees because it has the best performance (Termier et al., 2008) with respect to the kind of subtrees we consider. The authors of CMTreeMiner provided an implementation for mining unordered trees and another for ordered trees. We have first conceived a naive extension of CMTreeMiner computing interesting TARs from frequent, unordered, maximal subtrees.

### The CMTreeMiner Algorithm from a High-Level Point of View

The purpose of the CMTreeMiner (Chi et al., 2004) algorithm is to discover all closed frequent subtrees and maximal subtrees from a tree-shaped database. We have slightly modified the algorithm in order to return only subtrees which are both closed and maximal. Figure 5 shows a high-level description of the proposed variant of CMTreeMiner, in which the CM-Grow procedure is invoked to compute closed and maximal subtrees of an input tree *C*, by performing the following main steps:

- encoding the input tree in Depth First Canonical Form (DFCF): the DFCF represents a generic, unordered tree, as a univocally determined ordered tree, thanks to the definition of a weighted ordering of its nodes (Chi et al., 2004).
- analyzing structural properties of candidate subtrees of the input document *D* in order to quickly discard the portions of *D* that do not contain possible good candidates. In such way, it is possible to avoid the complete enumeration of all the possible subtrees of *D*, during the analysis. This step improves the performance of CMTreeMiner with respect to the other algorithms (e.g., PathJoin (Li, Xiao, Yao, & Dunham, 2003)).

Once the frequent subtrees have been mined from the original XML document, the set of interesting TARs must be extracted from them (the

*Figure 5. Sketch of the modified CMTreeMiner algorithm*

**Algorithm: CMTreeMiner**
**Input:** *D, minSupport*
**Output:** set of both closed and maximal subtrees

1: $CL \leftarrow \varnothing$, $MX \leftarrow \varnothing$ *//closed subtree set and maximal subtree set*
2: $C \leftarrow$ frequent 1-trees extracted from *D* *//a k-tree has k nodes*
3: *CM-Grow(C, CL, MX, minSupport)*
4: **return** $(CL \cap MX)$

basic steps of the algorithm are reported in Figure 6). Each frequent subtree $t$ will eventually be the consequent part (head) of a TAR, so the procedure must discover all the possible antecedent (body) parts that can be extracted from $t$. The process begins by analyzing $t$ from its lowest level leaves: the rightmost leaf of the lowest level of the tree is pruned generating the candidate tree $t_p$, then the support of the candidate tree $t_p$ is evaluated and, if the confidence of the rule in which that tree is the antecedent is greater than or equal to the minimum value, the rule is stated as feasible. The analysis loops by pruning the original frequent subtree $t$, level by level, until the confidence of the candidate rules is found unacceptable with respect to the minimum required; at this point, the process stops because no further improvement is possible: the process reduces the antecedent candidate size and, in this way, it possibly raises the support of the tree, which lowers the overall confidence of the rule (there is a monotone decrement of the confidence). At the end of the analysis, only the feasible rules remain and are stored.

## Storing TARs in XML

Once the TARs extraction process has been completed, the mined rules are stored in an XML file that can be queried later on by using the same language used to query the original XML document (e.g., XQuery). In particular, each rule is saved inside a Rule element which contains three attributes for the ID, support and confidence of the rule. Inside the Rule element, only the consequent of the rule is saved. In fact, we exploit the fact that the antecedent of the rule is a subtree of the consequent and use a reference attribute in each saved node to denote if the node also belongs to the antecedent of the rule. Finally, TARs are stored in the XML file sorted by the number of nodes in their antecedent; this feature is used to optimize the answering of queries containing a count operator. Figure 7 shows the XML document containing the iTARs in Figure 4.

In order to optimize the access to the stored TARs, we construct an index on them. Given a set $R$ of rules, the index associates, with every path $p$ present in at least one rule of $R$, the references to those rules that contain $p$. In particular, an index is an XML document containing a set of trees $T_1, \ldots, T_N$ such that each node $n$ of each tree $T_i$ contains a set of references to the rules containing the path from the root of $T_i$ to $n$. Antecedents and consequents of the rules are indexed separately.

*Figure 6. The TARs generation process*

```
Algorithm: RuleExtraction
Input: D, FT, minConfidence      //FT is the set of frequent subtrees
Output: set of TARs

1: R ← ∅
2: for all t ∈ FT do
3:     t_p ← prune the right-most leaf of the lowest level of t
4:     if support(t) / support(t_p) ≥ minConfidence then
5:         R ← R ∪ TAR(t, t_p)      //TAR(antecedent, consequent)
6:     else
7:         break
8:     endIf
9: return R
```

*Figure 7. Example of TAR document containing the iTARs of Figure 4*

```
<?xml version="1.0" encoding="UTF-8" standalone="no"?>
<Rules>
  <Rule ID = "1" support = "0.12" confidence = "1">
   <Incident body="true">
    <Incident_Type body="false"> violent crime </Incident_Type>
   </Incident>
  </Rule>
  <Rule ID = "2" support = "0.08" confidence = "0.67">
   <Incident body ="true">
    <Incident_Type body ="true"> violent crime </Incident_Type>
    <Crime_Details body ="false">
     <Injury_Sustained body ="false"> yes </Injury_Sustained>
    </Crime_Details>
   </Incident>
  </Rule>
</Rules>
```

During the first step, the index is composed by all antecedents (or consequents) annotated in such a way that each node contains the references to the ID of the rule it comes from. Then trees are scanned looking for those that have the same root; such trees are merged together, which means that the references of the root of tree $T_i$ are added to the references of the roots of the other trees and the same procedure is applied recursively to the children of the two roots. At the end, for each node $n$ of the resulting tree, a set of references is stored, pointing to the TARs that contain the path from the root of the tree to node $n$.

This procedure is applied separately to antecedents and consequents and the final index is the union of the two results, that is, a set of trees whose nodes contain references to one or more rules. The index is stored in an XML file and can be queried later using the same language used to query the original document (e.g., XQuery). Figure 8 shows the XML document containing the index of the TARs A and B in Figure 4.

Therefore, the intensional knowledge extracted from XML documents is represented by two XML files: the first one contains the mined TARs, while the second one contains an index constructed on such TARs which allows to speed up the access to them. The two XML documents in Figure 7 and Figure 8 represent the intensional knowledge extracted from the XML document containing the tree in Figure 2.

## Querying TARs

The second main contribution of this work is to allow users to query the intensional knowledge extracted from the data, rather than the data themselves. Such feature helps users to save time when the original dataset is so large that query processing becomes very slow or when the amount of results of a query is so large that it is hard to inspect it manually. Since intensional knowledge represents only frequent fragments of the original document, querying it will allow users to obtain mostly partial and approximate answers. This can give a satisfactory idea of the document content; however, the user who is interested in the exact list of results will use the result to formulate a more focused query, whose result will hopefully be smaller and thus more readable.

Since the stored intensional information is represented in a different way w.r.t. the original XML document (it is represented by means of two XML documents: one containing the index, the other containing the extracted TARs), queries formulated to be executed on the original dataset

*Figure 8. Example of XML document containing the index of the iTARs in Figure 4*

```xml
<?xml version="1.0" encoding="UTF-8" standalone="no"?>
<index>
 <antecedent>
  <Incident>
   <ref> 1 </ref>
   <ref> 2 </ref>
   <Incident_Type> violent crime
    <ref> 2 </ref>
   </Incident_Type>
  </Incident>
 </antecedent>
 <consequent>
  <Incident>
   <ref> 1 </ref>
   <ref> 2 </ref>
   <Incident_Type> violent crime
    <ref> 1 </ref>
    <ref> 2 </ref>
   </Incident_Type>
   <Crime_Details>
    <ref> 2 </ref>
    <Injury_Sustained> yes
     <ref> 2 </ref>
    </Injury_Sustained>
   </Crime_Details>
  </Incident>
 </consequent>
</index>
```

need to be appropriately rewritten, in order to be applied to the extracted intensional information. The TreeRuler tool implements an automatic rewriting algorithm that translates a user query directed to the original dataset into a query which can be applied to the TARs extracted from this dataset. Once the translation is completed, the rewritten query is applied: the index file is first accessed to retrieve the references to the rules satisfying the conditions imposed by the original query, then the file containing the iTARs is accessed to return the rules whose references were found in the previous step.

Since extensional and intensional data structures are quite different, not all queries lend themselves to such transformation. In the following we will explain in detail the three classes of queries currently implemented in the TreeRuler prototype.

- **Class 1: σ/π-queries.** This is used to impose a simple, or complex (containing AND and OR operators), restriction on the value of an attribute or the content of a leaf node, possibly ordering the result. For example "*Retrieve all incidents in which someone sustained injuries, ordered by type*". The corresponding XQuery, which can be applied on the extensional data, is as follows:

```
for $x in doc(''odyssey.xml'')/Nabis-
Db/Incident
where $x/Crime_Details/Injury_
Sustained[text()=''yes'']
order by $x/Incident_Type ascending
return $x
```

while the rewritten query, which can be executed on the intensional information, is:

```
let $RefI_1:= references(''/NabisDb/
Incident'', ''/Crime_Details/Injury_
Sustained[text()=''yes''] '')
let $Rules:= ruleset ($RefI_1)
for $r in $Rules/Rule
order by $r/NabisDb/Incident/Inci-
dent_Type ascending
return $r
```

Note that the rewritten query uses the reference function to access the intensional knowledge index and initialize variable $RefI_1 with the set of references to the iTARs containing the element /NabisDb/Incident/Crime_Details/Injury_Sustained with content yes. Then it uses function ruleset to access the file containing the iTARs and initialize variable $Rules with the rules whose reference is in $RefI_1. Finally, the iTARs in $Rules will be ordered according to the node Incident_Type.

- **Class 2: count-queries.** This is used to count the number of elements having a specific content. For example *"Retrieve the number of violent crimes"*. The corresponding XQuery, which can be applied on the extensional data, is as follows:

```
let $set:= (for $x in doc(''odyssey.
xml'')/NabisDb/Incident
              where $x/Incident_
Type[text()=''violent crime'']
              return $x)
return count($x)
```

while the rewritten query, which can be executed on the intensional information, is:

```
let $RefI_1:= referencesA(''/
NabisDb/Incident'',''/Incident_
Type[text()=''violent crime'']'')
let $Rules:= ruleset($RefI_1)
let $supp:= $Rules/Rule[1]@support
let $conf:= $Rules/Rule[1]@confidence
return $supp div $conf
```

The rewritten query uses the reference function to access the intensional knowledge index and initialize $RefI_1 with the set of references to the iTARs containing the element /NabisDb/Incident/Incident_Type with content violent crime in the antecedent. Then it uses function ruleset to access the file containing the iTARs and initialize variable $Rules with the rules whose reference is in $RefI_1. Finally, it returns the support of the first found rule divided by its confidence. In fact, to answer this class of queries, exploiting the property already introduced above, an association rule is used (if it exists) whose body exactly matches, in the body, the query conditions. Since for each association rule $X \Rightarrow Y$ it holds that $conf(X \Rightarrow Y) = supp(X \Rightarrow Y) / supp(X)$, it is possible to compute supp(X) (the exact number, up to approximation, of elements satisfying the conditions in X) as $supp(X \Rightarrow Y) / conf(X \Rightarrow Y)$. Moreover, since rules are stored ordered by the number of nodes they contain, if a rule whose body exactly matches the query conditions does not exist, an iTAR whose body partially matches the constraints (the body contains more constraints w.r.t. those required in the query) will be used. In this case, the answer of the query will not be exact but smaller or equal to the expected result.

- **Class 3: top-k queries.** This is used to select the best *k* answers satisfying a counting and grouping condition. For example "*Retrieve the k most frequent types of incident*". The corresponding XQuery, which can be applied on the extensional data, is as follows:

```
for $x in distinct-
values(doc(''odyssey.xml'')
                              /NabisDb/
Incident/Incident_Type)
let $set:= (for $y in doc(''odyssey.
xml'')/NabisDb/Incident
                 where $y/Incident_
Type[text()=$x/text()]
                 return $y)
order by count ($set) descending
return $x) [position() <= k]
```

while the rewritten query, which can be executed on the intensional information, is:

```
let $RefS:= references(''/NabisDb/In-
cidents/Incident_Type'', '' '')
let $Rules:= ruleset ($RefS)
(for $x in distinct-values($Rules/
NabisDb/Incident/Incident_Type)
  let $RefI_1:= referencesA(''/
NabisDb/Incident'', ''/Incident_
Type[text()=$x]'')
  let $RulesI:= ruleset($RefI_1)
  let $supp:= $RulesI/Rule[1]@support
  let $conf:= $RulesI/Rule[1]@confi-
dence
  order by $supp div $conf
  return $RulesI) [position() <= k]
```

The rewritten query uses the references function to access the intensional knowledge index and initialize the $RefS variable with the set of references to the TARs containing the element /NabisDb/Incident/Incident_Type. Then it uses function ruleset to access the file containing the iTARs and initialize variable $Rules with the rules whose reference is in $RefS. After this step, rules are scanned. In particular, for each distinct value of the element /NabisDb/Incident/Incident_Type, the index and then the iTARs are accessed looking for the rules which contain such value. For each found value, a rank is calculated as the support of the first found rule divided by its confidence. Finally, the first *k* rules are returned.

This class of rules encompasses both Class 1 and Class 2 queries, as it only adds a filter on the number of results which are first ordered according to a count condition. In fact, the query counts the occurrences of each distinct value of a certain variable in a desired set; then orders the variables with respect to their occurrences and returns the *k* most frequent.

Notice that, with the type of index we chose to use, the translation of the constraints required in the original query are straightforward, that is the index allows us to support XQuery and XPath constraints without any preprocessing.

## THE TREERULER PROTOTYPE APPLIED TO THE ODYSSEY SCENARIO

We have designed a tool that deals with both the relational and the XML data models, each with its own peculiarities. Although in this chapter we mainly focus our attention on XML data, we also learned some lessons from the challenges we faced due to the different data models involved.

In the relational scenario, the literature about data mining is wide (Agrawal, Imieliński, & Swami, 1993; Agrawal & Srikant, 1994; Agrawal & Srikant, 1995): well-known and efficient algorithms and tools for itemset and association rule extraction can be found. Moreover, much importance is given to the pre-processing of data while creating the set of itemset from the original database. Indeed, itemsets are usually mined from a single relation; if more expressive co-occurrences of data items must be extracted, the connections between data must be carefully reconstructed from the database schema by following foreign-key constraints. In this way, the designer can decide which relations (obtained by joins) must be analyzed, in order to discover meaningful association rules. This process does not seem to lend itself easily to automation given the complexity often reached by the schema of a relational database; moreover, applying data mining algorithms on the universal relation obtained by joining all the relations over the foreign keys is inefficient and risks to produce a lot of useless rules.

On the contrary, in the XML scenario, the relationships between data are much more explicit in their hierarchical organization. In the literature there are algorithms for mining frequent subtrees (Chi et al., 2004; Termier et al., 2008; Xiao, Yao, Li, & Dunham, 2003), but different notions of patterns/association rules can be found, because the structural information can be considered as a more or less strict constraint. Indeed, some approaches preserve the "parent-child" relationship between concepts, other focus on the "descendant" relationship when mining frequent subtrees. Moreover, due to the complexity of managing tree-based structure, in many proposals the designer has to decide which are the potentially interesting co-relations between subtrees, or at least the roots of the subtrees where the mining algorithms have to be applied.

With TreeRuler we want to discover unanticipated association rules, derived from frequent subtrees (mined without any input from the user) which contain also possibly complex structures. In fact, in the XML context, the structural relationships among the nodes of the tree-shaped documents can be considered as a guide to the document semantics. Indeed, when dealing with XML it is not possible to ignore the structure of data without losing a substantial part of the information, such as the ties of descent that also imply a semantic connection between concepts and not just syntax. This also implies that, since the data relationships are conveyed by the document structure, we do not have to resort to foreign keys to reconstruct the whole knowledge, and thus the preprocessing which is needed in the relational context is no more necessary here.

Keeping the structure information in the rules (i.e., the TARs in our framework) allows us to offer answers which, albeit summarized and partial, are certainly consistent with the initial knowledge; this facilitates the definition of an efficient translation of queries from extensional to intensional, due to the compatibility of the query models.

We have realized a Java prototype that implements all the features explained throughout the previous sections. TreeRuler develops three main steps that represent the entire analysis process:

1. XML frequent subtrees analysis, through the CMTreeMiner algorithm.
2. TARs generation, starting from the frequent subtrees evaluation.
3. Summarized query processing, developed to use the mined rules in order to provide intensional answers to the user's queries.

TreeRuler allows the user to choose an action among four:

- *Convert database* function, which represents a pre-processing step which allows users to input an XML document. Such document is then converted by the system into a format that can be easily managed during the phase of intensional knowledge extraction;
- *Analyze database* function, which allows users to extract intensional information (TARs) from the input XML document;
- *Query original database* and *Query intensional database* functions, allowing the users to formulate Xqueries on the original XML document and on the extracted intensional knowledge, respectively;

The core contributions of TreeRuler are the *Analyze* and *Query* functionalities. Once the first one is selected (Figure 9), allowing the user to select all the required inputs for intensional knowledge extraction. In particular, as shown in the figure, the user will be able to select: (1) the name of the input dataset where to apply the mining process, (2) the tag of the root of the tree where to discover frequent subtrees, and (3) the name of the XML files where to store mined TARs. Moreover, s/he will be required to define a support and confidence threshold for the rules to be mined. The first step of the analysis, i.e., the frequent subtrees analysis, provides the raw material to be processed during the rules generation. Once the TARs have been generated, the summarized knowledge is extracted from the original data and it is stored ready to be exploited later on. The generated rules represent the most common properties of the original dataset and, from a statistical point of view, the most interesting ones given the support and confidence parameters provided by the user.

The TARs' content summarizes the most relevant data and the data structure too, because it is always maintained during the analysis process. In accord with the original document, the rule structure is defined in XML: this choice allows for maintaining the same conceptual and structural richness of the original data. Once the analysis process has been completed, the user will be able to see the generated outputs (that is, the two XML files containing the extracted TARs and their index) and to query them.

The second main functionality of TreeRuler is the possibility to query both the original XML document and the extracted intensional knowledge. If the user chooses to query the original XML document (Figure 10), the prototype allows users to formulate any kind of XQuery and uses the Saxon XQuery processor to access the selected XML dataset and return the results.

On the other hand, if the user chooses to query the extracted intensional knowledge (Figure 11), the querying process provides a concise and fast alternative to traditional query answering on the original XML dataset. Rules can be efficiently exploited to answer general queries and present an overview of properties of the data to the user. The granularity of the answer is different, but in most cases it is enough to satisfy a wide range of generic queries. In some cases, a user interested in general features and common properties in the data can also receive a complete answer along with statistical information about the significance of the answer itself.

As it can be noted from Figure 11, the querying of intensional knowledge is managed differ-

*Figure 9. Rule generation screenshot*

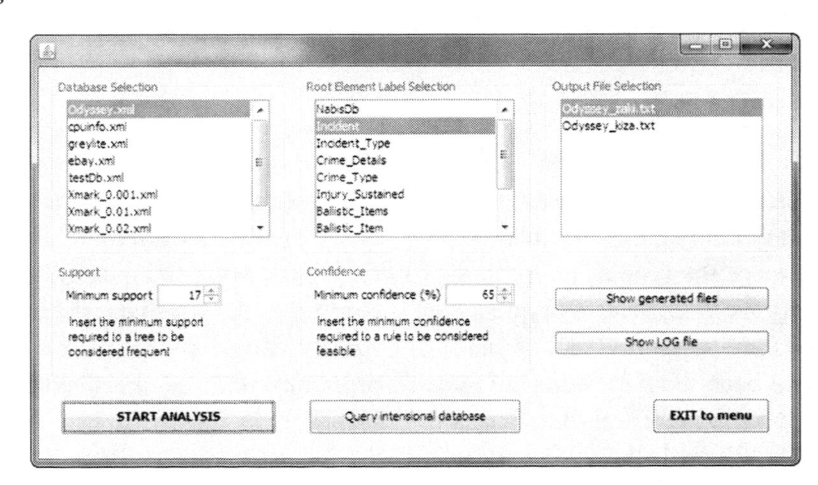

*Figure 10. A query over the original database*

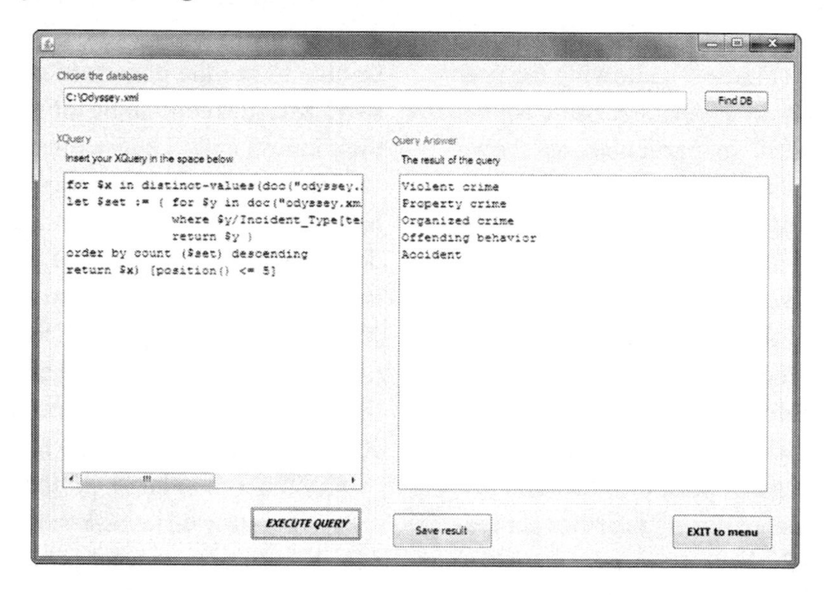


*Figure 11. A query over the intensional database*

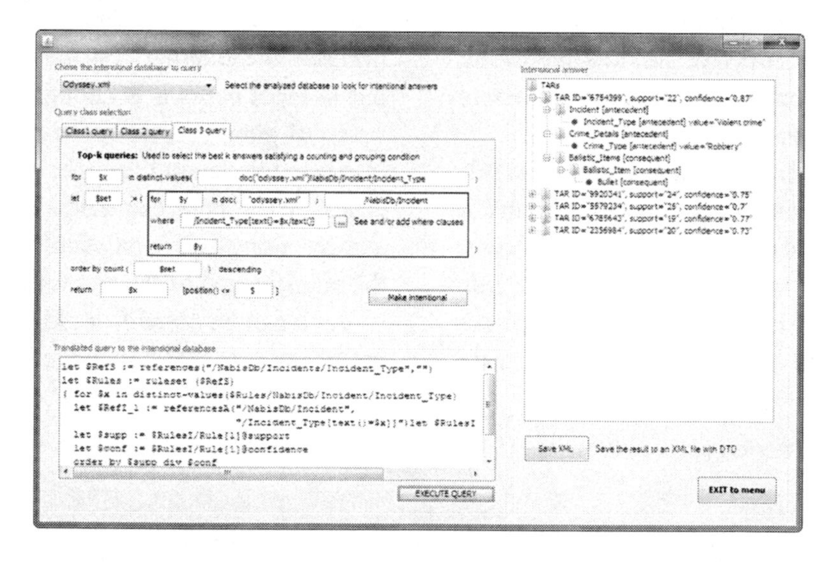


ently than the querying of the original XML document. In fact, in this case, users are not allowed to formulate any kind of XQuery; instead, they first have to choose the type of query they want to execute. Only the three classes of queries previously explained are supported at this time by the prototype and each class is managed by the system by using templates. Therefore, once a query class has been selected, the user will be able to insert the conditions required by such class. For example, Figure 11 shows the template of a query of class 3 used to formulate the "*Retrieve the 5 most frequent types of incident*" query. According to the template, the user will be able to specify that s/he is looking to count the number of occurrences of the distinct values of node NabisDB/Incident/Incident_Type and to return the 5 most frequent values.

## Experiments

As previously mentioned, the TreeRuler prototype is implemented in Java, wrapping and extending the CMTreeMiner frequent trees extraction algorithm, which is implemented in C++. The prototype was tested in both its main functionalities, that is, we have tested the time it takes to mine the intensional knowledge from different XML documents and the time it takes to answer user queries directed to the extracted information.

Concerning the TARs extraction time, we have tested TreeRuler on increasingly complex databases, most of them are real datasets found in the Washington XML public data repository[3] and some others have been generated by the benchmark tool XMark[4]. The test showed a linear dependency between the execution time of the TARs generation process and the number of nodes in the mined documents.

Figure 12 shows the dependency between the number of nodes in an XML documents and the time needed to extract intensional knowledge from such document. The time shown in the figure represents the execution time of the complete TARs generation process. In fact, the process of TARs generation is composed by three steps:

1. conversion of the input XML dataset into the DFCF compact representation accepted by CMTreeMiner;
2. frequent subtrees mining;
3. TAR generation.

The first step is a pre-processing phase, used to translate the original XML document to a more compact and handy representation. Such phase is required to use the CMTreeMiner algorithm, though the conversion itself is not strictly part of the TARs generation process. Therefore, Figure 13 shows the dependency between the number of nodes in an XML document and the time needed to perform steps 2 and 3 (mining time) of the TARs extraction process.

In order to obtain the list of frequent subtrees from CMTreeMiner, we have to comply with its support definition. In CMTreeMiner support refers to the trees which are represented in the forest to be analyzed, that is: a subtree is considered to be frequent if it is detected into a number of trees of the forest at least equal to the minimum support requested. The experiments setup was prepared taking into account such a behavior, so the support threshold requested was set near the 50% of the trees in each forest. This threshold requires that a subtree, to be considered a good candidate, be quite widespread among the trees in the dataset

*Figure 12. TreeRuler execution times (confidence = 0.9)*

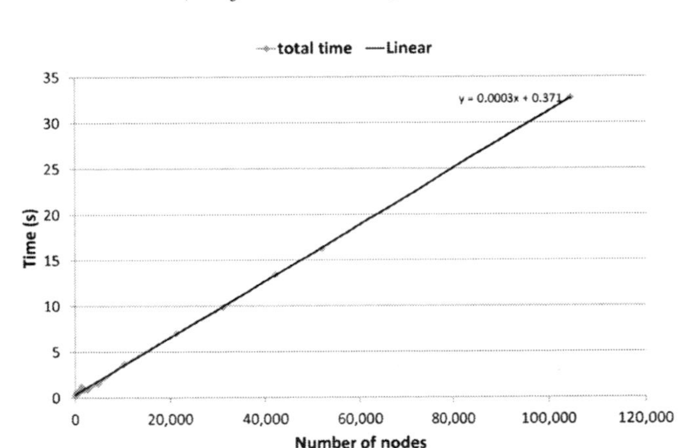

*Figure 13. TreeRuler execution time evidencing format conversions (confidence = 0.9)*

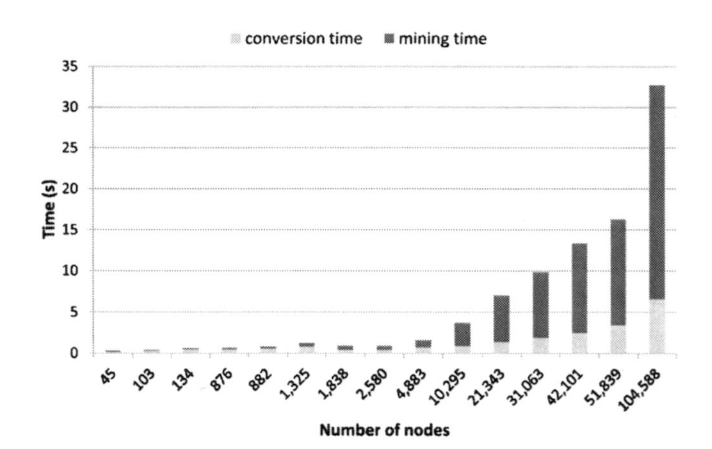


(i.e., in the 50% of trees), but it should be noticed that such a parameter is not too restrictive, because it represents the upper bound of the frequency, in the case that each of the trees in the dataset forest contains at most one occurrence of that subtree, while, in general, there could be none, one or more than one occurrence.

The chart in Figure 14 shows the execution time, without the initial dataset conversion, of the less complex datasets. From the stacked-histogram in Figure 13, it is possible to note that the conversion step influence is very low with respect to the whole process execution time, making the curve shift up but keeping its slope. During the performed tests, the number of mined rules was varied between 1 and 17, however it is also possible that no TARs are generated, depending on the XML document content and structure, but also on the values of confidence and support parameters.

At the end of the TARs extraction process, the mined rules are indexed and both the TARs and their index are stored in XML files, ready to be queried.

TreeRuler is able to compute both extensional answers to user queries, by using the original dataset, and intensional answers, by using the mined set of rules, if possible. The most interesting feature of the summarized view offered by

*Figure 14. TreeRuler execution time: Detail on the lower dimensions (confidence = 0.9)*

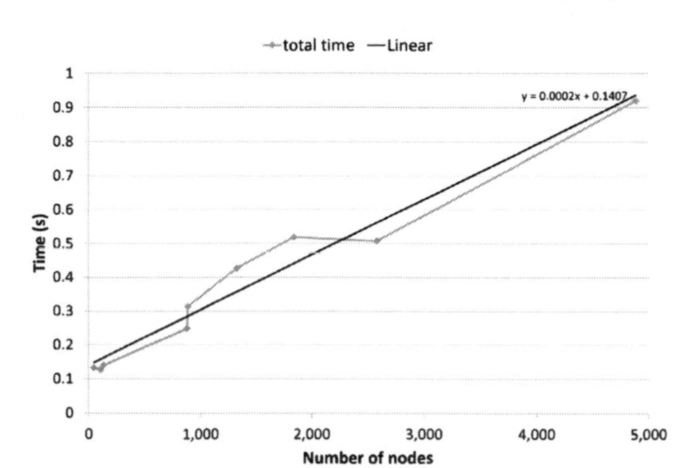

the TARs is the fast response time to a generic query. A user with little or no knowledge of the data will immediately gain an informative view of the content of the database and significant statistical properties of the database related to his/her input query.

Figure 15 shows the difference between extensional and intensional answers, in terms of time needed to compute the results of a user query. This corresponds to the response time[5] to general queries applied on both the original dataset and the related iTARs database. Each query applied to the original XML document has first been translated according to the previously explained process and then executed on the intensional knowledge mined from the corresponding XML document.

As it can be noted from the presented experimental results, the answering-time performance on the extracted rules is extremely interesting compared to the original database response times, especially in the case of general queries not imposing many conditions, but looking for generic elements (e.g., "all the properties of frequent incidents"); in fact, in this case TARs provide their best results because they suggest interesting relationships among the data and hints to better refine the query. In the lower part of the chart in Figure 15, response times are indistinguishable from the disk access times. The regular and uniform nature of the data contained into the databases usually provides few interesting rules and the execution time of the queries reflects this situation. In fact, although the dimension of a source database is increasing, the number of mined rules is almost similar, because significant and frequent alterations to a dataset must be performed in order to mine a wider set of TARs: this behavior provides quasi-constant query times on the rules generated from growing-but-uniform databases.

An example of query we have applied on the Odyssey dataset is "*find all robberies after which bullets were collected*". From the database of test incidents the system retrieved 33 subtrees in 23ms, while the TARs database required 8ms to retrieve 2 iTARs. Looking at the extensional answer, the user has to analyze each record at least once to gain an overview of the content and compare manually the data contained to gain information, making the post-search phase overwhelming and time consuming. TARs, instead, provide immediate access to the information contained: it is much more simple and straightforward to interpret a handful of probably small trees than a possibly huge list of XML records. Moreover, a TAR provides useful statistical meta-information such as the confidence related to the content and the support of the related subtree: it will take only a few moments to obtain

*Figure 15. TreeRuler query execution time*

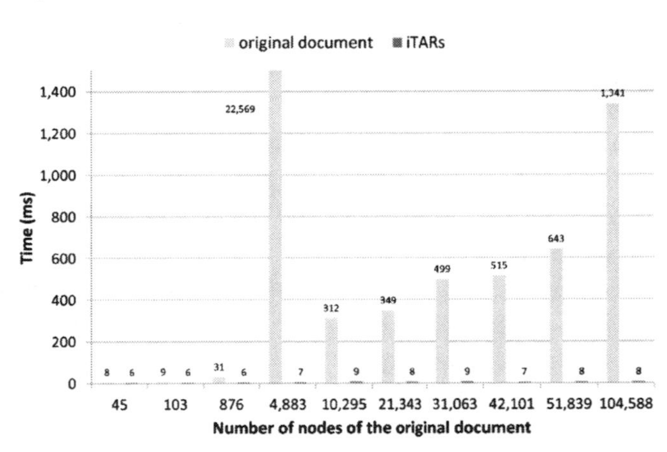

the order of magnitude of the tuples satisfying the same constraints of the retrieved rule, when considering a generic query, or their number in the case of counting query (applying the reverse support formula previously discussed).

The answers provided by querying the mined knowledge should not be always seen as a replacement of the extensional ones, especially when they are approximate. They constitute a useful enrichment of the traditional process and represent an expressive repository of statistical implications between trees, especially useful in the exploratory phase of a query. In Figure 15 we show that the overall performance degradation in terms of response time needed to associate the intensional answers to a query w.r.t. to the time required for the traditional results would be inexistent/very low with respect to the possible synthesis benefits.

As an example we could think about a dataset containing data related to bank robberies, and a generic query to "*find all the robberies happened in a certain period of time*". The extensional answer is a possibly long list of records related to the query conditions. A user, who is interested in gaining generic knowledge about robberies in a particular period, would have to analyze the answer-set record by record in order to find something statistically interesting. The association of intensional answers to the traditional query process enhances the usefulness of the answer-set by presenting immediately perceivable implications mined from the data (association rules) along with their statistical value, thus providing a very immediate access to some of the knowledge contained in the data; for example, we can think about a rule presented aside the traditional result set stating that a Ford red car is frequently related the robberies with a high level of confidence).

It is important to underline that while a generic XML dataset could be really messy (the spike in the chart refers to a relatively small dataset but difficult to analyze), a TARs database provides a well-defined structure which relieves the user from a possibly difficult interpretation of each dataset design, especially when a schema definition is not available.

## CONCLUSION

Query optimization, decision support and context-based data summarization are some of the application fields that can benefit from intensional answers. In fact, they provide summarized information, require short response times, help managing knowledge by emphasizing it from noise and making it easily available on mobile devices.

In this chapter we have described TreeRuler, a tool that helps the casual user to gain implicit knowledge about huge XML datasets, in terms of Tree-based Association Rules describing frequent correlations between subtrees satisfying a query. The summarized answers provided by TreeRuler allow the user to gain summarized knowledge about the context and structure of an XML dataset, and on the basis of such knowledge, refine his/her primitive request. TreeRuler has been developed in the context of a EU project dealing with information about crimes in Europe, and the obtained results in terms of quality and response time are encouraging. As a future work, we plan to study how to incrementally update mined TARs when the original XML datasets change and how to further optimize our mining algorithm.

## REFERENCES

Agrawal, R., Imieliński, T., & Swami, A. N. (1993). Mining association rules between sets of items in large databases. In P. Buneman, & S. Jajodia (Eds.), *Proceedings of the ACM SIGMOD International Conference on Management of Data*, (pp. 207-216). ACM.

Agrawal, R., & Srikant, R. (1994). Fast algorithms for mining association rules in large databases. In J. B. Bocca, M. Jarke, & C. Zaniolo (Eds.), *Proceedings of the 20th International Conference on Very Large Data Bases (VLDB)*, (pp. 487-499). Morgan Kaufmann.

Agrawal, R., & Srikant, R. (1995). Mining sequential patterns. *Proceedings of the 11th International Conference on Data Engineering (ICDE)*, (pp. 3-14). IEEE Computer Society.

Berzal, F., Jiménez, A., & Cubero, J. C. (2008). Mining induced and embedded subtrees in ordered, unordered, and partially-ordered trees. In *Proceedings of the 17th International Symposium on Methodologies for Intelligent Systems*, (pp. 111-120).

Boncz, P., Grust, T., van Keulen, M., Manegold, S., Rittinger, J., & Teubner, J. (2006). MonetDB/XQuery: A fast XQuery processor powered by a relational engine. In *Proceedings of the 2006 ACM International Conference on Management of Data (SIGMOD)*, (pp. 479-490). ACM.

Braga, D., Campi, A., & Ceri, S. (2005). XQBE (XQuery by example): A visual interface to the standard XML query language. *ACM Transactions on Database Systems*, *30*(2), 398–443. doi:10.1145/1071610.1071613

Braga, D., Campi, A., Klemettinen, M., & Lanzi, P. (2002). Mining association rules from XML data. In Y. Kambayashi, W. Winiwarter & M. Arikawa (Eds.), *Proceedings of the 4th International Conference on Data Warehousing and Knowledge Discovery (DaWaK) Lecture Notes in Computer Science: Vol. 2454* (pp. 133-156). Springer.

Chen, Q., Lim, A., & Ong, K. W. (2003). D(k)-index: An adaptive structural summary for graph-structured data. In *Proceedings of the 2003 ACM International Conference on Management of Data (SIGMOD)*, (pp. 134-144). ACM.

Chi, Y., Muntz, R. R., Nijssen S., & Kok, J. N. (2004). Frequent subtree mining – An overview. *Fundamenta Informaticae - Advances in Mining Graphs, Trees and Sequences, 66*(1-2).

Chi, Y., Yang, Y., Xia, Y., & Muntz, R. R. (2004). CMTreeMiner: Mining both closed and maximal frequent subtrees. *Proceedings of the 8th Pacific-Asia Conference on Advances in Knowledge Discovery and Data Mining (PAKDD)* [Springer.]. *Lecture Notes in Computer Science*, *3056*, 63–73. doi:10.1007/978-3-540-24775-3_9

Chung, C., Min, J., & Shim, K. (2002). APEX: An adaptive path index for XML data. In M. J. Franklin, B. Moon, & A. Ailamaki (Eds.), *Proceedings of the 2002 ACM International Conference on Management of Data (SIGMOD)*, (pp. 121-132) ACM.

Goethals, B., & Zaki, M. J. (2004). Advances in frequent itemset mining implementations: Report on FIMI'03. *SIGKDD Explorations*, *6*(1), 109–117. doi:10.1145/1007730.1007744

Harinarayan, V., Rajaraman, A., & Ullman, J. D. (1996). Implementing data cubes efficiently. In H. V. Jagadish, & I. S. Mumick (Eds.), *Proceedings of the 1996 ACM International Conference on Management of Data (SIGMOD)*, (pp. 205-216). ACM.

He, H., & Yang, J. (2004). Multiresolution indexing of XML for frequent queries. In *Proceedings of the 20th International Conference on Data Engineering (ICDE)*, (pp. 683-694). IEEE Computer Society.

Kawasoe, S., Arimura, H., Sakamoto, H., Asai, T., Abe, K., & Arikawa, S. (2002). Efficient substructure discovery from large semi-structured data. In *Proceedings of the SIAM International Conference on Data Mining (SDM)*. SIAM.

Kay, M. (2008). *Saxon: The XSLT and XQuery processor*. Retrieved from http://saxon.sourceforge.net/

Li, Z., Xiao, Y., Yao, J. F., & Dunham, M. H. (2003). Efficient data mining for maximal frequent subtrees. In *Proceedings of the 3rd IEEE International Conference on Data Mining (ICDM)*, (pp. 379-386). IEEE Computer Society.

Liu, H. C., & Zeleznikow, J. (2005). Relational computation for mining association rules from XML data. In *Proceedings of the 14th ACM Conference on Information and Knowledge Management (CIKM)*, (pp. 253-254). ACM.

Mazuran, M., Quintarelli, E., & Tanca, L. (2009). Mining tree-based frequent patterns from XML. In T. Andreasen, R. R. Yager, H. Bulskov, H. Christiansen, & H. L. Larsen (Eds.), *Proceedings of the 8th International Conference on Flexible Query Answering Systems (FQAS) Lecture Notes in Computer Science: Vol. 5822* (pp. 287-299). Springer.

Oliboni, B., Combi, C., & Rossato, R. (2005). Querying XML documents by using association rules. In *Proceedings of the 16th International Conference on Database and Expert Systems Applications (DEXA)*, (pp. 1020-1024). IEEE Computer Society.

Termier, A., Rousset, M., & Sebag, M. (2004). Dryade: A new approach for discovering closed frequent trees in heterogeneous tree databases. In *Proceedings of the 4th IEEE International Conference on Data Mining (ICDM)*, (pp. 543-546). IEEE Computer Society.

Termier, A., Rousset, M., Sebag, M., Ohara, K., Washio, T., & Motoda, H. (2008). DryadeParent: An efficient and robust closed attribute tree mining algorithm. *IEEE Transactions on Knowledge and Data Engineering, 20*(3), 300–320. doi:10.1109/TKDE.2007.190695

Wan, J. W. W., & Dobbie, G. (2003). Extracting association rules from XML documents using XQuery. In R. H. L. Chiang, A. H. F. Laender, & E.-P. Lim (Eds.), *Proceedings of the 5th ACM International Workshop on Web Information and Data Management (WIDM)*, (pp. 94-97). ACM.

Wang, K., & Liu, H. (2000). Discovering structural association of semistructured data. *IEEE Transactions on Knowledge and Data Engineering, 12*(3), 353–371. doi:10.1109/69.846290

Weigand, H., Feng, L., Dillon, T. S., & Chang, E. E. (2003). An XML-enabled association rule framework. In *Proceedings of the 14th International Conference on Database and Expert Systems Applications (DEXA) Lecture Notes in Computer Science: Vol. 2736* (pp. 88-97).

World Wide Web Consortium. (1999). *XML path language XPath* version 1.0. Retrieved March 15, 2006, from http://www.w3C.org/TR/XPath.html

World Wide Web Consortium. (2002). *XQuery: An XML query language*. Retrieved March 15, 2006, from http://www.w3C.org/TR/REC-xml

World Wide Web Consortium. (2004). *XML information set*. Retrieved from http://www.w3.org/TR/xml-infoset/

Xiao, Y., Yao, J., Li, Z., & Dunham, M. H. (2003). Efficient data mining for maximal frequent subtrees. In *Proceedings of the 3rd IEEE International Conference on Data Mining (ICDM)*, (pp. 379-386). IEEE Computer Society.

Yang, Y., Xia, Y., Chi, Y., & Muntz, R. R. (2004). Cmtreeminer: Mining both closed and maximal frequent subtrees. In *Proceedings of the 8th Pacific-Asian Conference on Knowledge Discovery and Data Mining (PAKDD)* [Springer.]. *Lecture Notes in Computer Science, 3056*, 63–73.

Youn, H. Y., Paik, J., & Kim, U. M. (2005). A new method for mining association rules from a collection of XML documents. In *Proceedings of International Conference on Computational Science and Its Applications (ICCSA)* [Springer.]. *Lecture Notes in Computer Science, 3481*, 936–945.

Zaki, M. J. (2005). Efficiently mining frequent trees in a forest: Algorithms and applications. *IEEE Transactions on Knowledge and Data Engineering, 17*(8), 1021–1035. doi:10.1109/TKDE.2005.125

## ENDNOTES

1. http://www.cs.waikato.ac.nz/ml/weka/
2. http://www.odyssey-project.eu/
3. http://www.cs.washington.edu/research/xmldatasets/www/repository.html
4. http://www.xml-benchmark.org/
5. All the measures were obtained through the Kernow project (http://kernowforsaxon.sourceforge.net/) using the XQuery sandbox

# Chapter 13
# Discovering Higher Level Correlations from XML Data

**Luca Cagliero**
*Politecnico di Torino, Italy*

**Tania Cerquitelli**
*Politecnico di Torino, Italy*

**Paolo Garza**
*Politecnico di Milano, Italy*

## ABSTRACT

*Association rule extraction is a widely used exploratory technique that allows the identification of hidden correlations among data. The problem of generalized association rule mining, originally introduced in the context of market basket analysis, exploits a taxonomy to drive the mining activity with the aim at discovering associations between data items at any level of the taxonomy. Since XML has become a standard for representing and exchanging information, the extraction of association rules from XML data is becoming appealing as it allows for identifying hidden and interesting patterns among data. Many approaches have been devoted to effectively mining association rules from both transactional and XML data. However, traditional association rule mining algorithms are sometimes not effective in mining valuable knowledge because of the excessive detail level of the mined information. Furthermore, the cardinality of the extracted knowledge may be too large to be effectively exploited in decision making processes.*

*This chapter proposes the XML-GERMI framework to support XML data analysis by automatically extracting generalized association rules (i.e., higher level correlations) from XML data. The proposed approach, which extends the concept of multiple-level association rules, is focused on extracting generalized rules from XML data. To drive the generalization phase of the extraction process, a taxonomy is exploited to aggregate features at different granularity levels. Experiments performed on both real and synthetic datasets show the adaptability and the effectiveness of the proposed framework in discovering higher level correlations from XML data.*

DOI: 10.4018/978-1-61350-356-0.ch013

## INTRODUCTION

During recent years, the eXtensible Markup Language (XML) has become a standard for representing, exchanging, and publishing information on the Web, by ensuring interoperability among software systems. XML data is commonly represented by either graph representations, e.g., GraphLog (Consens & Mendelzon, 1990), OEM (Papakonstantinou, Garcia-Molina, & Widom 1995), G-Log (Paredaens, Peelman, & Tanca, 1995), UnQL (Bunemann, Davidson, Fan, Hara, & Tan, 1996), or labeled trees (Damiani, Oliboni, Quintarelli, & Tanca, 2003; Baralis, Garza, Quintarelli, & Tanca, 2007). These representations allow for storing data that cannot be easily represented with traditional data models. Since nowadays a large amount of data is stored in XML, novel and more efficient data mining techniques are needed (2) to analyze large collections of semistructured data and (2) to discover useful and interesting knowledge. For example, discovering association rules (Agrawal & Srikant, 1994) allows the identification of hidden and interesting correlations among data. Originally introduced in the context of market basket analysis, this mining activity finds nowadays applications in a wide range of different contexts (e.g., network traffic characterization (Baldi, Baralis, & Risso, 2005), context-aware applications (Baralis, Cagliero, Cerquitelli, Garza, & Marchetti, 2009)). However, the suitability of data mining approaches for business decisions strictly depends on the granularity level of the available information. Traditional association rule mining algorithms (e.g., (Agrawal & Srikant, 1994)) are sometimes not effective in mining valuable knowledge because of the excessive detail level of the mined information. Consider, for instance, a business-oriented scenario in which orders submitted by customers are stored in an XML data repository. Traditional rule mining may discover occurrences concerning specific customers and orders. A minimum support threshold is enforced to discriminate with respect to the strength of the patterns (i.e., how patterns frequently occur). The discovery of higher level correlations regarding well-known categories of interest (e.g., order priority classes) may allow for better supporting business decisions by both (1) providing a higher level of the analyzed data, and (2) preventing relevant but infrequent knowledge discarding. For instance, a valuable occurrence about a low priority order category may be figured out even if each low priority order is infrequent with respect to the minimum support threshold (i.e., it would be discarded by a traditional rule miner). Indeed, our study is mainly focused on aggregating knowledge to discover and exploit valuable correlations, hidden in the analyzed data, at different levels of abstraction. To this aim, the mining task is driven by a conceptual taxonomy (i.e., a *is-a* hierarchy defined over items) to allow for discovering associations among data items at any aggregation level. This paper presents one of the first attempts to exploit generalized mining in a data mining framework oriented to XML data.

This chapter thoroughly describes the problem of generalized association rule mining from XML data. After a brief overview of related work that addresses the mining of hidden correlations from XML data, we present our framework called XML-GERMI (XML-GEneralized Rule MIner). The proposed framework first performs XML data pre-processing to tailor XML data to a transactional data format. Then, it performs the extraction of generalized association rules through the evaluation of a taxonomy built over data items. Although XML-GERMI is flexible in that it can easily integrate any rule mining algorithm, currently two algorithms, Cumulate (Agrawal & Srikant, 1995) and GenIO (Baralis, Cagliero, Cerquitelli, D'Elia, & Garza, 2010), are available in XML-GERMI to efficiently extract high level correlations. To effectively support end-users in exploring the extracted knowledge, mined patterns are stored in an XML data repository that can be queried by means of the XQuery language (XQuery, 2010). Experiments performed on both real and synthetic datasets show the effectiveness of the XML-GERMI framework in discovering higher level and interesting correlations from XML data.

## RELATED WORK

### Rule Mining from XML Data

The data mining research area focuses on discovering patterns that represent knowledge implicitly stored in massive data repositories. Data mining activities include studying correlations among data (e.g., association rules (Agrawal & Srikant, 1994)), extracting information for prediction (e.g., classification (Tan, Steibach, & Kumar, 2006; Yin, Li, Mei, & Han, 2009)), grouping data with similar properties (e.g., clustering (Newman, 2001)). In this chapter, we focus on association rule mining, which was originally introduced in (Agrawal & Srikant, 1994) in the context of market basket analysis. Plenty of techniques have been proposed to mine association rules from transactional data (Agrawal & Srikant, 1994; Han, Pei, & Yin, 2000; Park, Chen, & Yu, 1997; Zaki, 2002). Recently, the fast-growing amount of XML-based information has led to the development of novel and more efficient data mining techniques, which are able to (1) analyze large collections of semi-structured data in a large variety of application domains (e.g., network traffic domain, user and service profiling, social network analysis), and (2) discover higher level knowledge from data which can be effectively and efficiently exploited during decision making.

Many research activities in XML data mining have been devoted to identifying techniques to discover hidden correlations among data. Proposed approaches can be grouped in two classes: (1) discovering correlations hidden in a single XML document to support decision making, and (2) mining interesting patterns from a collection of XML documents.

The first approach is tailored to a single XML document. Since commonly used data mining algorithms often deal with transactional data, a straightforward approach to cope with XML mining is to map XML data to the transactional data format and exploit existing techniques proposed for transactional databases. In (Baralis et al., 2007), a preprocessing step performed on tree-based XML data representation allows for tailoring XML to a relational schema. This enables the exploitation of traditional association rule mining algorithms to produce a summarized representation of XML documents based on the concept of instance patterns, which can both provide succinct information and be directly queried. However, the devised approach has to deal with well-known association rule mining limitations (e.g., huge amounts of extracted knowledge hard to be analyzed and exploited).

A parallel effort on single XML document mining has been devoted to extending query languages to facilitate association rule mining (Imielinski & Virmani, 1999) in the XML context. (Braga, Campi, Ceri, Klemettinen, & Lanzi, 2003) proposed a framework to discover association rules in large amounts of XML data. The XQuery language (XQuery, 2010) has been properly extended with data mining and knowledge discovery capabilities by introducing association rules for native XML documents. Furthermore, an ad-hoc operator for specifying mining queries to extract a subset of interesting rules has also been defined. The syntax and an intuitive semantics for the operator has been formalized and some examples of complex association rules have also been presented. However, no algorithm for mining such complex rules is proposed. One step further towards discovering interesting correlation on XML data (Wan & Dobbie, 2004) is based on exploiting a set of functions in the XQuery language (World Wide Web Consortium, 2002) to perform the mining task by means of the Apriori algorithm (Agrawal & Srikant, 1994). This approach has been enhanced by exploiting the well-known FP-Growth mining algorithm (Han et al., 2000) for XML data (Ding & Sundarraj, 2006). However, in most of the above approaches the designer is asked to specify the structure of the desired rule in advance (Braga et al., 2003; Wan & Dobbie, 2004), which might not fit to many real-life contexts, in which documents are not associated with an explicit DTD or XML schema.

A relevant effort has been devoted to extending the SQL language by integrating traditional rule mining operators (Meo, Psaila, & Ceri, 1996) to efficiently select interesting rules. Different operators for specifying mining queries have been defined to extract interesting patterns, such as association rules, on a set of XML documents.

A second branch of study concerning XML mining has been devoted to mining association rules from collections of XML documents. The aim is to extract frequent structures from either graph-based data representations (Yan & Han, 2002; Washio & Motoda, 2003; Kuramochi & Karypis, 2004) or tree-based data representations (Termier et al., 2008; Zaki, 2005; Jiménez, Berzal, & Cubero, 2010). Each XML document corresponds to a database record, with a tree-like structure. The first algorithm, namely TreeMiner, to discover all frequent subtrees has been proposed in (Zaki, 2002). It exploits a data structure called the scope-list. Next, (Chang, Dillon, Feng, & Weigand, 2003) presented a general-purpose XML-enabled framework, which extends the notion of association item to an XML fragment (i.e., tree) and builds up associations among trees. Relevant extensions of the framework address two issues: (1) driving an XML mining process with constraints to tailor the extracted knowledge to user needs (Dillon & Feng, 2004), and (2) exploiting more effective data structures to enhance scalability in mining multiple XML documents (Paik et al., 2007). (Dillon & Feng, 2004) proposed a template to support XML-enabled association rule mining, while (Paik, Youn, & Kim, 2005) proposed a hierarchical data structure (HoPS) to extract XML association rules involving disjoint fragments of XML documents. Differently from the above XML mining approaches, we specifically address generalized association rule mining from a single XML document.

Traditional rule mining, driven by support and confidence thresholds, may entail both (1) generating a huge amount of patterns which may become difficult to be analyzed, and (2) pruning rare itemsets, even if their hidden knowledge might be relevant. To overcome the above issues, generalized patterns (Agrawal & Srikant, 1995) may be profitably exploited to provide a high level abstraction of the mined knowledge. By evaluating a taxonomy (i.e., a is-a hierarchy) over data items, items can be aggregated based on different granularity concepts. Generalized patterns can be used both to (1) give a higher level view of patterns hidden in the analyzed data, and (2) represent knowledge pruned by discarding infrequent lower level itemsets. Albeit several approaches investigate generalized association rule mining from structured or semistructured data (Agrawal & Srikant, 1995; Han & Fu, 1999; Pramudiono & Kitsuregawa, 2004; Baralis et al., 2010), to the best of our knowledge the problem of extracting generalized association rules from XML data has not been investigated so far.

## Taxonomy Construction

The generalized association rule mining is driven by the evaluation of a taxonomy built over the data items. A taxonomy, usually called conceptual taxonomy, is a hierarchical organizations of concepts, topics, and keywords in which is-a relationships among related concepts hold. The taxonomy can be either provided by a domain expert or automatically inferred from data of interest.

Most of the Semantic Web tools for taxonomy construction (e.g., the Web Ontology Language OWL (World Wide Web Consortium OWL, 2010)) heavily rely on human intervention. Nevertheless, the automatic construction of conceptual hierarchies is becoming an increasingly appealing topic in several research fields, including information retrieval, data summarization, association rule mining, and text categorization. To this aim, the discovering and the hierarchical organization of the most relevant keywords mined from text documents have been thoroughly discussed in the literature (Zamir, Etzioni, Madani, & Karp, 1997; Clifton, Cooley, & Rennie, 2004; Gates, Teiken, & Cheng, 2005; Ienco & Meo, 2008). The proposed algorithms mainly perform hierarchical clustering to provide a well-founded structuring of concepts of interest. The output diagram (called dendrogram) records the sequence of fusions of clusters into larger ones. Different greedy approaches have been defined to evaluate candidate solutions based on the computation of an overall goodness measure obtained by exploiting cluster cohesion measures (Tan et al., 2006). A similar approach has also been applied to the results of Web search engines to improve user browsing (Zamir et al., 1997), while (Hatzivassiloglou, Gravano, & Maganti, 2000) investigates its adoption in the context of document management. (Ienco & Meo, 2008) enriched the clustering-based approach by providing a concise description of each cluster through a keyword representative selected by PageRank ranking algorithm (Brin & Page, 1998). (Michalski & Stepp, 1983) proposed a different approach to induce the description of concepts by induction of a schematic pattern describing the concept rather than in terms of keywords.

To overcome well-known hierarchical clustering algorithm limitations (e.g., complexity and optimality issues), several alternative techniques have been devised in different application contexts. In (Hovy & Lin, 1999), the lexical database WordNet is exploited to generalize concepts and to identify the topics of the text in a summarization system. By contrast, in (Ou, Khoo, & Goh, 2005) a taxonomy is constructed to provide a structure for linking similar concepts in different dissertation abstracts. Gates, Teiken, and Cheng (2005) presented a system for the construction of taxonomies which yields high accuracy with automated categorization systems on the Web. Finally, (Tao & Sarabjot, 2009) proposed to exploit domain knowledge inferred by automated taxonomy generation in recommendation systems.

## DEFINITIONS AND NOTATION

Many efforts have been devoted to modeling XML data by means of graph representations, e.g., GraphLog (Consens & Mendelzon, 1990), OEM (Papakonstantinou et al., 1995), G-Log, (Paredaens et al., 1995) UnQL (Bunemann et al., 1996), where nodes denote either objects (i.e., abstract entities) or values (i.e., primitive values), and edges represent relationships between them. According to the definition reported in (Damiani et al., 2003), we represent an XML document by a labeled tree, as stated in the following definition:

**Definition 1 (XML document).** *An XML document is a labeled tree $<N, E, r>$, such that N is a set of nodes, $r \in N$ is the root of the tree (the root of the XML document), and E is a set of edges.*

A pictorial representation of a portion of the TPC-H XML order document (TPC-H, 2005) is reported in Figure 1. The document reports information about customer orders, where each order is characterized by several features, such as its corresponding identification key, priority level, submission date as well as the identification code and some eventual comments/questions raised by the customer who submitted the order. Attributes and elements are represented by empty circles, whereas the textual content of elements and the value of attributes are reported as a black-filled circle. The node labeled as *Orders* in Figure 1 is the root of all customer orders. The labeled tree rooted in the *Order* node is an example of customer order. In general, elements may be connected to their sub-elements, attributes, or leaf nodes, while attribute nodes may be connected to leaf nodes that represent their corresponding attribute values.

For the sake of simplicity, nodes characterized by empty circles in Figure 1 are all element nodes (e.g., the order key node labeled as *O_Key*), while connected text nodes are associated to their corresponding textual content (e.g., "*1*" for the order key node depicted in Figure 1). Moreover, the following properties on nodes and edges hold:

**Property 1.** *Each node $n_i$ has a tuple of labels $NL_i = \langle Ntag_i, Ntype_i, Ncontent_i \rangle$. The label type $Ntype_i$ indicates whether the node is the root, an element, text, or attribute, whereas the label $Ncontent_i$ can assume as value a PCDATA or $\perp$ (undefined, for non-terminals).*

For example, consider the node labeled as *O_priority* in Figure 1. It is an element node whose tuple of labels is <*O_priority*, *Element*, PCDATA>, which represents the order priority and assumes as value a PCDATA. For instance, its corresponding black-filled text node labeled as "*Low*" represents its textual content.

**Property 2.** *Each edge $e_i = \langle (n_h, n_k), EL_j \rangle$, with $n_h, n_k \in N$, has a label $EL_j = \langle Etype_j \rangle$, with $Etype_j \in \{$attribute-of, subelement-of$\}$.*

The nodes characterized by the tuple of labels <*O_comment*, *Element*, PCDATA> are subelements of the ones denoted as <*O_comments*, *Element*, PCDATA> because they represent the list of comments raised by the customer who submitted the order. Since our focus is to find high-level relationships among elementary values of XML documents, and such values may occur either as textual content of leaf elements or as attributes values, we only consider a single type of node and do not specify type labels.

Mostly used algorithms for association rule extraction consider a collection of transactions, each one containing a set of items. We refine the notion of transaction tailored to an XML document. In particular, an item is a couple (*data-element, value*), in which *data-element* is a label that provides a description of the element (e.g., element node labeled as "*O_date*" in Figure 1), whereas *value* is the content of the considered element (e.g., text node labeled as "*2010-06-20*" in Figure 1). The definition of transaction in the XML data format is given as follows.

**Definition 2 (XML Transaction).** *Let $\langle N, E, r \rangle$ be an XML document and $t_r \in N$ be a transaction root. A transaction is a subtree t rooted in a direct*

*Figure 1. A simplified labeled tree of a portion of the synthetically generated XML TPC-H order document*

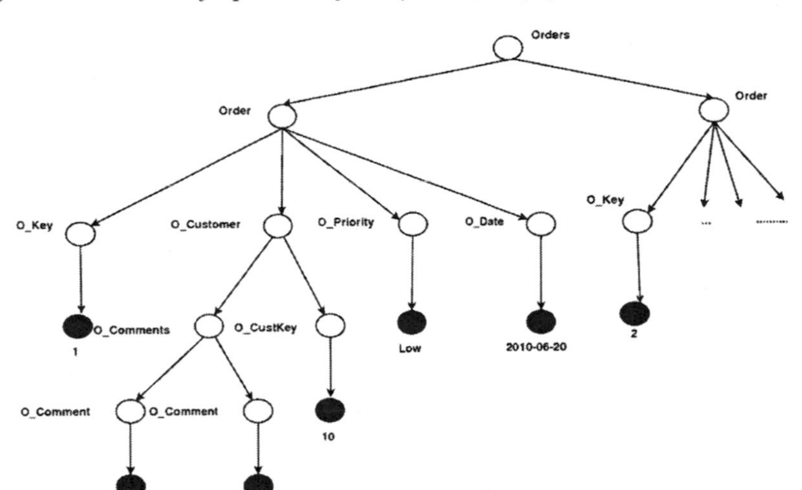

*descendant node* $n_{dr} \in N$ *of the transaction root* $t_r$. *Its items are represented by all the paths, belonging to t, that connect* $n_{dr}$ *to a leaf. Each path is an item such that:*

- *data-element* is the label of an element with a content rooted in $n_{dr}$ and defined as a sub-path from $n_{dr}$ to the element.
- *value* is the content of the considered element.

Consider for example an XML document, where each transaction is associated to an order and includes all the elements which characterize it (e.g., customer key, order key, order date). The node labeled as "*Orders*" is selected as transaction root. An order transaction may be depicted over the tree-based XML document representation, reported in Figure 1, as a subtree that connects a direct descendant of the transaction root node (e.g., the node labeled as "*Order*") to its corresponding leaves.

XML documents can be analyzed by different data mining techniques, such as association rule extraction (Braga et al., 2003), taxonomy inference (Clifton et al., 2004), and data summarization (Baralis et al., 2007), to effectively discover interesting occurrences among data items. To provide a high level view of the interesting patterns hidden in the analyzed data, generalized association rule mining (Agrawal & Srikant, 1995) can be efficiently used. Generalized association rule algorithms exploit a taxonomy (is-a hierarchy) to highlight high level occurrences among data items by aggregating features at different granularity levels. To this aim, preliminary notions of itemset and taxonomy are formally stated as follows.

**Definition 3 (Itemset).** *A k-itemset is a set of distinct items of size k.*

An example of a 2-itemset concerning a time occurrence of a specific customer order might be: {(*Customer key*, "*10*"), (*Order date*, "*2010-06-10*")}.

**Definition 4 (Taxonomy).** *Let <N, E, r> be an XML document and* $t_r \in N$ *be a transaction root. A taxonomy T is a conceptual hierarchy of aggregations built over transactional data items in <N, E, r>. Leaves are items belonging to the transactions generated from the XML document by fixing the transaction root* $t_r$. *Non-leaf nodes are aggregations of their children. The root node of the taxonomy, labeled as* $\perp$, *aggregates all the generated items.*

Figure 2 shows a simple example taxonomy built over order dates. The item (*Order date*, "*2010-06-10*") may be meaningfully aggregated into its corresponding month (*Order date*, "*June 2010*"), trimester (*Order date*, "*2nd trimester 2010*"), and year (*Order date*, "*2010*").

By evaluating a given taxonomy, items can be generalized into high level concepts.

**Definition 5 (Generalized item).** *Let T be a taxonomy. A generalized item (data-element, value_gen) assigns value value_gen to label data-element. (data-element, value_gen) is a non-leaf node in T. leaves(data-element, value_gen) defines the set of leaf nodes descendant of the value_gen in T.*

For instance, according to the taxonomy reported in Figure 2, if (*Order date*, "*June 2010*") is a generalized item, the item (*Order date*, "*2010-06-10*") is one of its corresponding leaf nodes.

Since the generalized association rule mining process is typically driven by well-known quality indexes, e.g., support and confidence (Agrawal and Srikant, 1994), in order to define the generalized itemset support we first introduce the concept of generalized itemset matching.

**Definition 6 (Generalized itemset matching).** *Let <N, E, r> be an XML document and T be a taxonomy over items in <N, E, r> given a transac-*

*Figure 2. A taxonomy over order date items*

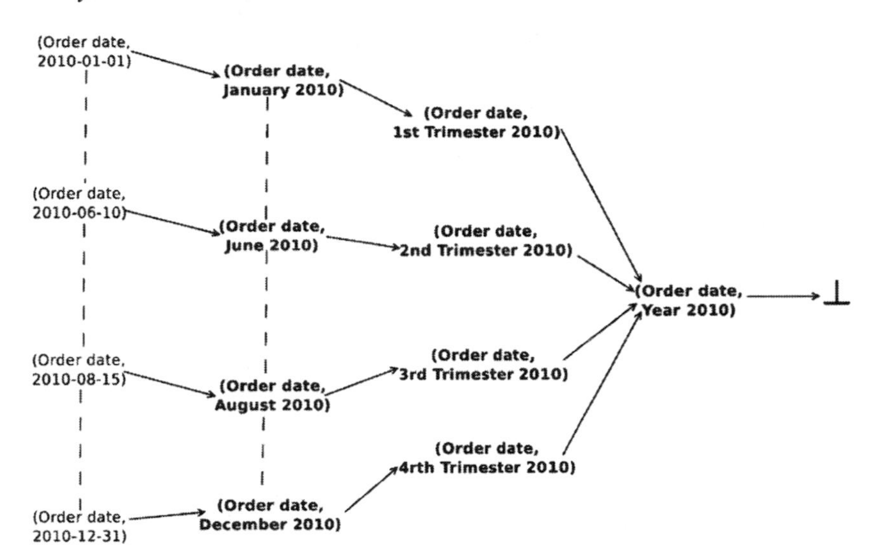


*tion root* $t_r \in N$. *A generalized itemset X matches an arbitrary transaction t in <N, E, r> if and only if each (possibly generalized) item (data-element, value_gen)* $\in X$:

- is a leaf node of $T$ and (*data-element, value_gen*) $\in t$, or
- is a non-leaf node of $T$ and there exists a node $i \in$ *leaves*($X$) such that $i \in X$.

The support of an itemset is defined as the observed frequency of an itemset into the XML document. Analogously, the support of a generalized item may be counted by summing the frequency of all leaf items in the XML document defined by the taxonomy including it.

**Definition 7 (Support of a generalized item).** *Let <N, E, r> be an XML document and T be a taxonomy over items in a transactional dataset D. Let (data-element, value_gen) be a generalized item. The support of (data-element, value_gen) is the sum of the (observed) frequencies of leaves(data-element, value_gen) in <N, E, r>.*

A generalized itemset may include both items and generalized items. Consider again the taxonomy reported in Figure 2. For instance, the itemset {(*Customer key*, "*10*"), (*Order date*, "*June 2010*")} is a generalized itemset and matches transactions containing both items (*Customer key*, "*10*") and (*Order date*, "*2010-6-10*") while it does not match transactions containing both items (*Customer key*, "*10*") and (*Order date*, "*2010-07-20*") since the latter is not a descendant of any of its items. If the itemset matches a hundredth of the transactions belonging to the source dataset, its support is 1%.

**Definition 8 (Generalized association rule).** *Let A and B be two generalized, disjoint itemsets. A generalized association rule is represented in the form A→ B, where A and B are the body and the head of the rule, respectively.*

*A* and *B* are also respectively denoted as antecedent and consequent of the generalized rule *A*→ *B*. For example, the generalized rule (*Customer key*, "*10*") → (*Order date*, "*June 2010*") represents a co-occurrence relationship among two itemsets of length 1 (Agrawal & Srikant, 1994; Agrawal & Srikant, 1995). Generalized association rule discovery is commonly driven by minimum rule support and confidence thresholds (Agrawal & Srikant, 1994), whose formal definitions follow.

**Definition 9 (Generalized association rule support).** *Let <N, E, r> be an XML document and A→ B be a generalized association rule. Its support is defined as the ratio s(A ∪ B) / |<N, E, r>|, where s(A ∪ B) is the support of the generalized itemset A ∪ B in <N, E, r> and |<N, E, r>| is the number of transactions in <N, E, r>.*

In general, support represents the prior probability of the generalized itemset *A* ∪ *B*, i.e., its observed frequency in the XML document.

**Definition 10 (Generalized association rule confidence).** *Let A→ B be a generalized association rule. Its confidence is defined as s(A ∪ B) / s(A).*

The confidence of a rule *A*→ *B* is the conditional probability of the generalized itemset *B* given the generalized itemset *A*. For example, the generalized rule {(*Customer key*, "*10*")→ (*Order date*, "*June 2010*")} *(support = 10%, confidence = 50%)* means that a specific customer, identified by his/her identification key "*10*", frequently submitted its orders in June 2010. The observed frequency of the rule over the XML document is 1% as the itemset {(*Customer key*, "*10*"), (*Order date*, "*June 2010*")} matches a hundredth of its transactions (cf. Definition 6). Confidence equal to 50% means that half of the time the customer submits his/her order in the specified time period (e.g., June 2010).

Given an XML document, a transaction root, a taxonomy, a minimum support threshold, and a minimum confidence threshold, the mining process discovers all the generalized association rules satisfying both constraints. The taxonomy drives the generalization process to discover a higher level knowledge through more abstract yet valuable correlations among data items.

## THE XML-GERMI FRAMEWORK

In this section, we present the XML-GERMI (XML Generalized Rule MIner) framework with the two-fold aim to efficiently discover generalized rules from XML documents and efficiently query the mined knowledge. The framework may be exploited to extract more abstract and valuable knowledge from XML data in different application domains (e.g., context-aware applications, market basket analysis, and network traffic analysis). Furthermore, the extracted knowledge can be efficiently queried to support decision making.

Figure 3 shows the building blocks of XML-GERMI, which mainly performs three activities:

1. **XML data pre-processing.** XML data to be analyzed is cleaned by removing irrelevant and redundant information as well as tailored to a transactional data format.
2. **Generalized association rule miner.** The rule mining block performs the extraction

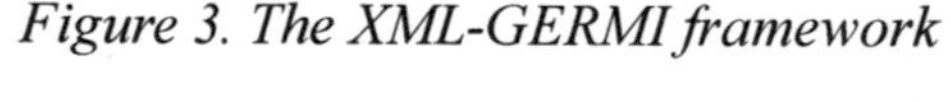
*Figure 3. The XML-GERMI framework*

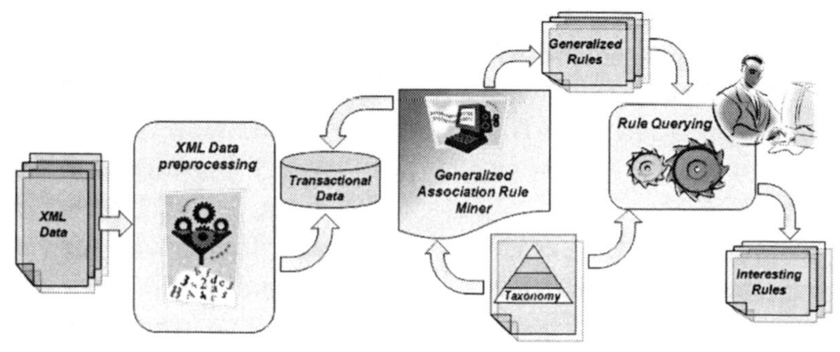

of generalized association rules through the evaluation of the input taxonomy. The mining activity can also be driven by different quality indexes (e.g., support, confidence, lift (Tan, Kumar, & Srivastava, 2002)) to reduce the knowledge space. Different generalized rule miners might be easily integrated into the framework. Currently, two implementations are available in the XML-GERMI framework: our implementation of a traditional generalized rule mining algorithm named *Cumulate* (Agrawal & Srikant, 1995), and a slight variation of the *GenIO* algorithm proposed in (Baralis et al., 2010).

3. **Rule querying.** Since end-users are often interested in efficiently exploiting the extracted knowledge during decision making, mined generalized rules are stored in an XML data repository, which may be queried by means of the XQuery language to efficiently retrieve only the interesting knowledge.

## XML Data Preprocessing

Due to their high manageability, mostly used mining algorithms to extract (generalized) association rules consider collections of transactions. To make our framework highly flexible and to take advantage of all the improvements achieved by data mining algorithms on transactional data, we first tailor XML data to a transactional data format. According to Definition 2, the transaction root is appropriately selected from the labeled tree. Each subtree of the transaction root is identified as a transaction. The item representation for data items yields a single item when the XML element contains a single data value. When the XML element has a textual content, the number of generated items depends on the semantic content of the element. The textual content can be considered either as a single data value (e.g., the order date in Figure 1) or a multiple value element (e.g., comments about orders in Figure 1). In the first case a single item is defined; in the second case, for each word of the element content, a couple (*data-element, value*) yields an item. Since in the textual data management many research efforts have been devoted to efficiently mining textual data, we integrated two functions to process textual elements in the XML data preprocessing, namely stopword removal (i.e., removal of very frequent and, possibly, noisy words) and word stemming (i.e., reduction of words to their lexical stem) (Porter, 1980; Porter, 1997).

Consider the tree reported in Figure 1, which represents a part of the order XML file. The order XML file is composed of a set of orders. In this case, the transaction root is the element "*Orders*", and each of its subtrees is a transaction. After preprocessing, the first subtree is represented by the following transaction:

```
{(Order/ O_Key, "1"), (Order/O_Prior-
ity, "Low"), (Order/O_Date, "2016-06-
20"), (Order/O_Customer/O_Comments/O_
Comment, "Acknowledgement of receipt
requested"), (Order/O_Customer/O_
Comments/O_Comment, "Fragile"),
(Order/O_Customer/O_CustKey, "10")}
```

One transaction composed of items (*data-element, value*) is generated for each subtree of the transaction root. Notice that *data-element* includes the full path for the transaction root to the considered element. This allows for distinguishing two different elements with the same label. Once the data have been transformed into a set of transactions, rules can be mined by using traditional itemset and rule mining algorithms.

## Generalized Association Rule Miner

This block takes as input the user-provided taxonomy, the transformed XML data, and some mining constraints (e.g., minimum support and confidence thresholds). It discovers the generalized association rule set satisfying the enforced constraints. To prevent discarding relevant but infrequent knowledge, the itemset generalization process of XML-GERMI is driven by a taxonomy defined over data items of interest. The taxonomy should be composed of aggregation hierarchies (e.g., the order date taxonomy reported in Figure 2) defined on most relevant data items. The user is asked to provide meaningful aggregations of items belonging to the transactional data into higher level concepts. Indeed, the user may be supported by domain experts to manually construct its own hierarchy based upon generalized concepts of interest, or trigger the automatic taxonomy construction over transactional data items through an existing taxonomy generation algorithm (e.g., (Clifton et al., 2004; Ienco & Meo, 2008)) and, next, validate its soundness with respect to its actual needs. The high flexibility of the XML-GERMI framework enables its use into a wide range of different application contexts in which meaningful taxonomies may be devised (e.g., network traffic analysis, context-aware profiling).

The mining task follows the usual two-step approach (Agrawal & Srikant, 1994): extraction of the frequent generalized itemsets, and generation of the corresponding generalized rules; since the first step is considered the most computationally intensive knowledge extraction task (Agrawal & Srikant, 1994), several algorithms, e.g., (Agrawal & Srikant, 1995; Han & Fu, 1999; Baralis et al., 2010) have been proposed to effectively perform this task. Next, generalized association rules may be mined by applying any traditional rule mining algorithm on the extracted itemsets. The flexibility of the framework allows for easily integrating any itemset mining algorithms that would better satisfy the analyst needs. Currently, in the XML-GERMI framework two different generalized itemset mining algorithms, among the ones available in the literature, have been integrated: the *Cumulate* algorithm, a traditional exhaustive generalized rule miner (Agrawal & Srikant, 1995), and the *GenIO* algorithm, a recently proposed support-driven approach to generalized itemset mining (Baralis et al., 2010). To perform rule generation, the XML-GERMI embeds our implementation of the Apriori rule mining algorithm (Agrawal & Srikant, 1994), hereinafter referred to as *Rule-Gen*. The main features of the aforementioned algorithms as well as main required modifications to successfully integrate the algorithms into the XML-GERMI framework are described in the following.

## Cumulate

Cumulate is a traditional generalized itemset mining algorithm proposed in (Agrawal & Srikant, 1995). It takes as input the dataset, a taxonomy, and a minimum support threshold, and extracts all the frequent generalized itemsets satisfying a minimum support constraint. Cumulate itemset mining step is based on the Apriori algorithm enriched by an exhaustive taxonomy evaluation (i.e., it extracts itemsets for all levels of the taxonomy) to produce generalized patterns as well.

Cumulate is a level-wise algorithm that, at each iteration, generates only the frequent, possibly generalized, itemsets of a given length. At arbitrary iteration *k*, three steps are performed: (1) *candidate generation*, in which all possible *k*-itemsets are generated from (*k*-1)-itemsets, (2) *taxonomy evaluation*, to trigger knowledge aggregation, and (3) *candidate generalized itemset support counting* through database scan. Once candidate itemsets of an arbitrary length are generated, in the second step a generalized version of those candidates is generated by evaluating the taxonomy. Finally, only those generalized itemsets that exceed the minimum support threshold are kept.

A pseudo-code that describes the generalization process of a (generalized) itemset is reported in Algorithm 1. The algorithm takes as input two parameters: a (generalized) itemset *it* and a taxonomy *T*. The generalization of an itemset *it* is performed by generalizing each item *i* belonging to *it* (lines 2-4). An item is generalized by climbing up the taxonomy stepwise (function *generalize_item*(*i*,*T*) in line 3). Since every ancestor node of *i* in the

*Algorithm 1. TaxonomyEvaluation*

```
Input: (generalized) itemset it, taxonomy T
Output: all generalizations Comb

1: Gen_items = ∅
2: for each item i in it do
3:   Gen_items = Gen_items U generalize_item(i, T)
4: end for
5: Comb = generate_comb(Gen_items)
6: return Comb
```

taxonomy is an item generalization, taxonomy climbing stops when the root of the taxonomy node is reached. All the itemsets obtained by replacing one or more items in *it* with their generalized versions are generalized itemsets of *it*. Indeed, the generalization of an itemset *it* may produce a set of generalized itemsets (line 5). The complete set of mined generalized itemsets is returned.

Consider, for example, the following itemset: {(*Customerkey,"10"*),(*Orderdate,"20/06/2010"*)} *(support=1%)*. Suppose that items characterized by the *Order date* data-element may be aggregated according to the taxonomy reported in Figure 2, while no aggregation hierarchy is available for items characterized by the *Customer key* data-element. Thus, the taxonomy evaluation described in Algorithm 1, may produce the two following generalized itemsets:

1. {(*Customer key, "10"*), (*Order date, "June 2010"*)} *(support=10%)*
2. {(*Customer key, "10"*), (*Order date, "2nd Trimester 2010"*)} *(support=27%)*

As expected, they are characterized by an increasingly higher support as they represent knowledge at a higher level of abstraction. More abstract correlations, like itemset (2), are characterized by a higher support than their respective descendants, e.g., itemset (1), because they aggregate a greater amount of knowledge in a single itemset.

However, the *Cumulate* algorithm may generate a possibly huge mined set, which might become unmanageable by domain experts. A post-pruning phase is often applied to prune redundant itemsets, and select only the interesting ones. However, this approach has a high computational complexity, especially when the mining process is driven by a low support threshold.

**Generalized Itemset Discoverer.** The *GenIO* algorithm (Baralis et al., 2010) discovers generalized itemset mining by performing a lazy user-provided taxonomy evaluation to drive the generalization process. Unlike *Cumulate*, instead of performing an exhaustive frequent generalized itemset extraction for all levels of the taxonomy followed by post-pruning, the *GenIO* algorithm performs a support-driven opportunistic itemset aggregation. More specifically, generalized itemsets are extracted only if items at a lower level in the taxonomy are below the support threshold (i.e., lazy taxonomy evaluation). Thus, *GenIO* may reach a good trade-off between itemset specialization and aggregation.

The pseudo-code of *GenIO* is reported in Algorithm 2. The *GenIO* algorithm takes as input a dataset *D* (i.e., a transformed XML dataset), a taxonomy *T*, and a minimum support threshold *s*. Analogously to *Cumulate*, the *GenIO* algorithm is based on Apriori, thus it is a level-wise algorithm that at each iteration generates all frequent itemsets of a given length. At arbitrary iteration *k*, two steps are performed: *candidate generation*, the most computationally and memory intensive step, in which all possible *k*-itemsets are generated from (*k*-1)-itemsets, and *candidate pruning*, which is based on the property that all subsets of frequent itemsets must also be frequent, to discard candidate itemsets which cannot be frequent. Actual candidate support is counted by scanning the dataset. Candidate *k*-itemsets that do not fulfill the minimum support threshold are not considered in the (*k*+1)-candidate generation. Furthermore, *GenIO* handles rare itemsets by lazily evaluating the taxonomy *T* (lines 7-10). Once the support of each candidate itemset in $C_k$ has been computed (line 7), generalized versions of infrequent ones are generated by evaluating the taxonomy (line 8) and inserted in the *Gen* set (line 9). The taxonomy evaluation procedure is the same one adopted in *Cumulate* and reported in Algorithm 1. It is lazily triggered to produce high level patterns having at least an infrequent descendant.

Next, infrequent (generalized) candidate $k$-itemsets are pruned. *GenIO* extracts both the frequent non-generalized itemsets and the set of generalized itemsets representing the generalization of the knowledge associated to infrequent non-generalized itemsets.

Consider again the following itemset: {(*Customer key*, "*10*"), (*Order date*, "*20/06/2010*")} *(support=1%)*. If the minimum support threshold is equal to 2%, then the pattern is infrequent and its generalization is triggered analogously to *Cumulate*. On the contrary, if the support threshold is equal to 0.5%, then the original pattern becomes frequent, thus its generalization is prevented since it does not provide any additional information with respect to its descendants. This support-driven approach to generalization prevents redundant knowledge extraction and reduces the mined knowledge set.

Since the original *GenIO* implementation (Baralis et al., 2010) only deals with relational data structures, we properly extended its implementation to the more general transactional data format. Accordingly, we generalized the notion of taxonomy built over data attributes by allowing the usage of multiple aggregations over a single (generalized) item as well. In particular, we generalized the concept of aggregation hierarchy over a specific data attribute by binding each taxonomy node to the corresponding couple (*data-element, value*), in which the attribute name corresponds to a specific data-element in the relational data format, and enabling multiple aggregations over a single item.

The new taxonomy definition complies with the one reported in Definition 4. This allows for generalizing the original version of the taxonomy evaluation procedure proposed in *GenIO* to the more general one proposed in Algorithm 1.

## RuleGen

The *RuleGen* algorithm generates the high-confidence generalized rules given the complete set of

*Algorithm 2. GenIO*

```
Input: minimum support min_sup, taxonomy T, XML transactional dataset D
Output: set L of generalized frequent itemsets

 1: k = 1, L = ∅
 2: C_1 = set of items in D
 3: repeat
 4:   scan D and count support for each c ∈ C_k
 5:   GenItemsets = ∅ // generalized itemset container
 6:   for all c ∈ C_k do
 7:     if support of c <min_sup then
 8:       newGenItemsets = TaxonomyEvaluation(T, c)
 9:       update GenItemsets with newGenItemsets
10:     end if
11:   end for
12:   if GenItemsets ≠ ∅ then
13:     scan D and count support for each itemset in GenItemsets
14:   end if
15:   L_k = {itemsets in C_k ∪ GenItemsets whose support ≥ min_sup}
16:   k = k + 1
17:   C_k = candidateGeneration(L_k-1)
18: until C_k ≠ ∅
19: return L
```

frequent generalized itemsets. Thus, it performs the second step of the rule mining step based on the Apriori algorithm. The Apriori rule generation algorithm (Algorithm 3) uses a level-wise approach for generating association rules, where each level corresponds to the number of items that belong to the rule consequent. Initially, all the high-confidence rules, i.e., rules that satisfy a minimum confidence constraint (cf. Definition 10), that have only one item in the rule consequent are extracted. These rules are used to generate new candidate rules. Since confidence of rules generated from the same itemset satisfies the anti-monotone property, candidate rules of length $k$ are generated by merging two ($k$-1)-length rules that share the same prefix in the rule consequent (Agrawal & Srikant, 1994). The pseudo-code of the rule generation algorithm is reported in Algorithm 3.

We adopted our implementation of the Apriori algorithm in which rule mining is constrained by a minimum confidence threshold (cf. Definition 10) to reduce the amount of generated rules. However, many different rule quality indexes may be easily integrated as well (e.g., lift (Tan et al., 2002)).

## Rule Querying

Analyst is commonly asked to perform generalized rule set querying tailored to his/her interest and to the type of analysis he/she is performing. Since XML is a widespread language to exchange data we use XML to store both the mined generalized rules and the taxonomy generated by our XML-GERMI framework. This allows use both to more easily share the mined knowledge with other systems and to exploit the powerfulness of XQuery language to query the mined rules.

In this section, we first describe the schemas of the XML files used to store rules and taxonomies. Then, we show some examples of queries that can be useful for selecting a subset of interesting rules from the complete mined rule set.

The DTD reported in Figure 4 describes the schema of the XML documents used to represent the mined rule set. Each mined generalized rule is represented by means of a (complex) rule element. Each rule element includes a body and a head element, respectively representing the rule antecedent and consequent. Both the body and the head elements are composed of items, where each

*Algorithm 3. Apriori RuleGen*

**Input:** frequent itemsets $F$, minimum rule confidence *min_conf*
**Output:** set of generated rules

1: **for all** frequent itemsets $f_k$ ($k \geq 2$) **do**
2: $H_1 = \{i \mid i \in f_k\}$
3: *ap-genrules*($f_k$, $H_1$)
4: **endFor**

procedure **ap-genrules**($f_k$, $H_m$)
1: $k = \mid f_k \mid$
2: $q = \mid H_m \mid$
3: **if** $k > q+1$ **then**
4: $H_{m+1}$ = apriori_gen($H_m$)
5: **for all** $h_{m+1} \in H_{m+1}$ **do**
6: *confidence* = *support*($f_k$) / *support*($f_k$ - $h_{m+1}$)
7: **if** *confidence* ≥ *min_conf* **then**
8: **output** the rule ($f_k$ - $h_{m+1}$) → $h_{m+1}$
9: **else**
10: **delete** $h_{m+1}$ from $H_{m+1}$
11: **endIf**
12: **endFor**
13: ap-genrules($f_k$, $H_{m+1}$)
14: **endIf**

item is a pair (*elementName, elementValue*). Each rule can also be characterized by a set of measure elements. Each measure element is composed of the name of the measure and its corresponding value. An example XML document that represents a rule set including two rules is reported in Figure 5.

XML is used in the XML-GERMI framework to represent the analyst-provided taxonomy as well. This allows for jointly querying the mined rule set and the taxonomy, thus enabling more complex and potentially useful queries. The taxonomy is stored by means of XML files conformed to the DTD schema reported in Figure 6. Each item represented in the taxonomy is characterized by an element name and an element value (cf. Definition 4). Optionally, an item may also be characterized by a set of child nodes (represented by the *listOfChildren* element). A child node represents a child of the current item in the taxonomy. Each child item may in turn be parent of other items (i.e., it may be a generalization of set of items).

*Figure 4. DTD of the XML documents used to store generalized association rules*

```
<?xml version="1.0" encoding="UTF-8"?>
<!ELEMENT ruleSet (rule*)>
<!ELEMENT rule (measure+, body, head)>
<!ELEMENT measure (#PCDATA)>
<!ATTLIST measure name CDATA #REQUIRED>
<!ELEMENT body (item+)>
<!ATTLIST body length CDATA #REQUIRED>
<!ELEMENT head (item+)>
<!ATTLIST head length CDATA #REQUIRED>
<!ELEMENT item EMPTY>
<!ATTLIST item elementName CDATA #REQUIRED
                    elementValue CDATA #REQUIRED>
```

*Figure 5. An example XML document representing a rule set composed of two generalized rules*

```
<ruleSet>
  <rule>
    <measure name="support">10.4</measure>
    <measure name="confidence">90</measure>
    <body length="1">
      <item elementName="user">Paolo</item>
    </body>
    <head length="2">
      <item elementName="place">Italy</item>
      <item elementName="university">Polytechnic of Turin</item>
    </head>
  </rule>
  <rule>
    <measure name="support">9.1</measure>
    <measure name="confidence">31.0</measure>
    <body length="1">
      <item elementName="user">Luca</item>
    </body>
    <head length="1">
      <item elementName="place">Turin</item>
    </head>
  </rule>
</ruleSet>
```

*Figure 6. DTD of the XML document used to store taxonomies*

```
<?xml version="1.0" encoding="UTF-8"?>
<!ELEMENT taxonomy (item+)>
<!ELEMENT item (elementName, elementValue, listOfChildren*)>
<!ATTLIST item elementName CDATA #REQUIRED
                 elementValue CDATA #REQUIRED>
<!ELEMENT listOfChildren (item+)>
```

Figure 7 reports part of a taxonomy representing an aggregation defined over geographical locations (*city*→ *state* → *region*) and an aggregation defined over items characterized by element "*university*" depending on the type of university (*university* → *type of university*).

By exploiting the XML representations of both the rule set and the taxonomy, the analyst can perform a wide range of different queries. For example, the analyst can select all rules in which a specific item or one of its generalizations appear. The query reported in

*Figure* 8 selects all the rules including the item (*place*, "*Turin*") or any of its generalizations. The first condition of the *where* clause checks whether the currently pointed item is the searched one.

*Figure 7. An example XML document representing a taxonomy defined over items including "place" and "university" elements*

```
<?xml version="1.0" encoding="UTF-8"?>
<taxonomy>
  <item elementName="place" elementValue="Europe">
    <listOfChildren>
      <item elementName="place" elementValue="Italy"/>
        <listOfChildren>
          <item elementName="place" elementValue="Turin"/>
          <item elementName="place" elementValue="Milan"/>
        </listOfChildren>
      <item elementName=" place" elementValue="France"/>
        <listOfChildren>
          <item elementName="place" elementValue="Paris"/>
          <item elementName="place" elementValue="Gap"/>
        </listOfChildren>
        ......
    </listOfChildren>
  </item>
  <item elementName="place" elementValue="America">
    <listOfChildren>
      <item elementName="place" elementValue="USA"/>
        <listOfChildren>
          <item elementName="place" elementValue="New York"/>
          ......
        </listOfChildren>
        ......
    </listOfChildren>
  </item>

  <item elementName="university" elementValue="PublicUniversity">
    <listOfChildren>
      <item elementName=" university" elementValue="Polytechnic of Turin"/>
      <item elementName=" university" elementValue="Polytechnic of Milan"/>
    </listOfChildren>
  </item>
  <item elementName="university" elementValue="PrivateUniversity">
    <listOfChildren>
      <item elementName=" university" elementValue="Bocconi University"/>
      .....
    </listOfChildren>
  </item>
  ........
</taxonomy>
```

Differently, the second part of the *where* clause verifies if the item (*place, "Turin"*) is a child of the currently pointed item (i.e., if the rule contains a generalization of the searched item). If one of the two conditions is satisfied, the current rule is selected. The files *MinedRules.xml* and *Taxonomy.xml* represent the extracted generalized rules and the exploited taxonomy respectively.

The query reported in Figure 8 is a simple introductory example of how the rule set and the taxonomy can be jointly queried to select specific rules of interest. More complex queries, involving different items and more complex operators, may easily be expressed by means of the XQuery language.

## EXPERIMENTAL EVALUATION

To assess the effectiveness of the proposed approach, in this section we report and describe experiments performed on both real and synthetic datasets. For each dataset, we analyze the number and the characteristics of the mined generalized rules. We also discuss the applicability and the usefulness of some of the mined rules from an end-user (analyst) point of view. Moreover, we thoroughly analyze the impact of the main parameter of the mining step, i.e., the minimum support threshold, on both the cardinality of the mined rule set and the quality of the extracted knowledge. To perform generalized itemset extraction we used our implementation of the *GenIO* (Baralis et al., 2010) and *Cumulate* (Agrawal & Srikant, 1995) mining algorithms. We also used our implementation of the Apriori algorithm (Agrawal & Srikant, 1994) to perform the rule set generation. Experiments were performed on a 3.0 GHz Intel Xeon system with 34 GB RAM, running Ubuntu 2.6.

### Evaluated Datasets

In Table 1, the main characteristics of the XML datasets exploited in the experimental session are reported. We used datasets characterized by different sizes in terms of number of transactions, file size, number of elements, and number of leaf nodes of the input XML files.

TPC-H is a suite of synthetic datasets generated from the TPC-H relational tables (TPC-H, 2005). We saved the generated relational tables in XML format. The TPC-H benchmark consists

*Figure 8. Selection of the rules including the item (place, "Turin") or any of its generalizations*

```
<resultSet> {
for $item in doc("MinedRules.xml")/ruleSet/rule//item
        let $children := doc("Taxonomy.xml")//item[@elementName=$item/@elementName and
        @elementValue=$item/@elementValue]
where $item[@elementName="place" and @elementValue="Turin"] or
        exists($children//item[@elementName="place" and @elementValue="Turin"])
return <rule> <body> { $item/../../body } </body> <head> { $item/../../head } </head> </rule>
} </resultSet>
```

*Table 1. Dataset characteristics*

| Dataset File | | Size (MB) | Description | Number of elements | Number of leaf nodes | Number of transactions |
|---|---|---|---|---|---|---|
| TPC-H 250 | *Orders* | 518 MB | order table in XML (1.0 scale factor) | 9 | 13,500,000 | 1,5000,00 |
| | *Part* | 59 MB | part table in XML (1.0 scale factor) | 8 | 160,000 | 20,000 |
| UCI | *Adult* | 10 MB | Census data | 15 | 488,415 | 32,561 |

of a synthetic data generator and a suite of business oriented ad-hoc queries. The queries and the data populating the database were chosen to have broad industry-wide relevance. By varying the scale factor parameter of the synthetic data generator, XML files with different sizes can be generated. We used the TPC-H data generator to generate large datasets (up to about 500 MB), and an UCI dataset to validate the usefulness of the mined generalized rules in a real-life context. For the TPC-H dataset, the *records* element was defined as transaction root (i.e., each record is a transaction). The UCI datasets include real-life data coming from different application domains; for example, the *Adult* dataset includes census data.

## Analyst-Provided Taxonomies

For each dataset, a taxonomy was defined by a domain expert. The provided taxonomies are exploited during the mining step to generalize infrequent items and itemsets. For the sake of uniformity, taxonomies provided by domain experts are denoted as "analyst-provided taxonomies" in the rest of the paper. We exploited the following analyst-provided taxonomies for the considered datasets.

### Orders Dataset

This represents orders performed by customers. Each order is characterized by 9 elements: an order identifier (Orderkey), its status (Orderstatus), the identifier of the customer who submitted the order (Custkey), its order date (OrderDate), its priority (OrderPriority), its shipping priority (ShipPriority), the clerk who managed the order (Clerk), the total price of the order (TotalPrice), and a comment (Comment). As reported in Table 1, the number of orders (i.e., number of transactions) is equal to 1,500,000. Hence, the generated tree, related to the XML file, is characterized by more than 13,000,000 leaf nodes; however, our approach is able to efficiently mine itemsets and rules of such an order of magnitude.

To allow an in-depth analysis on the orders depending on the place in which customers reside, a hierarchy was defined on the customer element of the orders dataset. The hierarchy is composed of 3 levels and aggregates customers depending on the place where they reside. By means of the defined hierarchy, customers can be aggregated in nations (e.g., "Italy") and nations in continents (e.g., "Europe"). The exploited hierarchy is hence represented by the following order: *Customer* → *Nation* → *Continent*. On the other elements any hierarchy has been defined.

### Part Dataset

This includes all the types of products that can be sold by a company. Each part is characterized by the following 8 elements: product key (PartKey), name (PartName), brand (PartBrand), type (PartType), size (PartSize), type of container (PartContainer), price (PartPrice), and comment (PartComment).

Each part is characterized by a brand and each brand is related to one manufacturer, while each manufacture can produce many brands. To allow an in-depth analysis on the number of parts depending on the manufacturer the domain expert proposed to define a hierarchy over the *brand* element. Each value of the brand element is generalized into the corresponding manufacturer. In such a way, the hierarchy is composed of the two following levels: *Brand* → *Manufacturer*.

### UCI Adult Dataset

The *Adult* dataset includes census data. For each people 15 characteristics are available. Each characteristic is stored by means of an XML element. The available elements span from age to marital status. For each people elements related to his/her education, occupation, marital status, race, sex, and many other census data are available.

A domain expert defined a taxonomy on four of the elements of the *Adult* dataset. In particular, the taxonomy over the items characterized by elements education, marital status, native country, and workclass has been devised. Specific values of each element are aggregated in higher level values as follows.

```
Education (1st grade,.., 12th grade,
Bachelors, Masters, Doctorate, Pre-
school) → No-College/College/Post-
College
Marital status (Divorced, Civil mar-
ried, Church married, Separated, Wid-
owed) → Married/Non-Married
Native country → Continent (Europe/
America/Asia/Oceania/Africa)
Work class (Never worked, Self-em-
ployed, Federal government employ,..)
→ Employed/Unemployed
```

For the other elements any meaningful hierarchies can be defined. Hence, the other elements are considered during the mining phase but any generalization is defined on them.

## Generalized Rule Mining

Given the analyst-provided taxonomies, the generalized rule mining process is performed. By performing generalized rule mining, domain expert finds himself to deal with a valuable set of correlations extracted from the XML data.

For all datasets, we performed a set of experiments by setting the minimum support threshold to different values and by considering the taxonomies previously described. A set of interesting generalized rules was obtained for all datasets and for all enforced minimum support thresholds.

Consider, as a representative example, the *Orders* dataset. By enforcing a minimum support threshold equal to 10% one of the mined generalized rules is the following: {(*Customer*, "*America*")} → {(*Ship priority*, "*0*")} *(support=20%, confidence=100%)*. The extracted itemset indicates that customers located in the American continent are always characterized by a ship priority equal to 0 (i.e., "high priority"). This information may be profitably exploited by clerks of the shipping department to organize the order's shipping depending on the customer's residence. Since both single customers and single nations are not frequent from their own, the generalization process performed by XML-GERMI allows for coming by interesting rules about American customers starting from the raw XML dataset. Without taxonomy evaluation, knowledge about single customers is not mined from the order table when the minimum support threshold is set to 10%. If lower minimum support threshold values are enforced (e.g., 1%), the customer membership nations become frequent, and hence lower level generalized itemset are mined. For example, two of the mined generalized rules are the following.

```
{(Customer, "Argentina"} → {(Ship
priority, "0")} (support=3.96%, con-
fidence=100%)
{(Customer, "United States of Ameri-
ca")} → {(Ship priority, "0")} (sup-
port=3.99%, confidence=100%)
```

Similar patterns are mined from other nations as well. The mined rules show a link between customer membership nation and ship-priority. With respect to the previous rule (the one representing the correlation between the American customer continent and the ship-priority value), in such a case a more detailed information is available.

If *Cumulate* is used to mine generalized itemsets by enforcing a minimum support threshold equal to 1%, even the high level generalized itemset {(*Customer*, "*America*")} → {(*Ship priority*, "*0*")} is mined since it satisfies the enforced minim support constraint. In contrast to *Cumulate*, *GenIO* does not mine such a rule because the single nations of the American continent are already frequent from their own with respect to the minimum support threshold (1%). Hence, the more general itemsets including item (*Customer*, "*America*") are considered redundant, and their generation is prevented.

Depending on the application domain, the XML-GERMI framework end-user may arbitrarily choose among *GenIO* and *Cumulate* to tailor the mined rule set to his/her own interests.

We also analyzed the rules mined by our framework from the *Adult* dataset. Analogously to the results obtained from the TPC-H datasets, the availability of the input taxonomy allows for mining also high level information, such as rules related to regions (e.g., "Europe") when the rules related to single status are not frequent, or other high level information (e.g., "married/non-married", "college/no-college"). The following are two of the rules mined from the *Adult* dataset by setting the minimum support threshold to 10%.

*{(Education, "no-college")} → {(Salary, "<=50.000$")} (support=39%, confidence=87%)*
*{(Education, "college")} → {(Work class, "employee")} (support=38%, confidence=86%)*

The two rules indicate high-level correlations between the educational level of the analyzed people and their salary or their employment status. Without any aggregation over the education element, no rules involving education and salary (or education and work class) are mined, because there are too many different education grades and any of them is characterized by a support lower than 10%. On the other hand, by aggregating the education grades into two high grained grades ("*college*" and "*no-college*") useful knowledge is mined by XML-GERMI.

## Effect of the Minimum Support Threshold

Minimum support threshold enforcement heavily affects both the complexity and the quality of the rule mining process. We analyzed the impact of the minimum support threshold on the number of extracted rules. In Figures 9 and 10, we respectively report the number of extracted rules for *Orders* and *Part* datasets; since the real-life *Adult* dataset is characterized by a similar trend, its results are not reported.

Similarly to traditional rule mining, even in the case of generalized rule mining the cardinality of the mined rule set increases when the

*Figure 9. Orders dataset: Number of rules*

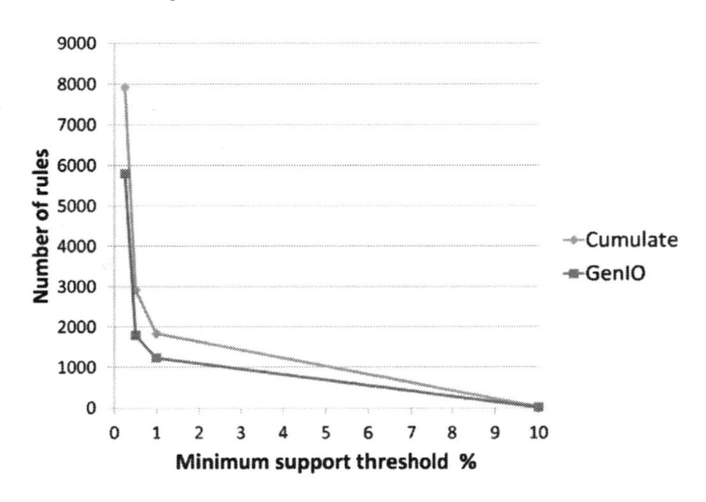

Figure 10. Part dataset: Number of rules

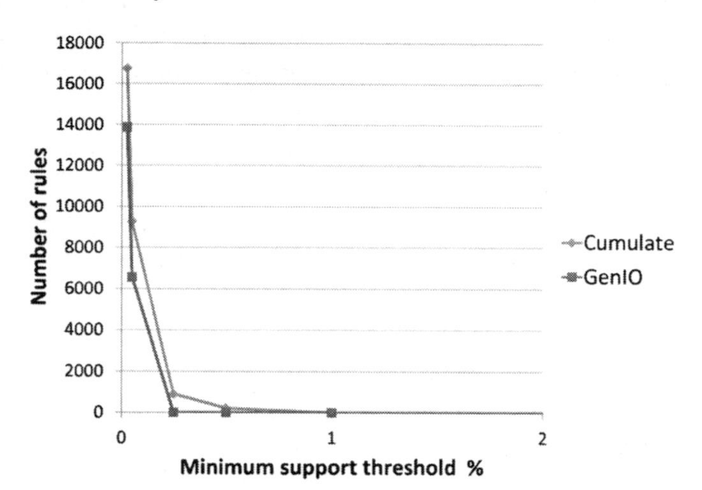


minimum support threshold decreases. In particular, the number of mined rules significantly increases when low support thresholds are enforced (e.g., lower than 0.5%).

By enforcing a high minimum support threshold (e.g., 10%), the majority of the mined rules is composed of generalized items (i.e., rules including at least one generalized item) for all the considered datasets. When a high support value is enforced, low level items are infrequent and only high level generalized items (and hence the rules composed of high level items) are frequent. Indeed, the availability of a taxonomy allows for mining interesting knowledge also when a high support threshold value is enforced. By contrast, when low values of the minimum support threshold are enforced a significant fraction of lower level items also becomes frequent, thus the fraction of generalized rules decreases with respect to the total number of mined rules.

As discussed in the previous sections, the set of generalized rules mined by *GenIO* is a subset of the generalized rules extracted by *Cumulate*. The difference between the two approaches is more evident when the majority of the low level rules are frequent (i.e., when low support threshold values are enforced). Since low level rules are frequent, *GenIO* does not generate (some of) their generalization because they do not provide more knowledge than that provided by non-generalized rules. In the extreme case, when all the possible non-generalized rules are frequent, *GenIO* mines exclusively non-generalized rules (i.e., it mines the same rules mined by a traditional non-generalized rule mining algorithm), while *Cumulate* anyway generates all the possible generalized rules.

## FUTURE RESEARCH DIRECTIONS

The widespread use of XML across the Web has guided the development of novel and ad-hoc techniques for both managing and mining XML data. Many research communities have significantly contributed to improve XML data representation, storage, and mining. The widespread exploitation of XML-based applications has prompted the development of methodologies, techniques, and systems to effectively and efficiently manage and analyze XML data. This has increasingly attracted the attention of different research communities, including database, information retrieval, pattern recognition, and data mining, from which several interesting approaches have been proposed to address research issues in XML data management and knowledge discovery.

Within the context of data mining and knowledge discovery from XML data, in this chapter we proposed a framework which entails generating generalized rule extraction driven by a user-provided taxonomy. The proposed approach can be extended in a number of directions, including: the automatic, or semi-automatic, inference of taxonomies from XML data, the inference of XML schema relationships by means of association rule mining, and the extension of XML frequent tree mining algorithms to generalized tree mining algorithms.

One input of our framework is a user-provided taxonomy that is exploited to generalize items to generate generalized itemsets and generalized rules. Taxonomies are representations of is-a relationships between concepts belonging to a given domain knowledge. Usually, the taxonomy is provided by a domain expert. Since the taxonomy creation process is a complex work, automatic or semi-automatic taxonomy generation algorithms would be needed. Some techniques are already available for the inference of ontologies (Lau et al., 2009); however, a general approach for automatic or semi-automatic taxonomy generation is not available. A possible direction in the context of XML data could be the application of well-founded data mining techniques (e.g., association rule mining, dependency discovering) to effectively support the discovering of most relevant is-a relationships hidden in both XML content and schema. The inference of is-a relationships between elements of XML documents could be exploited to create part of a possible taxonomy. A human validation is probably necessary to assess the soundness of the automatically inferred relationship. However, the validation of a potential taxonomy is easier than the creation from scratch of a taxonomy, and hence the automatic suggestion of a possible taxonomy is an interesting task.

Another interesting direction not already exploited in the context of XML data is the inference of schema relationships (i.e., dependency between XML elements) useful to identify key constraints or functional dependencies. This knowledge could be used to perform schema normalization. Our framework could be extended to extract schema relationships by appropriately changing the pre-processing module to deal with XML document schema (elements and attributes) and not on the content.

Finally, tree and graph mining algorithms could be used in the mining block of our framework to mine trees and graphs directly from XML data. However, current tree and graph mining algorithms do not take into consideration taxonomy and generalized items. The same advantages obtained by mining generalized association rules instead of traditional generalized rules, could be obtained by mining "generalized" trees and graphs. However, graph mining is already a complex and expensive task. The introduction of generalization in the current graph mining algorithms will significantly impact on the execution time of the mining process. Hence, new approaches are needed to early prune useless generalized trees during the mining phase.

## CONCLUSION

In this chapter we discussed the problem of generalized association rules from XML data by thoroughly describing the XML-GERMI framework. Generalized rules provide a high level representation of the analyzed data. They highlight interesting correlations at different levels of abstraction by exploiting a taxonomy built over XML data elements. The XML-GERMI framework provides a high flexibility in rule extraction from XML data by allowing the integration of any generalized rule mining algorithm. To effectively support end-users in exploring the extracted knowledge, mined patterns are stored in an XML data repository that can be queried by means of the XQuery language. The effectiveness of XML-GERMI in discovering higher level and interesting correlations has been experimentally evaluated on both real and synthetic datasets.

## REFERENCES


Agrawal, R., & Srikant, R. (1994). Fast algorithms for mining association rules in large databases. In J. B. Bocca, M. Jarke, & C. Zaniolo (Eds.), *Proceedings of the 20th International Conference on Very Large Data Bases (VLDB),* (pp. 487-499). Morgan Kaufmann.

Agrawal, R., & Srikant, R. (1995). Mining generalized association rules. In U. Dayal, P. M. D. Gray, & S. Nishio (Eds.), *Proceedings of the 21th International Conference on Very Large Data Bases (VLDB),* (pp. 407-419). Morgan Kaufmann.

Baldi, M., Baralis, E., & Risso, F. (2005). Data mining techniques for effective and scalable traffic analysis. In A. Clemm, O. Festor, & A. Pras (Eds.), *Proceedings of the International Symposium on Integrated Network Management* (pp. 105-118). IEEE Computer Society.

Baralis, E., Cagliero, L., Cerquitelli, T., D'Elia, V., & Garza, P. (2010). Support driven opportunistic aggregation for generalized itemset extraction. In *Proceedings of the 5th IEEE International Conference on Intelligent Systems* (pp. 102-107). IEEE Computer Society.

Baralis, E., Cagliero, L., Cerquitelli, T., Garza, P., & Marchetti, M. (2009). Context-aware user and service profiling by means of generalized association rules. In J. D. Velasquez, S. A. Rios, R. J. Howlett, & L. C. Jain (Eds.), *Proceedings of the 13th International Conference on Knowledge-Based and Intelligent Information & Engineering Systems (KES) Lecture Notes in Computer Science: Vol. 5712* (pp. 50-57). Springer.

Baralis, E., Garza, P., Quintarelli, E., & Tanca, L. (2004). Summarizing XML data by means of association rules. In W. Lindner, M. Mesiti, C. Turker, Y. Tzitzikas, & A. Vakali (Eds.), *Current Trends in Database Technology - EDBT Workshops Lecture Notes in Computer Science: Vol. 3268* (pp. 459-462). Springer.

Braga, B., Campi, A., Ceri, S., Klemettinen, M., & Lanzi P. L. (2003). Discovering interesting information in XML data with association rules. In *Proceedings of the ACM Symposium on Applied Computing (SAC),* (pp. 450-454). ACM.

Baralis, E., Garza, P., Quintarelli, E., & Tanca, L. (2007). Answering XML queries by means of data summaries. *ACM Transactions on Information Systems, 25*(3), 1–33. doi:10.1145/1247715.1247716

Brin, S., & Page, L. (1998). The anatomy of a large-scale hypertextual web search engine. *Computer Networks and ISDN Systems, 30*(1-7), 107-117.

Buneman, P., Davidson, S. B., Fan, W., Hara, C. S., & Tan, W. C. (2001). Reasoning about keys for XML. In G. Ghelli, and G. Grahne (Eds.), *Proceedings of the 8th International Workshop on Database Programming Languages (DBPL) Lecture Notes in Computer Science: Vol. 2397* (pp. 133-148). Springer.

Chang, E., Dillon, T. S., Feng, L., & Weigand, H. (2003). An XML-enabled association rule framework. In *Proceedings of the 14th International Conference on Database and Expert Systems Applications, Lecture Notes in Computer Science: Vol. 2736* (pp. 88-97). Springer.

Clifton, C., Cooley, R., & Rennie, J. (2004). TopCat: Data mining for topic identification in a text corpus. *IEEE Transactions on Knowledge and Data Engineering, 16*(8), 949–964.

Consens, M. P., & Mendelzon, A. O. (1990). GraphLog: A visual formalism for real life recursion. In *Proceedings of the 9th ACM Symposium on Principles of Database Systems (PODS),* (pp. 404-416). ACM.

Damiani, E., Oliboni, B., Quintarelli, E., & Tanca, L. (2003). Modeling semistructured data by using graph-based constraints. In Meersman, R., & Tari, Z. (Eds.), *On The Move to Meaningful Internet Systems 2003: OTM Workshops, Lecture Notes in Computer Science* (*Vol. 2889*, pp. 20–21). Springer. doi:10.1007/978-3-540-39962-9_9

Dillon, T. S., & Feng, L. (2004). Mining interesting XML-enabled association rules with templates. In *Proceedings of the 3rd International Workshop on Knowledge Discovery in Inductive Databases (KDID)* [Springer.]. *Lecture Notes in Computer Science, 3377*, 66–88.

Ding, Q., & Sundarraj, G. (2006). Association rule mining from XML. In S. F. Crone, S. Lessmann, & R. Stahlbock (Eds.), *Proceedings of the 2006 International Conference on Data Mining (DMIN),* (pp. 144-152). CSREA.

Gates, S. C., Teiken, W., & Cheng, K.-S. F. (2005). Taxonomies by the numbers: Building high-performance taxonomies. in O. Herzog, H.-J. Schek, N. Fuhr, A. Chowdhury, & W. Teiken (Eds.), *Proceedings of the ACM International Conference on Information and Knowledge Management (CIKM),* (pp. 568-577). ACM.

Han, J., & Fu, Y. (1999). Mining multiple-level association rules in large databases. *IEEE Transactions on Knowledge and Data Engineering, 11*(5), 798–805. doi:10.1109/69.806937

Han, J., Pei, J., & Yin, Y. (2000). Mining frequent patterns without candidate generation. In W. Chen, J. F. Naughton, & P. A. Bernstein (Eds.), *Proceedings of the ACM International Conference on Management of Data (SIGMOD),* (pp. 1-12). ACM.

Hatzivassiloglou, V., Gravano, L., & Maganti, A. (2000). An investigation of linguistic features and clustering algorithms for topical document clustering. In N. J. Belkin, P. Ingwersen, & M.-K. Leong (Eds.), *Proceedings of the 23rd ACM Conference on Research and Development in Information Retrieval (SIGIR),* (pp. 224–231). ACM.

Hovy, E., & Lin, C. (1999). Automated text summarization in SUMMARIST. In I. Mani, & M. T. MayBury (Eds.), *Advances in automatic text summarization* (pp. 81-94). Cambridge, MA: The MIT Press.

Ienco, D., & Meo, M. (2008). Towards the automatic construction of conceptual taxonomies. In I.-Y. Song, J. Eder, & T. M. Nguyen (Eds.), *Proceedings of the 10th International Conference on Data Warehousing and Knowledge Discovery (DaWaK) Lecture Notes in Computer Science: Vol. 5182* (pp. 327-336). Springer.

Imieliński, T., & Virmani, A. (1999). MSQL: A query language for database mining. *Data Mining and Knowledge Discovery, 3*(4), 373–408. doi:10.1023/A:1009816913055

Jiménez, A., Berzal, F., & Cubero, J. C. (2010). POTMiner: Mining ordered, unordered, and partially-ordered trees. *Knowledge and Information Systems, 23*(2), 199–224. doi:10.1007/s10115-009-0213-3

Kuramochi, M., & Karypis, G. (2004). An efficient algorithm for discovering frequent subgraphs. *IEEE Transactions on Knowledge and Data Engineering, 16*(9), 1038–1051. doi:10.1109/TKDE.2004.33

Lau, R. Y. K., Song, D., Li, Y., Cheung, T. C. H., & Hao, J.-X. (2009). Toward a fuzzy domain ontology extraction method for adaptive e-learning. *IEEE Transactions on Knowledge and Data Engineering, 21*(6), 800–813. doi:10.1109/TKDE.2008.137

Meo, R., Psaila, G., & Ceri, S. (1996). A new SQL-like operator for mining association rules. In T. M. Vijayaraman, A. P. Buchmann, C. Mohan, & N. L. Sarda (Eds.), *Proceedings of the International Conference on Very Large Data Bases (VLDB),* (pp. 122-133). Morgan Kaufmann.

Michalski, R. S., & Stepp, R. E. (1983). Automated construction of classifications conceptual clustering versus numerical taxonomy. *IEEE Transactions on Pattern Analysis and Machine Intelligence, 5*(4), 396–410. doi:10.1109/TPAMI.1983.4767409

Mohammadzadeh, R. A., Soltan, S., & Rahgozar, M. (2006). Template guided association rule mining from XML documents. In L. Carr, D. De Roure, A. Iyengar, C. A. Goble, & M. Dahlin (Eds.), *Proceedings of the 15th International Conference on World Wide Web (WWW),* (pp. 963-964). ACM.

Newman, M. E. J. (2001). Clustering and preferential attachments in growing networks. *Physical Review E: Statistical, Nonlinear, and Soft Matter Physics, 64*(2). doi:10.1103/PhysRevE.64.025102

Ou, S., Khoo, C. S. G., & Goh, D. H. (2005). Constructing a taxonomy to support multi-document summarization of dissertation abstracts. *Journal of Zhejiang University, 6A*(11), 1258-1267.

Paik, J., Lee, J. C., Nam, J., & Kim, U.-M. (2007). Mining maximally common substructures from XML trees with lists-based pattern-growth method. In Y. Wang, Y.-M. Cheng, Q. Zhang, & P. S. Wang (Eds.), *International Conference on Computational Intelligence and Security (CIS),* (pp. 209-213). IEEE Computer Society.

Paik, J., Youn, H. Y., & Kim, U.-M. (2005). A new method for mining association rules from a collections of XML documents. In O. Gervasi, M. L. Gavrilova, V. Kumar, A. Laganà, H. P. Lee, Y. Mun, D. Taniar, & C. J. K. Tan (Eds.), *Proceedings of the International Conference Computational Science and Its Applications (ICCSA) Lecture Notes in Computer Science: Vol. 3481* (pp. 936-945). Springer.

Papakonstantinou, Y., Garcia-Molina, H., & Widom, J. (1995). Object exchange across heterogeneous information sources. In P. S. Yu, and A. L. P. Chen (Eds.), *Proceedings of the 11th International Conference on Data Engineering (ICDE),* (pp. 251-260). IEEE Computer Society.

Paredaens, J., Peelman, P., & Tanca, L. (1995). G-Log: A declarative graph-based query language. *IEEE Transactions on Knowledge and Data Engineering, 7*(3), 436–453. doi:10.1109/69.390249

Park, J. S., Chen, M. S., & Yu, P. S. (1997). Using a hash based method with transaction trimming for mining association rules. *IEEE Transactions on Knowledge and Data Engineering, 9*(5), 813–825. doi:10.1109/69.634757

Porter, M. F. (1997). An algorithm for suffix stripping. In Jones, K. S., & Willet, P. (Eds.), *Readings in information retrieval* (pp. 313–316). San Francisco, CA: Morgan Kaufmann Publishers Inc.

Pramudiono, I., & Kitsuregawa, M. (2004). FP-tax: Tree structure based generalized association rule mining. In I. Pramudiono, & M. Kitsuregawa (Eds.), *Proceedings of the 9th ACM Workshop on Research Issues in Data Mining and Knowledge Discovery (DMKD),* (pp. 60-63). ACM.

Tan, P., Kumar, V., & Srivastava, J. (2002). Selecting the right interestingness measure for association patterns. In *Proceedings of the ACM International Conference on Knowledge Discovery and Data Mining (KDD),* (pp. 32-41). ACM.

Tan, P., Steinbach, M., & Kumar, V. (2006). *Introduction to data mining.* Addison-Wesley.

Tao, L., & Sarabjot, S. A. (2009). Exploiting domain knowledge by automated taxonomy generation in recommender systems. In T. Di Noia, and F. Buccafurri (Eds.), *Proceedings if the 10th International Conference on E-Commerce and Web Technologies (EC-Web) Lecture Notes in Computer Science: Vol. 5692* (pp. 120-131). Springer.

Termier, A., Rousset, M., Sebag, M., Ohara, K., Washio, T., & Motoda, H. (2008). DryadeParent, An efficient and robust closed attribute tree mining algorithm. *IEEE Transactions on Knowledge and Data Engineering, 20*(3), 300–320. doi:10.1109/TKDE.2007.190695

TPC-H. (2005). *The TPC benchmark H.* Transaction Processing Performance Council. Retrieved March 15, 2005, from http://www.tpc.org/tpch/default.asp

Uno, T., Kiyomi, M., & Arimura, H. (2004). LCM ver. 2: Efficient mining algorithms for frequent/closed/maximal itemsets. In R. J. Bayardo Jr., & B. Goethals (Eds.), *Proceedings of the IEEE ICDM Workshop on Frequent Itemset Mining Implementations (FIMI),* (pp. 32-41). CEUR-WS.org.

Wan, W. W. J., & Dobbie, G. (2004). Mining association rules from XML data using XQuery. In J. M. Hogan, P. Montague, M. K. Purvis, & C. Steketee (Eds.), *Australian Workshop on Data Mining and Web Intelligence (ACSW Frontiers),* (pp. 169-174). Australian Computer Society.

Washio, T., & Motoda, H. (2003). State-of-the-art of graph-based data mining. *SIGKDD Explorations, 5*(1), 59–68. doi:10.1145/959242.959249

World Wide Web Consortium OWL. (2010). *OWL: Web ontology language*. Retrieved July 15, 2010, from http://www.w3.org/TR/owl-features

XQuery. (2010). *An XML query language*. Retrieved September 1, 2010, from http://www.w3.org/TR/xquery

Yan, X., & Han, J. (2002). gSpan: Graph-based substructure pattern mining. In V. Kumar, S. Tsumoto, N. Zhong, P. S. Yu, & X. Wu (Eds.), *IEEE International Conference on Data Mining (ICDM),* (pp. 721-724). IEEE Computer Society.

Yin, Z., Li, R., Mei, Q., & Han, J. (2009). Exploring social tagging graph for web object classification. In J. F. Elder IV, F. Fogelman-Souliè, P. A. Flanch, & M. J. Zaki (Eds.), *Proceedings of the 15th ACM International Conference on Knowledge Discovery and Data Mining (KDD),* (pp. 957-966). ACM.

Zaki, M. J. (2002). Efficiently Mining frequent trees in a forest. In *Proceedings of the 8th ACM International Conference on Knowledge Discovery and Data Mining (KDD),* (pp. 1021-1035). ACM.

Zaki, M. J. (2005). Efficiently mining frequent trees in a forest. Algorithms and applications. *IEEE Transactions on Knowledge and Data Engineering, 17*(8), 1021–1035. doi:10.1109/TKDE.2005.125

Zamir, O., Etzioni, O., Madani, O., & Karp, R. M. (1997). Fast and intuitive clustering of web documents. In D. Heckerman, H. Mannila, & D. Pregibon (Eds.), *Proceedings of the 3rd International Conference on Knowledge Discovery and Data Mining (KDD),* (pp. 287–290). AAAI Press.

## ADDITIONAL READING

Arenas, M., & Libkin, L. (2004). A Normal Form for XML Documents. *ACM Transactions on Database Systems, 29*(1), 195–232. doi:10.1145/974750.974757

Baralis, E., Garza, P., Quintarelli, E., & Tanca, L. (2007). Using Mined Patterns for XML Query Answering. In Poncelet, P., Masseglia, F., & Teisseire, M. (Eds.), *Successes and New Directions in Data Mining* (pp. 39–66). Idea Group Inc. doi:10.4018/978-1-59904-645-7.ch003

Braga, B., Campi, A., Klemettinen, M., & Lanzi, P. L. (2002). Mining Association Rules from XML Data. In Y. Kambayashi, W. Winiwarter, and W. Arikawa (Eds.), *Proceedings of the International Conference on Data Warehousing and Knowledge Discovery (DaWaK): Vol. 2454. Lecture Notes in Computer Science* (pp. 21-30). Springer.

Braga, D., Campi, A., & Ceri, S. (2005). XQBE (XQuery By Example): A Visual Interface to the Standard XML Query Language. *ACM Transactions on Database Systems, 30*(2), 398–443. doi:10.1145/1071610.1071613

Ceri, S., Augurusa, E., Braga, D., & Campi, A. (2003). Design and Implementation of a Graphical Interface to XQuery. In *Proceedings of the ACM Symposium on Applied Computing (SAC),* (pp. 1163-1167). ACM.

Ceri, S., Hunt, E., Ives, Z. G., Rys, M., Bellahsene, Z., & Unland, R. (Eds.). (2005). *XSym. Database and XML Technologies, 3rd International XML Symposium.* Springer.

Chang, E., Tan, H., Dillon, T. S., Feng, L., & Hadzic, F. (2005). X3-Miner: Mining Patterns from XML Database. In *Proceedings of the 6th International Conference on Data Mining, Text Mining and their Business Applications* (pp. 287-296).

Dhillon, I. S., & Modha, D. S. (2001). Concept Decompositions for Large Sparse Text Data Using Clustering. *Machine Learning*, *42*(1/2), 143–175. doi:10.1023/A:1007612920971

Goethals, B. (2004). Implementation of the Apriori rule mining algorithm. Retrieved March 1, 2010, from http://adrem.ua.ac.be/~goethals.

Goethals, B., & Zaki, M. J. (2004). Advances in Frequent Itemset Mining Implementation: Report on FIMI'03. *SIGKDD Explorations Newsletter*, *6*(1), 109–117. doi:10.1145/1007730.1007744

Han, J. (2009). Data Mining. In Liu, L., & Tamer, M. (Eds.), *Encyclopedia of Database Systems* (pp. 595–598). Springer, US.

Hofmann, T. (1999). The Cluster-abstraction Model: Unsupervised Learning of Topic Hierarchies from Text Data. In T. Dean (Ed.), *Proceedings of the International Joint Conference on Artificial Intelligence (IJCAI)* (pp. 682-687). Morgan Kaufmann.

Khaing, M. M., & Them, N. (2006). An Efficient Association Rule Mining For XML Data. In *Proceedinga of the SICE-ICASE International Joint Conference* (pp. 5782-5786). Morgan Kaufmann.

Mazuran, M., Quintarelli, E., & Tanca, L. (2009). Mining Tree-based Frequent Patterns from XML. In T. Andreasen, R. R. Yager, H. Bulskov, H. Christiansen, and H. L. Larsen (Eds.), *Proceedings of the 8th International Conference on Flexible Query Answering Systems (FQAS): Vol. 5822. Lecture Notes in Computer Science* (pp. 287-299). Springer.

Neshati, M., & Hassanabadi, L. S. (2007). Taxonomy Construction Using Compound Similarity Measure. In R. Meersman, & Z. Tari (Eds.), *Proceedings of the OTM Confederated International Conference On the Move to Meaningful Internet Systems: Vol. 4803. Lecture Notes in Computer Science* (pp. 915-932). Springer.

Psaila, G. (2008). Virtual DOM: An Efficient Virtual Memory Representation for Large XML Documents. In A. M. Tjoa, and R. R. Wagner (Eds.), *Proceedings of the 19th International Workshop on Database and Expert Systems Applications (DEXA Workshops),* (pp. 233-237). IEEE Computer Society.

Sanderson, M., & Croft, W. B. (1999). Deriving Concept Hierarchies from Text. In F. Gey, M. Hearst, and R. Tong Tarra (Eds.), *Proceedings of the ACM Conference on Research and Development in Information Retrieval (SIGIR),* (pp. 206–213). ACM.

Segal, E., Koller, D., & Ormoneit, D. (2001). Probabilistic Abstraction Hierarchies. In Dietterich, T. G., Becker, S., & Ghahramani, Z. (Eds.), *Advances in Neural Information Processing Systems 14 (NIPS)* (pp. 913–920). The MIT Press.

Woon, W. L., & Madnick, S. E. (2009). Asymmetric Information Distances for Automated Taxonomy Construction. *Knowledge and Information Systems*, *21*(2), 91–111. doi:10.1007/s10115-009-0203-5

World Wide Consortium XML. (2010). Extensible Markup Language (XML) 1.0 (Second Edition) W3C Recommendation. Retrieved July 15, 2010 from http://www.w3.org/xml.

Yang, Y., Xia, Y., Chi, Y., & Muntz, R. R. (2004). CMTreeMiner: Mining both Closed and Maximal Frequent Subtrees. In H. Dai, R. Srikant, and C. Zhang (Eds.), *Proceedings of the 8th Pacific Asia Conference on Knowledge Discovery and Data Mining (PAKDD): Vol. 3056. Lecture Notes in Computer Science* (pp. 63-73). Springer.

Zhang, J., Ling, T. W., Bruckner, R. M., Tjoa, A. M., & Liu, H. (2004). On Efficient and Effective Association Rule Mining from XML Data. In F. Galindo, M. Takizawa, and R. Traunmuller (Eds.), *Proceedings of the 15th International Conference on Database and Expert Systems Applications (DEXA): Vol. 3180. Lecture Notes in Computer Science* (pp. 497-507). Springer.

Zhang, S., Zhang, J., Liu, H., & Wang, W. (2005). XAR-Miner: Efficient Association Rules Mining for XML Data. In A. Ellis, and T. Hagino (Eds.), *Proceedings of the 14th International World Wide Web Conference (WWW)*, (pp. 894-895). ACM.

# Section 4
# Semantics-Aware Mining

# Chapter 14
# XML Mining for Semantic Web

**Rafael Berlanga**
*Universitat Jaume I, Spain*

**Victoria Nebot**
*Universitat Jaume I, Spain*

## ABSTRACT

*This chapter describes the convergence of two influential technologies in the last decade, namely data mining (DM) and the Semantic Web (SW). The wide acceptance of new SW formats for describing semantics-aware and semistructured contents have spurred on the massive generation of semantic annotations and large-scale domain ontologies for conceptualizing their concepts. As a result, a huge amount of both knowledge and semantic-annotated data is available in the web. DM methods have been very successful in discovering interesting patterns which are hidden in very large amounts of data. However, DM methods have been largely based on simple and flat data formats which are far from those available in the SW. This chapter reviews and discusses the main DM approaches proposed so far to mine SW data as well as those that have taken into account the SW resources and tools to define semantics-aware methods.*

## INTRODUCTION

XML (Bray, Paoli, Sperberg-McQueen, & Maler, 2000) has been extensively used to represent and publish semistructured data across the Web both in the academic and business communities as it provides inter-operability and a well-defined, extensible and machine-readable format. The widespread adoption of XML as the de-facto standard has prompted the development of new techniques that address the problem of XML management and knowledge discovery. Many research efforts have been directed towards mining the structure of XML documents as a way to integrate data sources based on structure similarity. As a step forward, content features borrowed from the text mining field have been introduced to enrich the process of XML mining. However, the increase in volume and heterogeneity of XML-based applications demands new analysis techniques that consider semantic features in the process of

DOI: 10.4018/978-1-61350-356-0.ch014

knowledge discovery so that more meaningful analysis can be performed.

On the other hand, the Web of Data is currently coming into existence, as opposed to the classical Web of documents, through the Linked Data effort (Bizer, Heath, & Berners-Lee, 2009). The general idea is to extend the Web by creating typed entities and links between data resources in a way that is machine-readable and the meaning (i.e., semantics) is explicitly defined. This new data model, whose representation formats rely on XML, opens a new range of challenges and opportunities in the data mining and knowledge discovery area.

The aim of this chapter is to review the literature and discuss how semantic features have been incorporated and dealt with in the process of mining complex structured and semistructured data. From the data viewpoint, we provide a state-of-the-art review on approaches focused both on mining complex semistructured data (i.e., XML sources) and SW data. We conceive SW data as both formal knowledge resources that have been created with clear and well-defined semantics (e.g., an ontology conceptualizing the human anatomy) and also structured, semistructured or unstructured data that has been a posteriori enriched with semantics (i.e., linked to a semantic knowledge resource as claimed in the Linked Data effort) through the process of semantic annotation.

We believe the integration of heterogeneous data sources into a common semantic formalism, as is OWL-DL, provides a great asset for enhancing the knowledge discovery process. We discuss all the benefits provided by ontologies and knowledge representation formalisms (e.g., OWL-DL) and claim that semantics should be taken into account during the whole mining process.

Semantics-aware mining is a very young and novel field of research. The aim of this chapter is to show how well known statistics-based techniques from artificial intelligence (e.g., clustering, association rules, etc.) can benefit from inferred information coming from logic-based approaches followed in the Semantic Web. We provide a state-of-the-art review structured according to the mining phase in which semantics is incorporated.

The chapter is organized as follows. First we introduce the motivation of integrating knowledge resources and data mining algorithms. Afterwards, we introduce the semantic web scenario which serves as the technological platform for all the semantics-aware mining methods. Taking into account this scenario, we organize and discuss the existing literature according to the mining phase in which semantics is incorporated. Finally, we give some future trends and conclusions.

## INCORPORATING BACKGROUND KNOWLEDGE TO DATA MINING PROCESSES

Data Mining (DM) processes are aimed at discovering interesting patterns (data regularities) from huge amounts of data, which can be helpful for decision-making tasks such as classification, prediction and summarization. Basically, a DM algorithm takes as input a set of objects described with a fixed set of features, which are usually derived from the data structures (e.g., database schema). Most DM algorithms require input datasets to be clean, ho mogeneous in format and semantics, noise-free, non-redundant and complete (i.e., with no missing data). As a result, DM algorithms aimed at very large-scale scenarios, are usually implemented on top of a data warehouse, which homogeneously stores data facts under a simple well-defined schema (e.g., multidimensional schemas). In (Han & Kamber, 2006), a generic architecture for analysis over large databases is presented. In the Web scenario, the concept of data warehouse is still an open issue, for Web data (e.g., XML documents) present very heterogeneous structures and contents (Pérez, Berlanga, Aramburu, & Pedersen, 2008). In the SW scenario the problem of semantic heterogeneity is alleviated thanks to the existence of ontologies for vocabulary control, although SW data is also semistructured, dynamic and incomplete. The definition of data warehouses for SW data has been recently discussed in (Nebot, Berlanga, Pérez, Aramburu, & Pedersen, 2009) and (Nebot & Berlanga, 2010b).

The output of DM algorithms consists of data patterns which are usually expressed over the feature representation space of the dataset. Traditionally, these patterns have been divided into two main groups: *descriptive* and *predictive* patterns. In the Machine Learning (ML) area these groups refer to unsupervised and supervised methods, respectively. Descriptive patterns are aimed at giving a summary of the dataset by identifying its regular patterns. The main kind of descriptive patterns are those discovered by clustering and association rules. Predictive patterns, also known as learning models, are aimed at defining features from a given input dataset (called training set or examples), which allow either classifying new objects or predicting incomplete information in other datasets with the same structure and semantics. It is worth mentioning that both descriptive and predictive patterns have a fuzzy nature, that is, there is some kind of probability associated to the pattern (e.g., classification error, rule confidence, etc.) The fuzziness of discovered patterns contrasts with the crisp nature of deductive knowledge produced by the SW representation formalisms.

Another conflicting aspect between DM and SW formalisms is that existing between the *open world assumption* (OWA) and the *closed world assumption* (CWA). The CWA states that knowledge that is not known is assumed to be false. All database deductive systems (e.g., Datalog) assume the CWA, as well the majority of the DM methods (e.g., negative examples in ML methods). However, the CWA cannot be assumed in the SW due to its dynamicity and that unknown relationships are much larger than the known ones. Thus, SW formalisms assume the OWA, and therefore, unknown relationships are considered neither false nor true.

Background knowledge has been considered of great importance for improving the effectiveness of DM algorithms. However, its application has been limited to clustering and association analysis for pruning and generalizing the discovered patterns. Predictive methods have ignored background knowledge until very recently. So far, background knowledge has been expressed as small tree-like taxonomies, which are customized to the specific dataset to be mined. In the SW scenario, background knowledge is massively provided in form of domain ontologies and triplestores. These knowledge resources can present very different expressivity levels, running the gamut from lexical-like resources like WordNet[1] to formal logic ontologies like BioPax[2] ontologies. How to take profit from these resources will be for sure a challenging issue in the DM research area.

## THE SEMANTIC WEB SCENARIO

Semantic Web technology is aimed at providing the necessary representation languages and tools to express semantic-based metadata. Prior to SW, there were several efforts to provide metadata formats to the web contents, resulting in well-known metadata formats such as Dublin-Core, whose main purpose was to improve information discovery and retrieval. However, these formats were shown to be very limited mainly due to their very poor expressivity and little web-awareness. As a result, the W3C proposed new representation formats, all relying on XML, to overcome the limitations of existing metadata formats. The main idea behind these formats is that any concept or instance used for describing a web object must be referred through a unique resource identifier (URI). Thus, the most basic way to describe an object consists in creating a link to the URI that represents the intended semantics. With the resource description framework (RDF) (Beckett & McBride, 2004), we can create more complex metadata elements allowing the representation of relationships between descriptors (e.g., triples). Additionally, the RDFS (Brikley & Guha, 2004) extension allows users to define a conformant schema for RDF descriptions. It is worth mentioning that the semantics of RDFS are quite similar to frame-based and object-oriented formalisms. The Linked Data effort is based on the previous concepts. Later on, due to the demand of more expressivity in the semantic descriptions, logic-based frameworks were proposed: formerly DAML+OIL (Horrocks, van Harmelen, & Patel-Schneider, 2001), and more recently the ontology web language (OWL) (Dean et al., 2004). In contrast to RDFS, all these languages rely on description logics, which are tractable subsets of the first order logic (FOL). In this context, metadata is governed by logic axioms over both classes and instances (assertions). Like in RDFS, logic axioms in these formats must be defined over web-based references (i.e., URIs).

## SW Formats: RDF(S) and OWL

In RDF there are three kinds of elements: resources, literals, and properties. Resources are web objects (entities) that are identified through a URI, literals are atomic values such as strings, dates, numbers, etc., and properties are binary relationships between resources and literals. Properties are also identified through URIs. The basic building block of RDF is the triple: a binary relationship between two resources or between a resource and a literal. The resulting metadata can be seen as a graph where nodes are resources and literals, and edges are properties connecting them. As an example, let *corp* be the prefix for the local symbols we use in our metadata, and let *ext1* and *ext2* be the addresses of two external ontologies from which we borrow some symbols. Table 1 shows the triples that describe a car rental agreement (shadowed triples come from external ontologies).

In this example, we have used the anonymous node *_p0001*, called blank node in RDF notation, which expresses an unknown instance of Price. Figure 1 shows the XML serialization of the triples in Table 1.

RDFS extends RDF by allowing triples to be defined over classes and properties. In this way, we can describe the schema that rules our metadata within the same description framework. In Table 2 we show an example RDFS schema.

The ontology web language (OWL) mainly differs from RDFS in the underlying semantic formalism, which is founded in description logic (DL). Like in RDFS, DLs basic elements are concepts and individuals, concepts being the intentional representation of *individuals* sets. Concepts can be defined in terms of other concepts by using a series of constructors, which can be either set-oriented (i.e., union ($\sqcup$), intersection ($\sqcap$), and complement ($\neg$)) or relation-oriented (e.g., existential ($\exists$) and universal ($\forall$) restrictions). An OWL-formatted ontology consists of a series

*Table 1. Example of RDF triples*

| Subject | Predicate | Object |
|---|---|---|
| corp#Contract112 | rdf:type | corp#RentalAgreement |
| corp#Contract112 | corp#hasPrice | corp#_p0001 |
| corp#_p0001 | corp#hasCurrency | ext2#Euros |
| corp#_p0001 | corp#amount | "100"^^xsd:"float" |
| corp#Contract112 | corp#assignment | ext1#MMT34 |
| ext1#MMT34 | rdf:type | ext1#Car |
| ext2#Euros | rdf:type | ext2#Currency |

*Figure 1. Example of RDF statement for describing a rent-a-car transaction*

```
<rdf:RDF
  xmlns:rdf="http://www.w3.org/1999/02/22-rdf-syntax-ns#"
  xmlns:xsd="http://www.w3.org/2001/XMLSchema#"
  xmlns:euc="http://my-corporation/corp#"
  xmlns:ext1="http:/assets.org/taxonomy#"
  xmlns:ext2="http:/currency.org/taxonomy#">
<rdf:Description rdf:about="corp:Contract112">
   <corp:assignment  rdf:about="ext1:MMT34"/>
   <corp:price>
        <corp:hasCurrency rdf:about="ext2:Euros"/>
        <corp:amount rdf: datatype="&xsd:float">100</corp:amount>
   </corp:Price>
</rdf:Description>
</rdf:RDF>
```

*Table 2. Example of RDFS triples*

| Subject | Predicate | Object |
|---|---|---|
| corp#RentalAgreement | rdf:type | rdfs:Class |
| corp#Agreement | rdf:type | rdfs:Class |
| corp#RentalAgreement | rdfs:subClassOf | corp#Agreement |
| corp#hasCurrency | rdf:type | rdfs:Property |
| corp#hasCurrency | rdfs:range | ext2:Currency |
| corp#assignment | rdf:type | rdfs:Property |
| corp#assignment | rdfs:domain | corp:RentalAgreement |
| corp#assignment | rdfs:range | ext1:Car |

of axioms that semantically relate classes, properties and individuals.

In DL, the set of axioms describing concepts is called TBox (Terminological Box). There are two types of assertions in the TBox, namely subsumption ($C \sqsubseteq D$), and equivalence ($C \equiv D$). As an example, the following TBox axiom describes the concept Price as an equivalence axiom:

```
Price  ≡  1hasCurrency.Currency  ⊓
1amount.Float
```

The qualifier "1" of the roles hasCurrency and amount indicates that they represent functional relations for this concept definition, that is, they are one-to-one relationships. As examples of subsumption axioms, the RentalAgreement concept can be defined as follows:

```
RentalAgreement  ⊑  Commercial-
Transaction ⊓  ∃assignment.Asset  ⊓
1hasPrice.Price RentalAgreement  ⊑
∃hasCustomer.LegalEntity
```

The set of assertions over individuals is called ABox (Assertional Box). Table 1 shows the assertions related to a rental agreement instance as triples.

Unlike RDFS, not all the axioms of the ontology are to describe the "structure" of classes, properties, and instances. Some axioms can express the business logic over the ontology concepts.

For example, the following axiom may be used to identify taxed transactions according to their currency:

$\exists$hasPrice.($\exists$hasCurrency.(Currency $\sqcap$ $\exists$usedIn$^{-}$.($\neg$EuroZone)) $\sqsubseteq$ TaxedTransaction

In this way, we can encode implicit knowledge in our descriptions, resulting in much more concise metadata. For example, by just asserting that an instance $a$ is of type $\exists$hasPrice.($\exists$hasCurrency.Dollars), we can infer that "$a$ is an object having a 'price' (an 'amount' of 'money') expressed in the 'currency' used in 'USA', and therefore it is associated to a 'taxed transaction'". Afterwards, we will introduce the inference tasks that can be performed by means of *reasoning* mechanisms.

The previous axiom can be seen as a kind of logic rule of the form "body → head", because in DL the expression $C \sqcap D \sqsubseteq A$ is equivalent to the FOL expression $\forall x\ C(x) \wedge D(x) \rightarrow A(x)$. However, in DL we cannot express rules of the form: $\forall x\ \forall y\ C(x) \wedge R(x, y) \rightarrow P(x, y)$, which can be useful to describe concepts as well as transformation rules necessary for integration tasks. For example, consider the following rule for the running example:

$\forall x\ \forall y\ RentalAgreement(x) \wedge hasCustomer(x, y) \wedge NonUECustomer(y) \rightarrow TaxedCustomer(y)$

Several extensions of OWL have been proposed to support rules, mainly the semantic web rule language (SWRL) (Horrocks et al., 2004) and the recent integration between DL and rules (Motik & Rosati, 2010). However, these languages restrict the rule syntax in order to ensure they are safe: the variables of a safe rule can be only bound to individuals named explicitly in the ontology. As a consequence, data variables are not allowed, and therefore they are not suitable for data-oriented transformations as those required in some DM methods.

## Generating Semantic Annotations

An annotation is usually conceived as a comment attached to a section of a document, or more generally, an object. Annotations may be provided in different forms and formats, ranging from links to the information resources to embed in the annotated object and also as unstructured text or with formal structures. In general terms, *semantic annotation* is conceived as the process of discovering and assigning to the entities in the text links to their semantic descriptions, which are usually defined in a knowledge base (Kiryakov, Popov, Terziev, Manov, & Ognyanoff, 2004; Reeve & Han, 2005). In principle, semantic annotation is applicable to any kind of text – web pages, text documents, text fields in databases, and so on. It can be seen as a metadata acquisition process so that data can be leveraged into a more expressive semantic level. We put special emphasis in the language used to describe the schema of the annotation since the more formal the semantics of this language the more machine-processable are the annotations.

In recent years a lot of research and development has been carried out in the area of automatic *information extraction* (IE) from Web pages, text resources, semistructured data such as HTML tables or Wikipedia infoboxes. The main goal of these approaches is to provide a comprehensive knowledge base of facts about named entities, their semantic classes and their mutual relations. Most pattern-based approaches follow the basic method outlined in (Brin, 1998). In (Kiryakov et al., 2004; Maedche, Neumann, & Staab, 2003) extraction rules arise from an initial set of tagged entities. Other relevant approaches include (Cimiano, Handschuh, & Staab, 2004) which presents a tool for automatic pattern-based annotation based on the available knowledge on the Web, Text2Onto

(Cimiano & Völker, 2005), a tool for ontology learning with improved statistical assessment of fact candidates and patterns and Omnivore (Cafarella, 2009), which aims to extract arbitrary relations from natural language texts. Moreover, most research along these lines has considered Wikipedia as key asset for the extraction of knowledge. Examples of such efforts include (Atserias, Zaragoza, Ciaramita, & Attardi, 2008), which provides semantic annotations for the English Wikipedia, DBpedia (Auer et al., 2007), which harvests RDF subject-predicate-object triples from Wikipedia and similar sources, Kylin/KOG (Weld, Hoffmann, & Wu, 2008; Wu & Weld, 2007; Wu & Weld, 2008) an ambitious work whose goal is to extract arbitrary relations from natural language texts and Wikipedia *infobox* templates and YAGO (Suchanek, Kasneci, & Weikum, 2007, 2008), which integrates relational knowledge from Wikipedia with the WordNet taxonomy. The prevalent methods under these IE tools are a combination of rule-based pattern matching, natural language processing, and statistical ML.

Although one of the goals of the previous approaches is to leverage data with semantics (similar to the goal of semantic annotation) they conceive the harvesting of knowledge in a broad, universal way. They are domain-independent in the sense that they try to capture in an automatic way as many entities as possible and link them to knowledge resources mainly to advance the functionality of search engines to a more expressive semantic level. These differences w.r.t. the specific and domain-oriented nature of data mining processes along with the lack of standards and integration with formal knowledge hinders its usage for semantic annotation.

Most of the classic IE annotation tools require a complete syntactic analysis, and in some cases, a semantic analysis too, which is usually an expensive operation not affordable for even medium-sized document collections. Methods based on manual pattern definition do not suffer from these issues, but require human effort and intervention for updating and customizing patterns to each application scenario. Finally, ML methods usually rely on training corpora, which is not always available. As an alternative to the previous approaches, in (Danger & Berlanga, 2009) a tool for the extraction of complex instances from free text on the Web is presented. The approach is based on non-monotonic processing and uses a logic-based reference ontology, entity recognizers and disambiguators, in order to adequately create and combine instances and their relations. The complementary work in (Nebot & Berlanga, 2009) enables the customized use of available knowledge resources such as thesauri or ontologies to assist in the annotation process. The method allows the user to select and build tailored and logics-enabled ontologies from large knowledge repositories.

New research possibilities may arise if we consider the semantic descriptions delivered by the previous tools as a new type of data sources susceptible of being analyzed by DM methods. Along this line of research, we can find a few approaches aimed at analyzing semantic annotations encoded in logic languages such as RDF(S) and OWL. Nebot et al., (2009) propose a multidimensional framework for analyzing semantic annotations from a logical viewpoint using ontologies. In this approach semantic annotations are based on application and domain ontologies. The user can build a multidimensional integrated ontology (MIO) containing the required analysis measures and dimensions taken from the available ontologies.

The Linked Data project (Bizer et al., 2009) has already made available several billion of RDF triples, which could also be a potential source for applying knowledge discovery methods. The Linked Open Data (LOD) captures knowledge from diverse domains and is constantly growing. However, the development of applications based on LOD datasets faces some difficulties due to the need for schema-level mapping of the datasets, since links are mainly at the instance level. The DM community could contribute in this aspect since the area of ontology mapping has been extensively studied and is a hot topic in the community.

## Storing and Querying Semantic Annotations

An RDF store, also called *triplestore*, is a database management system in charge of storing huge amounts of RDF triples as well as of providing a query language for sub-graph retrieval. As RDF data is basically graph data expressed with triples of the form "subject-predicate-object" (SPO), the query language consists of sub-graph patterns also expressed as a set of triples containing variables over any of the triple arguments. Additionally, pattern variables can be restricted by filtering expressions. SPARQL (Prud'hommeaux & Seaborne, 2008) is the query language proposed by the W3C for RDF stores. Basically, a SPARQL statement is a SELECT-FROM-WHERE expression (Figure 2).

In a SPARQL query, variables start with "?", the WHERE clause contains triple patterns and filtering expressions over variables which are separated by ".", and the SELECT clause contains the variables that will be used in the result set. Result sets are just tuples with all the bindings of the variables that satisfy the WHERE clause. Although not yet part of the W3C Recommendation, several extensions have been proposed for SPARQL, e.g., by the ARQ query engine, that make it more applicable for analytical queries, including ORDERBY, DISTINCT and GROUP-BY clauses to manage resulting tuples. While SPARQL is the most prominent, other families of query languages capable of querying semantic web data exist, including XML query languages such as XQuery (Boag et al., 2007), topic map query languages, other RDF query languages such as RQL (Karvounarakis, Alexaki, Christophides, Plexousakis, & Scholl, 2002), and OWL query languages. A detailed survey of these is found in (Bailey, Bry, Furche, & Schaffert, 2009), which also notes that a drawback of SPARQL is the weak support for schema or ontology information.

RDF stores have the main drawback of lacking a conformant schema that facilitates its physical database design and query optimization techniques. The simplest way to implement an RDF store is to create a single relational table with three columns (S-P-O) and perform queries through self-join operations. This approach is clearly inefficient for both large triplestores and large graph queries. Several optimization approaches have been proposed in the literature, which have derived to different RDF store systems. A common optimization that still maintains a generic database schema is to put long text values such as URIs and string literals into separate tables. This is done, e.g., by the well-known triplestore 3store (Harris & Gibbins, 2003). A further optimization consists of grouping triples by predicate and then creating a table for each group. Jena (Wilkinson,

*Figure 2. SPARQL query example and its graph pattern representation*

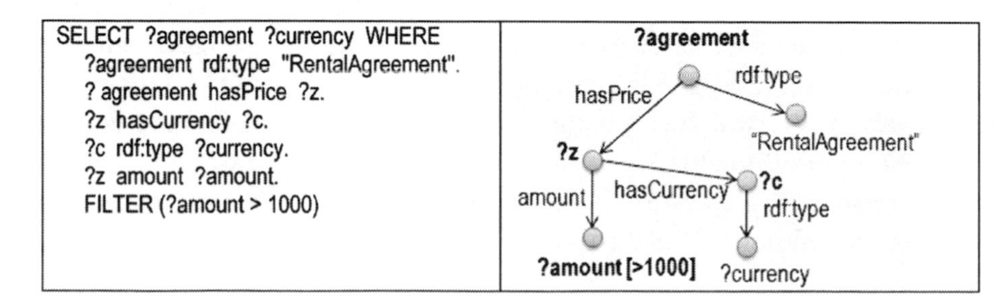

Sayers, Kuno, & Reynolds, 2003) and Sesame (Broekstra, Kampman, & van Harmelen, 2003) use this strategy in their implementations. More sophisticated ways of clustering triples have been proposed in order to facilitate the generation of materialized joint views, like in the Oracle-RDF and C-Store (Abadi, Marcus, Madden, & Hollenbach, 2007) implementations. The 3XL triplestore (Liu, Thomsen, & Pedersen, 2010) builds a specialized and optimized object-relational schema based on a supplied OWL-Lite ontology for the data in order to provide intelligent data partitioning, a strategy that proves very successful. Finally, the RDF-3X (Neumann & Weikum, 2010) and YARS2 (Harth, Umbrich, Hogan, & Decker, 2007) systems propose indexing the different SPO combinations under a B+-Tree, so that triple patterns can be solved through range queries.

The main issues addressed in query processing are the design of proper indexes for graph-pattern queries and gathering the most appropriate statistical information for join-order optimization. For the former, materialized join indexes, B+-trees and hash indexes have been proposed. For the latter, frequency statistics must go beyond S-P-O individual histograms and must take into account element co-occurrences for different graph shapes (Neumann & Weikum, 2010).

## Standard Reasoning Services

Logic-based systems can provide users with inference capabilities to manage the implicit knowledge derivable from the ontology axioms. Any inference can be expressed as $O \models \alpha$, where $\alpha$ is any axiom expressed with the same language as the ontology $O$. The typical inferences DL reasoning services usually provide are the following ones:

- Subsumption and equivalence inferences: $O \models C \sqsubseteq D$ and $O \models C \equiv D$
- Concept unsatisfiability: $O \models C \sqsubseteq \bot$
- Instance classification: $O \models C(a)$
- Instance inconsistency: $O \models \bot(a)$

Most of the DM methods regarding formal knowledge require the inferred closure of the ABox part of the knowledge base. In DL, this is called *realization*, and consists of asserting all the inferred triples, that is all the possible triples $(a, R, b)$, $(a, type, C)$ and $(b, type, D)$, such that $O \models C(a)$, $O \models D(b)$ and $O \models R(a, b)$. Notice that the ABox realization implies making explicit the transitive closure of all the transitive relationships (e.g., transitive roles and *is-a* taxonomies) and inverse roles, as well as the application of SWRL-like rules. Depending on the TBox expressiveness, this realization can be unfeasible and some kind of approximations should be done instead. Recently, in (Urbani, Kotoulas, Oren, van Harmelen, 2009; Urbani, Kotoulas, Maassen, van Harmelen, Bal, 2010) efficient methods to calculate the inferred closure for very large triplestores are proposed. These approaches are based on a map-reduce programming framework, where RDFS and a restricted subset of OWL can be expressed as *inference* rules that are executed under it.

### Reasoners

Major approaches to carry out these inferences mainly depend on the tableaux-based algorithms (Baader, 2009). A tableaux-algorithm is intended to incrementally build an ontology model (i.e., a finite interpretation of the ontology) by applying a series of transformation rules which express the semantics of each DL constructor in terms of models. Models in decidable DLs are always tree-shaped, where the branches represent relations between concepts (roles) and nodes represent interpretations of the involved concepts. Most of the popular reasoners for OWL-DL, like Pellet (Clark & Parsia, 2010), Racer (Haarslev &

Möller, 2001) and Fact++ (Horrocks, 1998), are implementations of these algorithms.

### Computational Complexity Issues

Unfortunately, most of the significant OWL1 languages proposed by the W3C (namely, OWL-DL and OWL-Lite) are actually coNP-hard in data complexity, i.e., when complexity is measured with respect to the size of the data layer only, which is indeed the dominant parameter in this context. This means that, in practice, computations over large amounts of data are prohibitively costly. A way to reduce the complexity of DLs is to impose restrictions on the ontology language, so as to guarantee that reasoning remains computationally tractable w.r.t. the TBox size. Possible restrictions that guarantee polynomial reasoning have been studied and proposed in the context of description logics, such as Horn SHIQ (Hustadt et al., 2005), EL++ (Baader, Brandt, & Lutz, 2005), DLP (Grosof, Horrocks, Volz, & Decker, 2003), and DL-Lite (Artale, Calvanese, Kontchakov, & Zakharyaschev, 2009), to mention a few.

Recently, the proposal of OWL2 (Calvanese et al., 2008; W3C, 2009) introduces three profiles aimed to perform specific reasoning tasks (e.g., classification, query/answering, etc.) with tractable computational cost, namely:

- OWL2-EL profile, which is intended to produce complete inferences in polynomial time for large terminological resources requiring a limited expressivity (e.g., life sciences ontologies),
- OWL2-QL profile, which is intended to efficiently perform queries over large databases with an expressivity equivalent to DL-Lite, and
- OWL2-RL, which is intended to make inferences over RDF (graph) data through rule-based query languages.

More details about these profiles can be found at the official W3C site. Currently, these profiles are supported by several reasoners: Mastro (previously known as QuOnto) is fully conformant to OWL2-QL, CEL (Baader, Lutz, & Suntisrivaraporn, 2006) and *snowrocket* are reasoners for the OWL2-EL profile, and systems like OWLRL (Herman, 2008) and *Jena* implement reasoners for the OWL2-RL profile.

Apart from these efforts, other recent approaches aim to implement efficient reasoners for the complete DL expressivity as well as new reasoning problems. For example, (Motik & Rosati, 2010) proposes an extension of the tableaux-algorithms, called hypertableux-algorithms, which allows reasoning with rules.

The HermiT reasoner implements this approach (Hermit, 2010).

## TOWARDS A SEMANTICS-AWARE KNOWLEDGE DISCOVERY FRAMEWORK

In this chapter we discuss the novel problem of mining semistructured data from a semantic point of view. We discuss the importance and feasibility of incorporating knowledge provided by ontologies during the whole knowledge discovery process by means of common standards and technologies emerged in the Semantic Web context.

Figure 3 shows a picture of how we conceive the DM process, where semantics is the connecting backbone. Data relevant to the study are collected from various heterogeneous sources (e.g., XML documents, databases, texts, etc). Semantics is added to the data sources through the process of semantic annotation with domain and application ontologies. Semantic annotation is the process by which data are mapped to a semantic space (which is usually represented as an ontology), and is accomplished by linking data to ontology classes and adding relationships among them.

*Figure 3. Semantics-aware knowledge discovery process*

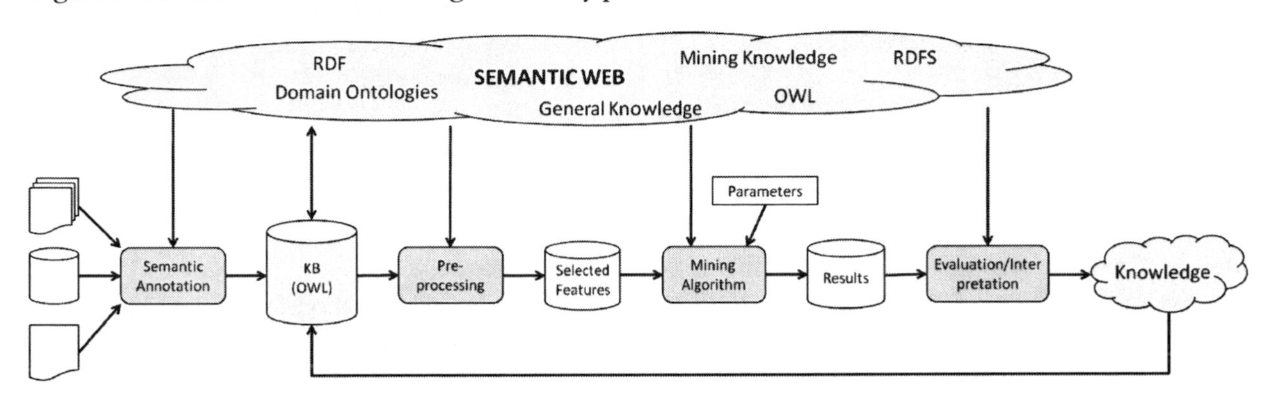


The main reason for using domain ontologies is to set up a common terminology and logic for the concepts involved in a particular domain. As a result, a large repository of semantic annotations (i.e., knowledge base) is created and the challenge of integrating heterogeneous data sources is addressed by the common semantic layer provided by the semantic annotations. As there is an upcoming trend towards moving data sources into a semantic space, we will review the literature on existing approaches and discuss the first promising results obtained for semantic annotation over both structured databases and semistructured data.

In the literature, we can distinguish three ways of exploiting knowledge during the mining process to enhance the mining results, which are: in the pre-processing phase, in the mining algorithm itself and in the interpretation phase. We will discuss the main benefits and drawbacks of each of these approaches.

The results of the mining process can be automatically formalized into the knowledge representation language used in order to enhance the knowledge base. Such a capability allows us to iteratively run the knowledge discovery process, using more complete domain knowledge after each iteration. Some approaches also emphasize ontology evolution and novelty detection.

In order to make the DM process more effective, we believe data to be mined should be integrated into a large knowledge base (KB), which consists of a triplestore concerning a specific domain (e.g., business, biomedicine, etc.) whose concepts and properties are described in a given ontology. Creating a large repository of semantic annotations has many benefits. The most obvious one is that heterogeneous sources are represented in an integrated way. Moreover, data have been abstracted from their syntactical representation into a conceptual level, where concepts along with their semantic relationships are described. Another benefit of having an integrated semantic representation of the data sources is the possibility of automatically incorporating domain knowledge or specific mining knowledge in order to exploit it during the mining process.

It is worth mentioning that Figure 3 shows a knowledge discovery framework where semantics are taken into account during the whole process. However, semantics-aware DM is a very young research field and the existing literature has mostly incorporated semantics only in some of the phases but not as the integrating factor as illustrated in the figure. Baring this in mind, we review the state-of-the-art of semantics-aware data mining of semistructured data and make a classification of the existing literature according to the data mining step in which semantics is introduced to enhance the knowledge discovery process. We distinguish the pre-processing phase, the mining phase and the interpretation phase.

## SEMANTICS-AWARE MINING OF COMPLEX DATA SOURCES

We say that a DM method is semantics-aware when it takes into account the semantics of the data during any of the mining phases, namely pre-processing, mining and post-processing. In the next section we will discuss the different semantics-aware approaches in the literature according to these three phases.

### Semantics in the Pre-Processing Mining Phase

Unlike traditional DM, in the SW scenario, the starting point is not a well-structured static data warehouse but a highly dynamic, heterogeneous and graph-like dataset. Consequently, the pre-processing phase is much more complex. We divide the pre-processing phase into three main steps: the data extraction step, the feature extraction and the feature selection step. In the former, a homogeneous, flat structured dataset is derived from the SW data, whereas in the second and third steps objects and features are defined and optionally selected to serve as input of the specific DM method to be applied.

#### Data Extraction Step

Traditional DM algorithms usually require as input data static, homogeneous and structured datasets, which contradicts the dynamic and graph-based structure of SW data. Therefore, users must define the *central entity type* (CET) to which instances subject to the analysis belong. Datasets will be then generated from the subgraph around each instance of the CET through a flattening process. However, since data have been leveraged to a conceptual level, this flattening process is guided by the semantics attached to the data, and the extracted dataset will be different from the initial relational set previous to the semantic annotation process. From the approaches of the literature, we can distinguish two main dataset extraction strategies:

1. Transaction-based methods, which aim at extracting sets of co-occurring data items within the sub-graph around each CET instance.
2. Tuple-based methods, which aim at extracting tuples that conform to a pre-defined data schema.

Methods based on transactions have the main advantage of handling the high heterogeneity of the SW data as well as missing elements, whereas methods based on tuples facilitate the definition of features by means of well-known DM methods used in relational databases.

Transaction-based methods have been defined in the context of mining highly heterogeneous XML databases (Tagarelli & Greco, 2010). In these approaches, the objective is to find *semantically* cohesive portions of XML documents so that they characterize properly the collection. In this context, semantics is defined in terms of compatible XML structures rather than the ontological perspective we propose in this chapter. Transactions can be obtained from XML documents by applying a series of interpretations about how data is structured. Thus, the lowest common ancestor (LCA) semantics (Li, Yu, & Jagadish, 2004) considers that data items should be organized under the closest common ancestor. More refined strategies are SLCA (Xu & Papakonstantinou, 2005) and that recently proposed in (Niemi, Näppilä, & Järvelin, 2009) for XML harmonization. In (Tagarelli & Greco, 2010) transactions are defined as sets of pairs (*path, data*), where each path appearing in the transaction must access a unique data item.

These approaches cannot be directly applied to SW datasets, as they consist of graphs instead of trees. In this context, (Grimnes, Edwards, & Preece, 2008) proposed the definition of *concise bounded description*, which captures a minimal *closed* RDF sub-graph around each instance of the central entity type. In this extraction approach, users must decide the optimal radius for extracting these sub-graphs. (Nebot & Berlanga, 2010a) proposed a method to extract transactions from RDF/OWL instances guided by the user information needs. The main idea is that the user specifies a *context* concept, reachable from the central entity concept, under which valid instance combinations generate the transactions. Similarly to the work of (Tagarelli & Greco, 2010), a valid combination is a set of co-occurring instances that is unique for the set of concepts participating in the DM process.

Tuple-based methods mainly rely on the specification of SPARQL queries. In (Kiefer, Bernstein, & Locher, 2008) an extension is proposed, called SPARQL-ML, which is aimed at extracting datasets that serve as input to predictive DM methods. More specifically, they propose a series of labels for the output tuples to indicate the attributes of the central entity to be considered for learning the model, and the classification target (i.e., the attribute to be predicted). Similarly, (Nebot & Berlanga, 2010a) proposes another extension of SPARQL for association mining tasks. It is worth mentioning that SPARQL queries do not account for the different structural variations the source data can present, and therefore the user must know all the possible sub-graph patterns the central entity type can involve. This problem is partially alleviated with extensions like SPARQLeR (Kochut & Janik, 2007) which allow including regular expressions over the paths between nodes in the RDF graph. In (Nebot & Berlanga, 2010a), the interpretation of the SPARQL-based pattern implicitly assumes that participating entities can be related with any kind of unique property chain.

In order to take profit from the knowledge expressed in the TBox, all the previous methods require the inferred closure of the ABox as mentioned in the previous section. Such a closure can be very expensive to obtain and can imply a high overload over the triplestore. Instead of generating the closure, other approaches are based on instance retrieval by means of, either specialized reasoners that deal with databases (e.g., Mastro for DL-Lite ontologies), or specialized compact indexes as those proposed in (Nebot & Berlanga, 2009).

## Feature Extraction Step

Once a dataset has been extracted from SW data, the next step consists in defining the feature set that will characterize each object (i.e., instance) for a particular DM method. The feature set (or feature vector) is usually a numerical summarized version of the raw data observation. Such reduced representation facilitates the mining process.

In the XML area, features for XML data are concerned with the structures and contents (tags and text) that better characterize the XML regions involved by each entity of interest. For example, in (Theobald, Schenkel, & Weikum, 2003), content features consist of pairs (*term, tf.idf*) and structural features comprise the tag names of the adjacent nodes. (Tagarelli & Greco, 2010) also considers content and structural features, but they add semantic information in the latter ones. Basically, structural features consist of paths, where each path has associated a semantic graph (synset graph), which is used in turn to bring unambiguous semantics to the involved tag names. Textual features consist of words weighted by a customized *tf-idf* and a measure of word rarity, which is related to words polysemy present in the lexical resource.

For SW data, features can be grouped in three main groups: those capturing content characteristics, those capturing structure characteristics and those capturing semantic properties of the data. Current DM approaches over SW data in the literature mainly focus on very simple structural features, basically taking the instances and data directly related to the central entity through object and data type properties. For example, in (Tresp, Huang, Bundschus, & Rettinger, 2009) the set of features consists of different combinations of the triple components (*s*, *p*, *o*), with which a matrix is built for statistical learning. In (Kiefer, Bernstein, & Locher, 2008), features consist of the attributes of the central entity plus multi-set attributes derived from the directly related instances (e.g., the ages of the members participating in a project). In (Rettinger, Nickles, & Tresp, 2009), a network of random variables is defined over the sub-graph surrounding the central entity, stating thus the variable dependencies that will be taken into account in the learning process. In (Grimnes, Edwards, & Preece, 2008), the set of features consists of the shortest paths and the values reached through them, both identified within the concise bounded descriptions of each instance.

Semantic-based features have been defined mainly in the context of clustering methods. Semantic feature vectors were proposed in (Kim & Candan, 2006) to characterize the concepts of a given taxonomy and then calculate its proximity with the cosine measure. These features were then used to cluster similar concepts in order to obtain more compact taxonomies for data summarization. More recently, (Fanizzi, d'Amato, & Esposito, 2008) proposes a semantic vector space whose components are calculated by inference over a given domain ontology. More specifically, given a set of DL concepts ($F_1$, …, $F_n$), the *i*-th component of the vector associated to the instance *a* is calculated as follows:

$$\pi_i(a) = \begin{cases} 1 & if\ O \models F_i(a) \\ 0 & if\ O \models \neg F_i(a) \\ \frac{1}{2} & otherwise \end{cases}$$

For example, instances of RentalAgreement can be characterized by the following feature vector:

```
(∃assignment.Car, ∃assignment.Book,
∃hasPrice. ∃hasCurrency.Dollar,
∃hasPrice. ∃hasCurrency.Euro)
```

The instance corp#Contract112 described in Table 1 has associated the vector (1, 0, 0, 1), whenever we have asserted that the concepts Car, Book, Euro and Dollar are disjoint pair wise. Notice that due to the OWA assumption, it is possible that we cannot infer if an assertion is either true or false. It is also worth mentioning that the inference of the negation is usually computationally expensive.

One interesting idea stemming from the ML area is that of *kernelizing* existing mining methods. The basic idea is to separate the object representation from the mining algorithm, which is especially useful for datasets with complex and heterogeneous structures. This is possible thanks to the concept of kernel function, which directly returns the inner product over (possible *unknown*) object vector spaces. Kernel functions are similarity functions that must satisfy a series of conditions to be well-defined, such as to be closed and positive semi-definite (Gärtner, Lloyd, Flach, 2004). In this way, kernelized DM algorithms can be applied to the kernel function instead of to the original dataset. Examples of algorithms that have been *kernelized* are: support vector machines (SVM) for classification, K-means for clustering and principal component analysis (PCA) for dimensionality reduction. In the case of the SW, the work of (Bloehdorn & Sure, 2007) proposes a series of kernel functions over an ontology *O*. As an example, the kernel function for measuring the semantic similarity of two instances *a* and *b* w.r.t. their common concepts is as follows:

$$K_{class}(a, b) = |\{C \in O \mid O \models C(a)\} \cap \{C \in O \mid O \models C(b)\}|$$

Other functions account for the instance similarity w.r.t. the common instances and literals they reference or are referenced by through properties, as well as a series of classical kernel functions for literal data types (e.g., integers, strings).

### Feature Selection

This technique is concerned with selecting a subset of relevant features for each object in order to reduce the computational complexity of the posterior mining algorithms. Most of the current approaches for SW data do not regard feature selection methods or dimensionality reduction techniques. This can be problematic in large domains because the number of potential features can be extremely high. For example, in the proposal of (Fanizzi, d'Amato, & Esposito, 2009) any DL expression can be part of the feature set. This implies a potentially infinite number of features if we do not limit the language grammar that generates these features.

Assuming that we have a finite set of potential features, traditional measures for weighting them can be used. Thus, (Fanizzi, d'Amato, & Esposito, 2009) proposes two measures: one based on data entropy and another based on variance of data. In (Kiefer, Bernstein, & Locher, 2008), for relational probability trees, features selected as data are partitioned using a statistical score like chi-square. Similarly, in (Danger & Berlanga, 2008) information gain is used to select those ontology named concepts that better discriminate instance data for multidimensional analysis.

## Semantics During the Mining Process

In this section, we mainly review the proposed DM approaches for analyzing SW datasets originally expressed in RDF/OWL formats.

### Clustering Methods

Most of the DM approaches that take into account semantics during the mining process are those performing clustering. This is because the notion of (dis-)similarity can accommodate easily semantic information of the objects to be compared. For example, the notion of semantic relatedness was formerly proposed in the natural language processing area to measure the similarity of two words given its synsets in WordNet. Semantic relatedness can be easily included into the similarity functions used in clustering algorithms (Tagarelli & Greco, 2010).

In the previous sections we have shown some approaches that represent objects as conceptual vectors, which can be compared with classical measures such as the cosine metric or, as proposed in (Fanizzi, d'Amato, & Esposito, 2009), a Minkowski's –like distance.

Most clustering approaches over XML and SW data have been designed as extensions of existing clustering algorithms such as K-means. The main reason is that classical clustering algorithms rely on metric spaces (usually Euclidean), which are far from the representations of SW data. For example, the notion of centroid used in K-means is very difficult to define for SW data. One solution is to adopt a kernelized version of the clustering algorithm, as mentioned in the previous section. Another solution is to apply a medoid-based clustering algorithm as proposed in (Fanizzi et al., 2009). In a medoid-based clustering approach, the problem is to determine the set of objects from the dataset that best represent the whole dataset. (Fanizzi et al., 2009) proposes a genetic algorithm to explore the search space.

### Machine Learning Methods

Most predictive DM methods do not apply background knowledge during the learning process. As previously mentioned, *kernelized* methods like the one proposed in (Bloehdorn & Sure, 2007) regard the learning and the prediction methods as black-boxes which are out of control of analysts. While this is a clear advantage with respect to applying vector-based ML algorithms to SW data, the counterpoint is that we cannot take profit from the learned model, as it is expressed in an unknown numerical space.

ML approaches such as statistical relational learning (SRL) methods, which have been recently proposed to deal with SW data, are able to take into account the background knowledge when designing the learning model. A good review can be found in (Tresp, Bundschus, & Rettinger, & Huang, 2008). Next paragraphs review some of these SRL approaches.

In the work presented in (Tresp, Huang, Bundschus, & Rettinger, 2009; Huang, Tresp, Bundschus, & Rettinger, 2010), the learning model consists of a matrix where each row represents an individual (statistical unit) and each column represents an observation over the input RDF dataset, which can be any of the combinations of the subject, predicate and object involving the corresponding individual. A cell of the matrix is initialized to 1 if the input RDF dataset contains the corresponding observation in the input dataset for the corresponding individual. The learning process consists of a matrix completion method such as singular value decomposition (SVD) or latent Dirichlet allocation (LDA). The resulting matrix provides the probability of those observations that were not present in the input dataset (e.g., missing attributes or relationships).

In (Rettinger, Nickles, & Tresp, 2009), an infinite hidden relational model is inferred from the input RDF dataset. Basically, this unsupervised method generates a set of hidden states which have associated a probabilistic distribution, which are estimated by sampling the input dataset and adjusting a series of parameters over the state-associated distributions. The resulting model induces a list of clusters over each concept and each role participating in the mining problem. One outstanding characteristic of this method is that the generated states are checked for consistency w.r.t. the ontology.

## Association Mining Methods

Background knowledge in form of concept taxonomies has been widely used in many approaches for association mining for both pruning and generalizing association rules. The former work presented in (Srikant & Agrawal, 1995) showed how to use the concept taxonomy to detect useless rules (i.e., those containing implications already stated in the taxonomy) as well as to generalize frequent itemsets and rules during the mining process. However, most of the research in this area has been focused on the post-mining phase as a means of filtering and exploring large sets of discovered rules. We will discuss these issues in the next section.

## Semantics for Interpreting the Results of the Mining Process

During the post-mining phase, the discovered patterns can be processed in different ways depending on their purposes and characteristics. In Figure 4, we show different tasks involved in the post-mining phase where domain knowledge is involved. Descriptive methods usually generate a large number of patterns that require post-processing in order to be filtered, summarized and visualized to end-users. Predictive methods produce instead learning models that are used to predict and classify data. In some cases, the learning model can be interpreted so that useful knowledge can be extracted and incorporated to the background knowledge (e.g., learning rules derived from decision trees). Notice that mining in the SW scenario has as the main goal to derive new knowledge from existing SW data so that it can be expressed and managed as the rest of the SW (i.e., using the same formats and tools as the input SW data).

*Figure 4. Semantics-aware tasks in the post-mining phase*

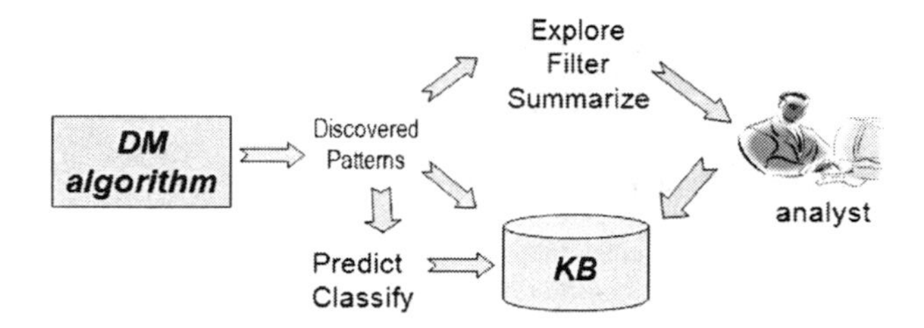


## Constraints Over Discovered Patterns

In order to manage the large amount of rules generated by association mining algorithms a series of approaches propose to filter, generalize and group the rules. Filtering through new interestingness measures like all-confidence aims at alleviating the problem of low-support thresholds usually required to capture useful rules. However, as indicated in (Liu, Hsu, Mun, Lee, 1999; Marinica & Guillet, 2010), statistical interestingness measures are not enough to both reduce the huge number of rules and to capture the user expectations about discovered rules. (Liu et al., 1999) proposed two kinds of rule matching patterns to express the user requirements, namely general impressions (*gi* patterns) and reasonably precise concepts (*rpc* patterns). These patterns regard item semantics through a pre-defined concept taxonomy, which is used to express matching elements with different detail levels. *Rpc*-patterns differ from *gi*-patterns in that they take into account the structure of the rule (i.e., the implication). As an example, consider the following patterns for the running example:

```
gi(<'ext1:Car', 'ext2:Euro',
'corp:ACMECorporation'>)
rpc(<'ext1:Car' → 'ext2:Euro')
```

Recently, (Marinica & Guillet, 2010) proposed a generalization of these patterns, called rule schemas, which allow the inclusion of concepts from an inferred taxonomy to specify matching rule elements. Furthermore, in this approach, authors propose a series of operators to apply these rule schemas in different post-mining tasks, namely filtering complying rules, and detecting unexpected rules as well as rule exceptions. For example, we can consider unexpected that the company "BookSellers Inc." is associated to commercial transactions involving "Cars", which is stated with the operator Up as follows:

```
Up(RS(<'ext1:Car'→'corp:BookSelle
rs_Inc'>)
```

## SPARQL Extensions for DM

Some approaches that apply DM to SW data have proposed extensions to SPARQL in order to store and query the discovered patterns. (Kiefer et al., 2008) proposes an extension called SPARQL-ML to specify ML problems on SW data as well as to query the resulting predictions and learned models. For this purpose, they also propose an application ontology, called mining ontology, which is used to store the parameter settings of the DM algorithms. In (Nebot & Berlanga, 2010a) a similar extension is proposed for association mining. In (Ławrynowicz, 2009) a CLUSTER-BY clause is proposed to group SPARQL results with some existing clustering algorithm. Finally, (Tresp, Huang, Bundschus, & Rettinger, 2009) proposes an extension to SPARQL for querying the probabilities of the induced relationships between instances through statistical relational learning methods. Table 3 shows two examples in our running scenario. The first one is aimed at estimating the probabilities of having transactions involving cars paid in Euros, and the second one

*Table 3. Example of SPARQL queries involving data mining tasks (the PREFIX sections are omitted)*

| SELECT ?trans WHERE<br>?trans assignment ?a.<br>?a rdf:type ''ext1:Car''.<br>?trans hasPrice ?p.<br>?p hasCurrency ''ext2:Euro'' WITH PROB ?pr.<br>ORDER BY ?pr | SELECT ?trans ?profit ?probability WHERE<br>?trans assignment ?a.<br>?a rdf:type ''ext1:Car''.<br>?trans hasCustomer ?c.<br>?c rdf:type ''corp:SpanishCorporation''.<br>(?profit ?probability)<br>sml:predict(<http://miningModels.org/transactionsPredict><br>?trans ?profit ?a ?c) |
|---|---|

is intended to predict the profit of transactions involving Spanish corporations and cars.

## Measuring the Impact of Semantics-Awareness in Results Quality

The XML data mining research community has proposed a series of large heterogeneous XML collections in order to measure both the performance and results quality of data mining algorithms (e.g., INEX competitions). Unfortunately, similar standard collections and quality assessment methods have not been proposed for semantics-aware and SW data mining. Several benchmarking collections for RDF/OWL are being proposed in the SW community, like the Lehigh University Benchmark (LUMB), but they are mainly oriented to data storage and querying tasks. As a consequence, most DM methods have been evaluated over small and specific datasets. Even so, some general conclusions can be drawn from these rather preliminary experiments. In (Tagarelli & Greco, 2010) it is shown that regarding semantics in clustering methods can improve the quality of resulting groups. In (Kiefer et al., 2008) experiments show that, in some cases, regarding inferred knowledge in the training dataset can improve the quality of classification tasks. In (Rettinger et al., 2009) it is shown that including semantic constraints during the learning process not only reduces the search space but also provides more precise statistical predictions. Despite these results, we cannot assert that inference from background knowledge usually improves DM results quality, until more comprehensive and large-scale experiments are conducted.

## FUTURE RESEARCH DIRECTIONS

Being an emerging field, DM for SW data has to address yet very challenging issues concerning the very large scale, uncertainty and implicitness of the managed information. We organize the discussion of some of these issues according to the mining phases.

Regarding the pre-processing DM step, future research must focus on more principled methods for extracting datasets and features, always guided by users' information requirements. Feature generation must be as much automated as possible also guided by users' requirements. As previously discussed, the number of potential features can be extremely high due to the different detail levels domain ontologies provide. On the other hand, existing knowledge resources must be enriched with knowledge that can be especially useful for DM methods, such as attribute discretization, summarization functions, similarity functions, and so on. It would be very valuable for the DM community to share those conceptualizations that are useful for extracting patterns in specific domain applications.

Regarding the mining phase, those methods that rely on complex (dis-)similarity or kernel functions to account for complex structures can also benefit from a more principled semantic conceptualization. Those conceptualizations could be afterwards evaluated against a series of benchmark datasets in order to assess when and how they can be effectively applied. An example of this kind of tools has been presented in (Sanz, Pérez, & Berlanga, 2008) for XML data.

With respect to the post-processing phase, three potential trends can be outlined, namely summarization, debugging, and evolution. Summarization has been shown as a good technique to manage very large RDF graphs (Zhang, Cheng, & Qu, 2007) and relational data (Yang, Procopiuc, & Srivastava, 2009). These summaries can be useful at both pre- and post-mining phases. (Danger & Berlanga, 2008) proposes a method to produce summarized OWL instances according to the user's requirements in form of multidimensional schema. Such data summaries are expressed under the same formalism as the original data so that they preserve as mush as possible their semantics. Furthermore, the ontology is enriched with metadata about which functions can be applied to each *summarizable* attribute. Another interesting trend concerning summarization is the combination of clustering and association mining algorithms, formerly introduced in (Fung, Wang, & Ester, 2003) with the Frequent Itemset based Hierarchical Clustering (FIHC). The main novelty of this algorithm is that it also provides brief descriptions for the generated clusters. Recently, Anaya-Sánchez, Pons-Porrata, and Berlanga (2010) presented another algorithm based on frequent item pairs that provides better descriptions and more homogeneous clusters than those obtained with FIHC.

Debugging consists of looking for potential errors in both the knowledge resources and mining algorithms. By comparing the induced knowledge from the ontology instances with that inferred from the ontology axioms we can detect wrong or underspecified conceptual descriptions. As an example of this kind of debugging process, (Jiménez-Ruiz, Cuenca Grau, Horrocks, & Berlanga, 2009) proposed to debug induced mappings between two ontologies by exploring the new inferences resulted from merging the ontologies and the mappings (expressed as axioms). As a result, a series of incompatible axioms between ontologies were detected as well as some errors in the golden-standard used for evaluating the mappings. Finally, the evolution trend is concerned with the capacity of a DM algorithm to manage, self-configure, or detect changes in the conceptual spaces represented by new incoming instances. One important notion in this context is that of *concept-drift*, deeply studied within DM approaches for data streams. However, in the SW context, concept-drift has been only treated in (Fanizzi et al., 2008). Concept novelty is also a relevant research issue that should be addressed in the SW scenario (Fanizzi et al., 2009).

## CONCLUSION

In this chapter we have introduced the main issues that are being addressed in a new emergent area, mining data with semantics. The eruption of the SW is producing huge amounts of semantic annotated data as well as large scale domain ontologies with inference capabilities. As a result, widely available background knowledge is now available to be exploited by current analytical tools, specifically DM methods. We classify these new methods as *semantics-aware data mining*, as they can take profit from existing knowledge at any stage of a DM process, namely pre-processing, data mining, and post-processing phases. We have introduced the main semantics-aware methods existing in the literature, and we have discussed the main results achieved so far. Although results are not yet conclusive, they are encouraging as they show potential improvements in all the mining process. Future trends we have presented in the chapter are focused on reinforcing the integration of deductive and inductive techniques which is the cornerstone of semantics-aware data mining.

## REFERENCES

W3C OWL Working Group (Eds.). (2009). *OWL 2 Web ontology language document overview*. Retrieved from http://www.w3.org/TR/owl2-overview/

Abadi, D. J., Marcus, A., Madden, S., & Hollenbach, K. J. (2007). Scalable Semantic Web data management using vertical partitioning. In C. Koch, J. Gehrke, M. N. Garofalakis, D. Srivastava, K. Aberer, A. Deshpande, D. Florescu, C. Y. Chan, V. Ganti, C.-C. Kanne, W. Klas, & E. J. Neuhold (Eds.), *Proceedings of the 33rd International Conference on Very Large Data Bases (VLDB)*, (pp. 411-422). ACM.

Anaya-Sánchez, H., Pons-Porrata, A., & Berlanga, R. (2010). A document clustering algorithm for discovering and describing topics. *Pattern Recognition Letters, 31*(6), 502–510. doi:10.1016/j.patrec.2009.11.013

ARQ. (n.d.). *A SPARQL processor for Jena*. Retrieved from http://jena.sourceforge.net/ARQ/

Artale, A., Calvanese, D., Kontchakov, R., & Zakharyaschev, M. (2009). The DL-lite family and relations. *Journal of Artificial Intelligence Research, 36*, 1–69.

Atserias, J., Zaragoza, H., Ciaramita, M., & Attardi, G. (2008). Semantically annotated snapshot of the English Wikipedia. *Proceedings of the International Conference on Language Resources and Evaluation (LREC)*. European Language Resources Association.

Auer, S., Bizer, C., Kobilarov, G., Lehmann, J., Cyganiak, R., & Ives, Z. (2007). Dbpedia: A nucleus for a Web of open data. In K. Aberer, K.-S. Choi, N. F. Noy, D. Allemang, K.-I. Lee, L. J. B. Nixon, J. Golbeck, P. Mika, D. Maynard, R. Mizoguchi, G. Schreiber, & P. Cudré-Maurou (Eds.), *Proceedings of the 6th International Semantic Web Conference (ISWC) Lecture Notes in Computer Science: Vol. 4825* (pp. 722-735). Springer.

Baader, F. (2009). Description logics. In Tessaris, S., Franconi, E., Eiter, T., Gutierrez, C., Handschuh, S., Rousset, M.-C., & Schmidt, R. A. (Eds.), *Reasoning Web. Semantic Technologies for Information Systems, 5th International Summer School, Lecture Notes in Computer Science* (*Vol. 5689*, pp. 1–39). Springer.

Baader, F., Brandt, S., & Lutz, C. (2005). Pushing the EL envelope. In L. P. Kaelbling, & A. Saffiotti (Eds.), *Proceedings of the 19th International Joint Conference on Artificial Intelligence (IJCAI)*, (pp. 364-369). Professional Book Center.

Baader, F., Lutz, C., & Suntisrivaraporn, B. (2006). CEL - A polynomial-time reasoner for life science ontologies. In *Proceedings Automated Reasoning, Third International Joint Conference (IJCAR)* [Springer.]. *Lecture Notes in Computer Science, 4130*, 287–291. doi:10.1007/11814771_25

Bailey, J., Bry, F., Furche, T., & Schaffert, S. (2009). Semantic Web query languages. In Liu, L., & Ozsu, M. (Eds.), *Encyclopedia of database systems* (pp. 2583–2586). Springer.

Beckett, D., & McBride, B. (Eds.). (2004). *RDF syntax specification* (revised). W3C Recommendation. Retrieved on 10th February 2004 from http://www.w3.org/TR/rdf-syntax-grammar/

Bizer, C., Heath, T., & Berners-Lee, T. (2009). Linked data - The story so far. *International Journal on Semantic Web and Information Systems, 5*(3), 1–22. doi:10.4018/jswis.2009081901

Bloehdorn, S., & Sure, Y. (2007). Kernel methods for mining instance data in ontologies. In K. Aberer, K.-S. Choi, N. F. Noy, D. Allemang, K.-I. Lee, L. J. B. Nixon, J. Golbeck, P. Mika, D. Maynard, R. Mizoguchi, G. Schreiber, & P. Cudré-Maurou (Eds.), *Proceedings of the 6th International Semantic Web Conference (ISWC), Lecture Notes in Computer Science: Vol. 4825* (pp. 58-71). Springer.

Boag, S., Chamberlin, D., Fernándex, M. F., Florescu, D., Robie, J., & Siméon, J. (2007). *XQuery 1.0: An XML query language*. Retrieved from http://www.w3.org/TR/xquery/

Bray, T. Paoli, J., Sperberg-McQueen, C.M., & Maler, E. (Eds.). (2000). *Extensible markup language (XML) 1.0* (2nd edition). Retrieved on October 6, 2010, from http://www.w3.org/TR/REC-xml/

Brickley, D., & Guha, R. V. (Eds.). (2004). *RDF vocabulary description language 1.0: RDF schema*. Retrieved from http://www.w3.org/TR/rdf-schema/

Brin, S. (1998). Extracting patterns and relations from the World Wide Web. In P. Atzeni, A. O. Mendelzon, & G. Mecca (Eds.), *The World Wide Web and Databases, International Workshop (WebDB) Lecture Notes in Computer Science: Vol. 1590* (pp. 172-183). Springer.

Broekstra, J., Kampman, A., & van Harmelen, F. (2003). Sesame: An architecture for storing and querying RDF Data and schema information. In D. Fensel, W. Wahlster, H. Lieberman, & J. Hendler (Eds.), *Spinning the Semantic Web* (pp. 197-222). MIT Press.

Cafarella, M. J. (2009). Extracting and querying a comprehensive web database. In *Proceedings of the Conference on Innovative Data Systems Research (CIDR)*.

Calvanese, D., Carroll, J., De Giacomo, G., Herman, I., Parsia, B., Patel-Schneider, P., & Ruttengerb, A. (2008). *OWL 2 Web ontology language: Profiles*. Retrieved from http://www.w3.org/TR/2008/WD-owl2-profiles-20081008/

Cimiano, P., & Völker, J. (2005). Text2Onto. In *Natural Language Processing and Information Systems, 10th International Conference on Applications of Natural Language to Information Systems (NLDB)* [Springer.]. *Lecture Notes in Computer Science*, *3513*, 227–238. doi:10.1007/11428817_21

Clark & Parsia. (2010). *Pellet: The OWL 2 reasoner*. Retrieved from http://clarkparsia.com/pellet/

Danger, R., & Berlanga, R. (2008). A Semantic Web approach for ontological instances analysis. In J. Filipe, B. Shishkov, M. Helfert, & L. Maciaszek (Eds.), *Software and data technologies: Vol. 22. Communications in computer and Information Science* (pp. 269-282). Springer.

Danger, R., & Berlanga, R. (2009). Generating complex ontology instances from documents. *Journal of Algorithms*, *64*(1), 16–30. doi:10.1016/j.jalgor.2009.02.006

Dean, M., Schreiber, G., Bechhofer, S., van Harmelen, F., Hendler, J., & Horrocks, I. … Stein, L. A. (2004). *OWL Web ontology language reference*. Retrieved from http://www.w3.org/TR/owl-ref/

Dublin Core. (n.d.). *Metadata initiative*. Retrieved from http://dublincore.org/

Fanizzi, N., d'Amato, C., & Esposito, F. (2008). Conceptual clustering and its application to concept drift and novelty detection. In S. Bechhofer, M. Hauswirth, J. Hoffmann, & M. Koubarakis (Eds.), *The Semantic Web: Research and Applications, 5th European Semantic Web Conference (ESWC) Lecture Notes in Computer Science: Vol. 5021* (pp. 318-332). Springer.

Fanizzi, N., d'Amato, C., & Esposito, F. (2009). Metric-based stochastic conceptual clustering for ontologies. *Information Systems*, *34*(8), 792–806. doi:10.1016/j.is.2009.03.008

Fung, B., Wang, K., & Ester, M. (2003). Hierarchical document clustering using frequent itemsets. In *Proceedings of the 3rd SIAM International Conference on Data Mining (SDM)*, (pp. 59-70). SIAM.

Gärtner, T., Lloyd, J. W., & Flach, P. A. (2004). Kernels and distances for structured data. *Machine Learning*, *57*(3), 205–232. doi:10.1023/B:MACH.0000039777.23772.30

Grimnes, G. A., Edwards, P., & Preece, A. D. (2008). Instance based clustering of Semantic Web Resources. In S. Bechhofer, M. Hauswirth, J. Hoffmann, & M. Koubarakis (Eds.), *The Semantic Web: Research and Applications, 5th European Semantic Web Conference (ESWC) Lecture Notes in Computer Science: Vol. 5021.* (pp. 303-317). Springer.

Grosof, B. N., Horrocks, I., Volz, R., & Decker, S. (2003). Description logic programs: Combining logic programs with description logic. In *Proceedings of the 12th International World Wide Web Conference (WWW),* (pp. 48-57). ACM.

Haarslev, V., & Möller, R. (2001). Description of the RACER system and its applications. In C. A. Goble, D. L. McGuinness, R. Möller, & P. F. Patel-Schneider (Eds.), *Working Notes of the 2001 International Description Logics Workshop (Description Logics). CEUR Workshop Proceedings.* CEUR-WS.org.

Han, J., & Kamber, M. (2006). *Data mining: Concepts and techniques*. Morgan Kauffmann.

Harris, S., & Gibbins, N. (2003). 3store: Efficient bulk RDF storage. In R. Volz, S. Decker, & I. F. Cruz (Eds.), *Proceedings of the 1st International Workshop on Practical and Scalable Semantic Systems (PSSS). CEUR Workshop Proceedings.* CEUR-WS.org.

Harth, A., Umbrich, J., Hogan, A., & Decker, D. (2007). YARS2: A federated repository for querying graph structured data from the Web. In *Proceedings of 6th International Semantic Web Conference and the 2nd Asian Semantic Web Conference*, (pp. 211-224). Springer.

Herman, I. (2008). *RDFS and OWL 2 RL generator service*. Retrieved from http://www.ivan-herman.net/Misc/2008/owlrl/

Hermit. (2010). *Hermit OWL reasoner*. Retrieved from http://hermit-reasoner.com/

Horrocks, I. (1998). Using an expressive description logic: FaCT or fiction? In *Proceedings of the 6th Conference on Principles of Knowledge Representation and Reasoning (KR)*, (pp. 636-649). Morgan Kaufmann.

Horrocks, I., Patel-Schneider, P. F., Boley, H., Tabet, S., Grosof, B., & Dean, M. (2004). SWRL: A Semantic Web rule language combining OWL and RuleML. Retrieved from http://www.w3.org/Submission/SWRL/

Horrocks, I., van Harmelen, F., & Patel-Schneider, P. (2001). *Reference description of the DAML+OIL ontology markup language*. Retrieved from http://www.daml.org/2000/12/reference.html

Huang, Y., Tresp, V., Bundschus, M., & Rettinger, A. (2010). Multivariate prediction for learning on Semantic Web. In *Proceedings of the 20th International Conference on Inductive Logic Programming (ILP)*. Springer.

Hustadt, U., Motik, B., & Sattler, U. (2005). Data complexity of reasoning in very expressive description logics. In L. P. Kaelbling, and A. Saffiotti (Eds.), *Proceedings of the 19th International Joint Conference on Artificial Intelligence (IJCAI)*, (pp. 466-471). Professional Book Center.

Jiménez-Ruiz, E., Cuenca Grau, B., Horrocks, I., & Berlanga, R. (2009). Ontology integration using mappings: Towards getting the right logical consequences. In *The Semantic Web: Research and Applications, 6th European Semantic Web Conference (ESWC)* [Springer.]. *Lecture Notes in Computer Science, 5554*, 173–187.

Karvounarakis, G., Alexaki, S., Christophides, V., Plexousakis, D., & Scholl, M. (2002). RQL: A declarative query language for RDF. In *Proceedings of the 11th International World Wide Web Conference (WWW)*, (pp. 592-603). ACM.

Kiefer, C., Bernstein, A., & Locher, A. (2008). Adding data mining support to SPARQL via statistical relational learning methods. In S. Bechhofer, M. Hauswirth, J. Hoffmann, & M. Koubarakis (Eds.), *The Semantic Web: Research and Applications, 5th European Semantic Web Conference (ESWC) Lecture Notes in Computer Science: Vol. 5021* (pp. 478-492). Springer.

Kim, J. W., & Candan, K. S. (2006). CP/CV: Concept similarity mining without frequency information from domain describing taxonomies. In *Proceedings of the 15th ACM International Conference on Information and Knowledge Management (CIKM)*, (pp. 483-492). ACM.

Kiryakov, A., Popov, B., Terziev, I., Manov, D., & Ognyanoff, D. (2004). Semantic annotation, indexing, and retrieval. *Journal of Web Semantics, 2*(1), 49–79. doi:10.1016/j.websem.2004.07.005

Klyne, G. Carroll, J., & McBride, B., (Eds.). (2004). *Resource description framework (RDF) concepts and abstract syntax*. Retrieved from http://www.w3.org/TR/rdf-concepts/

Kochut, K., & Janik, M. (2007). SPARQLeR: Extended Sparql for semantic association discovery. In E. Franconi, M. Kifer, & W. May (Eds.), *The Semantic Web: Research and Applications, 4th European Semantic Web Conference (ESWC) Lecture Notes in Computer Science: Vol. 4519* (pp. 145-159). Springer.

Ławrynowicz, A. (2009). Query results clustering by extending SPARQL with CLUSTER BY. In Meersman, R., Herrero, P., & Dillon, T. S. (Eds.), *On the Move to Meaningful Internet Systems (OTM Workshops) Lecture Notes in Computer Science* (*Vol. 5872*, pp. 826–835). Springer. doi:10.1007/978-3-642-05290-3_101

Li, Y., Yu, C., & Jagadish, H. V. (2004). Schema-free XQuery. In *Proceedings of the 30th International Conference on Very Large Data Bases (VLDB)*. (pp. 72-83). Morgan Kaufmann.

Liu, B., Hsu, W., Mun, L.-F., & Lee, H.-Y. (1999). Finding interesting patterns using user expectations. *IEEE Transactions on Knowledge and Data Engineering, 11*(6), 817–832. doi:10.1109/69.824588

Liu, X., Thomsen, C., & Pedersen, T. B. (2010). 3XL: Supporting efficient operations on very large OWL Lite triple-stores. Submitted for publication. *Information Systems*.

Maedche, A., Neumann, G., & Staab, S. (2003). Bootstrapping an ontology-based information extraction system. In Szczepaniak, P. S., Segovia, J., Kacprzyk, J., & Zadeh, L. A. (Eds.), *Intelligent exploration of the Web* (pp. 345–359). Physica-Verlag.

Marinica, C., & Guillet, F. (2010). Knowledge-based interactive postmining of association rules using ontologies. *IEEE Transactions on Knowledge and Data Engineering, 22*(6), 784–797. doi:10.1109/TKDE.2010.29

Motik, B., & Rosati, R. (2010). Reconciling description logics and rules. *Journal of the ACM*, *57*(5), 1–63. doi:10.1145/1754399.1754403

Nebot, V., & Berlanga, R. (2009). Efficient retrieval of ontology fragments using an interval labeling scheme. *Information Sciences*, *179*(24), 4151–4173. doi:10.1016/j.ins.2009.08.012

Nebot, V., & Berlanga, R. (2010a). Mining association rules from Semantic Web data. In *Proceedings of the 23rd International Conference on Industrial Engineering and Other Applications of Applied Intelligent Systems (IEA/AIE). Lecture Notes in Computer Science*, *6097*, 504–513. doi:10.1007/978-3-642-13025-0_52

Nebot, V., & Berlanga, R. (2010b). Building data warehouses with semantic data. In *Proceedings of the 1st International Workshop on Business Intelligence and the Web (BEWEB). ACM International Conference Proceeding Series.* Springer.

Nebot, V., Berlanga, R., Pérez, J. M., Aramburu, M., & Pedersen, T. B. (2009). Multidimensional integrated ontologies: A framework for designing semantic data warehouses. *Journal of Data Semantics*, *13*, 1–36.

Neumann, T., & Weikum, G. (2010). The RDF-3X engine for scalable management of RDF data. *The VLDB Journal*, *19*(1), 91–113. doi:10.1007/s00778-009-0165-y

Niemi, T., Näppilä, T., & Järvelin, K. (2009). A relational data harmonization approach to XML. *Journal of Information Science*, *35*(5), 571–601. doi:10.1177/0165551509104231

Oracle-RDF. (n.d.). *Oracle technical network, Semantic Technologies Center*. Retrieved from http://www.oracle.com/technology/tech/semantic_technologies/index.html

Pérez, J. M., Berlanga, R., Aramburu, M. J., & Pedersen, T. B. (2008). Integrating data warehouses with web data: A survey. *IEEE Transactions on Knowledge and Data Engineering*, *20*(7), 940–955. doi:10.1109/TKDE.2007.190746

Prud'hommeaux, E., & Seaborne, A. (2008). *SPARQL query language for RDF*. Retrieved from http://www.w3.org/TR/rdf-sparql-query/

Reeve, L., & Han, H. (2005). Survey of semantic annotation platforms. In H. Haddad, L. M. Liebrock, A. Omicini, & R. L. Wainwright (Eds.), *Proceedings of the 2005 ACM Symposium on Applied Computing (SAC)*, (pp. 1634-1638). ACM.

Rettinger, A., Nickles, M., & Tresp, V. (2009). Statistical relational learning with formal ontologies. In W. L. Buntine, M. Grobelnik, D. Mladenic, & J. Shawe-Taylor (Eds.), *Proceedings of the Machine Learning and Knowledge Discovery in Databases European Conference (ECML/PKDD (2)) Lecture Notes in Computer Science: Vol. 5782* (pp. 286-301). Springer.

Sanz, I., Pérez, M., & Berlanga, R. (2008). Designing similarity measures for XML. *In Proceedings of the 27th International Conference on Conceptual Modeling (ER). Lecture Notes in Computer Science*, *5231*, 514–515. doi:10.1007/978-3-540-87877-3_38

Srikant, R., & Agrawal, R. (1995). Mining generalized association rules. In U. Dayal, P. M. D. Gray, & S. Nishio (Eds.), *Proceedings of 21th International Conference on Very Large Data Bases (VLDB)*, (pp. 407-419). Morgan Kaufmann.

Suchanek, F. M., Kasneci, G., & Weikum, G. (2007). YAGO: A core of semantic knowledge. In C. L. Williamson, M. E. Zurko, P. F. Patel-Schneider, & P. J. Shenoy (Eds.), *Proceedings of the 16th International Conference on World Wide Web (WWW)*, (pp. 697-706). ACM.

Suchanek, F. M., Kasneci, G., & Weikum, G. (2008). YAGO: A large ontology from Wikipedia and WordNet. *Journal of Web Semantics*, *6*(3), 203–217. doi:10.1016/j.websem.2008.06.001

Tagarelli, A., & Greco, S. (2010). Semantic clustering of XML documents. *ACM Transactions on Information Systems*, *28*(1), 1–56. doi:10.1145/1658377.1658380

Theobald, M., Schenkel, R., & Weikum, G. (2003). Exploiting structure, annotation, and ontological knowledge for automatic classification of XML data. *In Proceedings of WebDB Workshop (WebDB)*, (pp.1-6).

Tresp, V., Bundschus, M., Rettinger, A., & Huang, Y. (2008). Towards machine learning on the Semantic Web. In P. C. G. da Costa, C. d'Amato, N. Fanizzi, K.n B. Laskey, K. J. Laskey, T. Lukasiewicz, M. Nickles, & M. Pool (Eds.), *Uncertainty Reasoning for the Semantic Web I, ISWC International Workshops (URSW) Lecture Notes in Computer Science: Vol. 5327* (pp. 282-314). Springer.

Tresp, V., Huang, Y., Bundschus, M., & Rettinger, A. (2009). Materializing and querying learned knowledge. In *Proceedings of the 1st ESWC Workshop on Inductive Reasoning and Machine Learning on the Semantic Web (IRMLeS)*. CEUR-WS.org.

Urbani, J., Kotoulas, S., Maassen, J., van Harmelen, F., & Bal, H. (2010). OWL reasoning with WebPIE: Calculating the closure of 100 billion triples. In L. Aroyo, G. Antoniou, E. Hyvönen, A. ten Teije, H. Stuckenschmidt, L. Cabral, & T. Tudorache (Eds.), *The Semantic Web: Research and Applications, 7th Extended Semantic Web Conference (ESWC) Lecture Notes in Computer Science: Vol. 6088* (pp. 213-227). Springer.

Urbani, J., Kotoulas, S., Oren, E., & van Harmelen, F. (2009). Scalable distributed reasoning using Mapreduce. In *Proceedings of the 8th International Semantic Web Conference (ISWC)*, (pp. 634-649). Springer.

Weld, D. S., Hoffmann, R., & Wu, F. (2008). Using Wikipedia to bootstrap open information extraction. *SIGMOD Record*, *37*(4), 62–68. doi:10.1145/1519103.1519113

Wilkinson, K., Sayers, C., Kuno, H. A., & Reynolds, D. (2003). Efficient RDF storage and retrieval in Jena2. In I. F. Cruz, V. Kashyap, S. Decker, & R. Eckstein (Eds.), *Proceedings of the 1st International Workshop on Semantic Web and Databases (SWDB)*, (pp. 131–150).

Wu, F., & Weld, D. S. (2007). Autonomously semantifying Wikipedia. In *Proceedings of the 16th ACM Conference on Information and Knowledge Management (CIKM)*, (pp. 41-50). ACM.

Wu, F., & Weld, D. S. (2008). Automatically refining the Wikipedia infobox ontology. In J. Huai, R. Chen, H.-W. Hon, Y. Liu, W.-Y. Ma, A. Tomkins, & X. Zhang (Eds.), *Proceeding of the 17th International Conference on World Wide Web (WWW)*, (pp. 635-644). ACM.

Xu, Y., & Papakonstantinou, Y. (2005). Efficient keyword search for smallest LCAs in XML databases. In F. Özcan (Ed.), *Proceedings of the ACM International Conference on Management of Data (SIGMOD)*, (pp. 527-538). ACM.

Yang, X., Procopiuc, C. M., & Srivastava, D. (2009). Summarizing relational databases. In *Proceedings of the 35th International Conference on Very Large Data Bases (VLDB)*, (pp. 634-645). Morgan Kaufmann.

Zhang, X., Cheng, G., & Qu, Y. (2007). Ontology summarization based on RDF sentence graph. In *Proceedings of the 16th International Conference on World Wide Web (WWW)*, (pp. 707-716). ACM.

## ADDITIONAL READING

Allemang, D. Hendler, K. (2008). *Semantic Web for the Working Ontologist*. Morgan Kaufmann.

Getoor, L., & Taskar, B. (Eds.). (2007). *Introduction to Statistical Relational Learning*. MIT Press.

Han, J., & Kamber, M. (2006). *Data Mining: Concepts and Techniques*. Morgan Kauffmann.

Maimon, O., & Rokach, L. (Eds.). (2010). *Data Mining and Knowledge Discovery Handbook*. Springer. doi:10.1007/978-0-387-09823-4

Pollock, J. T. (2009). *Semantic Web for Dummies*. Wiley.

Stumme, G., Hotho, A., & Berendt, B. (2006). Semantic Web Mining: State of the Art and Future Directions. *Journal of Web Semantics*, *4*(2), 124–143. doi:10.1016/j.websem.2006.02.001

Tan, P.-N., Steinbach, M., & Kumar, V. (2006). *Introduction to Data Mining*. Addison-Wesley.

Tresp, V., Bundschus, M., Rettinger, A., & Huang, Y. (2008). Towards Machine Learning on the Semantic Web. In *Uncertainty Reasoning for the Semantic Web I, ISWC International Workshops (URSW): Vol. 5327. Lecture Notes in Computer Science* (pp. 282-314). Springer.

## ENDNOTES

[1] http://wordnet.princeton.edu/

[2] http://www.biopax.org/

# Chapter 15
# A Component-Based Framework for the Integration and Exploration of XML Sources

**Pasquale De Meo**
*University of Messina, Italy*

**Antonino Nocera**
*University Mediterranea of Reggio Calabria, Italy*

**Domenico Ursino**
*University Mediterranea of Reggio Calabria, Italy*

## ABSTRACT

*Handling the interoperability issues in multiple, heterogeneous XML sources is central in XML data management and mining. In this chapter, we present a framework for the intensional integration and exploration of XML sources. Specifically, we propose a three-layer framework aimed at extracting interschema knowledge from the available sources, constructing a hierarchy based on the extracted knowledge to represent the sources at different abstraction levels, and finally organizing and exploring the sources through the constructed hierarchy. We also describe possible implementations of each of the three layers, focusing on the extraction of intensional interschema properties, the intensional integration of XML sources, and the clustering of XML schemas. In order to better handle the complexity of its activities, the proposed framework has been designed by means of the layers architecture patterns and the component-based development paradigm.*

## INTRODUCTION

The past years were characterized by an enormous increase of data available in electronic form, as well as by a proliferation of query languages, data models and data management systems. In such a scenario, traditional approaches to data management are not capable of guaranteeing the suitable level of access transparency to stored data and, at the same time, of preserving the autonomy of local data sources. This situation favored the development of new architectures for data source

DOI: 10.4018/978-1-61350-356-0.ch015

interoperability conceived to allow users to query pre-existing autonomous data sources to guarantee the maximum possible transparency, efficiency and effectiveness.

Developing modules that handle the reconciliation of involved information sources plays a relevant role in all architectures for data source interoperability. The definition of these modules strongly relies on *schema integration*, i.e., the construction of a global schema obtained by merging a set of related schemas (Chua, Chiang, & Lim, 2003; dos Santos Mello, Castano, & Heuser, 2002; McBrien & Poulovassilis, 2003). However, when the involved systems are numerous and/or large, schema integration often produces an over complex global schema, which could be not suited to supply a correct and complete description of the available data. In this case, it appears much more adequate the construction of a *source hierarchy*, representing the involved sources at different abstraction levels. Essentially, this hierarchy can be obtained as follows: initially, the involved schemas are organized into homogeneous groups by means of *data clustering* algorithms; for each cluster, the corresponding sources are integrated to obtain a global schema representing it and the obtained global schema are in turn grouped to construct second-level clusters, and a representative schema for each of these new clusters is obtained by performing an integration task. This process is iterated until a unique, highly abstract schema representing all the involved XML sources is obtained.

In order to carry out source integration and clustering correctly, the designer must clearly understand the semantics of the involved information sources. One of the most common ways of deriving and representing source semantics consists in detecting *interschema properties* (Bergamaschi, Castano, & Vincini, 1999; Castano, De Antonellis, & De Capitani di Virmercati, 2001; Palopoli, Saccà, Terracina, & Ursino, 2003; Rahm & Bernstein, 2001) or *source constraints*. Interschema properties are terminological and structural relationships involving concepts and objects belonging to different sources; examples of interschema properties are synonymies, homonymies and hyponymies. Source constraints are restrictions involving objects belonging to the same or different sources; examples of source constraints are domain constraints, functional dependencies and referential integrity constraints.

The increase in the number of available data sources favored the development of a large variety of possible data formats; in order to uniformly manage them, the adoption of a unified paradigm is compulsory. In this context, the most promising solution has revealed to be XML. Owing to its semistructured nature, XML can be exploited as a unifying formalism to handle the interoperability of information sources characterized by heterogeneous data representation formats. As a matter of fact, XML has become the *de facto* standard for information exchange. Most of the current information sources are XML-based or can be easily translated into XML.

The considerations outlined above were the premises for the development of the framework proposed in this chapter. Given an input set of XML sources, our framework is mainly designed to:

- identify interschema properties and/or constraints from the sources;
- exploit these properties and constraints to construct a hierarchy representing the involved sources at different abstraction levels; here, schema integration and clustering methods are essential to consolidate and organize the sources;
- exploring this hierarchy as the core of a cooperative information system (in particular, to implement the corresponding mediators) or a data warehouse (in particular, to handle the reconciled data level of a three-level data warehouse architecture). The presence of a hierarchy as the core of a cooperative information system allows the efficient exploration of a high number

of (possibly complex) XML sources. As a matter of fact, given a query, the hierarchy allows the XML sources involved in the query to be quickly identified in such a way as to submit the query only to them. In an analogous fashion, the presence of a hierarchy as the core of the reconciled data level of a data warehouse architecture allows the portions of the XML sources of interest to a reporting, OLAP or data mining task to be quickly identified and selectively used.

As for the implementation of the proposed framework, it is worth pointing out that, for each of the problems to be faced, it is possible to define different techniques; at the same time, the results obtained by solving one of these problems (e.g., interschema property extraction) could be exploited to solve another one (e.g., source integration). This suggests that the component-based development (hereafter, *CBD*) paradigm represents the best solution to be adopted in the framework construction. *CBD* organizes a software system into some subsystems called components; each component is seen as a black box which receives some information, processes it and returns the suitable results (Arlow & Neustadt, 2005). Moreover, since the previous problems are strictly related to each other, because the output of one of them is often the input for another one, it is reasonable to organize components into layers by following the ideas typical of the layers architecture pattern (Bussman, Meunier, Rohnert, Sommerlad, & Stal, 1996; Larman, 2002).

This chapter is organized as follows. In the next section we illustrate the general architecture of the proposed framework. In the subsequent three sections, we focus on the description of three modules that perform: (1) the extraction of intensional interschema properties, (2) the intensional integration of XML sources, and (3) the clustering of XML Schemas. As a matter of fact, in the past we have developed several approaches to face these three problems (De Meo, Quattrone, Terracina, & Ursino, 2006; De Meo, Quattrone, Terracina, & Ursino, 2007a; De Meo, Quattrone, Terracina, & Ursino, 2007b). In this chapter we present in detail one approach for each problem and, therefore, one approach for each module. In the last part of this chapter we present a comparison between each of the proposed approaches and related methods existing in the literature. Finally, we draw our conclusions and give some pointers for future work.

## ARCHITECTURE OF THE PROPOSED FRAMEWORK

The architecture of the proposed framework consists of three layers. In its turn, each layer consists of a set of components; these last ones generally cooperate with each other even if they perform complementary (or sometimes independent) activities. This architecture is shown in Figure 1. Due to layout reasons, in this figure we show the framework layers and the corresponding components along with their interfaces; we do not report the connections among components. These last ones will be reported in detail in the next figures.

The three layers of our framework are:

- *The Relationship/Constraint Extraction Layer*; it aims at extracting (both intensional and extensional) relationships and constraints existing among the concepts represented in the involved XML sources. The components currently defined for this layer are:
    - *The IPE (Interschema Property Extractor) component family*; each member of this family extracts interschema properties, i.e., intensional and extensional relationships existing among the concepts represented in the involved XML sources.

*Figure 1. The architecture of the proposed framework*

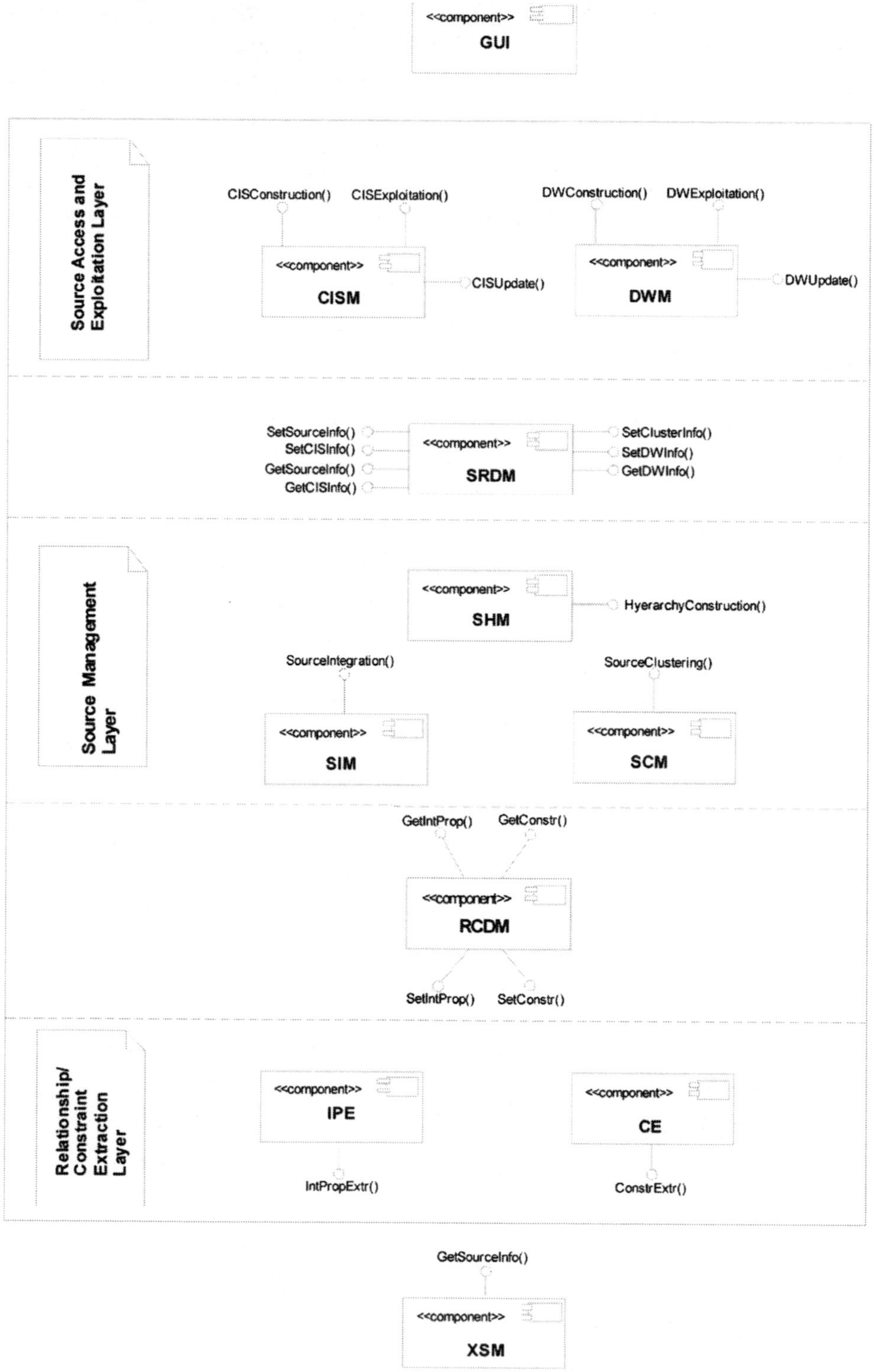

<<component>>
GUI

Source Access and Exploitation Layer

CISConstruction()
CISExploitation()
<<component>>
CISM
CISUpdate()

DWConstruction()
DWExploitation()
<<component>>
DWM
DWUpdate()

SetSourceInfo()
SetCISInfo()
GetSourceInfo()
GetCISInfo()
<<component>>
SRDM
SetClusterInfo()
SetDWInfo()
GetDWInfo()

Source Management Layer

<<component>>
SHM
HyerarchyConstruction()

SourceIntegration()
<<component>>
SIM

SourceClustering()
<<component>>
SCM

GetIntProp()
GetConstr()
<<component>>
RCDM
SetIntProp()
SetConstr()

Relationship/ Constraint Extraction Layer

<<component>>
IPE
IntPropExtr()

<<component>>
CE
ConstrExtr()

GetSourceInfo()
<<component>>
XSM

   - *The CE (Constraint Extractor) component family;* each member of this family extracts constraints existing among the concepts represented in the involved XML sources.

- *The Source Management Layer;* it aims at constructing complex structures to organize a large number of related sources in order to optimize their access and exploitation. The components currently defined for this layer are:
   - *The SIM (Source Integration Manager) component family;* each member of this family integrates a set of (possibly related) XML sources.
   - *The SCM (Source Clustering Manager) component family;* each member of this family clusters a set of (possibly related) XML sources.
   - *The SHM (Source Hierarchy Manager) component family;* each member of this family organizes a set of XML sources into a hierarchy on the basis of the interschema properties and the constraints detected by the components of the Relationship/Constraint Extraction layer.
- *The Source Access and Exploitation Layer;* it aims at constructing and maintaining systems (such as Cooperative Information Systems and Data Warehouses) allowing the access to, as well as the exploitation of, available XML sources. The components currently defined for this layer are:
   - *The CISM (Cooperative Information System Manager) component family;* each member of this family allows the construction, the maintenance, the access and the exploitation of a Cooperative Information System (hereafter, CIS).
   - *The DWM (Data Warehouse Manager) component family;* each member of this family allows the construction, the maintenance, the access and the exploitation of a Data Warehouse (hereafter, DW).

All extracted relationships and constraints are suitably organized and stored in a database, called *RCD* (*Relationship/Constraint Database*); it is handled by a component called *RCDM* (*RCD Manager*). Moreover, all information returned by *SIM*, *SCM*, *CISM* and *DWM* is suitably organized and stored in a database, called *SRD* (*Source Representation Database*), handled by a component called *SRDM* (*SRD Manager*).

A user can interact with our framework by means of a suitable *GUI* (*Graphical User Interface*) component. All involved XML sources can be accessed by the framework components through an *XSM* (*XML Source Manager*) component.

According to the Component-Based Development paradigm, the members of a component family receive the same inputs, perform the same task and return the same outputs. They differ from each other for the technique implemented by them to perform the task associated with their family. It is worth observing that, if desired, other component families could be added in our framework; they could solve problems someway related to those already handled by our framework.

## The Relationship/Constraint Extraction Layer

### The IPE (Interschema Property Extractor) Component Family

An *IPE* can be activated by a *SIM* or an *SCM*. It receives the set *SSet* of the XML sources to be analyzed and derives the interschema properties involving concepts and data instances represented in these sources. An *IPE* receives all data necessary to perform its task from *XSM* (if they concern the original sources) or from *SRDM* (if they concern the global sources derived from a previous integration process). It stores all derived properties into *RCD* through *RCDM*.

The structure of this component, along with its interfaces and its interactions with the other components, is reported in Figure 2.

Generally speaking, interschema properties can be intensional, if they regard the structures of the involved sources (e.g., the XML Schemas associated with XML sources), or extensional, if they concern the instances of the involved sources (e.g., the real XML documents). As a consequence, an *IPE* has two main sub-components, namely *IIPE*, which extracts intensional interschema properties, and *EIPE*, which derives extensional interschema properties. Clearly, there could exist many techniques to define an *IIPE* or an *EIPE*; in the following, we shall describe our approach to define an *IIPE*.

### The CE (Constraint Extractor) Component Family

A *CE* can be activated by a *SIM* or an *SCM*. It receives the set *SSet* of the XML sources to be analyzed and derives the constraints involving data represented in these sources. Analogously to an *IPE*, a *CE* receives all data necessary to perform its tasks from *XSM* or *SRDM*. It stores all derived constraints into *RCD* through *RCDM*.

The structure of this component, along with its interfaces and its interactions with the other components, is reported in Figure 3.

A *CE* is in charge of deriving constraints concerning XML sources. These are the evolutions of the classical constraints concerning relational databases, such as domain constraints, integrity constraints, functional dependencies, and so on. A particularly interesting constraint is that involving the notion of *tree tuple* which can be exploited to extend the notion of functional dependency to the XML setting (Arenas & Libkin, 2004; Flesca, Furfaro, Greco, & Zumpano, 2003). For instance, this notion can be exploited by a component of the *SCM* family to cluster XML sources (Tagarelli & Greco, 2010).

## The Source Management Layer

### The SIM (Source Integration Manager) Component Family

A *SIM* can be activated by a *SHM*. It receives the set *SSet* of the XML sources to be integrated. It requires information about the sources of *SSet* to

*Figure 2. Structure of the IPE component*

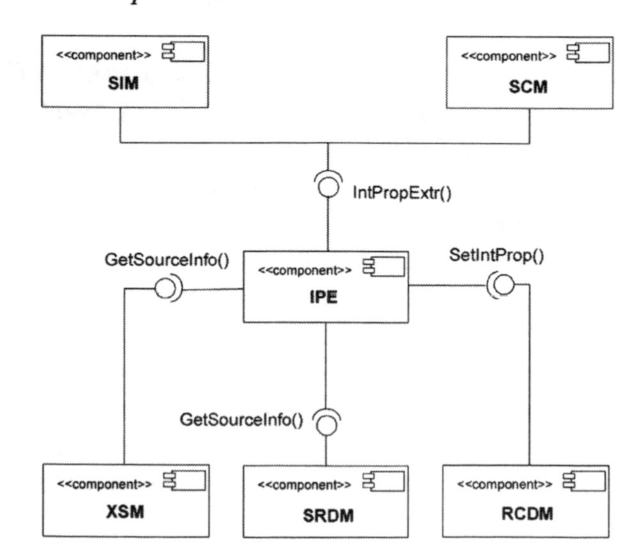

*Figure 3. Structure of the CE component*

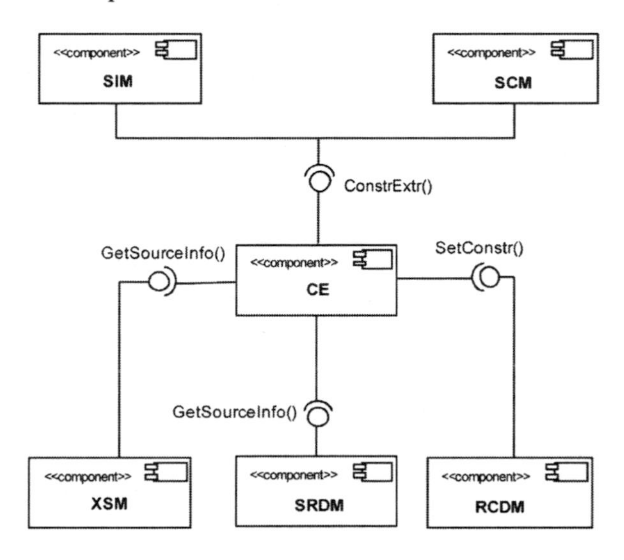


*XSM* or *SRDM*, and verifies if the interschema properties and/or the constraints involving concepts and/or data represented in the sources of *SSet* are already present in *RCD*. In the affirmative case, it queries this information to *RCDM*; in the negative case it activates *IPE* and/or *CE* and, when these last ones terminate, it queries the corresponding interschema properties and/or constraints to *RCDM*. It finally performs the integration of the sources of *SSet* and stores the corresponding global schema in *SRD* through *SRDM*.

The structure of this component, along with its interfaces and its interactions with the other components, is reported in Figure 4.

Generally speaking, integration can be performed both at the intensional and the extensional levels. In the former case it regards the structure of the involved sources; in the latter one it concerns the corresponding instances. As a consequence, a *SIM* has two sub-components, namely *ISIM*, which performs an intensional integration of the involved sources, and *ESIM*, which performs an extensional integration of them. Clearly, there could exist several techniques to define an *ISIM* or an *ESIM*; later in this chapter, we shall describe an approach we adopted to implement an *ISIM*. Some approaches that can be exploited to define an *ESIM* are described in

*Figure 4. Structure of the SIM component*

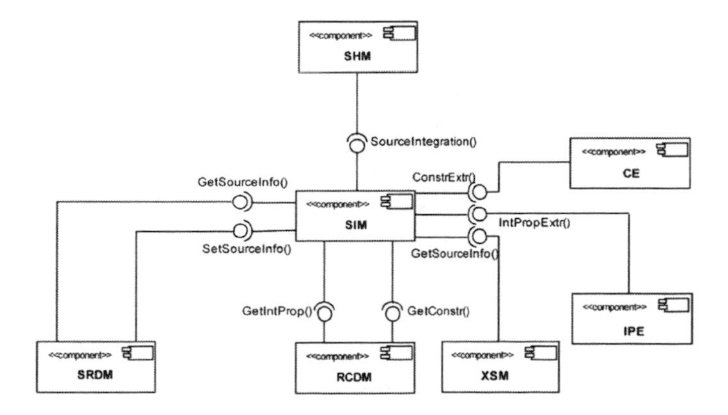

(Aggarwal, Ta, Wang, Feng, & Zaki, 2007) and in (Pontieri, Ursino, & Zumpano, 2003).

### The SCM (Source Clustering Manager) Component Family

An *SCM* can be activated by an *SHM*. It receives the set *SSet* of the XML sources to be clustered. It first collects all information necessary to its activity (source information, interschema properties and constraints) in an analogous way to *SIM*, then it groups the sources of *SSet* into homogeneous clusters and stores its results in *SRD* through *SRDM*.

The structure of this component, along with its interfaces and its interactions with the other components, is reported in Figure 5.

In the literature several approaches to cluster XML sources have been proposed (see, for instance, (Tagarelli & Greco, 2010)). According to the philosophy of the Component-Based Development paradigm, each component of the *SCM* family could implement a different clustering approach. Later in this chapter we shall describe our implementation of this task.

## The SHM (Source Hierarchy Manager) Component Family

An *SHM* can be activated by a *CISM* or a *DWM*. It receives the set *SSet* of the XML sources to be organized into a hierarchy. It is in charge of constructing this hierarchy. For this purpose, it first activates *SCM* to group the sources of *SSet* into homogeneous clusters; then, for each cluster, it activates *SIM* to integrate all the associated sources in order to obtain a global schema representing the cluster. At the end of this step, the bottom level of the hierarchy has been constructed.

*SHM* repeats the same process on the global schemas representing the clusters to obtain the second-level clusters and the associated global schemas. Finally, it iterates this process until a unique cluster and a unique global schema, representing all the sources of *SSet*, have been obtained.

The structure of this component, along with its interfaces and its interactions with the other components, is reported in Figure 6.

## The Source Access and Exploitation Layer

### The CISM (Cooperative Information System Manager) Component Family

A *CISM* can be activated by a user through the *GUI*. It allows the construction, the maintenance, the access and the exploitation of a Cooperative Information System (hereafter, *CIS*). A *CISM* has at least two sub-components, namely *CISC* (*CIS Constructor*), which constructs and maintains a *CIS* starting from the information stored in *SRD*,

Figure 5. Structure of the SCM component

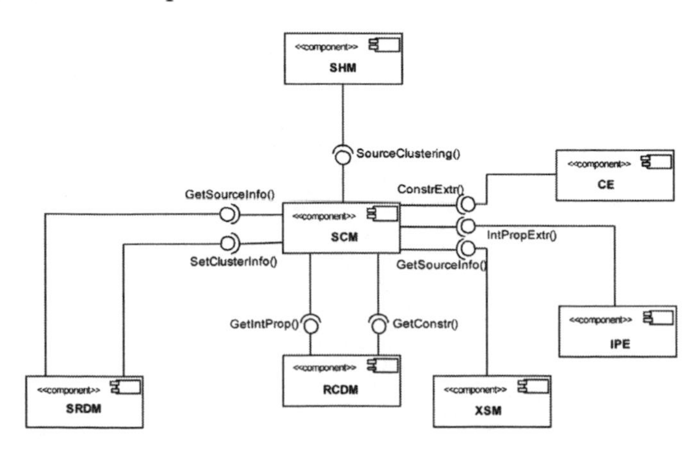

*Figure 6. Structure of the SHM component*

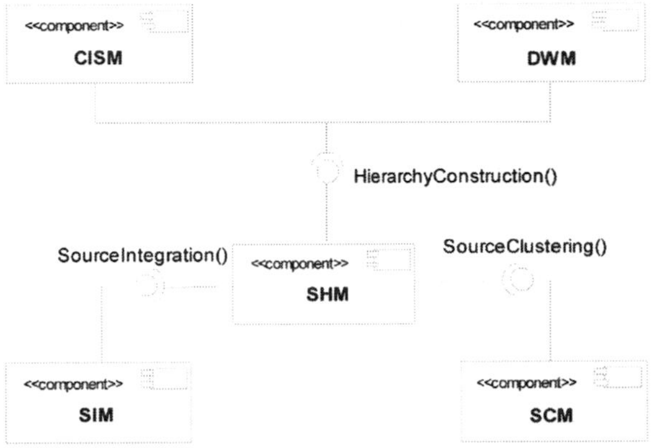

and *CISQM* (*CIS Query Manager*), which allows the querying of a *CIS* constructed by *CISC*.

*CISC* is activated by a user when he wants to construct a new *CIS* or to update an already constructed one. In the former case he must provide the set *SSet* of the sources forming the *CIS*; in the latter one he must specify the identifier of the *CIS* to be updated as well as the set *SSet* of the sources to be added, removed or updated in the specified *CIS*.

In order to construct a *CIS*, *CISC* defines the identifier of the new *CIS* and stores it into *SRD* through *SRDM*, activates *SHM* to construct the hierarchy representing the *CIS*, and finally derives the corresponding templates and mediators starting from the information registered in *SRD*. The update of a *CIS* is performed by *CISC* by means of an analogous, although incrementa procedure.

*CISQM* is activated by the user via the *GUI* when he wants to submit a query *q* on a given *CIS*. *CISQM* receives both the identifier of the involved *CIS* and *q*. It organizes the processing of *q* (for instance, it could decompose *q* into subqueries, could require the processing of these last ones and could compose the corresponding results) and returns the suitable answer to the user.

The structure of this component, along with its interfaces and its interactions with the other components, is reported in Figure 7.

## The DWM (Data Warehouse Manager) Component Family

A *DWM* can be activated by a user through the *GUI*. It allows the construction, the maintenance, the access and the exploitation of a Data Warehouse (hereafter, *DW*). A *DWM* has at least four sub-components, namely *DWC* (*DW Constructor*), which constructs and maintains a *DW* starting from the information stored in *SRD*, *DWR*, *DWOLAP* and *DWDM*, which allow reporting, OLAP and Data Mining tasks to be performed on a DW constructed by *DWC*.

*DWC* is activated by a user when he wants to construct a new *DW* or to update an already constructed one. In the former case, he must provide the set *SSet* of the sources which the *DW* consists of; in the latter one, he must specify the *DW* to be updated and the set *SSet* of the sources to be added, removed or updated in it.

If a *DW* construction is required, *DWC* defines the identifier of the new *DW* and stores it into *SRD* through *SRDM*, activates *SHM* to construct the hierarchy forming the reconciled data level of the *DW*, and finally derives the corresponding *DW* metadata starting from the information stored in *SRD*.

If a *DW* update is required, *DWC* carries out an analogous, even if incremental, procedure.

*Figure 7. Structure of the CISM component*

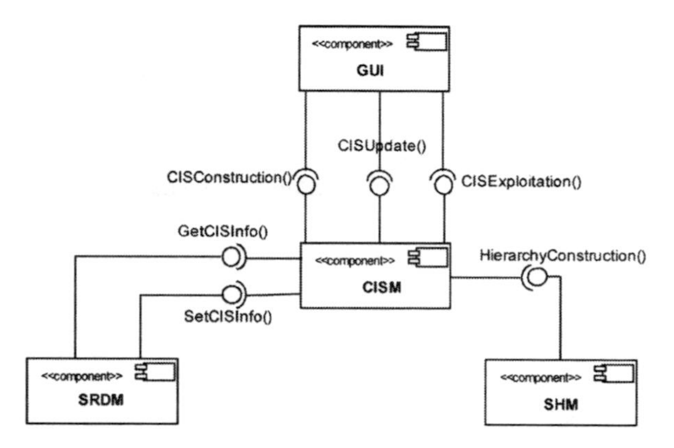


*DWR* (resp., *DWOLAP*, *DWDM*) is activated by the user via the GUI when he wants to perform reporting (resp., OLAP, Data Mining) activities on a given *DW*. It receives the identifier of the *DW* of interest and supports the user in the reporting (resp., OLAP, Data Mining) activity. Its implementation could also benefit of approaches for the construction of synopses and/or aggregated views over XML documents described in (Polyzotis & Garofalakis, 2002; Polyzotis, Garofalakis, & Ioannidis, 2004).

The structure of this component, along with its interfaces and its interactions with the other components, is reported in Figure 8.

## Database Managers

### The XSM (XML Source Manager) Component Family

An *XSM* provides *IPE*, *CE*, *SIM* and *SCM* with information about the involved XML sources.

The structure of this component, along with its interfaces and its interactions with the other components, is reported in Figure 9.

### The RCDM (Relationship Database Manager) Component Family

An *RCDM* handles the access to the *RCD* database. It can be activated by *IPE* when it must store derived interschema properties in *RCD*,

*Figure 8. Structure of the DWM component*

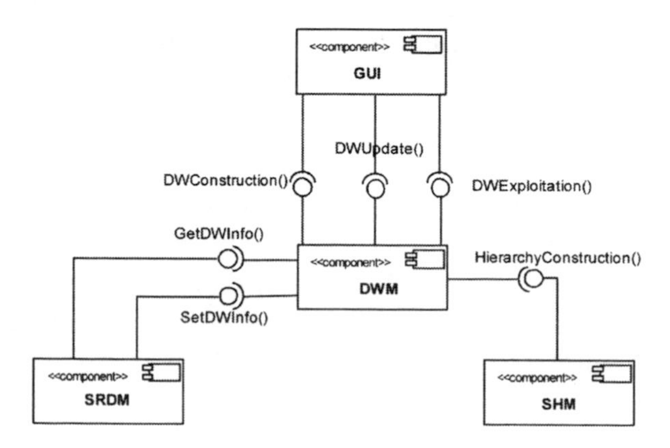

*Figure 9. Structure of the XSM component*

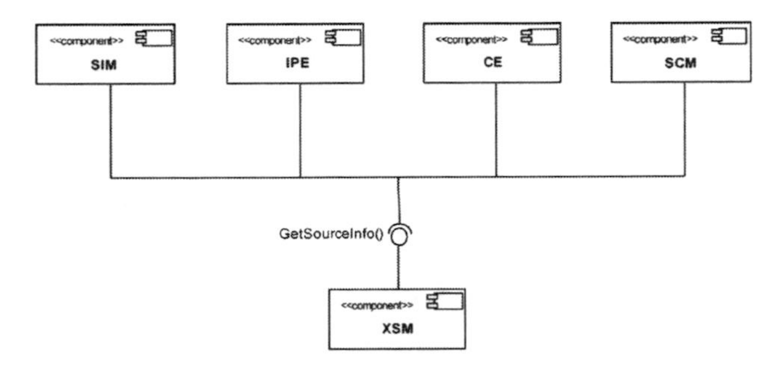


by *CE* when it must store derived constraints in *RCD*, by *SIM* and *SCM* when they need to know derived interschema properties and constraints.

The structure of this component, along with its interfaces and its interactions with the other components, is reported in Figure 10.

## The SRDM (Source Representation Database Manager) Component Family

An *SRDM* handles the access to the *SRD* database. It can be activated by: (1) *SIM*, when this must store the global sources obtained after the integration task or when it must gather information about previously derived global sources; (2) *SCM*, when this must store information about derived clusters or when it must gather information about previously derived global sources; (3) *CISM*, when this must store information about a new *CIS* or when it must gather information about an existing one; (4) *DWM*, when this must store information about a new *DW* or when it must gather information about an existing one; (5) *IPE* or *CE*, when these last ones must gather information about previously derived global sources.

The structure of this component, along with its interfaces and its interactions with the other components, is reported in Figure 11.

## The GUI (Graphical User Interface) Component

*GUI* represents the interface between a user and our framework. It can be activated by a user when he wants: (1) to construct a new *CIS*; (2) to update an existing *CIS*; (3) to submit a query on an existing *CIS*; (4) to construct a new *DW*; (5) to update an existing *DW*; (6) to perform reporting,

*Figure 10. Structure of the RCDM component*

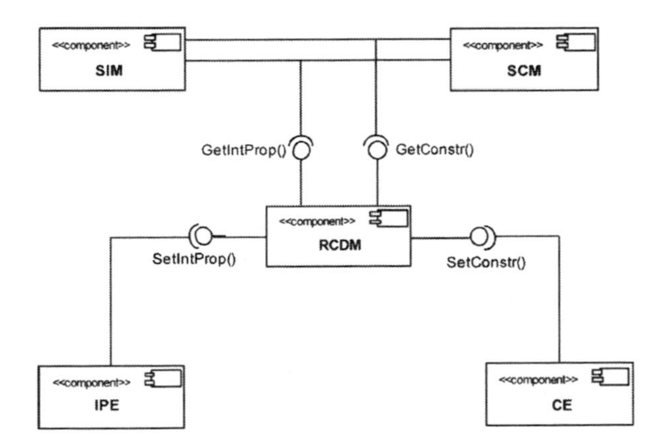

*Figure 11. Structure of the SRDM component*

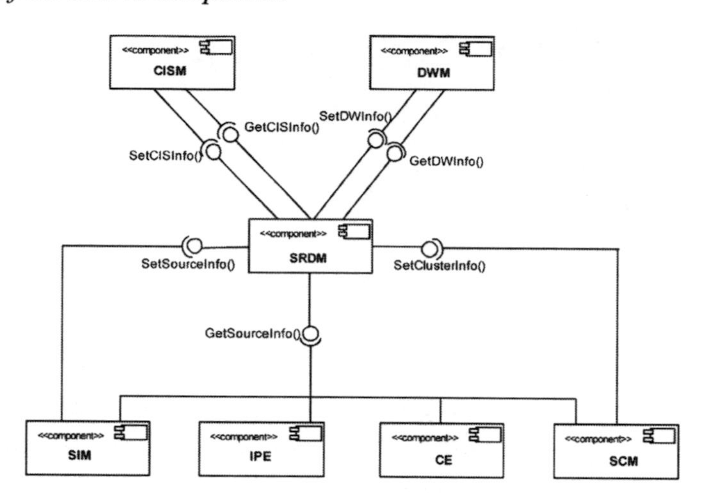


OLAP and Data Mining activities on an existing *DW*. In the first three cases *GUI* activates *CISM*; in the last three ones it activates *DWM*.

The structure of this component, along with its interfaces and its interactions with the other components, is reported in Figure 12.

## A POSSIBLE IMPLEMENTATION OF THE IIPE COMPONENT

As previously pointed out, *IIPE* is in charge of the extraction of intensional interschema properties. In particular, it extracts synonymies, homonymies, hyponymies/hyperonymies and overlappings. A *synonymy* between two concepts indicates that they have the same meaning. A *homonymy* between two concepts denotes that they refer to different meanings, yet having the same name. A concept $C_1$ is a *hyponym* of a concept $C_2$ (that is, in turn, $C_2$ a *hyperonym* of $C_1$) if $C_1$ has a more specific meaning than $C_2$. As an example, "PhD student" is a hyponym of "student". An *overlapping* holds between two concepts if they are not synonymous but share a significant set of properties.

Our intensional interschema property extraction approach is specialized for XML, almost automatic and semantic. It is based on the observation that, given two concepts belonging to different information sources, an interesting and powerful way to determine their semantics consists in the examination of their *neighborhoods*, since the concepts and the relationships which they are involved in contribute to define their meaning (Rahm & Bernstein, 2001). In addition, it exploits two further indicators to define the semantics of the involved data sources in a more precise fashion; these indicators are the *types* and the *cardinalities*

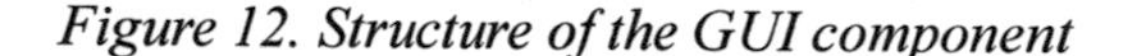

*Figure 12. Structure of the GUI component*

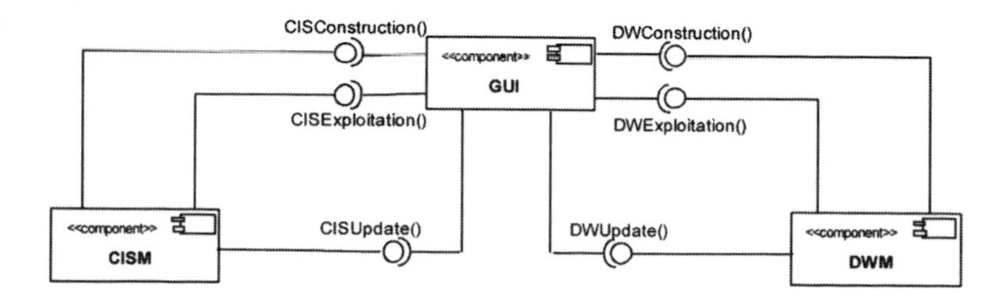

of the elements and the attributes belonging to the XML Schemas under consideration.

In XML Schemas concepts are expressed by means of elements or attributes. Since for the intensional interschema property extraction task it is not relevant to distinguish the concepts represented by elements from those represented by attributes, we introduce the term *x-component* to denote an element or an attribute in an XML Schema. An x-component is characterized by its name, its typology (stating if it is a simple element, a complex element or an attribute) and its possible data type.

In order to determine the neighborhood of an x-component it is necessary to define a "Semantic Distance" between two x-components of the same XML Schema; this distance considers how much the corresponding x-components are semantically related. For this purpose we introduce some boolean functions that allow the strength of the relationship existing between two x-components $x_\nu$ and $x_\mu$ of an XML Schema $S$ to be determined. These functions are:

- $veryclose(x_\nu, x_\mu)$, that returns *true* if and only if: $x_\mu = x_\nu$, or $x_\mu$ is an attribute of $x_\nu$, or $x_\mu$ is a simple sub-element of $x_\nu$;
- $close(x_\nu, x_\mu)$, that returns *true* if and only if: $x_\mu$ is a complex sub-element of $x_\nu$, or $x_\mu$ is an element of $S$ and there exists a keyref constraint stating that an attribute of $x_\nu$ refers to a key attribute of $x_\mu$;
- $near(x_\nu, x_\mu)$, that returns *true* if and only if either $veryclose(x_\nu, x_\mu) = true$ or $close(x_\nu, x_\mu) = true$;
- $reachable(x_\nu, x_\mu)$,that returns *true* if and only if there exists a sequence of *distinct* x-components $x_1, \ldots, x_n$ such that: $x_1 = x_\nu$, $near(x_1, x_2) = \ldots = near(x_{n-1}, x_n) = true$ and $x_n = x_\mu$.

The exploitation of the functions introduced above allows each pair $\langle x_\nu, x_\mu \rangle$ of an XML Schema to be associated with a coefficient called *Connection Cost*. It is a measure of the correlation degree existing between $x_\nu$ and $x_\mu$ and indicates how much the concept expressed by $x_\nu$ is semantically close to the one represented by $x_\mu$ ; in other words, it represents the ability of the concept associated with $x_\mu$ to characterize the concept associated with $x_\nu$. More formally, the Connection Cost from $x_\nu$ to $x_\mu$, denoted by $CC(x_\nu, x_\mu)$, is defined as shown in Exhibit 1.

Here $C_{\nu\mu} = \min(CC(x_\nu, x_\alpha) + CC(x_\alpha, x_\mu))$ for each $x_\alpha$ such that $reachable(x_\nu, x_\alpha) = reachable(x_\alpha, x_\mu) = true$.

Finally, given a non-negative integer $i$, we define the $i^{th}$ neighborhood of an x-component $x_\nu$ of an XML Schema $S$ as the set of the x-components of $S$ having a Connection Cost from $x_\nu$ less than or equal to $i$. More formally, the $i^{th}$ neighborhood of $x_\nu$ is defined as:

$$nbh(x_\nu, i) = \{x_\mu \mid x_\mu \textit{ is an x-component of } S, CC(x_\nu, x_\mu) \leq i\}$$

In order to verify if an intensional interschema property holds between two x-components, our approach compares their neighborhoods, their cardinalities and their data types. In addition, it

*Exhibit 1.*

$$CC(x_\nu, x_\mu) = \begin{cases} 0 & \textit{if } veryclose(x_\nu, x_\mu) = true \\ 1 & \textit{if } close(x_\nu, x_\mu) = true \\ C_{\nu\mu} & \textit{if } reachable(x_\nu, x_\mu) = true \textit{ and } near(x_\nu, x_\mu) = false \\ \infty & \textit{if } reachable(x_\nu, x_\mu) = false \end{cases}$$

exploits a thesaurus storing lexical synonymies holding among the terms of a language; specifically, it uses the English language and WordNet (Miller, 1995). If necessary, different (possibly already defined) domain-specific thesauri might be exploited.

Since neighborhood comparison plays a key role in our intensional interschema property extraction approach, we first introduce it and, then, illustrate our approach in detail.

## Neighborhood Comparison

Given two neighborhoods $nbh(x_\nu,v)$ and $nbh(x_\mu,v)$ of two x-components $x_\nu$ and $x_\mu$, three possible relationships, namely *similarity*, *comparability* and *generalization*, could exist between them. All of them are derived by computing suitable objective functions on the maximum cardinality matching associated with a bipartite graph obtained from the x-components of $nbh(x_\nu,v)$ and $nbh(x_\mu,v)$.

In the following we indicate by $BG(x_\nu, x_\mu, v) = \langle NSet(x_\nu, x_\mu, v), ESet(x_\nu, x_\mu, v)\rangle$ the bipartite graph associated with $nbh(x_\nu, v)$ and $nbh(x_\mu, v)$; when it is not confusing, we shall use the notation $BG(v)$ instead of $BG(x_\nu, x_\mu, v)$. In $BG(v)$, $NSet(v) = PSet(v) \cup QSet(v)$ represents the set of nodes; there is a node in $PSet(v)$ (resp., $QSet(v)$) for each x-component of $nbh(x_\nu, v)$ (resp., $nbh(x_\mu, v)$). $ESet(v)$ is the set of edges; there is an edge between $p \in PSet(v)$ and $q \in QSet(v)$ if: (1) a lexical synonymy between the names of the x-components $x_p$ and $x_q$, associated with $p$ and $q$, is stored in the reference thesaurus, and (2) the cardinalities of $x_p$ and $x_q$ are *compatible*, and (3) their data types are *compatible* (this last condition must be verified only if $x_p$ and $x_q$ are attributes or simple elements). Here, the cardinalities of two x-components are considered compatible if the intersection of the intervals defined by them is not empty. The compatibility rules associated with data types are analogous to the corresponding ones valid for high level programming languages.

The maximum cardinality matching for $BG(v)$ is the set $ESet'(v) \subseteq ESet(v)$ of edges such that, for each node $x \in PSet(v) \cup QSet(v)$, there is at most one edge of $ESet'(v)$ incident onto $x$ and $|ESet'(v)|$ is maximum (for algorithms solving the maximum cardinality matching problem see (Galil, 1986)).

### Neighborhood Similarity

Intuitively, two neighborhoods (and, more in general, two sets of objects) are considered similar if most of their components are similar. In order to determine if $nbh(x_\nu, v)$ and $nbh(x_\mu, v)$ are similar, we construct $BG(x_\nu, x_\mu, v)$ and, then, we define the objective function,

$$\phi_{BG(v)} = \frac{2\,|\,ESet'(v)\,|}{|\,PSet(v)\,| + |\,QSet(v)\,|}$$

associated with the maximum cardinality matching on $BG(v)$. Here $|ESet'(v)|$ represents the number of matches associated with $BG(v)$, i.e. the number of similarities involving $nbh(x_\nu,v)$ and $nbh(x_\mu,v)$. 2 $|ESet'(v)|$ indicates the number of matching nodes in $BG(v)$, i.e. the number of similar x-components present in $nbh(x_\nu,v)$ and $nbh(x_\mu,v)$. $|PSet(v)| + |QSet'(v)|$ denotes the total number of nodes in $BG(v)$, i.e. the total number of x-components associated with $nbh(x_\nu,v)$ and $nbh(x_\mu,v)$. Finally, $\phi_{BG(v)}$ represents the share of matching nodes in $BG(v)$, as well as the share of similar x-components present in $nbh(x_\nu, v)$ and $nbh(x_\mu, v)$.

We say that $nbh(x_\nu, v)$ and $nbh(x_\mu, v)$ are similar if, given the bipartite graph $BG(v)$, after the computation of the maximum cardinality matching on $BG(v)$, it holds that $\phi_{BG(v)} > 0.5$. Such an assumption derives from the consideration that two sets of objects can be considered similar if the number of similar components is greater than the number of the dissimilar ones or, in other words, if the number of similar components is greater than half of the total number of components.

It is possible to prove that the worst case time complexity to determine if $nbh(x_\nu, v)$ and $nbh(x_\mu, v)$ are similar is $O(p^3)$, where $p$ is the maximum between $|nbh(x_\nu, v)|$ and $|nbh(x_\mu, v)|$.

## Neighborhood Comparability

Intuitively, two neighborhoods $nbh(x_\nu, v)$ and $nbh(x_\mu, v)$ are comparable if there exist at least two (quite large) subsets $XSet_\nu$ of $nbh(x_\nu, v)$ and $XSet_\mu$ of $nbh(x_\mu, v)$ that are similar. Similarity between $XSet_\nu$ and $XSet_\mu$ is computed by constructing a bipartite graph $\overline{BG(XSet_\nu, XSet_\mu)}$ starting from the x-components of $XSet_\nu$ and $XSet_\mu$, and by computing $\phi$ in an analogous way to that we have previously seen. Comparability is a weaker property than similarity. As a matter of fact, if two neighborhoods are similar, they are also comparable. However, it could happen that two neighborhoods are not similar but they are comparable because they have quite large similar subsets.

More formally, two neighborhoods $nbh(x_\nu, v)$ and $nbh(x_\mu, v)$ are comparable if there exist two subsets, $XSet_\nu$ of $nbh(x_\nu, v)$ and $XSet_\mu$ of $nbh(x_\mu, v)$, such that: (i) $|XSet_\nu| > \frac{1}{2}|nbh(x_\nu, v)|$; (ii) $|XSet_\mu| > \frac{1}{2}|nbh(x_\mu, v)|$; (iii) $\varphi_{\overline{BG}}(XSet_\nu, XSet_\mu) > 0.5$. In this definition, conditions (i) and (ii) guarantee that $XSet_\nu$ and $XSet_\mu$ are representative (i.e., quite large); we assume that this happens if they involve more than half of the components of the corresponding neighborhoods; condition (iii) guarantees that $XSet_\nu$ and $XSet_\mu$ are similar.

It is possible to prove that the worst case time complexity to determine if $nbh(x_\nu, v)$ and $nbh(x_\mu, v)$ are comparable is $O(p^3)$, where $p$ is the maximum between $|nbh(x_\nu, v)|$ and $|nbh(x_\mu, v)|$; moreover, if $nbh(x_\nu, v)$ and $nbh(x_\mu, v)$ are similar then they are also comparable.

## Neighborhood Generalization

Consider two neighborhoods $\alpha$ and $\beta$ and assume that: (1) they are not similar; (2) most of the x-components of $\beta$ match with the x-components of $\alpha$; (3) most of the x-components of $\alpha$ do not match with the x-components of $\beta$. If all these conditions hold, then it is possible to conclude that the reality represented by $\alpha$ is richer than that represented by $\beta$ and, consequently, that $\alpha$ is more specific than $\beta$ or, conversely, that $\beta$ is more general than $\alpha$. The following definition formalizes this reasoning.

Let $x_\nu$ and $x_\mu$ be two x-components belonging to different XML Schemas. We say that $nbh(x_\nu, v)$ is more specific than $nbh(x_\mu, v)$ (and, consequently, that $nbh(x_\mu, v)$ is more general than $nbh(x_\nu, v)$) if: (1) they are not similar, and (2) the objective function,

$$\phi_{BG}(x_\nu, x_\mu, v) = \frac{|ESet'(v)|}{|QSet(v)|}$$

associated with the bipartite graph $BG(v)$, is greater than 0.5; here, $BG(v)$ has been previously defined, $ESet'(v)$ represents the set of the matching edges associated with $BG(v)$ whereas $QSet(v)$ is the set of the nodes of $BG(v)$ corresponding to the x-components of $nbh(x_\mu, v)$.

The reasoning underlying this definition derives from the observation that $\varphi_{BG}(x_\nu, x_\mu, v)$ represents the share of the x-components belonging to $nbh(x_\mu, v)$ matching with the x-components of $nbh(x_\nu, v)$. If this share is sufficiently high then most of the x-components of $nbh(x_\mu, v)$ match with the x-components of $nbh(x_\nu, v)$ (condition (2)) but, since $nbh(x_\nu, v)$ and $nbh(x_\mu, v)$ are not similar (condition (1)), most of the x-components of $nbh(x_\nu, v)$ do not match with the x-components of $nbh(x_\mu, v)$ (condition (3)). As a consequence, it is possible to conclude that $nbh(x_\nu, v)$ is more specific than $nbh(x_\mu, v)$.

It is possible to prove that the worst case time complexity to determine if $nbh(x_\nu, v)$ is more specific than $nbh(x_\mu, v)$ is $O(p^3)$, where $p$ is the maximum between $|nbh(x_\nu, v)|$ and $|nbh(x_\mu, v)|$.

## Intensional Interschema Property Derivation

Our approach for the derivation of intensional interschema properites (and, consequently, our approach for the intensional integration of a set of XML sources) is characterized by a specific feature that, to the best of our knowledge, has not been previously proposed in the literature; more specifically, it allows the choice of the "severity level" against which the interschema property extraction is performed. Such a feature derives from the consideration that applications and scenarios possibly benefiting of inteschema properties are numerous and extremely various. In some situations (e.g., in Public Administrations, Finance, and so on) the extraction process must be very severe in that two concepts must be considered equivalent only if their similarity is strengthened by more clues; in such a case a high severity level is required. In other situations (e.g., tourist Web pages) the extraction task can be looser and can consider equivalent two concepts having some similarities but presenting also some differences.

At the beginning of the extraction activity our approach asks the user to specify the desired severity level by means of a suitable, friendly wizard; this is the only information required to him until the end of the extraction task, when he has to validate obtained results. Interestingly enough, from the severity level point of view, a classical approach can be seen as a particular case of that presented in this chapter in which the severity level is fixed and the extraction of all intensional interschema properties is performed w.r.t. this level.

As previously pointed out, in order to verify if an intensional interschema property holds between two x-components $x_\nu$ and $x_\mu$, belonging to different XML Schemas, it is necessary to examine their neighborhoods. Specifically, first it is necessary to consider $nbh(x_\nu, 0)$ and $nbh(x_\mu, 0)$ and to verify if they are comparable. In the affirmative case, it is possible to conclude that $x_\nu$ and $x_\mu$ refer to analogous "contexts" and, presumably, define comparable concepts. However, observe that $nbh(x_\nu, 0)$ (resp., $nbh(x_\mu, 0)$) takes only the attributes and the simple sub-elements of $x_\nu$ (resp., $x_\mu$) into account; as a consequence, it considers quite a limited context. If a higher severity level is required, it is necessary to verify that other neighborhoods of $x_\nu$ and $x_\mu$ are comparable before marking the pair $\langle x_\nu, x_\mu \rangle$ as candidate. Such a reasoning is formalized by the following definition.

Let $S_1$ and $S_2$ be two XML Schemas. Let $x_\nu$ (resp., $x_\mu$) be an x-component of $S_1$ (resp., $S_2$). Let $u$ be a severity level. We say that *the pair* $\langle x_\nu, x_\mu \rangle$ *is comparable at the severity level* $u$ if $nbh(x_\nu, v)$ and $nbh(x_\mu, v)$ are comparable for each $v$ such that $0 \leq v \leq u$.

It is possible to prove that the worst case time complexity to verify if $\langle x_\nu, x_\mu \rangle$ is a candidate pair at the severity level $u$ is $O(up^3)$, where $p$ is the maximum between $|nbh(x_\nu, u)|$ and $|nbh(x_\mu, u)|$.

Now, in order to verify if a synonymy, a homonymy, a hyponymy or an overlapping holds at the severity $u$ for a *candidate pair* $\langle x_\nu, x_\mu \rangle$ it is necessary to examine the neighborhoods of $x_\nu$ and $x_\mu$ and to determine the relationship holding among them. Specifically:

- A homonymy holds between $x_\nu$ and $x_\mu$ at the severity level $u$ if $x_\nu$ and $x_\mu$ have the same name and the pair $\langle x_\nu, x_\mu \rangle$ is not comparable at the severity level $u$.
- A synonymy holds between $x_\nu$ and $x_\mu$ at the severity level $u$ if $nbh(x_\nu, v)$ and $nbh(x_\mu, v)$ are similar for each $v$ such that $0 \leq v \leq u$.
- $x_\nu$ is said a hyponym of $x_\mu$ at the severity level $u$ if $nbh(x_\nu, v)$ is more specific than $nbh(x_\mu, v)$ for each $v$ such that $0 \leq v \leq u$.
- An overlapping holds between $x_\nu$ and $x_\mu$ at the severity level $u$ if: $x_\nu$ and $x_\mu$ are not synonymous; neither $x_\nu$ is a hyponym of $x_\mu$ nor $x_\mu$ is a hyponym of $x_\nu$.

The previous assumptions derive from the following considerations: (i) if two x-components have the same name but they are not comparable at the severity level $u$, then it is possible to conclude that they represent different concepts and, consequently, they can be considered homonymous; (ii) if two x-components are comparable at the severity level $u$ and their neighborhoods are similar, then it is possible to conclude that they represent the same concept and, consequently, they can be considered synonymous; (iii) if two x-components are comparable at the severity level $u$ but the neighborhoods of one of them, say $x_\nu$, are more specific than the neighborhoods of the other one, say $x_\mu$, then it is possible to conclude that $x_\nu$ has a more specific meaning than $x_\mu$ or, in other words, that $x_\nu$ is a hyponym of $x_\mu$; (iv) if two x-components are comparable at the severity level $u$ but neither their neighborhoods are similar nor the neighborhoods of one of them are more specific than the neighborhoods of the other, then it is possible to conclude that they represent partially similar concepts and, consequently, that an overlapping holds between them.

As for the computational complexity of the intensional interschema property derivation, it is possible to state that the worst case time complexity to compute synonymies, homonymies, hyponymies and overlappings at the severity level $u$ is $O(up^3)$, where $p$ is the maximum between $|nbh(x_\nu, u)|$ and $|nbh(x_\mu, u)|$.

Finally, it is possible to prove that the worst case time complexity to derive all intensional interschema properties holding between two XML Schemas $S_1$ and $S_2$ at the severity level $u$ is $O(uq^3m^2)$, where $q$ is the maximum cardinality among all the neighborhoods of $S_1$ and $S_2$ and $m$ is the maximum between the number of complex elements of $S_1$ and the number of complex elements of $S_2$.

It could appear that a polynomial complexity for the intensional interschema property extraction is excessively high. Actually, this is not the case. Indeed, in many application contexts, the intensional component is much smaller than the extensional one; as a consequence, the number of involved x-components is generally very small. There are some very specific situations, e.g. biological contexts, where the intensional component could be much larger than the extensional one. However, we observe that, in any case, the computational complexity is polynomial. Moreover, the extraction of the intensional interschema properties must be carried out once and for all when the pair of XML Schemas is examined for the first time. Finally, a neighborhood (and, consequently, an interschema property) must be *modified* only if there is a change in the corresponding intensional component. With regard to this, we observe that: (i) changes of the intensional component of an information source are infrequent; (ii) the presence of a change does not imply the recomputation, but simply the incremental update, of the involved neighborhoods.

## A POSSIBLE IMPLEMENTATION OF THE ISIM COMPONENT

As previously pointed out, *ISIM* is in charge of performing the intensional integration of a set of XML sources to construct a global intensional representation of them. It receives two XML Schemas $S_1$ and $S_2$[1] and a severity level $u$ and returns the integrated XML Schema $S_G$. Our approach to implementing *ISIM* consists of two steps, namely: (1) construction of a *Merge Dictionary* $MD(u)$ and of a *Rename Dictionary* $RD(u)$; (2) exploitation of $MD(u)$ and $RD(u)$ to obtain $S_G$.

### Construction of Merge Dictionary and Rename Dictionary

At the end of the intensional interschema property derivation task, it could happen that an x-component of an XML Schema is synonymous with more x-components of the other XML Schema. The integration algorithm we are proposing here needs each x-component of an XML Schema to be synonymous with at most one x-component of the other XML Schema. In order to satisfy this requirement, it is necessary to construct a *Merge Dictionary* $MD(u)$ and a *Rename Dictionary* $RD(u)$ by suitably filtering previously derived synonymies and homonymies.

The construction of $MD(u)$ begins with the definition of a support bipartite graph $SimG(u) = \langle SimNSet_1(u) \cup SimNSet_2(u), SimASet(u)\rangle$. There is a node $n_{1j}$ (resp., $n_{2k}$) in $SimNSet_1(u)$ (resp., $SimNSet_2(u)$) for each complex element $E_{1j}$ (resp., $E_{2k}$) belonging to $S_1$ (resp., $S_2$). There is an arc $A_{jk} = \langle n_{1j}, n_{2k}\rangle \in SimASet(u)$ if $E_{1j}$ and $E_{2k}$ are synonymous at the severity level $u$.

Next, a maximum cardinality matching is computed on $SimG(u)$; it selects the subset $SimASubSet(u)$ of $SimASet(u)$ having the maximum cardinality. For each arc $A'_{jk} = \langle n'_{1j}, n'_{2k}\rangle \in SimASet(u)$ a tuple $\langle E'_{1j}, E'_{2k}\rangle$ is added to $MD(u)$. In addition, let $\langle E'_{1j}, E'_{2k}\rangle$ be a pair of complex elements such that $E'_{1j}$ belongs to $S_1$, $E'_{2k}$ belongs to $S_2$ and $\langle E'_{1j}, E'_{2k}\rangle \in MD(u)$; moreover, let $x'_{1j}$ (resp., $x'_{2k}$) be an attribute or a simple sub-element of $E'_{1j}$ (resp., $E'_{2k}$); then the tuple $\langle x'_{1j}, x'_{2k}\rangle$ is added to $MD(u)$ if $x'_{1j}$ and $x'_{2k}$ are synonymous at the severity level $u$ and the data types of $x'_{1j}$ and $x'_{2k}$ are compatible.

Finally, let $\langle x'_{1j}, x'_{2k}\rangle$ be a pair of attributes or of simple elements such that $x'_{1j}$ belongs to $S_1$ and $x'_{2k}$ belongs to $S_2$; the tuple $\langle x'_{1j}, x'_{2k}\rangle$ is inserted into $MD(u)$ (if not already present) if $x'_{1j}$ and $x'_{2k}$ have identical or synonymous names and compatible data types.

As for the construction of $RD(u)$, a pair of x-components $\langle x''_{1j}, x''_{2k}\rangle$ is inserted in this dictionary if $x''_{1j}$ and $x''_{2k}$ are both elements or both attributes and there exists a homonymy at the severity level $u$ between them.

## Construction of the Integrated XML Schema

The dictionaries $MD(u)$ and $RD(u)$ are exploited to construct the integrated XML Schema $S_G$. Our integration algorithm assumes that $S_1$ and $S_2$ are represented in the "Salami Slice" style. Actually, an XML Schema could be represented in several other ways (e.g., in the "Russian Doll" or in the "Venetian Blind" styles); however, there exist simple rules to translate it into the "Salami Slice" style (see (Thompson, Beech, Maloney & Mendelsohn, 2004) for more details on the various definition styles).

More formally, $S_1$ and $S_2$ can be represented as:

$$S_1 = \langle x_{1_1}, x_{1_2}, \ldots, x_{1_{n1}}, k_{1_1}, k_{1_2}, \ldots, k_{1_{f1}}, kref_{1_1}, kref_{1_2}, \ldots, kref_{1_{g1}} \rangle$$

$$S_2 = \langle x_{2_1}, x_{2_2}, \ldots, x_{2_{n2}}, k_{2_1}, k_{2_2}, \ldots, k_{2_{f2}}, kref_{2_1}, kref_{2_2}, \ldots, kref_{2_{g2}} \rangle$$

where $x_{11}, \ldots, x_{1n1}, x_{21}, \ldots, x_{2n2}$ are x-components, $k_{11}, \ldots, k_{1f1}, k_{21}, \ldots, k_{2f2}$ are keys and $kref_{11}, \ldots, kref_{1g1}, kref_{21}, \ldots, kref_{2g2}$ are keyrefs. A first, rough, version of $S_G$ can be obtained by constructing a list containing all the constructs of $S_1$ and $S_2$:

$$S_G = \langle x_{1_1}, x_{1_2}, \ldots, x_{1_{n1}}, k_{1_1}, k_{1_2}, \ldots, k_{1_{f1}}, kref_{1_1}, kref_{1_2}, \ldots, kref_{1_{g1}}, x_{2_1}, x_{2_2}, \ldots, x_{2_{n2}}, k_{2_1}, k_{2_2}, \ldots, k_{2_{f2}}, kref_{2_1}, kref_{2_2}, \ldots, kref_{2_{g2}} \rangle$$

This version of $S_G$ could present some redundancies and/or ambiguities. In order to remove them and, consequently, to refine $S_G$, $MD(u)$ and $RD(u)$ must be examined and some tasks must be performed for each tuple present therein. Specifically, let $\langle E_{1j}, E_{2k}\rangle \in MD(u)$ be a synonymy between two complex elements. $E_{1j}$ and $E_{2k}$ are merged into a complex element $E_{jk}$. The name of $E_{jk}$ is one between the names of $E_{1j}$ and $E_{2k}$. The set of sub-elements of $E_{jk}$ is obtained by applying the xs:sequence indicator to the sets of sub-elements of $E_{1j}$ and $E_{2k}$; the list of attributes of $E_{jk}$ is composed by the attributes of $E_{1j}$ and those of $E_{2k}$. Each xs:selector element referring to $E_{1j}$ or

$E_{2k}$ in a key or a keyref of $S_G$ must be updated in order to refer to $E_{jk}$.

Note that, after these tasks have been carried out, it could happen that:

- A tuple $\langle A'_{jk}, A''_{jk}\rangle$, such that $A'_{jk}$ and $A''_{jk}$ are attributes of $E_{jk}$, belongs to $MD(u)$. In this case $A'_{jk}$ and $A''_{jk}$ are merged into an attribute $A^*_{jk}$; the name of $A^*_{jk}$ is one between the names of $A'_{jk}$ and $A''_{jk}$; the data type of $A^*_{jk}$ is the most general one between those of $A'_{jk}$ and $A''_{jk}$. Each xs:field element referring to $A'_{jk}$ or $A''_{jk}$ in a key or a keyref of $S_G$ must be updated in order to refer to $A^*_{jk}$.
- A tuple $\langle E'_{jk}, E''_{jk}\rangle$, such that $E'_{jk}$ and $E''_{jk}$ are simple sub-elements of $E_{jk}$, belongs to $MD(u)$. In this case $E'_{jk}$ and $E''_{jk}$ are merged into an element $E^*_{jk}$ ; the name of $E^*_{jk}$ is one between the names of $E'_{jk}$ and $E''_{jk}$; the data type of $E^*_{jk}$ is the most general one between those of $E'_{jk}$ and $E''_{jk}$ ; the minOccurs (resp., the maxOccurs) indicator of $E^*_{jk}$ is the minimum (resp., the maximum) between the corresponding ones relative to $E'_{jk}$ and $E''_{jk}$. Each xs:field element referring to $E'_{jk}$ or $E''_{jk}$ in a key or a keyref of $S_G$ must be updated in order to refer to $E^*_{jk}$.
- A tuple $\langle E''_{jk}, A''_{jk}\rangle$, such that $E''_{jk}$ is a simple sub-element of $E_{jk}$ and $A''_{jk}$ is an attribute of $E_{jk}$, belongs to $MD(u)$. In this case, $A''_{jk}$ is removed since its information content is equivalent to the one of $E''_{jk}$ and the representation of an information content by means of an element is more general than that obtained by exploiting an attribute. Each xs:field element referring to $A''_{jk}$ in a key or a keyref of $S_G$ must be updated in order to refer to $E''_{jk}$.

It is worth observing that each sub-element $E'''_{jk}$ of $E_{jk}$ that is not considered in the three cases listed above derives from a sub-element of $E_{1j}$ (resp., $E_{2k}$) detected to be not similar with any attribute or sub-element of $E_{2k}$ (resp., $E_{1j}$). As a consequence, some instances of $E_{jk}$ might not have an instance of $E'''_{jk}$ as their sub-element; therefore, the minOccurs indicator associated with $E'''_{jk}$ must be set to 0. An analogous reasoning leads us to conclude that the use indicator of each attribute of $E_{jk}$ that is not considered in the three cases listed above must be set to optional.

All the references to $E_{1j}$ and $E_{2k}$ in $S_G$ are then transformed into references to $E_{jk}$; the minOccurs and the maxOccurs indicators associated with $E_{jk}$ are derived from the corresponding ones relative to $E_{1j}$ and $E_{2k}$. Owing to these operations, it could happen that two references to $E_{jk}$ are associated with the same element; in this case, one of them must be removed.

For each pair $\langle x_{1j}, x_{2k}\rangle$ of attributes (resp., simple elements) such that $\langle x_{1j}, x_{2k}\rangle \in MD(u)$ and the elements which they belong to are not synonymous (and, consequently, the pair has not been previously considered), $x_{1j}$ and $x_{2k}$ must be merged in the attribute (resp., simple element) $x_{Gjk}$; the merging rules are the same as those illustrated above.

After all x-components have been examined, it could happen that, in $S_G$, there exist two keys having the same xs:selector and the same xs:field. In this case one of these keys is removed and all its occurrences in the xs:refer attribute of keyrefs are transformed into occurrences of the other. Finally, if there exist in $S_G$ two keyrefs having the same xs:selector, xs:refer and xs:field, one of them is removed. After $MD(u)$ has been examined, it is necessary to consider $RD(u)$; in particular, let $\langle x_{1j}, x_{2k}\rangle$ be a tuple of $RD(u)$. In this case it is necessary to modify the name of $x_{1j}$ or $x_{2k}$, along with the corresponding references, keys and keyrefs.

Observe that, after all these activities have been performed, $S_G$ could contain two root elements. Such a situation occurs when the root elements $E_{1r}$ of $S_1$ and $E_{2r}$ of $S_2$ are not synonymous. In this case it is necessary to create a new root element $E_{Gr}$ in $S_G$ whose set of sub-elements is obtained by applying the xs:all indicator to $E_{1r}$ and $E_{2r}$. The occurrence indicators associated with $E_{1r}$ and $E_{2r}$ are minOccurs=0 and maxOccurs=1.

As for the computational complexity of our integration approach, it is possible to state that the worst case time complexity to integrate $S_1$ and $S_2$ into a global XML Schema $S_G$ is $O(mw^2)$, where $m$ is the maximum between the number of complex elements of $S_1$ and the number of complex elements of $S_2$, whereas $w$ is the maximum between $|ConstructSet(S_1)|$ and $|ConstructSet(S_2)|$, where $ConstructSet(S)$ denotes the set of the x-components, the keys and the keyrefs of $S$. As far as this computational complexity result is concerned, the considerations about the dimension of the intensional component of an XML document that we have drawn in the previous section are still valid. For an integration process, an important problem to face is the possible complexity of the global XML Schema. With regard to this, it could be interesting to predict the dimension of the global XML Schema from the dimensions of the XML Schemas to integrate; indeed, such a prediction could be used as a flag to determine the necessity of a schema integration. As far as this problem is concerned, it is possible to show that $|ConstructSet(S_G)| \leq |ConstructSet(S_1)| + |ConstructSet(S_2)| - |MD(u)|$.

As a final remark, we observe that in some application contexts, if a global XML Schema is too complex, it might be possible to perform an abstraction activity on it. Generally speaking, abstracting a global data source implies to group its concepts into homogeneous collections and to represent each collection by means of only one concept (Batini & Lenzerini, 1984; Rosaci, Terracina, & Ursino, 2004). The application of an abstraction activity to a global XML Schema allows the attention to be focused on the main concepts represented in it and avoids useless details to be considered.

The computational complexity results presented above and our reasoning about the possibility to apply abstraction techniques on the integrated XML Schema allow us to conclude that our approach is scalable. Indeed, the computation time is polynomial against the dimension of input XML Schemas; the dimension of the global XML Schema is reasonable and decreases when the number of existing similarities increases (with regard to this we observe that, if a user decides to integrate two XML Schemas then, presumably, many similarities hold between them). Finally, if the number and the dimension of the XML Schemas to integrate are too large, then an abstraction task can be applied on the integrated XML Schema; in this way, the user can examine the abstracted XML Schema to focus on the most relevant concepts; only when more details are necessary, the user must examine the (more complex) global XML Schema.

## A POSSIBLE IMPLEMENTATION OF THE SCM COMPONENT

As previously pointed out, *SCM* is in charge of clustering a set of possibly related XML sources. It receives a set $SchemaSet = \{S_1, S_2, \ldots, S_n\}$ of XML Schemas to cluster and the set of the intensional interschema properties involving concepts belonging to these Schemas. These properties, as a whole, form the so-called *Interschema Property Dictionary IPD*.

Before providing a detailed description of our approach to implementing *SCM*, we define $XCompSet(S_i)$ as the set of the x-components of $S_i$ and we denote with $P$ the total number of x-components belonging to the Schemas of *SchemaSet*, that is:

$$P = \sum_{i=1}^{n} | XCompSet(S_i) |$$

Now we define some functions that will be extremely useful in the following; they receive two x-components $x_\nu$ and $x_\mu$ and return a boolean value; these functions are:

- *identical*($x_\nu$, $x_\mu$), that returns *true* if and only if $x_\nu$ and $x_\mu$ are two synonymous x-components having the same name, the same typology and the same data type;
- *verystrong*($x_\nu$, $x_\mu$), that returns *true* if and only if $x_\nu$ and $x_\mu$ are two synonymous x-components having the same typology but different names or different data types;
- *strong*($x_\nu$, $x_\mu$), that returns *true* if and only if $x_\nu$ and $x_\mu$ are two synonymous x-components having different typologies;
- *hweak*($x_\nu$, $x_\mu$), that returns *true* if and only if $x_\nu$ and $x_\mu$ are related by a hyponymy property;
- *oweak*($x_\nu$, $x_\mu$), that returns *true* if and only if $x_\nu$ and $x_\mu$ are related by an overlapping property.

It is possible to prove that the computation of the functions *identical*($x_\nu$, $x_\mu$), *verystrong*($x_\nu$, $x_\mu$), *strong*($x_\nu$, $x_\mu$), *hweak*($x_\nu$, $x_\mu$), and *oweak*($x_\nu$, $x_\mu$) costs $O(\log P)$. Starting from the functions defined previously, it is possible to construct the following support dictionaries.

*Identity Dictionary ID*, defined as:

$$ID = \{\langle x_\nu, x_\mu \rangle \mid x_\nu, x_\mu \in \bigcup_{i=1}^{n} XCompSet(S_i),\ identical(x_\nu, x_\mu) = true\}$$

*Very Strong Similarity Dictionary VSSD*, defined as:

$$VSSD = \{\langle x_\nu, x_\mu \rangle \mid x_\nu, x_\mu \in \bigcup_{i=1}^{n} XCompSet(S_i),\ verystrong(x_\nu, x_\mu) = true\}$$

*Strong Similarity Dictionar SSD*, defined as:

$$SSD = \{\langle x_\nu, x_\mu \rangle \mid x_\nu, x_\mu \in \bigcup_{i=1}^{n} XCompSet(S_i),\ strong(x_\nu, x_\mu) = true\}$$

*HWeak Similarity Dictionary HWSD*, defined as:

$$HWSD = \{\langle x_\nu, x_\mu \rangle \mid x_\nu, x_\mu \in \bigcup_{i=1}^{n} XCompSet(S_i),\ hweak(x_\nu, x_\mu) = true\}$$

*OWeak Similarity Dictionary OWSD*, defined as:

$$OWSD = \{\langle x_\nu, x_\mu \rangle \mid x_\nu, x_\mu \in \bigcup_{i=1}^{n} XCompSet(S_i),\ oweak(x_\nu, x_\mu) = true\}$$

The construction of these dictionaries is carried out in such a way that they are always ordered w.r.t. the names of the involved x-components. It is possible to prove that the construction of the dictionaries *ID*, *VSSD*, *SSD*, *HWSD* and *OWSD* costs $O(P^2 \log P)$.

## Construction of the Dissimilarity Matrix

Most of the existing clustering algorithms are based on the knowledge of the Dissimilarity Matrix (Han & Kamber, 2006); once this structure has been constructed, it is possible to apply on it a large variety of clustering algorithms already proposed in the literature. In order to allow the application of the maximum possible number of clustering algorithms, we have decided to exploit a *metric* to measure the dissimilarity between two XML Schemas; in fact, many clustering algorithms require this feature.

Since involved XML Schemas could be semantically heterogeneous and since we want to group them on the basis of their relative semantics, the metrics we are defining must necessarily be very different from the classical ones; specifically, in our case, it must be strictly dependent on the intensional interschema properties that represent the basis of our strategy to define inter-source semantics.

Our notion of metrics is based on a suitable, multi-dimensional euclidean space. It has $P$ dimensions, one for each x-component of the involved XML Schemas; in the following it will be denoted by the symbol $\mathbb{R}^P$.

An XML Schema $S_i$ can be represented in $\mathbb{R}^P$ by means of a point $Q_i \equiv [q_1^i, q_2^i, \ldots, q_\nu^i, \ldots, q_P^i]$. The value of the generic coordinate $q_\nu^i$ is obtained by means of the following formula:

$$q_\nu^i = \xi(x_\nu) \cdot \psi(x_\nu, S_i, ID, VSSD, SSD, HWSD, OWSD)$$

$\xi(x_\nu)$ discriminates the complex elements w.r.t. the simple ones and the attributes. This is necessary because a complex element is presumably more characterizing than either a simple element or an attribute to define the semantics of a concept. $\xi(x_\nu)$ is defined in the following way:

$$\xi(x_\nu) = \begin{cases} 1 & \textit{if } x_\nu \textit{ is a complex element} \\ \gamma & \textit{if } x_\nu \textit{ is either a simple element or an attribute} \end{cases}$$

Here, $\gamma$ belongs to the real interval [0,1].

$\psi(x_\nu, S_i, ID, VSSD, SSD, HWSD, OWSD)$ indicates how much $S_i$ is capable of representing the semantics expressed by the concept associated with $x_\nu$; it is defined as shown in Exhibit 2.

Here, $\alpha_I$, $\alpha_{VS}$, $\alpha_S$, $\alpha_{HW}$, and $\alpha_{OW}$ belong to the real interval [0,1].

It is possible to prove that:

- the worst case time complexity to determine the point $Q_i$ associated with $S_i$ in $\mathbb{R}^P$ is $O(|XCompSet(S_i)|\ P \log P)$;
- the worst case time complexity to determine the points associated with all the Schemas of *SchemaSet* in $\mathbb{R}^P$ is

$$O\left(\left(\sum_{i=1}^{n} |\ XCompSet(S_i)\ |\right) P \log P\right) = O(P^2 \log P)$$

We are now able to introduce our notion of distance between two XML Schemas and, consequently, to construct the Dissimilarity Matrix. More specifically, the distance between two XML Schemas $S_i$ and $S_j$, belonging to *SchemaSet*, is computed by determining the euclidean distance between the corresponding points in $\mathbb{R}^P$ and by normalizing this distance to obtain a value in the real interval [0,1], as required by clustering algorithms. This is obtained by means of the following formula:

$$d(Q_i, Q_j) = \frac{\sqrt{\sum_{\nu=1}^{P} \left(q_\nu^i - q_\nu^j\right)^2}}{\sqrt{\sum_{\nu=1}^{P} \left(\xi(x_\nu)\right)^2}}$$

*Exhibit 2.*

$$\psi(x_\nu, S_i, ID, VSSD, SSD, HWSD, OWSD) = \begin{cases} 1 & \textit{if } x_\nu \in XCompSet(S_i) \\ \alpha_I & \textit{if } x_\nu \notin XCompSet(S_i), \exists\ x_\mu \in XCompSet(S_i) \mid \langle x_\nu, x_\mu \rangle \in ID \\ \alpha_{VS} & \textit{if } x_\nu \notin XCompSet(S_i), \exists\ x_\mu \in XCompSet(S_i) \mid \langle x_\nu, x_\mu \rangle \in VSSD \\ \alpha_S & \textit{if } x_\nu \notin XCompSet(S_i), \exists\ x_\mu \in XCompSet(S_i) \mid \langle x_\nu, x_\mu \rangle \in SSD \\ \alpha_{HW} & \textit{if } x_\nu \notin XCompSet(S_i), \exists\ x_\mu \in XCompSet(S_i) \mid \langle x_\nu, x_\mu \rangle \in HWSD \\ \alpha_{OW} & \textit{if } x_\nu \notin XCompSet(S_i), \exists\ x_\mu \in XCompSet(S_i) \mid \langle x_\nu, x_\mu \rangle \in OWSD \\ 0 & \textit{otherwise} \end{cases}$$

Here, the numerator represents the classical euclidean distance between two points of $R^P$; the denominator denotes the maximum distance possibly existing between two points of $R^P$ and is exploited to normalize the numerator[2].

It is possible to prove that the worst case time complexity to construct the Dissimilarity Matrix is $O(n^2P)$.

## Application of the Pre-Existing Clustering Algorithms on the Constructed Dissimilarity Matrix

Once the Dissimilarity Matrix has been defined, it is possible to apply on it a large variety of clustering algorithms previously proposed in the literature. These differ for their time complexity, for their result accuracy, as well as for their behaviour. Therefore, it is clear that the choice of the clustering algorithm to be adopted in a certain domain strictly depends on its main features. In order to evaluate this fact, we have considered three clustering algorithms, characterized by different features. For implementation purposes, we have chosen to apply three algorithms available in WEKA (Witten & Frank, 2000), one of the most popular Data Mining tools; specifically, we have chosen to apply K-Means, Expectation Maximization and Farthest First Traversal.

As previously pointed out, our clustering approaches operate on high-dimensional spaces, since the number of possible dimensions is $P$, i.e., the number of x-components of all the involved XML Schemas. In spite of this high dimensionality, all the three clustering algorithms adopted by us worked very well with all the test data. However, we cannot be sure that, in the future, when the number and the dimension of involved XML sources will be much greater than the current ones, these three algorithms will not show scalability problems.

If this happens then the clustering technique adopted could be substituted by techniques specifically devoted to cluster high-dimensional data. These approaches can be subdivided into two main categories, namely feature transformation and feature selection (Han & Kamber, 2006).

Feature transformation approaches, such as *principal component analysis* and *singular value decomposition*, transform the data into a smaller space while generally preserving the original relative distance between objects. They summarize data by creating linear combinations of the features, and may discover hidden structures in the data. However, such techniques do not actually remove any of the original features from analysis.

Feature subset selection approaches are generally used for data reduction by removing irrelevant or redundant dimensions. Given a set of features, feature subset selection finds the subset of features that are the most relevant to the clustering task.

A further possible way for handling high dimensional data is based on the exploitation of co-clustering approaches (Mirkin, 1996). However, they are difficult to be applicated in our context since they require the information necessary for clustering to be provided by means of the *object-by-variable* matrix, whereas our approach adopts the dissimilarity matrix for this purpose.

In this section, we provide a brief overview of the behaviour of these algorithms when applied to our reference context.

### K-Means

When applied to our reference context, K-Means (MacQueen, 1967) receives a parameter $k$ and partitions the set of points of $R^P$ in $k$ clusters. The worst case time complexity of K-Means is $O(n\ k\ t)$, where $n$ is the cardinality of *SchemaSet*, $k$ is the desired number of clusters and $t$ is the number of iterations necessary for the algorithm to converge. Typically, $k$ and $t$ are much smaller than $n$; therefore, the worst case time complexity of K-Means can be considered linear against the cardinality of *SchemaSet*; for this reason K-Means is relatively scalable to cluster large sets of XML Schemas.

A difficulty in the application of K-Means to our context regards its sensitivity to noise and outliers; this implies that, if there exist some XML Schemas semantically very different from the others, K-Means could return not particularly satisfactory results. Another drawback of K-Means consists of its necessity to preventively know the best value for $k$; if this information is not available, a try-and-check approach should be adopted to determine it. Clearly, this would increase the time necessary to the algorithm to provide the final results.

### Expectation-Maximization

Expectation-Maximization (EM) (Dempster, Laird, & Rubin, 1977; Xu & Jordan, 1996) models involved objects as a collection of $k$ Gaussians[3], where $k$ is the number of the clusters to be derived. For each involved object, *EM* computes a degree of membership to each cluster.

The implementation of *EM* is very similar to the one of K-Means. As with K-Means, *EM* begins with an initial guess of the cluster centers (*Expectation* step) and iteratively refines them (*Maximization* step). It terminates when a parameter, measuring the quality of obtained clusters, no longer shows significant increases. *EM* is guaranteed to converge to a local maximum, that often coincides with the global one.

An important feature of this algorithm is its capability of modelling quite a rich set of cluster shapes. Moreover, even if the user can directly specify the best number of clusters to be derived, *EM* can be instructed to determine it by itself.

The quite refined statistical model underlying *EM* allows it to often obtain optimal results; for this reason *EM* is frequently adopted in a large variety of application contexts. Moreover, its capability of automatically determining the best number of clusters makes it particularly suited for our reference context.

### Farthest First Traversal

The basic idea of Farthest First Traversal (*FFT*) (Hockbaum & Shmoys, 1985) is to get $k$ points out of $n$, that are mutually "far" from each other. *FFT* operates as follows. Initially, it randomly selects a point $Q_1$ and puts it into the so-called "Traversed Set" *TS*. Next, it performs $k$-1 iterations to construct *TS*: for this purpose, during each iteration it inserts into *TS* the point $Q_i$ having the maximum distance from *TS*; the distance of $Q_i$ from *TS* is defined as $d(Q_i,TS) = \min d(Q_i,Q_j)$ (with $Q_j \in TS$), where $d(Q_i,Q_j)$ could be any dissimilarity measure between two points (in our approach it is the dissimilarity measure defined previously).

After the construction of *TS*, *FFT* sets each point $Q_i \in TS$ as the centroid of a cluster; then, for each point $Q_k \notin TS$, it computes the distance of $Q_k$ from the various centroids and puts this point in the cluster whose centroid has the minimum distance from it.

*FFT* requires the user to specify the number $k$ of clusters to be constructed; moreover, the quality of its results might be influenced by the choice of the initial point $Q_1$ of *TS*. However, the worst case time complexity of this algorithm is $O(n\ k)$, where $n$ is the cardinality of *SchemaSet* and $k$ is the number of clusters to be obtained. As a consequence, it is scalable and particularly suited in application contexts, like ours, where objects to be clustered could be very numerous.

## RELATED WORK

In this section we compare the approaches we have defined to implement the *IIPE*, the *ISIM* and the *SCM* components of our framework with the corresponding ones already proposed in the literature. In the following, since interschema property extraction and source integration are often considered within the same approach in the literature, we analyze the approaches performing these tasks in a sub-section and those performing source clustering in another one.

## Intensional Interschema Property Extraction and Intensional Source Integration

In the literature many approaches to perform intensional interschema property extraction and intensional source integration have been proposed. Even if they are quite numerous and various, to the best of our knowledge, none of them guarantees the possibility to choose a "severity" level against which the various activities are carried out; this feature, instead, is very important in our approach. In this section we examine some of these approaches and highlight their similarities and differences w.r.t. our own.

### Approach of Passi, Lane, Madria, Sakamuri, Mohania, Bhowmick (2002)

In (Passi et al., 2002) an XML Schema integration framework, based on the extraction of interschema properties, is proposed. In order to perform its task this approach exploits an object-oriented data model called XSDM (XML Schema Data Model).

The approach of (Passi et al., 2002) is very close to our source integration approach. In particular, both of them are *rule-based* (Rahm & Bernstein, 2001) and assume that the global XML Schema is formulated in a *referenced style* rather than in an *inline style* (see (Thompson, Beech, Maloney, & Mendelsohn, 2004) for more details); moreover, the integration rules proposed in (Passi et al., 2002) are quite similar to those exploited by our approach.

As for the main differences existing between the two approaches we observe that: (1) the approach of (Passi et al., 2002) requires a preliminary translation of an XML Schema into an XSDM Schema; such a translation is not required by our approach; (2) the integration task in (Passi et al., 2002) is graph-based and object-oriented whereas, in our approach, it is directly based on the *examination of x-components*.

### Approach of Yang, Lee, & Ling (2003)

In (Yang, Lee, & Ling, 2003) an approach for the integration of XML data sources, based on the derivation of interschema properties, is proposed. It exploits a suitable data model called ORA-SS (Object Relationship Attribute Model for Semi-Structured Data).

This approach and ours share some similarities; in particular, both of them have been conceived to operate only on XML data sources and exploit graph-based algorithms to detect interschema properties.

However, there also exist some differences between them; indeed, (1) the approach of (Yang, Lee, & Ling, 2003) needs to translate input information sources into ORA-SS schemas; (2) it can produce more precise results than those returned by our approach but, on the other side, it is computationally more expensive.

### XClust

In (Lee, Yang, Hsu, & Yang, 2002) the system XClust, aiming at integrating XML data sources, is presented. XClust determines the similarity degrees of a group of DTDs by considering not only the corresponding linguistic and structural information but also their semantics, derived by the examination of the neighborhoods of their elements. In particular, a DTD is modeled as a tree and the neighborhood of an element consists of a set of ancestors and descendants. The computation of the similarity degrees among the DTDs allows their grouping into clusters; such a clustering activity is recursively applied on the DTDs of each generated cluster until a sufficiently small number of clusters has been obtained.

It is possible to recognize some similarities between our approach and XClust; in particular, (1) both of them have been specifically conceived to operate on XML data sources (even if our approach manages XML Schemas whereas XClust operates on DTDs); (2) both of them consider not only linguistic similarities but also semantic ones.

There are also several differences between them; more specifically, (1) to perform the integration activity, XClust requires the support of a hierarchical clustering whereas our approach adopts schema matching techniques; (2) XClust represents DTDs as trees; as a consequence, element and attribute neighborhoods are quite different from those constructed by our approach.

## Cupid

In (Madhavan, Bernstein, & Rahm, 2001) Cupid, a system to derive interschema properties among heterogeneous information sources, is presented. In this system property derivation is performed by carrying out two kinds of examinations, named *linguistic* and *structure* matchings.

Some differences can be detected between Cupid and our approach. In particular, (1) Cupid only derives interschema properties; (2) it has been conceived to handle a large variety of data source formats; (3) since the activities it performs to extract properties are numerous and sophisticated, the results it obtains could be more refined than those returned by our approach but the required time and user intervention are greater.

## Rondo

In (Melinik, Rahm, & Bernstein, 2003) Rondo, a system conceived to integrate and manipulate relational Schemas, XML Schemas and SQL views, is presented. Rondo exploits a graph-based approach to modeling information sources and the *Similarity Flooding Algorithm* (Melnik, Garcia-Molina, & Rahm, 2002) to perform schema matching.

Both Rondo and our approach are semi-automatic and exploit schema matching techniques.

The main differences existing between them are the following: (1) Rondo can handle several information source formats; (2) it models involved information sources as graphs whereas our approach directly operates on XML Schemas; (3) it exploits a sophisticated technique (i.e., the Similarity Flooding Algorithm) to perform schema matching activities; as a consequence, it obtains refined results but is time expensive and requires a heavy human feedback.

## Approach of dos Santos Mello, Castano, & Heuser (2002)

In (dos Santos Mello, Castano, & Heuser, 2002) an XML-based integration approach, capable of handling several source formats, is presented.

Both this approach and ours operate on XML sources and carry out a semantic integration. However, important differences between them can be found; indeed, (1) the approach of (dos Santos Mello, Castano, & Heuser, 2002) operates on DTDs and requires the translation of these DTDs in an appropriate formalism called ORM/NIAM (Halpin, 1998); vice versa, our approach operates directly on XML Schemas; (2) the global XML Schema constructed by the approach of (dos Santos Mello, Castano, & Heuser, 2002) is represented in the ORM/NIAM formalism whereas our approach returns directly a global XML Schema; (3) the approach of (dos Santos Mello, Castano, & Heuser, 2002) is quite complex to be applied when involved sources are numerous.

## SKAT

In (Mitra, Wiederhold, & Jannink, 1999) the system SKAT, exploiting first order logic rules to express match and mismatch relationships, as well as to derive new matches, is presented.

The approach of SKAT is similar to our own in that it is semi-automatic and looks at concept similarities to derive matchings.

The main differences between them are the following: (1) SKAT constructs a graph representation of the involved sources consisting of *one node per XML source*; vice versa, our approach derives *one graph representation per XML source*; in this way it obtains more refined representations of involved sources; (2) SKAT exploits first order logic rules to express derived matchings; this allows it to represent possibly complex relationships between concepts; however, a heavy intervention of human experts is necessary in the derivation of these relationships.

## DIXSE

In (Rodriguez-Gianolli & Mylopoulos, 2001) the DIXSE (Data Integration for XML based on Schematic Knowledge) system, aiming at supporting the integration of a set of XML documents, is presented.

Both DIXSE and our approach are semantic and operate on XML documents; both of them exploit structural and terminological relationships to carry out the integration activity.

The main differences between them regard the interschema property extraction technique; indeed, DIXSE requires the support of the user whereas our approach operates almost automatically. As a consequence, the results returned by DIXSE could be more refined than those provided by our approach but, when the number and/or the dimension of the sources to integrate are high, the effort DIXSE requires to the user might be particularly heavy.

## Approach of Lim & Ng (2001)

(Lim & Ng, 2001) describes an approach based on the exploitation of a suitable graph formalism named HDG, as well as on the extraction of interschema properties, to perform the integration of data sources characterized by different formats.

The approach of (Lim & Ng, 2001) and ours are similar in that: (1) both of them are semantic; (2) in both of them the integration is light, even if the approach of (Lim & Ng, 2001) requires a translation phase before it; (3) both of them are almost automatic and, finally, (4) both of them are *rule-based*.

They present also several differences; in particular: (1) the approach of (Lim & Ng, 2001) has been conceived to integrate information sources possibly having different formats; (2) it requires the translation of input data sources into the HDG formalism; (3) the interschema properties exploited to guide the integration activity are different in the two approaches; in particular, (Lim & Ng, 2001) is based on the relationship $_{>>}$, indicating if a concept is a hypernym or an ancestor of another one.

LSD. In (Doan, Domingos, & Halevy, 2001) a *machine learning* approach, named LSD (Learning Source Description), to perform schema matching activities on information sources, is proposed. It has been extended also to ontologies in GLUE (Doan, Madhavan, Domingos, Halevy, 2002).

During the initial phase, LSD requires quite a heavy support of the user to carry out training tasks; however, after this phase, no human intervention is required.

Both LSD and our approach operate mainly on XML sources. They differ especially in their purposes; in fact, LSD aims at deriving interschema properties whereas our approach first derives properties and, then, exploits them for the source integration activity. In addition, as far as property derivation is concerned, LSD is *learner-based* whereas our approach is *rule-based*. Finally, LSD requires a heavy human intervention at the beginning and, then, is automatic; vice versa, our approach does not need a pre-processing phase but requires the human intervention at the end to validate obtained results.

## Approach of He & Chang (2003)

In (He & Chang, 2003) a statistical framework for performing schema matching is proposed. In particular, the authors hypothesize the presence, for each application context, of a "hidden schema model" which acts as a unified generative model describing how schemas are generated from a finite vocabulary of attributes.

Both the approach of (He & Chang, 2003) and ours aim at integrating large Web sources and at performing schema matching almost automatically.

However, there are important differences between them; in particular, (1) the approach of (He & Chang, 2003) adopts statistical-based techniques; (2) it creates a hidden schema, which is both capable of fully describing a domain and useful as a mediated schema; however, as claimed by the authors, its complexity is exponential and, consequently, it can be adopted only if schema matching is carried out offline.

## Approach of Castano, De Antonellis, Ferrara, & Kuruvilla Ottathycal (2002)

In (Castano, De Antonellis, Ferrara, & Kuruvilla Ottathycal, 2002) an approach to carrying out the integration of XML sources with the support of interschema properties is proposed.

Our approach shares some similarities with this one. Indeed, both of them: (1) are *rule-based*; (2) derive interschema properties which are, then, exploited to perform the integration task; (3) are semi-automatic.

However, they have also several differences; in particular: (1) the approach proposed in (Castano, De Antonellis, Ferrara, & Kuruvilla Ottathycal, 2002) privileges result accuracy to the detriment of computational complexity; (2) the intervention of the human expert it requires is heavier than that needed by our approach.

## MOMIS

In (Bergamaschi, Castano, & Vincini, 1999) the MOMIS system, conceived to support information source integration and querying, is presented. MOMIS and our approach are similar in that both of them are semi-automatic and semantic; in addition, both of them first extract interschema properties and then exploit them to carry out the integration task.

However, there are also important differences between them; specifically, (1) MOMIS can handle several source formats; (2) in MOMIS the core of the interschema property derivation task is a cluster procedure, whereas our approach exploits graph matchings.

## COMA

In (Do & Rahm, 2002) COMA (COmbining MAtch), an interactive and iterative system to combine several schema matching approaches, is proposed.

The approach of COMA appears orthogonal to ours; in particular, our approach could inherit some features from COMA (as an example, the idea of operating iteratively) to improve the accuracy of its results. As for an important difference between them, we observe that COMA handles a large variety of information source formats; vice versa, our approach is specialized for XML sources. In addition, our approach requires the user to specify only the desired severity level; vice versa, in COMA, the user must specify the matching strategy (i.e., the desired matchers and the ways to combine their results).

## DIKE

In (Palopoli, Terracina, & Ursino, 2003a; Palopoli, Terracina, & Ursino, 2003b) DIKE (Database Intensional Knowledge Extractor), a system supporting the semi-automatic construction and management of Cooperative Information Systems and Data Warehouses from heterogeneous databases is presented. The input of DIKE consists of a set of relational databases. First this system derives intensional interschema properties among involved databases; then, it constructs a Data Repository representing a structured, integrated, hierarchical and consistent description of the information stored in the input databases. The

Data Repository thus constructed is, then, used as the core of a Cooperative Information System or a Data Warehouse.

The similarities between DIKE and our framework regard not only their integration approach but also some points of their overall behavior. Specifically: (1) both of them aim at deriving interschema properties, constructing a hierarchy and using it as the core of a Cooperative Information System or a Data Warehouse; (2) both of them adopt an intensional interschema property derivation approach based on neighborhoods; (3) in both of them the intensional integration activity strongly depends on derived intensional interschema properties.

However, there are several differences between DIKE and our framework. Specifically: (1) DIKE operates on structured databases whereas our framework considers XML sources; (2) DIKE handles only intensional information whereas our framework manages also the extensional one; (3) DIKE does not follow the Component-Based Development paradigm, which, instead, represents the core of our framework; (iv) DIKE does not consider severity levels in the derivation of the intensional interschema properties.

## Intensional Source Clustering and Related Semantic Approaches

### Approach of Qian, Zhang, Liang, Qian, & Jin (2000)

In (Qian, Zhang, Liang, Qian, & Jin, 2000) an approach to clustering DTDs is proposed. Initially, it applies any clustering algorithm to group elements of the involved DTDs in a set of clusters, then creates one array for each DTD, having one component for each cluster; the *i*-th component of the array indicates how many elements of the corresponding DTD belong to the *i*-th cluster. Finally, it applies any clustering algorithm on the set of constructed arrays.

There are some similarities between our approach and that described in (Qian, Zhang, Liang, Qian, & Jin, 2000). Specifically, both of them: (1) construct a "vector"-based representation of the involved schemas which, then, is provided in input to a clustering algorithm; (2) have been specifically conceived for XML.

The main differences between the two approaches are the following: (1) in (Qian, Zhang, Liang, Qian, & Jin, 2000) the computation of the similarity degree between two DTDs privileges their *structural* properties (i.e., the hierarchical organization of the corresponding elements); on the contrary, our approach considers interschema properties, that define a *semantic* information; (2) the clustering activity performed during the first phase allows the approach described in (Qian, Zhang, Liang, Qian, & Jin, 2000) to carry out a preliminary reduction of the number of involved elements; this feature is not present in our approach; however, errors possibly occurring during this initial clustering activity could negatively influence final results.

### XClust

As previously pointed out, XClust defines a clustering technique as a part of a more complex approach for DTD integration.

As for the main similarities between our clustering technique and the one underlying XClust we observe that both of them: (1) have been specifically conceived for XML; (2) operate on the intensional component of the involved information sources.

As for differences between them we observe that: (1) XClust considers only synonymies and does not take hyponymies and overlappings into account; (2) the clustering activity is performed as a support to the integration task in XClust whereas clustering and integration activities are independent and orthogonal in our framework.

## Approach of He, Tao, & Chen-Chuan Chang (2004)

In (He, Tao, & Chen-Chuan Chang, 2004) an approach to clustering structured information sources present in the Web is proposed. For each application domain, this approach assumes the existence of a *hidden model* containing a finite vocabulary of attributes; this assumption allows sources to be clustered by means of a specific algorithm called MD (*Model Differentiation*).

As for the main similarities between our approach and the one described in (He, Tao, & Chen-Chuan Chang, 2004) we observe that both of them: (1) define a suitable mechanism to represent involved sources; (2) exploit semantic information consisting of interschema properties in our approach and in the hidden model in the approach of (He, Tao, & Chen-Chuan Chang, 2004).

The main differences between the two approaches are the following: (1) the approach presented in (He, Tao, & Chen-Chuan Chang, 2004) requires a deep analysis of the extensional component of involved information sources; this analysis produces very satisfactory results but requires a significant pre-processing phase to construct, among the other things, the hidden model; (2) the approach proposed in (He, Tao, & Chen-Chuan Chang, 2004) has been specifically conceived to analyze structured information sources present in the Web; on the contrary, our approach is specialized for XML Schemas.

## SemXClust

In (Tagarelli & Greco, 2010) an approach to clustering semantically related XML documents is proposed. This approach estimates the semantical relatedness of the involved XML documents by analyzing both their structure and their content and by generating the so-called XML features with the support of a lexical ontology knowledge. An important characteristic of the approach of (Tagarelli & Greco, 2010) is the definition of an XML representation model that allows XML document trees to be mapped into transactional data called XML transactions. Each item of this model embeds a distinct combination of structure and content features. In order to capture different ways of associating the XML content with structure information, each considered XML document is preliminarily decomposed into smaller documents according to the notion of *tree tuple*. Obtained XML transactions are, then, provided as input to a suitable transactional clustering algorithm. As for the underlying clustering technique to be adopted, even if SemXClust has been conceived to be parametric w.r.t. any existing clustering algorithm, the authors propose two new ones; the former exploits a centroid-based partitional method, whereas the latter uses frequent (XML) itemsets to compute clusters and to build a hierarchy upon them.

There are some similarities between the approach of (Tagarelli & Greco, 2010) and ours. In particular, both of them: (1) have been specifically conceived for XML; (2) consider semantic relationships such as synonymies; (3) exploit a support lexical ontology (e.g., WordNet); (4) define a suitable strategy to handle the information encoded in the involved sources; (5) can operate with any clustering method.

As for the main differences between them we observe that: (1) SemXClust has been conceived to operate on XML documents; our approach, instead, is specialized for XML Schemas; (2) SemXClust performs also content analysis on textual elements (i.e., it analyzes the content of #PCDATA fields and the value of attributes); (3) in order to perform the clustering task, SemXClust exploits the notion of tree tuple; our approach, instead, considers interschema properties; (4) in order to compute the (dis)similarity matrix, SemXClust adopts a transactional representation; our approach, instead, considers a multi-dimensional euclidean space.

## CONCLUSION AND FUTURE WORKS

We presented a general framework for the intensional integration and exploration of XML sources. The architecture of the proposed framework consists of three layers, which aim at extracting interschema properties and constraints from the sources, integrating and organizing the sources based on an interschema knowledge-based hierarchy, and accessing and exploring the consolidated sources. Our framework follows the general philosophy of the layers architecture pattern, since it provides a layer for each of the three macro-activities mentioned above. Moreover, in order to guarantee a high flexibility and extensibility, the framework has been designed according to the component-based development paradigm.

We believe that the proposed framework should be considered as a starting-point of a more complex system for handling XML sources. Particularly, it could represent the first step towards a system for the management and mining of multiple, highly heterogeneous information sources, where heterogenity here may refer to different aspects, such as their semantics, their formats (e.g., XML documents, relational databases, unstructured information sources), the underlying models, and so forth. This system could consist of a central core (basically formed by the components presented in this chapter) which a large variety of plugins could be added to, in order to provide a catalogue of plugins specialized to solve various problems that are typical of distributed information sources. As a further research direction,it would be interesting to design an intelligent wizard, based on an underlying recommender system, which adaptively suggests the plugins to be added to the framework on the basis of users' needs.

## REFERENCES


Aggarwal, C. C., Ta, N., Wang, J., Feng, J., & Zaki, M. J. (2007). XProj: A framework for projected structural clustering of XML documents. In P. Berkhin, R. Caruana, & X. Wu (Eds.), *Proceedings of the 13th ACM SIGKDD International Conference on Knowledge Discovery and Data Mining (KDD),* (pp. 46-55). ACM.

Arenas, M., & Libkin, L. (2004). A normal form for XML documents. *ACM Transactions on Database Systems, 29,* 195–232. doi:10.1145/974750.974757

Arlow, J., & Neustadt, I. (2005). *UML 2 and the unified process* (2nd ed.). Addison-Wesley.

Batini, C., & Lenzerini, M. (1984). A methodology for data schema integration in the entity relationship model. *IEEE Transactions on Software Engineering, 10*(6), 650–664. doi:10.1109/TSE.1984.5010294

Bergamaschi, S., Castano, S., & Vincini, M. (1999). Semantic integration of semistructured and structured data sources. *SIGMOD Record, 28*(1), 54–59. doi:10.1145/309844.309897

Bussman, F., Meunier, R., Rohnert, H., Sommerlad, P., & Stal, M. (1996). *Pattern-oriented software architecture: A system of patterns.* Wiley.

Castano, S., De Antonellis, V., & De Capitani di Vimercati, S. (2001). Global viewing of heterogeneous data sources. *IEEE Transactions on Data and Knowledge Engineering, 13*(2), 277–297. doi:10.1109/69.917566

Castano, S., De Antonellis, V., Ferrara, A., & Kuruvilla Ottathycal, G. S. (2002). Ontology-based integration of heterogeneous XML datasources. In *Atti del Decimo Convegno Nazionale su Sistemi Evoluti per Basi di Dati* (pp. 27–41). SEBD.

Chua, C. E. H., Chiang, R. H. L., & Lim, E. P. (2003). Instance-based attribute identification in database integration. *The VLDB Journal*, *12*(3), 228–243. doi:10.1007/s00778-003-0088-y

De Meo, P., Quattrone, G., Terracina, G., & Ursino, D. (2006). Integration of XML schemas at various "severity" levels. *Information Systems*, *31*(6), 397–434. doi:10.1016/j.is.2004.11.010

De Meo, P., Quattrone, G., Terracina, G., & Ursino, D. (2007a). Semantics-guided clustering of heterogeneous XML schemas. *Journal on Data Semantics*, *9*, 39–81.

De Meo, P., Quattrone, G., Terracina, G., & Ursino, D. (2007b). An approach to extracting interschema properties from XML schemas at various "severity" levels. *Informatica*, *31*(2), 217–232.

Dempster, A. P., Laird, N. M., & Rubin, D. M. (1977). Maximum likelihood from incomplete data via the EM algorithm. *Journal of the Royal Statistical Society. Series B. Methodological*, *39*(1), 1–38.

Do, H., & Rahm, E. (2002). COMA - A system for flexible combination of schema matching approaches. In *Proceedings of the 28th International Conference on Very Large Databases (VLDB)*, (pp. 610-621).

Doan, A., Domingos, P., & Halevy, A. Y. (2001). Reconciling schemas of disparate data sources: A machine-learning approach. In *Proceedings of the ACM International Conference on Management of Data (SIGMOD)*, (pp. 509-520). ACM.

Doan, A., Madhavan, J., Domingos, P., & Halevy, A. Y. (2002). Learning to map between ontologies on the Semantic Web. In *Proceedings of the ACM International Conference on World Wide Web (WWW)*, (pp. 662-673). ACM.

dos Santos Mello, R., Castano, S., & Heuser, C. A. (2002). A method for the unification of XML schemata. *Information and Software Technology*, *44*(4), 241–249. doi:10.1016/S0950-5849(02)00014-9

Flesca, S., Furfaro, F., Greco, S., & Zumpano, E. (2003). Repairs and consistent answers for XML data with functional dependencies. In Z. Bellahsene, A. B. Chaudhri, E. Rahm, M. Rys, & R. Unland (Eds.), *Proceedings of the 1st International XML Database Symposium (XSym) Lecture Notes in Computer Science: Vol. 2824* (pp. 238-253). Springer.

Galil, Z. (1986). Efficient algorithms for finding maximum matching in graphs. *ACM Computing Surveys*, *18*(1), 23–38. doi:10.1145/6462.6502

Guha, S., Rastogi, R., & Shim, K. (2000). ROCK: A robust clustering algorithm for categorical attributes. *Information Systems*, *25*(5), 345–366. doi:10.1016/S0306-4379(00)00022-3

Halpin, T. (1998). Object-role modeling (ORM-NIAM). In Bernus, P., Mertins, K., & Schmidt, G. (Eds.), *Handbook on architectures of information systems* (pp. 81–102). Springer. doi:10.1007/3-540-26661-5_4

Han, J., & Kamber, M. (2006). *Data mining: Concepts and techniques* (2nd ed.). Morgan Kaufmann.

He, B., & Chang, K. C.-C. (2003). Statistical schema matching across Web query interfaces. In A. Y. Halevy, Z. G. Ives, & A. Doan (Eds.), *Proceedings of the ACM International Conference on Management of Data (SIGMOD)*, (pp. 217-228). ACM.

He, B., Tao, T., & Chang, K. C.-C. (2004). Organizing structured Web sources by query schemas: A clustering approach. In D. A. Grossman, L. Gravano, C. Zhai, O. Herzog, & D. A. Evans (Eds.), *Proceedings of the ACM International Conference on Information and Knowledge Management (CIKM)*, (pp. 22-31). ACM.

Hochbaum, D. S., & Shmoys, D. B. (1985). A best possible heuristic for the k-center problem. *Mathematics of Operations Research, 10*(2), 180–184. doi:10.1287/moor.10.2.180

Jolliffe, I. T. (2002). *Principal component analysis* (2nd ed.). Springer.

Larman, C. (2002). *Applying UML and patterns* (2nd ed.). Prentice-Hall.

Lee, M. L., Yang, L. H., Hsu, W., & Yang, X. (2002). XClust: Clustering XML schemas for effective integration. In *Proceedings of the ACM International Conference on Information and Knowledge Management (CIKM)*, (pp. 292-299). ACM.

Lim, S., & Ng, Y. (2001). Semantic integration of semistructured data. In *Proceedings of the International Symposium on Cooperative Database Systems and Applications (CODAS)*, (pp. 15-24). IEEE Computer Society.

MacQueen, J. B. (1967). Some methods for classification and analysis of multivariate observations. In *Proceedings of the 5th International Symposium on Mathematics, Statistics and Probability* (pp. 281-297). University of California Press.

Madhavan, J., Bernstein, P. A., & Rahm, E. (2001). Generic schema matching with Cupid. In P. M. G. Apers, P. Atzeni, S. Ceri, S. Paraboschi, K. Ramamohanarao, & R. T. Snodgrass (Eds.), *Proceedings of the International Conference on Very Large Data Bases (VLDB)*, (pp. 49-58). Morgan Kaufmann.

McBrien, P., & Poulovassilis, A. (2003). Data integration by bi-directional schema transformation rules. In U. Dayal, K. Ramamritham, & T. M. Vijayaraman (Eds.), *Proceedings of the International Conference on Data Engineering (ICDE)*, (pp. 227-238). IEEE Computer Society.

Melnik, S., Garcia-Molina, H., & Rahm, E. (2002). Similarity flooding: A versatile graph matching algorithm and its application to schema matching. In *Proceedings of the 18th IEEE International Conference on Data Engineering (ICDE)*, (pp. 117-128). IEEE Computer Society.

Melnik, S., Rahm, E., & Bernstein, P. A. (2003). Rondo: A programming platform for generic model management. In A. Y. Halevy, Z. G. Ives, & A. Doan (Eds.), *Proceedings of the International Conference on Management of Data (SIGMOD)*, (pp. 193-204). ACM.

Miller, A. G. (1995). WordNet: A lexical database for English. *Communications of the ACM, 38*(11), 39–41. doi:10.1145/219717.219748

Mirkin, B. (1996). *Mathematical classification and clustering*. Kluwer Academic Publishers.

Mitra, P., Wiederhold, G., & Jannink, J. (1999). Semi-automatic integration of knowledge sources. In *Proceedings of the 2nd International Conference on Information Fusion*.

Palopoli, L., Saccà, D., Terracina, G., & Ursino, D. (2003). Uniform techniques for deriving similarities of objects and subschemes in heterogeneous databases. [IEEE Computer Society.]. *IEEE Transactions on Knowledge and Data Engineering, 15*(2), 271–294. doi:10.1109/TKDE.2003.1185834

Palopoli, L., Terracina, G., & Ursino, D. (2003a). DIKE: A system supporting the semi-automatic construction of cooperative information systems from heterogeneous databases. *Software, Practice & Experience, 33*(9), 847–884. doi:10.1002/spe.531

Palopoli, L., Terracina, G., & Ursino, D. (2003b). Experiences using DIKE: A system for supporting cooperative information system and data warehouse design. *Information Systems, 28*(7), 835–865. doi:10.1016/S0306-4379(02)00101-1

Passi, K., Lane, L., Madria, S. K., Sakamuri, B. C., Mohania, M. K., & Bhowmick, S. S. (2002). A model for XML schema integration. In K. Bauknecht, A. Min Tjoa, & G. Quirchmayr (Eds.), *Proceedings of the International Conference on E-Commerce and Web Technologies (EC-Web) Lecture Notes in Computer Science: Vol. 2455.* (pp. 193-202). Springer.

Polyzotis, N., & Garofalakis, M. N. (2002). Statistical synopses for graph-structured XML databases. In M. J. Franklin, B. Moon, & A. Ailamaki (Eds.), *Proceedings of the ACM International Conference on Management of Data (SIGMOD)*, (pp. 358-369). ACM.

Polyzotis, N., Garofalakis, M. N., & Ioannidis, Y. E. (2004). Approximate XML query answers. In *Proc. of the ACM International Conference on Management of Data (SIGMOD)*, (pp. 263-274). ACM.

Pontieri, L., Ursino, D., & Zumpano, E. (2003). An approach for the extensional integration of data sources with heterogeneous representation formats. *Data & Knowledge Engineering*, *45*(3), 291–331. doi:10.1016/S0169-023X(02)00192-1

Qian, W., Zhang, L., Liang, Y., Qian, H., & Jin, W. (2000). A two-level method for clustering DTDs. In H. Lu, & A. Zhou (Eds.), *Proceedings of the 1st International Conference on Web-Age Information Management (WAIM) Lecture Notes in Computer Science: Vol. 1846.* (pp. 41-52). Springer.

Rahm, E., & Bernstein, P. A. (2001). A survey of approaches to automatic schema matching. *The VLDB Journal*, *10*(4), 334–350. doi:10.1007/s007780100057

Rodriguez-Gianolli, P., & Mylopoulos, J. (2001). A semantic approach to XML-based data integration. In *Proceedings of the International Conference on Conceptual Modelling (ER): Vol. 2224. Lecture Notes in Computer Science* (pp. 117-132). Springer.

Rosaci, D., Terracina, G., & Ursino, D. (2004). A framework for abstracting data sources having heterogeneous representation formats. *Data & Knowledge Engineering*, *48*(1), 1–38. doi:10.1016/S0169-023X(03)00092-2

Tagarelli, A., & Greco, S. (2010). Semantic clustering of XML documents. *ACM Transactions on Information Systems*, *28*(1), 1–56. doi:10.1145/1658377.1658380

Thompson, H. S., Beech, D., Maloney, M., & Mendelsohn, N. (Eds.). (2004). *XML schema part 1: Structures.* W3C Recommendation. Retrieved from http://www.w3.org/TR/xmlschema-1

Witten, I. H., & Frank, E. (2000). *Data mining: Practical machine learning tools and techniques with Java implementations*. Morgan Kaufmann.

Xu, L., & Jordan, M. I. (1996). On convergence properties of the EM algorithm for Gaussian mixtures. *Neural Computation*, *8*(1), 129–151. doi:10.1162/neco.1996.8.1.129

Yang, X., Lee, M.-L., & Ling, T. W. (2003). Resolving structural conflicts in the integration of XML schemas: A semantic approach. In I.-Y. Song, S. W. Liddle, T. Wang Ling, & P. Scheuermann (Eds.), *Proceedings of the International Conference on Conceptual Modeling (ER) Lecture Notes in Computer Science: Vol. 2813.* (pp. 520-533). Springer.

## ENDNOTES

1. Observe that this is not an actual limitation since if more than two XML Schemas must be integrated, it is possible to perform more integration steps.
2. Recall that $q_v^i = \xi(x_v) \cdot \psi(x_v, S_i, ID, VSSD, SSD, HWSD, OWSD)$ and that the maximum (resp., minimum) value of $\psi$ is equal to 1 (resp., 0).

[3] Although Gaussians are generally used distributions in *EM*, other different distributions might be considered.

# Chapter 16
# Matching XML Documents at Structural and Conceptual Level using Subtree Patterns

**Qi Hua Pan**
*Curtin University, Australia*

**Fedja Hadzic**
*Curtin University, Australia*

**Tharam S. Dillon**
*Curtin University, Australia*

## ABSTRACT

*Knowledge matching is an important problem for many emerging applications in many areas including scientific knowledge management, ontology matching, e-commerce, and enterprise application integration. Matching the concepts of heterogeneous knowledge representations is very challenging due to the difficulty of taking contextual information into account and detecting complex matches. In this chapter, we describe a knowledge matching approach that uses subtree patterns to utilize structural information for matching at the conceptual and structural level. Initially, the algorithm does not take any syntactic information into account, but rather forms candidate mappings according to their structural/contextual relationships in the knowledge structures, which are then validated using online dictionaries and string similarity measures. The approach will then automatically extract the knowledge structure that is shared among all the matched knowledge representations. Experimental evaluation is performed on a number of real world XML schemas, which demonstrates the effectiveness of the proposed approach.*

DOI: 10.4018/978-1-61350-356-0.ch016

## INTRODUCTION

Matching of heterogeneous knowledge sources has become an increasingly important problem in many areas such as e-commerce, enterprise application integration, schema matching, ontology matching/merging/alignment, knowledge management related tasks and many emerging semantic web applications. For example, many web services use XML as a unified exchange format, since it provides the extensibility and language neutrality that is the key for standards–based interoperability between different software applications (Alesso & Smith, 2006; Fensel et al., 2007). The process of discovering particular web services, composing them together and associating semantics with them in order to accomplish a specific goal is an important step toward the development of 'semantic web services' (Alesso & Smith, 2006; Fensel et al., 2007; Paolucci, Kawamura, Payne, & Sycara, 2002). In this process, being able to detect common knowledge structures between the information presented by the services to be integrated will be a useful step toward automation. Some other common uses of knowledge matching are to produce a shared knowledge representation for one domain or to produce a knowledge representation encompassing aspects from many domains at the same time.

Most of the current techniques used for the knowledge matching problem rely on user interaction and there are only a few methods that approach the task in a close to automatic manner. The main difficulty in this process is caused by the fact that each particular community or organization may name the same concepts differently and structure their knowledge in a unique organization-specific way. The lexical ambiguity of a word or phrase increases the difficulty of knowledge matching, which as a research topic has attracted academic contribution from the 1950's (Ide & Véronis 1998). A recent work of Tagarelli, Longo, and Greco (2009) investigates an unsupervised word sense disambiguation method to identify the semantic relationship among the concepts underlying the constituents of structure information by referring to the WordNet. The first, and the most complex, step in the knowledge matching process is finding semantically correct matches among the concepts from heterogeneous knowledge representations. This is often referred to as the problem of *conceptual level matching*. Once correct mappings between the concepts have been determined, one can choose a common name to represent the concepts representing the same aspect of the domain. The next step in the knowledge matching process is that of *structural level matching*, which is concerned in detecting the common structure in which the concepts of the domain at hand are organized in the knowledge representation considered. In this chapter we focus on both the conceptual level and the structural level knowledge matching.

We propose a unique approach to this problem based on the utilization of previously developed tree mining algorithms (Tan, Dillon, Hadzic, Feng, & Chang, 2006; Tan, Hadzic, Dillon, & Chang, 2008; Hadzic, Tan, & Dillon, 2008) to approach the problem in a fully automated manner. The work presented in this chapter is an extension of our previously developed method for concept matching presented in (Pan, Hadzic, & Dillon, 2010). The conceptual level matching problem is addressed by utilizing the substructures of the knowledge representations to first determine the similarity of the concepts based upon their position in the knowledge substructures and the structural properties of the substructures in which they occur. This will enable us to detect candidate simple and complex matches among the concepts in the domain, by taking into account the context in which they are used. These formed mappings are evaluated for validity using online dictionaries and string similarity metrics including string edit distance and sound similarity. Once the correct matches have been identified the labels of the concepts from the formed matches are updated so that the same name is used to represent the same aspect of the domain at hand. This enables us to focus on finding similarities in which the concepts of the domain are organized in the heterogeneous knowledge structures considered.

By using a tree mining approach to knowledge matching at the structural level, many of the structural differences among the knowledge representations can be detected more easily and the largest common structure automatically extracted. When considering different knowledge representations (KR), each KR is most likely to differ in the way the knowledge is structured and the amount of concept granularity. However, since they are describing the same domain there are usually parts of knowledge equivalent among the KRs considered. This is where the tree mining algorithms will prove useful as they are capable of efficiently extracting common sub-structures from large tree databases, this has been previously demonstrated in works such as (Tan, Hadzic, Dillon, Chang, & Feng, 2008; Hadzic, Tan, & Dillon, 2008; Zaki, 2005a). The obtained common substructure that is valid among all different organizations' KRs could be less specific than the KR from a particular data source, but it is therefore valid for all the organizations in a domain. Furthermore, each of the different organizations could have their own specific part of knowledge which is only valid from their perspective, and which can be added to the shared KR so that every aspect for that organization is covered. Hence, the shared KR can be used as the basis for structuring the knowledge for that particular domain and different communities of users can extend this model when required for their own organization-specific purposes.

The rest of this chapter is organized as follows. The related work in this problem area is overviewed in the "Background" section. We formulate the knowledge matching problem at both conceptual and structural levels, and define some tree related concepts in the "Problem Definition" section. In the "Motivation of the proposed approach" section, we justify the direction taken in the development of the proposed knowledge matching technique. The proposed knowledge matching method is presented in detail in the "Method Description" section, which also describes a running example. In the "Experimental Evaluation" section, we evaluate our method using real world knowledge representations of the same domain. We then discuss our future work in this area and conclude the chapter.

## BACKGROUND

The main challenge during matching of heterogeneous knowledge representations is that of finding semantically correct matches among the concepts. This problem is analogous to schema matching in databases. Schema matching takes the semantic information as well as the positions of nodes in the conceptual models (graph or tree) into account. Regarding the tree structure matching, tree edit distance is a basic approach to describe difference between two trees. Touzet (2007) describes a linear algorithm for comparing two similar ordered rooted trees with node labels by using tree edit distance. Hao and Zhang (2007) has employed the concept of tree edit distance to match web-service operations. The TreeMatch algorithm (Giunchiglia & Shvaiko, 2007) computes the similarity of contexts in which the two concepts occur in the two schemas. It utilizes schema information and the representative tree structure. More related works to matching of tree structured knowledge representations can be found in (Bille, 2005).

*String similarity* and *semantic similarity* are the most often used measures in the field of concept matching (Melnik, Molina-Garcia, & Rahm, 2002; Doan, Madhavan, Dhamankar, Domingos, & Halevy, 2003; Amarintrarak, Runapongsa, Tongsima, & Wiwatwattana, 2009). String similarity compares concept names based on string edit distance and English pronunciation similarity using a phonetic indexing scheme (Cohen, Ravikumar, & Fienberrg, 2003). Semantic similarity is the measurement to identify the information which semantically corresponds to another piece of information from different datasets based on a linguistic resource, such as an online dictionary. WordNet (Miller, 1995; Fellbaum, 1998) is an online lexical reference system and it organizes English nouns, verbs, adjectives and adverbs into synonym sets, each representing one underlying lexical concept. Different semantic relations link the synonym sets. WordNet is well-suited for semantic similarity measures, since it provides relations of words (Liu, Zhao, & Yu, 2006). There are more works which have been done on the topic of measuring the semantic similarity using textual information. The most popular approach is to utilize WordNet to measure the semantic relatedness (Pedersen, Banerjee, & Patwardhan, 2005; Pedersen, Patwardhan, & Michelizzi, 2004; Patwardhan, Banerjee, & Pedersen, 2007). For example, a method to use Wikipedia to compute semantic relatedness on various benchmarking datasets has been proposed in (Strube & Ponzetto, 2006). More recent methods using Wikipedia to aid in the semantic matching process can be found in (Gabrilovich & Markovitch, 2007; Mohler & Mihalcea, 2009). However, because both WordNet and Wikipedia give semantic relatedness of different concepts, there are some methods which provide mappings between WordNet and Wikipedia (Ponzetto & Navigli, 2009; Navigli & Ponzetto, 2010), that offer a better and more complete semantic similarity comparison.

Some other schema matching methods are built on matching graph structures. A similarity flooding (SF) algorithm (Melnik, Molina-Garcia, & Rahm, 2002) utilizes a hybrid matching algorithm based on the idea of the similarity update among adjacent nodes of an initial match. At first, it converts the schemas into directed labeled graphs which will be used in an iterative *fixpoint* computation. The user can then find a node in one graph which is similar to a node in another graph, based on the string-based comparison. SF is based on the assumption that the nodes corresponding to same concepts of the domain will have similar adjacent elements in the schemas considered. The important concept of SF is the spreading of similarities in the matched models which is similar to the way that IP packets flood the network in broadcast communication. However, SF is a semi-automatic schema-matching tool which needs human involvement to check and adjust the results of the algorithm. The Anchor-PROMPT algorithm (Noy, 2004) takes as input a set of similar terms (anchors) and determines the sets of other related terms by analyzing the paths in the subgraph limited by the anchor points. It is based on the notion that if two pairs of concepts in the source ontologies are similar, and there are paths connecting those two concepts, then the concepts in those paths are often similar as well. The method proposed in (Giunchiglia & Shvaiko, 2007) performs element and structure-level semantic matching among the elements of two graphs. Schema information is used to produce semantic relations among all the concepts and the structure is then traversed to construct the propositional formulas among concepts (equality, overlap, mismatch, granularity).

Cupid (Madhavan, Bernstein, & Rahm, 2001) is a schema matching tool developed by Microsoft, which combines an element name matcher and a structure-based matcher. By comparing the linguistic meanings of elements with the assistance of a domain-specific thesaurus, it categorizes the elements of schemas by calculating the similarities of names, data types, and domains. It then transforms the schemas into a tree structure and applies a bottom-up structure matching. The purpose of this step is to obtain the structural similarity between pairs of elements, which is based on the similarity of their leaf node sets. With the linguistic and structural similarities of each pair of elements, Cupid calculates a weighted mean of these two values and generates a final alignment by choosing pairs of schema elements with weighted similarity coefficients which are higher than a set threshold. Cupid allows users to be involved in adjusting this threshold. COMA (Combination of Matching

Algorithms) (Do & Rahm, 2002) is a composite schema matching tool which represents schemas by graph nodes connected by directed links. Similar to Cupid, it calculates the similarity between two elements according to their element names, data types and structures. The difference is that COMA calculates the structural similarity based on the path while Cupid focuses on the structural similarity of the leaf node set of the elements. Additionally, it provides an extensible library of matching algorithms with different matchers. In COMA++ (Aumueller, Do, Massmann, & Rahm, 2005), the authors have improved COMA in that it supports more data models, such as relational schema and OWL. Many-to-many matches are possible in COMA++, while COMA only supports one-to-one matches. COMA++ can further cope with large schemas by implementing the fragment-based matching processing framework mentioned in (Madhavan, Bernstein, & Rahm, 2001). Bernstein, Melnik, and Churchill (2006) proposed a schema matching system that suggests candidate matches to the user for a selected schema element and allows user navigation between the candidates. The candidate matches are chosen with higher ranking of match candidates based on lexical similarity, schema structure, element types, and the history of prior matching actions. There are more methods which need manual configuration (Drumm, Schmitt, Do, & Rahm, 2007; Amarintrarak et al., 2009). In the context of schema concept matching, Sheth and Larson (1990) have argued that full automation is not feasible due to insufficient information currently provided by the database schema, which motivated the use of the additional semantics provided through ontologies in many of the newly developed methods. Das, Chong, Eadon, & Srinivasan (2004) addressed the issues of supporting ontology-based semantic matching in RDBMS and introduces a set of SQL operators for ontology-based semantic matching. This approach enables users to reference ontology data directly from SQL using the semantic match operators. However, it strongly depends on the assumption that the ontologies are stored in the RDBMS which may not be the common case in real-world applications. Ge and Qiu (2008) presents a concept similarity matching method based on semantic distance, and it considers the inheritance relations and semantic distance relations between concepts, and measures the degree of matching between concepts through semantic similarity. By consulting WordNet, the fragment of the ontology hierarchy concerning concepts can be obtained. However, the problems of this method are the effort made to get the ontology and whether it supports phrase semantic similarity. Extensive surveys and comparisons of some existing approaches to concept matching have been provided in (Shvaiko & Euzenat, 2005; Noy, 2004; Doan & Halevy, 2005).

A related field, where many research works exist, is *ontology matching* (Euzenat & Shvaiko, 2007; Shvaiko & Euzenat, 2008). Ontology has been defined as a formal, explicit specification of a shared conceptualization (Gruber, 1993). An ontology should hence be machine-readable, concepts and their constraints should be explicitly defined, while conceptualization refers to the definition of concepts and their relationships that occur in a particular domain (Gruber 1993, 1995). The important distinguishing factor to other formal and explicit domain knowledge conceptualizations is that it captures consensual knowledge, in the sense that the conceptualization is accepted by a large community of users. Hence, the consensual knowledge can be shared and reused across applications and groups of users. Due to the clear structural and linguistic representation of ontologies, it has been widely used in many applications, such as database integration, peer-to-peer systems, e-commerce, semantic web services and social networks. Ontology matching deals with the *semantic heterogeneity* problem by finding correspondences between semantically related entities of ontologies, which can be used for different tasks, such as ontology merging, query answering and data translation.

Thus, matching ontologies enables the knowledge and data expressed in the matched ontologies to interoperate (Euzenat & Shvaiko, 2007). GLUE (Doan et al., 2003) describes machine learning techniques, especially multi-strategy learning, for computing concept similarities in ontologies. GLUE applies statistical analysis to the data and exploits information in concept instances and taxonomic structure of ontologies by applying multiple learners to it. A probabilistic model is then used to combine the results from different learners, and a relaxation labeling approach is utilized to search for the mapping configuration. Ritze, Völker, Meilicke, & Svab-Zamazal (2010) integrate linguistic techniques into a pattern-based approach for detecting complex correspondences. It presents correspondence patterns and defines a set of matching conditions for each pattern. However, this approach is only using the linguistic information of ontologies. Cruz, Antonelli, & Stroe (2009) present the AgreementMaker system for schema and ontology matching, which is an integrated evaluation engine that depends on inherent quality measures and semi-automatic and automatic methods. It comprises some matching algorithms to match the source and target ontologies taking the structural and string similarities into account. However, it requires the end users of the system to be sophisticated domain experts whose needs have driven the design and implementation of the system.

As we have discussed above, there are a number of tools or algorithms that have been developed in the field of concept matching. Generally speaking, knowledge matching can be applied to data integration and message translation in the e-commerce domain (Rahm & Bernstein, 2001). Data migration is the task of transforming and integrating data that originates from one or more applications or databases into a new system. The requirement to migrate data between these systems arises when the original system or application needs to be replaced by a new one or the application is required to be merged with another application. During the migration process, data and concepts need to be extracted from the source systems, transformed and then loaded into the target system. Concept matching is essential for this data integration process because it identifies similar or semantically related concepts between the source and target systems. Once the matched elements are detected, one is capable of determining the mapping between two systems and transforming instance data from the source format to the target format (Drumm et al., 2007). In the e-commerce domain, trading partners frequently exchange messages describing business transactions. Usually, each trading partner uses its own message format which comes from different applications, so they may use different message schemas. To exchange the message between different trading partners from different organizations or companies, application developers need to convert messages between different schemas. Although messages are in the same format, the message schemas may use different names or different logics which represent the same concepts in different ways when they were built. Fields are also grouped into structures that may differ between the two message knowledge representations (Berners-Lee, Hendler, & Lassila, 2001).

The method proposed in this chapter can be seen as similar to the previously mentioned SF method (Melnik, Molina-Garcia, & Rahm, 2002). In SF, the similarity is propagated among the adjacent nodes of an initial match, while in our method it is propagated across all nodes found in an embedded structure. The sibling and ancestor-descendant node relationships are taken into account over several levels. This additional property enables us to detect candidate complex matches which are not dealt with in the similarity flooding process of SF. In addition, if the initial match is not provided by a user, our method will not use the string match operator as in SF but will rather take the root nodes of the knowledge structures to form the initial match. Hence, our method does not use any string similarity operators or online dictionaries to form the initial matches but rather completely utilizes the structural information. Taking structural position of the nodes into account including their ancestor-descendant and sibling/cousin relationships is a promising way to be able to take the context in which the concept is used into account. The candidate formed mappings are completely based on structural information, they are then verified using WordNet and a combination of string similarity metrics. In addition, SF only detects one-to-one matches while the proposed method can also detect complex matches (one-to-many and many-to-one).

## PROBLEM DEFINITION

This section provides the definitions of the problems considered in this chapter with respect to knowledge matching. It starts with the problem of conceptual level matching and then formulates the problem of structural level matching. Knowledge representations in general follow a tree or graph structure, and in this chapter we focus on knowledge representations where the underlying structure is a tree, i.e., no cycles are allowed. However, the proposed method could be applied to graph-structured knowledge representations if we first convert the underlying graph structure into the tree structure where the information regarding cycles is preserved in some manner. For example, the work presented in (Feng, Chang, & Dillon, 2002) dealt with the transformation from semantic networks (graph with cycles) to XML Schema (tree). To enable the transformation, the approach taken is to break the cycles, and turn a cyclic directed graph into an equivalent acyclic directed graph (i.e., tree) without loss of semantics. Whenever a cycle occurs ($n_1$, $n_2$, $n_3$, ..., $n_m$), where node $n_1$ points to $n_2$, $n_2$ to $n_3$, and so on until $n_m$ points to $n_1$ again, a new leaf node $n_x$ is introduced so that $n_m$ points to $n_x$. Referential integrity constraint is applied on $n_x$ so that its key refers to node $n_1$ (Feng, Chang, & Dillon, 2002). This ensures that the information contained in the original graph structure is preserved in the transformed tree structure. Hence, if a similar method could be applied for transforming graph-structured social network data or other graph-structured data on the Web, the applicability of frequent subtree mining would extend to Web data originally in graph-structured form. At the end of the section we define some tree related concepts that are necessary for understanding our knowledge matching method.

### Concept Matching

The concept term matching problem is the problem of finding a mapping between the concept terms of two (or more) knowledge representations (*KR*). Since knowledge representations commonly differ in the amount of specific/general knowledge stored about some aspect of the domain, the number of concept terms will differ among them and the mappings will not just be restricted to simple one-to-one (1:1) but to complex matches, many-to-one (M:1), one-to-many (1:M) and many-to-many (M:M). The last case does not occur so often because it can usually be considered as two mappings. Representing M:M as a 1:M and M:1 match gives a better indication of the point in the structure where the difference in the knowledge level of detail occurs. A complex match generally indicates that while one *KR* uses a singular concept term to represent some aspect of the domain, the second *KR* uses multiple concept terms or stores more detailed information about that aspect of the domain.

As a simple example, consider Figure 1 (schemas obtained from www.ontologymatching.org) where the concept with label 'ShipTo' in $KR_2$ corresponds to two concepts in $KR_1$ namely 'DeliverTo' and 'Address' (the same holds for the concept 'BillTo'). We refer to this kind of a 1:M match as a *true* 1:M match in the sense that there is no additional information in $KR_1$ that is not present in $KR_2$, as it is essentially just a dif-

*Figure 1. XML schema structures for describing a post order*

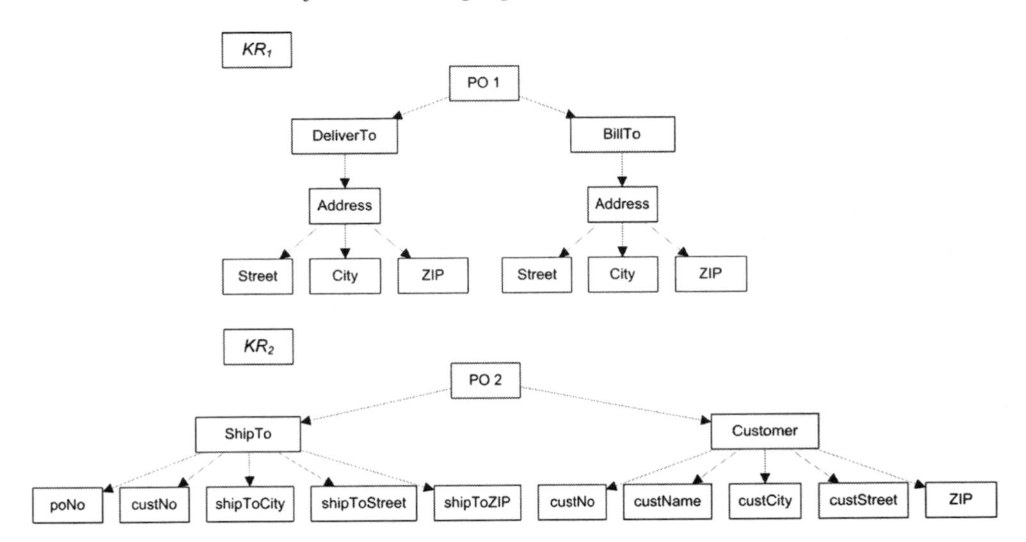


ferent way of representing the information. The 'ShipTo' and ('DeliverTo', 'Address') concept terms both describe one concept or aspect of the domain, which is where to deliver the goods.

The problem of concept matching can be generally stated as: Let $KR_1$ and $KR_2$ correspond to two knowledge representations, and let $C_1 = \{_1c_1, _1c_2, ..., _1c_n\}$ (where $n = |C_1|$) and $C_2 = \{_2c_1, _2c_2, ..., _2c_p\}$ (where $p = |C_2|$) denote the complete sets of concept terms used in $KR_1$ and $KR_2$, respectively. The task of concept matching is to find a mapping $M = \{m_1, m_2, ..., m_{|M|}\}$, where every element $m \in M$ is a 2-tuple denoted as $(e, f)$ such that $e$ and $f$ are sets of 1 or more concepts and $e \subseteq C_1$ and $f \subseteq C_2$.

Most of the sets $e$ and $f$ from the mappings $m$ will consist of a single concept, but in cases of a complex match, a number of concept terms will be present in one of the sets. In an ideal case, the set $M$ would contain all concept terms from $C_1$ and $C_2$ in all the sets $e$ and $f$ from its elements, respectively. However, due to the many different ways in which knowledge is represented by different organizations, there may remain some elements from $C_1$ and/or $C_2$ which are not present in the respective element sets ($e$ and $f$) of the found mappings ($m$). This usually occurs in cases where the extent to which the domain knowledge is covered by one organization is much larger, and there are some aspects of the domain totally unaccounted for by the other organization. If we let $C_1$ correspond to the concept terms from $KR_1$, and $C_2$ to concept terms from $KR_2$ from Figure 1, the set of correct mappings found for the example structures are $M$= {({'PO1'}, {'PO2'}), ({'DeliverTo', 'Address'}, {'ShipTo'}), ({'BillTo', 'Address'}, {'Customer'}), ({'City'}, {'shipToCity'}), ({'Street'}, {'custStreet'}), ({'Zip'}, {'custZip'}), ({'City'}, {'custCity'}), ({'Street'}, {'custStreet'}), ({'Zip'}, {'custZip'})}. Please note that the concepts appearing on the left of the knowledge representations are listed first. In this case all the concept terms from set $C_1$ are contained in the concept terms of sets $e$ in all $m \in M$, while the set $C_2$ is not contained completely in the concepts of sets $f$ in all $m \in M$. While we said that the above mapping is correct, if the unmatched concepts from $C_2$ would be part of one of the mappings for either 'custCity', 'custStreet' and 'custZip', these would not essentially be incorrect, as they indicate that there is a difference in granularity at a particular position in the knowledge representation. This information may be more useful to the user as opposed to not having any information relating to the unmatched concepts.

The concept matching problem has been formulated here for two knowledge representations, but the definitions can be extended when more knowledge representations are considered by performing the task for each pair separately. We next describe the structural level matching problem, and at this stage of the problem, the assumption is that the concept term matching has been performed and the same concept terms are used for representing the same domain concepts. The aim is to find the largest common knowledge substructure $KS$ among the knowledge representations $KR_i$ considered, which we denote as $KS \cap KR_i$. The problem can be stated as: Given $n$ tree structured knowledge representations $KR_i$ (where $i = \{1, \ldots, n\}$), find the largest substructure $KS$ such that $KS \cap KR_i$, for each $KR_i$.

Semistructured documents, such as XML, can be effectively modeled using a rooted ordered labeled tree. We next provide some definitions of tree related concepts that lay the groundwork for understanding our approach to the knowledge matching problem. A graph consists of a set of nodes (or vertices) that are connected by edges. Each edge has two nodes associated with it. A path is defined as a finite sequence of edges. A rooted tree has its top-most node defined as the root that has no incoming edges and there is a single unique path between any two nodes. A node $u$ is said to be a parent of node $v$, if there is a directed edge from $u$ to $v$. Node $v$ is then said to be a child of node $u$. Nodes with the same parent are called siblings. The ancestors of a node $u$ are the nodes on the path between the root and $u$, excluding $u$ itself. The descendants of a node $v$ can then be defined as those nodes that have $v$ as their ancestor.

A rooted labeled tree can be denoted as $T(v_0, V, L, E)$, where: $v_0 \in V$ is the *root* vertex, $V$ is the set of *vertices* or *nodes*, $L$ is the set of *labels* of vertices, for any vertex $v \in V$, $L(v)$ denotes the label of $v$; and $E = \{(x, y) \mid x, y \in V\}$ is the set of *edges* in the tree. In an ordered tree, there is an ordering specified for the children of each vertex, or in other words the children of each node are ordered from left to right. When using the above notation, in this paper we will always refer to ordered trees unless otherwise specified. Please note, the $T_{DB}$ can either correspond to a collection of independent trees (often referred to as transactions) or a single large tree. The term *transaction*, as used in the data mining community, corresponds to a set of one or more items obtained from a finite item domain, and a dataset is a collection of transactions (Bayardo, Agrawal and Gunopulos, 1999). A tree database transaction would correspond to a fragment of the database tree whereby an independent instance (or record) is described. The problem of frequent subtree mining can be generally stated as: Given a tree database, $T_{DB}$, and minimum support ($\sigma$), find all subtrees that occur at least $\sigma$ times in $T_{DB}$.

Driven by different application needs, there are a number of different subtrees that can be sought after in the general tree mining framework defined above. We reserve the explanation of instances where the different types of subtrees are the most appropriate for the knowledge matching task when we discuss the motivation behind our approach in next section. The most commonly mined subtree types are induced and embedded, as defined next.

Given a tree $S = (vs_0, V_S, L_S, E_S)$ and tree $T = (vt_0, V_T, L_T, E_T)$, $S$ is an *ordered induced subtree* of $T$, if and only if (1) $V_S \subseteq V_T$; (2) $L_S \subseteq L_T$ *and* $L_S(v) = L_T(v)$; (3) $E_S \subseteq E_T$; and (4) the left to right ordering of sibling nodes in the original tree is preserved.

Given a tree $S = (vs_0, V_S, L_S, E_S)$ and tree $T = (vt_0, V_T, L_T, E_T)$, $S$ is an *ordered embedded subtree* of $T$, if and only if (1) $V_S \subseteq V_T$; (2) $L_S \subseteq L_T$ *and* $L_S(v) = L_T(v)$; (3) *if* $(v_1,v_2) \in E_S$ *then* $parent(v_2) = v_1$ in $S$ and $v_1$ is ancestor of $v_2$ in $T$; and (4) the left to right ordering of sibling nodes in the original tree is preserved.

If $S = (vs_0, V_S, L_S, E_S)$ is an embedded subtree of $T = (vt_0, V_T, L_T, E_T)$, and two vertices $p \in V_S$ and

$q \in V_S$ form ancestor-descendant relationship, the *level of embedding* (Tan, Dillon, Hadzic, Feng, & Chang, 2006), between $p$ and $q$, denoted by $\Delta(p,q)$, is defined as the length of the path between $p$ and $q$. With this observation a *maximum level of embedding constraint* ($\delta$) can be imposed on the subtrees extracted from $T$, such that any two ancestor-descendant nodes present in an embedded subtree of $T$, will be connected in $T$ by a path that has the maximum length of $\delta$. In this regard, we could define an induced subtree $st_I$ as an embedded subtree where the *maximum level of embedding* that can occur in $T$ is equal to 1, since the level of embedding of two nodes that form a parent-child relationship is 1.

The subtrees defined above take into account the order among the child nodes of a vertex (siblings) and a requirement is that this ordering is preserved as detected in the original tree. This is what makes them *ordered* subtrees. In an *unordered subtree*, the left-to-right ordering among the sibling nodes does not need to be preserved. Hence, if we were defining the induced and embedded subtrees for the unordered case, then condition 4 could be removed from the definition. Therefore, the main difference when it comes to the mining of unordered subtrees is that the order of sibling nodes of a subtree can be exchanged and the resulting tree is still considered the same.

The transactional support of a subtree $st$ (denoted as $\sigma(st)$) in a tree database $T_{DB}$ is equal to the number of transactions in $T_{DB}$ that contain at least one occurrence of subtree $st$. Let the notation $st \prec tr$, denote the support of subtree $st$ by transaction $tr$, then, $st \prec tr = 1$ whenever $tr$ contains at least one occurrence of $st$, and 0 otherwise. Suppose that there are $N$ transactions $tr_1$ to $tr_N$ of tree in $T_{DB}$, the $\sigma(st)$ in $T_{DB}$ is defined as:

$$\sum_{i=1}^{N} st \prec tr_i$$

To illustrate the difference in different subtree types, please consider Figure 2, which represents two subtrees ($st_1$ and $st_2$) from a tree database ($T_{DB}$) with two transactions $tr_1$ and $tr_2$. The positions of the nodes in each of the transactions are numbered according to the pre-order traversal of that particular transaction tree. A *pre-order traversal* can be defined as follows: If ordered tree $T$ consists only of a root node $r$, then $r$ is the pre-order traversal of $T$. Otherwise let $st_1$, $st_2$,..., $st_n$ be the subtrees occurring at $r$ from left to right in $T$. The pre-order traversal begins by visiting $r$ and then traversing all the remaining subtrees in pre-order starting from $st_1$ and finishing with $st_n$.

In Figure 2, the label of each node is shown as a single-quoted symbol inside the circle, whereas its pre-order position is shown as an index on the left side of the circle. The term 'occurrence coordinate(s) (*oc*)' is used to refer to the occurrence(s) of a particular node or a subtree in the tree database. In the case of a node, *oc* corresponds to the pre-order position of that node in the tree database, whereas for a subtree, *oc* is a sequence of *oc* from nodes that belong to that particular subtree. On the right side of Figure 2, the *oc* of each subtree are presented with the corresponding transaction that they occur in. If ordered induced subtrees are mined, $st_1$ occurs only once in $tr_1$ with *oc*:125; whereas, if unordered induced subtrees are mined, the order of node *'c'* and *'e'* can be exchanged, and hence, now $st_1$ also occurs in $tr_2$ with *oc*:132 (note: the order of occurrence coordinates is exchanged since the order of corresponding nodes is exchanged). If embedded subtrees are mined, a parent in $st_1$ subtree can be an ancestor in $T_{DB}$, and hence, many more occurrences of $st_1$ are counted as can be seen in the top right corner of Figure 2. Similarly, counting the occurrences of subtree $st_2$ in $T_{DB}$, in the case of induced (ordered or unordered) subtree mining it occurs only once in $tr_2$ with *oc*:04567. However, if we consider ordered embedded subtrees, then there are additional occurrences of $st_2$ in $tr_2$ with *oc*:02567, *oc*:02568, *oc*:04568, since we

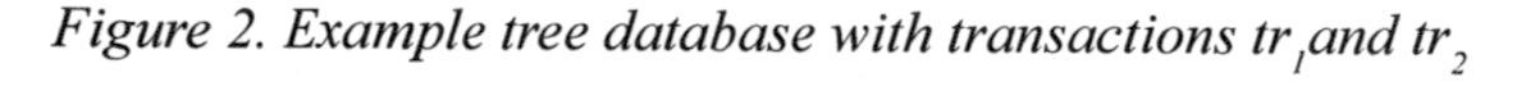

*Figure 2. Example tree database with transactions $tr_1$ and $tr_2$*

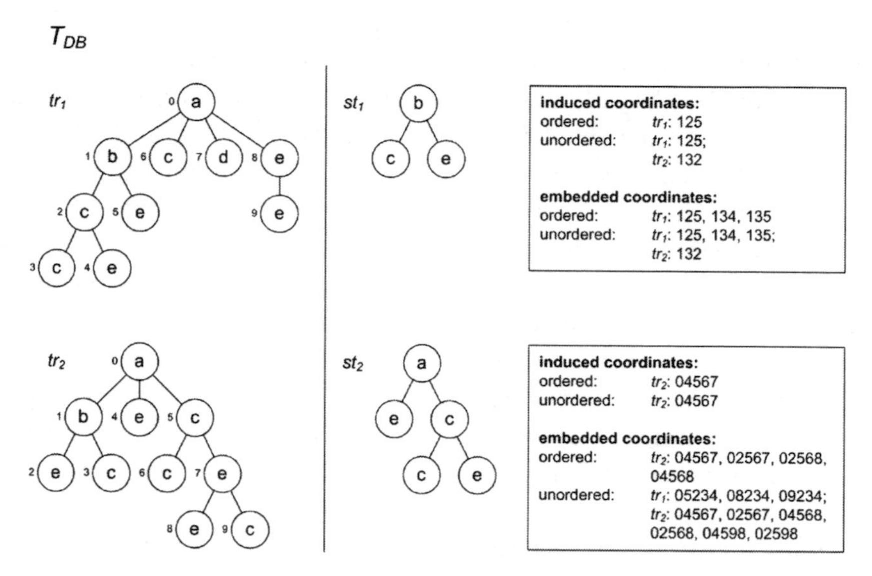


allow the extra ancestor-descendant relationship between the nodes. Once the ordering among the siblings can be exchanged, there are many more instances of the $st_2$ subtree as shown on the bottom right corner of Figure 2.

Driven by different application needs, many frequent subtree mining algorithms have been developed, and the main difference is the type of subtree being mined (Chi, Nijssen, Muntz, & Kok, 2005; Cserkuti, Levendovszky, & Charaf, 2006; Jiménez, Berzal, & Cubero, 2008). For example, FREQT (Asai et al., 2002), IMB3-Miner (Tan et al., 2006; Tan et al., 2008), AMIOT (Hido & Kawano, 2005) and PrefixTreeISpan (Zou, Lu, Zhang, Hu, & Zhou, 2006) are some of the algorithms that mine induced ordered subtrees, while TreeMiner (Zaki, 2005a), XSpanner (Wang et al., 2004) and MB3-Miner (Tan et al., 2005) mine ordered embedded subtrees. In regards to mining unordered subtrees, some of the existing algorithms for mining in induced context are: HybridTreeMiner (Chi, Yang, & Muntz, 2004), the method presented by Nijssen and Kok (2003) and UNI3 (Hadzic, Tan, & Dillon, 2007), while for the embedded case TreeFinder (Termier et al., 2002), SLEUTH (Zaki, 2005b) and U3 (Hadzic, Tan, & Dillon, 2008) have been proposed. Katsaros et al. (2005) describes a method to achieve fast frequent subtree mining by hashing and indexing and a recent work in (Tatikonda & Parthasarathy, 2010) gives an overview of the methods for hashing tree-structured data and their applications. A frequency counting based on frequent occurrence of similar subtrees is explored in (Tosaka, Nakamura, & Kudo, 2007). The similarity measure used is based on the tree edit/alignment distance, and hence an occurrence of a subtree is counted for not only equivalent, but similar subtrees. For an extensive overview of the frequent subtree mining methods, we refer the interested reader to works such as (Chi et al., 2005; Tan et al., 2008; Hadzic, Tan, & Dillon, 2011), where different approaches to the problem, various implementation issues, and applications are discussed in detail.

Several works have focused on enabling effective querying over tree structured data (Feng & Dillon, 2005; Wang, Park, Fan, & Yu, 2003; Rao & Moon, 2004; Kimelfeld & Sagiv, 2006). Twig patterns are often used in tree-structured queries for XML documents. It includes three basic language elements, namely, arbitrary node conditions, parent-child edges and ancestor-descendant edges. It provides easier queries with only a limited knowledge of the XML hierarchy, the names of elements and the precise data stored under each element (Kimelfeld & Sagiv, 2006). TwigStack (Bruno, Koudas, & Srivastava, 2002) and TwigStackList (Lu & Ling, 2004) algorithms are based on region encoding *<start, end, level>* labeling of the XML tree to provide a structural query. Twig patterns are used in XML filtering for the XPath matching of the incoming documents (Lu, Chen, Ling, Chan, & Chen, 2005). Candan, Hsiung, Chen, Tatemura, & Agrawal (2006) propose AFilter, an adaptable, and thus scalable, path expression filtering approach. The FiST system (Kwon, Rao, Moon, & Lee, 2005) transforms twig patterns expressed in XPath and XML documents into Prüfer sequences and performs holistic matching of twig patterns on user profiles with incoming documents. It is focused on matching twig patterns where the order must conform to the document order in XML, and the filtering algorithm involves a progressive subsequence matching and refinement phase to ensure the absence of false positives and false negatives.

## MOTIVATION OF THE PROPOSED APPROACH

A number of ways and criteria exist for forming the mappings, many of these are based on comparing the concept terms using string similarity measures, online dictionaries and thesauruses. In this case, the actual string label used for describing a concept of the domain is used as the basis for comparison. In the example given in Figure 1, the concept terms describing the same aspect of the domain are represented by different labels and there is a different level of granularity amongst the representations. While the WordNet and string similarity measures may detect some of the valid matches by performing label to label comparisons, the nodes with labels 'Street', 'City' and 'Zip' occur twice in the $KR_1$ in different contexts. Unless the structure in which the concept terms are presented is analyzed, it is difficult to automatically determine the correct matches with respect to the context in which they were used. Generally speaking, approaches based on string similarity and online dictionaries work well, but they are not always reliable as different naming conventions are used among knowledge representations and the same name may refer to different concepts or be used in different contexts.

In the work presented in this chapter, the aim is to analyze the structure in which the concept terms are presented rather than make initial comparisons based on string labels. We aim to approach the problem in a different manner from most existing approaches in order to see how close to the correct set of mappings one can get without considering the labels. Hence, the main aim is to use the structural information in which concept terms occur in a particular knowledge representation. The position of the concept terms in the representational structure can often indicate the context in which the concepts are used. It is important to take the context into account during the concept matching phase, as it is possible that multiple concepts exist with the same label, but in parts of the knowledge representation they are used in different contexts or have different meanings. Furthermore, there is usually some indication of the possible complex matches which are more difficult to obtain by label comparison. The way that these issues are handled will be explained in the next section. The basic idea of the approach is to consider all of the substructures from the given knowledge structure and from an initial match propagate the similarity among other nodes within the substructures of same size and structural properties where both concepts from the initial match have occurred. Additionally, as opposed to the SF algorithm (Melnik, Molina-Garcia, & Rahm, 2002), by considering substructures that can be of embedded subtree type, the similarity is propagated among the nodes situated several levels away from the matched node, rather than to only adjacent nodes as is the case in SF. This is a useful property especially in the cases when many concepts from one knowledge representation correspond to a single concept in another knowledge representation, as it allows us to detect candidate complex matches as will be explained in the next section. Hence, our method starts by extracting substructures (embedded subtrees) of all sizes from a given knowledge representation. Next, we discuss how the knowledge matching at the structural level will be approached.

Suppose that we have two document structures used by different organizations for representing the knowledge from the same domain. The aim is to merge them into one representation which captures the general knowledge for that specific domain. Each knowledge structure is most likely to differ in the way the knowledge is represented and the amount of concept granularity. However, since they are describing the same domain, there will be some common parts of knowledge. This is where a tree mining approach will prove useful since sub-structures from large tree databases can be automatically extracted. The way that the experiment is set up can be explained as follows. Given $n$ tree structured documents $D_i$ (where $i = \{1, \ldots, n\}$) to be matched, which can be modeled as rooted ordered labeled trees $KS_i$ (where $i = \{1, \ldots, n\}$), set up a tree database ($T_{DB}$) so that each $KS_i$ is represented as an independent subtree (i.e., a separate transaction) in $T_{DB}$. The root of each $KS_i$ will be a child of the root node of $T_{DB}$. Since the order of sibling nodes is irrelevant, and the knowledge structures can differ in the level of detail stored about a concept, it was decided that the application of an algorithm for the mining of unordered embedded subtrees is most suitable for this problem. Hence, the U3 algorithm (Hadzic, Tan, & Dillon, 2008, 2010) will be applied to the database using the transactional support definition of $n$ (i.e., the number of documents to be matched). The detected set of frequent patterns corresponds to the common sub-structures of the documents being compared. The largest frequent $k$-subtree (i.e., largest common unordered embedded subtree among all $KS_i$ in $T_{DB}$) is selected to represent the shared knowledge structure among the documents compared. It should be noted that this subtree actually corresponds to the largest frequent maximal subtree.

The structural level matching problem as defined in previous section can now be reformulated as follows. If tree $T_S$ is the largest unordered embedded subtree of a tree $T_K$, the following notation will be used $T_S \cap_{UE} T_K$. The problem of knowledge structure matching among $n$ number of tree-structured knowledge representations can be stated as: Given a set of trees $T = \{T_1, T_2, \ldots, T_n\}$ find a tree $T_S$ such that for each $T_i \in T$, where $i = \{1, \ldots, n\}$, $T_S \cap_{UE} T_i$.

## METHOD DESCRIPTION

This section starts with an overview of the proposed method for knowledge matching as a whole, and then provides more detail regarding the conceptual and structural matching tasks. It concludes with a running example to illustrate the working mechanism of the method as a whole. To match at the conceptual level, the method takes as input two tree-structured knowledge representations, represented as rooted ordered labeled trees. The conceptual matching process as a whole is illustrated in Figure 3. The initial match is preferably supplied by the user, or otherwise, the root nodes of the knowledge representations are good candidates for the initial match (the latter is the default and occurs in all of our experiments provided later). As mentioned earlier, the method starts without considering the labels and utilizes only the structural properties of the compared knowledge representations to form candidate mappings. We use a previously developed algorithm for mining ordered induced/embedded subtrees (Tan et al., 2006) to extract all of the substructures from the given knowledge representations. We extract all possible subtrees of each knowledge

*Figure 3. High level overview of the method for conceptual level matching*

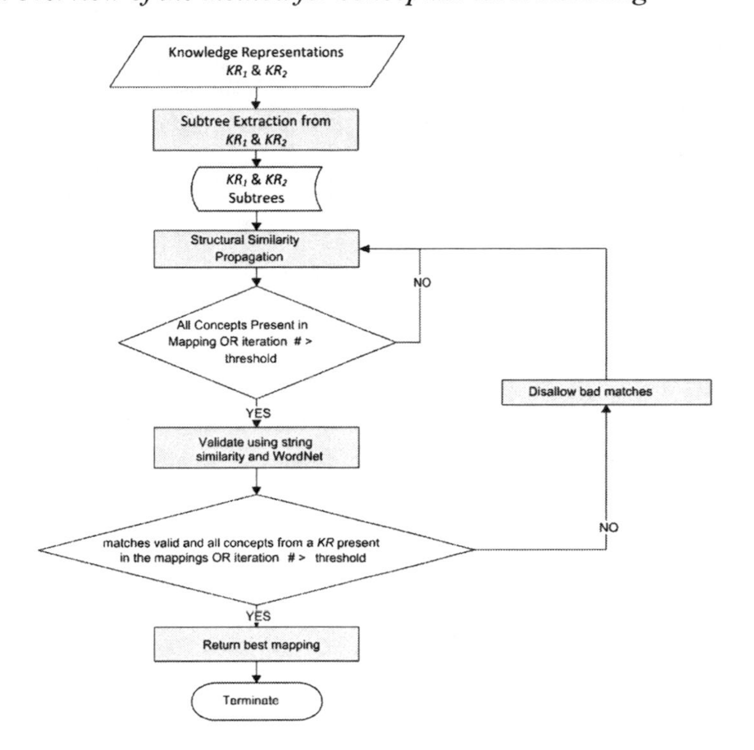


representation separately (i.e., the minimum support threshold is set to 1). Please note, for some more complex knowledge representations, it may not be feasible to extract the complete set of embedded subtrees that exist in the knowledge representation. In these scenarios, we restrict the size of the embedded subtrees extracted, and for example focus only on those consisting of 2 to 5 nodes. The embedded relationships are still captured in such smaller subtrees, and hence the general working mechanism of the method will not be greatly affected.

The process continues by traversing the subtree sets from each knowledge representation in which the matched concepts occur. Whenever a pair of subtrees (one from $KR_1$ and one from $KR_2$) of the same size are similar in structure and the matched concepts occur at the same position, the similarity value between the remaining concept terms in those subtrees is increased. Once the similarity value between two concepts exceeds a chosen threshold, they become part of a new match and the process of subtree traversal and similarity update repeats. This process is repeated until either all concepts from one of the knowledge representations are present in the found matches, or the number of iterations exceeds a chosen threshold. The reason for using this approach first is that by utilizing the structural properties, the method can detect candidate 1:M matches and it is likely to form candidate mappings with the context in which the concepts are taken into account. However, once the mappings are formed it is still important that they are verified by certain measures, as it is also likely that different concepts of the domain are represented in different order or level in the compared knowledge representations. Therefore, we validate the formed mapping using string similarity measures (Cohen, Ravikumar, & Fienberrg, 2003) and WordNet, and repeat the process by not allowing any matches that were previously determined to be invalid. Please note, in all our discussion we assume two knowledge representations, but in cases where there are more knowledge representations, the method will be performed for each pair separately. Once the correct concept mappings have been identified and a common label is now used in all representations, to extract the common substructure among all the knowledge representations considered, we extract the largest unordered embedded subtree that occurs in all the knowledge representations, as was discussed in the previous section.

Each of the steps presented in Figure 3 is now described in more detail. We focus more on the structural similarity propagation, as it is the core process of the method that provides candidate mappings which are then evaluated using some standard string and semantic comparison techniques. The subtrees extracted from the knowledge representations are of embedded subtree type, and the IMB3 algorithm (Tan et al., 2006) is used. The reason for choosing to extract embedded subtrees is that when propagating similarity among the substructures, it is important to propagate the similarity not only for all the immediate nodes in the subtrees (i.e., children) but also to all the descendants, as it is possible that additional nodes may exist in one of the representations in the form of additional children/descendants of a matching node (concept). If only induced subtrees were considered, the similarity would not be propagated among all of the descendants of the matched node, if the immediate child nodes do not match, and the candidate 1:M matches would not be formed.

Please note, at implementation level a unique integer to label mapping is performed for all concepts, as this enables faster processing by the tree mining algorithms (Tan et al., 2008), but in our explanation we will talk about labels, as remapping is always performed as necessary (i.e., for validation purposes using WordNet and string similarity). Also, any available algorithm for mining of ordered embedded subtrees, such as TreeMiner (Zaki, 2005a), could have been used to extract the subtrees for the purpose of similarity propagation. The reason for choosing the IMB3 algorithm (Tan et al., 2006), is that it can mine both embedded and induced ordered subtrees through the use of the level of embedding constraint. We have mentioned earlier that for the sake of detecting complex matches, it may be necessary to consider structural relationships between the concepts that are situated deep in the tree, and go beyond propagating similarity to adjacent nodes by propagating similarity among ancestor-descendant nodes. The maximum level of embedding constraint allows one to restrict the level of embedding between the nodes in the extracted embedded subtrees. In certain scenarios, allowing the extra embeddings can result in unnecessary and misleading information, but in other cases, it proves useful as it detects common structures in spite of the difference in concept granularity. Hence, to make the change from mining embedded subtrees where the allowed level of embedding is equal to the depth of the tree to induced subtrees where the level is limited to one, is quite significant and many valid complex matches could be missed. In this sense, the maximum level of embedding constraint would allow for some compromise as similarity would be propagated among the concepts that are still within the reasonable distance (level of embedding) of each other within the knowledge structures. This, however, is left for future considerations when optimizations of the method are being investigated.

## Substructure Similarity Propagation Process

This process in its simplified form can be described by the flowchart represented in Figure 4.

A similarity matrix (*SM*) is set up where all the concept terms from $KR_1$ and $KR_2$ are organized into rows and columns in pre-order traversal of the underlying tree structures. We use the tree notation (see "Problem Definition" section for definitions of tree related concepts) for the knowledge representations, i.e., $KR_1(v1_0, V_1, L_1, E_1)$ and $KR_2(v2_0, V_2, L_2, E_2)$. Let $CT_1 = \{L(v1_0), \ldots, L(v1_n)\}$ $(n = |V_1|-1)$ and $CT_2 = \{L(v2_0), \ldots, L(v2_p)\}$ $(p =$

*Figure 4. High level overview of similarity propagation phase*

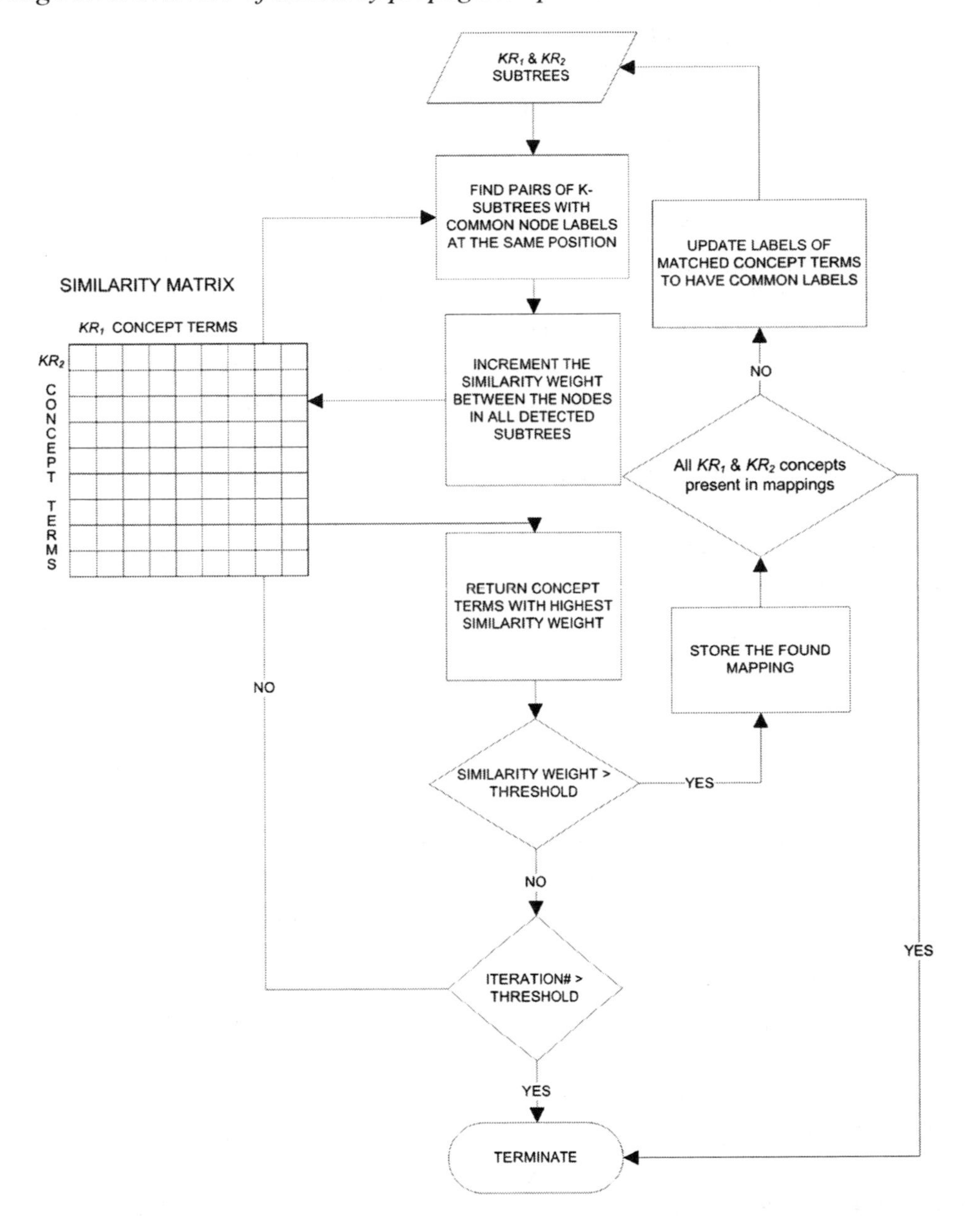


$|V_2|$-1), denote the concept terms of $KR_1$ and $KR_2$, respectively, listed according to the pre-order traversals of the underlying trees. An entry in the similarity matrix $SM(i,j)$ $(i = \{0,..., n\text{-}1\}; (j = \{0,..., p\text{-}1\})$ stores the similarity value between $L(v1_i)$ and $L(v2_j)$. Let $ST_1$ and $ST_2$ contain all the ordered embedded $k$-subtrees ($k \geq 2$) from $KR_1$ and $KR_2$, respectively. Initially $SM(i,j) = 0$, for each $i = \{0, ..., n\text{-}1\}; j = \{0,..., m\text{-}1\}$).

To represent the subtrees at the implementation level, the pre-order string encoding ($\varphi$) as used in (Zaki, 2005a) is utilized. It is a sequential representation of the nodes of a tree as encountered during the pre-order traversal of that tree. In addition, the backtrack symbol ('/') is used when moving up a node in the tree during the pre-order traversal. The encoding of a subtree $st$ is denoted as $\varphi(st)$, and as an example consider Figure 2 again. The string encoding of $st_1$ is, $\varphi(st_1)$: '*b c / e /*', and of $st_2$ is $\varphi(st_2)$: '*a e / c c / e / /*' The backtrack symbols can be omitted after the last node. Further, let $\varphi(st)_r$ denote the $r_{th}$ element (label or '/') of $\varphi(st)$, and hence $\varphi(st)_0$ corresponds to the label of the root node of *st*.

The similarity propagation process starts by taking in an initial match that is either supplied by the user, or the root nodes of the knowledge representations are used to form the initial match (i.e., $m=(L(v1_0),L(v2_0))$. The process continues by traversing the subtree sets from each knowledge representation in which the matched concepts occur. Whenever a pair of *k*-subtrees (subtrees consisting of *k* nodes), one from $KR_1$ and one from $KR_2$, have the same or a similar structure and the matched concepts occur at the same position, the similarity value between the remaining concept terms in those subtrees is increased in the corresponding entry in the *SM*. Considering that we have taken the root nodes to form the initial match, many subtrees will satisfy this condition, and hence the similarity value will be updated among many nodes, including all the nodes that are situated at different levels in the knowledge representation. This is because embedded subtrees are considered. However, the similarity between the nodes that are situated near the matched concepts of each knowledge representation would be higher than the nodes further away from the matched concepts, because the nearer nodes will occur in more embedded subtrees in which the matched concepts occurs. Since we are dealing with pre-order string representations of the subtrees to find the candidate subtrees that are used to update the similarity matrix, we consider only those subtrees that are of the same size and contain the matched concepts at the same position in the string encoding.

Let us denote a *k*-subtree as $k\text{-}st_x$ (where $k\text{-}st_x \in ST_x$, $x = 1$ or 2). Hence, given a match $m(e,f)$, two *k*-subtrees, $k\text{-}st_1$ and $k\text{-}st_2$ will be candidates for updating the similarity matrix if and only if there exists *r*, such that $e = \varphi(k\text{-}st_1)_r$ AND $f = \varphi(k\text{-}st_2)_r$. Both $\varphi(k\text{-}st_1)$ and $\varphi(k\text{-}st_2)$ become input to another method (*UpdateSimilarityMatrix*($\varphi(k\text{-}st_1),\varphi(k\text{-}st_2)$)) which ensures that the updates only occur among the nodes that are structurally in the same position with respect to the concept of the match being processed. The labels and backtracks from the encodings are traversed sequentially and for every pair of labels encountered the value in the corresponding entry in SM is updated (incremented). The value of the update (denoted as *updateVal*) for incrementing the value in an entry *SM*(*i,j*) is worked out with respect to the total number of subtrees and concepts in the knowledge representation with largest number of concepts. Let us assume that $KR_1$ has more concepts than $KR_2$; then $updateVal = 1 / ((2 * |ST_1|) * |V_1|)$. The *UpdateSimilarityMatrix*($\varphi(k\text{-}st_1),\varphi(k\text{-}st_2)$) will stop as soon as we have encountered a '/' symbol in one of $\varphi(k\text{-}st_1)$ or $\varphi(k\text{-}st_2)$ while encountering a label in the other encoding, as this indicates a structural mismatch. Whenever a similarity value between two concept terms exceeds a predetermined threshold value (denoted as *matchThr*), it becomes a new match and the process is repeated using the newly matched concepts.

Furthermore, the possibility of complex matches is checked during the process. For example, these matches occur between the concept terms from $KR_1$ in the similarity matrix which do not have a sufficiently high similarity value to any of the concept terms in $KR_2$ to exceed the threshold, but usually have a number of neighboring concept terms from $KR_1$ that have close similarity values with a particular concept term in $KR_2$. In this example, complex matches can occur between a set of neighboring concept terms from $KR_1$ that all have close similarity values with a single concept term in $KR_2$. To implement this logic two thresholds are used, namely *complexMatchThr* which is the minimum similarity value that an entry in the *SM* needs to have for it to become a candidate of a complex match, and *complexMatchDifThr* which is the allowed difference (in %) between consecutive values in the *SM* for them to be considered

*Figure 5. Logic for detecting and forming complex matches from a similarity matrix (SM)*

```
Algorithm: CHECKFORCOMPLEXMATCH
Input: similarity matrix SM
Output: Boolean value

 1: for every row i and column j in SM do
 2:   if (SM(i,j)>complexMatchThr AND DIF(SM(i,j),SM(i,j+1)) < complexMatchDifThr) then
 3:     for (c=1 to |col| in SM) do
 4:       while (DIF(SM(i,j),SM(i, j+c)) < complexMatchDifThr
               AND SM(i, j+c) ≥ ( complexMatchThr / 2)) do
 5:           f_j = f_j + L(v2_{j+c})    //forming the many side of complex match
 6:       newMatch = (L(v1_i), f_j)
 7:       M = M ∪ newMatch
 8:       return true
 9:   else if (SM(i,j) > complexMatchThr AND DIF(SM(i,j),SM(i+1,j)) < complexMatchDifThr) then
10:     for (c =1 to |row| in SM) do
11:       while (DIF(SM(i,j),SM(i+c, j)) < complexMatchDifThr
               AND SM(i+c, j) ≥ (complexMatchThr / 2))) do
12:           e_i = e_i + L(v1_{i+c})
13:     newMatch = (e_i, L(v2_j))
14:     M = M ∪ newMatch
15:     return true
16: return false
```

as part of the complex match. Also, a consecutive value needs to be at least *complexMatchThr* / 2 to be considered for addition to the corresponding concept on the many side of the match. Hence, a method is called for the purpose of detecting and forming a complex match, pseudo code of which is provided in Figure 5.

When a complex match (many-to-one or one-to-many) is determined, the same process can be applied for similarity update except that the 'many' side of a match is considered as a single concept term. Hence, in case of M:1, rather than comparing $k$-subtrees from $KR_1$ and $KR_2$, a $((k-1)+c_n)$-subtree from $KR_1$ is compared with a $k$-subtree from $KR_2$, where $c_n$ is equal to the number of concept terms in $KR_1$ which constitutes the many side of the match. The same method *UpdateSimilarityMatrix*($\varphi(k\text{-}st_1)$, $\varphi(k\text{-}st_2)$) explained earlier is called, with the difference being that the string encodings have been updated so that they are of the same size. This is achieved by removing all the constituents of the match, i.e., the single node (label) from the one side and the set of nodes (labels) from the many side. Please note, when we check for the existence of many labels (i.e., for a complex match) in the string encoding, the backtrack symbols are taken into account, to ensure that any occurrence of the many match is considered as long as there is no more than one edge separating each consecutive item of the many side of the complex match.

The whole process of similarity propagation and new match forming is continued until either all the concept terms in the $KR_1$ and/or $KR_2$ are present in the found mapping or a predetermined number of iterations have been exceeded (denoted as *iterThr*). More formally, the process of checking whether all concepts of at least one knowledge representation are covered in the found mapping $M$, is true when:

*Figure 6. Similarity propagation pseudo code*

```
Algorithm: SimilarityPropagation
Input: sets ST_1, ST_2 containing the ordered embedded k-subtrees (k ≥ 2) from KR_1 and KR_2
Output: mapping M

 1: M = {m_1}, m_1 = (L(v1_0), L(v2_0))
 2: while (iterCounter < iterThr AND allMappingsFound(M) = false) do
 3:    for each unprocessed match m_i(e_i,f_i) ∈ M do
 4:       if m_i is 1:1 match then
 5:          for every pair of k-subtrees, k-st_1 in ST_1 and k-st_2 in ST_2 do
 6:             if (∃r, e_i = φ(k-st_1)_r AND f_i = φ(k-st_2)_r) then
 7:                UpdateSimilarityMatrix(φ(k-st_1), φ(k-st_2))
 8:       if m_i is a complex match then
 9:          if m_i is M:1 match then
10:             for every pair of ((k-1) + |e_i|)-subtree ((k-1) + |e_i|)-st_1 in ST_1
                   and k-subtree k-st_2 in ST_2 do
11:                if (∃r,e_i=(φ(((k-1) + |e_i|)-st_1)_r + φ(((k-1) + |e_i|)-st_1)_(r+1) +...
                      ...+ φ(((k-1) + |e_i|)-st_1)_(r+ |ei|-1)) AND f_i=φ(k-st_2)_r) then
12:                   φ(k-st_1)' = φ(k-st_1) - e_i // remove many labels
13:                   φ(k-st_2)' = φ(k-st_2) - f_i // remove one label
14:                   UpdateSimilarityMatrix(φ(k-st_1)',φ(k-st_2)')
15:          if m_i is 1:M match then
16:             for every pair of k-subtree k-st_1 in ST_1
                   and ((k-1)+|f_i|)-subtree ((k-1)+ |f_i|)-st_2 in ST_2 do
17:                if (∃r,e_i=φ(k-st_1)_r AND f_i=(φ(((k-1)+ |f_i|)-st_2)_r + φ(((k-1)+ |f_i|)-st_2)_(r+1) + ...
                      ... + φ(((k-1)+ f_i|)-st_2)_(r+ |fi|-1)) then
18:                   φ(k-st_1)' = φ(k-st_1) - e_i // remove one label
19:                   φ(k-st_2)' = φ(k-st_2) - f_i // remove many labels
20:                   UpdateSimilarityMatrix(φ(k-st_1)', φ(k-st_2)')
21:    SetMatchAsProcessed(m_i)
22:    if (matchThr < MAX(SM(i,j)) (with i = (0, ..., n-1); j = (0, ..., m-1)) then
23:       M = M ∪ (L(v1_i), L(v2_j)) // add new match
24:       reset iterCounter
25:    else if (CheckForComplexMatch(SM)) then
26:       reset iterCounter
27:    else
28:       increment iterCounter
29:    SetAllMatchesAsUnprocessed(M)
30: endWhile
31: return M
```

- either for every $L(v1_i) \in CT_1$ ($i = \{0, \ldots, n\}$), there exists $e_i \in m_i$ ($m_i \in M$) such that $L(v1_i) \subseteq e_i$
- or for every $L(v2_j) \in CT_2$ ($j = \{0, \ldots, m\}$), there exists $f_j \in m_j$, ($m_j \in M$) such that $L(v2_j) \subseteq f_j$.

The above check is denoted as *allMappingsFound*(*M*) in the pseudo code of the similarity propagation process as a whole given in Figure 6.

Please note, in addition to the logic for forming simple and complex matches, if an index in

*SM* was already processed as part of another match it is disallowed to form part of a new match, whether simple or complex.

## Validating the Candidate Mappings

Once the mappings have been formed, the WordNet online dictionary and string similarity comparisons are used to validate the mappings. WordNet allows us to detect whether the concept names compared are synonyms or use different naming conventions, while the string similarity compares concept names based on string edit distance and similarity in English pronunciation (Cohen, Ravikumar, & Fienberrg, 2003), and handles abbreviations and different order of name components. Furthermore, whenever one of the compared strings ends or starts with the other string, we consider it as a valid match. We have used the open source library for implementing the string similarity metric based on edit distance and sound (Chapman, 2006).

Each of these validating methods returns a similarity value and the highest one is used to validate the candidate match. However, there is a difference in the range of values returned and we use a threshold for each method. For the WordNet we use the similarity threshold of 0.7 for considering a match as valid, while for the string similarity we use the threshold 0.9, as the measures used (string edit and soundex) often return values that range from 0.5 to 1.0. Hence, if the similarity value is below a chosen threshold, the candidate match will be considered incorrect and remembered so that, when new candidate matches/mappings are formed through structural similarity propagation, the particular match will not be allowed. However, there are exceptions to this, as at times both measures could consider a match incorrect, when it is in fact a correct match. For example, the 'BillTo' and 'Customer' are in fact valid matches, even though both validation methods would consider them as incorrect. Hence, extra logic is integrated in the validating process so that if the children (and optionally some close descendants) of two nodes have been determined to match, and their parent (or ancestor) is considered as a match by the structural similarity propagation method, then it will be considered as a valid match, and will not be disallowed to be formed again in the next substructure similarity propagation step. The reason for implementing this logic is that if completely different naming conventions are used, neither WordNet nor string similarity would consider them as valid matches. The logic implemented can be described as follows. Each knowledge representation is represented using the pre-order string encoding as described earlier, i.e., $\varphi(KR_1)$ *and* $\varphi(KR_2)$, where $\varphi(KR_1)_r$ denotes the element at the position $r$ (either a label or a backtrack symbol) of $\varphi(KR_1)$. Let us say we are considering a candidate match $m_i(e_i, f_i)$, and $e_i$ occurs at position $r1$ in $\varphi(KR_1)$, while $f_i$ occurs at position $r2$ in $\varphi(KR_2)$. The level of each node/label in the $\varphi(KR_1)$ and $\varphi(KR_2)$ is known as, during the scanning of the encoding the level is incremented when a label is encountered and is decremented when a backtrack symbol is encountered (root node starts at level 0). Given that the node corresponding to label $e_i$ has level $l_1$ and the node corresponding to label $f_i$ has level $l_2$, we traverse the $\varphi(KR_1)$ and $\varphi(KR_2)$ in both directions to determine the parent node(s) and the child node(s) of $e_i$ and $f_i$, respectively. The parent nodes of $e_i$ and $f_i$ are determined as the first encountered nodes with level $l_1 - 1$ and $l_2 - 1$, respectively, during the scanning of the $\varphi(KR_1)$ and $\varphi(KR_2)$, from $\varphi(KR_1)_{r1}$ and $\varphi(KR_2)_{r2}$ to the left (i.e., starting from $\varphi(KR_1)_{r1-1}$ and $\varphi(KR_2)_{r2-1}$). The child nodes of $e_i$ and $f_i$ are determined as the first encountered nodes with level $l_1 + 1$ and $l_2 + 1$, respectively, during the scanning of the $\varphi(KR_1)$ and $\varphi(KR_2)$, from $\varphi(KR_1)_{r1}$ and $\varphi(KR_2)_{r2}$ to the right (i.e., starting from $\varphi(KR_1)_{r1+1}$ and $\varphi(KR_2)_{r2+1}$). However, in the latter if we encounter a backtrack symbol first we know that the current node has no children, in which case the logic is not applied. The traversal of $\varphi(KR_1)$ and $\varphi(KR_2)$ stops as soon as the parent nodes and child nodes of $e_i$ and $f_i$ have been determined. We then check whether the pair of parent nodes and the pair of child nodes of $e_i$ and $f_i$ are part of any currently formed matches and if so we consider the candidate match $m_i$ as a valid match.

Another exception to the general rule is when a 1:M match is evaluated, which as we have distinguished in the "Background" section can be either a true 1:M match or a granular 1:M match. Essentially, if the term from the one side has a sufficiently high similarity value to only one of the terms from the many side, then the formed match will not be considered as invalid as it is potentially a granular 1:M match, or even a true 1:M match, as in some cases the name of the additional concept (e.g., 'Address' from $KR_1$ of Figure 1) will not be similar to the concept name on the one side (e.g., 'Customer' from $KR_2$ of Figure 1). Alternatively, if the term on the one side has a high similarity value to all the terms on the many side, then it will be definitely considered as a true match. Hence, by default we parse both labels from the many side of a complex match to the WordNet as a phrase. If the method terminates because all of the matches in a found mapping have been determined to be correct, then that found mapping is returned. When the method terminates because the number of iterations has reached the threshold, mappings formed need to be evaluated. The criteria used are as follows. Given that there is a mapping that contains the highest number of valid matches, then this mapping is returned, and if there are more than one such mappings then we take into consideration the number of invalid matches in the mapping, and hence a further criterion will be the mapping that has least invalid matches. Additional criterion used is for a mapping to contain the least number of unmatched concepts (i.e., concepts not present in any of the formed matches). The mappings that have unmatched concepts from only a single knowledge representation, but have matched all the concepts from the other knowledge representation would take the priority. Furthermore, we give high priority to mappings containing a complex match (1:M or M:1) as opposed to a mapping containing the same number of valid matches but where the number of concepts present in the matches is smaller. In fact these criteria would be handled by the logic above, since the mapping that has the largest number of concepts on the many side of a valid complex match would also have the least unmatched concepts. Furthermore, if the concepts for which the formed match was invalid or which simply were not present in the formed matches of the chosen best mapping, and these concepts are present in another mapping's valid match, then this match can be added to the best mapping.

## Running Example

We will use the two knowledge representations from Figure 7 as a running example to aid the understanding of the method. They correspond to the left-hand sides of the $KR_1$ and $KR_2$ for schemas corresponding to a simple post order displayed earlier in Figure 1. The process would be fairly similar if complete knowledge representations from Figure 1 were considered because the left-hand side and the right-hand side of each $KR_1$ and $KR_2$ are similar with respect to the structural position of the concepts considered. Hence, the concepts would be matched in the similar way as explained for the left-hand side in this section. Please refer back to all the notations introduced in previous sections as they will be used to aid the explanation.

### Step 1: Frequent Subtree Generation

The first step consists in extracting all possible ordered embedded subtrees from each knowledge representation, and we have used the IMB3 (Tan et al., 2006) algorithm, with no constraint on the level of embedding and the minimum support set to 1 for each knowledge representation separately in order to extract all embedded subtrees. For the ease of explanation, we will explain the process

*Figure 7. Trees $KR_{L1}$ and $KR_{L2}$ are the left parts of $KR_1$ and $KR_2$ in Figure 1*

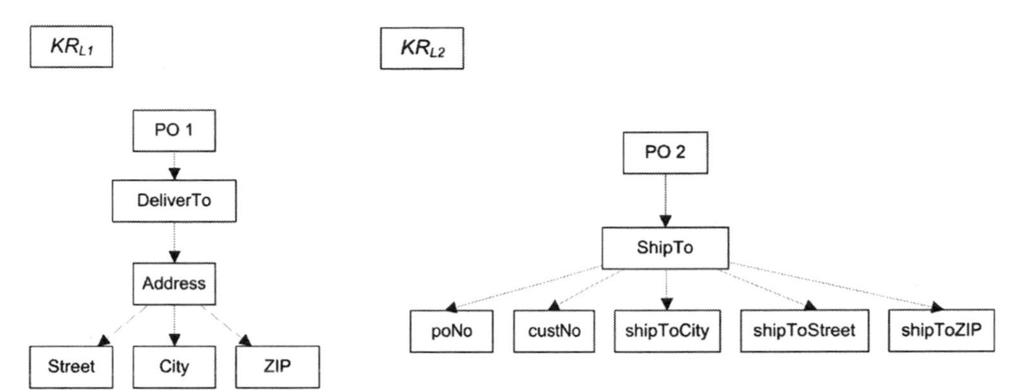


where the size of the embedded subtrees (i.e., number of nodes) ranges from 2 to 5, for $KR_{L1}$ and $KR_{L2}$ in Figure 7.

We will use the pre-order string encoding ($\varphi$) to represent subtrees. The embedded 2-subtrees are given in Table 1, 3-subtrees in Table 2, 4-subtrees in Table 3, and 5-subtrees in Table 4. The identifier of each subtree is displayed on the left of the subtrees, i.e., $x\text{-}st1_i$ denotes subtrees from $KR_{L1}$ while $x\text{-}st2_i$ denotes subtrees from $KR_{L2}$.

## Step 2: Similarity Propagation

The root nodes of $KR_{L1}$ and $KR_{L2}$ are taken to form the first match, and hence the set of mappings $M$ initially contains $m_1$ = ({'PO1'}, {'PO2'}) (i.e., $e_1$ = {'PO1'} and $f_1$ = {'PO2'}). The next step is to traverse the subtree sets to detect structurally similar subtree pairs where the matched nodes/concepts occurred in the same position, and propagate the similarity among the remaining node/concept pairs in the subtrees. As we are dealing with a one-to-one match, we check for pairs of subtrees having the same size. We mentioned earlier that subtrees considered as candidate subtree pairs for

*Table 1. 2-Subtrees from $KR_{L1}$ and $KR_{L2}$*

| $KR_{L1}$ 2-subtrees | | $KR_{L2}$ 2-subtrees | |
|---|---|---|---|
| 2-$st1_1$ | PO1 DeliverTo | 2-$st2_1$ | PO2 ShipTo |
| 2-$st1_2$ | PO1 Address | 2-$st2_2$ | PO2 poNo |
| 2-$st1_3$ | PO1 Street | 2-$st2_3$ | PO2 custNo |
| 2-$st1_4$ | PO1 City | 2-$st2_4$ | PO2 shipToCity |
| 2-$st1_5$ | PO1 Zip | 2-$st2_5$ | PO2 shipToStreet |
| 2-$st1_6$ | DeliverTo Address | 2-$st2_6$ | PO2 shipToZip |
| 2-$st1_7$ | DeliverTo Street | 2-$st2_7$ | ShipTo poNo |
| 2-$st1_8$ | DeliverTo City | 2-$st2_8$ | ShipTo custNo |
| 2-$st1_9$ | DeliverTo Zip | 2-$st2_9$ | ShipTo shipToCity |
| 2-$st1_{10}$ | Address Street | 2-$st2_{10}$ | ShipTo shipToStreet |
| 2-$st1_{11}$ | Address City | 2-$st2_{11}$ | ShipTo shipToZip |
| 2-$st1_{12}$ | Address Zip | | |

*Table 2. 3-Subtrees from $KR_{L1}$ and $KR_{L2}$*

| $KR_{L1}$ **3-subtrees** | | $KR_{L2}$ **3-subtrees** | |
|---|---|---|---|
| 3-$st1_1$ | PO1 DeliverTo Address | 3-$st2_1$ | PO2 ShipTo poNo |
| 3-$st1_2$ | PO1 DeliverTo Street | 3-$st2_2$ | PO2 ShipTo custNo |
| 3-$st1_3$ | PO1 DeliverTo City | 3-$st2_3$ | PO2 ShipTo shipToCity |
| 3-$st1_4$ | PO1 DeliverTo Zip | 3-$st2_4$ | PO2 ShipTo shipToStreet |
| 3-$st1_5$ | PO1 Address Street | 3-$st2_5$ | PO2 ShipTo shipToZip |
| 3-$st1_6$ | PO1 Address City | 3-$st2_6$ | PO2 poNo / custNo |
| 3-$st1_7$ | PO1 Address Zip | 3-$st2_7$ | PO2 poNo / shipToCity |
| 3-$st1_8$ | PO1 Street / City | 3-$st2_8$ | PO2 poNo / shipToStreet |
| 3-$st1_9$ | PO1 Street / Zip | 3-$st2_9$ | PO2 poNo / shipToZip |
| 3-$st1_{10}$ | PO1 City / Zip | 3-$st2_{10}$ | PO2 custNo / shipToCity |
| 3-$st1_{11}$ | DeliverTo Address Street | 3-$st2_{11}$ | PO2 custNo / shipToStreet |
| 3-$st1_{12}$ | DeliverTo Address City | 3-$st2_{12}$ | PO2 custNo / shipToZip |
| 3-$st1_{13}$ | DeliverTo Address Zip | 3-$st2_{13}$ | PO2 shipToCity / shipToStreet |
| 3-$st1_{14}$ | DeliverTo Street / City | 3-$st2_{14}$ | PO2 shipToCity / shipToZip |
| 3-$st1_{15}$ | DeliverTo Street / Zip | 3-$st2_{15}$ | PO2 shipToStreet / shipToZip |
| 3-$st1_{16}$ | DeliverTo City / Zip | 3-$st2_{16}$ | ShipTo poNo / custNo |
| 3-$st1_{17}$ | DeliverTo Street /City | 3-$st2_{17}$ | ShipTo poNo / shipToCity |
| 3-$st1_{18}$ | Address Street / City | 3-$st2_{18}$ | ShipTo poNo / shipToStreet |
| 3-$st1_{19}$ | Address Street / Zip | 3-$st2_{19}$ | ShipTo poNo / shipToZip |
| 3-$st1_{20}$ | Address City / Zip | 3-$st2_{20}$ | ShipTo custNo / shipToCity |
| | | 3-$st2_{21}$ | ShipTo custNo / shipToStreet |
| | | 3-$st2_{22}$ | ShipTo custNo / shipToZip |
| | | 3-$st2_{23}$ | ShipTo shipToCity / shipToStreet |
| | | 3-$st2_{24}$ | ShipTo shipToCity / shipToZip |
| | | 3-$st2_{25}$ | ShipTo shipToStreet / shipToZip |

update of similarity matrix are those that satisfy the pre-condition there exists $r$, such that $e_i = \varphi(k\text{-}st1)_r$ AND $f_i = \varphi(k\text{-}st2)_r$, where $r$ corresponds to the $r$-th position in the pre-order string encoding ($\varphi$) of a subtree. Hence for $m_1$ = ({'PO1'}, {'PO2'}), the precondition becomes there exists $r$, such that 'PO1' = $\varphi(k\text{-}st1)_r$ AND 'PO2' = $\varphi(k\text{-}st2)_r$). Since 'PO1' and 'PO2' are root nodes, they will always be listed first in any subtree (encoding). From Table 1, the pairs of 2-subtrees that satisfy this pre-condition are {(2-$st1_1$, 2-$st2_1$), (2-$st1_1$, 2-$st2_2$), …, (2-$st1_1$, 2-$st2_6$), (2-$st1_2$, 2-$st2_1$), (2-$st1_2$, 2-$st2_2$), …, (2-$st1_2$, 2-$st2_6$), (2-$st1_3$, 2-$st2_1$), (2-$st1_3$, 2-$st2_2$), …, (2-$st1_3$, 2-$st2_6$), (2-$st1_4$, 2-$st2_1$), (2-$st1_4$, 2-$st2_2$), …, (2-$st1_4$, 2-$st2_6$), (2-$st1_5$, 2-$st2_1$), (2-$st1_5$, 2-$st2_2$), …, (2-$st1_5$, 2-$st2_6$)}, while from Table 2 the pairs of 3-subtrees satisfying the condition are: {(3-$st1_1$, 3-$st2_1$), (3-$st1_1$, 3-$st2_2$), …, (3-$st1_1$, 3-$st2_{15}$), (3-$st1_2$, 3-$st2_1$), (3-$st1_2$, 3-$st2_2$), …, (3-$st1_2$, 3-$st2_{15}$), …, (3-$st1_{10}$, 3-$st2_1$), (3-$st1_{10}$, 3-$st2_2$), …, (3-$st1_{10}$, 3-$st2_{15}$). Similarly, in Table 3 every 4-subtree of $KR_{L1}$ that contains 'PO1' (i.e., 4-$st1_1$, 4-$st1_2$, …, 4-$st1_{10}$) is paired up with every other 4-subtree of $KR_{L2}$ that contains 'PO2' (i.e., 4-$st2_1$, 4-$st2_2$, …, 4-$st2_{20}$), and from Table 4 every 5-subtree of $KR_{L1}$ that contains 'PO1' (i.e., 5-$st1_1$, 5-$st1_2$,

*Table 3. 4-Subtrees from $KR_{L1}$ and $KR_{L2}$*

| $KR_{L1}$ 4-subtrees | | $KR_{L2}$ 4-subtrees | |
|---|---|---|---|
| 4-$st1_1$ | PO1 DeliverTo Address Street | 4-$st2_1$ | PO2 ShipTo poNo / custNo |
| 4-$st1_2$ | PO1 DeliverTo Address City | 4-$st2_2$ | PO2 ShipTo poNo / shipToCity |
| 4-$st1_3$ | PO1 DeliverTo Address Zip | 4-$st2_3$ | PO2 ShipTo poNo / shipToStreet |
| 4-$st1_4$ | PO1 DeliverTo Street / City | 4-$st2_4$ | PO2 ShipTo poNo / shipToZip |
| 4-$st1_5$ | PO1 DeliverTo Street / Zip | 4-$st2_5$ | PO2 ShipTo custNo / shipToCity |
| 4-$st1_6$ | PO1 DeliverTo City / Zip | 4-$st2_6$ | PO2 ShipTo custNo / shipToStreet |
| 4-$st1_7$ | PO1 Address Street / City | 4-$st2_7$ | PO2 ShipTo custNo / shipToZip |
| 4-$st1_8$ | PO1 Address Street / Zip | 4-$st2_8$ | PO2 ShipTo shipToCity / shipToStreet |
| 4-$st1_9$ | PO1 Address City / Zip | 4-$st2_9$ | PO2 ShipTo shipToCity / shipToZip |
| 4-$st1_{10}$ | PO1 Street / City / Zip | 4-$st2_{10}$ | PO2 ShipTo shipToStreet / shipToZip |
| 4-$st1_{11}$ | DeliverTo Address Street / City | 4-$st2_{11}$ | PO2 poNo / custNo / shipToCity |
| 4-$st1_{12}$ | DeliverTo Address Street / Zip | 4-$st2_{12}$ | PO2 poNo / custNo / shipToStreet |
| 4-$st1_{13}$ | DeliverTo Address City / Zip | 4-$st2_{13}$ | PO2 poNo / custNo / shipToZip |
| 4-$st1_{14}$ | Address Street / City / Zip | 4-$st2_{14}$ | PO2 poNo / shipToCity / shipToStreet |
| | | 4-$st2_{15}$ | PO2 poNo / shipToCity / shipToZip |
| | | 4-$st2_{16}$ | PO2 poNo / shipToStreet / shipToZip |
| | | 4-$st2_{17}$ | PO2 custNo / shipToCity / shipToStreet |
| | | 4-$st2_{18}$ | PO2 custNo / shipToCity / shipToZip |
| | | 4-$st2_{19}$ | PO2 custNo / shipToStreet / shipToZip |
| | | 4-$st2_{20}$ | PO2 shipToCity / shipToStreet / shipToZip |
| | | 4-$st2_{21}$ | ShipTo poNo / custNo / shipToCity |
| | | 4-$st2_{22}$ | ShipTo poNo / custNo / shipToStreet |
| | | 4-$st2_{23}$ | ShipTo poNo / custNo / shipToZip |
| | | 4-$st2_{24}$ | ShipTo poNo / shipToCity / shipToStreet |
| | | 4-$st2_{25}$ | ShipTo poNo / shipToCity / shipToZip |
| | | 4-$st2_{26}$ | ShipTo poNo / shipToStreet / shipToZip |
| | | 4-$st2_{27}$ | ShipTo custNo / shipToCity / shipToStreet |
| | | 4-$st2_{28}$ | ShipTo custNo / shipToCity / shipToZip |
| | | 4-$st2_{29}$ | ShipTo custNo / shipToStreet / shipToZip |
| | | 4-$st2_{30}$ | ShipTo shipToCity / shipToStreet / shipToZip |

5-$st1_3$) is paired up with every other 5-subtree of $KR_{L2}$ that contains 'PO2' (i.e., 4-$st2_1$, 4-$st2_2$, …, 4-$st2_{20}$). As there are no structural mismatches between the candidate 2-subtree pairs, they all update the similarity matrix. Alternatively, for candidate 3-subtree pairs, a structural mismatch, if it occurs, is found after reading the third symbol of the encoding. As mentioned earlier, the *UpdateSimilarityMatrix*($\varphi(k\text{-}st_1), \varphi(k\text{-}st_2)$) method will stop updating the similarity matrix as soon as a '/' symbol in one of $\varphi(k\text{-}st_1)$ or $\varphi(k\text{-}st_2)$ is encountered while encountering a label in the other encoding. In this case, the similarity value between the second pairs of symbols read is still updated, but no update occurs afterwards. This structural mismatch occurred between candidate

*Table 4. 5-Subtrees from KRL1 and KRL2*

| $KR_{L1}$ 5-subtrees | | $KR_{L2}$ 5-subtrees | |
|---|---|---|---|
| 5-$st1_1$ | PO1 DeliverTo Address Street / City | 5-$st2_1$ | PO2 ShipTo poNo / custNo / shipToCity |
| 5-$st1_2$ | PO1 DeliverTo Address Street / Zip | 5-$st2_2$ | PO2 ShipTo poNo / custNo / shipToStreet |
| 5-$st1_3$ | PO1 DeliverTo Address City / Zip | 5-$st2_3$ | PO2 ShipTo poNo / custNo / shipToZip |
| 5-$st1_4$ | PO1 Address Street / City / Zip | 5-$st2_4$ | PO2 ShipTo poNo / shipToCity / shipToStreet |
| 5-$st1_5$ | DeliverTo Address Street / City / Zip | 5-$st2_5$ | PO2 ShipTo poNo / shipToCity / shipToZip |
| | | 5-$st2_6$ | PO2 ShipTo poNo / shipToStreet / shipToZip |
| | | 5-$st2_7$ | PO2 ShipTo custNo / shipToCity / shipToStreet |
| | | 5-$st2_8$ | PO2 ShipTo custNo / shipToCity / shipToZip |
| | | 5-$st2_9$ | PO2 ShipTo custNo / shipToStreet / shipToZip |
| | | 5-$st2_{10}$ | PO2 ShipTo shipToCity / shipToStreet / shipToZip |
| | | 5-$st2_{11}$ | PO2 poNo / custNo / shipToCity / shipToStreet |
| | | 5-$st2_{12}$ | PO2 poNo / custNo / shipToCity / shipToZip |
| | | 5-$st2_{13}$ | PO2 poNo / custNo / shipToStreet / shipToZip |
| | | 5-$st2_{14}$ | PO2 poNo / shipToCity / shipToStreet / shipToZip |
| | | 5-$st2_{15}$ | PO2 custNo / shipToCity / shipToStreet / shipToZip |
| | | 5-$st2_{16}$ | ShipTo poNo / custNo / shipToCity / shipToStreet |
| | | 5-$st2_{17}$ | ShipTo poNo / custNo / shipToCity / shipToZip |
| | | 5-$st2_{18}$ | ShipTo poNo / custNo / shipToStreet / shipToZip |
| | | 5-$st2_{19}$ | ShipTo poNo / shipToCity / shipToStreet / shipToZip |
| | | 5-$st2_{20}$ | ShipTo custNo / shipToCity / shipToStreet / shipToZip |

*Table 5. State of the similarity matrix after $m_1$ = ({'PO1'}, {'PO2'}) is processed*

| | PO1 | DeliverTo | Address | Street | City | Zip |
|---|---|---|---|---|---|---|
| PO2 | 1.0 | 0.0 | 0.0 | 0.0 | 0.0 | 0.0 |
| ShipTo | 0.0 | 0.09213 | 0.04648 | 0.01743 | 0.00498 | 0.00083 |
| poNo | 0.0 | 0.05395 | 0.05478 | 0.02739 | 0.01245 | 0.00249 |
| custNo | 0.0 | 0.02822 | 0.03237 | 0.01992 | 0.01328 | 0.00747 |
| shipToCity | 0.0 | 0.01245 | 0.0166 | 0.01411 | 0.01743 | 0.01411 |
| shipToStreet | 0.0 | 0.0016 | 0.0064 | 0.00747 | 0.01494 | 0.02324 |
| shipToZip | 0.0 | 0.00083 | 0.00166 | 0.00249 | 0.01245 | 0.03237 |

subtree pairs that are formed between any (3-$st1_1$, 3-$st1_2$, …, 3-$st1_7$) and (3-$st2_6$, 3-$st2_7$, …, 3-$st2_{15}$), and between any (3-$st1_8$, 3-$st1_9$, 3-$st1_{10}$) and (3-$st2_1$, 3-$st2_2$, …, 3-$st2_5$). For example, when updating the similarity matrix by the candidate pair 3-$st1_4$ and 3-$st2_{11}$ (i.e., *UpdateSimilarityMatrix*($\varphi$(3-$st1_5$),$\varphi$(3-$st2_{11}$)) is called), the similarity between 'DeliverTo ' and 'custNo' will be updated but not between 'Zip' and 'shipToStreet'. While this is not correct as such, we allow for this kind of update because when larger patterns are considered it may be the case that the structural mismatch occurs at the end of the considered subtrees. Updating the similarity between other concepts which are structurally positioned in the same way with respect to the matched concept is still important. With same reasoning, there were a total of 130 instances of structural mismatch when the total of 200 candidate 4-subtree pairs were considered, and for 5-subtrees a structural mismatch occurred in 50 out of 60 candidate subtree pairs (i.e., only 5-$st1_4$ was structurally the same as first 10 5-subtrees from $KR_{L2}$ (5-$st2_1$, ..., 5-$st2_{10}$). Here the importance of updating nodes before any structural mismatch occurs is evident, as for example the 5-subtrees have a large fragment that is similar in structure, and even though the nodes in the candidate subtree pairs are not all structurally positioned in the same way, it is important to update the similarity between the nodes that are structurally positioned in the same way with respect to the matched concept.

Since we are only considering a subset of the subtrees, we will work out the amount of update (*updateVal*) for incrementing the value in SM entry accordingly. As mentioned earlier, we use $updateVal = 1 / ((2 * |ST|) * |V|)$, where $ST$ is the subtree set and $V$ the node set from the knowledge representation containing most concepts. In the running example this corresponds to $KR_{L2}$, and hence $updateVal = 1 / ((2 * |ST_2|) * |V_2|) = 1 / ((2 * (11+25+30+20) * 7)) \approx 0.00083$. To reduce the number of steps in this illustrative example, we want the matches to be formed faster, and hence we choose much smaller thresholds for the remaining parameters as *matchThr* = 0.1, *complexMatchDifThr* = 0.05 and *complexMatchThr* = 0.075. As mentioned earlier, any candidate concept for forming a complex match needs to have the corresponding similarity value of at least *complexMatchThr* / 2 (i.e., 0.0375). After processing the entire candidate subtree pairs listed in the previous paragraph, the state of the similarity matrix is displayed in Table 5.

Before moving onto the next step, let us discuss some of the values of the similarity matrix. If we look down the column of 'Street', 'City' and 'Zip', we notice that 'City' has the highest similarity value to 'shipToCity', and 'Zip' has the highest value to 'shipToZip', which is a desired outcome. However, the 'Street' has a very low value to its correct match of 'shipToStreet'. This can be explained by referring back to the Figure 7. In both $KR_{L1}$ and $KR_{L2}$, 'Zip' and 'shipToZip' are listed as the right-most leaf nodes of the left-hand side of each tree structure. This causes a high similarity value as they are to some extent structurally positioned the same way with respect to the matching concept 'PO1' and 'PO2'. Similarly, 'City' and 'shipToCity' are both positioned similarly as the middle leaf node (however $KR_{L2}$ has extra 2 nodes on each side of 'shipToCity' node), which again causes the similarity propagation to update their similarity value the most with respect to other candidates. However, node 'Street' from $KR_{L1}$ and node 'shipToStreet' are very different in the way that they are organized among the other sibling nodes, i.e., 'Street' appears as the left-most leaf node in $KR_{L1}$ while 'shipToStreet' appears next to the right-most leaf node of $KR_{L2}$. This is what causes a low similarity value. Generally speaking, when the order of sibling nodes substantially differs, the similarity propagation may incorrectly suggest another match which is the exact reason why formed matches are validated using semantic (WordNet) and syntactic string similarity.

Going back to the running example, we are at the stage now where the similarity matrix is scanned to form a new match. As one can see from Table 5, no similarity value reaches *matchThr* of 0.1 to form a one-to-one match. The next check is regarding the complex matches. Please refer back to pseudo code in Figure 5 for the detailed logic behind it. As we see in the first row, the pre-condition is satisfied between 'DeliverTo', 'Addresss' from $KR_{L1}$ and 'ShipTo' from $KR_{L2}$, since $SM(1,1) = 0.09213 > complexMatchTh$, and $SM(1,2) = 0.04648 > complexMatchThr / 2$, and $SM(1,1) - SM(1,2) = 0.04565 < complexMatchDifThr$. The candidate complex match is formed $m_2$ = ({'DeliverTo', 'Address'}, {'ShipTo'}) (i.e., $e_2$ = {'DeliverTo', 'Address'} and $f_1$ = {'ShipTo'}).

When verifying the complex matches by WordNet the whole part of the many side of a complex match is considered as a phrase and the similarity of the phrase as a whole to the matched single concept is used. From our experiments, we have determined the suitable threshold below which the matched concepts are discarded as invalid matches as 0.7. The semantic similarity as returned by WordNet between 'DeliverToAddress' and 'ShipTo' equals 0.7071, and hence the match $m_2$ is considered valid and is added to the set of mappings $M$. Hence, at this stage $M$ = {({'PO1'}, {'PO2'}), ({'DeliverTo', 'Address'}, {'ShipTo'}). Please note, as we traverse the similarity matrix in a certain way, we have detected this complex match first. Looking at column 2 of Table 5, one can see that the pre-condition for a complex match is also satisfied between 'DeliverTo' from $KR_{L1}$ and 'ShipTo' and 'poNo' from $KR_{L2}$. However, even if this candidate complex match was detected first, it would have been discarded as an invalid match since the semantic similarity between 'DeliverTo' and 'ShipTo poNo' as returned by WordNet is 0.5 which is below our threshold set at 0.7.

As explained earlier, the process of updating the similarity matrix differs for complex matches. The $m_2$ is a many-to-one match, where the many labels come from $KR_{L1}$, i.e., $|e_2| = 2$. Hence, by referring back to the pseudo code from Figure 6, we will be matching every pair of $((k\text{-}1) + |e_i|)$-subtree (i.e., $((k\text{-}1) + |e_i|)\text{-}st_1$ in $ST_1$ and $k$-subtree $k\text{-}st_2$ in $ST_2$). Since $|e_2| = 2$, we will be matching every pair of $(k+1)\text{-}st_1$ in $ST_1$ and $k\text{-}st_2$ in $ST_2$ (contents of $ST_1$ and $ST_2$ are displayed in Tables 1-4). Hence, the 2-subtrees from $KR_{L1}$ are not candidates to propagate similarity. We first detect the candidate subtrees for the change if and only if they satisfy the condition if there exists $r$, such that $e_i = (\varphi(((k\text{-}1) + |e_i|)\text{-}st_1)_r + \varphi(((k\text{-}1) + |e_i|)\text{-}st_1)_{(r+1)} + \ldots + \varphi(((k\text{-}1) + |e_i|)\text{-}st_1)_{(r+|ei|-1)}$ AND $f_i = \varphi(k\text{-}st_2)_r$) (see Figure 6). In other words the set of nodes from the many side $e_2$ must start at the same position in a $(k+1)\text{-}st1$ subtree as the single node from $f_2$ in a $k\text{-}st2$ subtree. For example, considering 3-subtrees from $KR_{L1}$ and 2-subtrees from $KR_{L2}$ the candidate subtree pairs satisfying this condition are as follows: {(3-$st1_1$, 2-$st2_1$), (3-$st1_{11}$, 2-$st2_7$), (3-$st1_{11}$, 2-$st2_8$), (3-$st1_{11}$, 2-$st2_9$), (3-$st1_{11}$, 2-$st2_{10}$), (3-$st1_{11}$, 2-$st2_{11}$), (3-$st1_{12}$, 2-$st2_7$), (3-$st1_{12}$, 2-$st2_8$), (3-$st1_{12}$, 2-$st2_9$), (3-$st1_{12}$, 2-$st2_{10}$), (3-$st1_{12}$, 2-$st2_{11}$), (3-$st1_{13}$, 2-$st2_7$), (3-$st1_{13}$, 2-$st2_8$), (3-$st1_{13}$, 2-$st2_9$), (3-$st1_{13}$, 2-$st2_{10}$), (3-$st1_{13}$, 2-$st2_{11}$)}. Looking at the candidate subtree pairs between 4-subtrees from $KR_{L1}$ and 3-subtrees from $KR_{L2}$, the subtrees 4-$st1_1$, 4-$st1_2$, 4-$st1_3$ are each paired up with every single subtree 3-$st2_1$, 3-$st2_2$, ..., 3-$st2_5$, while 4-$st1_{11}$, 4-$st1_{12}$, 4-$st1_{13}$ are each paired with each 3-$st2_{16}$, 3-$st2_{17}$, ..., 3-$st2_{25}$. Looking at the candidate subtree pairs between 5-subtrees from $KR_{L1}$ and 4-subtrees from $KR_{L2}$, the subtrees 5-$st1_1$, 5-$st1_2$, 5-$st1_3$ are each paired up with every single subtree 4-$st2_1$, 4-$st2_2$, ..., 4-$st2_{10}$, while 5-$st1_5$ is paired with each 4-$st2_{21}$, 4-$st2_{22}$, ..., 4-$st2_{30}$. For each of those candidate subtree pairs the similarity matrix is updated, but before this is done each string encoding is updated so that the actual labels corresponding to the formed complex match are removed. For example, if the method *UpdateSimilarityMatrix*($\varphi$(4-$st1_{13}$),$\varphi$(3-$st2_{24}$)) is called, then labels 'DeliverTo' and 'Address' will be removed from $\varphi$(4-$st1_{13}$) resulting in 'City / Zip', while 'ShipTo' label will be removed from $\varphi$(3-$st2_{24}$)) resulting in 'shipToCity / shipToZip', and the similarity between nodes/concept pairs 'City' and 'shipToCity', 'Zip' and 'shipToZip' is incremented. The fact that after the labels have been removed the string representation does not correspond to a valid subtree does not matter, as we are only interested in updating the nodes that were structurally the same. Since the backtrack symbol separated both pairs of nodes, a structural mismatch did not occur, and the update occurred.

After the similarity propagation process was done using the newly formed complex match $m_2$, the state of the similarity matrix is displayed in Table 6. Note that the similarity between already matched nodes/concepts is not updated. For example, the candidate subtree pair (3-$st1_1$, 2-$st2_1$) will have no effect, since 'PO1' and 'PO2' are

*Table 6. State of the similarity matrix after $m_2$ = ({'DeliverTo', 'Address'}, {'ShipTo'}) is processed*

| | PO1 | DeliverTo | Address | Street | City | Zip |
|---|---|---|---|---|---|---|
| PO2 | 1.0 | 0.0 | 0.0 | 0.0 | 0.0 | 0.0 |
| ShipTo | 0.0 | 0.09213 | 0.04648 | 0.01743 | 0.00498 | 0.00083 |
| poNo | 0.0 | 0.05395 | 0.05478 | 0.04731 | 0.02158 | 0.00415 |
| custNo | 0.0 | 0.02822 | 0.03237 | 0.03403 | 0.02407 | 0.01245 |
| shipToCity | 0.0 | 0.01245 | 0.0166 | 0.02324 | 0.02905 | 0.02324 |
| shipToStreet | 0.0 | 0.0016 | 0.0064 | 0.01245 | 0.02573 | 0.03735 |
| shipToZip | 0.0 | 0.00083 | 0.00166 | 0.00415 | 0.02075 | 0.05229 |

already part of the match $m_1$. We have shaded the entries in Table 6, where no update occurs. As one can see from Table 6, no similarity value reaches 0.1 to form a one-to-one match, or 0.75 to even be a candidate for forming a complex match. Hence, the similarity propagation is repeated starting from the first match $m_1$ again.

After the similarity was propagated based on match $m_1$, there were still no candidates for a new match, and hence the similarity is then updated based on $m_2$, and the resulting similarity matrix is shown in Table 7. As we can see, the entry corresponding to the similarity between 'Zip' and 'shipToZip' is larger than *matchThr*, and hence a new candidate match $m_3$ = ({'Zip'}, {'shipToZip'}) is formed. The match $m_3$ is then validated and as the WordNet semantic similarity measure between 'Zip' and 'shipToZip' equals 0.7017 and the string similarity check returns 0.97, $m_3$ is considered valid and is added to the set of mappings whose snapshot is now $M$= {$m_1$, $m_2$, $m_3$} = {({'PO1'}, {'PO2'}), ({'DeliverTo', 'Address'},{'ShipTo'}), ({'Zip'}, {'shipToZip'})}. Please note again that the string similarity measure of 0.97 is not a value returned by the string edit distance calculation or soundex function, but rather it is a default value returned when one of the compared strings either ends or starts with the other string. As mentioned earlier this is part of the logic implemented so that abbreviations of name would be taken into account as well as cases such as these.

As there are no other candidate matches to be formed, the similarity propagation step is now performed based on the new match $m_3$. Referring back to Tables 1-4, no candidate 2-subtree pairs will be considered as the node 'Zip' always occurs with a node that is already a part of a formed match. Hence, we consider pairs of $k$-subtrees that satisfy the pre-condition that there exists $r$,

*Table 7. State of the similarity matrix after $m_1$ and $m_2$ are processed for the 2nd time*

| | PO1 | DeliverTo | Address | Street | City | Zip |
|---|---|---|---|---|---|---|
| PO2 | 1.0 | 0.0 | 0.0 | 0.0 | 0.0 | 0.0 |
| ShipTo | 0.0 | 0.09213 | 0.04648 | 0.01743 | 0.00498 | 0.00083 |
| poNo | 0.0 | 0.05395 | 0.05478 | 0.09462 | 0.04316 | 0.0083 |
| custNo | 0.0 | 0.02822 | 0.03237 | 0.06806 | 0.04814 | 0.0249 |
| shipToCity | 0.0 | 0.01245 | 0.0166 | 0.04648 | 0.0581 | 0.04648 |
| shipToStreet | 0.0 | 0.0016 | 0.0064 | 0.0249 | 0.05146 | 0.0747 |
| shipToZip | 0.0 | 0.00083 | 0.00166 | 0.0083 | 0.0415 | 0.10458 |

such that 'Zip' = $\varphi(k\text{-}st1)_r$ AND 'shipToZip' = $\varphi(k\text{-}st2)_r$ and contain other nodes than those that have already been matched. Note that in this case this precondition already enforces structural similarity. This is because the nodes 'Zip' and 'shipToZip' occur at the end of the string encodings, and hence if one subtree encoding has more backtrack symbols due to structural difference, than the precondition will not be satisfied because the position $r$ will be different. For example, subtrees 5-$st1_2$, 5-$st1_3$ will not be paired up with 5-subtree from $KR_{L2}$ because each 5-subtree from $KR_{L2}$ where the 'shipToZip' occurs, has more backtrack symbols, and hence is structurally different. Looking at the candidate subtree pairs between 3-subtrees from $KR_{L1}$ and 3-subtrees from $KR_{L2}$, the subtrees 3-$st1_9$, 3-$st1_{15}$, 3-$st1_{16}$, 3-$st1_{19}$, 3-$st1_{20}$ are each paired up with every single subtree 3-$st2_9$, 3-$st2_{12}$, 3-$st2_{14}$, 3-$st2_{15}$, 3-$st2_{19}$, 3-$st2_{22}$, 3-$st2_{24}$, 3-$st2_{25}$. Considering 4-subtree pairs, the subtrees 4-$st1_5$, 4-$st1_6$, 4-$st1_8$, 4-$st1_9$, 4-$st1_{12}$, 4-$st1_{13}$ are each paired up with every single subtree 4-$st2_4$, 4-$st2_7$, 4-$st2_9$, 4-$st2_{10}$, while 4-$st1_{10}$, 4-$st1_{14}$ are each paired up with every single subtree 4-$st2_{13}$, 4-$st2_{15}$, 4-$st2_{16}$, 4-$st2_{18}$, 4-$st2_{19}$, 4-$st2_{20}$, 4-$st2_{23}$, 4-$st2_{25}$, 4-$st2_{26}$, 4-$st2_{28}$, 4-$st2_{29}$, 4-$st2_{30}$. In regard to 5-subtree pairs, the subtrees 5-$st1_4$, 5-$st1_5$ are each paired up with every single subtree 5-$st2_3$, 5-$st2_5$, 5-$st2_6$, 5-$st2_8$, 5-$st2_9$, 5-$st2_{10}$. The state of the similarity matrix after updating based on each candidate subtree pair according to match $m_3$ is shown in Table 8.

The candidate match where the corresponding value has exceeded *matchThr* is ({'Street'}, {'poNo'}). When validated by WordNet (similarity value equal to 0.0) and string similarity measures (similarity value equal to 0.6), the match is determined to be invalid and is flagged as a 'bad' match so that the same match is not formed on the next run. Please note, for the WordNet similarity threshold we use the value 0.7 for considering a match to be valid, whereas for the string similarity we set it to 0.9, as the measures used (string edit and soundex) return values that range from 0.5 to 1.0. No other entry in the similarity matrix exceeds the *matchThr*, and hence the next check performed is for the pre-conditions of a complex match. This is satisfied between entries corresponding to similarity value between 'Street' and 'custNo', and 'City' and 'custNo'. Hence a candidate complex match is formed ({'Street', 'City'}, {'custNo'}). When verified with WordNet the semantic similarity value returned is 0, and hence the match is flagged as a 'bad' match, so it is not formed again later. Another candidate complex match that satisfies the pre-conditions is ({'Street'}, {'custNo', 'shipToCity'}), but similarly it is discarded and flagged as a 'bad' match since the WordNet semantic similarity value was 0. As there are no other candidate matches, the similarity is propagated again starting from match $m_1$ again. The state of the similarity matrix after $m_1$ has been processed is shown in Table 9. The candidate one-to-one match that was determined

*Table 8. State of the similarity matrix after $m_3$= ({'Zip'}, {'shipToZip'}) is processed*

| | PO1 | DeliverTo | Address | Street | City | Zip |
|---|---|---|---|---|---|---|
| PO2 | 1.0 | 0.0 | 0.0 | 0.0 | 0.0 | 0.0 |
| ShipTo | 0.0 | 0.09213 | 0.04648 | 0.01743 | 0.00498 | 0.00083 |
| poNo | 0.0 | 0.05395 | 0.05478 | 0.11703 | 0.04897 | 0.0083 |
| custNo | 0.0 | 0.02822 | 0.03237 | 0.08549 | 0.05893 | 0.0249 |
| shipToCity | 0.0 | 0.01245 | 0.0166 | 0.05893 | 0.07387 | 0.04648 |
| shipToStreet | 0.0 | 0.0016 | 0.0064 | 0.03237 | 0.07221 | 0.0747 |
| shipToZip | 0.0 | 0.00083 | 0.00166 | 0.0083 | 0.0415 | 0.10458 |

*Table 9. State of the similarity matrix after $m_1$ is processed for the 3[rd] time*

| | PO1 | DeliverTo | Address | Street | City | Zip |
|---|---|---|---|---|---|---|
| PO2 | 1.0 | 0.0 | 0.0 | 0.0 | 0.0 | 0.0 |
| ShipTo | 0.0 | 0.09213 | 0.04648 | 0.01743 | 0.00498 | 0.00083 |
| poNo | 0.0 | 0.05395 | 0.05478 | 0.11703 | 0.06142 | 0.0083 |
| custNo | 0.0 | 0.02822 | 0.03237 | 0.10541 | 0.07221 | 0.0249 |
| shipToCity | 0.0 | 0.01245 | 0.0166 | 0.07304 | 0.0913 | 0.04648 |
| shipToStreet | 0.0 | 0.0016 | 0.0064 | 0.03984 | 0.08715 | 0.0747 |
| shipToZip | 0.0 | 0.00083 | 0.00166 | 0.0083 | 0.0415 | 0.10458 |

as a 'bad' match is shaded black in the matrix, and no update occurs between these concepts. As we can see from Table 9, the next value reaching beyond *matchThr* of 0.1 occurs between concepts 'Street' and 'custNo', and WordNet returns a similarity value of 0 and string similarity of 0.5, and hence the match is flagged as a 'bad' match.

As there are no other candidate matches, we continue updating the similarity matrix by processing $m_2$. The state of the similarity matrix after another update with $m_2$ is shown in Table 10 (note that only non-shaded fields are updated.

As can be seen from Table 10, a new candidate match $m_4$ = ({'City'}, {'shipToCity'}) is formed because the corresponding value (i.e., 0.10292) exceeded the *matchThr* of 0.1. When the match is validated WordNet returns a similarity value of 0.57735 and hence, according to our threshold used for WordNet it would be considered as a 'bad' match. However, the similarity value returned from the string similarity approach we are using is 0.97, since string 'shipToCity' ends with the string 'City'. Hence, the new match $m_4$ = ({'City'}, {'shipToCity'}) is added to the set of mappings whose snapshot is now $M = \{m_1, m_2, m_3, m_4\}$ = {({'PO1'}, {'PO2'}), ({'DeliverTo', 'Address'},{'ShipTo'}), ({'Zip'}, {'shipToZip'}), ({'City'}, {'shipToCity'})}. At this stage we are left with only a single unmatched concept from $KR_{L1}$, namely 'Street'. The similarity propagation would continue with the new match $m_4$, and will repeat propagating the similarity with all matches if necessary. In fact, only a single cell similarity matrix would be updated, i.e., the one between 'Street' and 'shipToStreet', since the other possible matches of concept 'Street' have either been flagged as bad or are already part of another valid match (e.g., $m_4$). Eventually, the value between 'Street' and 'shipToStreet', which would become a candidate once the correspond-

*Table 10. State of the similarity matrix after $m_2$ is processed for the 3[rd] time*

| | PO1 | DeliverTo | Address | Street | City | Zip |
|---|---|---|---|---|---|---|
| PO2 | 1.0 | 0.0 | 0.0 | 0.0 | 0.0 | 0.0 |
| ShipTo | 0.0 | 0.09213 | 0.04648 | 0.01743 | 0.00498 | 0.00083 |
| poNo | 0.0 | 0.05395 | 0.05478 | 0.11703 | 0.07055 | 0.0083 |
| custNo | 0.0 | 0.02822 | 0.03237 | 0.10541 | 0.083 | 0.0249 |
| shipToCity | 0.0 | 0.01245 | 0.0166 | 0.08217 | 0.10292 | 0.04648 |
| shipToStreet | 0.0 | 0.0016 | 0.0064 | 0.04482 | 0.09794 | 0.0747 |
| shipToZip | 0.0 | 0.00083 | 0.00166 | 0.0083 | 0.0415 | 0.10458 |

ing value in the similarity matrix reached beyond *matchThr*. Another option is to evaluate it immediately as it is the only possibility left, and only updates to this cell are allowed anyway. Hence a new match $m_5$ = ({'Street'}, {'shipToStreet'}) is formed whose semantic similarity as returned by WordNet is 0.57735, but as the default value of 0.97 is returned by string similarity, it is considered as a valid match and added to the mappings. The final set of mappings obtained is $M$= {({'PO1'}, {'PO2'}),({'DeliverTo', 'Address'},{'ShipTo'}), ({'Zip'}, {'shipToZip'}), ({'City'}, {'shipToCity'}), ({'Street'}, {'shipToStreet'})}. At this stage the similarity propagation step is complete since all concepts terms of at least one knowledge representation are present in the mapping found, or as defined in the method description, for every $L(v1_i) \in CT_1$ $(i = (0, \ldots, n))$ there exists $e_i$, $(e_i \in m_i, m_i \in M)$ such that $L(v1_i) \subseteq e_i$.

## Step 3: Extracting the Shared Knowledge Representation

The next step of our method is to label the matched concepts of the knowledge representation $KR_{L1}$ and $KR_{L2}$ so that they share the same label. We choose the labels from $KR_{L1}$ to be the common labels and Figure 8 shows the two knowledge representations again. The final step of the method is to extract the shared knowledge representation, which is obtained as follows. First the two knowledge representations are taken to represent an individual transaction within a tree database. We have used the U3 (Hadzic, Tan, & Dillon, 2008, 2010) algorithm which mines unordered embedded subtrees and the minimum support was set to 2 (i.e., number of knowledge representations considered). The largest unordered embedded subtree is shown in Figure 9, and this corresponds to the shared knowledge representation. As can be seen in Figure 9, the sibling node order has changed in the shared representation. An algorithm for mining unordered subtree has to use a canonical form of a subtree (Hadzic, Tan, & Dillon, 2010; Hadzic, Tan, & Dillon, 2011; Chi, Yang, & Muntz, 2004; Zaki, 2005b), according to which candidate subtrees are first ordered before being grouped. In the canonical form used by the U3 algorithm, the sibling nodes are ordered alphabetically and the nodes considered smaller are placed to the left of the subtree (as shown in the shared representation of Figure 9). This process ensures all the subtrees with different order of sibling nodes that have the same labels, are still grouped to one candidate. The subtree from Figure 9 actually corresponds to a maximal unordered embedded subtree, and hence the algorithm for extracting such subtrees is preferably used on larger knowledge representations, to avoid the unnecessary generation of smaller subtrees.

*Figure 8. $KR_{L1}$ and $KR_{L2}$ after matched concepts are updated to share the common label*

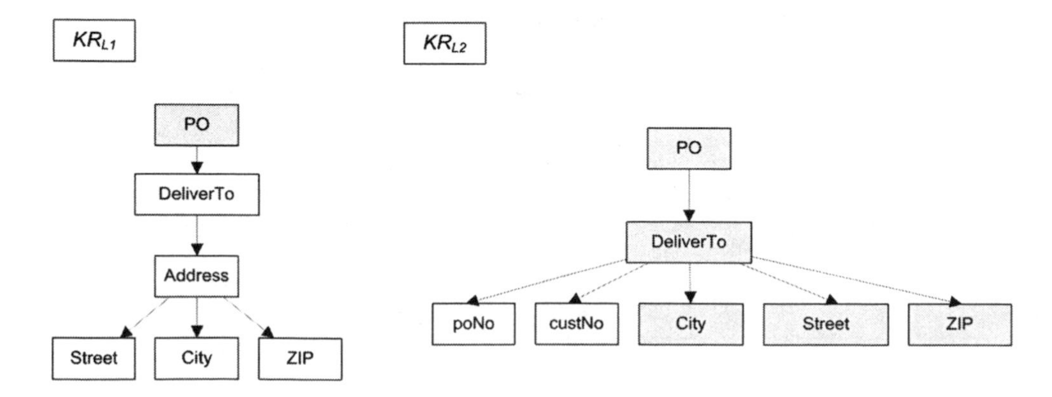

*Figure 9. Shared knowledge representation of $KR_{L1}$ and $KR_{L2}$*

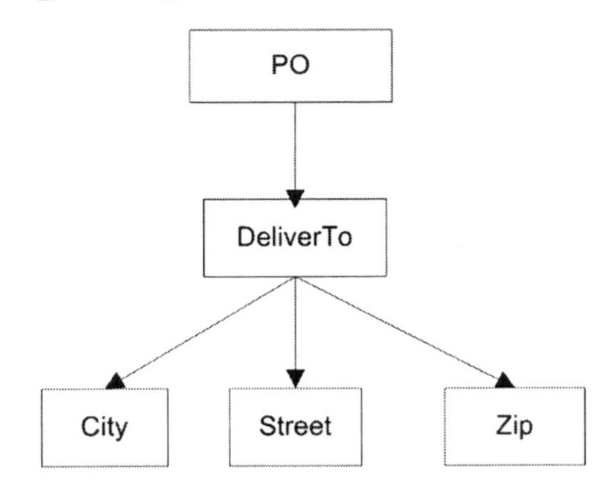


## EXPERIMENTAL EVALUATION

The method is implemented in Java, and Themis (Polyvyanyy & Kuropka, 2007) is used to determine the semantic similarity of two concepts. Themis is an Information Retrieval framework which uses the Enhanced Topic-based Vector Space Model (eTVSM) and is powered by Wordnet. To construct an ontology which will represent word relations, the eTVSM uses concepts of terms, interpretations and topics. A hierarchical, non-cyclic directed graph structure is used to represent these concepts (Gross & Yellen, 2003). Edges of the graph are to specify semantic relations of concepts of the same class, as well as inter-conceptual semantic relations. Themis has been used as an external API to measure the semantic similarity of two concepts with the text pre-processing functionalities such as stemming and stop-words removal.

When running the application, users only need to identify the two (or more) source XML schemas which need to be mapped. There is no further user involvement and this method will provide its best set of mappings found. At the same time, the method will optionally output the top set of mappings found as well as all of the matches detected to be valid during mapping evaluation phase. Hence, optionally the users can also investigate the similarity value of individual matches in the set of mappings. This is done in the cases when a user involvement is preferred for verifying the correctness of the detected mappings.

We present two experiments to evaluate the approach and discuss some interesting properties. The XML Schemas from www.ontologymatching.org were used. In Experiment 1, schemas of "Accounts" has been analyzed, while we use "Amazon vs Yahoo" in Experiment 2. In the first experiment, the thresholds of the methods have been set to the default values, because the knowledge representations in Experiment 1 are comparatively simple. In the second experiment of this section, since more complex knowledge representations are considered, we investigate the effects of different thresholds in 12 test cases. For each experiment, the results are compared with SF (Melnik, Molina-Garcia, & Rahm, 2002) because SF is a schema matching tool that takes an initial mapping followed by similarity propagation. As mentioned earlier, our method will optionally provide the detail of top mappings found in addition to all of the matches considered valid during mapping evaluation. This can be useful in cases when user interaction is preferred to verify the formed mappings and compose the best mapping from the available information.

### Experiment 1

The proposed method analyzes and builds the mappings between two XML schemas shown in Figure 10, of which the underlying tree structures are shown in Figure 11.

A total of 7 mappings were found using the similarity propagation among the substructures and Table 11 presents the detailed measurement of those mappings. It examines the number of matches, number of valid matches, percentages of valid matches, number of invalid matches and average of the semantic similarity in each mapping. The *recall* and *precision* ratios are used to evaluate the performance of the proposed method

*Figure 10. Two schemas for the 'Accounts' domain: Left.xml and Right.xml*

```
<?xml version="1.0"?>
<Schema>
  <Root>
    <ElementType name="CustomerAddress">
      <element type="Street"/>
      <element type="City"/>
      <element type="USState"/>
      <element type="PostalCode"/>
    </ElementType>
    <ElementType name="Customer">
      <element type="Cname"/>
      <element type="CAddress"/>
      <element type="CPhone"/>
    </ElementType>
  </Root>
</Schema>
```

```
<?xml version="1.0"?>
<Schema>
  <Root>
    <ElementType name="Address">
      <element type="Street"/>
      <element type="City"/>
      <element type="State"/>
      <element type="ZIP"/>
    </ElementType>
    <ElementType name="AccountOwner">
      <element type="Name"/>
      <element type="Address"/>
      <element type="Birthdate"/>
      <element type="TaxExempt"/>
    </ElementType>
  </Root>
</Schema>
```

with various values in these three thresholds. If we define that $A$ stands for the number of retrieved correct matches, $B$ for the number of returned incorrect matches, $C$ for the number of the correct matches which are not retrieved, then the total number of the correct matches equals $A+C$, while the total number of retrieved matches equals $A+B$. The precision ($p$) and recall ($r$) are defined as $p = A/(A+B)$ and $r = A/(A+C)$. From Table 11, the highest precision is achieved in the last mapping, which has the same recall value as mappings 4 and 6. The difference occurred in the fact that the mapping 4 and 6 have an additional match which is in fact invalid causing a decrease in their precision.

Let us look at some properties of unsuccessful mappings, and take mapping 2 and 3 whose details are shown in Figure 12 as an example. Both mappings contain M:1 or 1:M matches. Although the percentage of valid matches in each mapping is the same, one can see that mapping 3 has more potential than mapping 2 because there is a 3:1

*Figure 11. Tree structured representations of schemas from Figure 10*

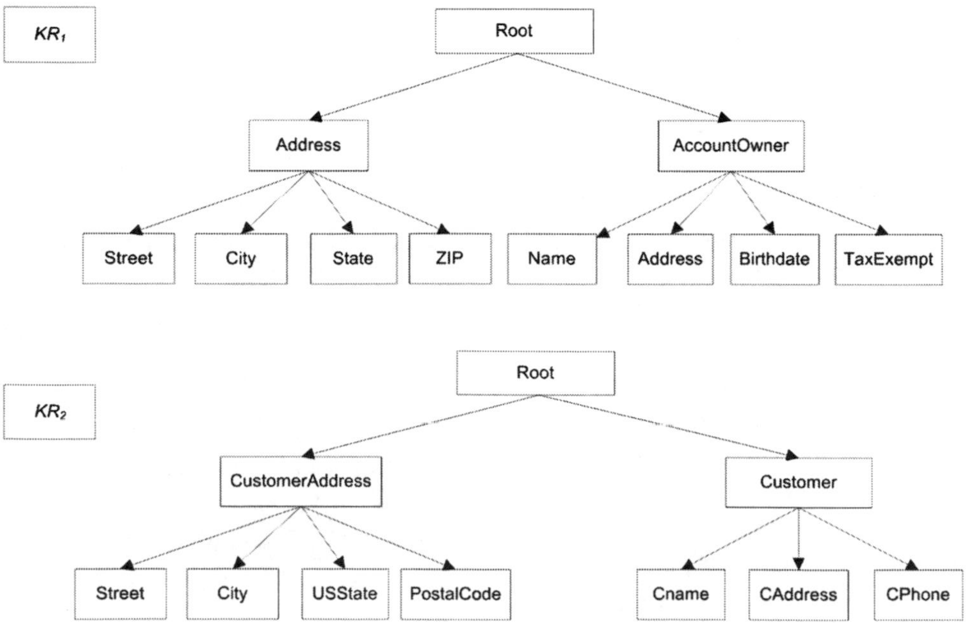

*Table 11. Mapping results for accounts schemas*

| Mapping No. | No. of Matches | No. of Valid Matches | No. of Invalid Matches | Avg. of Similarity | Precision | Recall |
|---|---|---|---|---|---|---|
| 1 | 10 | 7 | 3 | 0.63 | 70% | 77% |
| 2 | 8 | 6 | 2 | 0.73 | 75% | 67% |
| 3 | 8 | 6 | 2 | 0.75 | 75% | 67% |
| 4 | 9 | 8 | 1 | 0.73 | 89% | 89% |
| 5 | 9 | 7 | 2 | 0.65 | 78% | 78% |
| 6 | 9 | 8 | 1 | 0.73 | 89% | 89% |
| 7 | 8 | 8 | 0 | 0.82 | 100% | 89% |

match which has valid match between the item ('CAddress', 'Address'), while the other mapping contains two 1:2 matches where similarity of only one match is more than 0. Additionally, the similarity of the complex match in mapping 3 is much higher than the one in mapping 2.

Additionally, it is necessary to mention that the validation phase in our method does not detect the match between 'AccountOwner' from $KR_1$ and 'Customer' from $KR_2$ in Figure 11, because Themis and string similarity could not connect these two elements and find the semantic/syntactic similarity between them. However, two of their children 'Name' and 'Address' from $KR_1$, match with 'Cname' and 'CAddress' from $KR_2$ (Figure 11). Thus, 'AccountOwner' and 'Customer' are considered as a match according to the structural information and the matching of their children, as was explained in the previous section.

Let us compare our results with the matching result of SF. Table 12 shows all of the matches found and compares the similarity values of each pairs between the proposed method and SF. The average similarity of the valid matches found from the proposed method is 0.83 with the range of values from 0.71 to 1.0, while the average similarity from SF is 0.21 and the range of values is from 0.05 to 0.4 (Melnik, Molina-Garcia, & Rahm, 2002). Although the similarity values from different concept matching methods are not comparable, we can still notice the distribution of the similarity values is very large in SF even after it is normalized to (0, 1). Some matching pairs with very high similarity values from our methods receive comparatively low similarity values from SF such as ('Zip', 'PostalCode'). Please note that the similairty values from the proposed method in Table 12 correspond to the highest value from the ones returned by WordNet and string similarity comparison. The similarity values in columns 1, 5 and 6, correspond to the

*Figure 12. Two mappings which uncover that the number of valid matches is not the only way to determine the validity of a mapping*

| Mapping No. 2 | Mapping No. 3 |
|---|---|
| Sim(Root, Root) = 1.0 | Sim(Root, Root) = 1.0 |
| Sim(Address, CustomerAddress) = 0.89 | Sim(Address, CustomerAddress) = 0.89 |
| Sim(Street, Street) = 1.0 | Sim(Street, Street) = 1.0 |
| Sim(City, City) = 1.0 | Sim(City, City) = 1.0 |
| Sim(State, USState) = 0.72 | Sim(State, USState) = 0.72 |
| Sim(ZIP, PostalCode) = 0.707 | Sim(ZIP, PostalCode) = 0.707 |
| Sim(Name, Customer Cname) = 0.447 | Sim(Name, Customer) = 0.0 |
| Sim(Birthdate, CAddress CPhone) = 0.0 | Sim(Address Birthdate TaxExempt, CAddress) = 0.707 |

*Table 12. Comparison of similarity values between the proposed method and SF*

| Tag in $KR_1$ | Tag in $KR_2$ | Similarity from Proposed Method | Similarity from SF |
|---|---|---|---|
| Address | CAddress | 0.97 | 0.11 |
| Street | Street | 1.0 | 0.4 |
| City | City | 1.0 | 0.4 |
| AccountOwner | Customer | 0.71 | 0.24 |
| Name | Cname | 0.97 | 0.15 |
| State | USState | 0.97 | 0.14 |
| Zip | PostalCode | 0.71 | 0.05 |

default value used since those tags in $KR_2$ end with the corresponding tags in $KR_1$.

Once the knowledge representations have been updated to contain the same label, we have extracted the largest unordered embedded subtree that occurs in both representations. This tree reflects the shared knowledge representation (displayed in Figure 13). Note the change in the order of sibling nodes, which is caused by the fact that in unordered subtrees, the sibling nodes are ordered according to lexicographical ordering of their labels.

## Experiment 2

The purpose of the second experiment is to show the result of the proposed method when applied on the domain of Amazon and Yahoo Digital Camera Schemas. The underlying tree structure of the XML schemas are shown in Figure 14.

We adjust the values of different thresholds to test if a certain combination of thresholds (see the "Method Description" section) can provide better results. Figure 15 summarizes the precision and recall of the obtained mappings for varying values of different thresholds.

For the chart (a) in Figure 15, the *matchThr* parameter values range from 0.6 to 0.9 while *complexMatchThr* = 0.5 and *complexMatchDifThr* = 0.02. As shown in the figure, when *matchThr* = 0.78 recall reaches 95% while the precision is at its lowest point. In chart (b), the *complexMatchThr* parameter ranges from 0.5 to 0.8 while *matchThr* = 0.75 and *complexMatchDifThr* = 0.02. As indicated in the figure, match recall and precision reach the highest point when *complexMatchThr* = 0.7. In chart (c), the *complexMatchDifThr* parameter ranges from 0.2 to 0.002 while *complexMatchThr* = 0.7 and *matchThr* = 0.9. It shows that when *complexMatchDifThr* = 0.002, recall and precision reach the highest points. Figure 15

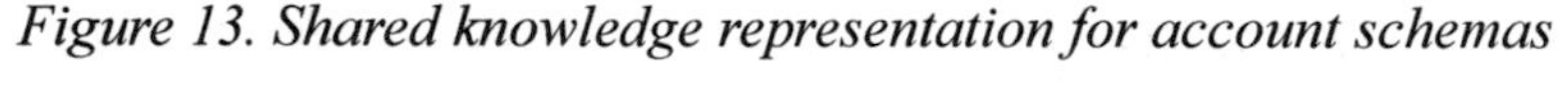

*Figure 13. Shared knowledge representation for account schemas*

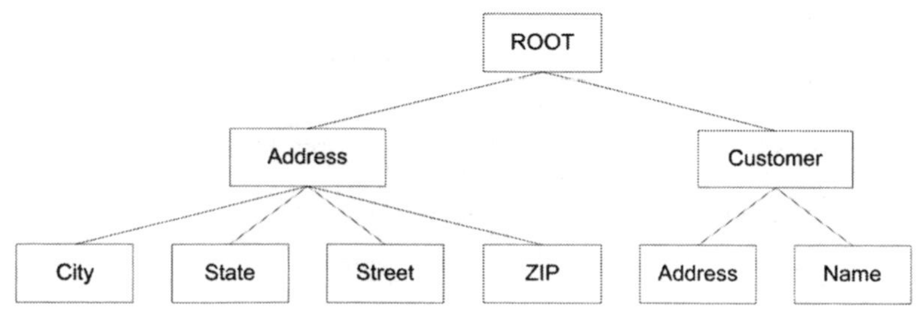

*Figure 14. Tree structured representations of Amazon and Yahoo schemas*

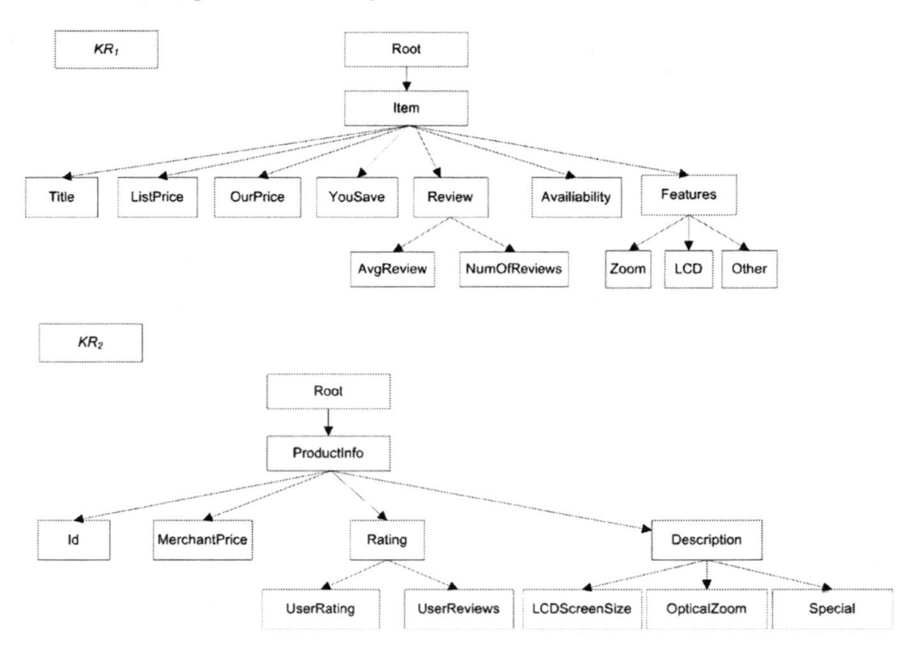


*Figure 15. Precision and recall summary for mappings obtained using different threshold values*

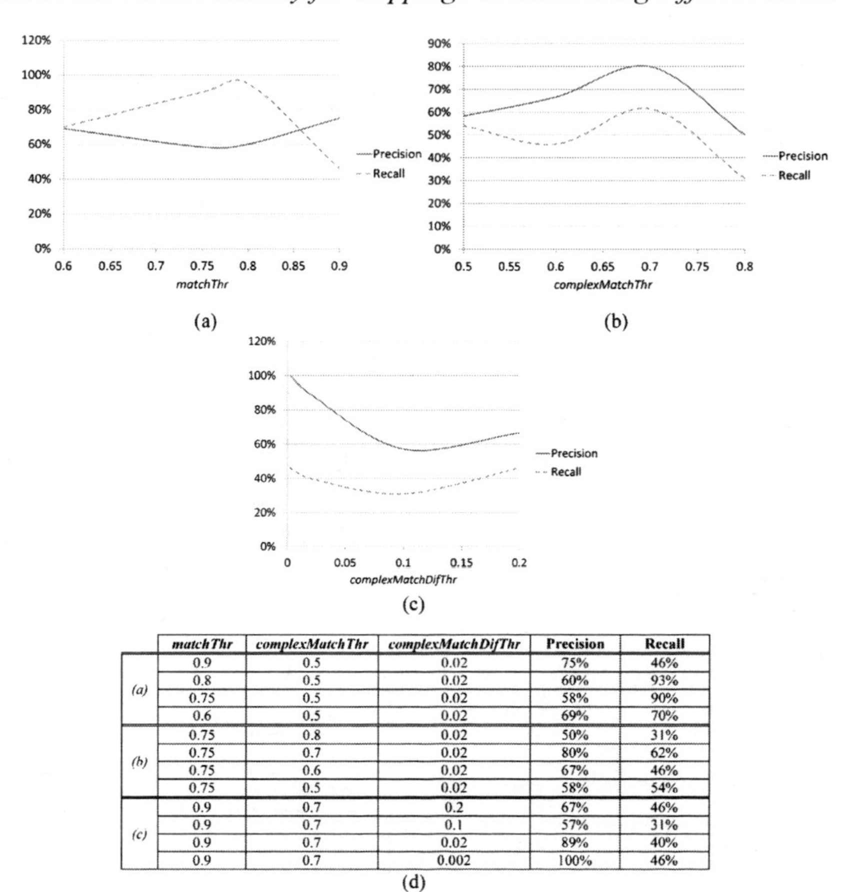


| | matchThr | complexMatchThr | complexMatchDifThr | Precision | Recall |
|---|---|---|---|---|---|
| (a) | 0.9 | 0.5 | 0.02 | 75% | 46% |
| | 0.8 | 0.5 | 0.02 | 60% | 93% |
| | 0.75 | 0.5 | 0.02 | 58% | 90% |
| | 0.6 | 0.5 | 0.02 | 69% | 70% |
| (b) | 0.75 | 0.8 | 0.02 | 50% | 31% |
| | 0.75 | 0.7 | 0.02 | 80% | 62% |
| | 0.75 | 0.6 | 0.02 | 67% | 46% |
| | 0.75 | 0.5 | 0.02 | 58% | 54% |
| (c) | 0.9 | 0.7 | 0.2 | 67% | 46% |
| | 0.9 | 0.7 | 0.1 | 57% | 31% |
| | 0.9 | 0.7 | 0.02 | 89% | 40% |
| | 0.9 | 0.7 | 0.002 | 100% | 46% |

(d)

(d) shows the impact of the different thresholds on the matching result. One can find that precision and recall are inversely related with *matchThr* and directly related with *complexMatchThr* and *complexMatchDifThr*. The purpose of this method is to detect as many valid matches as possible. However, if we consider *matchThr*, to achieve a high recall we must lower precision. So, the best results are provided if we set *matchThr* = 0.78, *complexMatchThr*=0.7 and *complexMatchDifThr* = 0.002. This detected 9 valid matches out of the 12 matches that were found. The average of similarity is 0.982 with 75% precision and 100% recall. This mapping is shown in Table 13 (note that 'Yahoo' and 'Amazon' have the high similarity of 1.0, because they are root nodes and are taken as the initial match).

For this experiment, the proposed method detects 9 matches (Table 13) while SF detects 10 matches (Table 14) with the similarity threshold of 0.05 as described in (Melnik, Molina-Garcia, & Rahm, 2002). However, our method has found one complex match ({'Review', 'AvgReview', 'NumOfReviews'}, {'UserReviews'}) which is not included in the result from SF. This explains why our method detects fewer mappings than SF, as every concept from both knowledge representations can only appear once in the mapping result of our method. This restriction does not occur in SF, demonstrated in Table 14, as the concept 'MerchantPrice' is present in two matches from the obtained mapping. This is because SF calculates the similarities of all the possible matching pairs and it causes the ambiguous mapping result, which can cause difficulties when merging two knowledge representations. As mentioned in the last experiment, the similarity measurement of SF is scattered from 0.06 to 0.27 while in the proposed method, the condensed similarity values from 0.5 to 1.0 show the matches with the highest recommendation.

After the labels of matched nodes in both subtrees have been replaced by a common label, the largest unordered embedded subtree has been extracted to represent the shared knowledge structure, and it is displayed in Figure 16.

## FUTURE RESEARCH DIRECTIONS

The proposed method for knowledge matching was developed with the motivation to initially ignore the labels by which the concepts are represented

*Table 13. Mapping result of the proposed method for Yahoo and Amazon schemas*

| Tag in Yahoo.xml | Tag in Amazon.xml | Similarity from Proposed Method |
|---|---|---|
| Yahoo | Amazon | 1.0 |
| Item | ProductInfo | 0.5 |
| Title | Id | 0.5 |
| ListPrice | MerchantPrice | 1.0 |
| Features | Description | 0.5 |
| Zoom | OpticalZoom | 1.0 |
| LCD | LCDScreenSize | 0.8 |
| Other | Special | 0.5 |
| Review, AvgReview, NumOfReviews | UserReviews | 0.985 |

*Table 14. Mapping result of the SF method for Yahoo and Amazon schemas*

| Tag in Yahoo.xml | Tag in Amazon.xml | Similarity from SF |
|---|---|---|
| Yahoo | Amazon | 0.20 |
| Item | ProductInfo | 0.27 |
| Zoom | OpticalZoom | 0.18 |
| Features | Description | 0.12 |
| OurPrice | MerchantPrice | 0.11 |
| ListPrice | MerchantPrice | 0.11 |
| Title | Id | 0.09 |
| NumOfReviews | UserReviews | 0.08 |
| LCD | LCDScreenSize | 0.06 |
| Other | Special | 0.07 |

*Figure 16. Shared knowledge representation for Amazon and Yahoo schemas*

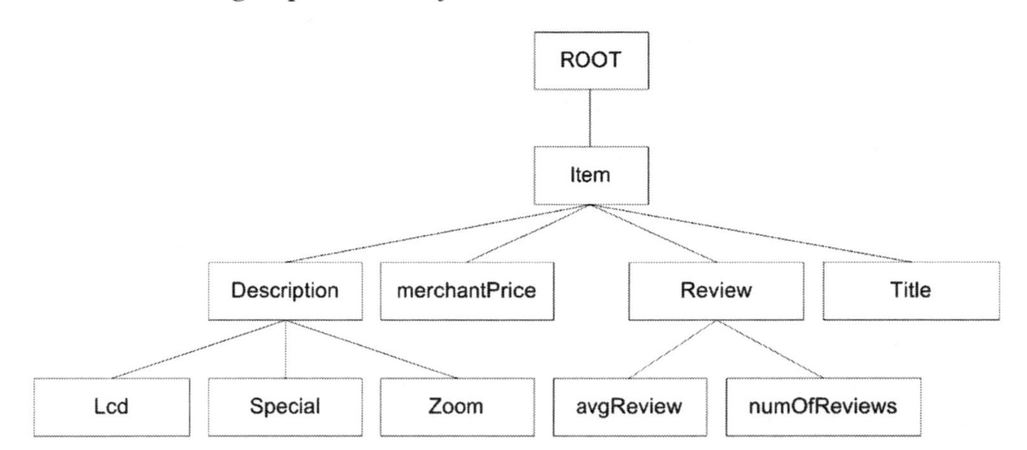


in different knowledge structures and utilize the structural properties instead to form the initial set of mappings. The experimental evaluation has indeed shown that this is useful in the cases of complex matches and different naming conventions. We have also seen that using the WordNet and syntactic matching approach is useful to validate the formed mappings, but in certain cases it can still not provide full validation at which point we need to turn back to investigate the structural relationships between the concepts. This has occurred in Experiment 1 where Themis and string similarity could not connect 'AccountOwner' and 'Bank Customer' nodes, but they were matched because of their structural similarity as their child nodes are part of a valid match. This may not always be the case in very complex knowledge representations, and it is here that one can see the limitation of using online dictionaries and syntactic/string similarity approaches for validating the mappings. Hence, one of our future extensions will be to populate the knowledge representations with related instances from the domain and utilize this information to validate the mappings. This is motivated by the observation that in many cases similar instance information will be assigned to similar concepts in the knowledge representations. This will add another level of certainty in the formed mappings, as if mapping are structurally, syntactically and semantically similar and also cover the same or similar instance information, then one can be very confident that those concepts form a valid match. Another type of information useful for validation purposes corresponds to the schema information such as element types, value constraints, etc., and we will consider the utilization of those as well. Furthermore, while in this chapter we have used some fairly simple XML schemas to demonstrate the complex aspects that one encounters during the knowledge matching task, in the future we will obtain much larger knowledge representations (optionally accompanied with instances) to further evaluate and refine the method in regard to the efficiency and scalability.

The proposed method itself is to undergo several improvements. For example, in our experimental section we have indicated the effect of the varying input parameter values on the quality of the results obtained. While we have developed an intuitive way of setting the update value based on the number of subtrees and concepts, there is a need to derive a more intuitive way for setting the remaining parameters. For example, the threshold at which a match is formed should also be worked out with respect to the number of subtree pairs that are likely to update the similarity matrix. From another perspective, not all subtree pairs may be useful for updating the similarity matrix. This could potentially be dependent on the position of the concepts from a match based upon which the similarity values are updated. Furthermore, it may not be necessary to consider all embedded subtrees, and studying the minimum size of the embedded subtree that should be considered will also be a part of our future investigation. Last but not least, the maximum level of embedding constraint (Tan et al., 2006) (see the "Problem Definition" section) can be utilized to alleviate the complexity of the similarity propagation, as we may not be interested in updating the similarity between concepts that are situated at substantially different levels in the knowledge representations being compared. For example, it may be sufficient to only consider embedded subtrees where the allowed level of embedding is 4 as one may not expect such a large number of additional concepts in one domain, so that the similarity needs to be propagated across 4 levels. However, this may be dependent on the domain and a careful study is required to find an optimal setting.

In this work, the focus was placed on tree-structured/hierarchical knowledge representations, and subtree patterns were used as a basis for incorporating structural and contextual information during the concept matching phase. We have mentioned earlier how the method would also be applicable to graph-structured knowledge representations where cycles are allowed if one first simplifies a graph structure into a tree. However, from another perspective, the method could be extended in such a way that the same idea is used to process graphs directly. Hence, rather than incorporating structural/contextual information through the use of subtree patterns, one would use subgraph patterns instead, and the shared knowledge structure would be the largest subgraph that occurs in all of the knowledge representations being matched. This would be a more complex task since the graph mining and traversal problem is much more complex, and many optimizations would need to take place for the similar idea to be applied.

## CONCLUSION

This chapter has presented an automatic method for knowledge matching at the conceptual and structural levels, driven mainly by the application of frequent subtree mining algorithms to utilize contextual information during matching. The method was evaluated using real-world knowledge representations in form of XML schemas. The chosen datasets had some interesting differences regarding the contextual information and the granularity of representation, which made them suitable for highlighting some of the common difficulties encountered during matching of heterogeneous knowledge representations. The results indicate the effectiveness of the proposed method in taking contextual information into account and detecting complex matches.

## REFERENCES

Agrawal, R., Imielinski, T., & Swami, A. (1993). Mining association rules between sets of items in large databases. In *Proceedings of the ACM International Conference on Management of Data (SIGMOD)*, (pp. 207-216). ACM.

Alesso, H. P., & Smith, C. F. (2006). *Thinking on the Web: Berners-Lee, Gödel, and Turing*. John Wiley & Sons, Inc.

Amarintrarak, N., Runapongsa, S. K., Tongsima, S., & Wiwatwattana, N. (2009). SAXM: Semi-automatic XML schema mapping. In *Proceedings of the 24th International Technical Conference on Circuits/Systems, Computers and Communications, (ITC-CSCC)*, July 5-8, Jeju Island, Korea.

Asai, T., Abe, K., Kawasoe, S., Arimura, H., Sakamoto, H., & Arikawa, S. (2002). Efficient substructure discovery from large semi-structured data. In R. L. Grossman, J. Han, V. Kumar, H. Mannila, & R. Motwani (Eds.), *Proceedings of the 2nd SIAM International Conference on Data Mining (SDM)*, (pp. 158-174). SIAM.

Asai, T., Arimura, H., Uno, T., & Nakano, S. (2003). Discovering frequent substructures in large unordered trees. In G. Grieser, Y. Tanaka, and A. Yamamoto (Eds.), *Proceedings of the 6th International Conference on Discovery Science, Lecture Notes in Computer Science: Vol. 2843.* (pp. 47-69). Springer.

Aumueller, D., Do, H., Massmann, S., & Rahm, E. (2005). Schema and ontology matching with COMA++. In F. Özcan (Ed.), *Proceedings of the ACM International Conference on Management of Data (SIGMOD)*, (pp. 906-908). ACM.

Bayardo, R. J., Agrawal, R., & Gunopulos, D. (1999). Constraint-based rule mining on large, dense databases. In *Proceedings of the International Conference on Data Engineering (ICDE)*, (pp. 188-197). IEEE Computer Society.

Berners-Lee, T., Hendler, J., & Lassila, O. (2001). The Semantic Web. *Scientific American Magazine, 284*(5), 34–43. doi:10.1038/scientificamerican0501-34

Bernstein, P. A., Melnik, S., & Churchill, J. E. (2006). Incremental schema matching. In U. Dayal, K.-Y. Whang, D. B. Lomet, G. Alonso, G. M. Lohman, M. L. Kersten, S. Kyun Cha, & Y.-K. Kim (Eds.), *Proceedings of the 32nd International Conference on Very Large Data Bases (VLDB)*, (pp. 1167-1170).

Bille, P. (2005). A survey on tree edit distance and related problems. *Theoretical Computer Science, 337*(1-3), 217–239. doi:10.1016/j.tcs.2004.12.030

Bruno, N., Koudas, N., & Srivastava, D. (2002). Holistic twig joins: Optimal XML pattern matching. In M. J. Franklin, B. Moon, & A. Ailamaki (Eds.), *Proceedings of the ACM International Conference on Management of Data (SIGMOD)*, (pp. 310-321). ACM.

Candan, K., Hsiung, W., Chen, S., Tatemura, J., & Agrawal, D. (2006). AFilter: Adaptable XML filtering with prefix-caching suffix-clustering. In U. Dayal, K.-Y. Whang, D. B. Lomet, G. Alonso, G. M. Lohman, M. L. Kersten, S. Kyun Cha, & Y.-K. Kim (Eds.), *Proceedings of the 32nd International Conference on Very Large Data Bases (VLDB)*, (pp. 559-570). ACM.

Chapman, S. (2006). *String similarity metrics for information integration*. Retrieved March 20, 2010, from http://staffwww.dcs.shef.ac.uk/people/S.Chapman/stringmetrics.html

Chi, Y., Nijssen, S., Muntz, R. R., & Kok, J. N. (2005). Frequent subtree mining - An overview. *Fundamenta Informaticae. Special Issue on Graph and Tree Mining, 66*(1-2), 161–198.

Chi, Y., Yang, Y., & Muntz, R. R. (2004). HybridTreeMiner: An efficient algorithm for mining frequent rooted trees and free trees using canonical forms. In *Proceedings of the 16th International Conference on Scientific and Statistical Database Management (SSDBM)*, (pp.11-20). IEEE Computer Society.

Cohen, W. W., Ravikumar, P., & Fienberrg, S. E. (2003). A comparison of string distance metrics for name-matching tasks. In S. Kambhampati, & C. A. Knoblock (Eds.), *Proceedings of the IJCAI-03 Workshop on Information Integration (IIWeb)*, (pp. 73-78).

Cruz, I. F., Antonelli, F. P., & Stroe, C. (2009). AgreementMaker: Efficient matching for large real-world schemas and ontologies. In *Proceedings of the 35th International Conference on Very Large Data Bases (VLDB)*, (pp. 1586-1589).

Cserkuti, P., Levendovszky, T., & Charaf, H. (2006). Survey on subtree matching. In *Proceedings of the International Conference on Intelligent Engineering Systems (INES)*, (pp. 216-221). IEEE Computer Society.

Das, S., Chong, E. I., Eadon, G., & Srinivasan, J. (2004). Supporting ontology-based semantic matching in RDBMS. In *Proceedings of the 30th International Conference on Very Large Data Bases (VLDB)*, (pp. 1054-1065). ACM.

Do, H., & Rahm, E. (2002). COMA: A system for flexible combination of schema matching approaches. In *Proceedings of the 28th International Conference on Very Large Data Bases (VLDB)*, (pp. 610-621).

Doan, A., Madhavan, J., Dhamankar, R., Domingos, P., & Halevy, A. (2003). Learning to match ontologies on the SemanticWeb. *VLDB Journal: Very Large Data Bases*, *12*(4), 303–319. doi:10.1007/s00778-003-0104-2

Drumm, C., Schmitt, M., Do, H. H., & Rahm, E. (2007). QuickMig - Automatic schema matching for data migration projects. In *Proceedings of the 16th ACM Conference on Information and Knowledge Management* (*CIKM*), (pp. 107-116). ACM.

Euzenat, J., & Shvaiko, P. (2007). *Ontology matching*. Springer.

Fellbaum, C. (Ed.). (1998). *WordNet: An electronic lexical database*. Massachusetts, USA: MIT Press.

Feng, L., Chang, E., & Dillon, T. S. (2002). A semantic network-based design methodology for XML documents. *ACM Transactions on Information Systems*, *20*(4), 390–421. doi:10.1145/582415.582417

Feng, L., & Dillon, T. S. (2005). An XML-enabled data mining query language XML-DMQL. *International Journal of Business Intelligence and Data Mining*, *1*(1), 22–41. doi:10.1504/IJBIDM.2005.007316

Fensel, D., Lausen, H., Polleres, A., Bruijn, J. D., Stollberg, M., Roman, D., & Domingue, J. (2007). *Enabling Semantic Web services: The Web service modeling ontology*. Springer.

Gabrilovich, E., & Markovitch, S. (2007). Computing semantic relatedness using Wikipedia-based explicit semantic analysis. In M. M. Veloso (Eds.), *Proceedings of the 20th International Joint Conference on Artificial Intelligence (IJCAI)*, (pp. 6-12).

Ge, J., & Qiu, Y. (2008). Concept similarity matching based on semantic distance. In *Proceeding of the 4th International Conference on Semantics, Knowledge and Grid (SKG)*, (pp. 380-383). IEEE Computer Society.

Giunchiglia, F., & Shvaiko, P. (2007). Semantic matching: Algorithms and implementation. [Springer.]. *Journal on Data Semantics*, *9*, 1–38.

Gross, J. L., & Yellen, J. (2003). *Handbook of graph theory*. CRC Press.

Gruber, T. R. (1993). A translation approach to portable ontology specifications. *Knowledge Acquisition*, *5*(2), 199–220. doi:10.1006/knac.1993.1008

Gruber, T. R. (1995). Toward principles for the design of ontologies used for knowledge sharing. *International Journal of Human-Computer Studies*, *43*(5-6), 907–928. doi:10.1006/ijhc.1995.1081

Hadzic, F., Tan, H., & Dillon, T. S. (2007). UNI3 - Efficient algorithm for mining unordered induced subtrees using TMG candidate generation. In *Proceedings of the IEEE Symposium on Computational Intelligence and Data Mining (CIDM)*, (pp. 568-575). IEEE Computer Society.

Hadzic, F., Tan, H., & Dillon, T. S. (2008). U3 – Mining unordered embedded subtrees using TMG candidate generation. In *Proceedings of the IEEE/WIC/ACM International Conference on Web Intelligence (WI-IAT)*, (pp. 285-292). IEEE Computer Society.

Hadzic, F., Tan, H., & Dillon, T. S. (2010). Model guided algorithm for mining unordered embedded subtrees. *Web Intelligence and Agent Systems: An International Journal*, *8*(4), 413–430.

Hadzic, F., Tan, H., & Dillon, T. S. (2011). *Mining of data with complex structures*. Springer.

Hao, Y., & Zhang, Y. (2007). Web services discovery based on schema matching. In G. Dobbie (Ed.), *Proceedings of the 30th Australasian Conference on Computer Science - Volume 62 (ACSC)*, (pp. 107-113). Australian Computer Society.

Hido, S., & Kawano, H. (2005). AMIOT: Induced ordered tree mining in tree-structured databases. In *Proceedings of the 5th IEEE International Conference on Data Mining (ICDM)*, (pp. 170-177). IEEE Computer Society.

Ide, N., & Véronis, J. (1998). Introduction to the special issue on word sense disambiguation: The state of the art. *Computational Linguistics*, *24*(1), 1–40.

Jiménez, A., Berzal, F., & Cubero, J. (2008). Mining induced and embedded subtrees in ordered, unordered, and partially-ordered trees. In *Foundations of Intelligent Systems* [Springer.]. *Lecture Notes in Computer Science*, *4994*, 111–120. doi:10.1007/978-3-540-68123-6_12

Katsaros, D., Nanopoulos, A., & Manolopoulos, Y. (2005). Fast mining of frequent tree structures by hashing and indexing. *Information and Software Technology*, *47*(2), 129–140. doi:10.1016/j.infsof.2004.06.006

Kimelfeld, B., & Sagiv, Y. (2006). Twig patterns: From XML trees to graphs. In *Proceedings of the 9th International Workshop on the Web and Databases (WebDB)*.

Kwon, J., Rao, P., Moon, B., & Lee, S. (2005). FiST: Scalable XML document filtering by sequencing twig patterns. In *Proceedings of the 31st International Conference on Very Large Data Bases (VLDB)*, (pp. 217-228).

Liu, P., Zhao, T., & Yu, X. (2006). Application-oriented comparison and evaluation of six semantic similarity measures based on Wordnet. In *Proceedings of the International Conference on Machine Learning and Cybernetics,* (pp.2605-2610).

Lu, J., Chen, T., & Ling, T. W. (2004). Efficient processing of XML twig patterns with parent child edges: A look-ahead approach. In *Proceedings of the 130th ACM International Conference on Information and Knowledge Management (CIKM)*, (pp. 533-542). ACM.

Lu, J., Chen, T., Ling, T. W., Chan, C. Y., & Chen, T. (2005). From region encoding to extended Dewey: On efficient processing of XML twig pattern matching. In K. Böhm, C. S. Jensen, L. M. Haas, M. L. Kersten, P. Larson, & B. Chin Ooi (Eds.), *Proceedings of the 31st International Conference on Very Large Data Bases (VLDB),* (pp. 193-204). ACM.

Madhavan, J., Bernstein, P. A., & Rahm, E. (2001). Generic schema matching with Cupid. In P. M. G. Apers, P. Atzeni, S. Ceri, S. Paraboschi, K. Ramamohanarao, & R. T. Snodgrass (Eds.), *Proceedings of the 27th International Conference on Very Large Data Bases (VLDB)*, (pp. 49-58). Morgan Kaufmann.

Melnik, S., Molina-Garcia, H., & Rahm, E. (2002). Similarity flooding: A versatile graph matching algorithm and its application to schema matching. In *Proceedings of the 18th International Conference on Data Engineering (ICDE)*, pp. (117-128). IEEE Computer Society.

Miller, G. A. (1995). WordNet: A lexical database for English. *Communications of the ACM, 38*(11), 39–41. doi:10.1145/219717.219748

Mohler, M., & Mihalcea, R. (2009). Text-to-text semantic similarity for automatic short answer grading. In *Proceedings of the 12th Conference of the European Chapter of the Association for Computational Linguistics (EACL)*, (pp. 567-575). The Association for Computational Linguistics.

Navigli, R., & Ponzetto, S. P. (2010). BabelNet: Building a very large multilingual semantic network. In *Proceedings of the 48th Annual Meeting of the Association for Computational Linguistics (ACL)*, (pp. 216-225). The Association for Computational Linguistics.

Nijssen, S., & Kok, J. N. (2003). Efficient discovery of frequent unordered trees. In *Proceedings of the 1st International Workshop Mining Graphs, Trees, and Sequences (MGTS)*, (pp. 55-64).

Noy, N. F. (2004). Semantic integration: A survey of ontology-based approaches. *SIGMOD Record, 33*(4), 65–70. doi:10.1145/1041410.1041421

Pan, Q. H., Hadzic, F., & Dillon, T. S. (2010). Discovering concept mappings by similarity propagation among substructures. In *Proceedings of the 11th International Conference on Intelligent Data Engineering and Automated Learning (IDEAL)* [Springer.]. *Lecture Notes in Computer Science, 6283*, 324–333. doi:10.1007/978-3-642-15381-5_40

Paolucci, M., Kawamura, T., Payne, T. R., & Sycara, K. P. (2002). Semantic matching of Web Services capabilities. In I. Horrocks & J. A. Hendler (Eds.), *Proceedings of the 1st International Semantic Web Conference (ISWC)*, (pp. 333-347). Springer.

Patwardhan, S., Banerjee, S., & Pedersen, T. (2007). UMND1: Unsupervised word sense disambiguation using contextual semantic relatedness. In *Proceedings of the 4th International Workshop on Semantic Evaluations (SemEval)*, (pp. 390-393). The Association for Computational Linguistics.

Pedersen, T., Banerjee, S., & Patwardhan, S. (2005). Maximizing semantic relatedness to perform word sense disambiguation. In *Research Report UMSI 2005/25, University of Minnesota Supercomputing Institute, March 2005*.

Pedersen, T., Patwardhan, S., & Michelizzi, J. (2004). WordNet: Similarity - Measuring the relatedness of concepts. In *Proceedings of Human Language Technology Conference of the North American Chapter of the Association for Computational Linguistics Demonstrations (HLT-NAACL)*, (pp. 38-41). The Association for Computational Linguistics.

Polyvyanyy, A., & Kuropka, D. (2007). *A quantitative evaluation of the enhanced topic-based vector space model*. Universitätsverlag Potsdam.

Ponzetto, S. P., & Navigli, R. (2009). Large-scale taxonomy mapping for restructuring and integrating Wikipedia. In H. Kitano (Ed.), *Proceedings of the 21st International Joint Conference on Artificial Intelligence (IJCAI)*, (pp. 2083-2088). Morgan Kaufmann.

Rahm, E., & Bernstein, P. A. (2001). A survey of approaches to automatic schema matching. *The VLDB Journal, 10*(4), 334–350. doi:10.1007/s007780100057

Rao, P., & Moon, B. (2004). PRIX: Indexing and querying XML using Prufer sequences. In *Proceedings of the 20th International Conference on Data Engineering (ICDE)*, (pp. 288-299). IEEE Computer Society.

Ritze, R., Völker, J., Meilicke, C., & Svab-Zamazal, O. (2010). Linguistic analysis for complex ontology matching. In *Proceedings of the 5th International Workshop on Ontology Matching (OM)*. CEUR-WS.org.

Sheth, A. P., & Larson, J. A. (1990). Federated database systems for managing distributed, heterogeneous, and autonomous databases. *ACM Computing Surveys, 22*(3), 183–236. doi:10.1145/96602.96604

Shvaiko, P., & Euzenat, J. (2005). A survey of schema-based matching approaches. *Journal on Data Semantics, 4*, 146–171.

Shvaiko, P., & Euzenat, J. (2008). Ten challenges for ontology matching. In R. Meersman, & Z. Tari (Eds.), *Proceedings of OTM 2008 Confederated International Conferences, Lecture Notes in Computer Science: Vol. 5332* (pp. 1164-1182). Springer.

Strube, M., & Ponzetto, S. P. (2006). WikiRelate! Computing semantic relatedness using Wikipedia. In *Proceedings of the 21st National Conference on Artificial Intelligence - Volume 2 (AAAI)*, (pp. 1419-1424). AAAI Press.

Tagarelli, A., Longo, M., & Greco, S. (2009). Word sense disambiguation for XML structure feature generation. In *Proceedings of the 6th European Semantic Web Conference on The Semantic Web: Research and Applications (ESWC)* [Springer.]. *Lecture Notes in Computer Science, 5554*, 143–157. doi:10.1007/978-3-642-02121-3_14

Tan, H., Dillon, T. S., Hadzic, F., & Chang, E. (2008). State of the art of data mining of tree structured information. *International Journal of Computer Systems Science and Engineering, 23*(4), 255–270.

Tan, H., Dillon, T. S., Hadzic, F., Feng, L., & Chang, E. (2006). IMB3-Miner: Mining induced/embedded subtrees by constraining the level of embedding. In W. K. Ng, M. Kitsuregawa & J. Li (Eds.), *Proceedings of the 10th Pacific-Asia Conference on Advances in Knowledge Discovery and Data Mining (PAKDD) Lecture Notes in Computer Science: Vol. 3918* (pp. 450-461). Springer.

Tan, H., Hadzic, F., Dillon, T. S., Chang, E., & Feng, L. (2008). Tree model guided candidate generation for mining frequent subtrees from XML documents. *ACM Transaction Knowledge Discovery Data, 2*(2), 1–43. doi:10.1145/1376815.1376818

Tan, H., Hadzic, F., Feng, L., & Chang, E. (2005). MB3-miner: Mining eMBedded subTREEs using tree model guided candidate generation. In *Proceedings of the 1st International Workshop on Mining Complex Data in Conjunction with ICDM.* IEEE Computer Society.

Tatikonda, S., & Parthasarathy, S. (2010). Hashing tree-structured data: Methods and APPLICATIONS. In *Proceedings of the 26th International Conference on Data Engineering (ICDE)*, (pp. 429-440). IEEE Computer Society.

Termier, A., Rousset, M.-C., & Sebag, M. (2002). TreeFinder: A first step towards XML data mining. In *Proceedings of the 2nd IEEE International Conference on Data Mining (ICDM)*, (pp. 450-457). IEEE Computer Society.

Tosaka, H., Nakamura, A., & Kudo, M. (2007). Mining subtrees with frequent occurrence of similar subtrees. In V. Corruble, M. Takeda, and E. Suzuki (Eds.), *Proceedings of the 10th International Conference on Discovery science (DS) Lecture Notes in Computer Science: Vol. 4755* (pp. 286-290). Springer.

Touzet, H. (2007). Comparing similar ordered trees in linear-time. *Journal of Discrete Algorithms, 5*(4), 696–705. doi:10.1016/j.jda.2006.07.002

Wang, C., Hong, M., Pei, J., Zhou, H., Wang, W., & Shi, B. (2004). Efficient pattern-growth methods for frequent tree pattern mining. In H. Dai, R. Srikant, & C. Zhang (Eds.), *Proceedings of the 8th Pacific-Asia Conference Advances in Knowledge Discovery and Data Mining (PAKDD) Lecture Notes in Computer Science: Vol. 3056* (pp. 441-451). Springer.

Wang, H., Park, S., Fan, W., & Yu, P. S. (2003). ViST: A dynamic index method for querying XML Data by tree structures. In A. Y. Halevy, Z. G. Ives, & A. Doan (Eds.), *Proceedings of the ACM International Conference on Management of Data (SIGMOD)*, (pp. 110-121). ACM.

Zaki, M. J. (2005a). Efficiently mining frequent trees in a forest: Algorithms and applications. *IEEE Transactions on Knowledge and Data Engineering, 17*(8), 1021–1035. doi:10.1109/TKDE.2005.125

Zaki, M. J. (2005b). Efficiently mining frequent embedded unordered trees. *Fundamentae Informaticae*, *66*(1-2), 33–52.

Zhang, S., Zhang, J., Liu, H., & Wang, W. (2005). XAR-miner: Efficient association rules mining for XML data. In A. Ellis, & T. Hagino (Eds.), *Proceedings of the 14th International Conference on World Wide Web (WWW)*, (pp. 894-895). ACM.

Zou, L., Lu, Y., Zhang, H., Hu, R., & Zhou, C. (2006). Mining frequent induced subtrees by prefix-tree-projected pattern growth. In *Proceedings of the 7th International Conference on Web-Age Information Management Workshops (WAIMW)*, (p. 18). IEEE Computer Society.

## ADDITIONAL READING

Feng, L., & Dillon, T. S. (2005). Mining Interesting XML-Enabled Association Rules with Templates. In B. Goethals, and A. Siebes (Eds.), *Proceedings of the Third International Workshop on Knowledge Discovery in Inductive Databases (KDID): Vol 3377. Lecture Notes in Computer Science* (pp. 66-88). Springer.

Feng, L., Dillon, T. S., & Liu, J. (2001). Inter-transactional Association Rules for Multi-dimensional Contexts for Prediction and their Application to Studying Meteorological Data. *Data & Knowledge Engineering*, *37*(1), 85–115. doi:10.1016/S0169-023X(01)00003-9

Hadzic, F. (2008). *Advances in Knowledge Learning Methodologies and their Applications*. Perth: Curtin University of Technology.

Hadzic, F., Dillon, T. S., & Chang, E. (2007). Tree Mining Application to Matching of Heterogeneous Knowledge Representations. In *Proceedings of the IEEE International Conference on Granular Computing (GrC)*, (pp. 351-361). IEEE Computer Society.

Hadzic, F., Dillon, T. S., Sidhu, A. S., Chang, E., & Tan, H. (2006). Mining Substructures in Protein Data. In *Proceedings of the 6th IEEE International Conference on Data Mining (ICDM)*, (pp. 213-217). Tree Mining Application to Matching of Heterogeneous Knowledge Representations.

Hadzic, F., Tan, H., & Dillon, T. S. (2008). *Mining Unordered Distance-constrained Embedded Subtrees*, Paper presented at the 11th International Conference on Discovery Science (DS*)*, Budapest, Hungary.

Hadzic, F., Tan, H., Dillon, T. S., & Chang, E. (2007). Implications of Frequent Subtree Mining Using Hybrid Support Definition. In *Proceedings of International Conference on Data Mining & Information Engineering*, The New Forest, UK.

Hadzic, M., Hadzic, F., & Dillon, T. S. (2008). *Tree Mining in Mental Health Domain*. Paper presented at the 41st Hawaii International Conference on System Sciences (HICSS), January 7-10, Waikola, Hawaii, USA.

Pan, Q. H., Hadzic, F., & Dillon, T. S. (2008). Conjoint Data Mining of Structured and Semi-structured Data. In *Proceedings of the 4th International Conference on the Semantics, Knowledge and Grid (SKG)*, (pp. 87-94). IEEE Computer Society.

Sestito, S., & Dillon, T. S. (1994). *Automated Knowledge Acquisition*. Sydney: Prentice Hall.

Shaharanee, I. N. M., Hadzic, F., & Dillon, T. S. (2009). Interestingness of Association Rules using Symmetrical Tau and Logistic Regression. In A. E. Nicholson, and X. Li (Eds.), *Proceedings of the 22nd Australasian Joint Conference on Advances in Artificial Intelligence (AI): Vol. 5866. Lecture Notes in Computer Science* (pp.422-431). Springer.

Shasha, D., Wang, J. T. L., & Zhang, S. (2004). Unordered Tree Mining with Applications to Phylogeny. In *Proceedings of the 20th International Conference on Data Engineering (ICDE)*, (pp. 708-719). IEEE Computer Society.

Tan, H., Dillon, T. S., Feng, L., Chang, E., & Hadzic, F. (2005). X3-Miner: Mining Patterns from XML Database. In *Proceedings of the 6th International Conference on Data Mining, Text Mining and their Business Applications* (pp. 287-296).

Tan, H., Dillon, T. S., Hadzic, F., & Chang, E. (2006). *Razor: Mining Distance-constrained Embedded Subtrees.* In *Workshops Proceedings of the 6th IEEE International Conference on Data Mining (ICDM)*, (pp. 8-13). IEEE Computer Society.

Tan, H., Dillon, T. S., Hadzic, F., & Chang, E. (2006). SEQUEST: Mining Frequent Subsequences using DMA Strips. In *Proceeding of the 7th International Conference on Data Mining and Information Engineering* (pp. 315-328). WIT Press.

Zaki, M. J., & Aggarwal, C. C. (2003). XRules: An Effective Structural Classifier for XML Data. In *Proceedings of the 9th International Conference on Knowledge Discovery and Data Mining (KDD)*, (pp. 316-325). ACM.

# Section 5
# Applications

# Chapter 17
# Geographical Map Annotation with Significant Tags Available from Social Networks

**Elena Roglia**
*University of Turin, Italy*

**Rosa Meo**
*University of Turin, Italy*

**Enrico Ponassi**
*University of Turin, Italy*

## ABSTRACT

*In this chapter we describe how to extract relevant information on a geographical area from information that users share and provide by means of their mobiles or personal digital assistants, thanks to Web 2.0 applications such as OpenStreetMap, Geonames, Flickr, and GoogleMaps. These Web 2.0 applications represent, store, and process information in an XML format. We analyze and use this information to enrich the content of the cartographic map of a given geographical area with up-to-date information. In addition we provide a characterization of the map by selection of the annotations that differentiate the given map from the surrounding areas. This occurs by means of statistical tests on the annotations frequency in the different geographical areas. We present the results of an experimental section in which we show that the content characterization is meaningful, statistically significant, and usefully concise.*

## INTRODUCTION

Today most of the data available for spatial data mining can be found on the Web. Web 2.0 technologies enable users to add information to Internet pages, allowing a two-way flow of information, from the producer to users, and vice versa (O'Reilly, 2010). Thus, the users and producers, whether as experts or amateurs, were transformed to producers of geo-data (Budhathoki, Bruce, & Nedovic-Budic, 2008). Wikipedia, the first major application of Web 2.0, together with Geonames, Flickr, OpenStreetMap and other blogs and social networks are freely available tools that provide

DOI: 10.4018/978-1-61350-356-0.ch017

information coming from the community of their users on the geographical domain. Information is updated frequently and can be shared as a free source of information (Wikipedia; Geonames; Flickr; OpenStreetMap). In addition, most of the mentioned sites provide API - Application Programming Interfaces - to end users. These sets of procedures allow programmers to retrieve and manipulate data in different formats, including XML (W3C XML), KML (OGC KML) or other XML-based formats, as in the case of OpenStreetMap, which offers its own data format: OSM. This type of data representation enabled the scientific community to integrate traditional spatial data mining techniques with XML mining techniques.

In this chapter we focus on the content characterization of geographical areas using OpenStreetMap tag elements. This need arises from two observations.

1. The cartographic maps describing the territory are rich of detailed information, but are costly and get outdated very soon. For instance, unfortunately, in Italy there are only a few regional departments that maintain an updated and detailed cartography of their region. Many other regions have an outdated cartography that does not respond anymore to the users' needs. Furthermore, a cartographic map is often thematic and does not contain all the information that is needed by any user. For instance, there are maps devoted to tourists, maps of trasportation services, maps for military activities, etc.
2. On the Internet, there exists very often a large amount of information on the geographical areas generated by the everyday experience of people. People provide geographical information through handhelds, pocket PCs or mobile phones connected to Internet while traveling or simply while moving. This information is frequently updated by the active users of social networks. The idea to enrich the cartography with these fresh annotations arises immediately.

Information is generally inserted by users of social networks for free and are not always strictly controlled by a system moderator. Suppliers are allowed to annotate any location or spatial object they wish by associating it with a tag. OpenStreetMap helps the users in annotating locations by providing them an ontology of spatial objects. For each object class a tag is provided. Tags have the form of a *key:value* pair, such as *historic:monument* or *historic:castle* in which the key (*historic*, in the example) represents the object broad concept and the value (*monument* or *castle*) specializes it. The annotation system also allows the specification of additional information that the user considers useful. For instance, with an annotation like *amenity:restaurant* a user might provide an additional attribute: *cuisine:Chinese*. Usually, users provide annotations on commodities (like a bike shop or a mountain trail), on general interest locations (like airports or tourists' attractions) or on spatial objects by their purpose (hospital or zoo).

This chapter describes how we obtain a content characterization of a geographical area. The characterization occurs in terms of the concepts corresponding to the tags provided as annotation by the users on that area. A problem might arise in this process if a big number of tags might be provided by users, especially in certain metropolitan areas. In addition, some of the tags could not be relevant or interesting or be the result of a mistake. We look at this misleading result like the effect of the superimposition of noise on the valuable information.

In order to eliminate the noisy effects and validate the users annotation process we propose to apply a *filter* to the tags. The filter consists in the extraction of the tags that appear to be significant by a statistical validation method. This validation method compares the frequency of occurrence of each tag encountered in the given area, with the distribution of the frequencies of the same tag in the surrounding geographical areas. The tags that we expect that will be selected by the filter process will be:

1. the tags on which the majority of the users agree (they will be the most frequent ones) and will not be the result of some isolated cases;
2. the tags that annotate really typical features of the given area. We expect that the typical features of an area do not appear with the same frequency also in the surrounding areas. In this case, the tag frequency in the given area will be an outlier of the tag frequency distribution in the surrounding areas.

The method that we propose in this chapter identifies as significant features the tags whose frequency in the given area is an outlier of the tags frequency distribution in the neighboring areas. We will see from the results of the experimental section that the concepts that emerge from this filter process allow for identifying the typical, significant features of a given geographical area and constitute as a whole a concise description of it.

This procedure is suitable as a preprocessing step on XML spatial data, in preparation to further KDD tasks. Its outcome can be given in input to other, more advanced XML mining algorithms designed for XML document classification, clustering, indexing and retrieval.

## BACKGROUND

This section summarizes some basic concepts of XML, spatial data mining, XML mining, OpenStreetMap tags, and related works. This summarization cannot be a comprehensive description of these themes and only some of the related projects will be mentioned due to the space limits of this chapter.

### XML-Based Spatial Encoding

One of the most significant activities of the World Wide Web Consortium (W3C) is centered in the Extensible Markup Language XML specification. The work on XML started around 1996, with the goal to develop a simplified Web-adapted version of the widely accepted Standard Generalized Markup Language SGML (W3C SGML), a language defining a mark-up syntax for structured text documents. The XML specification became an official W3C Recommendation in February 1998 (W3C Recommendation).

XML is a text-based format for representing structured information that is applicable for sharing information between programs, between people or between computers and people, both locally and across networks. XML supports text document processing and generic data transmission. It can be applied to structure, store and exchange information. It is both human- and machine-readable. An XML document that follows all the syntactic rules defined by its schema specification is said to be well-formed. An XML document is valid if it is well-formed and it conforms to the rules of a Document Type Definition (DTD). DTD specifies the allowed element hierarchy and indicates the mandatory and optional descriptive attributes of the elements. Definitions in a DTD are expressed in a meta-language.

Tags, together with few other constructs, are called the markup, which essentially describe the logical structure of the XML document. The rest of the content of an XML document is called its character data.

XML enables structured data from different sources to be combined in an efficient manner. Considering the advantages offered by such language, the Open Geospatial Consortium (OGC) has started working on an XML-based language for encoding geographical information in order to facilitate the storage and the interchange of geographical features over the web. This work has produced the Geography Markup Language

(GML) in 1999 (OGC GML). GML allows users and developers to describe generic geographical data sets that contain points, lines and polygons. In addition to the encoding of geographical features, different vendors have identified the strong potential offered by XML for both vector rendering in a browser and geographical data encoding in Geographical Information Systems projects. The most significant example on this matter is the Keyhole Markup Language (OGC KML).

KML was originally created as a file format used to display geographical data in an Earth browser (KML Google) such as Google Earth (Google Earth), Google Maps (Google Maps), and Google Maps for mobile (Google Mobile). KML was supported by a gradually increasing number of suppliers and products. For this reason Google submitted KML to the Open Geospatial Consortium to be evolved within the OGC consensus process. KML Version 2.2 has been adopted as an OGC implementation standard in 2008. Ascolta Trascrizione fonetica KML provides a way to link the existing geospatial information stored in a geographical database directly to Google Earth. KML is largely inspired to GML. The difference is that GML is a pure data description language, leaving styling to SLDs and to context documents. KML, instead, merges both data and portrayal instructions into a single file. By means of KML, users are allowed using both a set of predefined tags, proper of KML, or to define custom tags as the attributes of the objects. Once described, the objects can be uniformly interpreted. This is an opportunity for the annotation of spatial objects and the addition of semantics to locations. This functionality, however, is in contrast to GML.

In addition to KML and GML, in recent years the OpenStreetMap file format – OSM – is spreading. OpenStreetMap is the best example of the Volunteered Geographic Information (VGI) phenomenon. VGI is a collection of tools that have the purpose to create, assemble and disseminate geographical data provided voluntarily by individuals (Goodchild, 2007). OpenStreetMap primary goal is to generate a free map of the world through volunteered effort. Any user around the world can contribute either by collecting their own GPS data tracks, digitally tracing aerial images from Yahoo Imagery, or by obtaining data from other free sources. The collected spatial data is made publicly available and may be used for other purposes as well, since one of the key motivations behind this project is to provide free access to current digital geographical information, often considered to be expensive by other sources (Haklay & Weber, 2008).

## Web Feature Service (WFS)

The Open Geospatial Consortium Web Feature Service (OGC WFS) returns original geographic data semantics in GML. It offers a direct fine-grained access to the geographic information at the feature level. It allows the user to manipulate and retrieve features from a map, find a feature definition (feature proper name and type) and lock features to prevent modification. WFS allows client to only retrieve or modify the data that is needed rather than retrieving the content of an entire file. It operates at a level of *source code* of the geographical information.

In WFS, objects are called spatial WFS Features. They have an identifier, one or more geometry types and attributes (Simple Features). WFS provides a *DescribeFeatureType* function that describes the FeatureType structure and a *GetFeature* function that extracts features of one or more FeatureType. The *GetCapabilities* function describes which operations are supported on each feature type. In addition it can carry out transactional operations on features like insertions, updates and deletions.

## Spatial Data Mining

Spatial data mining is a knowledge discovery process aimed to the extraction of implicit, interesting knowledge, spatial relationships or other patterns not explicitly stored in databases (Koperski, Adhikary, & Han, 1996). Spatial data mining works concentrate in spatial clustering and outlier detection, predictive models and spatial models based on co-location rules.

Spatial clustering is the process of grouping a set of spatial objects into groups called clusters. Objects within a cluster show a high degree of similarity, whereas the clusters are as much dissimilar as possible (Shekhar, Zhang, Huang, & Vatsavai, 2004). A large number of heuristic methods for clustering exist in literature. Traditional partitioning methods such as *k-means* and the *expectation-maximization* (EM) method can capture simple distance relationships and are therefore available for massive spatial databases. Density-based methods define clusters as regions of space with a relatively large number of spatial objects; unlike other methods, these ones can find arbitrarily shaped clusters. Constraints-based methods can capture spatial restrictions on clusters or the relationships that define them. An example is clustering with obstructed distance algorithm that can account for geographical obstacles such as rivers, borders or mountains. A survey of clustering methods for spatial datasets can be found in (Kamber, Han, & Tung, 2001). Clustering methods are sometimes accompanied by outlier detection. The goal of outlier detection is to discover data points, which are often viewed as noise, error, deviations or exceptions. A spatial outlier is a spatially referenced object whose non-spatial attribute values are significantly different from the values of other spatially referenced objects in the spatial neighbourhood (Shekhar & Chawla, 2003). Several outlier detection algorithms are based on visualization tools. See for instance: (Cheng & Li, 2004), (Haslett, Brandley, Craig, Unwin, & Wills, 1991) (Luc, 1995). Other algorithms use statistical tests to discover local inconsistencies (Lu, Shekhar, & Zhang, 2003) or consider both the spatial relationships and the semantic relationships among neighbours (Adam, Janeja, & Atluri, 2004).

Statistical methods are often used to create predictive models for events occurring at particular geographical locations. These methods combine different statistical techniques (Jhung & Swain, 1996), (Vatsavai, Wu, Shekhar, Schrater, & Chawla, 2002) and are used to predict natural disasters, vegetation diseases, earthquakes and forest fire hazardous area (Han, Ryu, Chi, & Yeon, 2003).

Predictive models are also developed and analyzed by the geostatistics science.

Geostatistics can be defined as a branch of statistics that is specialized in the analysis and interpretation of any spatially (and temporally) referenced data (Journel, 1986). It is a collection of techniques and theories that can be used to build statistical models, make spatio-temporal predictions at unvisited locations, extract spatio-temporal patterns in the data and validate them. Among the basic components of geostatistics there are: the variogram analysis for the characterization of spatial/temporal correlation of a phenomenon; the kriging techniques for the optimal linear prediction of a phenomenon value at any location; the stochastic simulation for the generation of multiple equiprobable images of random variables. It is important to remember that geostastics is limited to set of points analysis or polygonal subdivisions and often deals with a unique variable. Under these conditions, it constitutes a good tool for spatial and spatio-temporal trend analysis.

Works in spatial co-location rules focused on the discovery of co-location patterns. They consist in subsets of spatial objects that are frequently located together. The spatial co-location rule problem is different from the association rule problem (Agrawal & Srikant, 1994). Even though boolean spatial features (also called spatial events) may correspond to item types in association rules over market-basket datasets, in the spatial domain there is not a natural notion of transaction. The transactions in the classical problem of association rules are independent of each other. Transactions are disjoint in the sense that they do not share the same instances of the item types. In contrast, the instances of boolean spatial features are embedded in a continuous space and share a variety of spatial relationships (e.g., neighborhood) with each other (Shekhar, Zhang, Huang, & Vatsavai, 2004). This creates difficulty in using traditional measures (e.g., support, confidence) and applying association rule mining algorithms which use support based pruning (Shekhar & Huang, 2001). Existing work in this field concentrates on discovering spatial association rules and spatial co-location patterns in geographical information databases (Koperski & Han, 1995), (Munro, Chawla, & Sun, 2003). Co-location rules are often used to describe dependencies in spatial data. Spatial dependency follows the Tobler's first law of geography: "everything is related to everything else, but near things are more related than distant things" (Tobler, 1970).

## XML Mining

XML mining is usually categorized in XML structure and XML content mining. The first essentially consists in mining the XML schema and includes *intra-structure mining* and *inter-structure mining* (Nayak, Witt, & Tonev, 2002). Intra-structure mining is concerned with the internal structure of an XML document, whereas inter-structure mining is concerned instead with the relationship between the structures of XML documents, such as between subjects, organizations and nodes on the Web. For both types of structure mining, classification and clustering are essential tasks: in fact, the first aims to assign a new XML document to a predefined class of documents, and the second aims to identify similarities among XML documents and detect how such documents can be grouped together according to their structural similarities.

Association rule discovery can also be applied to *intra-structure* mining in order to describe relationships between tags that tend to occur together in XML documents. The tree structure of XML is transformed into a set of pseudo-transactions; then, it becomes possible to generate association rules (Nayak, Witt, & Tonev, 2002). Association rule mining techniques are used to build up associations among trees rather than items as in traditional data mining techniques. These techniques are used to extract subtrees, which occur frequently among a set of XML documents or within an individual XML document.

XML content mining essentially consists in mining the textual content interleaved with the structure in XML data. As XML represents hierarchical-structured information, XML content mining is more difficult than traditional plain-text mining (the various hierarchy levels in which text content is present need to be taken into account), thus identifies new challenges and opportunities. Formica (2008) defined a method for determining semantic similarity of XML-Schema elements in the presence of type hierarchies; it compares the structural components of type declarations, by a method inspired by the maximum weighted matching problem in bipartite graphs. Particularly, semantic ambiguity problems in XML data (e.g., XML documents with similar content may have schemas that appear dissimilar for the problem of synonymy of terms) are being explored (Tagarelli & Greco, 2010; Nayak, 2009).

# OPENSTREETMAP

OpenstreetMap (OSM) is a collaborative project whose aim is to create a free editable map of the whole world. It follows the same peer production model that has been used in many other well-known initiatives such as Wikipedia. The set of map data are free to use, editable, and licensed under new copyright schemes. The project, born at University College London (UCL) in July 2004, was founded by Steve Coast. Although Coast moved on to start his own company, UCL still supports and hosts the main server infrastructure (Haklay et al. 2008). All data in the main server infrastructure have been collected and uploaded by users who have registered on the OSM website. Users can produce data using handheld GPS devices or Yahoo Imagery or other free map sources. Users can actively add data to the map using either a light-weight online Flash-based editor, named Potlatch, or using the more advanced offline editing suite of Java OpenStreetMap Editor (JOSM). A database implemented in MySql stores the data. OSM map features are exchanged and exported with other web applications in the XML-like format OSM.

### OpenStreetMap Tags

OpenStreetMap maps are made up of three basic elements: nodes, ways and relations that correspond to the entities stored in the OSM database. Each element may have an arbitrary number of properties (tags) which are key-value pairs, such as *highway="primary"*.

A node is the basic element of the OSM scheme and represents a map feature or a standalone entity. A node must have at least one tag. It consists of the latitude and longitude of the location in the geocentric coordinate system, the user name who provided the data and a timestamp.

Along with the geographical coordinates of map features, feature attributes are recorded for each node as semicolon-separated key-value pairs (for example, *type="pub"*; *name="The Bull"*). This tagging schema, which is increasingly being developed into a complex taxonomy of real-world feature classes and objects, is a core part of the OSM initiative and is community-driven. Any member of the community can contribute to an update the schema by proposing new key-value pairs (Haklay & Weber, 2008).

Nodes can be used also to represents ways which are ordered list of nodes (at least 2 and at most 2000) and are used to describe linear features such as a street, or similar. Nodes can be members of multiple ways. Closed ways are used to represent areas or polygons. Area entities are defined by a particular condition on the way: the first and the last node of the list are the same and the tag *area="yes"*.

Relations are used to describe complex objects (such as nested polygons). A relation groups objects that are geographically related. It can group together nodes, ways, and maybe even other relations. These geographical elements are therefore the *members* of a relation. A membership has a *role* that describes the role of an element in the relationship. Examples of relation include bus routes, cycle routes, numbered highways and turn restrictions.

## RELATED WORK

Several works deal with geographical concept characterization and data quality for geo-referenced data.

As regards the first topic we mention (Nothegger, Winter, & Raubal, 2004) that proposed a formal measure for the salience of geographical feature for route directions based on their visual properties and (Tezuka & Tanaka, 2005) that proposed the concept of salience for landmarks extraction in a web mining approach extending existing methods of text mining. Both approaches focused on the identification of salient spatial objects regardless of the surrounding.

Contrary to this approach, (Ester, Frommelt, Kriegel, & Sander, 1998) presented two algorithms for the characterization and the detection of trends in spatial databases. They defined a spatial characterization of a given set of target objects with respect to the database containing these targets. The spatial characterization is a description of the spatial and non-spatial properties which are typical for the target objects but not for the whole database. In particular the task of spatial characterization aims at discovering the properties of targets as pairs (attribute, value). Significant properties occur in target objects and in their neighbors in such a way that their frequency is significantly different from their frequency in the database. More recently, (Tomko & Pulves, 2009) proposed a method to calculate the descriptive prominence of categories of spatial objects in a given region. They selected the most prominent categories for inclusion in the characteristic description of the region. The descriptive prominence of a spatial object is computed using the concept of contrast from background. In particular, they used the frequency of occurrence of a category in a given region and in the surroundings to evaluate if a category is over- or under-represented. A category is relatively over-represented in a region if the probability that the category occurs in a region is higher that the probability it occurs in a containing region. Analogously for the under-represented categories. In their work they assess the descriptive prominence of a category of spatial objects using the combinations of over- and under-represented concepts in three nested regions.

The method proposed in this chapter, similar to what was done in the two previous works, estimated the spatial characterization of an area considering the surrounding. The underlying assumption for all these works is that the spatial features are spatially correlated. In other terms, a feature is expected to occur more frequently in the nearby locations than in distant ones. A possible reason for this phenomenon is that whatever causes produces an observation in one location also produces similar observations in nearby locations. According to this consideration, the spatial categories that are judged interesting are those ones that are in contrast to this assumption: they occur in the given region differently than in the neighborhood.

On the contrary to these previous works, our proposal automatically extracts the characteristic features without imposing a priori any knowledge on the geographical area. In facts, it does not require the identification of categories of objects, as it occurs in (Tomko & Pulves, 2009), or the definition of a set of targets, as in (Ester, Frommelt, Kriegel, & Sander, 1998). Target categories are instead automatically identified in the tags content of the examined XML files.

In addition, in order to determine the significance of a spatial feature, our method does not require the specification of any parameter value from the user. (Tomko & Pulves, 2009) and (Ester, Frommelt, Kriegel, & Sander, 1998) require from the user a threshold of significance but often the user does not know how to set it or sets it arbitrarily. Instead, in our method, significance is automatically detected by means of a sound, theoretical procedure that comes from the statistical analysis of hypothesis tests and confidence intervals. The statistical analysis guarantees that it is unlikely that a significant feature occurs by chance in the region. The error in this inference is controlled by the significance level of the test.

As regards the topic of data quality, we mention (Flanagin & Metzger, 2008) and (Haklay, 2010) that posed the problem of the quality and reliability of the VGI data as source of information. Our method can also be used as a method to filter noisy tags or users errors. If a user enters an incorrect description of a particular object its frequency will be significantly lower than the other tags corresponding to any real object situated in that location. If the tag frequency is below a minimal frequency threshold decided by the statistical test itself, the tag will not be recognized as a descriptive tag of the area. Thus the proposed method is applicable to very general conditions, without having a priori any knowledge on the geographical area or knowing the reliability of the processed data or their intrinsic characteristics.

## MAP ANNOTATION WITH TAGS FROM SOCIAL NETWORK APPLICATIONS

The main focus of the work described in this chapter is to provide additional information on the locations included in cartographic maps. Such information on locations is checked by the system in order to guarantee statistical significance and as such, an increased level of reliability as we will describe later in this section. Locations are represented in XML OSM format. OSM files are retrieved by means of web services provided by the OpenStreetMap project.

In Figure 1 we show an example of a cartographic map of the city of Torino, Italy. The map has been enriched with annotations taken from OpenStreetMap on historical locations. On the left side of the window the user can observe a list of annotations ordered by key type. As already said, an annotation has the form of a pair *key:value*, where *key* is the class of the spatial object and *value* represents a subclass that further specializes the class description. Each annotation on the left corresponds to an icon correctly geo-referenced in the map on the right. The map is interactive: the user can zoom on the map by means of the vertical bar and can click on specific annotations in the list. As a consequence, a message box opens showing additional and descriptive information on the specific locations.

In the example shown in Figure 1, the Castello del Valentino, a famous historical target place in Torino, is modeled in OpenStreetMap as a polygon represented by a closed way. The excerpt of the XML file containing this information is shown in Figure 2. Notice that the node representing the Castello del Valentino is identified by a certain *id* (equal to 28156946). The XML file reports also other useful details, such as the user who provided the information (named apetro), the timestamp of the storage in the system of the annotation, etc. The way element reports also a list of nd tags. Each of them refers to a node representing the information of a geographical point (with the latitude and longitude spatial coordinates). As regards the annotation information, it consists of the tags of type K (key). In this case, we find the key tag building that represents the homonymous fact referred to the spatial object. A second key tag represents the fact that the spatial object is a historic castle. Finally, it specifies the name. Usually, while parsing the annotations contained into the key tags, the key name is retained only for the purposes of display of useful information in the message box. However, the name is expected to be a unique identification of the spatial location, and as such, it is not a recurrent spatial feature. Therefore, no statistical

*Figure 1. Particular of the map of Torino enriched with annotations retrieved from OpenStreetMap*

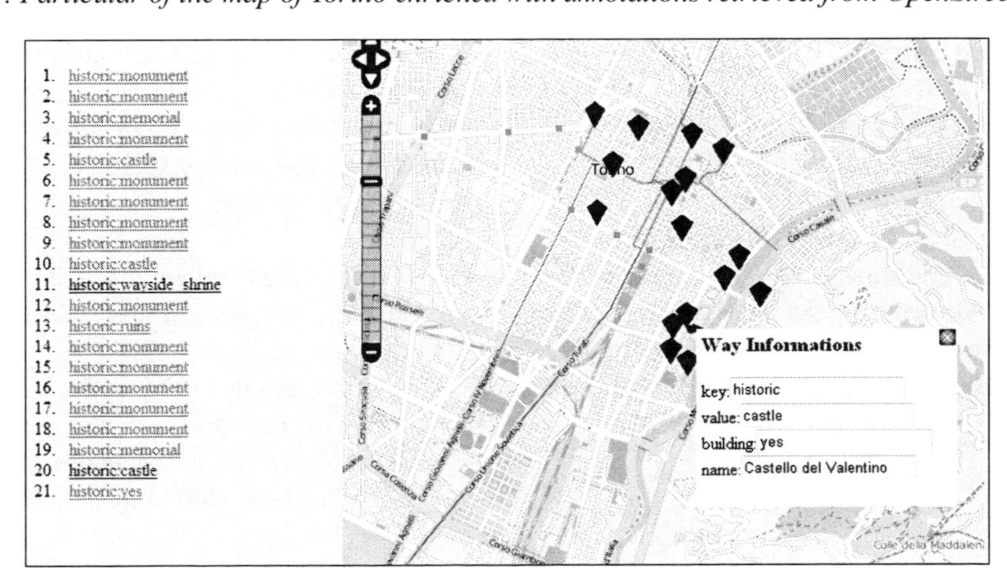

*Figure 2. Excerpt of the XML file describing the polygon representing the historical site "Castello del Valentino" shown in Figure 1*


```
<way id="28156946" user="apetro" ... timestamp="2008-11-01T22:01:03Z">
   <nd ref="309274254"/>
   <nd ref="309274255"/>
      ...
   <tag k="building" v="yes"/>
   <tag k="created_by" v="Potlatch 0.10f"/>
   <tag k="historic" v="castle"/>
   <tag k="name" v="Castello del Valentino"/>
</way>
...
<node id="309274254" lat="45.0541276" lon="7.6853507" user="apetro" ... timestamp="2008-11-01T22:01:03Z"/>
<node id="309274255" lat="45.0536668" lon="7.6868527" user="apetro" ... timestamp="2008-11-01T22:01:02Z"/>
```


elaboration is performed on the frequency of this tag.

In order to get to an annotated map like the one shown in Figure 1, the system and the user need to perform certain preparatory steps. We discuss them in the following section.

## XML Data Analysis and Annotation Preparation

The system initially presents to the user a geographical map using one of the web services exported by OpenStreetMap. The map is initialized to a certain location. The user is allowed to change the geographical position shown in the map interactively. Once the map is located in the desired geographical position, the user can define the interested area.

### Identification of the Geographical Area of Interest

This operation can be done either by inserting the geographical coordinates of the vertices of the bounding box enclosing the interested area or by dragging the mouse around the interested area. In this way the target geographical map is identified.

### Retrieval of the Map

The system downloads the metadata on the map from the OpenStreetMap services in a number of ways. In the case of our project, we construct an API request by means of a URL where the region of interest is specified by a bounding box. The bounding box is identified by the coordinates of the vertices of a square region. Vertices are defined in terms of their latitude and longitude. In the URL, the bounding box is expressed as four comma-separated numbers, in this order: left, bottom, right, top. Left is the westernmost side of the bounding box, bottom is the southernmost side of the bounding box, right is the easternmost side of the bounding box and top is the northernmost side of the bounding box.

For example, if we are interested in a geographical area surrounding the Torino airport, with the following URL: http://api.openstreetmap.org/api/0.6/map?bbox=7.639,45.190,7.643,45.192 it is possible to retrieve:

- All the nodes that are inside the bounding box and any relation that makes reference to them.
- All the ways that refer to at least one node inside the bounding box; any relations that refer to the ways; any nodes outside the bounding box referred by the ways.

- All the relations that refer to one of the nodes or ways included in the result set due to the above rules.

### Parsing the Map

All this information is exported in an XML file in the OSM format. We parse the file with *javax.xml.parsers.SAXParser* with the goal of extracting key:value pairs for ways and node points, their name and their geographical coordinates. These ones are needed in order to correctly position the annotation later on the map.

## Statistical Description of the Region

We describe here a preprocessing task that acts as a filter on annotations. This filter is motivated by the following considerations.

We observed that in certain regions, especially in metropolitan areas, the annotations are abundant. The user then risks getting lost in the volume of reported annotations. Thus, there is a number of possibilities to organize them. A first possibility is to order the annotations by their type and make them accessible by means of an index. As shown in Figure 1, we exploited this possibility in the visualization of the annotated map. Another possibility is to show only some representative annotations. Representatives are generated by means of a clustering step that identifies a prototypical annotation of a given type in a certain area; then, at a first glance, only the prototypical annotations are shown instead of all the annotations in the cluster and this simplifies the initial presentation of the annotated map. A drawback is that it would be complex for the user to infer the correct position of the desired annotations from the position of the prototypes unless the position of each of them is again restored.

As mentioned before, OpenStreetMap provides the users with a well-defined and structured hierarchy of annotation tags from which the user can choose the correct one and further enrich the annotation with his own descriptions. However, there is a possibility that a user makes a mistake in the selection of the tag. In order to clean the annotations, we propose a statistical method which is described in the following.

When we look at a geographical map we would like to observe the characteristic features of that particular region disregarding those features that occur commonly also in the neighborhood. The proposed method identifies the typical features of an area as those ones that distinguish the given geographical area from the nearby regions. In fact, we know that features occurring in a given spatial area tend by default to replicate also in the neighborhood. There exists a sort of inertia in how features change in space. This is the reason why we compare the features occurring in the given area with the neighborhood. If we find them, it means that these features are strong enough in that area to introduce a discontinuity with the neighborhood and to compensate for the spatial inertia. We now explain in detail the method we used to detect these characteristic features.

In Figure 3 we show the whole map of the city of Torino. Suppose that we take into consideration a specific area of the map that is located at the center, in the shaded central area. We wish to determine the characteristic features of the center of Torino in comparison with the neighborhood.

We build a grid around the central area, placed like a sort of square ring around it. The grid is composed of a total of 49 cells, all having equal surface area of the central, target cell. In this way, all the neighborhood of the central area can be monitored. Each key tag that represents an annotation associated to a certain spatial location by a user corresponds to a feature of the area. The aim is to monitor the frequency of occurrence of each feature in the central cell of the grid and compare it with the frequency of the same feature in the neighboring cells. We perform a standard, statistical test on the frequency of observation of each feature. The rationale of this test is discussed in the following section. At the end of the proce-

*Figure 3. The central map of Torino and its surrounding areas taken for comparative analysis*

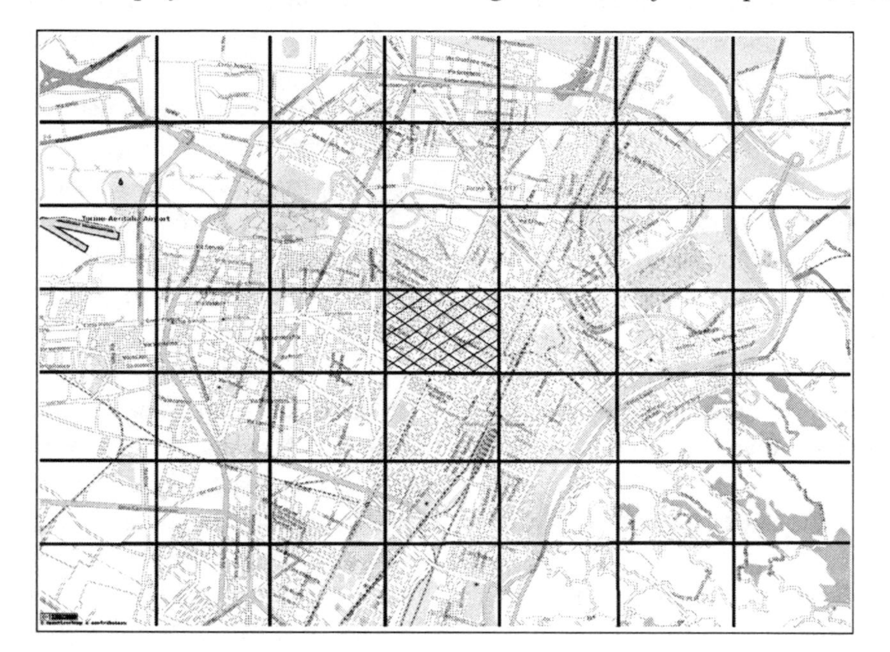

dure, only the features that will pass the filter will be presented to the user as statistical significant features for that geographical area.

## Statistical Test

We make use of a statistical test on the mean (Devore, 2008) with the aim to make a hypothesis test on the frequency of occurrence of each feature from the cells of the grid. We make the hypothesis that, given the spatial neighborhood of the cells of the grid, all the cells have the same law of feature distribution. If all the cells came from the same population we would expect that the features were present in the cells with the same frequency or with a very close one. This behavior is the most likely one when the cells constitute a random sample drawn from the same population. By means of inferential statistics, it is possible to compute the probability with which we expect to observe in a cell of the same population certain values for the feature frequency, given the frequencies observed for that feature in the sample. Thus, if we observe a marked difference in the feature frequency between the central cell and the frequencies observed in the neighborhood, and the difference is statistically significant, it is likely that either the difference is observed by chance (but this chance occurs with a quantifiable, extremely low probability) or the central cell comes from a different population for which the observed frequency is more probable. This means that the central cell is an outlier with respect to the neighborhood.

The statistical test is justified in cases in which the observations are random independent cases drawn from the same population of examples. If the sample is constituted by a sufficiently large number of cases (at least 30-40 cases), even if the original population is not distributed according to the normal distribution, the law of large numbers applies. It tells us that the statistics on the sample observations are distributed according to the normal distribution. In our case, each observation is constituted by the frequency with which a certain feature occurs in one of the cells of the grid. Suppose that the observations from the sample are distributed normally according to the

*Figure 4. In black the normal distribution (mean equal to 0.3 and standard deviation equal to 0.15); in grey the corresponding cumulative probability function that, for each value x, gives the probability with which an observation f>x exists in the same population.*

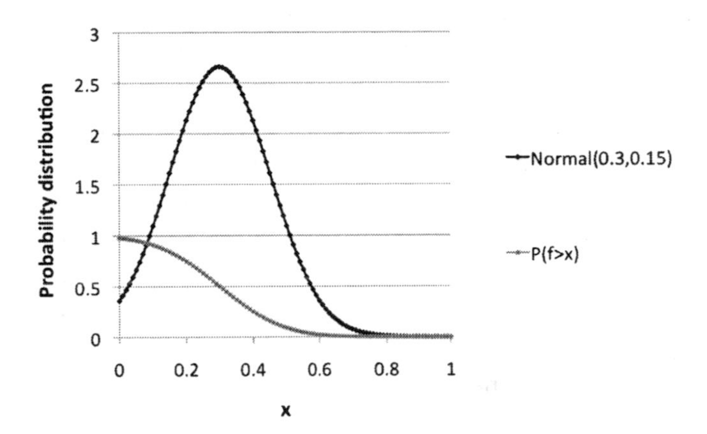


normal distribution with mean $m$ equal to 0.3 and standard deviation $\sigma$ equal to 0.15: *Normal*(0.3, 0.15). This function is shown in black in Figure 4. In grey we show, for each $x$, $P(f>x)$, i.e., the probability that exists from the same population an observation $f$ such that $f>x$. We observe that, for values of $x$ close to 0, this probability is almost 1 (there is a high probability that the observed frequency will be higher than $x\approx0$). Instead, when $x$ approaches to extreme values that differ from the mean $m$, $P(f>x)$ starts to decrease. In particular, when $x>m+3\sigma$, then $P(f>x)<0.01$. This latter probability quantifies the probability that we observe from the same spatial area a spatial cell having for a certain feature a so marked difference in frequency.

The proposed filter is applied to the features appearing in the central cell. For each of these features we apply the test described above. We compute the frequency of the same feature in all the cells of the grid. The sample is constituted by the neighboring cells, placed in the square ring around the central cell. The central cell itself is excluded from the sample. We compute the mean $m$ and the standard deviation $\sigma$ of the feature frequency from the cells in the sample. Then we compare the frequency $f$ of the same feature in the central cell with the distribution of frequencies in the sample. The statistical test determines if the feature frequency in the central cell is statistically significant. The significance level is set to 99%. This means that a feature is statistically significant only if the frequency $f$ in the central cell is such that $f>m+3\sigma$, where $m$ and $\sigma$ are computed from the frequency distribution of the feature in the neighborhood cells.

## CASE STUDIES

In this section we present the results of the statistical tests executed in four experiments.

1. The first experiment considers the map of Torino city and its neighborhood. The aim is to extract and recognize the typical features of a metropolitan area in contrast with those ones of the suburbs.
2. The second experiment considers narrower sub-areas in the center of the city with the purpose to distinguish the characteristics features of the single districts.
3. In the third experiment we considered a completely different map, located in a non-

metropolitan area, but in the middle of a natural environment: the Everest. The purpose was to check the ability of the method to detect features even in different locations in which the density of annotations is much lower.

4. In the last experiment, we checked the filter of features on maps extracted at random from the earth's surface. The aim was to check the robustness of the method and validate its propensity to recognize the situations in which there is not the presence of any typical feature. In fact, if the area is selected at random it is not expected to have any feature that distinguishes that area from the neighborhood.

In all the experiments we considered only the annotations that occurred in a cell at least a minimum amount of times. We set this minimum amount of times to 2. Notice that this limit does not influence in any way the soundness of the statistical procedure. It was set in order to reduce the total number of annotations and to eliminate the rare annotations that could be noisy with a higher probability. In the next section we present results of the tests and discuss them.

## Test Results

### Results of Experiment 1 on Torino City and its Neighborhood

The map that we took on Torino city and its neighborhood was large 63 km$^2$. We found a total of 102 distinct tags occurring at least 2 times. Of these tags, only 44 (corresponding to 43% of the total) resulted statistically significant if the frequency of each tag is compared to the frequency of the same tag in the neighborhood cells. In Table 1 we report some of the most significant tags found in this experiment. It is interesting to list here at least some of these tags.

We can find almost all the specializations of the highway tag, with values like secondary, pedestrian, cycleway and footway. Many other typical tags of a touristic city exist, like historic:monument, leisure:garden, amenity:fountain, amenity:restaurant. Other tags are typical of all the big cities that offer a variety of services like amenity:parking, amenity:atm, amenity:school, amenity:car_sharing, amenity:hospitals, railway:station, shop:supermarket.

As a single example case from this experiment we discuss in detail the tag highway:cicleway. The curve of Figure 5 shows the distribution of frequencies of this tag in the neighborhood areas placed in the square ring around the center of Torino's map. Notice that the curve follows the power law: there is a large number of maps that have a low number of occurrences of this tag and there is a low number of maps that have a large number of occurrences of this tag. Notice, in particular, that the rightmost outlier at frequency 62 represents just the center of Torino's map. It is clear that the frequency of this tag in this particular central map is surprising if we expect to observe the same frequency of the neighboring areas.

In Figure 6 we show with the grey curve the normal distribution of the tag highway:cicleway as observed in the neighborhood areas. The normal distribution has been obtained by the pair of the parameters mean frequency and standard deviation obtained from all the observations of the sample. The point placed at frequency 40 corresponds to the critical point at $3\sigma$ over the mean frequency; after this critical point any frequency is an outlier and corresponds to statistically significant features (with a significance level of at least 99%). The black point at frequency 62 represents the frequency of highway:cicleway observed in the central cell. This tag is a significant feature that contributes to distinguish the center of Torino's map from the neighborhood.

*Table 1. Some of the most significant tags found in Experiment 1*

| Tag name | Frequency in central map | Frequency mean in surrounding maps | Standard deviation in surrounding maps |
|---|---|---|---|
| highway:secondary | 158 | 16,93877551 | 26,15451536 |
| highway:pedestrian | 101 | 3,367346939 | 14,81931999 |
| highway:footway | 76 | 3,816326531 | 12,26898778 |
| highway:cycleway | 63 | 3,387755102 | 11,21348951 |
| leisure:garden | 54 | 1,285714286 | 7,721722606 |
| amenity:parking | 47 | 5,183673469 | 11,65953378 |
| railway:tram | 41 | 1,244897959 | 6,074299041 |
| amenity:restaurant | 26 | 0,918367347 | 3,812461665 |
| amenity:school | 21 | 0,816326531 | 3,066441133 |
| railway:station | 20 | 2 | 4,072263908 |
| amenity:pharmacy | 19 | 0,959183673 | 2,828126468 |
| amenity:fountain | 16 | 0,326530612 | 2,285714286 |
| shop:supermarket | 14 | 0,775510204 | 2,123924298 |
| historic:monument | 13 | 0,326530612 | 1,875141718 |
| leisure:playground | 11 | 0,448979592 | 1,744768663 |
| natural:water | 10 | 1,183673469 | 2,048103486 |
| shop:bicycle | 9 | 0,326530612 | 1,328968195 |
| amenity:atm | 9 | 0,244897959 | 1,299528957 |
| amenity:university | 9 | 0,224489796 | 1,311254268 |
| amenity:car_sharing | 9 | 0,183673469 | 1,285714286 |
| amenity:hospital | 9 | 0,346938776 | 1,331525134 |
| amenity:library | 7 | 0,163265306 | 1,007201957 |
| railway:construction | 7 | 0,142857143 | 1 |
| .... | .... | .... | .... |

*Figure 5. The distribution of frequency of the tag highway:cicleway in the central map of Torino and its surrounding areas*

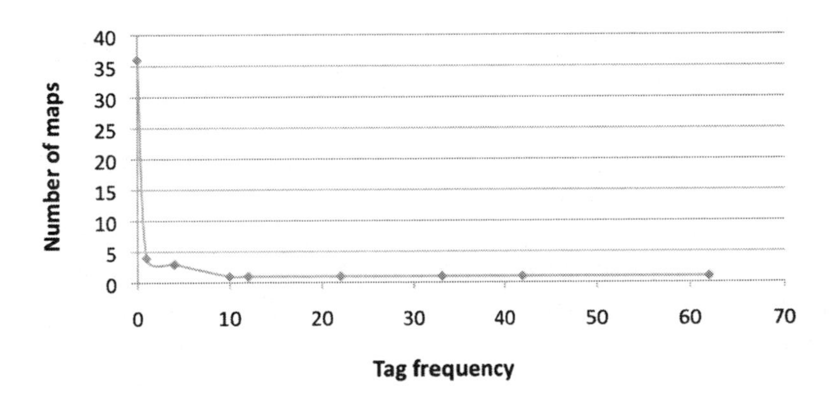

*Figure 6. Application of the statistical hypothesis test on the tag frequency*

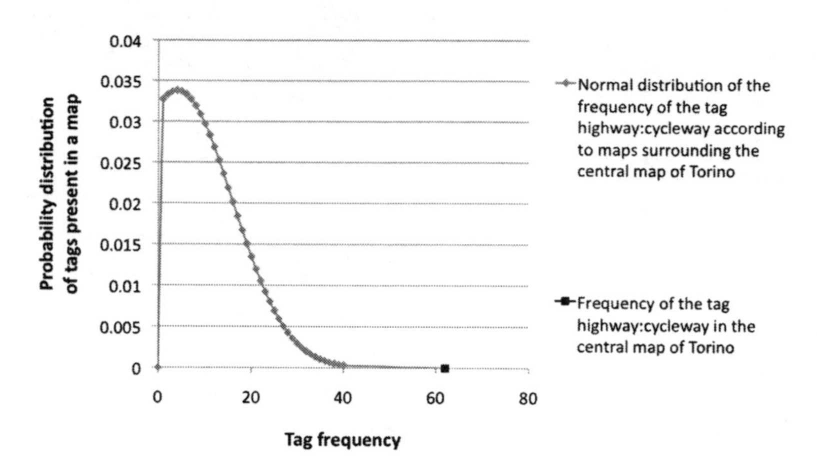


## Experiment 2 on Districts in Torino City

The map that we took on a very central, elegant and touristic district of Torino was narrower than the map in the Experiment 1 and was large only 1.7 km$^2$. We found a total of 28 distinct tags occurring at least twice. Of these tags, only 10 (corresponding to 35% of the total) resulted statistically significant if the frequency of each tag is compared to the frequency of the same tag in the neighboring districts of the city. Some of them are: amenity:fountain, amenity:parking, amenity:theatre, amenity:place_of_worship, historic:monument, tourism:museum, railway:tram, highway:pedestrian, amenity:bicycle_rental, amenity:restaurant. They confirm that these are the typical characteristics of the touristic center of the city. Notice that the other significant tags related to services that we found in the experiment 1 on the whole city are not present anymore in this touristic part. (Examples are amenity:atm, amenity:university, amenity:school, amenity:library, amenity:car_sharing, amenity:hospitals, amenity:pharmacy, railway:station, railway:construction, shop:supermarket, shop:bicycle). In fact, the majority of the annotations on services is common also to the other districts of the city and therefore they do not discriminate between this area and the neighboring ones.

## Experiment 3 on Everest

The map that we took on the area on the Everest, was large 2,227 km$^2$. We found a total of 14 tags occurring at least twice. As expected, the total number of tags was much lower than in a metropolitan area. This is due to the fact that, even though the area surface was much larger, the area itself offered few services and activities, is less populated and therefore few persons insert annotations. Of these tags 6 resulted statistically significant at the significance level of 99% with respect to the neighborhood. Some of these tags are typical of those natural landings, like: natural:water, natural:peak, natural:glacier, tourism:camp_site, highway:path and waterway:stream. Instead, the other tags that did not result significant with respect to the neighborhood are waterway:river and others that were related to human activity such as tourism:alpine_hut, place:village and tourism:guest_house.

## Experiment 4 on Random Maps

In this experiment, we checked the features in maps extracted at random from the earth's surface (for simplicity we restricted ourselves to the European area). We selected at random a sample of 30 maps but we took care that their extension was as large as Torino's city as in the experiment 1 (the area was large 63 $km^2$). As already said the aim of this experiment was to check the robustness of the method and validate its propensity to recognize features even in random maps. The obtained results confirmed our expectations: in maps located randomly it is difficult to find significant features. Generally, the features do not represent distinctive features that distinguish the area from the nearby ones.

## Conclusive Comparisons

In Figure 7 we report the distribution of the percentages of significant features found in three different types of map: the random maps, the Torino's city map and the Everest map. The curve in light grey of Figure 7 represents the percentages of significant features in the random maps. It is evident that the mean of these percentages is very low (close to 10%). With respect to this distribution, both Torino's map and Everest's map are outliers (shown by the black square and dark grey triangle). Both Torino's and Everest's maps have been selected ad-purpose by the humans in a way that they include a meaningful area for the human reasoning. Thus it is more probable that these maps contain distinctive features. On the opposite, even maps of the same extension of Torino's city, but with vertices extracted casually, did not include any significant piece of information. And indeed, the filter recognized this.

## Relationship Between Tag Frequency and Statistical Significance

We noticed, with a certain interest, the following phenomenon that could be of interest also to other researchers in the field of itemsets mining. There was an evident correlation between the frequency of the tags and their statistical significance. In Figure 8 we report the relationship observed in the results of experiment 1 on Torino's map. The shown relationship is between the minimum frequency threshold of the tags in a map (*Minsup*) and two quantities:

1. the total number of tags found in the map with a frequency higher than *Minsup*
2. the percentage of statistical significant tags in the map.

We recall that *Minsup* is a minimum threshold on frequency of observed elements that works as a filter and helps the data mining algorithms to reduce the volume of elements to be considered. We can observe that, as *Minsup* increases, the

*Figure 7. Application of the statistical hypothesis test on the percentage of significant features in maps*

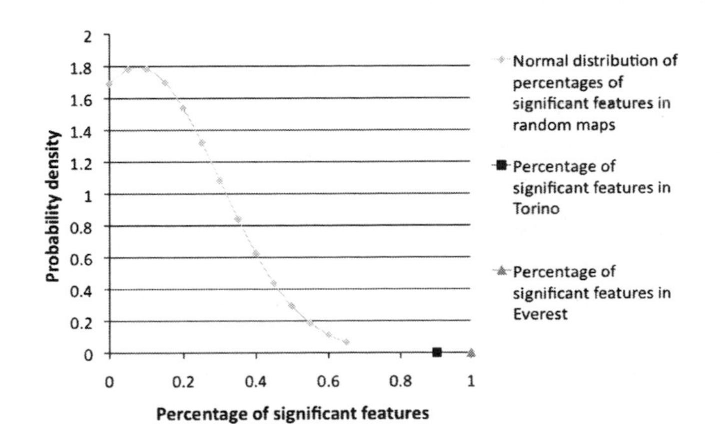

*Figure 8. Number of tags and percentage of significant tags in relationship with Minsup frequency threshold in experiment 1*

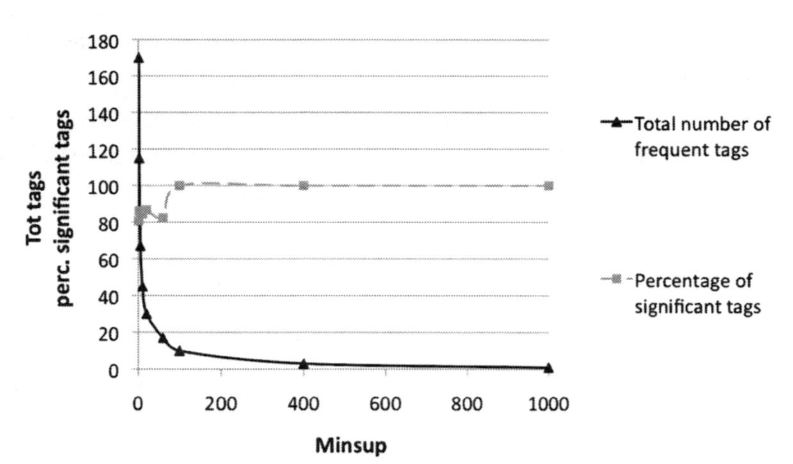


number of tags whose frequency is higher than the threshold decreases. This is a typical phenomenon that occurs also in the field of itemsets mining. In the specific field of spatial data mining, despite the total number of selected tags reduces, the percentage of the tags that are statistically significant tends to increase. As Figure 8 shows the statistical significance occurs more in highly frequent tags than in less frequent ones. This is because the statistically significant tags are just the tags that result more frequent in the map of interest than in the neighboring maps. Thus the imposition of a frequency threshold works as a sort of filter for statistical significant elements. This result could be considered as a meaningful observation that supports and justifies the adoption of a minimum frequency in feature selection and frequent itemsets mining in the spatial context.

However, the high frequency cannot be considered neither a sufficient nor a necessary condition for a tag to be considered as significant. First of all, it should be clear that statistical significant tags could be present even at lower frequencies. This is the case of the 80-90 tags that occur once or twice in Torino's map and nevertheless these few occurrences constitute a statistical significant observation. Secondarily, even high frequent tags might not result statistically significant. In this respect, consider Figure 9 that shows the relationship between Minsup and the percentage of significant tags in experiment 2 on sub-areas in Torino's map. These sub-areas are all metropolitan areas that share many common characteristics. They are less different from their neighborhood than Torino is different from its neighborhood – the suburbs. In fact, we can notice that the range of percentages of significant tags (50%-65%) has values much lower than in experiment 1 (80%-100%). This means that even at the highest frequencies some tags still result non-significant because they are the tags that are common to all the sub-areas. A similar observation occurs also for the remaining experiments on the Everest area and in random maps.

We conclude that a high frequency does not guarantee that the tag is statistically significant with respect to the neighborhood. To confirm this fact a statistical test cannot be avoided and should be conducted in any case.

## Integration of the Proposed Statistical Tag Filter into a Spatial Knowledge Discovery Process

We consider the proposed statistical test on spatial features as a filter in support of the feature selec-

*Figure 9. Number of tags and percentage of significant tags in relationship with Minsup in Experiment 2*

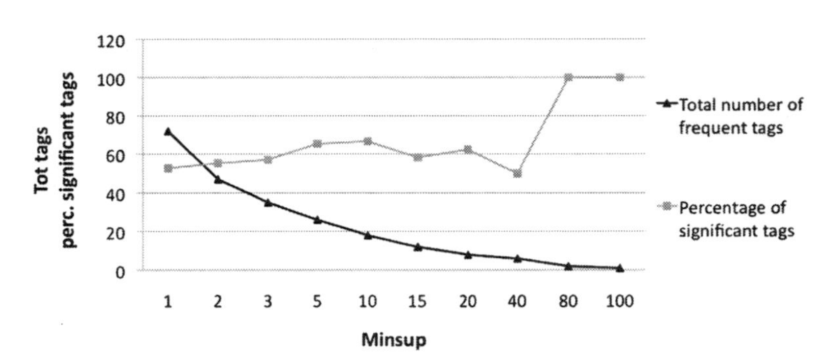


tion task in a spatial context. It could be adopted as a pre-processing task in the KDD process on spatial data because it allows identifying the typical features of a certain geographical area, given the property of spatial auto-correlation of the features. The qualitative evaluation on the tags found in the experiments and shown in Table 1 confirms that these tags are really typical of the studied area.

Moreover, we ask ourselves if the knowledge of the relationship between tag frequency and statistical significance can help in facilitating the frequent itemset mining. In particular, if it could give a computational advantage to the data mining algorithms and help in the early elimination of certain elements. An answer consists in the identification of the best trade-off between a value of *Minsup* that allows the elimination of a sufficiently high number of spatial features but still retains a sufficiently high percentage of statistically significant features. The evaluation of the desired value of *Minsup* could be done on a preliminary sample, composed of random maps in a region of interest where the spatial features of each random map are evaluated. All the possible values of *Minsup* are considered and a graph like the one in Figure 9 is generated. The value of the trade-off parameter could be chosen as a function of the two evaluation measures, *Minsup* and the percentage of statistically significant features (here called *SigPerc*):

$$MinSupf \times SigPerc > MinFeatN$$

*MinSupf* is a function that returns the number of features whose frequency is higher than *Minsup*; it can be extrapolated or fitted on the curve that relates *Minsup* and the number of extracted features and can be drawn on the sample. *MinFeatN* is the minimum number of features that the user wants to allow. Its value could be driven by the capabilities of the storage system or by the necessity to obtain a clear visualization of the features on the map.

As a final observation on the work we performed in the context of OSM data, we conclude that it is rare to find a number of tags associated to the same spatial element, at least in the geographical regions in which we performed experiments. This would make impossible to perform a frequent itemset mining task based on the users' annotations to the single spatial objects but more sophisticated approaches of grouping of nearby spatial objects need to be performed like in (Koperski & Han, 1995), (Munro, Chawla, & Sun, 2003) with the aim to discover the spatial co-located patterns.

## FUTURE RESEARCH DIRECTIONS

The future research directions of the work consist in the integration of the annotations coming from a multiplicity of information sources, social networks and Web 2.0 applications. Notice that not all of these systems provide the same, well-structured ontology of annotation tags like it occurs in OpenStreetMap. The most promising techniques for data integration can exploit one of the following possibilities:

1. Adopting the tag ontology provided by a unique system (e.g., OpenStreetMap) as a referential knowledge base and then try to learn the correspondences between tags in the different systems. The problem of finding the best match between the keywords provided by different systems can be thought of as a predictive task.
2. Maintain the multiplicity of tags of the original systems, provided that these ones refer to the same spatial object, identified on the basis of the spatial coordinates.

As a conclusion, spatial objects would be annotated, according to a unique tagging system.

A second research direction is to exploit the semantic web. According to the semantic web research field, objects can be described and queried according to their semantics and the relationships between them and other objects. Thus tags are only one of the elements that form the complex and structured knowledge description. The integration of the information sources could be made according to their proximity in the semantic knowledge network.

## CONCLUSION

Web 2.0 applications provide opportunities to update the available information. In particular, in this chapter we showed how it is possible to extract relevant information on a geographical area from the annotations that users provide on locations by means of OpenStreetMap. OpenStreetMap and the majority of Web 2.0 applications represent information in the XML format with the use of tags. We analyzed and used the tags in the XML files with the purpose to enrich of new content the cartographic maps.

In this chapter we showed that it is possible to provide a characterization of the content of a certain geographical area by means of a set of features that are selected by statistical tests as significant in contrast to the surrounding areas. We presented some results in an experimental section on a specific geographical area and in random areas, as well. The conclusion is that the content characterization of a geographical map corresponds to the actual, more frequent features of the geographical area. The features turn out to be statistically significant and provide a usefully concise descriptive summary. Furthermore, the application of this statistical technique could be used to improve the annotation process as a sort of cleaning. It might help to eliminate the noisy tags provided by users by mistake or being not enough relevant.

## REFERENCES

W3C. (1995). Overviwe of SGML resources. Retrieved October 5, 2010, from http://www.w3.org/MarkUp/SGML/

W3C. (n.d.). *Website of the World Wide Web Consortium*. Retrieved October 5, 2010, from www.w3c.org

W3C Recommendation. (1998). *XML 1.0*. Retrieved October 5, 2010, from http://www.w3.org/TR/1998/REC-xml-19980210

W3C XML. (n.d.). *XML standards*. Retrieved 10 05, 2010, from W3C: http://www.w3.org/standards/xml/

Adam, N. R., Janeja, V. P., & Atluri, V. (2004). Neighborhood based detection of anomalies in high dimensional spatio-temporal sensor datasets. In H. Haddad, A. Omicini, R. L. Wainwright, & L. M. Liebrock (Eds.), *Proceedings of the 2004 ACM Symposium on Applied Computing (SAC)*, (pp. 576–583). ACM.

Agrawal, R., & Srikant, R. (1994). Fast algorithms for mining association rules in large databases. In J. B. Bocca, M. Jarke, & C. Zaniolo (Eds.), *Proceedings of the 20th International Conference on Very Large Data Bases (VLDB)*, (pp. 487-499). Morgan Kaufmann.

Budhathoki, N. R., Bruce, B., & Nedovic-Budic, Z. (2008). Reconceptualizing the role of the user of spatial data infrastructure. *GeoJournal*, *72*(3-4), 149–160. doi:10.1007/s10708-008-9189-x

Cheng, T., & Li, Z. (2004). A hybrid approach to detect spatial-temporal outliers. In *Proceedings of the 12th International Conference on Geoinformatics Geospatial Information Research*, (pp. 173-178).

Devore, J. L. (2008). *Probability and statistics for engineering and the sciences*. Brooks/Cole.

Ester, M., Frommelt, A., Kriegel, H.-P., & Sander, J. (1998). Algorithms for characterization and trend detection in spatial databases. In R. Agrawal, P. E. Stolorz, & G. Piatetsky-Shapiro (Eds.), *Proceedings of the 4th International Conference of Knowledge Discovery and Data Mining (KDD)*, (pp.44-50).

Flanagin, A. J., & Metzger, M. J. (2008). The credibility of volunteered geographic information. *GeoJournal*, *72*(3-4), 137–148. doi:10.1007/s10708-008-9188-y

Flickr. (n.d.). *Website*. Retrieved October 5, 2010, from http://www.flickr.com/

Formica, A. (2008). Similarity of XML-schema elements: A structural and information content approach. *The Computer Journal*, *51*(2), 240–254. doi:10.1093/comjnl/bxm051

Geonames. (n.d.). *Website*. Retrieved October 5, 2010, from http://www.geonames.org/

Goodchild, M. (2007). Citizens as sensors: The world of volunteered geography. *GeoJournal*, *69*(4), 211–221. doi:10.1007/s10708-007-9111-y

Google, K. M. L. (n.d.). *KML tutorial*. Retrieved October 5, 2010, from http://code.google.com/intl/it-IT/apis/kml/documentation/kml_tut.html

Google Earth. (n.d.). *Website*. Retrieved October 5, 2010, from http://earth.google.com/intl/it/

Google Maps. (n.d.). *Website*. Retrieved October 5, 2010, from http://maps.google.it/

Google Mobile. (n.d.). *Website*. Retrieved October 5, 2010, from http://www.google.it/mobile/gmm/

Haklay, M. (2010). How good is volunteered geographical information? A comparative study of OpenStreetMap and ordnance survey datasets. *Environment and Planning. B, Planning & Design*, *37*(4), 682–703. doi:10.1068/b35097

Haklay, M., & Weber, P. (2008). Openstreetmap: User-generated street maps. *IEEE Pervasive Computing / IEEE Computer Society [and] IEEE Communications Society*, *7*(4), 12–18. doi:10.1109/MPRV.2008.80

Han, J. G., Ryu, K. H., Chi, K. H., & Yeon, Y. K. (2003). Statistics-based predictive geo-spatial data mining: Forest fire hazardous area mapping application. In X. Zhou, Y. Zhang, & M. E. Orlowska (Eds.), *Proceedings of the 5th Asia-Pacific Web Conference on Web Technologies and Applications (APWeb)*, (pp. 370–381).

Haslett, J., Brandley, R., Craig, P., Unwin, A., & Wills, G. (1991). Dynamic graphics for exploring spatial data with application to locating global and local anomalies. *The American Statistician, 45*(3), 234-242. Jhung, Y., & Swain, P. H. (1996). Bayesian contextual classification based on modified m-estimates and Markov random fields. *IEEE Transactions on Geoscience and Remote Sensing, 34*(1), 67–75.

Journel, A. G. (1986). Mining geostatistics. *Mathematical Geology*, 119–140. doi:10.1007/BF00897658

Kamber, M., Han, J., & Tung, A. K. (2001). Spatial clustering methods in data mining: A survey. In Miller, H., & Han, J. (Eds.), *Geographic data mining and knowledge discovery* (pp. 201–231). Taylor and Francis.

Koperski, K., Adhikary, J., & Han, J. (1996). Spatial data mining: Progress and challenges. In *Workshop on Research Issues on data Mining and Knowledge Discovery (DMKD),* (pp. 1-10).

Koperski, K., & Han, J. (1995). Discovery of spatial association rules in geographic information databases. In M. J. Egenhofer, & J. R. Herring (Eds.), *Proceedings of the 4th International Symposium Advances in Spatial Databases (SSD) Lecture Notes in Computer Science: Vol. 951.* (pp. 47-66). Springer.

Lu, C., Shekhar, S., & Zhang, P. (2003). A unified approach to detecting spatial outliers. *GeoInformatica, 7*(2), 139–166. doi:10.1023/A:1023455925009

Luc, A. (1995). Local indicators of spatial association: Lisa. *Geographical Analysis, 27*(2), 93–115.

Munro, R., Chawla, S., & Sun, P. (2003). Complex spatial relationships. In *Proceedings of the Third IEEE International Conference on Data Mining (ICDM)*, (pp. 19-22).

Nayak, R. (2009). The process and application of XML data mining. In Song, M., & Wu, Y. B. (Eds.), *Handbook of research on text and web mining technologies* (pp. 249–272). Hershey, PA: IGI Global.

Nayak, R., Witt, R., & Tonev, A. (2002). Data mining and XML documents. In *International Conference on Internet Computing*, (pp. 660-666).

Nothegger, C., Winter, S., & Raubal, M. (2004). Computation of the salience of features. *Spatial Cognition and Computation, 4*, 113–136. doi:10.1207/s15427633scc0402_1

O'Reilly, T. (2005). *What is Web 2.0: Design patterns and business models for the next generation of software.* Retrieved October 5, 2010, from http://www.oreillynet.com/lpt/a/6228

OGC. (n.d.). *Open Geospatial Consortium.* Retrieved October 5, 2010, from http://www.opengeospatial.org/

OGC. (n.d.). *GML*. Retrieved October 5, 2010, from http://www.opengeospatial.org/standards/gml

OGC. (n.d.). *KML*. Retrieved October 5, 2010, from http://www.opengeospatial.org/standards/kml

OpenStreetMap. (n.d.). *The free wiki world map*. Retrieved October 5, 2010, http://www.openstreetmap.org/

OpenStreetMap. (n.d.). *Wiki: Element*. Retrieved October 5, 2010, from http://wiki.openstreetmap.org/wiki/Elements.

OpenStreetMap. (n.d.). *Wiki: Export*. Retrieved October 5, 2010, from http://wiki.openstreetmap.org/wiki/Export.

Shekhar, S., & Chawla, S. (2003). Introduction to Spatial Data Mining. In *Spatial Databases: A Tour* (pp. 21–44). Prentice Hall.

Shekhar, S., & Huang, Y. (2001). Discovering spatial co-location patterns: A summary of results. In C. S. Jensen, M. Schneider, B. Seeger, & V. J. Tsotras (Eds.), *Proceedings of the 7th International Symposium on Advances in Spatial and Temporal Databases (SSTD) Lecture Notes in Computer Science: Vol. 2121* (pp. 236-256). Springer.

Shekhar, S., Zhang, P., Huang, Y., & Vatsavai, R. (2004). Trends in spatial data mining. In Kargupta, H., Joshi, A., Sivakumar, K., & Yesha, Y. (Eds.), *Data mining: Next generation challenges and future directions*. AAAI/MIT Press.

Tagarelli, A., & Greco, S. (2010). Semantic clustering of XML documents. *ACM Transactions on Information Systems*, *28*(1), 1–56. doi:10.1145/1658377.1658380

Tezuka, T., & Tanaka, K. (2005). Landmark extraction: A Web mining approach. In Gohn, A. G., & Mark, D. M. (Eds.), *Spatial Information Theory* (*Vol. 3693*, pp. 379–396). Lecture Notes in Computer Science. doi:10.1007/11556114_24

Tobler, W. R. (1970). A computer movie simulating urban growth in the Detroit region. *Economic Geography*, *46*(2), 234–240. doi:10.2307/143141

Tomko, M., & Pulves, R. S. (2009). Venice, city of canals: Characterizing regions through content classification. *Transactions in GIS*, *13*(3), 295–314. doi:10.1111/j.1467-9671.2009.01165.x

Vatsavai, R. R., Wu, W., Shekhar, S., Schrater, P. R., & Chawla, S. (2002). Spatial contextual classification and prediction models for mining geospatial data. *IEEE Transactions on Multimedia*, *4*(2), 174–188. doi:10.1109/TMM.2002.1017732

*Wikipedia*. Retrieved October 5, 2010, from www.wikipedia.org/

## ADDITIONAL READING

Candillier, L., Tellier, I., & Torre, F. (2005). Transforming XML Trees for Efficient Classification and Clustering. In N. Fuhr, M. Lalmas, S. Malik, and G. Kazai (Eds.), *Proceedings of the Workshop of the Initiative for the Evaluation of XML Retrieval (INEX): Vol. 3977. Lecture Notes in Computer Science* (pp. 469-480). Springer.

Chi, Y., Nijssen S., Munts, R., Nijssen, S., & Kok, J. N. (2005). Frequent Subtree Mining – An Overview. *Fundamenta Informaticae - Advances in Mining Graphs, Trees and Sequences*, 66(1-2).

Dalamagas, T., Cheng, T., Winkel, K., & Sellis, T. (2004). Clustering XML Documents Using Structural Summaries. In W. Lindner, M. Mesiti, C. Türker, Y. Tzitzikas, and A. Vakali (Eds.), *Workshops on Current Trends in Database Technology (EDBT): Vol. 3268. Lecture Notes in Computer Science* (pp. 547-556). Springer.

Dalamagas, T., Cheng, T., Winkel, K. J., & Sellis, T. (2006). A Methodology for Clustering XML Documents by Structure. *Information Systems*, *31*(3), 187–228. doi:10.1016/j.is.2004.11.009

Flesca, S., Manco, G., Masciari, E., Pontieri, L., & Pugliese, A. (2005). Fast Detection of XML Structural Similarity. *IEEE Transactions on Knowledge and Data Engineering*, *17*(2), 160–175. doi:10.1109/TKDE.2005.27

Khaing, M. M., & Them, N. (2006). An Efficient Association Rule Mining for XML Data. In *SICE-ICASE, 2006. International Joint Conference*, (pp. 5782-5786).

Lian, W., Cheung, D. W., Mamoulis, N., & Yiu, S. (2004). An Efficient and Scalable Algorithm for Clustering XML Documents by Structure. *IEEE Transactions on Knowledge and Data Engineering*, *16*(1), 82–96. doi:10.1109/TKDE.2004.1264824

Mazuran, M., Quintarelli, E., & Tanca, L. (2009). Mining Tree-based Frequent Patterns From XML. In *Proceedings of the 8th International Conference on Flexible Query Answering Systems (FQAS): Vol. 5822. Lecture Notes in Computer Science* (pp. 287-299). Springer.

Nierman, A., & Jagadish, H. V. (2002). Evaluating Structural Similarity in XML Documents. In M. F. Fernandez, and Y. Papakonstantinou (Eds.), *Proceedings of the 5th International Workshop on the Web and Databases (WebDB),* (pp. 61-66).

Paik, J., Nam, J., Kim, W. Y., Ryu, J. S., & Kim, U. M. (2009). Mining Association Rules in Tree Structured XML Data. In S. Sohn, L. Chen, S. Hwang, K. Cho, S. Kawata, K. Um, F. I. S. Ko, K.-D. Kwack, J. H. Lee, G. Kou, K. Nakamura, A. C. M. Fong, and P. C. M. Ma (Eds.), *Proceedings of the 2nd International Conference on Interaction Sciences: Information Technology, Culture and Human (ICIS)*, (pp. 807-811). ACM.

Termier, A., Rousset, M., & Sebag, M. (2002). TreeFinder: A First Step towards XML Data Mining. In *Proceedings of the 2002 IEEE International Conference on Data Mining (ICDM)*, (pp. 450-457). IEEE Computer Society.

Tran, T., Kutti, S., & Nayak, R. (2009). Utilizing the Structure and Content Information for XML Document Clustering. In *Advances in Focused Retrieval* (*Vol. 5631*, pp. 460–468). Lecture Notes in Computer Science. doi:10.1007/978-3-642-03761-0_48

Worboys, M. F., & Duckham, M. (2004). *GIS: A Computing Perspective* (2nd ed.). CRC Press.

Zielstra, D., & Zipf, A. (2010). A Comparative Study of Proprietary Geodata and Volunteered Geographic Information for Germany. In 13th AGILE International Conference on Geographic Information Science.

# Chapter 18
# Organizing XML Documents on a Peer-to-Peer Network by Collaborative Clustering

**Francesco Gullo**
*University of Calabria, Italy*

**Giovanni Ponti**
*ENEA, Italy*

**Sergio Greco**
*University of Calabria, Italy*

## ABSTRACT

*XML and peer–to–peer (P2P) technologies are nowadays increasingly being combined in many application scenarios. Indeed, while XML is the standard for representing and exchanging data, P2P networks offer innovative opportunities to users to share and locate distributed data over the Internet. This synergistic coupling of XML and P2P networks becomes particularly appealing in mining contexts, such as document clustering. Clustering XML documents is extensively used to discover meaningful groups in large collections of XML documents according to structure and/or content information. However, despite the growing availability of distributed XML sources and the variety of high-demand environments, existing methods for clustering XML documents work only in a centralized way.*

*In this chapter we address the problem of clustering XML documents in a collaborative distributed environment. We developed a clustering framework for XML sources distributed on a P2P network. XML documents are modeled based on a transactional representation which uses both XML structure and content information. The clustering method employs a centroid-based partitional scheme suitably adapted to work on a P2P network. Each peer is enabled to compute a clustering solution over its local repository and to exchange the resulting cluster representatives with the other peers. The exchanged cluster representatives are hence used to compute the global clustering solution in a collaborative way.*

DOI: 10.4018/978-1-61350-356-0.ch018

*Effectiveness and efficiency of the framework were evaluated on real XML document collections varying the number of peers. Experimental results have shown significant improvements of our collaborative distributed algorithm with respect to the centralized clustering setting in terms of execution time, achieving clustering solutions that still remain accurate with a moderately low number of nodes in the network.*

## INTRODUCTION

The extensibility of its markup functionalities along with its natural capability of representing complex real-world objects and their relationships are the keys of success of XML in enabling the development of domain-specific markup languages. This has had a strong impact on the role of XML in the Internet, where XML languages have been developed for a large variety of domain applications, ranging from multimedia and networking to Web content syndication and rendering, from scientific data representation and literature to business processes.

In recent years, the use of XML for data representation and exchange has become central in *high-demand environments*. On the one hand, the growing availability of large XML document repositories has raised the need for fast and accurate organization of such data. In this respect, research on *XML document clustering* has produced a variety of approaches and methods, with different focuses on aspects such as the structure and/or content type of XML features, the XML data representation and summarization model, the XML similarity measures, and the strategy of clustering that was able to such special requirements as dealing with large document collections and high dimensionality, ease for browsing, meaningfulness of cluster descriptions (Candillier, Tellier, & Torre, 2005; Denoyer & Gallinari, 2008; Doucet & Lehtonen, 2006; Kutty, Tran, Nayak, & Li, 2008; Lian, Cheung, Mamoulis, & Yiu, 2004; Nayak & Xu, 2006; Tran, Nayak, Bruza, 2008; Tagarelli & Greco, 2010).

On the other hand, the inherently distributed nature of XML repositories is also calling for adequate distribute processing techniques that can aid the efficient management and mining of XML data. As an example, think of some Web news services that are in charge of very frequently gathering up-to-date information spanning over thousands of news sources: if such services aim to highlight (new) hot topics through the news channels or provide the users with a (personalized) view on the news headlines, they might be required to apply clustering algorithms to the news articles with a frequency of few minutes.

Clustering XML documents in such high-demand environments is hence challenging as the algorithms developed are to be able to face tight requirements on both processing power and space resources. Existing methods for clustering XML documents are instead designed as centralized systems, which is mainly due to the difficulty of decentralizing most clustering strategies and, additionally, to a number of issues arising in the development of a convenient yet effective summarization of both XML structure and content information in XML documents.

XML distributed applications are increasingly being demanded in several domains, such as software and multimedia sharing, product rating, personal profiling, and many others. A great merit of such an extensive use of XML in distributed applications is due to the popularity of *peer–to–peer* (P2P) networks. A P2P network is a distributed system with the following main properties (Rodrigues & Druschel, 2010). It has a high degree of decentralization, since processing power, bandwidth and space resources are contributed by the peers, which implement both client and server functionalities of the system. In general, there can be a high heterogeneity of resources, in terms of hardware and software architecture, power supply, geographic location.

A P2P is mostly self-organizing, since any newly introduced peer node requires little or no manual configuration for the system maintenance. Multiple administrative domains usually characterize the system as the peers are not owned or controlled by a single organization. The deployment costs of a P2P system are typically lower than client-server systems, thanks to its independence of dedicated infrastructure, while the upgrade of the system components is made easier. Because there are few if any peers with centralized state, the P2P system is also more resilient to faults and attacks.

XML is being coupled with P2P networks (Koloniari & Pitoura, 2005; Abiteboul, Manolescu, & Taropa, 2006; Rao & Moon, 2009; Antonellis, Makris, & Tsirakis, 2009), thanks to the merits of P2P in enabling innovative services. Hence, devising a distributed approach to XML clustering based on a P2P system arises as a new challenge in efficient XML data management and mining. Ideally, a distributed approach to efficiently clustering XML documents might satisfy at least the following special requirements:

- **High level of resource distribution:** the decentralization should involve both the data objects and the other data needed to perform clustering.
- **Collaborativeness:** this should be a major advantageous aspect resulting from the establishment of the clustering approach on a P2P network, in order to develop a distributed system that is reliable, resource sharing-aware, and able to effectively and efficiently exchange the processed information.
- **Limited network load:** a summarized data structure should be devised to suitably represent structure and content information in XML data, and to ensure an efficient exchange of information.
- **Ease of implementation:** because each peer in the network is easy to maintain, the clustering strategy adopted by the network nodes and the processing information exchanged between the nodes needs to be feasible on a large-scale system.

This chapter addresses the problem of clustering XML documents on a distributed, peer-to-peer network. A framework recently proposed in (Greco, Gullo, Ponti, & Tagarelli, 2009) is presented. Such a framework exploits the approach in (Tagarelli & Greco, 2010; Tagarelli & Greco, 2006) for modeling and clustering XML documents. That approach allows for transforming XML documents into *transactional data* based on the notion of *tree tuple*, which aims to model any XML document according to a flat, relational-like representation. XML tree tuples are well-suited for clustering XML documents according to both structure and content information.

The distributed environment underlying the framework assumes that only a portion of the input collection of XML documents to be clustered can be accessed by each node in the network. The clustering task is performed according to a collaborative model, where each node communicates with all the other ones. In particular, according to the well-known paradigm of *centroid-based partitional clustering* (Jain & Dubes, 1988), the information exchanged among the nodes has the form of *cluster centroids*. Summarizing the clustered data based on cluster centroids is highly desirable, especially in scenarios where the input data is spread across a network. Indeed, cluster centroids provide an accurate as well as compact representation of the information to be exchanged among the various nodes in the network. In this way, the exchanged data is highly representative and, at the same time, the network load is maintained relatively small.

The collaborative clustering approach in the distributed framework essentially acts as follows. Each node in the network is responsible for computing a local clustering solution (a partition of its own set of XML data), whose clusters are summarized by "local" centroids that are sent to the other nodes in the network. The nodes are also responsible of computing a subset of the "global" centroids by taking into account the information stored in the corresponding "local" centroids received from the other nodes. The global centroids are eventually sent back to all the nodes to be used for updating the local clustering solution. The process ends when no global centroid changes with respect to the previous iteration.

Experiments were conducted on large, real-world collections of XML documents, whose features are particularly suitable for assessing the validity of distributed collaborative clustering of XML documents. The experiments were performed by varying the number of nodes in the network while keeping the communication among nodes minimized. Results have shown that, although accuracy is typically lower than in the centralized case, a relatively small number of nodes is sufficient for drastically improving the efficiency of the clustering task.

This chapter is organized as follows. Section "Background" briefly discusses related work. Section "XML Transactional Representation" introduces the transaction model used for representing structure and content information from XML documents. Section "Collaborative Clustering of XML Documents" describes the XML transactional similarity measure and the collaborative clustering algorithm. Section "Experimental Evaluation" reports experimental results achieved by our approach from both effectiveness and efficiency viewpoint. Section "Conclusion and Future Research" contains concluding remarks and our pointers for future research directions.

## BACKGROUND

In the past few years, there has been a great interest in XML data management in distributed environments. In this respect, early research studies focused on efficient distributed query processing and optimization. (Abiteboul, Manolescu, & Taropa, 2006) describes an extension of the Active XML (AXML) language used to embed service call specification in XML documents, by which XML applications can easily be specified and deployed in complex distributed systems. Antonellis, Makris, and Tsirakis (2009) propose a distributed clustering-based approach to efficiently locate XML documents over a P2P network for the purpose of improving time performance of querying systems. This problem is also studied in (Rao & Moon, 2009), where XML documents and XML query patterns are mapped into algebraic signatures, and distributed hash tables are used to index the document signatures.

XML allows for publishing information that can be edited and reorganized in a distributed collaborative way. (Ignat & Oster, 2008) investigates the problem of XML document reconciliation in a P2P network by proposing an environment in which users perform an off-line editing of XML documents, and their edits are committed and synchronized with the ones performed by the other users as they reconnect to the network. In order to guarantee consistency, a tombstone operational transformation based approach has been employed to merge XML structures of the edited XML document.

Data mining algorithms are traditionally designed to work with data located in a centralized system and/or memory. However, with the development of large-scale systems, there has been an increasing demand for data mining methods that can work in parallel and distributed environments. This is challenging for two main reasons: data mining algorithms usually require large resources in terms of storage systems, and it is highly inefficient to transfer the huge amount of data stored in several (distributed) databases and analyze them in a single centralized site. Early proposals on distributed data mining exploited agent-based architectures. Kargupta, Hamzaoglu, and Stafford (1997) design a distributed system in which each agent is able to model its local world and the global solution is cooperatively obtained by exploiting agent communication exchange. Dhillon and Modha (2000) define a parallel implementation of the k-Means algorithm based on the message passing model. Cesario and Talia (2008) focus on distributed data mining as WSRF services by exploiting the Grid infrastructure. Other examples of distributed data mining can be found in (Cannataro, Congiusta, Pugliese, Talia, & Trunfio, 2004; Kargupta, Park, Hershberger, & Johnson, 1999; Prodromidis, Chan, & Stolfo, 2000).

As regards distributed document clustering in P2P networks, (Eisenhardt, Muller, & Henrich, 2003) discusses the efficiency of partitional clustering approaches like k-Means based on centroids in the task of distributed clustering of documents. Here, local clustering solutions are improved taking into account recommendations exchanged among the peers, whereas clusters are summarized as keyphrases. A very recent P2P approach to distributed document clustering is presented in (Papapetrou, Siberski, & Fuhr, 2010). Here the clustering strategy is again based on a k-Means-like scheme, whereas the main novelty lies in the cluster summary indexing and in the 2-step document-to-cluster assignment, which are probabilistically controlled. Despite the P2P scenario, this approach however ignores any notion of "collaborativeness" in the computation and/or exchange of cluster centroids/summaries, which might improve the efficiency (and parallelism) of the distributed clustering process.

To the best of our knowledge, Hammouda and Kamel are the only authors that have addressed the problem of distributed clustering of (plain) documents from a *collaborative* fashion (Hammouda & Kamel, 2006). They had the intuition that recommendations exchanged between the peers in the network may improve the accuracy of document clustering in a distributed environment. In their work, document cluster summaries in the form keyphrases are also exploited. Our proposed work also exploits a notion of collaborativeness in a distributed environment; however, besides dealing with the more complex case of semistructured (XML) documents, in our approach we devise different strategies for summarizing clusters and exchanging information between the peers. In fact, our XML cluster summaries are defined as transactions that are comprised of items containing highly representative structure and content information present in that cluster of XML documents. Moreover, XML information exchanged among peers is not supplied in the form of recommendations, but in a simpler way that exploits "meta-representatives", which guide the construction of the global clustering solution.

## XML TRANSACTIONAL REPRESENTATION

Tagarelli and Greco (2010, 2006) originally introduced an XML representation model that allows for mapping XML document trees into *transactional data*. In a generic application domain, a transaction dataset is a multi-set of variable-length sequences of objects with categorical attributes; in the XML domain, a transaction is devised as a set of items, each of which embeds a distinct combination of structure and content features from the original XML data. Within this view, XML documents are not directly transformed to transactional data, rather they are initially decomposed on the basis of the notion of *tree tuple*. Intuitively, given any XML document, a tree tuple is a tree representation of a complete set of distinct concepts that are correlated according to the structure semantics of the original document tree. Tree tuples extracted from the same tree maintain similar or identical structure while reflect different ways of associating content with structure as they can be naturally inferred from the original tree.

### XML Tree Tuple Extraction

Tree tuple resembles the notion of tuple in relational databases and has been proposed to extend functional dependencies to the XML setting

(Arenas & Libkin, 2004; Flesca, Furfaro, Greco, & Zumpano, 2003). In a relational database, a tuple is a function assigning each attribute with a value from the corresponding domain.

Given an XML tree *XT*, an *XML tree tuple* $\tau$ derived from *XT* is a maximal subtree of *XT* such that, for each (tag or complete) path *p* in *XT*, the size of the answer of *p* on $\tau$ is not greater than 1. We denote with $T_{XT}$ and *T* the set of tree tuples that can be derived from any given tree *XT* and from the collection ***XT***, respectively. Also, we use $P_\tau$ to denote the set of complete paths in a tree tuple $\tau$. Intuitively, a tree tuple is a (sub)tree representation of a set of distinct concepts that are correlated according to the structure semantics of the original tree. Tree tuples extracted from the same tree maintain identical structure while reflect different ways of associating content with structure as they can be naturally inferred from the original tree.

Consider the XML document tree shown in Figure 1, which represents two software tools. Any internal node has a unique label denoting a tag name, whereas each leaf node is labeled with either name and value of an attribute, or symbol *S* and a string corresponding to the #PCDATA content model. Path answers can be easily computed: for example, the path software.tool.name yields the set of node identifiers $\{n_8, n_{20}\}$, and the path software.tool.developer.*S* yields the set of strings {*"software's developer 1"*, *"software's developer 2"*}.

Four tree tuples can be extracted from the example tree; in Figure 2, nodes belonging to the same tree tuple are shaded the same. Two distinct tree tuple are extracted starting from the left

*Figure 1. Example XML document and its tree XML*

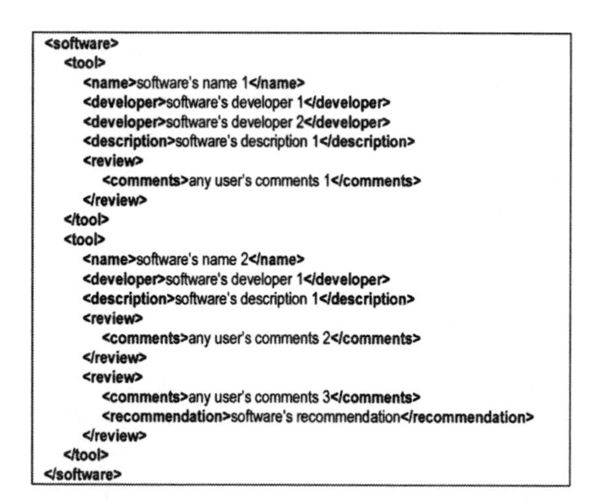

```
<software>
  <tool>
    <name>software's name 1</name>
    <developer>software's developer 1</developer>
    <developer>software's developer 2</developer>
    <description>software's description 1</description>
    <review>
      <comments>any user's comments 1</comments>
    </review>
  </tool>
  <tool>
    <name>software's name 2</name>
    <developer>software's developer 1</developer>
    <description>software's description 1</description>
    <review>
      <comments>any user's comments 2</comments>
    </review>
    <review>
      <comments>any user's comments 3</comments>
      <recommendation>software's recommendation</recommendation>
    </review>
  </tool>
</software>
```

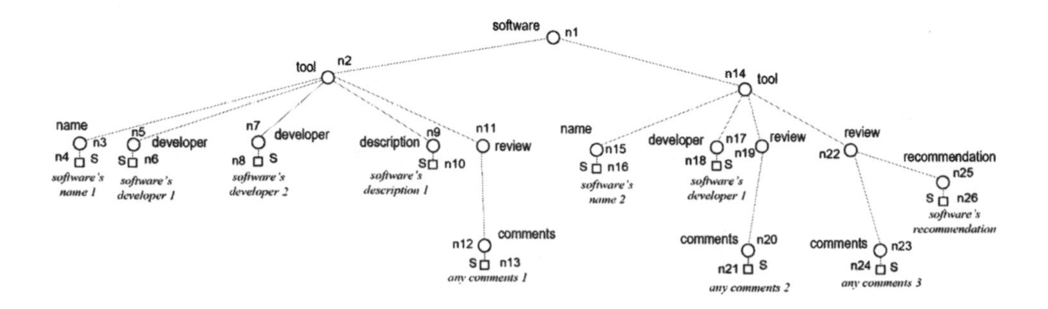

*Figure 2. The tree tuples extracted from the XML tree of Figure 1*

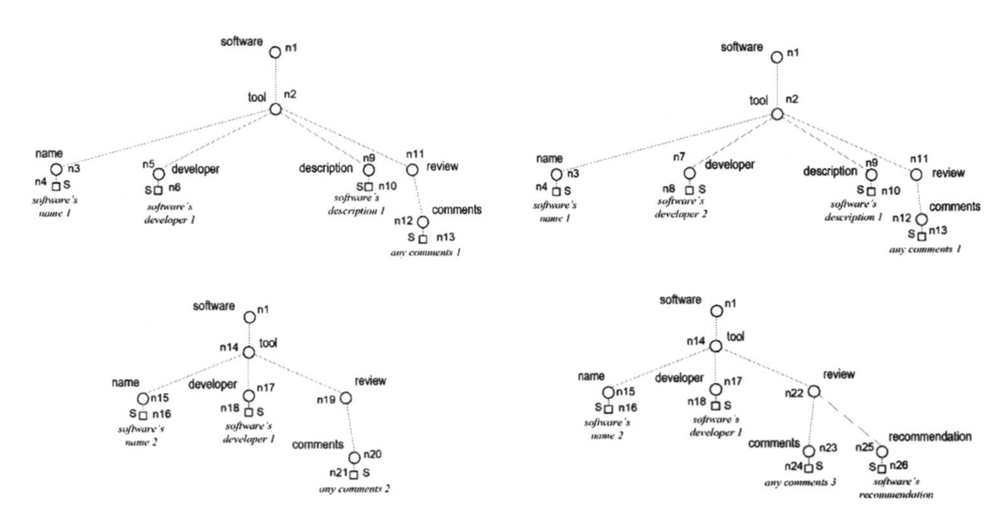


subtree rooted in the software element, as here there are two paths software.tool.developer. Two other distinct tree tuples are instead extracted starting from the right subtree rooted in software, as here there are two paths software.tool.review, each of which yields a distinct path answer corresponding to a tool.

## Transactional Modeling of XML Tree Tuples

In the huge amount of available structured data, a relevant portion is represented by *transactional data*, that is, variable-length sequences of objects with categorical attributes. Given a set $I = \{e_1, ..., e_m\}$ of distinct categorical values, or *items*, a transactional database is a multi-set of transactions $tr \subseteq I$. The item domain is built over all the leaf elements in a given collection of XML tree tuples, that is the set of distinct answers of complete paths applied to the tree tuples. A transaction is then modeled with the set of items associated to the leaf elements of a specific tree tuple. The intuition behind such a model lies mainly on the definition of XML tree tuple itself: each path applied to a tree tuple yields a unique answer, thus each item in a transaction indicates information on a concept that is distinct from that of other items in the same transaction.

Formally, given an XML tree tuple $\tau$ and a path $p \in P_\tau$, an *XML tree tuple item* in $\tau$ is a pair $e = \langle p, A_\tau(p) \rangle$, where $A_\tau(p)$ denotes the answer of $p$ on $\tau$. The *XML transaction* corresponding to $\tau$ is the set of XML tree tuple items of $\tau$.

# COLLABORATIVE CLUSTERING OF XML DOCUMENTS

## XML Tree Tuple Item Similarity

XML features are represented by tree tuple items. Therefore, in order to compare XML data in our transactional domain, we define a measure of similarity between tree tuple items according to their structure and content features. Given two tree tuple items $e_i$ and $e_j$, the *tree tuple item similarity* function is defined as:

$$sim(e_i, e_j) = f \times sim_S(e_i, e_j) + (1 - f) \times sim_C(e_i, e_j)$$

where $sim_S$ (resp. $sim_C$) denotes the structural (resp. content) similarity between the items, and $f \in [0, 1]$ is a factor that tunes the influence of the structural part to the overall similarity. Since the combination of structure and content information characterizes an XML tree tuple item, it is advisable to take tolerance on computing similarity between XML tree tuple items. For this purpose, we introduce a similarity threshold $\gamma \in [0, 1]$ that represents the minimum similarity value for considering two XML tree tuple items as similar. According with this, two XML tree tuple items $e_i$ and $e_j$ are said to be *γ-matched* if $sim(e_i, e_j) \geq \gamma$.

## Similarity by Structure

Structural similarity between two tree tuple items $e_i$ and $e_j$ is evaluated by comparing their respective tag paths. Computing the similarity between any two paths is essentially accomplished by referring to it as a simple case of string matching of their respective element names, and finally averaging the (weighted) matchings. To this end, given any two tags $t_1$ and $t_2$, the Dirichlet function (Δ) is applied in such a way that $\Delta(t_1, t_2)$ is equal to one if the tags match, otherwise $\Delta(t_1, t_2)$ is equal to zero.

Given two XML tree tuple items $e_i$ and $e_j$, let $p_i = t_{i1}.t_{i2}. \ldots .t_{in}$ and $p_j = t_{j1}.t_{j2}. \ldots .t_{jm}$ be their respective tag paths. The *structural similarity* between $e_i$ and $e_j$ is defined as,

$$sim_S\left(e_i, e_j\right) = \frac{1}{n+m}\left(\sum_{h=1}^{n} s\left(t_{ih}, p_j, h\right) + \sum_{k=1}^{m} s\left(t_{jk}, p_i, k\right)\right)$$

such that, for each tag $t$ and path $p = t_1.t_2. \ldots .t_L$, $s(t, p, a) = \max_{\{l=1..L\}} (1+|a-l|)^{-1} \times \Delta(t, t_l)$.

Above, the tag matchings are corrected by a factor which is inversely proportional to the absolute difference of location of the tags in their respective paths. Essentially, this factor penalizes the similarity of two paths that have the same tags but are differently located.

## Similarity by Content

A *textual content unit* (for short, TCU) is referred to as the preprocessed text of a tree tuple item, that is, a #PCDATA element content or an attribute value. To weight the relevance of terms in TCUs, an adaptation of the popular *tf.idf* (term frequency - inverse document frequency) to the XML transactional domain is defined.

Given a collection ***XT*** of XML trees, let $w_j$ be an index term occurring in a TCU $u_i$ of a tree tuple $\tau$ belonging to T extracted from a tree *XT* belonging to ***XT***. The *ttf.itf* (*Tree tuple Term Frequency - Inverse Tree tuple Frequency*) weight of $w_j$ in $u_i$ with respect to $\tau$ is defined as,

$$ttf.itf\left(w_j, u_i|_\tau\right) = tf\left(w_j, u_i\right) \times \exp\left(\frac{n_{j,\tau}}{N_\tau}\right) \times \frac{n_{j,XT}}{N_{XT}} \times \ln\left(\frac{N_\mathrm{T}}{n_{j,\mathrm{T}}}\right)$$

where $tf(w_j, u_i)$ denotes the number of occurrences of $w_j$ in $u_i$, and the other symbols denote the number of TCUs appearing in $\tau$ ($N_\tau$) and in the portion containing $w_j$ ($n_{j,\tau}$), in *XT* ($N_{XT}$) and in the portion containing $w_j$ ($n_{j,XT}$), in T ($N_\mathrm{T}$) and in the portion containing $w_j$ ($n_{j,\mathrm{T}}$). Note that the *ttf.itf* weight increases by increasing each of the factors in the function, namely the term frequency within the specific TCU, the term popularity across the TCUs of the same XML transaction and across the TCUs of the same document tree, and the term rarity across the whole collection of TCUs.

Content similarity between two tree tuple items is computed by measuring the text similarity of their respective TCUs. A vector-space model to represent the TCUs is adopted, therefore any TCU $u_i$ is modeled with a vector whose *j*-th component corresponds to an index term $w_j$ and contains the *ttf.itf* relevance weight. To measure the similarity between TCU vectors, the well-known *cosine similarity* (Strehl, Ghosh, & Mooney, 2000) is used.

## The Centralized Approach: XK-means Algorithm

XML tree tuples modeled as transactions can be efficiently clustered by applying a centralized partitional algorithm devised for the XML transactional domain. A partitional clustering problem consists in partitioning a set $\{x_1, ..., x_n\}$ of objects in $k$ non-empty groups each containing a homogeneous subset of objects.

In (Tagarelli & Greco, 2010; Tagarelli & Greco, 2006), a centroid-based partitional clustering algorithm, called XK-means, was developed as a variant of the $k$-Means algorithm for the XML transactional domain. XK-means embeds novel notions of proximity among XML transactions, and XML cluster representative (centroid). The basic idea underlying the algorithm is to search for the "shared" items when comparing any two XML transactions. Following one of the commonly used measures for categorical data, the similarity of two XML transactions could be computed as directly proportional to the number of common items and inversely proportional to the number of different items. However, computing exact intersection between XML transactions will likely lead to very poor results, since two XML (tree tuple) items may share relevant structural or content information even though they are not identical. Therefore, the notion of standard intersection between sets of items was enhanced with one able to capture similarities, rather than strictly exact matching, from content and structure features of XML elements.

Let $tr_1$ and $tr_2$ be two transactions, and $\gamma \in [0,1]$ be a similarity threshold. The set of *$\gamma$-shared items* between $tr_1$ and $tr_2$ is defined as,

$$match^{\gamma}(tr_1, tr_2) = match^{\gamma}(tr_1 \rightarrow tr_2) \cup match^{\gamma}(tr_2 \rightarrow tr_1)$$

where $match^{\gamma}(tr_i \rightarrow tr_j) = \{e \in tr_i \mid \exists e_h \in tr_j, sim(e, e_h) \geq \gamma, \neg\exists e' \in tr_i, sim(e', e_h) > sim(e, e_h)\}$. The set of $\gamma$-shared items resembles the intersection between transactions at a degree greater than or equal to a similarity threshold $\gamma$. This notion of (enhanced) intersection is also at the basis of the *XML transaction similarity* function:

$$sim_J^{\gamma}(tr_1, tr_2) = \frac{|match^{\gamma}(tr_1, tr_2)|}{|tr_1 \cup tr_2|}$$

The above function is used in *XK-means* to measure the proximity among transactions. Moreover, given a cluster $C$, its centroid $c$ is computed by starting from the set of $\gamma$-shared items among all the transactions within C. More precisely, for each transaction in $C$, the union of the $\gamma$-shared item sets with respect to all the other transactions in $C$ is obtained; this guarantees no dependence of the order of examination of the transactions. Then, the set of $\gamma$-shared items is involved to compute a centroid having the form of a tree tuple. According to such a function, a raw centroid is firstly defined by selecting the items from these union sets with the highest frequency: the raw centroid, however, may not have the form of a tree tuple, as some items therein may refer to the same path but with different answers. Any raw centroid is transformed into a tree tuple. This step involves a set $I$ of items and yields a tree tuple composed by all the distinct paths $p$ involved into the items in $I$; the content associated to each path $p$ is the union of the contents of the items in $I$ having $p$ as a path. A greedy heuristic refines the current centroid by iteratively adding the remaining most frequent items until the sum of pair-wise similarities between transactions and centroid cannot be further maximized. Performing again this step, any refinement guarantees that the resulting centroid satisfies the requirements presented above.

## The Distributed Approach: CXK-means Algorithm

The main novelties and intuitions introduced in *XK-means*, such as XML transaction proximity measure and cluster centroid for a set of XML transaction, are exploited by the *CXK-means* XML transactional clustering algorithm for a distributed collaborative environment (Greco, Gullo, Ponti, & Tagarelli, 2009). The pseudo-code of *CXK-means* is sketched in Figure 3.

In the *CXK-means* algorithm, document data are distributed over $m$ nodes and each node communicates with all the other ones sending "local" centroids and receiving "global" centroids. An initial process corresponding to a node $N_0$ defines a partition of the set $\{1, ..., k\}$ of cluster identifiers into $m$ subsets. Each set contains the identifiers of the clusters for which the node $N_j$ has the responsibility of computing the global centroids (i.e., the *responsibility assignments*). It should be noted that the presence of node $N_0$ does not contrast the collaborative nature of the *CXK-means* algorithm. Indeed, $N_0$ is not responsible of summarizing the information coming from the various peers (nodes $N_1$, ..., $N_m$) and, therefore, does not act as a coordinator; rather, $N_0$ performs only trivial startup operations which, in principle, can be performed by any other peer node $N_1$, ..., $N_m$.

Each node $N_i$ is in charge of computing local clusters $C^i_1$, ..., $C^i_k$ and local centroids $l^i_1$, ..., $l^i_k$, but also a subset $g_j$ of the global centroids; this is performed by looking at its own responsibility assignment and the local centroids computed by all nodes. Each node has a process that executes a classic $k$-Means-like partitional clustering scheme on its local data in $S^i$ ($S^i$ is the subset of the whole set $S$ of transactions available from the original distributed dataset stored into node $N_i$). The clustering process employs global centroids received from each other node in the network and terminates when transaction assignments to

*Figure 3. The CXK-means clustering algorithm*

**Algorithm: CXK-MEANS**
**Input:** set $S$ of XML transactions distributed over $m$ nodes,
number $k$ of clusters, similarity threshold $\gamma$
**Output:** partition **C** of $S$ in $k$ clusters distributed over $m$ nodes

**Process $N_0$**
1: define a partition of $\{1, ..., k\}$ into $m$ subsets $\{Z_1, ..., Z_m\}$
*// $Z_i$ is the responsibility assignment of node $N_i$*
2: **send** the chosen *responsibility assignments* to each node

**Process $N_i$**
3: select a global centroid $g_j$ for each $j \in Z_i$
4: **repeat**
5: **send** global centroids $g_j$ for each $j \in Z_i$ to all other nodes
6: **receive** the remaining global centroids from all the other nodes
7: set the initial local centroids $l^i_j$ as equal to the global centroids
8: assign each transaction to the cluster with the closest local centroid
(according to the $sim^\gamma_J$ function)
9: re-compute local centroids $l^i_j$ of each cluster $C^i_j$
10: **if** each $l_j$ does not change **then**
11: **send** a *termination signal* to all other nodes
12: **else**
13: **send** a *continuation signal* and local centroids to all the other nodes
14: **receive** local centroids from all the other nodes
15: **if** there exists a node that does not terminate **then**
16: compute global centroids $g_j$
for each $j \in Z_i$ employing local ones received by the other nodes
17: **until** each node terminates

local clusters do not change. For each node $N_i$, the local centroid of a cluster $C^i_j$ is computed by starting from the set of $\gamma$-shared items among all the transactions within $C^i_j$. The procedure followed is the one employed by *XK-means*.

The global centroid $g_j$ of a cluster $C_j$ is computed in a way similar to that employed for local centroids. A major difference is that global centroids are computed by considering the $m$ local centroids $l^1_j, ..., l^m_j$ (computed by each node $N_1, ..., N_m$) along with their respective weights $|C^1_j|, ..., |C^m_j|$, which are needed for taking also into account the size of the cluster summarized by each node. The rationale in this respect is that the greater the weight $|C^i_j|$ (i.e., the greater the number of transactions belonging to the cluster $C_j$ stored into the local repository $S^i$ at node $i$), the more reliable the local centroid $l^i_j$ in summarizing cluster $C_j$ is – in other terms, $l^i_j$ is more reliable than any other local centroid $l^{i'}_j$ outputted by a node $i' \neq i$ such that $|C^{i'}_j| < |C^i_j|$.

Nodes communicate their local state by sending a flag to other nodes in the network. In particular, a node sends a termination signal if, at the end of its local clustering process, all its local cluster centroids do not change with respect to the ones computed in the previous execution. In this way, the collaborative clustering process continues until each node in the network reaches a stable clustering solution.

## EXPERIMENTAL EVALUATION

### Experimental Setting

The experimental evaluation was mainly conceived to evaluate the performance of *CXK-means* with respect to *XK-means* in terms of both efficiency and effectiveness. In this respect, the number of nodes in the peer-to-peer distributed environment was varied from 1 to a maximum of 19, where a network size equal to 1 clearly refers to the baseline case represented by the centralized case (i.e., *XK-means* algorithm).

### Data Description

Two real-world document collections were involved into the evaluation. Figure 2 illustrates the XML DTDs that can be inferred from each of the evaluation datasets. Note that these schemas are presented only for purposes of description of the datasets involved into the experiments, that is, they were not used during the evaluation since the approach at hand does not require the availability of XML schemas.

The *DBLP* dataset is a subset of the DBLP archive,[1] a digital bibliography on computer science which contains citations on journal articles, conference papers, books, book chapters, and theses. *DBLP* is comprised of 3,000 documents which correspond to 5,884 transactions and 8,231 items. *DBLP* is characterized by a small average depth (3), whereas the number of leaf nodes is 13,209 and the maximum fan out is 20. According to its element type definition (Figure 2(a)), exhibits short text descriptions (e.g., author names, paper titles, conference names), and a moderate structural variety which corresponds to 4 main structural categories, namely "journal articles" (*article*), "conference papers" (*inproceedings*), "books" (*book*), and "book chapters" (*incollection*). Also, 6 topical classes are identified in *DBLP*, which are "multimedia", "logic programming", "web and adaptive systems", "knowledge based systems", "software engineering", and "formal languages". If both content and structure information are taken into account, 16 classes are identified.

The *IEEE* dataset refers to the IEEE collection version 2.2, which has been used as a benchmark in the INEX document mining track 2008[2]. *IEEE* consists of 4,874 articles originally published in 23 different IEEE journals from 2002 to 2004. Such articles follow a complex schema which includes front matter, back matter, section headings, text formatting tags and mathematical formulas. We kept most of the logical structure elements and removed the stylistic markups, as shown in the DTD of Figure 2(b). In our XML transactional domain, the *IEEE* collection has 211,909 transactions and 135,869 items. Also, the number of leaf nodes is 228,869, the maximum fan out is 43, and the average depth is about 5. In *IEEE*, the article journals determine the categories that were used to partition the collection, which strictly follow the original INEX categorization. Precisely, two structural categories correspond to "Transactions" and "non-Transactions" articles, respectively, whereas the classification by content organizes the articles by the following 8 topic-classes: "Computer", "Graphics", "Hardware", "Artificial Intelligence", "Internet", "Mobile", "Parallel", and "Security". Moreover, 14 hybrid classes are identified according to these structural and content classes.

## Cluster Validity Measures

The quality of clustering solutions for the datasets was assessed by exploiting the availability of reference classifications for XML documents. The objective was to evaluate how well a clustering fits a predefined scheme of known classes (natural clusters). For this purpose, the evaluation employed the well-known *F-measure* (Larsen, & Aone, 1999), which is defined as the harmonic mean of values that express two notions from Information Retrieval, namely *Precision* and *Recall*. F-measure ranges within [0,1], where higher values refer to better quality results. Since tree tuple decomposition of XML documents and then transactional modeling were performed as preliminary phases, the evaluation process take into account the set $S$ of XML transactions.

Given a set $S = \{tr_1, ..., tr_m\}$ of XML transactions, let $\Gamma = \{\Gamma_1, ..., \Gamma_H\}$ be the reference classification of the objects in $S$, and $\mathbf{C} = \{C_1, ..., C_K\}$ be the output partition yielded by a clustering algorithm. *Precision* of cluster $C_j$ with respect to class $\Gamma_i$ is the fraction of the objects in $C_j$ that has been correctly classified, whereas *Recall* of cluster $C_j$ with respect to class $\Gamma_i$ is the fraction of the objects in $\Gamma_i$ that has been correctly classified. Formally,

$$P_{ij} = \frac{|C_j \cap \Gamma_i|}{|C_j|} \quad R_{ij} = \frac{|C_j \cap \Gamma_i|}{|\Gamma_i|} \quad F_{ij} = \frac{2P_{ij}R_{ij}}{(P_{ij} + R_{ij})}$$

In order to score the quality of $C$ with respect to $\Gamma$ by means of a single value, the overall F-measure $F(\mathbf{C}, \Gamma)$ is computed using the weighted sum of the maximum $F_{ij}$ score for each class $\Gamma_i$.

$$F(\mathbf{C}, \Gamma) = \frac{1}{|S|} \sum_{i=1}^{H} |\Gamma_i| \max_{j \in [1..K]} F_{ij}$$

## Results

### Effectiveness

Table 1(a–b) illustrates accuracy performances obtained on (a) *DBLP* an (b) *IEEE* by *CXK-means* when data are equally partitioned over the nodes. Experiments have been performed for each of the clustering type (i.e., content-, structure-, and content/structure-driven) by varying the number of nodes. For each dataset and clustering setting, results refer to multiple (10) runs of the algorithm and correspond to F-measure scores averaged over the range of $f$ values specific of the clustering setting. Moreover, the best setting of parameter $\gamma$ was found to be close to high values (typically above 0.85), for each dataset and type of clustering (Tagarelli & Greco, 2010).

As it is reasonable to expect, the centralized case corresponds to an upper bound in terms of clustering quality for the distributed collaborative approach. While the focus here is not on the effectiveness evaluation of the centralized case, it can be noted how the clustering accuracy decreases as the number of nodes increases, regard-

*Table 1. Clustering accuracy results for data equally distributed over the nodes: (a) DBLP and (b) IEEE*

| (a) DBLP | | |
|---|---|---|
| **Clustering type (#clusters)** | **#nodes** | **avg F-measure** |
| $f \in [0, 0.3]$ (content-driven similarity) (6 clusters) | 1 | 0.795 |
| | 3 | 0.730 |
| | 5 | 0.701 |
| | 7 | 0.639 |
| | 9 | 0.574 |
| $f \in [0.4, 0.6]$ (structure/content-driven similarity) (16 clusters) | 1 | 0.803 |
| | 3 | 0.750 |
| | 5 | 0.716 |
| | 7 | 0.641 |
| | 9 | 0.585 |
| $f \in [0.7, 1]$ (structure-driven similarity) (4 clusters) | 1 | 0.991 |
| | 3 | 0.971 |
| | 5 | 0.935 |
| | 7 | 0.855 |
| | 9 | 0.751 |
| **(b) IEEE** | | |
| **Clustering type (#clusters)** | **#nodes** | **avg F-measure** |
| $f \in [0, 0.3]$ (content-driven similarity) (8 clusters) | 1 | 0.629 |
| | 3 | 0.552 |
| | 5 | 0.514 |
| | 7 | 0.440 |
| | 9 | 0.396 |
| $f \in [0.4, 0.6]$ (structure/content-driven similarity) (14 clusters) | 1 | 0.598 |
| | 3 | 0.524 |
| | 5 | 0.478 |
| | 7 | 0.423 |
| | 9 | 0.375 |
| $f \in [0.7, 1]$ (structure-driven similarity) (2 clusters) | 1 | 0.655 |
| | 3 | 0.572 |
| | 5 | 0.527 |
| | 7 | 0.453 |
| | 9 | 0.406 |

less of the dataset and the type of clustering. However, this performance degradation remains relatively acceptable for a distributed environment, which is partly due to the model of cluster centroid in achieving good quality summaries for the clusters. Indeed, loss of accuracy of *CXK-means* with respect to *XK-means* was always lower than 0.2 in relation to the number of nodes leading to the stabilization of efficiency performance determined in the previous paragraph (i.e., 4 and 6 for *DBLP* and *IEEE*, respectively); particularly, the decrease in accuracy were roughly equal to 0.08 (*DBLP*) and 0.14 (*IEEE*).

## Efficiency

Figure 4 shows time performances on the four evaluation datasets by increasing the number of nodes. The dataset size was also varied in order to consider the whole datasets and reduced-size (50%) datasets and show the scalability of *CXK-means*. Results refer to structure/content-driven clustering experiments ($f \in [0.4,0.6]$) and data equally distributed in the network.

Here a noteworthy remark is that the performance of *CXK-means* takes major advantages with respect to *XK-means* in terms of runtime behavior. In fact, a higher number of nodes in the network leads to more parallelism, which results in a drastic reduction of the overall time needed for the clustering task. However, when the number of nodes grows up, the data exchanged among nodes grow up as well. This fact clearly affects negatively the network traffic (i.e., the centroid exchange) which might not be negligible anymore. Indeed, as it can be noted in Figure 3 for both the datasets, after a drastic reduction of the runtime due to the use of just a few nodes, the runtime remains roughly constant for a certain range, then it starts to slightly increase when the number of

*Figure 4. Clustering time performances varying the number of nodes and the dataset size:(a) DBLP, and (b) IEEE*

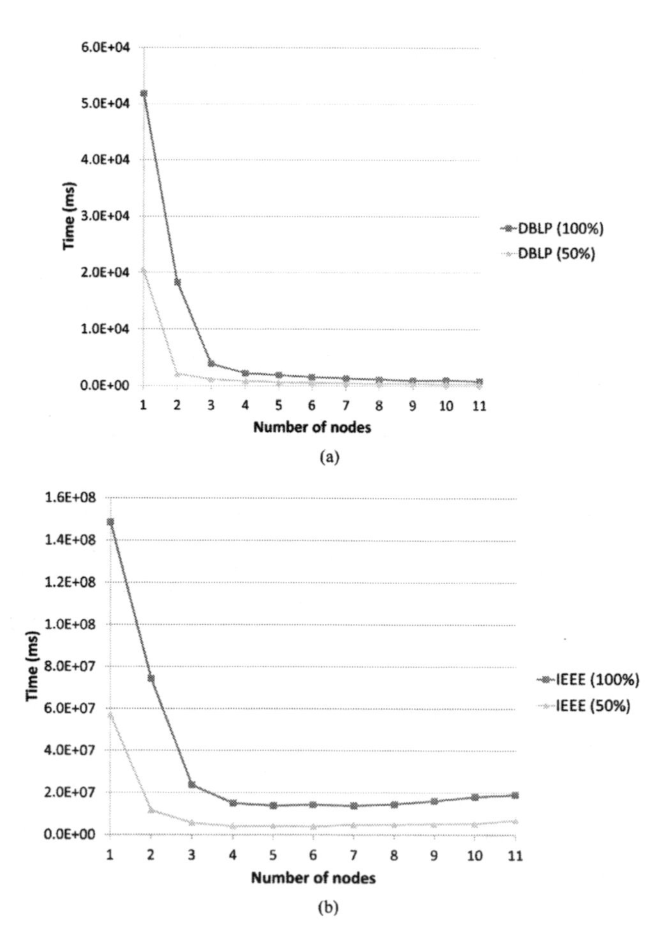

nodes becomes significantly higher. Regarding the evaluation of the stabilization (saturation) points, it can be noted that time performances on *IEEE* tend to stabilize for 6 and 4 nodes, respectively in the case of full and halved dataset; on *DBLP*, time performances tend to stabilize for a smaller number of nodes (4 and 2, respectively) which is due to a smaller size of *DBLP* with respect to *IEEE*, in terms of both transactions and vocabulary of terms.

Another important remark is that, as the dataset size is halved, the minimum number of nodes to bring down the clustering times tends to decrease. This further confirms that the advantage of the distributed collaborative approach with respect to the centralized one tends to become less significant as the dataset size is reduced.

## CONCLUSION AND FUTURE RESEARCH

In this chapter we presented a collaborative clustering approach to organizing XML documents in P2P networks. The framework is based on a distributed, centroid-based partitional clustering algorithm, where cluster centroids are used to describe local and global clusters of the input document collection. Each node yields a local clustering solution, whose clusters are represented by local centroids. These centroids are exchanged with the other nodes in the network in a collaborative way; the ultimate goal is to exploit such local centroids for computing global clusters that form the overall clustering solution. Experimental results have shown that XML distributed collaborative clustering is more efficient than the corresponding centralized clustering setting, though paying a slight decrease in accuracy.

There are several directions that are worthy of investigation. Some of them involve enhancements of the framework we have proposed in this chapter. For instance, semantic information of both structural and content type from XML data could be integrated in our framework at different levels, following the study provided in (Tagarelli & Greco, 2010). Other future research directions regard in general the impact of using a distributed approach to XML document clustering in such contexts as data integration and information retrieval. Collaborative distributed clustering of XML documents can in fact efficiently support the integration and classification of heterogeneous XML sources, but the extent to which this can be useful need to be thoroughly investigated. The summarization and extraction of information from the Web and the consequent organization of selectively structured information (wrapped data) represent real-world scenarios in which collaborative distributed clustering of XML documents can help in different ways. For instance, it clustering can be used to preliminarily filter subsets of documents that are cohesive with respect to a specific domain of interest for the user who needs to summarize, extract and organize the extracted data. Also, distributed clustering can easily be applied to the result of summarization and extraction of heterogeneous Web sources without requiring any effort of centralization of resources.

## REFERENCES

Abiteboul, S., Manolescu, I., & Taropa, E. (2006). A framework for distributed XML data management. In Y. E. Ioannidis, M. H. Scholl, J. W. Schmidt, F. Matthes, M. Hatzopoulos, K. Böhm, A. Kemper, T. Grust, & C. Böhm (Eds.), *Proceedings of the 10th International Conference on Extending Database Technology (EDBT) Lecture Notes in Computer Science: Vol. 3896.* (pp. 1049-1058). Springer.

Antonellis, P., Makris, C., & Tsirakis, N. (2009). Utilizing XML Clustering for Efficient XML Data Management on P2P Networks. In S. S. Bhowmick, J. Küng, & R. Wagner (Eds.), *Proceedings of the 20th International Conference on Database and Expert Systems Applications (DEXA) Lecture Notes in Computer Science: Vol. 5690.* (pp. 68-82). Springer.

Arenas, M., & Libkin, L. (2004). A normal form for XML documents. *ACM Transactions on Database Systems*, *29*(1), 195–232. doi:10.1145/974750.974757

Baeza-Yates, R., & Ribeiro-Neto, B. (1999). *Modern information retrieval*. Addison Wesley.

Candillier, L., Tellier, I., & Torre, F. (2005). Transforming XML trees for efficient classification and clustering. In N. Fuhr, M. Lalmas, S. Malik, & G. Kazai (Eds.), *Proceedings of the 4th International Workshop of the Initiative for the Evaluation of XML Retrieval (INEX) Lecture Notes in Computer Science: Vol 3977.* (pp. 469-480). Springer.

Cannataro, M., Congiusta, A., Pugliese, A., Talia, D., & Trunfio, P. (2004). Distributed data mining on Grids: Services, tools, and applications. *IEEE Transactions on Systems, Man, and Cybernetics. Part B*, *34*(6), 2451–2465.

Cesario, E., & Talia, D. (2008). Distributed data mining models as services on the Grid. In *Workshops Proceedings of the 8th IEEE International Conference on Data Mining (ICDM)*, (pp. 486-495). IEEE Computer Society.

Costa, G., Manco, G., Ortale, R., & Tagarelli, A. (2004). A tree-based approach to clustering XML documents by structure. In J.-F. Boulicaut, F. Esposito, F. Giannotti, & D. Pedreschi (Eds.), *Proceedings of the 8th European Conference on Principles and Practice of Knowledge Discovery in Databases (PKDD) Lecture Notes in Computer Science: Vol. 3202* (pp. 137-148). Springer.

Denoyer, L., & Gallinari, P. (2008). Report on the XML mining track at INEX 2007: Categorization and clustering of XML documents. *SIGIR Forum*, *42*(1), 22–28. doi:10.1145/1394251.1394255

Dhillon, I. S., & Modha, D. S. (2000). A data-clustering algorithm on distributed memory multiprocessors. In M. Javeed Zaki, & C.-T. Ho (Eds.), *Proceedings of the Workshop on Large-Scale Parallel KDD Systems (KDD) Lecture Notes in Computer Science: Vol. 1759* (pp. 245-260). Springer.

Dhillon, I. S., & Modha, D. S. (2001). Concept decompositions for large sparse text data using clustering. *Machine Learning*, *42*(1/2), 143–175. doi:10.1023/A:1007612920971

Doucet, A., & Lehtonen, M. (2006). Unsupervised classification of TextCentric XML document collections. In *Proceedings of the 5th International Workshop of the Initiative for the Evaluation of XML Retrieval (INEX)* [Springer.]. *Lecture Notes in Computer Science*, *4518*, 497–509. doi:10.1007/978-3-540-73888-6_46

Eisenhardt, M., Muller, W., & Henrich, A. (2003). Classifying documents by distributed P2P clustering. In K. R. Dittrich, W. König, A. Oberweis, K. Rannenberg, W. Wahlster (Eds.), *Proceedings of the INFORMATIK 2003 - Innovative Informatikanwendungen (GI Jahrestagung, 2) Lecture Notes in Informatics: Vol. 35* (pp. 286-291). GI.

Flesca, S., Furfaro, F., Greco, S., & Zumpano, E. (2003). Repairs and consistent answers for XML data with functional dependencies. In Z. Bellahsene, A. B. Chaudhri, E. Rahm, M. Rys, & R. Unland (Eds.), *Proceedings of the 1st International XML Database Symposium (XSym) Lecture Notes in Computer Science: Vol. 2824* (pp. 238-253). Springer.

Greco, S., Gullo, F., Ponti, G., & Tagarelli, A. (2009). Collaborative clustering of XML documents. In *Proceedings of the International Workshop on Distributed XML Processing: Theory and Practice (ICPPW)* (pp. 579-586). IEEE Computer Society.

Hammouda, K., & Kamel, M. (2006). Collaborative document clustering. In J. Ghosh, D. Lambert, D. B. Skillicorn, & J. Srivastava (Eds.), *Proceedings of the SIAM International Conference on Data Mining (SDM)*, (pp. 451-461). SIAM.

Ignat, C.-L., & Oster, G. (2008). Peer-to-peer collaboration over XML documents. In *Proceedings of the 5th International Conference on Cooperative Design, Visualization, and Engineering (CDVE,)* (pp. 66-73). Springer.

Jain, A., & Dubes, R. (1988). *Algorithms for clustering data*. Prentice-Hall.

Kargupta, H., Hamzaoglu, I., & Stafford, B. (1997). Scalable, distributed data mining using an agent based architecture. In *Proceedings of the European Conference on Principles and Practice of Knowledge Discovery in Databases (PKDD),* (pp. 211-214).

Kargupta, H., Park, B. H., Hershberger, D., & Johnson, E. (1999). Collective data mining: A new perspective toward distributed data mining. In *Proceedings of Advances in Distributed and Parallel Knowledge Discovery* (pp. 133-184).

Koloniari, G., & Pitoura, E. (2005). Peer-to-peer management of XML data: Issues and research challenges. *SIGMOD Record, 34*(2), 6–17. doi:10.1145/1083784.1083788

Kutty, S., Tran, T., Nayak, R., & Li, Y. (2008). Clustering XML documents using closed frequent subtrees: A structural similarity approach. In N. Fuhr, J. Kamps, M. Lalmas, and A. Trotman (Eds.), *Focused Access to XML Documents, 6th International Workshop of the Initiative for the Evaluation of XML Retrieval (INEX) Lecture Notes in Computer Science: Vol. 4862.* (pp. 183-194). Springer.

Larsen, B., & Aone, C. (1999). Fast and effective text mining using lineartime document clustering. In *Proceedings of the 5th ACM SIGKDD International Conference on Knowledge Discovery and Data Mining (KDD),* (pp. 16-22). ACM.

Lian, W., Cheung, D., Mamoulis, N., & Yiu, S. (2004). An efficient and scalable algorithm for clustering XML documents by structure. *IEEE Transactions on Knowledge and Data Engineering, 16*(1), 82–96. doi:10.1109/TKDE.2004.1264824

Nayak, R., & Xu, S. (2006). XCLS: A fast and effective clustering algorithm for heterogeneous XML documents. In W. Keong Ng, Masaru Kitsuregawa, J. Li, and K. Chang (Eds.), *Proccedings of the Pacific-Asia Conference on Knowledge Discovery and Data Mining (PAKDD) Lecture Notes in Computer Science: Vol. 3918.* (pp. 292-302). Springer.

Nierman, A., & Jagadish, H. (2002). Evaluating structural similarity in XML documents. In *Proceedings of the ACM SIGMOD International Workshop on the Web and Databases (WebDB),* (pp. 61-66).

Papapetrou, O., Siberski, W., & Fuhr, N. (2010). Text clustering for peer-to-peer networks with probabilistic guarantees. In C. Gurrin, Y. He, G. Kazai, U. Kruschwitz, S. Little, T. Roelleke, S. M. Rüger, & K. van Rijsbergen (Eds.), *Proceedings European Conference on Information Retrieval Research (ECIR) Lecture Notes in Computer Science: Vol. 5993.* (pp. 293-305). Springer.

Polyzotis, N., & Garofalakis, M. (2002). Structure and value synopses for XML data graphs. In *Proceedings of the International Conference on Very Large Data Bases (VLDB),* (pp. 466-477). Morgan Kaufmann.

Prodromidis, A. L., Chan, P. K., & Stolfo, S. J. (2000). Metalearning in distributed data mining systems: Issues and approaches. In *Proceedings of the Advances in Distributed and Parallel Knowledge Discovery* (pp. 81-87).

Rao, P. R., & Moon, B. (2009). Locating XML documents in a peer–to–peer network using distributed hash tables. *IEEE Transanctions On Knowledge and Data Engineering, 21*(12), 1737–1752. doi:10.1109/TKDE.2009.26

Rodriguez, R., & Druschel, P. (2010). Peer–to–peer systems. *Communications of the ACM, 53*(10), 72–82.

Steinbach, M., Karypis, G., & Kumar, V. (2000). A comparison of document clustering techniques. In *Proceedings of the KDD Workshop on Text Mining.*

Strehl, A., Ghosh, J., & Mooney, R. (2000). Impact of similarity measures on web-page clustering. In *Proceedings of the AAAI Workshop on AI for Web Search* (pp. 58-64). AAAI.

Tagarelli, A., & Greco, S. (2006). Toward semantic XML clustering. In J. Ghosh, D. Lambert, D. B. Skillicorn, & J. Srivastava (Eds.), *Proceedings of the SIAM International Conference on Data Mining (SDM),* (pp. 188-199). SIAM.

Tagarelli, A., & Greco, S. (2010). Semantic clustering of XML documents. *ACM Transactions on Information Systems, 28*(1), 1–56. doi:10.1145/1658377.1658380

Tran, T., Nayak, R., & Bruza, P. (2008). Combining structure and content similarities for XML document clustering. In J. F. Roddick, J. Li, P. Christen, & P. J. Kennedy (Eds.), *Proceedings of the 7th Australasian Data Mining Conference (AusDM): Vol. 87. CRPIT* (pp. 219-226). Australian Computer Society.

Vercoustre, A. M., Fegas, M., Gul, S., & Lechevallier, Y. (2005). A flexible structured-based representation for XML document mining. In N. Fuhr, M. Lalmas, S. Malik, & G. Kazai (Eds.), *Advances in XML Information Retrieval and Evaluation, 4th International Workshop of the Initiative for the Evaluation of XML Retrieval (INEX) Lecture Notes in Computer Science: Vol. 3977* (pp. 443-457). Springer.

Zhao, Y., & Karypis, G. (2004). Empirical and theoretical comparison of selected criterion functions for document clustering. *Machine Learning, 55*(3), 311–331. doi:10.1023/B:MACH.0000027785.44527.d6

## ENDNOTES

[1] http://dblp.uni-trier.de/xml/

[2] http://www.inex.otago.ac.nz/data/documentcollection.asp

# Chapter 19
# Incorporating Qualitative Information for Credit Risk Assessment through Frequent Subtree Mining for XML

**Novita Ikasari**
*Curtin University, Australia & University of Indonesia, Indonesia*

**Fedja Hadzic**
*Curtin University, Australia*

**Tharam S. Dillon**
*Curtin University, Australia*

## ABSTRACT

*Credit risk assessment has been one of the most appealing topics in banking and finance studies, attracting both scholars' and practitioners' attention for some time. Following the success of the Grameen Bank, works on credit risk, in particular for Small Medium Enterprises (SMEs), have become essential. The distinctive character of SMEs requires a method that takes into account quantitative and qualitative information for loan granting decision purposes. In this chapter, we first provide a survey of existing credit risk assessment methods, which shows a current gap in the existing research in regards to taking qualitative information into account during the data mining process. To address this shortcoming, we propose a framework that utilizes an XML-based template to capture both qualitative and quantitative information in this domain. By representing this information in a domain-oriented way, the potential knowledge that can be discovered for evidence-based decision support will be maximized. An XML document can be effectively represented as a rooted ordered labelled tree and a number of tree mining methods exist that enable the efficient discovery of associations among tree-structured data objects, taking both the content and structure into account. The guidelines for correct and effective application of*

DOI: 10.4018/978-1-61350-356-0.ch019

*such methods are provided in order to gain detailed insight into the information governing the decision making process. We have obtained a number of textual reports from the banks regarding the information collected from SMEs during the credit application/evaluation process. These are used as the basis for generating a synthetic XML database that partially reflects real-world scenarios. A tree mining method is applied to this data to demonstrate the potential of the proposed method for credit risk assessment.*

## INTRODUCTION

The emerging need for methods of credit risk assessment for Small Medium Enterprises' loan applications presents a unique challenge to the knowledge discovery and data mining field. The present credit scoring methods are considered not viable for SMEs since they are constructed from characteristics and risks pertaining to large scale business. In addition, SMEs are known for their imprecise management style, having non-systematic bookkeeping and organization of the business. This leads to a lack of valid and reliable financial information in traditional form (Berger, Klapper, & Udell, 2001; Berger & Udell, 1995) which is currently needed for the assessment of loan applications. In order to overcome the problem, loan staffs are required to collate data using a qualitative data collection method, namely interviews and observations. Therefore, a good portion of information on loan applications is available in a qualitative rather than quantitative form.

The abundant studies on credit scoring have contributed to credit risk methods being constructed using statistical and machine learning techniques. Aside from these mainstream techniques, our survey of the existing literature shows that a small number of researches have conducted studies using hybrid methods. Although each method shows respectable performance in classifying good and bad loan applications, each has inherent weaknesses. This, among others, is due to the fact that they are constructed using quantitative data which results in limited applicability of such a method in the real world of SMEs. Recent studies on credit risk assessment of SMEs highlight the necessity of incorporating qualitative information into the method (e.g., Dinh & Kleimeier, 2007). The level of qualitative data on SMEs loan applications is variable in both quality and quantity. There are elements which could impact upon decisions regarding loan applications which are conspicuously higher in qualitative nature than others; these are goodwill, competency and integrity. These three characteristics require adequate elaborations since answers to these questions can only be understood by inference rather than a direct response.

This qualitative information is mainly available in free form text, which poses additional complications as most of the well developed and explored statistical and machine learning (data mining) methods are applied mainly to relational data with a well-defined structure. The task at hand is to develop a technique that incorporates and analyses qualitative information in tandem with quantitative information so that it accurately discloses applicants' credit risks. We propose a way to capture the qualitative information in a domain oriented way by defining an XML based template. We will show how the relevant information from the documents used by the banks for assessing credit risk for SME loan applications can be effectively captured using the proposed template. Within this context, preliminary results of the pre-defined XML template that are generated from a small number of textual document instances will be presented.

The main problem in association rule mining of semi-structured documents such as XML, is that of frequent pattern discovery, where a pattern in this case corresponds to a subtree. This is known as the *frequent subtree mining* problem, in which given a tree database $T_{DB}$ and minimum support threshold ($\sigma$), the goal is to find all subtrees that occur at least $\sigma$ times in $T_{DB}$. Driven by different application needs, several frequent subtree mining algorithms have been proposed in the literature that can mine different subtree types using different support definitions and constraints (Chi, Yang, & Muntz, 2005; Hadzic, Tan, & Dillon, 2010; Nijssen & Kok, 2003; Tan, Dillon, Hadzic, Feng, & Chang, 2006; Tan, Hadzic, Dillon, Feng, & Chang, 2008b; Zaki, 2005). We provide guidelines for a correct and effective application of frequent subtree mining methods and the implications of using different frequent parameters (i.e., subtree types and support definitions) in the credit risk assessment domain. The documents from the banks are used to generate the synthetic XML database to demonstrate the usefulness and potential of the proposed approach.

The end product of our presented methodology is a set of rules that can support decision making, based on the historical data. The rules can then be applied to new SMEs loan applications lodged within a particular timeframe and validated by comparing the decisions made according to these rules with the actual decisions made by loan officers on these subsequent loan applications. After substantial validation, the rules can be of great assistance to loan officers during the credit risk assessment and decision making process. Based on the previous discussion, our contribution to XML data mining is the development of a conceptual framework for incorporating qualitative information and quantitative data during the knowledge discovery process. The discovery of patterns and interesting rules using data mining techniques undoubtedly adds value to business knowledge management. Banks will be able to strategize their lending activities with regard to SMEs in order to maintain expected financial performance. Furthermore, banks are provided with feedback on determinants of SMEs' credit risk with regards to current practices. Taking into account the construction of the method, the underlying framework can also be useful when applied to other similar domain-specific databases.

The remainder of the chapter is organized as follows. In the next section, we provide the contextual background of the problem to be addressed and methodically establish the significance of qualitative information in the credit risk assessment domain. We then give an overview of the extensive existing studies related to credit risk assessment methods, highlighting the strengths and weaknesses of each method. Afterwards, we discuss the proposed framework for incorporating qualitative and quantitative information for credit scoring using XML-based data mining. We rationalise the use of XML and the construction of the proposed XML template for capturing qualitative and quantitative information from a textual document. We proceed by defining the frequent subtree mining related concepts necessary to understand our methodology, discussing the various implications regarding the appropriate use of existing tree mining algorithms in this domain and reviewing some of the existing algorithms. We then provide a preliminary experiment using the proposed method and discuss some of the knowledge patterns found. The future research directions are discussed before concluding the chapter by highlighting significant points as well as our contribution to the field.

## BACKGROUND

Small Medium Enterprises have become an essential element of the global economy and countries around the world have benefited from the existence of these small businesses. Across the 25 countries of the European Union (European Commission, 2010), United States (United States International Trade Commission, 2010) and Asia-Pacific countries (Asia-Pacific Economic Cooperation, 2010), SMEs constitute 99% of the total number of firms operating in each of these regions, significantly contributing to job creation, productivity and business innovation. In Africa, the number is somewhat similar, with SMEs constituting 90% of the nation's industry; however, they have managed to contribute to only 50% of the Gross Domestic Product (GDP) (UNEP Finance Initiative, 2007). Across nations, therefore, there are highly significant numbers of these particular enterprises.

These staggering facts, nevertheless, are often overlooked as big companies continuously exert their excessive business power and corporate public policy in order to maximise profits. Multinational firms, encouraged by inadequate supervision from relevant governing bodies, utilise their abundant monetary and non-monetary resources to such an extent that it led to the global economic crises in 1996 and 2006. As nations were unexpectedly caught up in such vicious cycles, many have survived the economic turmoil by recognising the positive value of having SMEs within their economic structure.

The growing appreciation of SMEs increased in 2005, which the United Nations declared as the International Year of Microcredit. Although closely related, microcredit is different from microfinance in that the former incorporates social mission, while the latter does not. The most prominent example of a financial institution providing microcredit is the Grameen Bank, established by 2006 Nobel Prize winner Muhammad Yunus in 1976. This bank relies on social networks and strong kinships between the credit provider and recipients to alleviate the economic welfare of borrowers. Microfinance relates to financial transactions between lender and borrower for purely economic purposes. Financial institutions, such as banks, grant credit to eligible applicants based on risk assessment conducted by the institutions. Banks provide the loaned money at a price, or interest rate, which not only reflects the risk level of the borrower, but also covers the cost of lending. Within this context, the nature of relationship between credit provider and recipients is that of supplier and consumer. Throughout this chapter, we address the issue of microfinance rather than microcredit.

The main purpose of credit assessment is to create a reliable risk profile of the prospective borrower. This is vital to ensure the full repayment of money granted to the debtor. If banks are unable to accurately ascertain the comprehensive risk attached to the loan applicant, but nevertheless accept the application, they are at risk of creating non-performing or default loans in their business portfolio. 'Non-performing' loans are those where there are discontinuous instalments within the existing loan periods, causing banks to incur expenses including collection costs. 'Default' refers to the borrower's inability to repay the loan altogether, resulting in loss from both unrecovered loan principal and interest. On the other hands, banks may reject applications that will actually have been performing loans they should have accepted. In this case, banks lose potential profits which can be described as a "lose-lose situation".

From the banks' perspective, borrowers can be categorised as Multinational Corporations (MNC), Medium to Large National Companies, SMEs and Individuals. Each group has its own characteristics in terms of business strategies and management. MNCs perform economic transactions both within their country of residence and worldwide. This requires systematic and standardised bookkeeping as they have to comply with local and international laws, and 'head office' rules and regulations. This is important as financial performance has to be comparable among offices. The difference between MNCs and Medium to Large National Companies is the extent of the business' scope. These latter firms operate within a country where they have their offices with possible expansion to several other countries, though not globally. Similar to MNCs, Medium to Large National companies have a strong track of financial records, mature accounting systems and orderly documentation.

Credit assessment methods, for the two types of companies described above, are well-established and standardized. The method of credit scoring is constructed around the risk profile of big companies. Thus, banks do not encounter significant problems in evaluating these companies' credit applications. The situation is similar to an individual loan, i.e., a loan application lodged by a person rather than an entity. Banks can use the systematic credit scorings with adjustments to reflect individual risk. One way to compensate for personal risk is the heavy reliance on collateral. Banks determine the value of the collateral to a degree that it ensures coverage of at least the principal loan amount.

SMEs, on the other hand, are companies with business activities limited by their capital and human resources. In general, SMEs' business is affected by factors similar to those affecting larger companies. These factors include, among others, changes in macroeconomic indicators such as GDP, Gross National Product (GNP), inflation rate and foreign exchange conversion rate. With the exception of foreign exchange conversion rate, which is relevant only for firms with export-import activities, other indicators have an effect on enterprises of every size and across sectors. In addition, there are internal and non-systematic risks that differ according to industry characteristics and firms' business strategies. SMEs' reaction to these types of risks is different. Here, it is crucial for banks to understand and foresee these risks in order to ensure performing loans. Within this context, banks are not equipped to make accurate credit risk assessments of SMEs.

Information used for credit assessment of SMEs is extracted from primary and secondary data. As briefly introduced earlier, SMEs are by and large unmethodical in their record keeping practices, resulting in vague and unreliable documented representation of the state of their business. In order to obtain a comprehensive and reliable description of SMEs' business risks, loan staffs conduct a series of interviews and observations with prospective borrowers as well as people within their business environment. Information gathered from these processes is used to construct risk profiles or verify facts and figures recorded in company books. This reflects the significant amount of qualitative information that needs to be incorporated into the risk assessment process.

The most well-used credit assessment method, namely credit scoring, presents problems when applied to SMEs. One obvious issue is the fact that credit scoring is constructed from historical credit performance of big companies that have a more systematic approach to record keeping. Throughout the years, studies have been conducted to improve the accuracy of credit scoring in particular and the credit risk assessment method in general. The next section explores these efforts in more detail.

## STUDIES OF RELEVANT WORKS

As mentioned earlier, credit assessment methods have been developed and perfected over the years. A well-functioning credit risk analysis is an integral part of a bank's business. Banks exercise credit management with the ultimate goal of maximizing their profits. Profits are acquired as a result of sound loan pricing, while losses are incurred when loan delinquency or default occurs. In order to ensure their profitability, banks perform rigorous procedures on relevant information related to potential borrowers that will lead to loan approval or rejection. As outlined earlier, credit scoring is the most preferred credit risk assessment method used. Benefits of credit scoring include low information cost (Frame, Srinivasan, & Woosley, 2001), faster decision making (Dinh & Kleimeier, 2007), consistency (Abdou, Pointon, & El-Masry, 2008; Yu, Wang, Wen, Lai, and He, 2008) and objectivity (Chye, Chin, & Peng, 2004; Yu, Wang, Wen, Lai, & He, 2008). However, this well-established credit scoring has imperfections when applied to information opaque companies such as SMEs. A majority of work addressing issues of credit scoring for SMEs has covered the development of credit scoring (e.g., Tsaih,

Liu, Liu, & Lien, 2004; Bensic, Sarlija, & Zekic-Susac, 2005; Šušteršič, Mramor, & Zupan, 2009) and the role of such techniques on small business lending (e.g., Longenecker, Moore, & Petty, 1997; de Young, Glennon, & Nigro, 2008). Aside from credit scoring, banks have been known to apply relationship lending on SMEs' loan applications, which depends heavily on nurtured relationships between the bank and customers. Advantages of this type of credit assessment relate to lower loan rates as well as credit rationing (Berger & Udell, 1995; Elsas & Krahnen, 1988), and less monitoring costs (Lehmann & Neuberger, 2001). However, the need to establish a working relationship over time is dependent on staffs' experience that results in a certain degree of subjectivity (Abdou, Pointon, & El-Masry, 2008; Dinh & Kleimeier, 2007). With respect to the aforementioned points of views, mainstream studies on credit risk assessment tend to focus on quantitative data collected from big companies. Nevertheless, the role of qualitative data on SMEs' credit risk assessment is crucial as expressed by Lehmann (2003). This qualitative data, which consists of, among others things, quality of management, subjective financial analysis, and business positioning, has limited value to add to credit ratings from a cost-benefit perspective. While there are limited studies on credit risk analysis performed either on qualitative data or on SMEs, the extensive studies on credit risk assessment, spanning the period from 1941 to 2010, can be categorised into three fields of study based on the methods applied: (1) statistical, (2) machine learning, and (3) hybrid.

## Statistical Methods

An evaluation of loan applications was carried out using judgmental lending before any move was made to standardize the process. Applicants were required to answer a set of questions delivered by loan officers to ascertain the applicants' character, capacity to pay, and their collateral (i.e., 3Cs). In other words, credit was granted (or declined) based on assessment on the 3Cs (Durand, 1941; Thomas, 2000) by experts such as loan staff. In subsequent years, the 3Cs evolved to the 4Cs and 5Cs, adding capital and conditions of economy as factors influencing the decisions. However, the need to pass on this expertise to non-experts and the competition amongst lenders (Hand & Henley, 1997) have forced the industry to consider applying statistical methods to produce an evaluation tool that best represents the experts' skills, i.e., credit scoring. Credit scoring is an estimation of a borrower's credit risk based on a number of quantifiable borrower characteristics (Dinh & Kleimeier, 2007). It is understood that credit scoring can be used individually or jointly with other types of lending assessment for decision making purposes. Some of these characteristics reflect the company's future financial ability and its prospect of going concern. Studies on financial distress have contributed to this field by proposing variables and techniques to foresee financial difficulties.

In the statistical field, the first attempt to formalise the credit scoring method was made by Durand (1941). The object of the study, which is personal loans, emulates features of SMEs' loans in loan amount (mostly less than USD 500) and non-bankable collateral. Durand applied a simple Efficiency Index (EI) on several risk characteristics that he reclassified into financial and non-financial factors. These classifications are formed based on two different surveys he conducted on banks and finance agencies. The results of these surveys showed that banks give a higher weighting to moral characteristics over others (financial, employment, personal and loan). The financial agencies put employment and past payment record above loan characteristics. Durand eliminated items under moral characters (including past payment record) due to unavailability of data. EI represents the number of bad loans that can be foregone without affecting good loans. This provides an insight into a characteristics' power to control credit risk. Later, Durand developed three rating formulas from these characteristics using simple statistical techniques. However, the author recognized the limitations of EI, amount of data, and number of samples. The formulae were derived from pre-calculated risk analysis, thereby limiting the applicability of the formulae. The failure to collect data about payment history and moral character raised issues about the study's reliability, particularly since further research (Hassler, 1963) showed that payment history is a significant factor in distinguishing performing from non-performing loans. Lastly, due to the small sample used in the study, namely a 100 good loans and 100 bad loans, the results would have limited generalisation ability. Nevertheless, the study instigated research on risks pertaining to credit. As a pioneer, Duran's work contributed to: (1) the selection of risk indicators relevant to consumer instalment credit from lenders, and (2) the development of credit rating formulae.

Within the next 30 years, work in related fields has been produced by various researchers. Initially, studies were more concerned with credit risks as a concept with applications of statistical measurement, while later they focused more on the accuracy of the credit rating method. The statistical methods that are commonly used include discriminant analysis, logistic (logit) regression, and others such as k-nearest neighbour (Yu, Wang, Lai, & Zhou, 2008). Each of the methods is briefly described below.

## Discriminant Analysis

Discriminant analysis is used to categorise or discriminate between two groups based on a set of variables. In the case of credit scoring, discriminant analysis is applied to distinguish good from bad borrowers. This method recognises the error that may arise from classifying a good applicant as a bad and vice versa. In the former case, banks reject the applicant and lose a possible profit, while the latter means that banks accept the applicant and incur a definite loss from loan delinquency or default. This method follows a linear rule; thus, it is often called linear discriminant analysis.

It is important to highlight a handful of studies due to their significant contributions to the field. One notable study by Myers (1963) considered rejected loans in the samples. These were included in order to test the ability of numerical scoring system as a decision-making tool for non-experts, in particular in the extreme cases of 'accept or reject' loans. In a further study, Myers proposed a four weighting system based on discriminant analysis applied to items that are scored using judgmental numerical scoring (Myers & Forgy, 1963). He concluded that discriminant analysis is as good a predictor as is an experienced loan officer and recommended further development of the method. Since then, discriminant analysis has proved to be a perennial method for assessing risks related to loans to the extent that it provides lenders with a tool to predict delinquent loans due to borrowers' financial difficulties.

Two other studies, arguably the most prominent in the financial distress domain, were performed by Beaver (1966) and Altman (1968). Beaver established the grounds for Altman and subsequent researchers by presenting an understanding on financial ratios as predictive tools for firms' performance. While Beaver concentrated on dealing with each ratio as a single feature, Altman offered a more systemic view. Using discriminant analysis, Altman used ratios in combination and was able to identify five financial ratios as main predictors of a company's financial distress. The fact that Altman used data collected from firms one year prior to their going bankrupt, as opposed to Beaver' five years, presents an indispensable applicability boundary. This implied that the model can perform best in short-term cases while companies are more likely to show signs of financial deterioration in the medium- to long-range time horizon. Despite this, the Z-Score theory and its variation, see (Altman, Haldeman, & Narayanan, 1977), remains as one of the most utilized models for assessing companies' distress (Altman, 1984) and contributes significantly to credit risk assessment. In subsequent years, financial distress was being used as a complementary tool for credit risk analysis.

Discriminant analysis has been criticised at length by Eisenbeis (1977), mainly on the assumption of multivariate normal distribution data, which is an unrealistic expectation in finance studies. Other apparent weaknesses include unequal dispersion, a priori population probability, unequal covariance matrices, preselected sample analysis, and effective measurement of discriminant analysis.

### Logistic Regression

Logistic regression was developed to overcome the binary problem of linear discriminant analysis. While the independent variables can comprise values from minus to positive infinite, the dependent variable is limited to a value of 0 to 1. Therefore, a logarithmic function is applied to the dependent variable, creating a logistic regression approach. While many studies use logistic regression in comparison with other statistical and/or machine learning methods, one particular work of Wiginton (1980) stands out as the pioneer. In his study, Wiginton used maximum likelihood with logistic regression and compared this with discriminant analysis. Wiginton argued that maximum likelihood is a more appropriate technique for discrete data such as demographic information than is the linear discriminant model. The result showed that logistic regression outperformed discriminant analysis. One important finding from this study was the notion that qualitative information plays a role in credit granting decision making.

### Others

Other statistical methods include the k-nearest-neighbour (k-NN) method, a nonparametric pattern recognition approach. According to Henley and Hand (1996), the method is appropriate for credit assessment problems due to its ability to model risk irregularities over feature space, fitness to handle multidimensional data, and practicality. The researchers recognised the importance of establishing a metric to define the distance between two points that will improve classification performance, and suggested the adjusted standard Euclidean metric for this study. The result of this work shows that k-NN was able to produce the lowest expected bad risk rate.

## Machine Learning Methods

The rapid development of Machine Learning has generated interest, since it provides solutions to the aforementioned statistical limitations, including linearity problems, and offers a more efficient and accurate process. Discussions on machine learning methods are categorised as those on Neural Networks, Support Vector Machines, Decision Tree, and Hybrid Methods and confined to the use of these techniques on credit risk assessment. For further information on the technical aspects of these techniques, we refer interested readers to books on Machine Learning (e.g., Michalski, Carbonell, & Mitchell, 1983; Mitchell, 1997) and Support Vector Machines (e.g., Cristianini & Shawe-Taylor, 2000; Alpaydin, 2004).

### Neural Networks (NN)

Neural Networks (NN) is a method inspired by the way that the human brain performs. It comprises neurons that are working in layers where information is communicated. Studies in the application of NN to the financial sector can be found as early as 1990 (Wong, Bodnovich, & Selvi, 1997), with many of them focusing on financial distress detection. One of the earlier works on credit risk was done by Jensen (1992), showing the classification ability of Back-propagation Neural Networks (BPN) at around 80%. Jensen compared this result with that from the credit scoring model, i.e., discriminant analysis. He applied relevant variables to develop a credit scoring method, namely type of home ownership, years of employment, type of occupation, financial standing in commercial stores and banks, as well as credibility with credit bureau. At this first attempt, it was found that NN is better at classifying good loans than bad ones. However, at later stages, the results were ambivalent with some showing NN superiority in classifying bad loans (Angelini, di Tollo, & Roli, 2008; Desai, Crook, & Overstreet, 1996; Malhotra & Malhotra, 2003), while other results indicate traditional statistical methods, such as LDA, have better predictive ability on good loans (Yobas, Crook, & Ross, 2000). Over the course of time, studies comparing traditional statistical methods with NN have a definite preference towards one over the other. While some clearly indicate the prevalence of statistical techniques, as described before, others incline towards NN (Abdou, Pointon, & El-Masry, 2008; Malhotra & Malhotra, 2003; West, 2000) and a small number of studies show mixed results (Desai, Crook, & Overstreet, 1996; Lee & Sung-Chang, 2000).

Throughout the years, there are studies on credit scoring carried out to improve NN performance. Among others, Gao, Zhou, Gao, and Shi (2006) utilized a Structuring Particle Swarm Optimization approach and found that it increased the classification accuracy performance of NN in comparison to Back-propagation (BP) and Genetic Algorithm (GA). In addition, Rui, Li, and Jun (2010) developed an improved BP algorithm to increase the NN' robustness and performance on personal credit scoring.

## Support Vector Machines

The Multilayer Perceptron (MLP) and Support Vector Machine (SVM) for credit classification emerged as favourable techniques over NN for credit classification. The use of SVM, in particular, is intended to overcome the over-fitting drawbacks of NN (Lee, 2007; Li, Shiue, & Huang, 2006). Aside from SVM, a neuro-fuzzy application, with its 'IF-THEN' rules, is also suggested (Piramuthu, 1999) to curtail the black-box limitation, i.e., the inability of NN to provide justification to decisions they produced. SVM outperforms both traditional statistics methods (Bellotti & Crook, 2009; Lee, 2007) and other machine learning techniques (Chen & Shih, 2006; Li, Shiue, & Huang, 2006; Huang, 2004; Zhang & Hui, 2009). Nevertheless, SVM has its limitations related to the small input feature and parameter setting (Zhou, Lai, & Yu, 2010), sensitivity to noise and outliers (Wei, Li, & Chen, 2007), and complex computation (Wei, Li, & Chen, 2007; Yu, Lai, Wang, & Zhou, 2007). In order to overcome these drawbacks, Wei, Li, and Chen (2007) suggested the use of mixture of kernels, while others (Hao, Chi, Yan, & Yue, 2010; Wang, Wang, & Lai, 2005; Yu, Lai, Wang, & Zhou, 2007) proposed a least squares fuzzy approach to SVM. These studies demonstrated the satisfactory performance of SVM on credit assessment. Taking into account the existing boundaries related to each method, knowledge within this field has advanced to hybrid techniques with better performance.

## Decision Tree Learning

Decision tree learning (DT) is an effective tool for decision making processes. It comprises nodes with attributes and leaf nodes that reflect the classifications involved. This particular method is useful for generating rules that eventually can be utilised to explain black-box models (Yu, Wang, Lai, & Zhou, 2008). Within this context, Daubie (2002) applied DT and rough sets to reconfirm credit decisions made by the bank. DT performed better in comparison with the rough sets method.

## Hybrid Methods

Hybrid methods are applied with the emphasis on assembling the "perfect" combination of methods that produce the best result. Hybrid methods that have been proven as improved techniques are the hybrid neural discriminant model (Lee, Chiu, Lu, & Chen, 2002), GA-BP based hybrid NN (Wang, Yin, & Jiang, 2008), hybrid SVM (Chen, Ma, & Ma, 2009), a combination of logistic regression with neural networks (Tsai & Chen, 2005), artificial NN and multivariate adaptive regression splines (Zhou, Zhang, & Jiang, 2008), rough sets and DT, and integration of rough set theory and SVM (Yu, Wang, Wen, Lai, & He, 2008). Others have produced promising results, including models such as Genetic Algorithms-SVM (Huang, Chen, & Wang, 2007).

Many of the hybrid methods are designed to test features that will improve the method's accuracy. Lee, Chiu, Lu, & Chen (2002) aimed to provide statistically supported input to NN. Wang, Yin, and Jiang (2008) strove to advance NN learning ability. Chen, Ma and Ma (2009) and Lee and Chen (2005) focused on feature selection. Lastly, Zhou, Zhang and Jiang (2008) used rough sets and DT to extract association rules efficiently.

## Discussions

The aforementioned studies were carried out using quantitative data from financial institutions that have big companies as clients. In addition, due to the experimental nature of this machine learning research, the number of variables tested is small, from as few as 3 to a maximum of 24 variables. Most variables are either financial ratios or a combination of financial and non-financial performance indicators. They are neither justified nor utilised as an instrument to measure credit risk.

Studies on SMEs' credit risk assessment have been scarce and relatively balanced with regards to the methods applied, with both statistical (Altman & Sabato, 2007; Dinh & Kleimeier, 2007) and machine learning (Derelioğlu, Gürgen, & Okay, 2009; Wu & Wang, 2000) methods demonstrating good predictive ability. In order to overcome the problem of non-systematic bookkeeping practices and lack of valid and reliable financial information problem, Wu and Wang (2000) proposed the use of NN. Another study that employed NN for SMEs was carried out by Dima and Vasilache (2009), focusing on the non-performing loans. Using MLP, NN application showed moderate accuracy in classifying micro and small enterprises that managed make repayments on time and those that failed to do so.

Altman and Sabato (2007) recognized the role of qualitative data when evaluating SME portfolios, suggesting that banks should use a combination of methods (i.e., scoring systems with judgemental) specifically developed for SMEs. Dinh and Kleimer (2007) provided a thorough overview on using qualitative information together with quantitative information in predicting loan default. This qualitative information encompasses aspects such as gender, types of collateral and duration of loan as well as factors which are country-specific. Nevertheless, this qualitative information is different to that suggested by Berger. Berger was referring to data collected and presented in accordance with loan officers' subjectivity that will complement the credit scoring. Dinh and Kleimer, on the other hand, refer to non-numerical data.

Based on the literature survey, both statistical and machine learning methods have shown excellent ability in classifying good/accepted and bad/rejected loans from historical data. The models were effectively applied to transactional lending type with quantitative data such as those related to firms' financial performance and credit history. On the other hand, judgmental lending such as that performed by banks with regards to SMEs' loan applications has not been well-represented in existing studies. As described at the beginning, this particular lending type relates to qualitative data, which is unstructured and complex. Hence, the challenge is to develop a technique that incorporates and analyses qualitative information together with quantitative information so that the credit risk of loan applicants (SMEs) can be accurately determined. Because qualitative data is available mainly in free form text (often referred to as unstructured data), this creates complications, since most of the well developed and explored statistical and machine learning/data mining methods are mainly applicable to relational data with well-defined structure. Moreover, the available data mining techniques for analysing free form text are still underdeveloped with many unresolved challenges.

## PROPOSED METHOD

In this section, we describe the process for presenting qualitative information together with quantitative information in one format. First, we rationalise our use of XML to represent both types of information in a domain-oriented way. Next, we highlight the particular credit parameters applied by Indonesian banks to lay the groundwork for subsequent sections. We then describe the problem of frequent subtree mining, discussing the different subtree types and support definitions. The section concludes with an overview of some existing frequent subtree mining algorithms.

### Motivation for Using XML

The loan application forms are designed to provide relevant information for the loan granting process. In addition to personal information (e.g., company's name, address, contact details, etc), these forms also capture the essence of applicants' creditworthiness. Banks follow certain guidelines when ascertaining the level of risk, which will be explored in more detail in the next section. However, they have autonomy when designing their own forms regarding the information details that they require. In the case of SMEs' loan applications, assessment is performed on information drawn from not only administrative documents, but also from observations of interactions and interviews. This emphasizes the role of subjectivity and qualitative information within this particular type of business. Thus, relationships between data have to be preserved since they have particular meaning as a whole. Within this context, XML can represent the relationships better than the tabular form. As we have established, data on loan applications can be found in both relational and textual databases, which represent the data objects in structured and unstructured form, respectively. The structured form has discrete (e.g., financial values and ratios) as well as continuous (e.g., income) values. There is a need to represent qualitative information found in textual (unstructured) form in a data format where some structure may be expected. In order to represent the qualitative information found in text, together with quantitative information available in a structured form, we use XML to capture domain specific terms and effectively organize (contextualise) the available information. This will maximize the information that is expressed by the document and the potential knowledge that can be discovered through analysis.

In this work we have generated the XML template by analysing the existing textual documents containing loan applications in order to determine the factors that are usually assessed in such documents. The template was then developed with the guidance of the loan officers and the structure and the information will be discussed in the next section. The XML was chosen because it is an intermediate representation between structured and unstructured data. It is referred to as semi-structured because it may embed unstructured data into a partial structure (commonly known as XML Schema). In our future work we will investigate a means by which the related unstructured information from text can be automatically converted into the XML format. There are several text-to-XML Annotators such as UIMA (Ferrucci & Lally, 2004), GLOSS (Kaye, 2006), PCFG parser (Klein & Manning, 2003), and XI (Marchal, 2002). Typically, such annotators use a data dictionary or a gazette for information extraction from a text of named entities (e.g., persons, organizations) and simple relations between terms (e.g., works-for). We aim to use the PCFG parser (Klein & Manning, 2003) backend that uses both statistical and rule-based annotators and can produce phrase structure trees that can be effectively presented in XML. To enhance their capability, techniques such as PCFG can be enhanced by further annotating the documents based on domain ontology. This permits disambiguation of terms through concept relationships in the same segment of text. The annotators will extract relevant tokens from a document and these will be mapped to a small subset of the attributes for determining matches in semi-structured data (defined XML template). To summarise, the benefits of representing the available qualitative and quantitative information using XML format are: the available information is enriched and organized in a domain-specific way, the related attributes are contextualised under a common domain aspect, partial unstructured information can be embedded within the predefined structure (template) and text to XML annotators can be used to automatically arrive at an intermediate representation of the available unstructured information.

## Construction of XML Template

As stated earlier, this section introduces the distinct types of information that banks collect with regard to loan applications. Banks are required to collate financial and non-financial data that best depict the prospective borrowers' ability to maintain loan repayments throughout the loan duration. The information as a whole is not limited to determining the present financial capacity of an applicant; it can also predict the longevity of the applicant's business. From previous sections, it is understood that large and small size companies have different business styles. Large companies operate using an organised and established system, while small companies rely on leadership and organisational adaptability to change. Thus, banks can utilise valid and reliable data from large companies, but have to perform more rigorous risk assessment of non-standard data collected from interviews and observations. This type of data is subjective in nature and needs to be structured in order to be assessed in a consistent manner for all applicants.

In this chapter, we utilise selected information from Indonesian banks. The Republic of Indonesia Law Number 10 Year 1998 on Banking Practices requires Indonesian banks to apply the 5Cs good lending concept to all assessments of loan applications submitted by prospective borrowers. The concept is applied regardless of the size of the firm which means that it is applied equally to both large and small companies. These 5Cs are: *character*, *capacity*, *capital*, *collateral*, and *conditions* (of economy). Of these five Cs, four are quantitative data, while Character is considered as qualitative information about prospective borrowers. Nevertheless, banks are relying on character more than on any other Cs when they perform credit risk assessment for SMEs. The characteristics of the 5Cs as determined by the Central Bank of Indonesia are as follows:

1. "Character" provides a comprehensive profile of the prospective borrower's personal qualities and traits. Assessment is based on customers' positive characteristics. Loan officers should clearly describe applicants' willingness to work hard, attitude towards responsibilities, openness, honesty, persistence, moral, sparing, efficient, not having gambling habits, consultative and other traits that the officer considers relevant for decision making. The comprehensive profile of applicants' characters is constructed from various interviews with business partners, neighbours, employees and, to some extent, members of their family. Loan staffs are required to record their understanding and perception of the applicant's character once this rigorous interview process has been concluded. The level of soundness of this information depends on the type of loan staff as well. A prudent and meticulous staff member may produce a different profile for

the same prospective borrower in comparison to an imprudent and inaccurate loans officer.

2. "Capacity" represents applicants' managerial skills, in particular their ability to manage the firms' resources and direct them into income generating activities. This information is extracted from the company's financial statements, namely Profit and Loss Statement and Balance Sheet. Loan officers perform the necessary analysis that will measure applicants' ability to repay the loan. As mentioned earlier, most SMEs cannot provide the bank with systematic financial records, therefore loan staff has to construct the numbers based on site interviews and observations. For this capacity element, banks have to show the applicants' financial performance, expressed in ratios, within the last three years. This will be used to predict applicants' future financial capacity. Banks also take into account the industry and sub-industry in which companies are operating. Thus, separate standards for the ratios are determined for each sub-industry. There are 9 industries and 41 sub-industries identified in Indonesia with 6 financial ratios as proxy to financial performance. These ratios are current ratio, total debt to equity ratio, earnings before interest, tax, depreciation and amortization (EBITDA) to total debt ratio, EBITDA to interest ratio, earnings after tax (EAT) to sales ratio and sales growth ratio. For example, the cut-off point for EBITDA to total debt ratio for food crops SMEs is 39.7, while for plantation SMEs is 49.03. Both agriculture and mining arc sub-industries of the agriculture industry.
3. "Capital" refers to prospective borrowers' dependency on external financing. Capital, as presented on the Balance Sheet, is divided into three categories, namely Stockholders' Equity/Owners' Capital, Bank Loan and Third-Party Loan. The capital structure of a company reflects management's responsibility and attitude to risks. In principal, loan staffs perform a similar evaluation process as with "capacity". Ratios that are used to describe "capital" are included in the "capacity"; thus they are not displayed separately in most cases. The value of these ratios is also sub-industry sensitive. For example, acceptable debt to equity ratio for oil and gas SMEs is 2.75, while it is 10 for leasing SMEs.
4. "Collateral" indicates the debtors' ability to repay their loans in case of default. Collateral is categorised as principal and additional. Principal collateral is mandatory and commonly in the form of objects or projects that are financed by the loan. Additional collateral is non-mandatory and is decided based on loan officers' discretion. Information on collateral is divided into type and value of collateral. When collateral includes the applicant's personal assets such as house, vehicle or land, it is accepted as such only when accompanied by relevant documents or licenses. Banks have a standardised requirement for values of collateral. For example, for a loan amount above IDR 100 million, a full-licensed house has to have a market value that covers 120% of the principal loan amount requested. Vehicles with a market value that covers 70% of the principal loan amount are accepted.
5. "Condition of Economy" is an analysis performed by loan officers to ascertain the possibility of certain economic events which may impact on the borrowers' business. These economic events include national and international monetary, banking and financial policies. Conditions of economy is rarely presented in the loan application form; nevertheless, the loan officer has to consider condition of economy when s/he prepares the report.

We have used the small number of document instances provided by our industry partner (Indonesian bank) to produce an XML template. These instances are also used as the basis for generating the synthetic XML database, in addition to some constraints on the allowed attribute value combinations (credit parameters) obtained from the loan officers of the bank. A portion of the XML template is shown in Figure 1. In the developed XML template, there are a total of 53 attributes which store additional and more specific information (e.g., industry, sub-industry, marketing strategies, etc.), and therefore we have reported in Figure 1 a simplification of the actual template. It shows some of the stored information and the possible set of values each attribute can have, but of course each XML instance will only have one of those values for each attribute. Please note that the ratios within the financial report in the document instances have actually specific values that correspond to the standard for a particular industry and corresponding sub-industry, and these were obtained from the bank.

In Figure 1, we present a small section of the XML template that best represents the issue at hand. The three elements, personalinfo, customerprofile and financialreport are significant since they depict the consumer's profile related to funds requirements, business and financial performance of the company. These are three major factors that must be considered before arriving at a loan granting decision. Each contains attributes that are only partially presented here due to space constraints. In our original XML template, personalinfo has 9 attributes, while customerprofile and financialreport have 34 and 8 attributes, respectively. Element personalinfo is associated with business risk and requested loan scheme. Most of the information is available from the loan application form, such as the principal loan amount, loan period, purpose of loan and industry in which prospective borrowers do business. Based on these written

*Figure 1. XML template (part of), indicating sets of possible values for each attribute separated by commas*

```
<?xml version="1.0" encoding="UTF-8" ?>
<creditapplication>
  <creditriskindicators>
    <personalinfo>
      <industryrisk>very low,low,moderate,high,very high</industryrisk>
      <creditinformation>
        <principal>up to IDR 50 million,more than IDR 50 million up to IDR 100 million</principal>
        <duration>up to 1 year,more than 1 year to 2 years,more than 2
                  years to 3 years,more than 3 years to 4 years,more than 4 years to 5 years
        </duration>
      </creditinformation>
    </personalinfo>
      ...
    <customerprofile>
        ...
      <integrity>high,medium,low</integrity>
      <capacity>
        <salesperyear>below IDR 300 million,above IDR 300 million to IDR
                      2.5 billion,above IDR 2.5 billion to IDR 50 billion
        </salesperyear>
        <eatpermonth>less than 0.2 of sales,between 0.2 to 0.4 of sales,more than 0.4 of sales
        </eatpermonth>
      </capacity>
    </customerprofile>
    <financialreport>
      <currentratio>below standard,above standard</currentratio>
      ...
      <salesgrowthratio>below standard,above standard</salesgrowthratio>
    </financialreport>
  </creditriskindicators>
  <creditriskassessment>accept,accept with considerations,reject</creditriskassessment>
</ creditapplication >
```

facts, supplied by applicants, loan officers categorize each according to a pre-defined value. These categorisations differ from one bank to another. With regard to industry risk, loan officers are guided by sets of indicators developed in accordance with industry and sub-industry business features.

A customer profile reflects the borrower's capacity and willingness to fulfil his/her loan repayment obligations. The value of attribute "integrity" for each applicant is assigned after various interviews with the applicant, his/her family and business partners. Loan officers must be able to refer to their written report to validate their choice. This attribute is the one most prone to subjectivity where emotions could play a role. Another attribute that contributes to a customer profile is his/her capacity to repay the loan as shown by the company's annual sales and monthly EAT. Assessment on capacity is basically carried out on the basis of sales as can be seen from values of EAT per month. This is due to the significant role of having a business that is capable of maintaining its selling power in order to ensure the continuous flow of cash.

The financial report provides a picture of what the company was and is financially capable of. As mentioned earlier, five financial ratios are used. Loan officers can obtain this data from financial statements when they are available. In the case of unreliable or unavailable data, loan officers have to generate the numbers based on their on-site visit and third party valuation. In these cases, the ratios can be inconsistent and misleading.

Based on the above illustration, the element customerprofile is the one with the most qualitative information. Loan staffs are required to explore and ascertain the level of integrity of prospective borrowers. In fact, for SMEs, integrity is the most important factor in determining the success of an application. Although the applicant is unable to show good standing in terms of financial capacity, banks are willing to give credit provided that the applicant has high integrity. Therefore, it is in the banks' best interest to ensure that interviews are carried out in a standardized manner. In our case, this was done through the pre-defined XML template so that the loan officers are able choose the values from the set of predetermined standardized values.

## Frequent Subtree Mining

The purpose of this section is to introduce the reader to tree-related concepts necessary for understanding the data mining part of the proposed method. For a more detailed overview of the frequent subtree mining field including various implementation issues and algorithm comparisons, we refer the interested reader to (Chi, Muntz, Nijssen, & Kok, 2004; Tan, Hadzic, Dillon, & Chang, 2008a; Hadzic, Tan, & Dillon, 2011). We will use the simplified example of the XML template from Figure 1 for illustrative purposes. To see the parallelism between an XML document and a tree structure, and how all of the information in a n XML document can be effectively modelled using a rooted ordered labelled tree please refer to (Feng, Dillon, Weigand, & Chang, 2003). In Figure 2, we represent the XML template (part of) from Figure 1 as a tree. Please note that for the attributes which can have a value associated with them we use '(x)' after the name which corresponds to any value from the set of possible values from Figure 1.

A *tree* is a special type of graph where no cycles are allowed. It consists of a set of *nodes* (or vertices) that are connected by *edges*. Each edge has two nodes associated with it. A *path* is defined as a finite sequence of edges and in a tree there is a single unique path between any two nodes. A *rooted tree* has its top-most node defined as the *root* that has no incoming edges and for every other node there is a path between the root and that node. A node $u$ is said to be a *parent* of node $v$, if there is a directed edge from $u$ to $v$. Node $v$ is then said to be a *child* of node $u$. Nodes with no children are referred to as *leaf nodes* and

*Figure 2. XML template from Figure 1 as a tree*

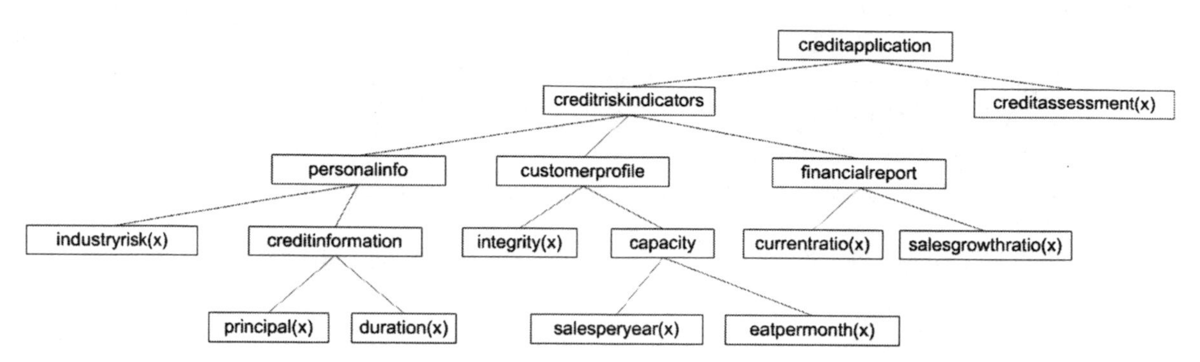


are also called internal nodes. Nodes with the same parent are called *siblings*. The *ancestors* of a node $u$ are the nodes on the path between the root and $u$, excluding $u$ itself. The *descendants* of a node $v$ can then be defined as those nodes that have $v$ as their ancestor. A tree is *ordered* if the children of each internal node are ordered from left to right.

The problem of *frequent subtree mining* can be generally stated as: given a tree database $T_{DB}$ and minimum support threshold ($\sigma$), find all subtrees that occur at least $\sigma$ times in $T_{DB}$. A rooted labelled tree can be denoted as $T(v_0, V, L, E)$, where: $v_0 \in V$ is the *root* vertex, $V$ is the set of *vertices* or *nodes*, $L$ is the set of *labels* of vertices, for any vertex $v \in V$, $L(v)$ denotes the label of $v$; and $E = \{(x,y) \mid x,y \in V\}$ is the set of *edges* in the tree. In an ordered tree, there is an ordering specified for the children of each vertex, or in other words, an order is imposed on all the sibling nodes in the tree. When using the above notation in this paper, we will always refer to ordered trees unless otherwise specified. Please note that the $T_{DB}$ can correspond either to a collection of independent trees (often referred to as transactions) or a single large tree. In the data mining field, a transaction corresponds to a set of one or more items obtained from a finite item domain, and a dataset is a collection of transactions (Bayardo, Agrawal, & Gunopulos, 1999). Hence, in the context of a tree database, a transaction would correspond to a fragment of the database tree whereby an independent instance (or records) is described. In the context of work in this paper, a transaction would correspond to the XML document instance that describes a single loan application. Some properties of the tree from Figure 2 are as follows:

- $v_0$ = 'creditapplication'
- $L$ = {creditapplication, creditsikindicators, personalinfo, …, eatpermonth(x), creditassesement(x)}, $|L| = 16$;
- $E$ = {(creditapplication, credistriskindicators), (creditriskindicators, personalinfo), (personalinfo, industryrisk(x)), …, (creditapplication, creditassesement(x))}, $|E| = 15$;
- The parent of node 'capacity' is 'customerprofile', while node 'creditriskindicators' and 'creditapplication' are its ancestors;
- The leaf nodes are: 'industryrisk(x)', 'principal(x)', 'duration(x)', integrity(x)', 'salesperyear(x)', 'eatpermonth(x)', 'currentratio(x)', 'salesgrowthratio(x)' and 'creditassessment(x)';
- The internal nodes are: 'creditriskindicators', 'personalinfo', 'creditinformation' 'customerprofile', 'capacity' and 'financialreport'.

Driven by different application needs, there are number of different subtrees that can be sought in the general frequent subtree mining framework defined above. The two most commonly mined types of subtrees are induced and embedded. An induced subtree preserves the parent-child relationships of each node in the original tree, while an embedded subtree allows a parent in the subtree to be an ancestor in the original tree. Formal definitions follow:

Given a tree $S = (V_S, L_S, E_S)$ and tree $T = (V_T, L_T, E_T)$, $S$ is an *ordered induced subtree* of $T$, if and only if (1) $V_S \subseteq V_T$; (2) $L_S \subseteq L_T$ and $L_S(v) = L_T(v)$; (3) $E_S \subseteq E_T$; and (4) the left to right ordering of sibling nodes in the original tree is preserved.

Given a tree $S = (V_S, L_S, E_S)$ and tree $T = (V_T, L_T, E_T)$, $S$ is an *ordered embedded subtree* of $T$, if and only if (1) $V_S \subseteq V_T$; (2) $L_S \subseteq L_T$ and $L_S(v) = L_T(v)$; (3) *if* $(v_1,v_2) \in E_S$ *then* $parent(v_2) = v_1$ in $S$ and $v_1$ is ancestor of $v_2$ in $T$; and (4) the left to right ordering of sibling nodes in the original tree is preserved.

In an *unordered subtree*, the left-to-right ordering among the sibling nodes does not need to be preserved. Hence, if we were defining the induced and embedded subtrees for the unordered case, then condition 4 can be removed from the definitions above. Examples of different subtree types of the tree from Figure 2 are given in Figure 3. Please note that induced subtrees are also embedded but not vice versa.

Within the current frequent subtree mining framework to determine a support of a subtree $st$, generally denoted as $\sigma(st)$, two support definitions have been used, namely, transaction-based support and occurrence match support (also referred to as weighted support) (Zaki, 2005; Chi, Muntz, Nijssen, & Kok, 2004). Another more recently proposed support definition is hybrid support (Hadzic, Tan, Dillon, & Chang, 2007) that combines both support definitions to extract more specialized subtree patterns with respect to the chosen support threshold.

When using the *transaction-based support* (*TS*) definition, the support ($\sigma$) of a subtree $st$, denoted as $\sigma_{tr}(st)$ in a tree database $T_{DB}$ is equal to the number of transactions (records or instances) in $T_{DB}$ that contain at least one occurrence of subtree $st$. Let the notation $st \prec tr$, denote the support of subtree $st$ by transaction $tr$, then, $st \prec tr = 1$ whenever $tr$ contains at least one occurrence of $st$, and 0 otherwise. Suppose that there are $N$ transactions $tr_1$ to $tr_N$ of tree in $T_{DB}$, the $\sigma(st)$ in $T_{DB}$ is defined as:

$$\sum_{i=1}^{N} st \prec tr_i$$

The *occurrence-match support* (*OC*) takes the repetition of items in a transaction into account and counts the subtree occurrences in the database as a whole. Hence, for *OC*, the support ($\sigma$) of a

*Figure 3. Example subtrees of the tree from Figure 2*

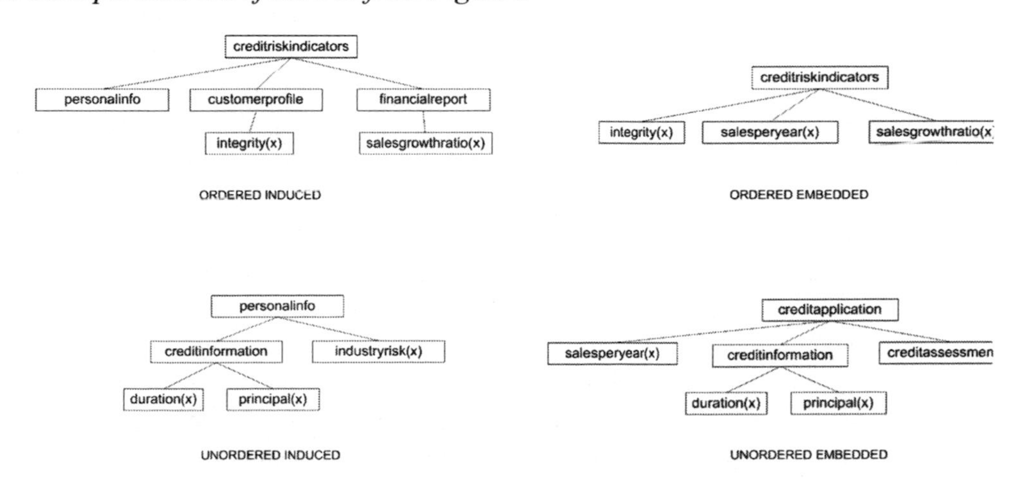

subtree *st*, in a tree database $T_{DB}$ is equal to the total number of occurrences of *st* in all transactions in $T_{DB}$.

The *hybrid support* (*HS*) definition can be seen as a transactional support that also takes into account the intra-transactional occurrence of a subtree. The support threshold is set as $x|y$, where $x$ denotes the minimum number of transactions that must support subtree *st*, and $y$ denotes the minimum number of times that *st* has to occur in those $x$ transactions. *HS* provides extra information about the intra-transactional occurrences of a subtree. Hence, using *HS* threshold of $x|y$, a subtree is considered frequent if it occurs in $x$ transactions and it occurs at least $y$ times in each of the $x$ transactions. Therefore, while two values $x$ and $y$ are used as input, the support of a subtree is determined based upon the single value $x$ that corresponds to the number of transactions in which that subtree has occurred at least $y$ times.

To alleviate the complexity problem and reduce the number of candidate subtrees that need to be enumerated, some work has shifted toward the mining of maximal and closed subtrees (Chehreghani, Rahgozar, Lucas, & Chehreghani, 2007; Chi, Yang, & Muntz, 2005). A closed subtree is a subtree for which none of its proper supertrees has the same support, while for a maximal subtrees, no supertrees exist that are frequent. No information is lost since the complete set of frequent subtrees can be obtained from closed subtrees (including support information) and maximal subtrees. We next provide some formal definitions for maximal and closed subtrees, and the term subtree used here can correspond to any of the different subtree types as defined earlier.

A subtree $st_1$ is a proper superset of another (sub)tree $st_2$, denoted as $st_2 \subset st_1$, if and only if (1) $st_2 \prec st_1$ (i.e., $st_2$ is a subtree from $st_1$ and (2) $size(st_1) > size(st_2)$.

Given a set of frequent subtrees, *ST* from a tree database $T_{DB}$, a subtree $st \in ST$ is a frequent *maximal* subtree if there are no proper supersets of *st* in *ST*. For a given support, the set of all frequent subtrees can be obtained from the set of maximal frequent subtrees, but the support information will not be available.

Given a set of frequent subtrees, *ST* from $T_{DB}$, where a support of a subtree $st_1$ is indicated as $sup(st_1)$, a subtree $st_1 \in ST$ is a frequent *closed* subtree if and only if there is no other subtree $st_2$ in *ST*, where $st_2$ is a proper superset of *S* and $sup(st_1) = sup(st_2)$.

## Choosing the Right Subtree Types and Support Definitions

This section discusses the differences and implications behind mining different subtree types under different support definitions for the credit scoring application domain. A more detailed discussion about general knowledge management can be found in (Hadzic, Dillon, & Chang, 2008). It is largely governed by the way in which the available information is organized in an XML document and several different scenarios are discussed. Here, we focus on scenarios where the data comes from a single financial institution, i.e., bank, while individual bank locations are referred to as branches. We start with the difference in the subtree types chosen.

Generally speaking, the mining of ordered or unordered subtree types depends on whether the information in the XML document is known to be stored in a particular order. While most XML documents can be modelled using an ordered labelled tree, in many applications the order of the sibling-nodes is considered irrelevant to the task and is often not available. If one is interested in comparing different document structures, it is very common for the order of sibling nodes to differ while the information contained in the structure is essentially the same. In these cases, the mining of unordered subtrees is much more suitable. All matching sub-structures will be returned with the only difference being that the order of sibling nodes is not used as an additional candidate grouping criterion. Hence, the main difference when it comes to the mining of unordered subtrees is that the order of sibling nodes of a subtree can be changed and the resulting tree is still considered the same. On the other hand, in an ordered subtree, the left-to-right ordering of the sibling nodes in the original tree has to be preserved and is used as an additional candidate subtree grouping criterion. In the current application domain, the format and ordering of the information contained in individual loan application data coming from one branch is expected to be the same, which means that mining of ordered subtrees will be most suitable. However, if the collected data originates from different branches, then it is possible that the information contained in individual loan applications from different branches is found in different format or order, or did not follow the same standard. It is likely that this can occur especially if the information representation has not been standardized across branches. Given this uncertainty, it would be more suitable to mine unordered subtrees, because if a frequent relationship between data object characteristics exists, it will be detected (grouped to the same candidate subtree) even if the order of sibling nodes reflecting that relationship is different. The common characteristics of a particular type of loan application would still be found, while if there were a restriction on the order of sibling nodes being the same, then this common characteristic could be missed if the support threshold is not low enough. Even if detected, it may give the wrong information about the frequency of the detected relationship, as we would not know whether the same relationship occurred in different loan applications in different order.

Another choice to be made is whether one should be mining induced or embedded subtrees. The main trade-off is that while embedded subtrees may detect some relationships/associations that exist deep within a tree structure, some important contextual information could be lost. Even though in our simplified example in Figures 1-3, there are no repetitions of nodes with the same label, it may well be the case that the same financial ratio is present for both capacity and financial report information. In this case, if an association were found without the nodes (capacity and financial report) that indicate the particular context, then one would not know which ratios the detected association is referring to and the pattern would be considered as unreliable for decision support. Hence, in this case the mining of induced subtrees would be preferred as the context information would be preserved in the pattern as no ancestor-descendant relationships are allowed (see definitions provided earlier). On the other hand, if one of the nodes that lies on the path between an ancestor and a descendant node is itself unlikely to be frequent, then the potentially frequent associations between the two nodes lying at different levels would not be detected from the induced subtree set. In this case, embedded subtrees would be preferred. In our template this is not the case and hence, the mining of induced subtrees is sufficient.

We now discuss the implications behind choosing different support definitions. The transactional support would be the most preferred choice as naturally the data would be organized in such a way that each loan application is represented as a separate transaction (record) within the XML database. This is typically the case when analyzing a set of loan applications from a single branch, as the aim is to discover any particular relationship or association that occurs in a sufficient number of transactions. Occurrence match support is not particularly useful as, even if there are repetitions of relationships in a transaction, one would desire an indication of the number of cases that support that relationship. On the other hand, hybrid support can be useful if the information from multiple branches of the same bank are stored in a single database, and the records from one branch are all captured in one transaction. In this case, a user may be interested in finding associations that have occurred in all of the branches and are repeated at least in a number of cases in each branch. For example, if there were 200 branches, and the user wants to find all associations that occurred in at least 15 cases in each branch, the hybrid support threshold would be set to 200|15 to satisfy the user query.

## Overview of Some Existing Closed/ Maximal Subtree Mining Algorithms

In this section, we overview some of the existing algorithms for mining closed/maximal subtrees, as such an algorithm is used in our experimental study. Similarly to frequent itemset/sequence mining, closed/maximal subtree mining is driven by the complexity issues associated with the enumeration of a complete set of frequent subtrees. This paper is more focused on the application of such algorithms, rather than on the theoretical and implementation issues that must be considered when developing frequent subtree mining algorithms. For further insight into these, please refer to (Chi, Muntz, Nijssen, & Kok, 2004; Tan et al., 2008a, Hadzic, Tan, & Dillon, 2011), where a number of popular algorithms are described in detail and various theoretical and implementation issues are discussed.

The first algorithm that appeared in the context of closed/maximal subtree mining was Pathjoin (Xiao, Yao, Li, & Dunham, 2003), developed to extract all maximal ordered induced subtrees. The algorithm works by first extracting all maximal frequent paths and the joining of the paths to form the set of frequent subtrees. The frequent subtrees that have a superset in the set (i.e., are not maximal) are pruned. Pathjoin uses a compact data structure, FST-Forest, which is a compressed representation of the tree and is used for finding the maximal paths. CMTreeMiner algorithm (Chi, Yang, Xia, & Muntz, 2004) is an algorithm developed for mining both closed and maximal ordered induced subtrees without first discovering all frequent subtrees. It uses a data structure called the *enumeration DAG* (Directed Acyclic Graph) to represent the subtree/supertree relationships on the set of all frequent subtrees. Each level in this data structure consists of the frequent subtrees, the size of which (number of nodes) is equal to the level number. The neighbouring levels are then connected by directed edges which emanate from the subtree to the supertree to represent a subtree/supertree relationship between two frequent subtrees in the neighbouring levels. The purpose of the enumeration DAG is to determine whether a given frequent subtree is maximal or closed, and to prune away trees that do not correspond to frequent closed or maximal subtrees. The traversal of the enumeration DAG is further optimized by removing any branches in the DAG that cannot possibly contain any closed/maximal subtrees. The Dryade algorithm (Termier, Rousset, & Sebag, 2004) was developed to deal with highly heterogeneous tree data with varying structures. It discovers frequent unordered closed embedded subtrees in level-wise fashion and it enables frequency test with propositional algorithms by intensive task decomposition and reformulation of several search strategies in a propositional language. As such, it does not use the classical 'generate and test' strategy for subtree enumeration, and achieves good time performance. The tree inclusion definition used was appropriate for highly heterogeneous data and in (Termier, Rousset, & Sebag, 2008) it has been generalized to the standard inclusion definition and an extended algorithm, DryadeParent for mining frequent closed attribute trees (no two sibling nodes with the same label), was proposed.

In (Ozaki & Ohkawa, 2006), the differences in the search strategies are discussed with respect to the mining of closed ordered subtrees. Two algorithms are presented: one which uses a breadth-first enumeration strategy, and the other which uses depth-first/breadth-first enumeration strategies. These two versions correspond to adjustments to the AMIOT (Hido & Kawano, 2005) and TreeMiner (Zaki, 2005) algorithms so that closed subtrees are obtained by applying pruning strategies. SCCMETreeMiner algorithm (Ji & Zhu, 2008) mines frequent closed and maximal ordered embedded subtrees using length-decreasing support constraint. It uses the right-most path extension enumeration strategy and a projection technique to construct the candidate subtree set. The branches of the enumeration tree that do not correspond to closed and/or maximal subtrees under the length-decreasing constraint are pruned. The length-decreasing constraint is motivated by noting that in applications, small subtrees with high support are considered interesting, while the larger subtrees may be considered interesting even when their support is relatively small. Hence, the length-decreasing support constraint reduces the support threshold as the length of the tree increases. SEAMSON (Scalable and Efficient Algorithm for Maximal frequent Subtree extractiON) algorithm (Paik, Nam, Hwang, & Kim, 2008) discovers frequent maximal ordered embedded subtrees by using their newly proposed L-dictionary structure which is essentially a compressed representation of the database. L-dictionary is created by storing the label, pre-order position, parent positions, and tree (transaction) indexes, for each node in the database tree in form of lists. The frequency of each label is worked out from the number of lists, and lists from frequent labels are joined together through the parent node information and tree index in order to arrive at maximal subtrees. Exit-B algorithm (Paik, Nam, Won, & Kim, 2005) extracts frequent maximal ordered embedded subtrees; here, the novel idea is to represent trees with bit sequences, store them in specialized data structures, and extract all maximal subtrees. The main purpose is to increase time performance and space efficiency by avoiding disadvantages caused by storing string labels. The TDU approach (Chehreghani, Rahgozar, Lucas, & Chehreghani, 2007) is a top-down approach for extracting all frequent maximal embedded unordered subtrees. It starts by computing the set of all frequent nodes by incrementing their count in a 1-dimensional array and an intermediate representation tree is constructed. Each tree that is infrequent is fragmented into its *k*-1-subtrees until a frequent subtree is reached. This subtree is then checked for a subset/superset relationship with other frequent subtrees, to eliminate any subtrees of an already frequent maximal subtree.

## PRELIMINARY EXPERIMENTS

This section elaborates on the application of the proposed method. It begins with a discussion of the way in which the experimental XML database was set up. Next, we discuss the algorithm used to extract interesting associations. Finally, we present preliminary results of the experiment and the contributions to this specific issue.

### XML Database Creation

As mentioned earlier, the number of textual documents that were available from our financial industry partner was very limited. In addition, these recorded only those cases where the loan application was approved as they do not retain records of rejected applications. Regardless of the importance of understanding banks' coverage rate in terms of SMEs financing, these documents are destroyed once the prospective borrower has understood that his or her loan application has been rejected. Banks make their decisions according to a set of standards that have been determined by the management. However, data provided by SMEs – and later verified by loan staff – tends to show variance from the standard norm. Therefore, loan staffs are allowed to exercise some discretion when they encounter applications with borderline values or anomalies.

We have conducted several interviews with the loan officers form the bank in order to obtain some domain knowledge about rules that reflect realistic credit parameters and the corresponding assessment decision. This background knowledge is not a full reflection of real-life practice, although it is a fair representation of real cases. The instances where officer have used discretion are too many to capture and may cause inefficiency in the experimental process. Taking this into consideration, some rules that lead to negative decisions have resulted from precedents set by previous applications, while others are formed through implicit knowledge provided by the domain expert. These rules are comprised of 9 attributes: integrity, sales per year, EAT per month, current ratio, debt to equity ratio, EBITDA to total debt ratio, EBITDA to interest ratio, EAT to sales ratio and sales growth ratio (please refer to the previous section for abbreviation explanation). These rules apply exclusively to loan amounts up to IDR 100 million. Loan applications above that amount need one other attribute, namely collateral. However, we have excluded this type of loan for two reasons. First, the sums of money that Indonesian SMEs usually borrow from the bank tend to be less than IDR 100 million. This predominantly applies to micro and small size enterprises. Second, the addition of collateral has not significantly altered the decision profile. With regards to SMEs, the main indicator is character followed by capacity to make loan repayments. Regardless of the type and value of collateral, loan officers still rely on the integrity of applicants.

The Indonesian Central Bank has established a database where debtors with a default history are listed. Thus, all applicants have to submit a reference letter from the central bank confirming the fact that they are not listed on that database. If an applicant fails to provide the letter, or if loan staff find that applicant's name on that database during the verification process, then the loan application has to be rejected. This is considered to be the lowest form of integrity, and therefore it is not included as a possible case in our database.

In Table 1, we present examples of rules that are applied to 3 different circumstances and lead to a particular decision in each case. Since loan officers have the authority to grant or refuse loan applications, these decisions may vary in real life. In addition, many more rules apply for the same decisions. The set value "above standard" and "below standard" refers to a standard that is set by the bank in relation to the industry and sub-industry as explained previously.

To summarize, 50,000 XML instances were automatically created using the pre-defined XML template (Figure 1) for the overall structure of an instance. The values for credit parameters (i.e., attribute values) of each instance were randomly chosen from the known set of possible values. However, please note that for related attributes, after an initial value was randomly chosen, the values for other related attributes would be chosen from only those values that are applicable to that

*Table 1. Example rules provided by domain expert*

| Descriptions | Accept | Accept with considerations | Reject |
|---|---|---|---|
| Integrity (High), sales per year (above IDR 2.5 billion to IDR 50 billion), EAT per month (more than 0.4 of sales), Current Ratio (above standard), Debt to Equity Ratio (above standard), EBITDA to Debt ratio (above standard), EBITDA to interest ratio (above standard), EAT to sales ratio (above standard), sales growth ratio (above standard) | √ | | |
| Integrity (Medium), sales per year (above IDR 2.5 billion to IDR 50 billion), EAT per month (less than 0.2 of sales), Current Ratio (below standard), Debt to Equity Ratio (below standard), EBITDA to Debt ratio (above standard), EBITDA to interest ratio (above standard), EAT to sales ratio (above standard), sales growth ratio (above standard) | | √ | |
| Integrity (Low), sales per year (below IDR 300 million), EAT per month (less than 0.2 of sales), Current Ratio (below standard), Debt to Equity Ratio (below standard), EBITDA to Debt ratio (below standard), EBITDA to interest ratio (below standard), EAT to sales ratio (below standard), sales growth ratio (below standard) | | | √ |

case. For example, when an industry is randomly chosen, we can select only from a set of valid sub-industries, and then from the different financial ratios (e.g., EAT to sales ratio, Debt to Equity Ratio, etc.), that apply for that particular industry/sub-industry combination. Each instance (transaction) reflects a single loan application. The rules provided by domain experts were then incorporated on top of those instances, to ensure that the attribute value combinations within each instance were realistic as well as the corresponding credit assessment decision. There were 63 rules in total applied to the initially generated 50,000 XML instances and a total of 26,637 instances were modified. As mentioned, these rules were general with respect to the financial ratios, indicating that a ratio is above or below a standard for a particular industry/sub-industry. However, in our generated database, real ratios were used for the corresponding industry/sub-industry, giving a total of 41 possible variations where a general rule can apply. Hence, while on average a single rule would have modified 400 instances, the rule itself will not be present in 400 instances because specific ratios apply to the randomly chosen industry and sub-industry. Therefore, the rules themselves will not be present in the extracted patterns as this would require us to set a very low support threshold (i.e., approximately 0.02% of the database).The structural characteristics of the created XML document are: 502 unique labels (attributes and their values when applicable), 54 nodes in each tree instance (transaction), and the height and fan-out of each tree instance were 5 and 9 respectively.

## XML Frequent Subtree Mining Algorithm

As explained in the previous section, each loan application instance is represented as a separate transaction in the tree database, and all information in each transaction is organized in the same way. Furthermore, in this domain it may be possible that attributes with the same name (e.g., financial amounts) may be referring to different attributes are used in a different context. Hence, after the investigation of the nature of the resulting XML database, it was decided that mining for ordered induced subtrees (previously discussed) under the transactional support definition was most suitable. To extract patterns of interest, lower support thresholds need to be used, and due to the complex nature of the data being considered, the algorithms for extracting all frequent subtrees could not complete the task due to the large memory consumption. We have therefore used the CMTreeMiner algorithm presented in (Chi et al., 2004), which efficiently extracts all ordered induced closed and maximal frequent subtrees under the transactional support definition. In our experiment, we have used the CMTreeMiner algorithm to extract both closed and maximal subtrees that have occurred at least in 250 transactions (i.e., minimum support threshold was set to 250). The total run time was 35110 seconds and a total of 18,998,995 closed and 14,842,201 maximal subtrees were extracted. From these numerous patterns, we decided to focus on closed subtrees that contain the class value within the detected frequent relationship (total of 638,299 subtrees). The long run time and the large number of frequent subtrees extracted are caused by the complex structural characteristics of each document instance.

In what follows we discuss a number of selected patterns that potentially reflect interesting relationships in this domain. Before these results can be confidently used in the decision making process, one needs to determine the confidence of each pattern and represent them as association rules with support and confidence values. Please note that since many of the attribute values were randomly assigned during the database creation, the results do not completely reflect real-world situations. However, as mentioned previously, we have established several constraints that should be imposed on the allowed combination of attribute values so that the real-world scenario is reflected to some extent, at least in parts of the generated document instances. The example patterns will be presented using the pre-order string encoding (Zaki, 2005), as the frequent subtree mining algorithms often use the pre-order string encoding to represent trees at the implementation level, and this is the case for the algorithms used in this paper. Basically, in the pre-order string encoding, the node labels are listed following the pre-order traversal of the tree being represented. Additionally, a special symbol ("/" in this paper) is used to indicate the going back up the tree during the pre-order traversal. As an example, the pre-order string encoding of the first tree (ordered induced) from Figure 3 is "credititriskindicators personalinfo / customerprofile integrity(x) / / financialreport salesgrowthratio", and from the second tree (ordered embedded) is "creditriskindicators integrity(x) / salesperyear(x) / salesgrowthratio(x)".

## Preliminary Results

As discussed earlier, the term "capacity" captures the prospective borrower's ability to perform continuous repayment of the loan that is reflected by financial ratios. Within the context of SMEs, banks consider current ratio as the primary one, since it reveals the SME's liquidity level. We present several patterns that describe the relationship between the current ratio and debt to equity ratio. The first ratio helps banks to assess SMEs' likelihood of fulfilling their future settlement obligations, while the latter provides information on SMEs' financing preference, i.e., if they tend to have external financing through loans or internal financing by accumulating retained earnings. It is important to note that the higher the debt to equity ratio, the higher is the company's leverage. This means the ratio has an inverse relationship to performance. If debt to equity ratio is above the standard, this means the company is struggling since it has more debt than equity. The examples below are for SMEs that are conducting business in the agriculture sector. We first discuss the current ratio as a single attribute and then show how the current ratio interacts with the debt to equity ratio.

### Example 1

```
creditapplication() creditris-
kindicators() personalinfo()
industry(agriculture) / creditin-
formation() principal(more than
IDR 50 million / / / customerpro-
file() marketing() strategies() /
/ management() / financial() cash-
flows() / / capacity() / / collat-
eral() / rating() / financialre-
port() currentratio(above 1.5) / / /
creditassessment(accept)
support = 448
```

```
creditapplication() creditris-
kindicators() personalinfo()
industry(agriculture) / creditin-
formation() principal(more than
IDR 50 million / / / customerpro-
file() marketing() strategies() /
/ management() / financial() cash-
flows() / / capacity() / / collat-
eral() / rating() / financialre-
port() currentratio(above 1.5) / / /
creditassessment(accept with consid-
erations) support=337
```

```
creditapplication() creditris-
kindicators() personalinfo()
industry(agriculture) / creditin-
formation() principal(more than
IDR 50 million / / / customerpro-
file() marketing() strategies() /
/ management() / financial() cash-
flows() / / capacity() / / collat-
eral() / rating() / financialre-
port() currentratio(below 1.5) / / /
creditassessment(accept)
support=263
```

```
creditapplication() creditris-
kindicators() personalinfo()
industry(agriculture) / creditin-
formation() principal(more than
IDR 50 million / / / customerpro-
file() marketing() strategies() /
/ management() / financial() cash-
flows() / / capacity() / / collat-
eral() / rating() / financialre-
port() currentratio(below 1.5) / / /
creditassessment(accept with consid-
erations)
support=415
```

```
creditapplication() creditris-
kindicators() personalinfo()
industry(agriculture) / creditin-
formation() principal(more than
IDR 50 million / / / customerpro-
file() marketing() strategies() /
/ management() / financial() cash-
flows() / / capacity() / / collat-
eral() / rating() / financialre-
port() currentratio(below 1.5) / / /
creditassessment(reject)
support=369
```

From the above patterns, we can see how the current ratio performs on credit assessment. The more liquid the ratio of the prospective borrowers, the more likely that banks will grant the requested loan. In the first pattern, the current ratio is above the standardised level for the agriculture business; thus, a positive decision is expected. The decision may be slightly changed given the same values of other attributes as is shown by the second pattern. A negative decision (reject) will not apply to the case when the current ratio has a value above the standard. On the other hand, a current ratio with a value below the standard shows a pattern that reflects prudent banking practice. A loan application showing liquidity issues is least likely to be accepted, even though acceptance can still be expected. The highest support of 415 that is generated by the next pattern reflects the real-life situation where loan officer is required to gather additional information in order to complete the liquidity profile of the applicant. Lastly, an applicant is likely to be rejected when the current ratio is below the standard value set for this specific industry. The current ratio as a single ratio is not sufficient to produce an accurate decision. With the inclusion of more ratios, as briefly illustrated by the next example, the credit granting decision will be made using a more comprehensive financial profile.

## Example 2

```
creditapplication() creditris-
kindicators() personalinfo()
industry(agriculture) / cred-
itinformation() / / customerpro-
file() marketing() strategies() /
/ management() / financial() cash-
flows() / / capacity() / / col-
lateral() / rating() / financial-
report() currentratio(above 1.5) /
debttoequityratio(above 2.0) / / /
creditassessment(accept with consid-
erations)
support=334
```

```
creditapplication() creditris-
kindicators() personalinfo()
industry(agriculture) / cred-
itinformation() / / customerpro-
file() marketing() strategies() /
/ management() / financial() cash-
flows() / / capacity() / / col-
lateral() / rating() / financial-
report() currentratio(above 1.5) /
debttoequityratio(below 2.0) / / /
creditassessment(accept)
support=366
```

```
creditapplication() creditris-
kindicators() personalinfo()
```

```
industry(agriculture) / cred-
itinformation() / / customerpro-
file() marketing() strategies() /
/ management() / financial() cash-
flows() / / capacity() / / col-
lateral() / rating() / financial-
report() currentratio(below 1.5) /
debttoequityratio(below 2.0) / / /
creditassessment(reject)
support=431
```

The patterns in Example 2 demonstrate the appropriateness that the current ratio has over debt to equity ratio. When the current ratio is above the predefined standard for the agriculture business, even when the debt to equity ratio shows that the applicant prefers debt rather than equity financing, the decisions to accept a loan application is still supported by 334 instances. The decision becomes more positive when both ratios reflect a strong financial performance for the debtor, i.e., above the standard current ratio and below the standard debt to equity ratio. This means that a loan application from a company that has liquidity and low leverage is more likely to be accepted by banks. The decision is unambiguous when both ratios indicate a low level of liquidity as well as high preference for external financing. This shows that applicant tends to look for fresh capital from outside and may have accumulated debt without the apparent capacity of fulfilling his/her obligations to the third party. We have emphasised the importance of qualitative information to credit assessment. The next example will demonstrate the effect of integrity on the decision.

## Example 3

```
creditapplication() creditris-
kindicators() personalinfo()
industry(agriculture) / creditin-
formation() principal(up to IDR 50
million) / / / customerprofile()
marketing() strategies() / / manage-
ment() / financial() cashflows() / /
integrity(high) / capacity() / / col-
lateral() / rating() / financialre-
port() currentratio(above 1.5) / / /
creditassessment(accept)
support = 275

creditapplication() creditris-
kindicators() personalinfo()
industryrisk(high) / creditinfor-
mation() principal(up to IDR 50
million) / / / customerprofile()
marketing() strategies() / / manage-
ment() / financial() cashflows() / /
integrity(medium) / capacity() / /
collateral() / rating() / financial-
report() currentratio(above 1.5) / /
/ creditassessment(accept with con-
siderations)
support = 340

creditapplication() creditris-
kindicators() personalinfo()
industryrisk(high) / creditinfor-
mation() principal(up to IDR 50
million) / / / customerprofile()
marketing() strategies() / / manage-
ment() / financial() cashflows() / /
integrity(low) / capacity() / / col-
lateral() / rating() / financialre-
port() currentratio(above 1.5) / / /
creditassessment(reject)
support = 321
```

The patterns in Example 3 have now incorporated qualitative information, i.e., integrity, derived from various interviews and observations. Here we combine both quantitative and qualitative information as measured by the current ratio and integrity, respectively. An applicant with the same liquidity capacity, as shown by the current ratio value above the industry standard, receives different decisions depending on the integrity assessed by the loan officer. A prospective borrower with high integrity poses less risk in comparison with those with medium and low integrity. Thus, loan officers are most likely to reject applications based on the low level of integrity of the applicant. The trend as shown by example 3, is representative of real-world practice where the lower the integrity level, the more likely that the application will not be approved. Hence, medium integrity requires that banks make an effort to gather more information.

## Contributions of Results

This experimental section has shed light on the method for generating a loan granting decision based on qualitative and quantitative information about the prospective borrower. We have concluded from our survey that methods applied to credit risk assessment for SMEs have overlooked the important role of "soft" information such as an applicant's character, the business' marketing strategy and management. In other words, existing techniques become problematic when they are used on applications from small businesses with a significant portion of information collated in a consultative manner. In the case of Indonesian SMEs' loan applications, interviews and observations are without doubt the key means of data collection, demanding a considerable amount of staff time. The proposed method offers a logical construction for developing a data structure comprising both types of information to be mined. This, with some refinements that we propose in the next section, will provide a useful guideline that can be applied to other similar domain-specific databases.

Based on selected patterns presented above, the role of qualitative information is most clearly evident in the last scenario. For medium scale enterprises in particular, financial performance is not the best predictor of risk, even though key financial indicators are most likely to be available. When making a decision, loan officers have to consider, among other things, character, business strategy, and management style. Officers have to manage an abundance of data available in unstructured form and when subjectivity or human error comes into play, they may decide against a potentially good loan or approve a potentially bad loan application. The method could enable loan officers to make better decisions by alerting them to doubtful applications, as shown by the last pattern.

# FUTURE RESEARCH DIRECTIONS

This study has demonstrated the prospect of discovering useful associations from loan applications containing both quantitative and qualitative information. In order to have comprehensive and productive results in the future, the loan applications need to be systematically categorised based on their subsequent performance as performing loans, delinquent loans, default loans and rejected loans. Rules extracted from each group will shed light on risk parameters of applicants with respect to their business activities and management style. We expect that this kind of categorization, together with the inclusion of rejected applications, will provide us with more specific association rules. Further, a thorough observation of grounds for loan rejection should enrich these risk parameters of prospective borrowers.

The distinction is further emphasised when recognizing the influence of industry and sub-industry. The more comprehensive the instances, the more likely are we able to add rules, in particular those that can accurately classify the borrower as a timely "good" or "bad" debtor. This means ascertaining a borrower's present credit risk as well as foreseeing his or her credit performance in the future. At the moment, due to the imperfect credit assessment method, there is the chance that banks are refusing good debtors. This possibility merits a more detailed investigation into each application without reservations as there are likely to be other characteristics of SMEs that are currently not being taken into account. Information from rejected loan applications, in particular, will enrich the risk parameter and advance the analysis.

Therefore, we also highlight the importance of collecting information on loan applications that have been refused. Overall, some of the currently used assessment rules are likely to be refined and lead to a correct, more confident decision.

From the data mining perspective, we have seen that the loan application data that captures both quantitative and qualitative information tends to be very complex. This can be largely a result of the number of attributes that are likely to be present in every instance or transaction. In our example, these attributes correspond to the attributes important for contextualising some of the information, and they correspond to all the internal nodes from the our XML template tree. These attributes are themselves not as useful for the decision making process, but they significantly increase the complexity of the frequent subtree mining task due to the combinatorial complexity. In these scenarios, it is likely that the traditional frequent subtree mining based approach may not be applicable, and there is a need to develop alternative data mining methods for tree-structured data to directly mine for discriminative patterns with respect to the classification task. Some work has already been initiated in this direction (Kim, Kim, Weninger, Han, & Abdelzaher, 2010). In addition, the frequent subtree patterns themselves may be so large in number that they cause significant delays in the analysis and interpretation of the results. Many of the patterns may not be useful for the application at hand and/or are redundant, or of no interest to the user. One immediate task is to form association rules from the discovered patterns based on the support and confidence framework. Furthermore, we will also apply and extend the method proposed in (Shaharanee, Hadzic, & Dillon, 2010) to filter out any irrelevant, redundant or uninteresting rules using a statistical heuristic-based approach to ascertain the discovered association rules.

Last, but not least, we mentioned that in our future work we will investigate the means by which the related unstructured information from text can be automatically converted into the XML format. Several text-to-XML Annotators exist and we propose to use the PCFG parser (Klein & Manning, 2003) back-end that uses both statistical and rule-based annotators for text. It works our grammatical structure of sentences and can output various analysis formats, including part-of-speech tagged text, phrase structure trees and grammatical relations. The phrase structure trees could bee effectively represented in XML format, and this conversions form unstructured text to phrase structure trees will allow for easier analysis. To enhance the capability of the parser, we also aim to extend the technique based on domain ontology/concept. This permits disambiguation of terms through concept relationships in the same segment of text. The annotators will be used to extract relevant tokens from a document and map them to a small subset of the attributes for determining matches in structured data. For example, by applying Named Entity Extraction techniques in an annotator one can extract names from a document, and match them against the customer and product name attributes of the transaction table. One could also extract chunked text such as noun clauses by using a part of speech tagger for matching. This allows us to determine a score for an entity in a document. The highest scoring entity or best matching one can be found without computing explicit scores for all entities. A ranked list of possible entities can be obtained by performing fuzzy matching on each extracted token. The resultant entities and relationships can be used to define the XML profiles for those documents. The extraction methods can be used to determine the values for each tag for an instance document. We will use a combination of approaches namely (1) ontology-based (Embley, Campbell, Smith, & Liddle, 1998; Alani, Kim, Millard, Weal, Hall, Lewis, & Shadbolt, 2003) ones that extract terms from text and map them to concepts in an ontology to produce semantics and (2) ontology-driven (Handschuh, Staab, & Maedche, 2001; Vargas-Vera et al., 2002) ones that make active use of an ontology to guide or constrain the analysis.

## CONCLUSION

In this chapter we have proposed a method that combines qualitative and quantitative information into a single data source based on a predefined XML template. This will essentially maximise the information content and enhance the knowledge patterns that can be assist in the decision making process in the credit scoring domain. We have presented a case study based on SMEs loan application, but the method is likely to prove useful in the general credit assessment context. The appropriate use of the tree mining methods was discussed in relation to a number of scenarios that are likely to occur in this domain. The experimental results indicate the potential of the proposed method in aiding banks to make reliable and sound decisions when assessing the loan applications of SMEs.

## REFERENCES


Abdou, H. A., Pointon, J., & El-Masry, A. (2008). Neural nets versus conventional techniques in credit scoring in Egyptian banking. *Expert Systems with Applications*, *35*(3), 1275–1292. doi:10.1016/j.eswa.2007.08.030

Alani, H., Kim, S., Millard, D. E., Weal, M. J., Hall, W., Lewis, P. H., & Shadbolt, N. (2003). Automatic ontology-based knowledge extraction from web documents. *IEEE Intelligent Systems*, *18*(1), 14–21. doi:10.1109/MIS.2003.1179189

Alpaydin, E. (2004). *Introduction to machine learning*. MIT Press.

Altman, E., & Sabato, G. (2007). Modelling credit risk for SMEs: Evidence from the U.S. market. *Abacus*, *43*(3), 332–357. doi:10.1111/j.1467-6281.2007.00234.x

Altman, E. I. (1968). Financial ratios, discriminant analysis and the prediction of corporate bankruptcy. *The Journal of Finance*, *23*(4), 589–609. doi:10.2307/2978933

Altman, E. I. (1984). The success of business failure prediction models: An international survey. *Journal of Banking & Finance*, *8*(2), 171–198. doi:10.1016/0378-4266(84)90003-7

Altman, E. I., Haldeman, R. G., & Narayanan, P. (1977). ZETA™ analysis: A new model to identify bankruptcy risk of corporations. *Journal of Banking & Finance*, *1*(1), 29–54. doi:10.1016/0378-4266(77)90017-6

Angelini, E., di Tollo, G., & Rolli, A. (2008). A neural network approach for credit risk evaluation. *The Quarterly Review of Economics and Finance*, *48*(4), 733–755. doi:10.1016/j.qref.2007.04.001

Asia-Pacific Economic Cooperation (Ed.). (2010). *SME market access and internationalization: Medium-term KPIs for the SMEWG strategic plan*. Singapore: APEC Secretariat.

Beaver, W. H. (1966). Financial ratios as predictors of failure. *Journal of Accounting Research*, *4*, 71–111. doi:10.2307/2490171

Bellotti, T., & Crook, J. (2009). Support vector machines for credit scoring and discovery of significant features. *Expert Systems with Applications*, *36*(2), 3302–3308. doi:10.1016/j.eswa.2008.01.005

Bensic, M., Sarlija, N., & Zekic-Susac, M. (2005). Modelling small-business credit scoring by using logistic regression, neural networks and decision trees. *Intelligent Systems in Accounting. Financial Management*, *13*(3), 133–150.

Berger, A. N., Klapper, L. F., & Udell, G. F. (2001). The ability of banks to lend to informationally opaque small businesses. *Journal of Banking & Finance*, *25*(12), 2127–2167. doi:10.1016/S0378-4266(01)00189-3

Berger, A. N., & Udell, G. F. (1995). Relationship lending and lines of credit in small firm finance. *The Journal of Business*, *68*(3), 351–381. doi:10.1086/296668

Berger, A. N., & Udell, G. F. (2006). A more complete conceptual framework for SME finance. *Journal of Banking & Finance*, *30*(11), 2945–2966. doi:10.1016/j.jbankfin.2006.05.008

Chehreghani, M. H., Rahgozar, M., Lucas, C., & Chehreghani, M. H. (2007). Mining maximal embedded unordered tree patterns. In *Proceedings of the 2007 IEEE Symposium on Computational Intelligence and Data Mining (CIDM)*, (437-443). IEEE Computer Society.

Chen, W., Ma, C., & Ma, L. (2009). Mining the customer credit using hybrid support vector machines technique. *Expert Systems with Applications*, *36*(4), 7611–7616. doi:10.1016/j.eswa.2008.09.054

Chen, W.-H., & Shih, J.-Y. (2006). A study of Taiwan's issuer credit rating systems using support vector machines. *Expert Systems with Applications*, *30*(3), 427–435. doi:10.1016/j.eswa.2005.10.003

Chi, Y., Muntz, R. R., Nijssen, S., & Kok, J. N. (2004). Freequent subtree mining – An overview. *Fundamenta Informaticae. Special Issue on Graph and Tree Mining*, *66*(1-2), 161–198.

Chi, Y., Yang, Y., & Muntz, R. R. (2005). Canonical forms for labelled trees and their applications in frequent subtree mining. *Knowledge and Information Systems*, *8*(2), 203–234. doi:10.1007/s10115-004-0180-7

Chi, Y., Yang, Y., Xia, Y., & Muntz, R. R. (2004). CMTreeMiner: Mining both closed and maximal frequent subtrees. In H. Dai, R. Srikant, & C. Zhang (Eds.), *Proceedings of the 8th Pacific Asia Conference on Knowledge Discovery and Data Mining (PAKDD) Lecture Notes in Computer Science: Vol. 3056*. (pp. 63-73). Springer.

Chye, K. H., Chin, T. W., & Peng, G. C. (2004). Credit scoring using data mining techniques. *Singapore Management Review*, *26*(2), 25–47.

Cristianini, N., & Shawe-Taylor, J. (2000). *An introduction to support vector machines and other kernel-based learning methods*. UK: Cambridge University Press.

Daubie, M., Levecq, P., & Meskens, N. (2002). A comparison of the rough sets and recursive partitioning induction approaches: An application to commercial loans. *International Transactions in Operational Research*, *9*(5), 681–694. doi:10.1111/1475-3995.00381

De Young, R., Glennon, D., & Nigro, P. (2008). Borrower-lender distance, credit scoring, and loan performance: Evidence from informational-opaque small business borrowers. *Journal of Financial Intermediation*, *17*(1), 113–143. doi:10.1016/j.jfi.2007.07.002

Derelioğlu, G., Gürgen, F., & Okay, N. (2009). A neural approach for SME's credit risk analysis in Turkey. In Perner, P. (Ed.), *Machine Learning and Data Mining in Pattern Recognition, Lecture Notes in Computer Science* (*Vol. 5632*, pp. 749–759). Springer. doi:10.1007/978-3-642-03070-3_56

Desai, V. S., Crook, J. N., & Overstreet, G. A. (1996). A comparison of neural networks and linear scoring models in the credit union. *European Journal of Operational Research*, *95*(1), 24–37. doi:10.1016/0377-2217(95)00246-4

Dima, A. M., & Vasilache, S. (2009). ANN model for corporate credit risk assessment. In *Proceedings of the 2009 International Conference on Information and Financial Engineering (ICIFE)*, (pp. 94-98). IEEE Computer Society.

Dinh, T. H. T., & Kleimeier, S. (2007). A credit scoring model for Vietnam's retail banking market. *International Review of Financial Analysis*, *16*(5), 471–495. doi:10.1016/j.irfa.2007.06.001

Durand, D. (1941). *Risk elements in consumer installment financing*. New York, NY: The National Bureau of Economic Research.

Eisenbeis, R. A. (1977). Pitfalls in the application of discriminant analysis in business, finance and economics. *The Journal of Finance*, *32*(3), 875–900. doi:10.2307/2326320

Elsas, R., & Krahnen, J. P. (1988). Is relationship lending special? Evidence from credit-file data in Germany. *Journal of Banking & Finance*, *22*(10-11), 1283–1316. doi:10.1016/S0378-4266(98)00063-6

Embley, D. W., Campbell, D. M., Smith, R. D., & Liddle, S. W. (1998). Ontology-based extraction and structuring of information from data-rich unstructured documents. In G. Gardarin, J. C. French, N. Pissinou, K. Makki, & L. Bouganim (Eds.), *Proceedings of the 7th International Conference on Information and Knowledge Management (CIKM)*, (pp. 52-59). ACM.

European Commission (Ed.). (2010). *European SMEs under pressure*. European Commission.

Feng, L., Dillon, T. S., Weigand, H., & Chang, E. (2003). An XML-enabled association rule framework. In *Proceedings of the 14th International Conference on Database and Expert Systems Applications* [Springer.]. *Lecture Notes in Computer Science*, *2736*, 88–97. doi:10.1007/978-3-540-45227-0_10

Ferrucci, D., & Lally, A. (2004). UIMA: An architectural approach to unstructured information processing in the corporate research environment. *Natural Language Engineering*, *10*(3-4), 327–348. doi:10.1017/S1351324904003523

Frame, W. S., Srinivasan, A., & Woosley, L. (2001). The effect of credit scoring on small-business lending. *Journal of Money, Credit and Banking*, *33*(3), 813–825. doi:10.2307/2673896

Gao, L., Zhou, C., Gao, H.-B., & Shi, Y.-R. (2006). Credit scoring model based on neural network with particle swarm optimization. In L. Licheng Jiao, X. Wang, J. Gao, J. Liu, & F. Wu (Eds.), *Proceedings of the 2nd International Conference on Advances in Neural Computation (ICNC, 1), Lecture Notes in Computer Science: Vol 4221* (pp. 76-79). Springer.

Hadzic, F., Dillon, T. S., & Chang, E. (2008). Knowledge analysis with tree patterns. In *Proceedings of the 41st Annual Hawaii International Conference on System Sciences (HICSS)*, (p. 369). IEEE Computer Society.

Hadzic, F., Tan, H., & Dillon, T. S. (2010). Model guided algorithm for mining unordered embedded subtrees. *Web Intelligence and Agent Systems: An International Journal*, *8*(4), 413–430.

Hadzic, F., Tan, H., & Dillon, T. S. (2011). *Mining of data with complex structures*. Springer.

Hadzic, F., Tan, H., Dillon, T. S., & Chang, E. (2007). Implications of frequent subtree mining using hybrid support definition. In *Proceedings of the Data Mining & Information Engineering*.

Han, J., & Kamber, M. (2006). *Data mining: Concepts and techniques*. Morgan Kaufmann Publishers.

Hand, D. J., & Henley, W. E. (1997). Statistical classification methods in consumer credit scoring: A review. *Journal of the Royal Statistical Society. Series A, (Statistics in Society)*, *160*(3), 523–541. doi:10.1111/j.1467-985X.1997.00078.x

Handschuh, S., Staab, S., & Maedche, A. (2001). Cream: Creating relational metadata with a component-based, ontology-driven annotation framework. In *Proceedings of the 1st International Conference on Knowledge Capture (K-CAP)*, (pp. 76-83). ACM.

Hao, Y., Chi, Z., Yan, D., & Yue, X. (2010). An improved fuzzy support vector machine for credit rating. In Li, K., Jesshope, C., Jin, H., & Gaudiot, J.-L. (Eds.), *Network and Parallel Computing (NPC) Lecture Notes in Computer Science* (*Vol. 4672*, pp. 495–505). Springer.

Hassler, H. W., Myers, J. H., & Seldin, M. (1963). Payment history as a predictor of credit risk. *The Journal of Applied Psychology*, *47*(6), 383–385. doi:10.1037/h0044308

Henley, W. E., & Hand, D. J. (1996). A k-nearest-neighbour classifier for assessing consumer credit risk. *Journal of the Royal Statistical Society, Series D (. The Statistician*, *45*(1), 77–95. doi:10.2307/2348414

Hido, S., & Kawano, H. (2005). AMIOT: Induced ordered tree mining in tree-structured databases. In *Proceedings of the 5th IEEE International Conference on Data Mining (ICDM)*, (pp. 170-177). IEEE Computer Society.

Huang, C.-L., Chen, M.-C., & Wang, C.-J. (2007). Credit scoring with a data mining approach based on support vector machines. *Expert Systems with Applications*, *33*(4), 847–856. doi:10.1016/j.eswa.2006.07.007

Huang, Z., Hsinchun, C., Hsu, C.-J., Chen, W.-H., & Wu, S. (2004). Credit rating analysis with support vector machines and neural networks: A market comparative study. *Decision Support Systems*, *37*(4), 543–558. doi:10.1016/S0167-9236(03)00086-1

Jensen, H. L. (1992). Using neural networks for credit scoring. *Managerial Finance*, *18*(6), 15–26.

Ji, G.-L., & Zhu, Y.-W. (2008). Mining closed and maximal frequent embedded subtrees using length-decreasing support constraint. In *Proceedings of the 7th International Conference on Machine Learning and Cybernetics* (pp. 268-273).

Kaye, R. (2006). The GLOSS system for transformations from plain text to XML. In *Proceedings of 2006 Mathematical User-Interfaces Workshop.*

Kim, H., Kim, S., Weninger, T., Han, J., & Abdelzaher, T. F. (2010). NDPMine: Efficiently mining discriminative numerical features for pattern-based classification. In Balcázar, J., Bonchi, F., Gionis, A., & Sebag, M. (Eds.), *Machine Learning and Knowledge Discovery in Databases, Lecture Notes in Computer Science* (*Vol. 6322*, pp. 35–50). Springer. doi:10.1007/978-3-642-15883-4_3

Klein, D., & Manning, C. D. (2003). Accurate unlexicalized parsing. In *Proceedings of the 41st Meeting of the Association for Computational Linguistics (ACL)*, (pp. 423-430).

Lee, T.-S., & Chen, I. F. (2005). A two-stage hybrid credit scoring model using artificial neural networks and multivariate adaptive regression splines. *Expert Systems with Applications*, *28*(4), 743–752. doi:10.1016/j.eswa.2004.12.031

Lee, T.-S., Chiu, C.-C., Lu, C.-J., & Chen, I. F. (2002). Credit scoring using the hybrid neural discriminant technique. *Expert Systems with Applications*, *23*(3), 245–254. doi:10.1016/S0957-4174(02)00044-1

Lee, T.-S., & Sung-Chang, J. (2000). Forecasting creditworthiness: Logistic vs. artificial neural net. *Journal of Business Forecasting Methods and Systems*, *18*(4), 28–30.

Lee, Y.-C. (2007). Application of support vector machines to corporate credit rating prediction. *Expert Systems with Applications*, *33*(1), 67–74. doi:10.1016/j.eswa.2006.04.018

Lehmann, E., & Neuberger, D. (2001). Do lending relationships matter?: Evidence from bank survey data in Germany. *Journal of Economic Behavior & Organization*, *45*(4), 339–359. doi:10.1016/S0167-2681(01)00151-2

Li, S.-T., Shiue, W., & Huang, M.-H. (2006). The evaluation of consumer loans using support vector machines. *Expert Systems with Applications*, *30*(4), 772–782. doi:10.1016/j.eswa.2005.07.041

Longenecker, J. G., Moore, C. W., & Petty, J. W. (1997). Credit scoring and the small business: A review and the need for research. In *Proceedings of the 1997 United States Association for Small Business and Entrepreneurship*.

Malhotra, R., & Malhotra, D. K. (2003). Evaluating consumer loans using neural networks. *Omega*, *31*(2), 83–96. doi:10.1016/S0305-0483(03)00016-1

Marchal, B. (2002). *XI: Open-source conversion of legacy text files to XML*. Retrieved June 4, 2010, from http://www.ananas.org/xi/index.html

Michalski, R. S., Carbonell, J. G., & Mitchell, T. M. (1983). *Machine learning: An artificial intelligence approach*. Morgan Kaufmann.

Mitchell, T. M. (1997). *Machine learning*. USA: The McGraw-Hill Companies, Inc.

Myers, J. H. (1963). Predicting credit risk with a numerical scoring system. *The Journal of Applied Psychology*, *47*(5), 348–352. doi:10.1037/h0049168

Myers, J. H., & Forgy, E. W. (1963). The development of numerical credit evaluation systems. *Journal of the American Statistical Association*, *58*(303), 799–806. doi:10.2307/2282727

Nijssen, S., & Kok, J. N. (2003). Efficient discovery of frequent unordered trees. In *Proceedings of the 1st International Workshop on Mining Graphs, Trees, and Sequences (MGTS)*.

Ozaki, T., & Okhawa, T. (2006). Efficient mining of closed induced ordered subtrees in tree-structured databases. In *Workshops Proceedings of the 6th IEEE International Conference on Data Mining (ICDM Workshops)*, (pp. 279-283). IEEE Computer Society.

Paik, J., Nam, J., Hwang, J., & Kim, U. M. (2008). Mining maximal frequent subtrees with list-based pattern-growth method. In Y. Zhang, G. Yu, E. Bertino, & G. Xu (Eds.), *Proceedings of the 10th Asia-Pacific Web Conference (APWeb) Lecture Notes in Computer Science: Vol. 4976* (pp. 93-98). Springer.

Paik, J., Won, D., Fotouhi, F., & Kim, U. M. (2005). EXiT-B: A new approach for extracting maximal frequent subtrees from XML data. In M. Gallagher, J. Hogan & F. Maire (Eds.), *Proceedings of the 6th International Conference on Intelligent Data Engineering and Automated Learning (IDEAL) Lecture Notes in Computer Science: Vol. 3578* (pp. 1-8). Springer.

Piramuthu, S. (1999). Financial credit-risk evaluation with neural and neurofuzzy systems. *European Journal of Operational Research*, *112*(2), 310–321. doi:10.1016/S0377-2217(97)00398-6

Rui, Q., Li, L. L., & Jun, X. (2010). *An application of improved BP neural network in personal credit scoring*. In *Proceedings of the 2nd International Conference on Computer Modeling and Simulation* (pp. 238-341).

Shaharanee, I. N. M., Hadzic, F., & Dillon, T. S. (2010). A statistical interestingness measures for XML based association rules. In B.-T. Zhang, & M. A. Orgun (Eds.), *Proceedings of the 11th Pacific Rim International Conference on Artificial Intelligence (PRICAI) Lecture Notes in Computer Science: Vol. 6230*. (pp. 194-205). Springer.

Šušteršič, M., Mramor, D., & Zupan, J. (2009). Consumer credit scoring models with limited data. *Expert Systems with Applications*, *36*(3), 4736–4744. doi:10.1016/j.eswa.2008.06.016

Tan, H., Dillon, T. S., Hadzic, F., Feng, L., & Chang, E. (2006). IMB3-Miner: Mining induced/embedded subtrees by constraining the level of embedding. In W. K. Ng, M. Kitsuregawa & J. Li (Eds.), *Proceedings of the 10th Pacific-Asia Conference on Advances in Knowledge Discovery and Data Mining (PAKDD) Lecture Notes in Computer Science: Vol. 3918* (pp. 450-461). Springer.

Tan, H., Hadzic, F., Dillon, T. S., & Chang, E. (2008a). State of the art of data mining of tree structured information. *International Journal of Computer Systems Science and Engineering, 23*(4), 255–270.

Tan, H., Hadzic, F., Dillon, T. S., Feng, L., & Chang, E. (2008b). Tree model guided candidate generation for mining frequent subtrees from XML. *ACM Transactions on Knowledge Discovery from Data, 2*(2).

Thomas, L. C. (2000). A survey of credit and behavioural scoring: Forecasting financial risk of lending to consumers. *International Journal of Forecasting, 16*(2), 149–172. doi:10.1016/S0169-2070(00)00034-0

Tsai, C.-F., & Chen, M.-L. (2010). Credit rating by hybrid machine learning techniques. *Applied Soft Computing, 10*(2), 374–380. doi:10.1016/j.asoc.2009.08.003

Tsaih, R., Liu, Y.-J., Liu, W., & Lien, Y.-L. (2004). Credit scoring system for small business loans. *Decision Support Systems, 38*(1), 91–99. doi:10.1016/S0167-9236(03)00079-4

UNEP Finance Initiative (Ed.). (2007). *Innovative financing for sustainable small and medium enterprises in Africa.* (2007). Paper presented at the International Workshop Geneva, Switzerland

United States International Trade Commission (Ed.). (2010). *Small and medium-sized enterprises: U.S. and EU export activities, and barriers and opportunities experienced by U.S. firms*. (Investigation no. 332-509). Washington, DC: USITC Secretariat

Vargas-Vera, M., Motta, E., Domingue, J., Lanzoni, M., Stutt, A., & Ciravegna, F. (2002). MNM: Ontology driven semi-automatic and automatic support for semantic markup. In *Proceedings of the 13th International Conference on Knowledge Engineering and Knowledge Management (EKAW)* [Springer.]. *Lecture Notes in Computer Science, 2473*, 379–391. doi:10.1007/3-540-45810-7_34

Wang, S., Yin, S., & Jiang, M. (2008). Hybrid neural network based on GA-BP for personal credit scoring. In *Proceedings of the 4th International Conference on Natural Computation- Volume 03 (ICNC)*. IEEE Computer Society.

Wang, Y., Wang, S., & Lai, K. K. (2005). A new fuzzy support vector machine to evaluate credit risk. *IEEE Transactions on Fuzzy Systems, 13*(6), 820–831. doi:10.1109/TFUZZ.2005.859320

Wei, L., Li, J., & Chen, Z. (2007). Credit risk evaluation using support vector machine with mixture of kernel. In Y. Shi, G. van Albada, J. Dongarra & P. Sloot (Eds.), *Proceedings of the 7th International Conference on Computational Science (ICCS (2) Lecture Notes in Computer Science: Vol. 4488* (pp. 431-438). Springer.

West, D. (2000). Neural network credit scoring models. *Computers & Operations Research, 27*(11-12), 1131–1152. doi:10.1016/S0305-0548(99)00149-5

Wiginton, J. C. (1980). A note on the comparison of logit and discriminant models of consumer credit behavior. *Journal of Financial and Quantitative Analysis, 15*(3), 757–770. doi:10.2307/2330408

Wong, B. K., Bodnovich, T. A., & Selvi, Y. (1997). Neural network applications in business: A review and analysis of the literature (1988-1995). *Decision Support Systems, 19*(4), 301–320. doi:10.1016/S0167-9236(96)00070-X

Wu, C., & Wang, X.-M. (2000). A neural network approach for analyzing small business lending decisions. *Journal Review of Quantitative Finance and Accounting, 15*(3), 259–276. doi:10.1023/A:1008324023422

Xiao, Y., Yao, J.-F., Li, Z., & Dunham, M. H. (2003). Efficient data mining for maximal frequent subtrees. In *Proceedings of the 3rd IEEE International Conference on Data Mining (ICDM),* (pp. 379-386). IEEE Computer Society.

Yobas, M. B., Crook, J. N., & Ross, P. (2000). Credit scoring using neural and evolutionary techniques. *IMA J Management Math, 11*(2), 111–125. doi:10.1093/imaman/11.2.111

Yu, L., Lai, K., Wang, S., & Zhou, L. (2007). A least squares fuzzy SVM approach to credit risk assessment. In B.-Y. Cao (Ed.), *Proceedings of the 2nd International Conference of Fuzzy Information and Engineering (ICFIE) Advances in Soft Computing: Vol. 40* (pp. 865-874). Springer.

Yu, L., Wang, S., Lai, K. K., & Zhou, L. (2008). *Bio-inspired credit risk analysis: Computational intelligence with support vector machines*. Springer.

Yu, L., Wang, S., Wen, F., Lai, K. K., & He, S. (2008). Designing a hybrid intelligent mining system for credit risk evaluation. *Journal of Systems Science and Complexity, 21*(4), 527–539. doi:10.1007/s11424-008-9133-7

Zaki, M. J. (2005). Efficiently mining frequent trees in a forest: algorithms and applications. *IEEE Transactions on Knowledge and Data Engineering, 17*(8), 1021–1035. doi:10.1109/TKDE.2005.125

Zhang, L., & Hui, X. (2009). Application of support vector machines method in credit scoring. In H. Wang, Y. Shen, T. Huang & Z. Zeng (Eds.), *Proceedings of the 6th International Symposium on Neural Networks (ISNN) Advances in Soft Computing: Vol. 56* (pp. 283-290). Springer.

Zhou, L., Lai, K. K., & Yu, L. (2010). Least squares support vector machines ensemble models for credit scoring. *Expert Systems with Applications, 37*(1), 127–133. doi:10.1016/j.eswa.2009.05.024

Zhou, X., Zhang, D., & Jiang, Y. (2008). A new credit scoring method based on rough sets and decision tree. In Washio, T., Suzuki, E., Ting, K., & Inokuchi, A. (Eds.), *Advances in Knowledge Discovery and Data Mining, Lecture Notes in Computer Science* (*Vol. 5012*, pp. 1081–1089). Springer. doi:10.1007/978-3-540-68125-0_117


## ADDITIONAL READING


Abe, K., Kawasoe, S., Asai, T., Arimura, H., & Arikawa, S. (2002). Optimized Substructure Discovery for Semistructured Data. In *Proceedings of the 6th European Conference on Principles of Data Mining and Knowledge Discovery (PKDD): Vol. 2431. Lecture Notes in Computer Science* (57-100). Springer.

Asai, T., Abe, K., Kawasoe, S., Arimura, H., Sakamato, H., & Arikawa, S. (2002). Efficient Substructure Discovery from Large Semi-structured Data. In *Proceedings of the 2nd SIAM International Conference on Data Mining (SDM)*. SIAM.

Bayardo, R. J., Agrawal, R., & Gunopulos, D. (1999). Constraint-based Rule Mining in Large, Dense Databases. In *Proceedings of the 15th International Conference on Data Engineering (ICDE),* (pp. 188-197). IEEE Computer Society.

Feng, L., Chang, E., & Dillon, T. S. (2002). A Semantic Network-based Design Methodology for XML Documents. *ACM Transactions on Information Systems, 20*(4), 390–421. doi:10.1145/582415.582417

Feng, L., & Dillon, T. S. (2004). Mining XML-Enabled Association Rules with Templates. In *Proceedings of the 3rd International Workshop on Knowledge Discovery in Inductive Databases (KDID).*

Feng, L., & Dillon, T. S. (2005). An XML-Enabled Data Mining Query Language XML-DMQL. *International Journal of Business Intelligence and Data Mining*, *1*(1), 22–41. doi:10.1504/IJBIDM.2005.007316

Feng, L., Dillon, T. S., & Liu, J. (2001). Inter-transactional Association Rules for Multi-dimensional Contexts for Prediction and their Application to Studying Meteorological Data. *Data & Knowledge Engineering*, *37*(1), 85–115. doi:10.1016/S0169-023X(01)00003-9

Hadzic, F. (2008). *Advances in knowledge learning methodologies and their applications*. Perth: Curtin University of Technology.

Hadzic, F., Dillon, T. S., & Chang, E. (2007). Tree Mining Application to Matching of Heterogeneous Knowledge Representations. In *Proceedings of the IEEE International Conference on Granular Computing (GrC),* (pp. 351-357). IEEE Computer Society.

Hadzic, F., Dillon, T. S., Sidhu, A. S., Chang, E., & Tan, H. (2006). Mining Substructures in Protein Data. In *Workshops Proceedings of the 6th IEEE International Conference on Data Mining (ICDM Workshops),* (pp. 213-217). IEEE Computer Society.

Hadzic, F., Tan, H., & Dillon, T. S. (2007). UNI3 - Efficient Algorithm for Mining Unordered Induced Subtrees using TMG Candidate Generation. In *Proceedings of the IEEE Symposium on Computational Intelligence and Data Mining (CIDM),* (pp. 568-575). IEEE Computer Society.

Hadzic, F., Tan, H., & Dillon, T. S. (2008). Mining Unordered Distance-constrained Embedded Subtrees. In *Proceedings of the 11th International Conference on Discovery Science (DS): Vol. 5255. Lecture Notes in Computer Science (pp. 272-283).* Springer.

Hadzic, F., Tan, H., & Dillon, T. S. (2008). U3 – Mining Unordered Embedded Subtrees Using TMG Candidate Generation. In *Proceedings of the IEEE/WIC/ACM International Conference on Web Intelligence (WI-IAT),* (pp. 285-292). IEEE Computer Society.

Hadzic, M., Hadzic, F., & Dillon, T. S. (2008). Tree Mining in Mental Health Domain. In *Proceedings of the 41st Hawaii International Conference on System Sciences (HICSS),* (p. 230). IEEE Computer Society.

Pan, Q. H., Hadzic, F., & Dillon, T. S. (2008). Conjoint Data Mining of Structured and Semi-structured Data. In *Proceedings of the 4th International Conference on the Semantics, Knowledge and Grid (SKG),* (pp. 87-94). IEEE Computer Society.

Sestito, S., & Dillon, T. S. (1994). *Automated Knowledge Acquisition*. Sydney: Prentice Hall.

Shaharanee, I. N. M., Hadzic, F., & Dillon, T. S. (2009). Interestingness of Association Rules using Symmetrical Tau and Logistic Regression. In *Proceedings of the 22nd Australasian Joint Conference on Advances in Artificial Intelligence (AI): Vol. 5866. Lecture Notes in Computer Science* (pp. 422-431). Springer.

Shasha, D., Wang, J. T. L., & Zhang, S. (2004). Unordered Tree Mining with Applications to Phylogeny. In *Proceedings of the 20th International Conference on Data Engineering (ICDE),* (pp. 708-719). IEEE Computer Society.

Tan, H., Dillon, T. S., Feng, L., & Chang, E. (2005). Tree Model Guided Candidate Generation Approach for XML Data Mining. In *Proceedings 1st International Conference on Pattern Recognition and Machine Intelligence (PReMI).*

Tan, H., Dillon, T. S., Feng, L., Chang, E., & Hadzic, F. (2005). X3-Miner: Mining Patterns from XML Database. In *Proceedings of the 6th International Conference on Data Mining, Text Mining and their Business Applications* (pp. 287-296).

Tan, H., Dillon, T. S., Hadzic, F., & Chang, E. (2006). *Razor: Mining Distance-constrained Embedded Subtrees.* In *Workshops Proceedings of the 6th IEEE International Conference on Data Mining (ICDM),* (pp. 8-13). IEEE Computer Society.

Tan, H., Dillon, T. S., Hadzic, F., & Chang, E. (2006). SEQUEST: Mining Frequent Subsequences using DMA Strips. In *Proceeding of the 7th International Conference on Data Mining and Information Engineering* (pp. 315-328). WIT Press.

Tan, H., Hadzic, F., Feng, L., & Chang, E. (2005). MB3-Miner: Mining eMBedded subTREEs Using Tree Model Guided Candidate Generation. In *Proceedings of the 1st International Workshop on Mining Complex Data in conjunction with ICDM.* IEEE Computer Society.

Zaki, M. J., & Aggarwal, C. C. (2003). XRules: An Effective Structural Classifier for XML Data. In *Proceedings of the 9th International Conference on Knowledge Discovery and Data Mining (KDD)*, (pp. 316-325). ACM.

Zhang, S., Zhang, J., Liu, H., & Wang, W. (2005). *XAR-Miner: Efficient Association Rules Mining for XML Data.* In A. Ellis, and T. Hagino (Eds.), *Proceedings of the 14th International World Wide Web Conference (WWW)*, (pp. 894-895). ACM.

# About the Contributors

**Andrea Tagarelli** is an Assistant Professor of Computer Science with the Department of Electronics, Computer and Systems Sciences, University of Calabria, Italy. He graduated in Computer Engineering, in 2001, and obtained his Ph.D. in Computer and Systems Engineering, in 2006. He was visiting researcher at the Department of Computer Science & Engineering, University of Minnesota at Minneapolis, USA. His research interests include topics in knowledge discovery and text/data mining, information extraction, Web and semistructured data management, spatio-temporal databases, and bioinformatics. On these topics, he has coauthored journal articles, conference papers, and book chapters and developed practical software tools. He has served as a reviewer as well as a member of program committee for leading journals and conferences in the fields of databases and data mining, information systems, knowledge and data management, and artificial intelligence. He has been a SIAM member since 2008 and an ACM member since 2009.

***

**Panagiotis Antonellis** is a Computer Engineer and a PhD student at the Department of Computer Engineering and Informatics University of Patras, Greece. He graduated in Computer Engineering, in 2005, and obtained his MSc in Computer Science, in 2007. His research interests include topics in knowledge discovery and text/data mining, XML data management, and software quality assessment.

**Rafael Berlanga Llavori**, Ph.D., is an Associate Professor of Computer Science at University Jaume I (UJI), Spain. His main research concerns the analysis and mining of semi-structured and semantic data in the context of the (Semantic) Web. He is the current leader of the Temporal Knowledge Group of the Computer Languages & Systems department (UJI). He is author of several articles in international journals of high impact, such as *Decision Support Systems, BMC Bioinformatics, Information Processing & Management* and *Information Science*, as well as more than 70 papers published in international conferences and workshops (DEXA, EDBT, ICDE, SIGMOD, etc.). He has served as PC member in several international workshops and congresses. More information of the research group is available at http://krono.act.uji.es.

**Albert Bifet** is a Postdoctoral Research Fellow at the Machine Learning Group at the University of Waikato in Hamilton, New Zealand. He obtained a Ph.D. from UPC-Barcelona Tech. He is the author of a book on Adaptive Stream Mining and Pattern Learning and Mining from Evolving Data Streams. Albert is one of the core developers of MOA (Massive Online Analysis) software environment for implementing algorithms and running experiments for online learning from evolving data streams.

MOA is designed to deal with the challenging problem of scaling up the implementation of state of the art algorithms to real world dataset sizes.

**Luca Cagliero** received the Master's degree in Computer and Communication Networks from the Politecnico di Torino in 2008. Since January 2009, he has been a PhD student in computer engineering in the Dipartimento di Automatica e Informatica, Politecnico di Torino. His current research interests are in the areas of data mining and database systems. In particular, he is investigating the application of novel classification and association rule mining approaches to very large databases as well the exploitation of generalized patterns to support analyst decision making in different application contexts. He has been a Teaching Assistant in different databases and data mining courses at the Politecnico di Torino since academic year 2009-2010.

**Tania Cerquitelli** got the Master degree in Computer Engineering and the PhD degree from the Politecnico di Torino, Torino, Italy, and the Master degree in Computer Science from the Universidad De Las Américas Puebla. She has been a postdoctoral researcher in computer engineering in the Dipartimento di Automatica e Informatica, Politecnico di Torino since January 2007. Her research interests include the design of innovative algorithms to efficiently perform large-scale data mining, novel and efficient data mining techniques for sensor readings, and innovative algorithms to extract high level abstraction of the mined knowledge (e.g., generalized association rules). She has been a teaching assistant in different databases and data mining courses at the Politecnico di Torino since academic year 2004-2005.

**Pasquale De Meo** received the MsC Degree in Electrical Engineering from the University of Reggio Calabria in May 2002 and the PhD in System Engineering and Computer Science from the University of Calabria in February 2006. Since January 2011 he is an Assistant Professor at the University of Messina. His research interests include user modeling, intelligent agents, e-commerce, e-government, e-health, machine learning, knowledge extraction and representation, scheme integration, XML, cooperative information systems, folksonomies, and social internetworking.

**Tharam Dillon** is an expert in the field of software engineering, data mining XML based systems, ontologies, trust, security, and component-oriented access control. Professor Dillon has published five authored books and four co-edited books. He has also published over 750 scientific papers in refereed journals and conferences. Over the last fifteen years, he has more than 4500 citations. Many of his research outcomes have been applied by industry worldwide. This indicates the high impact of his research work. He is the distinguished research Professor and Head of R&D in DEBI Institute in Curtin University and the Head of the IFIP International Task Force WG2.12/24 on Semantic Web and Web Semantics, and the IEEE/IES Technical Committee on Industrial Informatics.

**Qin Ding** is currently an Assistant Professor in the Department of Computer Science at East Carolina University, Greenville, North Carolina, USA. She received her Ph.D. in Computer Science from North Dakota State University, Fargo, North Dakota, M.S. and B.S. in Computer Science from Nanjing University, Nanjing, China. She was a faculty member at Pennsylvania State University at Harrisburg before joining East Carolina University. Her research interests include data mining, database, and bioinformatics. She has published more than 50 peer-reviewed papers in these areas. She has also served as program committee member and reviewer for multiple conferences and journals in her research fields.

**Giacomo Fiumara** is Assistant Professor at the Faculty of Sciences of the University of Messina since 2008. He graduated in Physics in 1989 and took his Ph.D. in Physics in 1992 at the University of Messina. His scientific areas of interest cover Semantic Web, automatic extraction of data from Web sources, reasoning on Web data and social networks.

**Paolo Garza** received the Master's and PhD degrees in Computer Engineering from the Politecnico di Torino. He has been an Assistant Professor (with non-tenure track position) at the Dipartimento di Elettronica e Informatica, Politecnico di Milano, since June 2010. Prior to that, he was a postdoctoral fellow in the Dipartimento di Automatica e Informatica, Politecnico di Torino. His current research interests include data mining and database systems. In particular, he has worked on the classification of structured and unstructured data, compact representation of XML documents by means of association rules, outlier detection, and itemset mining algorithms. He has published several papers in journals and conference proceedings.

**Ricard Gavaldà** received his Degree (1987) and Ph.D. (1992) in Computer Science from Universitat Politècnica de Catalunya, UPC. He has had a permanent position at the Departament de Llenguatges i Sistemes Informŕtics of UPC since 1993, where he became Full Professor in 2008. His main research field was initially computational complexity theory, and has gradually evolved towards computational learning theory, and algorithmic aspects of machine learning and data mining. He has recently started working on applications of machine learning to autonomic computing.

**Sergio Greco** is Full Professor of Computer Science at the Faculty of Engineering at the University of Calabria, chair of the Dept. of Electronics, Computer and Systems Sciences and associated researcher at the Institute of High Performance Computing and Networks of the Italian National Research Council. He was researcher at CRAI, a research consortium of informatics. He was visiting researcher at the Microelectronics and Computer Center (MCC) of Austin, Texas, and at the Computer Science Dept. of University of California at Los Angeles, USA. He has published more than 150 papers including 40 journal papers and about 80 papers published in the proceedings of international conferences. His primary research interests include database theory, logic programming, logic and deductive database, nonmonotonic reasoning, data integration, Web search engines, and mining and querying semistructured data. He is a member of the IEEE Computer Society and ACM and associated Editor of IEEE TKDE.

**Francesco Gullo** is currently a research Fellow with the Department of Electronics, Computer and Systems Sciences at University of Calabria, Italy. He received his M.Sc. degree in Computer Engineering in December 2005 and his Ph.D. in Computer and Systems Engineering in January 2010. He was visiting scholar at the Department of Computer Science, George Mason University, Fairfax, Virginia, USA, where he conducted research activity in collaboration with the Carlotta Domeniconi's data mining research group. His research interests are in the fields of databases, particularly falling into the areas of data mining and knowledge discovery, and XML data management. In particular, he is concerned with research topics including clustering ensembles, uncertain and probabilistic data mining, spatio-temporal data management, bioinformatics, and XML document clustering.

**Fedja Hadzic** received his PhD from Curtin University of Technology in 2008. His PhD thesis is entitled: “Advances in Knowledge Learning Methodologies and their Applications.” He is currently a Research Fellow at the Digital Ecosystems and Business Intelligence Institute of the Curtin University. He has contributed in a number of fields of data mining and knowledge discovery and their applications. His work has been published in a number of refereed conferences and journals, and he has authored a recent book on mining of data with complex structures. His research interests include data mining, machine learning, and AI in general with more focus on tree mining, graph mining, neural networks, knowledge matching, and ontology learning.

**Markus Hagenbuchner** holds a PhD (Computer Science, University of Wollongong, Australia). He is currently a Senior Lecturer in the School of Computer Science and Software Engineering at the University of Wollongong. He joined the machine learning research area in 1992, and started to focus his research activities on neural networks for the graph structured domain in 1998, and pioneered the development of self-organizing maps for structured data. He is the team leader of the machine learning group at the University of Wollongong.

**Novita Ikasari** has business background both in theoretical and practical sense. She received her Bachelor degree in Business Administration from University of Indonesia and Master of Commerce from University of Sydney. She has been teaching accounting and finance units for more than 10 years and was Head of Finance and Banking Program at Diploma Program University of Indonesia for four years. During this time she developed her interests on microfinance and microcredit. She is currently pursuing her doctorate degree from Curtin University with research topic in microcredit. Her research will contribute to the extensive application of data mining in business context and a better provision of financial support for small enterprises in Indonesia.

**Milly Kc** is an early career researcher working in the field of machine learning and information retrieval. She graduated from Bachelor of Information and Communication Technology with a first class Honor in 2004. She then proceeded into research in the areas of machine learning and web-based information retrieval. In 2009, she earned a PhD in Computer Science and Software Engineering from University of Wollongong. She worked as a Research Associate in University of Wollongong, in the Informatics Faculty’s School of Computer Science and Software Engineering, from 2008 to 2010. Her research focuses on the distributed estimation or calculation of centralized ranking algorithms such as PageRank. During her employment, she has collaborated and presented her work to research partners in Australia, Italy, and Hong Kong. She has also been actively involved in teaching subjects in her research area such as artificial intelligence, reasoning and learning, distributed computing, and markup languages.

**Evgeny Kharlamov** is a PhD candidate at the Free University of Bozen-Bolzano (FUB) and Inria Saclay, France where he has been working under the supervision of Diego Calvanese, Werner Nutt, and Pierre Senellart. He is expected to graduate in April 2011. In 2009 he did a six-month internship at Inria Saclay with Serge Abiteboul. He got his European M.Sc. degree in Computer Science from both Dresden University of Technology and FUB in 2006. He is an alumni of the Novosibirsk State University, the Russian leading research school, where he studied mathematics. His research interests focus around theoretical and algorithmic aspects of database management systems and the semantic side of the World Wide Web. More specifically, the focus is on integration, aggregation, and updates for (i) uncertain and probabilistic databases and (ii) ontologies in the context of the Semantics Web. Evgeny has published several papers in top-tier conferences (VLDB, ICDT, ISWC).

**Michal Kozielski** graduated and received the Ph.D. degree in Computer Science, both from the Silesian University of Technology, Gliwice, Poland, in 2003 and 2008, respectively. He is an Assistant Professor with the Institute of Informatics, Faculty of Automatic Control, Electronics and Computer Science of the Silesian University of Technology. His research interests include data mining, especially clustering and soft computing with application to complex data such as semistructured data, biological data, and social networks.

**Sangeetha Kutty** is a currently working as a research fellow and is a completing PhD student working under the supervision of Dr.Richi Nayak in Queensland University of Technology (QUT), Brisbane, Australia. She has published 10 refereed research articles in conferences, workshops, and books since 2006. She has completed her Master's in Information Technology from Auckland University of Technology (AUT), Auckland, New Zealand. Her current research is mainly focused in the area of XML mining and Information Retrieval (IR).

**Fei Li** is an undergraduate student in Harbin Institute of Technology. He has worked as a research assistant in Data and Knowledge Engineering Research Center since 2009. His research interests include XML data management, graph mining, and database usability. During his undergraduate study, he won many honors and awards including National Encouragement Scholarship, First Prize of China Undergraduate Math Contest, Honorable Mention in American Mathematical Contest in Modeling, Second Prize of China Undergraduate Mathematical Contest in Modeling, and Student Travel Award in International Workshop on XML Data Management. He will receive his B.S from Harbin Institute of Technology in July, 2011.

**Jianzhong Li** is a Professor in the Department of Computer Science and Technology at the Harbin Institute of Technology, China. In the past, he worked as a visiting scholar at the University of California at Berkeley, as a staff scientist in the Information Research Group at the Lawrence Berkeley National Laboratory, and as a Visiting Professor at the University of Minnesota. His research interests include data management systems, data mining, data warehousing, sensor networks, and bioinformatics. He has published extensively and been involved in the program committees of all major database conferences, including SIGMOD, VLDB, and ICDE. He has also served on the boards for varied journals, including the IEEE *Transactions on Knowledge and Data Engineering*. He is a member of the IEEE.

**Sanjay Kumar Madria** received his Ph.D. in Computer Science from Indian Institute of Technology, Delhi, India in 1995. He is an Associate Professor, Department of Computer Science, at the Missouri University of Science and Technology (formerly, University of Missouri-Rolla), USA. He has published more than 140 Journal and conference papers in the areas of mobile computing, sensor networks, security, XML, web data warehousing, and databases in general. He co-authored a book entitled "Web Data Management: A Warehouse Approach" published by Springer-Verlag. He guest edited *WWW Journal*, several data and knowledge engineering sp. issues on web data management and data warehousing. He was founding Program Chair for EC&WEB conferences held in UK and Germany. He is regular invited panelist in NSF, NSERC (Canada), Hong Kong Research Council and Sweden Council of Research. He has served as invited/keynote speakers in conferences. He received UMR faculty excellence award in 2007, Japanese Society for Promotion of Science invitational fellowship in 2006, and Air Force Research Lab's visiting faculty fellowship from 2008-2010. His research is supported by grants from NSF, DOE, AFRL, ARL, UM research board, and from industries such Boeing and Hengsoft. He is IEEE Senior Member and also a speaker under IEEE Distinguished Visitor program for 3 years (2007-2010).

**Mirjana Mazuran** was born on August 23rd, 1982 in Sarajevo (BiH). In 2008 she received her M.Sc. in Computer Science Engineering from Politecnico di Milano. She spent six months as a research assistant in Information Technology at Politecnico di Milano, working on a project for the extraction of relevant information from XML documents. Since January 2009 she is a PhD student in Computer Science at Politecnico di Milano. Her main topic of research is the application of data mining techniques to support advanced database functionalities. In particular, she is currently working on mining and querying tree-based patterns from XML documents and on mining violations to relax relational database constraints.

**Rosa Meo** took her Master degree in Electronic Engineering in 1993 and her Ph.D. in Computer Science and Systems Engineering in 1997, both at the Politecnico di Torino, Italy. From 2005 she is Associate Professor at the Department of Computer Science in the University of Turin, where she works in the database and data mining research field. From 2000 to 2003 she was responsible for the University of Torino the cInQ Project (consortium on knowledge discovery by Inductive Queries) funded by the V EU Funding Framework. She is active in the scientific activity in the field of database and data mining in which she published more than 40 papers. She served in the Program Committee of many international and national conferences on databases and data mining, among which VLDB, ACM KDD, IEEE ICDM, SIAM DM, ACM CIKM, ECML/PKDD, ACM SAC, DEXA, and DaWak.

**Richi Nayak** received her PhD degree in Computer Science in 2001 from QUT, Brisbane, Australia. She is a Senior Lecturer in the Faculty of Science and Technology at QUT. Her research interests are data mining, information retrieval, and Web intelligence. She conducts both theoretical and applied research and has published 50+ refereed research articles in quality journals, conferences, and books since 1999.

**Victoria Nebot** received her BSc+MSc degree in Computer Science from Universitat Jaume I, Spain, in 2008. She joined the Temporal Knowledge Bases Group (TKBG) at Universitat Jaume I as a PhD Student. Her main research is focused on analyzing and exploiting semi-structured and complex data derived mainly from the Semantic Web. In particular, she is interested in researching new techniques that exploit the rich knowledge encoded in the ontologies associated to the data in order to make it available to data mining and OLAP tools and enhance decision support tasks and knowledge discovery.

**Antonino Nocera** received the MSc Degree in Telecommunication Engineering from the University of Reggio Calabria in July 2009. Currently he is a PhD Student in Information Engineering. His research interests include scheme integration, XML, Cooperative Information Systems, folksonomies, and social internetworking.

**Qi Hua Pan** received her Master Degree in Information Technology from La Trobe University in Melbourne. She has three years working experience in industries mainly in charge of database management and software development. She was involved in a few projects including managing the production information of warehouse, retail, and market promotion. She also developed online learning system evaluation website and JAVA project of knowledge sharing. Currently, she is studying as a PhD student in Curtin University in Perth. Her research interest is in XML data mining, semantic matching, schema matching, and frequent pattern mining from relational data, and XML data conjointly.

**Enrico Ponassi** graduated with a Bachelor degree in Computer Science at the University of Torino in 2007. From March 2008 he is a Master student in Computer Science at the same University. In October 2010 he won a research scholarship in the context of the SMAT-F1 project, funded by the Piedmont Region and whose goal is the monitoring of the territory with advanced systems. His task in the project is the development of the metadata retrieval system component for geo-referenced systems and the extraction of relevant features.

**Giovanni Ponti** is currently a researcher at ENEA, the Italian National Agency for New Technologies, Energy, and Sustainable Economic Development. He received his M.Sc. degree in Computer Engineering on December 2005 and his Ph.D. in Computer and Systems Engineering on January 2010. He was research fellow with the Department of Electronics, Computer and Systems Sciences at University of Calabria, Italy, from 2006 to 2010. His research interests concern the fields of databases, with special attention to problems of knowledge discovery, data mining, and XML data management. His research topics regard text mining, probabilistic topic modeling, uncertain and probabilistic data mining, spatio-temporal data management, bioinformatics, and XML document clustering.

**Elisa Quintarelli** received her Master's degree in Computer Science from the University of Verona, Italy. On January 2002 she completed the Ph.D. program in Computer and Automation Engineering at Politecnico di Milano and is now an Assistant Professor at the Dipartimento di Elettronica e Informazione, Politecnico di Milano. Her main research interests concern the study of efficient and flexible techniques for specifying and querying semistructured and temporal data, the application of data-mining techniques to provide intensional query answering. More recently, her research has been concentrated on context aware data management.

**Angelo Rauseo** was born in 1985 in Elizabeth, NJ (US). He is attending the Ph.D. in Computer Engineering from the Politecnico di Milano since January 2010 under direction of Prof. Letizia Tanca, from the same university he gained his Master Degree in Computer Engineering in December 2009 and his Bachelor Degree in Computer Engineering in July 2007 and in July 2004 he obtained the high school degree from the Liceo Scientifico Statale Bonaventura Cavalieri of Verbania (VB). His main research interests relate to data mining in XML and relational systems, logic programming, and context applied to data and applications.

**Elena Roglia** took her degree in mathematics science at Mathematics Science Department of Turin University. Her thesis focuses on Hopfield neural networks and Boltzmann machine. She is a PhD student in Computer Science and High Technology at Department of Computer Science of Turin University. Her research topics include machine learning techniques for classification and regression with particular emphasis on neural networks, data mining techniques for features selection, and geographical information systems. She has held a contract for project collaboration with the Department of Computer Science of Turin University, where she was involved in the design and implementation of the control station for the project SMAT-F1 promoted by Piedmont Region for the development of innovative technologies for territorial monitoring by means of Unmanned Aerial Vehicle. In addition, she worked for the annotation of geographical map with social metadata, in order to enrich the information content of the mission data.

**Pierre Senellart** is an Associate Professor in the DBWeb team at Télécom ParisTech, the French leading engineering school specialized in information technology. He is an alumnus of the École normale supérieure and obtained his M.Sc. (2003) and his Ph.D. (2007) in computer science from Université Paris-Sud, studying under the supervision of Serge Abiteboul. Pierre Senellart has published articles in internationally renowned conferences and journals (*PODS, AAAI, VLDB Journal, Journal of the ACM*, etc.). He has been a member of the program committee and participated in the organization of various international conferences and workshops (including WWW, CIKM, ICDE, VLDB, SIGMOD, ICDT). He is also the Information Director of the *Journal of the ACM*. His research interests focus around theoretical aspects of database management systems and the World Wide Web, and more specifically on the intentional indexing of the deep Web, probabilistic XML databases, and graph mining.

**Gnanasekaran Sundarraj** was born in Dindigul, India. He received Bachelor of Engineering degree in Electrical and Electronics from Madurai Kamaraj University in 1992 and Master of Science degree in Computer Science from Pennsylvania State University in 2005. His main research interests include computational complexity, graph theory, algorithms, and databases. He is currently working as a software engineer.

**Letizia Tanca** worked for four years as a software engineer and then obtained her Ph.D. in Computer Science in 1988. She is currently a full Professor at Politecnico di Milano, where she has held the chair of the degree and Master courses in Computer Science and Engineering at the Leonardo campus, from 2000 to 2006. She has taught and teaches mainly courses on Databases and Information System Technologies. She is the author of more than a hundred papers on databases and database theory, published in international journals and conferences, and co-author of the book "Logic Programming and Databases." Recently, she has edited the book "Semantic Web Information Management." Her research interests range over deductive and active databases, graph-based languages for databases, semantic-web information management, semistructured information. Her most recent research interests concern context-aware knowledge management. She is in the board of the Informatics Europe association.

**Tien Tran** is a PhD student at QUT, Brisbane, Australia. She has published in conferences, journal, and workshops about XML data mining and its application in transforming the XML documents.

**Ah-Chung Tsoi** was born in Hong Kong and lived there until 1969. He studied Electronic Engineering at the Hong Kong Technical College (graduated in 1969); Electronic Control Engineering (graduated in 1970) and Control Engineering (graduated in 1972) at University of Salford, England. Since graduation, he worked as a post doctoral fellow at the Inter-University Institute of Engineering Control at University College of North Wales, Bangor, North Wales, a lecturer at Paisley College of Technology, Paisley, Scotland, before emigrating to New Zealand. He worked as a Senior Lecturer in Electrical Engineering in the Department of Electrical Engineering, University of Auckland, before emigrating to Australia. He worked as a Senior Lecturer in Electrical Engineering, University College, University of New South Wales for 5 years. He then served as Professor of Electrical Engineering at University of Queensland,

Australia; Dean, and simultaneously Director of Information Technology Services, and then foundation Pro-Vice Chancellor (Information Technology and Communications) at University of Wollongong; before joining the Australian Research Council as an Executive Director, Mathematics, Information and Communications Sciences. He was Director, Monash e-Research Centre, Monash University in Melbourne, Australia. In April 2007, Professor Tsoi took up the position of Vice President (Research and Institutional Advancement), Hong Kong Baptist University, Hong Kong and held the position until August 2010. Since September 2010, he has been Dean Faculty of Information Technology, Macau University of Science and Technology, Macau. Professor Tsoi works in the area of artificial intelligence in particular neural networks and fuzzy systems in recent years. He has published widely in neural network literature. In more recent years, Professor Tsoi works in the application of neural networks to graph domains, with applications to the World Wide Web searching, ranking problems, and sub-graph matching problem.

**Domenico Ursino** received the MSc Degree in Computer Engineering from the University of Calabria in July 1995. From September 1995 to October 2000 he was a member of the Knowledge Engineering group at DEIS, University of Calabria. He received the PhD in System Engineering and Computer Science from the University of Calabria in January 2000. From November 2000 to December 2004 he was an Assistant Professor at the University Mediterranea of Reggio Calabria. Since January 2005 he is an Associate Professor at the University Mediterranea of Reggio Calabria. His research interests include user modeling, intelligent agents, e-commerce, knowledge extraction and representation, scheme integration and abstraction, semi-structured data and XML, Cooperative Information Systems, folksonomies, and social internetworking.

**Waraporn Viyanon** received a Ph.D. in Computer Science in 2010 from Missouri University of Science and Technology (formerly University of Missouri-Rolla). She obtained her Master's degree in Applied Computer Science from Illinois State University, and a Bachelor's degree in computer science from Srinakharinwirot University. Her research interest lies at the intersection of the XML, Semantic Web, database systems, data mining, information retrieval, and service computing.

**Hongzhi Wang** received his BS, MS, and PhD in Computer Science from Harbin Institute of Technology, Harbin, China, in 2001, 2003, and 2008, respectively. He is currently an Associate Professor of the Department of Computer Science and Engineering at Harbin Institute of Technology. His research interests include XML data management, data quality, and information integration. He is the author of more than 70 research papers published at national and international journals and conference proceedings. He has been involved in the program committees of many international conferences. He has also served as reviewers for varied journals. He has been awarded Microsoft Fellow, IBM PHD Fellowship, and Chinese Excellent Database Engineer.

**Guangming Xing** received the BS degree in computer science from Nankai University, Tianjing, China, in 1996, and the Ph.D. degree in computer science from the University of Georgia, Athens, in 2001. He is currently an Associate Professor of Computer Science at Western Kentucky University, Bowling Green, Kentucky. His research interests include XML data management, finite automata theory and implementation, and data mining. He is also actively involved in the projects at the Center for Water Resource Studies at Western Kentucky University.

**Mohammed J. Zaki** is a Professor of Computer Science at Rensselaer Polytechnic Institute, Troy, New York. He received his Ph.D. degree in computer science from the University of Rochester in 1998. His research interests focus on developing novel data mining techniques, especially in bioinformatics. He has published over 200 papers and book-chapters on data mining and bioinformatics. He is the founding co-chair for the BIOKDD series of workshops. He is currently Area Editor for *Statistical Analysis and Data Mining,* and an Associate Editor for *Data Mining and Knowledge Discovery*, *ACM Transactions on Knowledge Discovery from Data*, *Knowledge and Information Systems*, ACM Transactions on Intelligent Systems and Technology, *Social Networks and Mining*, and *International Journal of Knowledge Discovery in Bioinformatics*. He was the program co-chair for SDM'08, SIGKDD'09, and PAKDD'10. He received the National Science Foundation CAREER Award in 2001 and the Department of Energy Early Career Principal Investigator Award in 2002. He is a senior member of the IEEE, and was named an ACM Distinguished Scientist in 2010.

**Shu Jia Zhang** is currently a final-year PhD student in University of Wollongong, Australia (UoW). She started her research work by participating in a Summer Scholarship Program in UoW in 2006. She developed an early interest in Automatic Web Search Service Testing project, and earned Bachelor of Information Communication Technology Honor Degree from UoW, majored in Software Engineering, in 2007. She continued her research on search engine testing area for one year when she worked as Research Assistant in UoW. She started PhD study since July 2008 and her thesis topic is "Impact Sensitive Ranking of Structured Documents." The main research interest is to provide alternative ranking scheme by utilizing machine learning methods to encode structural information of the documents.

# Index

## D

## E



## F

## G



## H



## I

J



K



L



M



N

## O



## P



## Q



## R



## S

## X



## Z

CPSIA information can be obtained at www.ICGtesting.com
Printed in the USA
BVOW051637050412

286899BV00007B/15/P

9 781613 503560